THE GREAT DOMAINES OF BURGUNDY

REMINGTON NORMAN

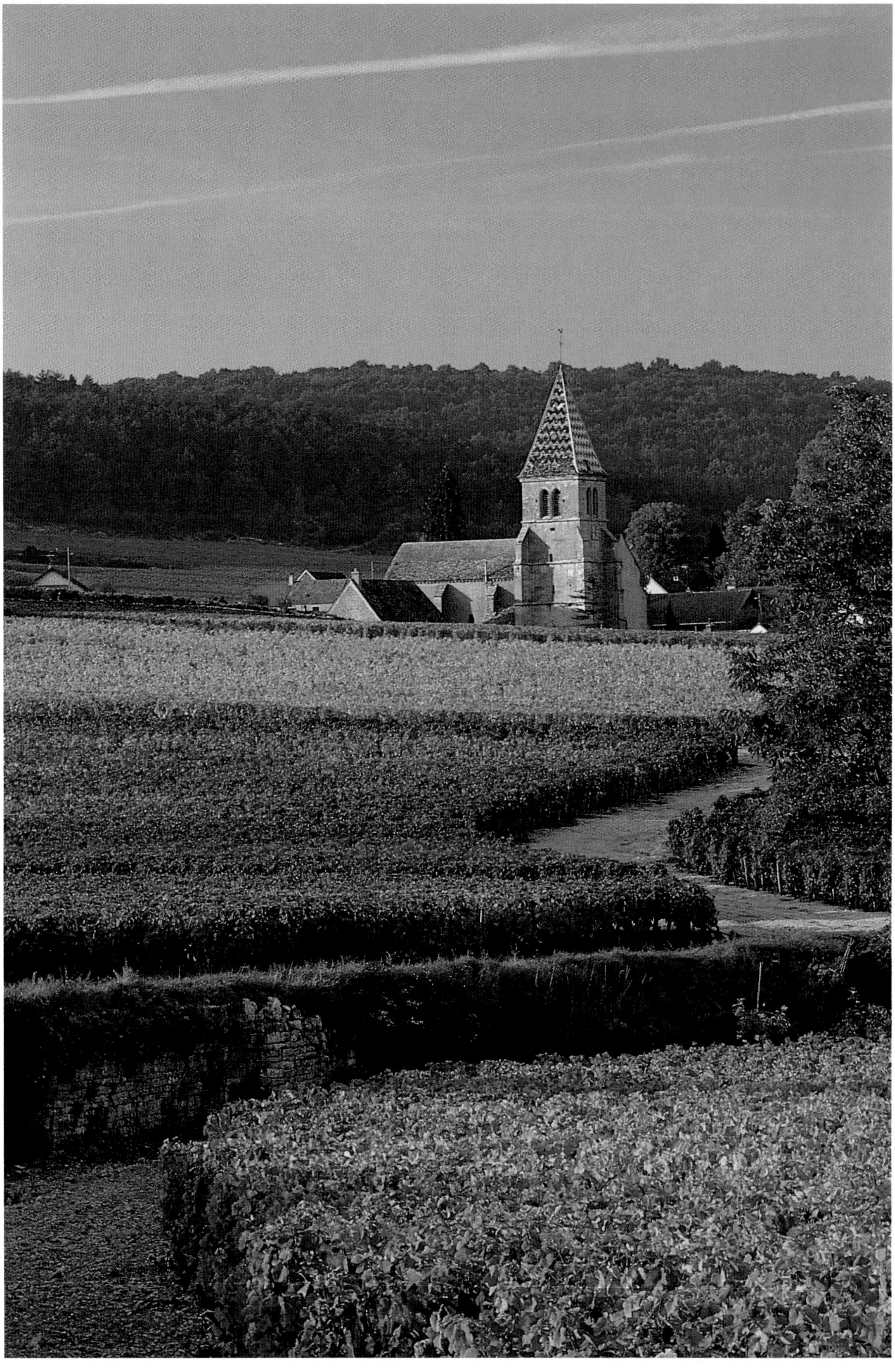

THE GREAT DOMAINES *of* BURGUNDY

A Guide to the Finest Wine Producers of the Côte d'Or

REMINGTON NORMAN

with a foreword by
MICHAEL BROADBENT

photographs by Janet Price

HENRY HOLT AND COMPANY
NEW YORK

For Geraldine

First published in the United States in 1993 by Henry Holt and Company, Inc., 115 West 18th Street, New York, New York 10011.
Originally published in Great Britain in 1992 by Kyle Cathie Ltd.

Library of Congress Cataloging-in-Publication data is available on request.

ISBN 0 - 8050 - 2463 - 8

Henry Holt books are available at special discounts for bulk purchases for sales promotions, premiums, fund-raising, or educational use. Special editions or book excerpts can also be created to specification.

For details contact:
Special Sales Director
Henry Holt and Company, Inc.
115 West 18th Street
New York, New York 10011

First American Edition – 1993

Editors: Jean Maund and Caroline Taggart
Designed by Geoff Hayes
Maps by Eugene Fleury

Printed in Great Britain
10 9 8 7 6 5 4 3 2 1

Abbreviations

Throughout the text and, in particular, in the tables, the following abbreviations have been used:
BGO. *Bourgogne Grande Ordinaire.*
Bourg. *Bourgogne.* C. *Centigrade.* C/S. *Cases.*
F. *Fermier.* G.C. *Grand Cru.* Ha. *Hectare.*
Hl. *Hectolitre.* Hl./Ha. *Hectolitres per hectare.*
M. *Metayeur.* P. *Proprietaire.* P.C. *Premier Cru.*
PTG. *Passe-tout-Grains.* R. *Regional Appellation.*
V. *Village Appellation.*

Explanation of Tables

1. Grands Crus: at the foot of the relevant commune chapter, for each commune which has one or more Grands Crus, a table is given, giving the name, area, number of proprietors and approximate annual yield in cases of each Grand Cru.

2. Domaines: the vineyard holdings of each profiled Domaine are tabulated at the end of the profile. These tables are taken from information supplied by the Domaine and include the commune, name and status – Grand Cru, Premier Cru etc. – of each vineyard, the Domaine's holding, expressed in hectares and 100ths of a hectare, the average vine age(s) or date of planting, and the status under which the Domaine exploits the vines – Proprietor, *Metayeur* or *Fermier.*

In reading these it shuld be remembered that a Domaine which exists as a company may farm or share-crop vines belonging to its individual owners – so F. or M. beside an entry does not necessarily mean that those vines are owned by some third party. Equally, where a Domaine is a *Metayeur*, the land holding shown may in some cases represent the total area worked by the Domaine; if it has to cede half the crop to the landlord, then the figure will not truly reflect its own production. Domaines were asked to list vineyard areas which correspond to their own production.

This information was collected between October 1990 and February 1991.

Contents

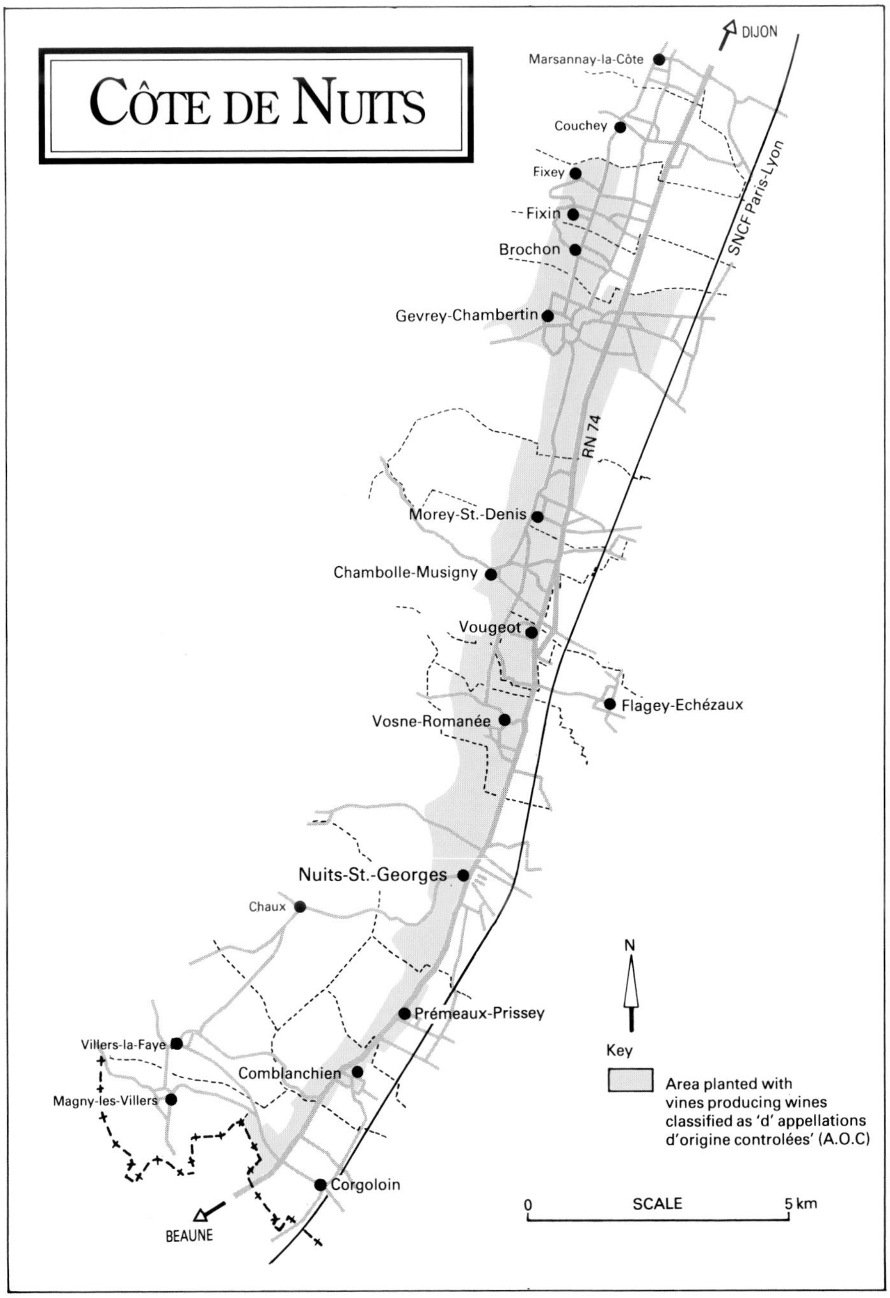

CÔTE DE NUITS
DIJON
Marsannay-la-Côte
Couchey
Fixey
Fixin
Brochon
Gevrey-Chambertin
SNCF Paris-Lyon
RN 74
Morey-St.-Denis
Chambolle-Musigny
Vougeot
Flagey-Echézaux
Vosne-Romanée
Nuits-St.-Georges
Chaux
Prémeaux-Prissey
Villers-la-Faye
Comblanchien
Magny-les-Villers
Corgoloin
BEAUNE
N
Key
Area planted with vines producing wines classified as 'd' appellations d'origine controlées' (A.O.C)
0
SCALE
5 km

Côte de Beaune

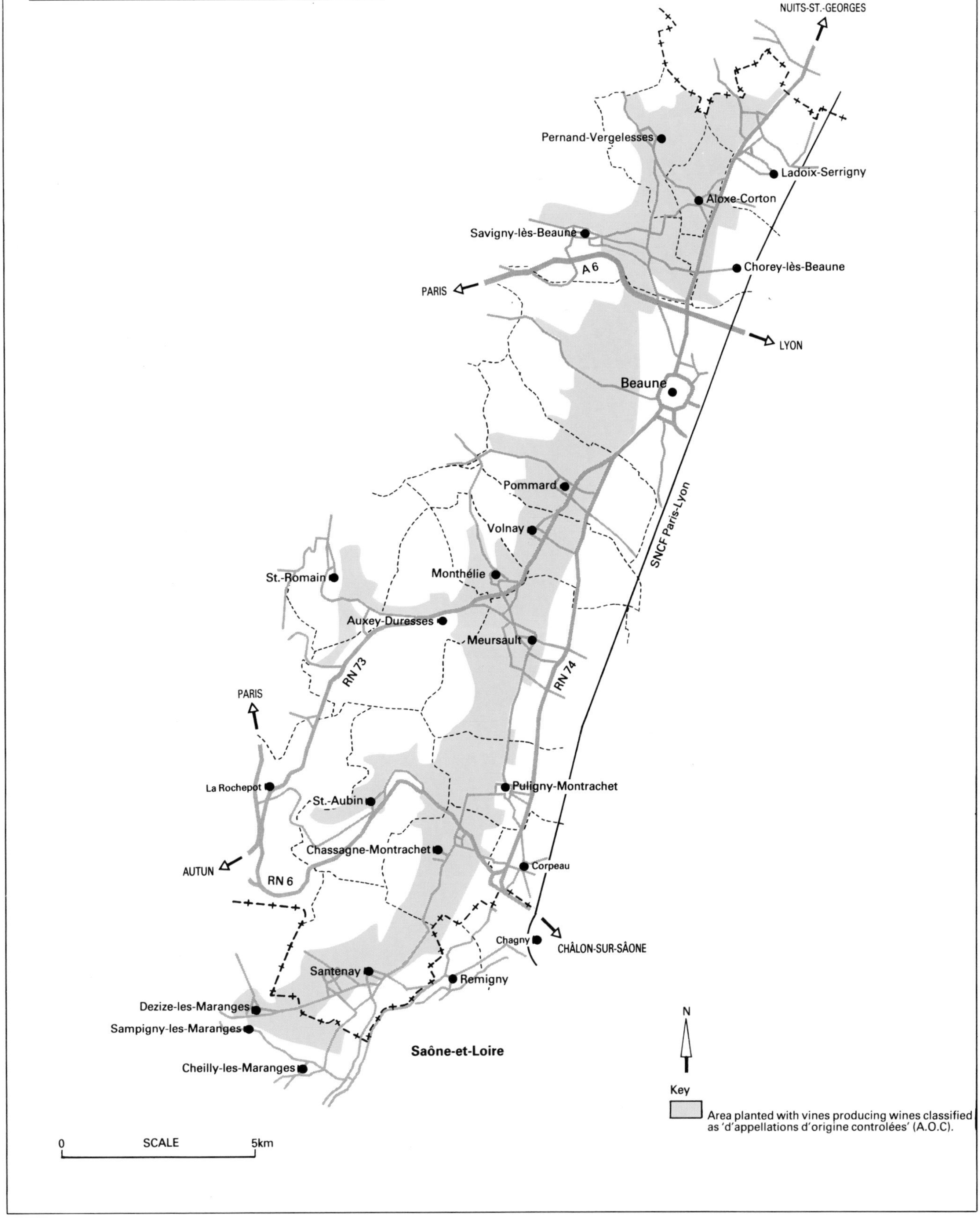
NUITS-ST.-GEORGES
Pernand-Vergelesses
Ladoix-Serrigny
Aloxe-Corton
Savigny-lès-Beaune
Chorey-lès-Beaune
A 6
PARIS
LYON
Beaune
Pommard
SNCF Paris-Lyon
Volnay
Monthélie
St.-Romain
Auxey-Duresses
Meursault
RN 73
RN 74
PARIS
La Rochepot
St.-Aubin
Puligny-Montrachet
Chassagne-Montrachet
Corpeau
AUTUN
RN 6
Chagny
CHÂLON-SUR-SÂONE
Santenay
Remigny
Dezize-les-Maranges
Sampigny-les-Maranges
Cheilly-les-Maranges
Saône-et-Loire
N
Key
Area planted with vines producing wines classified as 'd'appellations d'origine controlées' (A.O.C).
0
SCALE
5km

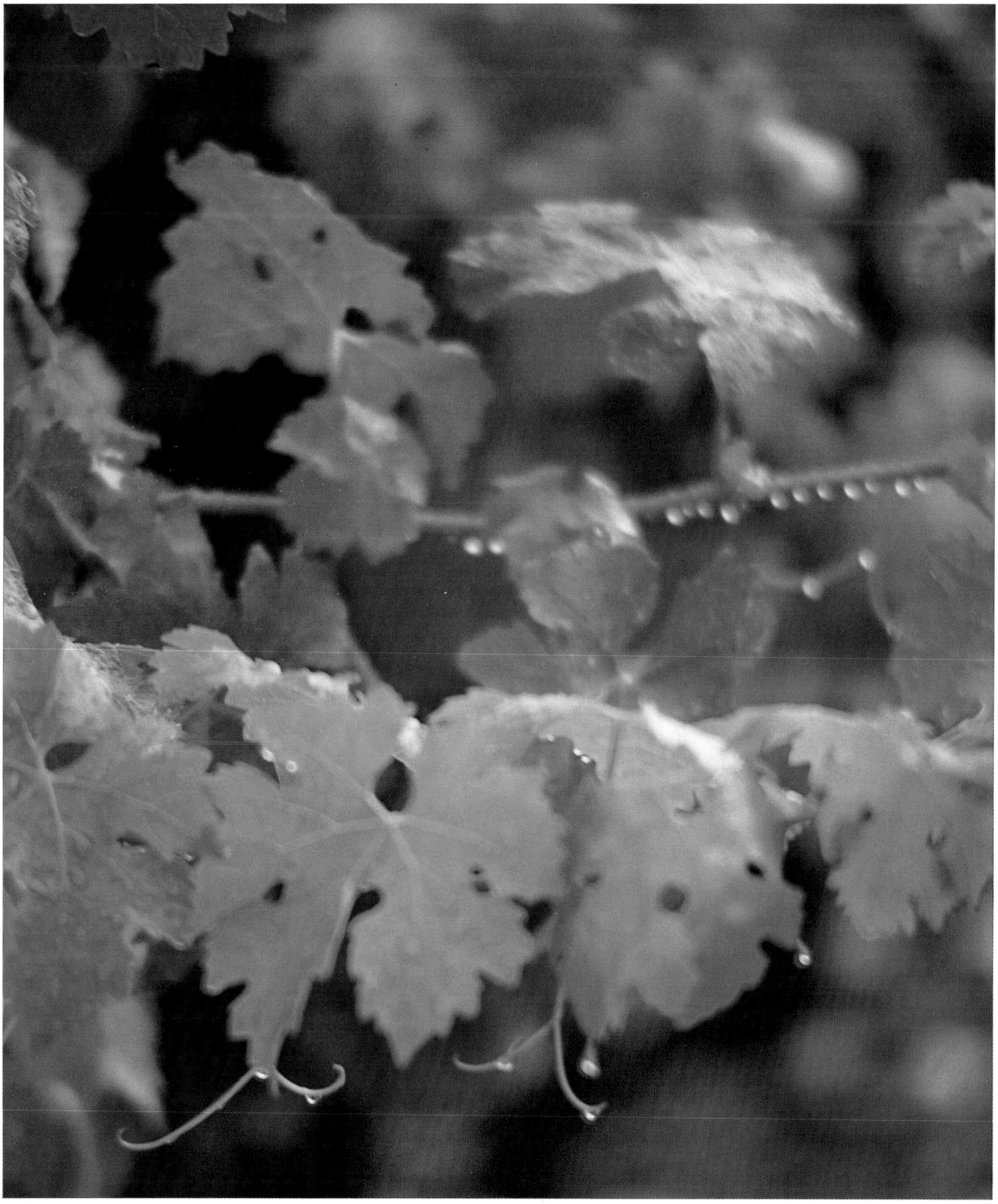

FOREWORD

There is no more heart-warming sight than the almost unbroken vista of vines carpeting the lower slopes of the Côte de Beaune. One drives, in a leisurely but careful way (the RN74 is notoriously dangerous), from Dijon to Beaune, a route punctuated by the most evocative signs to villages, the names of which sound like a roll call of the most voluptuous red wines of the world: Chambolle-Musigny, Vougeot, Vosne-Romanée . . . The vineyards themselves form a rhythmic pattern of parallel lines changing from the brown of winter, the light, bright green of the spring and early summer, the lush green of September and autumn russet after the harvest: one huge park more akin to a series of expensive individually-owned allotments.

Beyond the ancient walled town of Beaune, the expanse of vineyards continues, the view to the right being broader, the slopes further from the main road. But the rows of vines are endless, and the list of famous village names goes on: Volnay, Pommard, Meursault, Puligny, Chassagne . . .

It is within these villages that the growers live and maintain their cellars. Their way is quite different from Bordeaux. The countryside is different. The vineyards of Bordeaux, particularly in the Médoc, are smugly self-contained; each has its own château and chai within the confines of the property; each property has one resident or absentee proprietor. In Burgundy there is no equivalent to the 'château' of Bordeaux. The word 'Domaine' is proprietorial yet more nebulous – a personal or *société anonyme* estate made up of small vineyard parcels, often mere strips of vines, individually tended, the wines very individually made.

The man who introduced me to fine wine almost half a century ago, when asked what was the difference between Bordeaux and Burgundy, answered 'about 400 miles': the differences were too vast to explain. They are different worlds: different climate – one maritime, the other continental; different soils, different vine varieties but, above all, different people. I have always felt that Burgundians are closer to the soil. The vineyards are but a step outside each village boundary, some only a few minutes walk from the centre of that lovely, old – and very rich – town of Beaune.

The people and their 'domaines': these are the keys to Burgundy and the subjects of this book.

In Burgundy, the name of the grower is as significant as that of the parcel of vines he tends, no matter how grand the *grand cru*. To get to know the maker and his domaine is to know the wine.

Not everyone, even nowadays, realises that there can be an immense difference in style and quality between one Nuits-St.-Georges – or Pommard or Meursault – and another; those more knowledgeable do know that wines made from vines grown in an individual but sub-divided, named vineyard can vary markedly. This book explains how and why.

There is no wine on earth as elevating as a great Burgundy: richness of 'robe', intensity of bouquet, a velvety liquid that expands in the mouth, reaching – flooding – the head and heart. This sort of wine does not make itself. It is made by individuals, by stalwart characters dedicated to making the best wine their well-tended vines can produce following an invariably unpredictable growing season. Burgundy is easy to drink, speciously easy to criticise, fiendishly difficult to make.

And what about the author? Remington Norman is not a writer new to wine. He is a fellow Master of Wine, with a lifetime in the wine trade. Based in London, principally as a retailer, he gained long experience buying and selling the wines of Burgundy, as well as those of Alsace and the Rhône valley, selecting the real thing for his most discerning clientèle from a mass of familiar and not so familiar names being touted by importers and *négociants*. He has been driven, inexorably, to explore the villages of Burgundy, to talk at length to the wine-makers and investigate their methods, discovering for himself first hand who, at the foot of those 'golden slopes', is making the best and the true.

Remington combines the soul of an artist, the level head of a businessman and an enquiring mind. No other book on Burgundy deals so thoroughly and approachably with the philosophy and techniques of individual growers and wine-makers. He writes lucidly, unpretentiously and with authority. What he has discerned and written about will add greatly to our understanding as well as our knowledge of one of the most complex and, at best, unsurpassed wines of the world.

Michael Broadbent
Christie's, London
December 1991

Introduction

Of all the world's great wine-producing regions Burgundy is widely seen as one of the most difficult to understand. This reputation reflects both the impression that it is unpredictable – there seems to be no certainty that one bottle of a given appellation will taste anything like another – and the feeling that, all too frequently, price seems to bear little relation to quality. If, to these frustrations, one adds the difficulty of getting to grips with an apparently structureless plethora of appellations, vineyards and growers, it is hardly surprising that amateurs and professionals alike are deterred from further exploration. Even seasoned wine-lovers, faced with a range of Burgundies on a shop shelf or restaurant wine-list, may turn towards the more predictable attractions of Bordeaux or elsewhere, rather than risk an expensive disappointment, whilst many restaurateurs and wine-merchants who would like to discover more, find it hard to know where to start.

This state of affairs is unfortunate, but understandable. Burgundy has unquestionably suffered from comparison with Bordeaux, where the uncluttered structure of a few clearly defined appellations and a relatively small number of large estates, each producing one or two wines, has undeniable appeal. There, knowing the appellation or the property gives a measure of security and predictability which Burgundy seems to lack.

Burgundy has also suffered needless, self-inflicted harm from giving its name to far too much mediocre wine. Poor quality blurs differences between appellations, making wine from one commune taste much like that from any other, and when expensive Grand Cru turns out dilute and meagre compared with Village wine at one-fifth of the price, the credibility of the grading system crumbles and the image of the region is inevitably tarnished. It only takes a handful of indifferent wines to goad a confused buyer into enquiring whether Vosne-Romanée really differs from Vougeot or Volnay, and whether producers' names have anything more than a tangential bearing on the contents of the bottle. He might even be tempted to conclude that appellations are merely distinctions without differences and that Burgundy is nothing more than a disorderly patchwork of variegated brands.

This irritating unpredictability leaves many struggling to make sense of the appellation system while wondering what it is about Burgundy that seems to generate such excitement. Do the opulent, sensuous wines they have read so much about really exist, or are these simply the figments of wine-writers' over-stimulated imaginations?

Faced with such an unrewarding lottery, some abandon the quest for this elusive Grail; others soldier on, often limiting their researches to a favourite appellation or producer because of a bottle once enjoyed. In both cases the best of Burgundy eludes them.

Fortunately, as this book demonstrates, great Burgundy still exists – and not just within the confines of a few famously expensive Domaines. Furthermore, despite its apparent complexity, the region is not particularly complicated. However, to understand Burgundy properly it is essential to know how it is structured and to appreciate its rather unusual and fragmented system of production.

The primary purpose of this book is to de-mystify Burgundy and to enable those who have either lost heart, or found the entire subject too intimidating to embark upon at all, to navigate the minefield with confidence. By presenting this greatest of wine regions through the perspective of the entities which really matter – the Domaines – one can separate the real magic of the wines from the rather interwoven structures which define them.

The rest of this introduction provides background to what follows; it summarises the scope and aims of the book, describes the structure of the Côte d'Or and explains the basis upon which the 111 great Domaines included here were selected. It also outlines some important recent trends, setting Burgundy into its modern context.

Scope and Outline

Viticultural Burgundy extends over a large area of eastern France, comprising, from north to south: Chablis, the Côte d'Or, the Côte Chalonnaise, the Maconnais and the Beaujolais. Since covering all this thoroughly would far outcompass a single volume, the present scope is limited to the heart of Burgundy – the Côte d'Or, a narrow 55 km. strip of land extending south, from the outskirts of Dijon to just beyond Santenay. Here are to be found the world-famous villages and vineyards which produce most of the region's finest wines.

In this book, the Côte d'Or is viewed from three different perspectives. First, the finest Domaines and the people who run them are profiled in detail together with an account of how they handle their vines and grapes, in order to discover how great wine is made and why some estates consistently out-perform others. Second, a short account is given of each of the Côte's principal communes – its history, wine and most important vineyards. These, accompanied by newly-drawn, detailed maps, are designed to show how each commune fits into the overall context of the Côte. Third, a section of background chapters draws together several important threads influencing viticulture and wine-making and reflects on matters related to buying, tasting and enjoying Burgundy; included is an assessment of vintages from 1945 to 1991. These chapters show that tasting – important as it undoubtedly is – is only one element in true wine appreciation; one also needs to understand how wine is put together and the many factors which contribute to quality. A glossary of technical terms is included, defining words italicised in the main text. Some French terms translate poorly, but every effort has been made to render them intelligible.

In writing this book, I have tried to keep in view the 'typical reader' – someone, whether amateur or professional, who is interested in broadening their knowledge and appreciation of Burgundy. If the book is to have any permanent value for them beyond mere anecdote, some technical explanation is inevitable; this I have made as assimilable as possible without sacrificing important detail. There is nothing here which should baffle an intelligent reader, even with a non-technical background.

The Structure of the Côte d'Or

Geographically the Côte is subdivided into 28 villages or communes – in effect, small parishes. Those comprising the northerly sector, from Marsannay to Corgolion, are collectively known as the Côte de Nuits – based on the town of Nuits-St.-Georges – whilst those adjoining it to the south, from Ladoix-Serrigny to Santenay, form the Côte de Beaune – based on the rather larger town of Beaune.

Surrounding each village is an area of vineyards which, as the maps show, is relatively small and heavily subdivided into individually named vineyard sites. Although to the passing visitor there is little to distinguish one patch of vines from another, all have been meticulously measured and mapped, and their borders precisely delineated. With very few exceptions, each vineyard

is divided among several different growers, each the proprietor of designated vines, from which he makes his own wine. For example, the Bâtard-Montrachet vineyard has some 49 individual owners and the Clos de Vougeot no fewer than 82. So, it would be possible, in theory at least, to line up 49 bottles of Bâtard-Montrachet and 82 of Clos de Vougeot in any given vintage, each bearing the name of a different producer. Although there might be broad similarities in taste between such bottles of 'the same' wine, these would be eclipsed by the differences, particularly in quality, reflecting the differing competence of individual vignerons, It is this fragmentation and diversity which vitiates the Bordeaux comparison – there is only one Château Latour 1991, whilst there are at least as many Bâtard-Montrachet 1991s or Clos de Vougeot 1991s as there are owners of these vineyards; and it is this which makes Burgundy so frustrating and yet such a fascinating challenge.

The skill of the grower is not the only determinant of quality. The vineyards themselves also differ significantly in quality potential – a fact reflected in the Appellation Contrôlée system which grades each vineyard into one of four categories: Régionale, Village, Premier Cru and Grand Cru, in ascending order (see Appellations and Quality Control, p.244, for a more detailed explanation of this system).

Superimposed on the differences between vineyards and growers are important differences in style (largely due to soils) between the wines of the communes themselves. So, whilst for example a Volnay Premier Cru can be expected to outclass a Volnay Village wine, both should differ in character from the wines of neighbouring Pommard. The pattern is thus complex – but logical.

Individual land-holdings are small – often no more than a fraction of a hectare in any one vineyard. So to establish a viable business, a grower (or Domaine) will generally own a portfolio of plots in several sites – a few rows here, half a hectare there etc. – not only within the home commune, but often further afield. These are likely to be spread over different quality levels. From each individual appellation, a different wine will be produced, vinified and bottled separately. This again contrasts vividly with Bordeaux, where Châteaux have a few large chunks of vines in a single appellation, all contributing to one or two wines. By comparison, the Côte d'Or is highly fragmented in its pattern of production and ownership.

The prospective buyer is therefore theoretically faced with a vast array of wine – 28 communes, 4 separate levels of quality, innumerable individual vineyard sites and several thousand growers – from which to choose. Fortunately, it is neither necessary, nor realistic, to expect to know even a fraction of these first-hand. Anyone looking for reliable Burgundy of better than average quality needs only to concentrate on the relatively small number of estates for whom quality is the top priority. Domaines differ considerably: some consistently produce magnificent wine, some manage excellence now and then, and for others one keeps the proverbial barge-pole permanently to hand.

The Côte d'Or must therefore be seen as a fragmented patchwork of small, individual estates, each producing a range of wines – from basic quality Régionale to Premier or Grand Cru. Within this framework, the name of the producer is the single most reliable indicator of quality, transcending even the grading of the vineyard or the vintage. The grower/Domaine is therefore the key to unlocking Burgundy.

Selection

Selecting just over 110 Domaines from the Côte's rich array was no easy task. The basis upon which it was done needs some explanation and, since no selection will please everyone, some justification.

The principles of selection were dominated by the determination that the final choice should reflect merit rather than either land-holdings or reputation – a lavish marketing budget and the consequent high profile are not always matched by wine quality. In deciding who to include, I have been influenced by two overriding considerations: firstly, absolute quality – the ability to produce something especially fine, in its class; and secondly, consistency – that dimension of year-on-year excellence which gives one the impression that a bottle from this Domaine, whatever its Appellation or vintage, would rarely, if ever, disappoint. The Domaines profiled here fulfil both these criteria.

Although this book is devoted to the best, it is not entirely a paean of praise. There are several Domaines, some of high repute, which regularly turn out disgracefully poor wine. Some recognise their shortcomings, and are striving to put things right; others shrug off their mediocrity, seemingly content to enjoy the lavish profits which even poor Grands and Premiers Crus are still capable of generating. Within the bounds of fair comment, these Domaines are identified. Their continuing prosperity is, however, in doubt, as ever more value-conscious markets baulk at exorbitant asking-prices for indifferent quality.

As well as already knowing many of the Domaines visited, the fortune of a trio of excellent vintages – 1988, 1989 and 1990 – made the timing of my visits fortuitous and the task of assessment much easier. Furthermore, the more difficult 1987 vintage proved useful as a diagnostic – an additional comparator. Whilst it is relatively easy to produce a respectable wine given fine land and a good, ripe growing season (although some even manage to fail this test), it is the skill at dealing with the lesser vintages which usually sorts out the great from the good. This observation must be tempered with the realisation that even the finest wine-maker is not immune from mistakes – sometimes even disasters. These growers would be the first to admit to imperfection – and would probably ascribe to their failures some of the motivation which keeps them striving for excellence.

The logistics of selection were straightforward. A short list of Domaines was compiled, helped by some 20 years experience of buying Burgundy. These were approached and, with a few exceptions, visited between October 1990 and February

1991. All, whether good or less good, were treated on equal terms, both to ensure fairness and to provide useful reference points on the quality scale.

Each of the 170 visits followed a similar pattern: an in-depth interview covering history, viticultural and vinification practices and as extensive a tasting as possible – recent vintages on the spot, with samples of 1987s being taken back to London for further, comparative, assessment. From this, the list was whittled down to the 111 Domaines included here.

Of the Domaines originally solicited, almost all were most co-operative, with two, unfortunately important, exceptions – the Domaine de la Pousse d'Or in Volnay, where M. Potel broke a long-standing appointment which could not be reinstated, and Domaines Leroy in Auxey-Duresses and Charles Noëllat in Vosne-Romanée where permission to visit was refused by the owner, Mme. Bize-Leroy. I regret these omissions, and recognise the gaps that they create.

For the rest, I have deliberately omitted the Hospices de Beaune, since all its wine is dispersed in barrel at the famous Hospices auction each November, making the final quality of its wines dependent upon the skill in *élevage* of each purchaser. The estate therefore has no real identity beyond its vineyards. Also excluded are estates whose wines are normally made by others, such as Baron Thenard and the Duc de Magenta.

However, I have deliberately included assessments of a couple of less than excellent Domaines, since I believe that their failings are useful illustrations of what can go wrong, in spite of genuine efforts towards quality.

Although the aim was to cover the Côte d'Or, this was done with no prima facie idea of how the final selection would be distributed between the communes. No attempt was made to massage standards so that equal numbers of Domaines appeared under each commune chapter. As they fell out, so they appear.

There are a few other factors affecting the final selection, which merit specific comment. It is generally recognised that some communes are inherently capable of producing better wine than others – Volnay than Monthelie or Puligny than St.-Aubin, for example – a matter of *terroir*. Even a moderately good Puligny Premier Cru will probably outclass a St.-Aubin Premier Cru, however well-made. I have therefore allowed for such relative strengths and weaknesses, in assessing the Domaines.

No attempt has been made to put the Domaines into any order of merit – since I believe these to serve no useful purpose, especially in a region where a single estate may produce a score, or more, of wines in a single vintage. The fact that the profiles vary widely in length reflects nothing more than the intrinsic interest of the Domaine being discussed – some vignerons are distinctly more innovative or loquacious than others – and should not be taken as an indication of status. Conversely, from the fact that a Domaine is omitted altogether, it would be wrong to conclude that it produces poor wine. This selection simply represents the finest from the Côte; there are many other meritorious Domaines producing excellent wines, if not at the topmost level.

In the end, whether a Domaine or an individual wine is considered great rather than just good, is a matter of personal opinion. Nevertheless, in making such an invidious selection, there are bound to be omissions and injustices – not least because it is impossible, try as one may, to eradicate completely the accumulated impressions of 20 years buying, tasting and drinking. I hope that these are few, and that those who feel hard done by will appreciate the difficulties.

Recent trends (welcome)

The Côte d'Or is a collection of strong-minded individuals who have their own perceptions of what fine wine should be and their own methods of realising them. From these deep-rooted convictions they are not easily shaken. However, recent years, in particular the decade of the 1980s, have seen developments which are important in the broader context of Burgundy and its wines – not specific events perhaps, but welcome evolutions which are precursors of better all-round quality.

The most significant changes are those in the collective mentality of growers; in particular, the novel discovery that greater openness, instead of making one vulnerable, can be of mutual benefit. The older guard is now ceding responsibility to a younger, formally trained generation of vignerons, who are used to discussing wine-making problems openly, with friends, and to tasting each others' wines critically, together. This was virtually unheard of after the last war, when wines were made behind closed doors and when you were left alone to cover up any mistake, preferably without anyone knowing it had happened.

This trend has come in the wake of another: much greater technological knowledge and control of wine-making. So now, even modest-sized Domaines have both the knowledge of what can be done, and the technical means at their disposal to implement their ideas. Today, technically incompetent wines are fewer and growers have little excuse for sloppy wine-making. Much of what passed for 'tradition' was no more than the slavish adherence to antiquated practices, both because they worked with acceptable frequency and also because there was no

alternative. Now that research has enabled growers who want to, to understand how means relate to ends, tradition is being replaced by flexibility – a willingness to adapt vinification to the character of the vintage – and the accumulated dogmatic baggage of generations is, albeit with some nostalgic reluctance, being slowly discarded.

Growers are also realising that quality pays. They are aware of an enticingly vast international market, but realise that, with the advent of substantial quantities of excellent, attractively-priced wines from outside France, the competition for the consumer is severe.

Enlightened growers are adapting to this trend. They are prepared to make short-term sacrifices by declassifying substandard wine or by selling it in bulk, to harvest late and restrict yields, and to adopt vinification practices designed to produce wines of concentration and quality. They realise that the long-term advantages of such a policy far outweigh any immediate pecuniary gains. If you are recognised as a 'no compromise on quality' Domaine, then you can charge high prices and still have no difficulty in selling your wine.

As more and more Domaines produce better quality, they also realise the financial advantages of marketing their own wines, rather than of selling them in bulk to négociants. The great négociant houses of Beaune and Nuits, which effectively dominated the market in Burgundy until the 1970s, are finding their regular sources of supply drying up. Those really dedicated to quality have secured their future with the purchase of vineyards and will continue to produce excellent, reliable wines. Others, however, drift steadily downwards in quality, supplying that sector of the market which is only concerned with label and price. As a result, the market is becoming polarised, with the serious sector concentrating on the finest Domaines, for whose wines buyers prepared to pay top prices.

These trends have led to great prosperity, with Domaines becoming sufficiently profitable to attract the younger generation back to the Côte, either to take over family Domaines or to establish their own, even though wine-making might not have been a family tradition. In the well-established Domaines, parents and grandparents are increasingly prepared to hand over responsiblity to their successors before they retire, and the 'patron to the end' mentality is definitely in decline.

Recent trends (unwelcome)

Not all recent trends are beneficial. Many a vigneron trying to run his small estate, helped by his wife and a worker or two, finds himself beset by an ever-increasing administrative workload. Selling in bulk was easy – one invoice, a few appellation certificates and that was it. Now, on top of a general increase in declarations of this or records of that, every bottle sale has to be accounted for individually and many more customers and their enquiries dealt with, which is leading some growers to lament that they are becoming glorified bureaucrats, spending more time shovelling paper round their offices than out in their vineyards.

By far the worst trend to have hit the Côte's vignerons in recent years is the phenomenal increase in land values, brought about by a heavy demand, in particular from wealthy corporations, for the little good vineyard land offered for sale. Insurance companies, pension funds and banks seem willing to pay exorbitant prices, especially for Premiers and Grands Crus, which bear no sensible relation to economic return – now estimated at 1–2% on notional capital value. So, whilst on paper even a modest Domaine may be worth several million francs, this is of little benefit to the owner, since it has no bearing whatsoever on how he calculates his wine prices and thus no impact on his annual income.

What these often exaggerated values do bear upon are inheritance and capital taxes. The former, levied when the owner of the Domaine dies, presents heart-rending difficulties since, although notionally of high net worth, the inheritor(s) will rarely have enough disposable cash to meet their tax liabilities, and there is then no alternative to selling part of the family patrimony to pay the bill.

High vineyard values also affect annual taxes levied on capital assets – the 'wealth tax' – which, in France, is charged both on vineyards and on stock. This mitigates against quality in two ways: the less cash a vigneron has, the more he is tempted to cut corners; also, obliged to pay tax on any stock in the cellars, many growers will submit to the attractions of producing quick-maturing, early-selling wines to minimise their inventory.

On top of everything, the Code Napoléon, which governs inheritance in France, requires that assets, including land, be split equally between surviving children. This further subdivides estates, unless the legatees can be persuaded to keep their vines within a single exploiting company.

The more enlightened growers now operate under a corporate structure which provides a limited buffer against eventual taxation and subdivision, since it is only the shares which are valued and change hands. However, this is no more than a short-term palliative. There is a strong case for the French government acting to make a special case of viticulture, both to allow vignerons to keep their Domaines intact, and also to prevent this unique vineyard land from falling into the hands of remote banks and insurance companies, which may not always have the production of fine wine as their top priority.

These trends and evolutions further complicate the already fragmented pattern of the Côte and add to the difficulty of getting to grips with its Domaines.

The outlook of the wine-maker

How a wine-maker, wherever he happens to be, sets about making his wine, depends to a great extent on his philosophy – how he sees his role. For most if not all of these Great Domaines, the primary concern is to preserve, in each wine, the typicity of the vineyard which produced the grapes. This typicity is indissolubly linked to the concept of *terroir* – to the idea that soil and microclimate contribute significantly to the individual qualities, and the quality, of a wine. This is the anchor premise on which the entire appellation system is founded.

Although the notion of *terroir* is controversial and has yet to gain wide acceptance in much of the New World, where the grape variety and fruit ripeness seem to take precedence, there are few honest tasters who would deny its importance in the Côte d'Or where genuine differences exist between the wine of one commune or vineyard and that of its neighbours.

This contrast points up two entirely different wine-making perspectives, both of which are to be found in Burgundy. There are those who regard themselves as mere intermediaries between *terroir* and wine – vinous midwives, whose role is to assist the grapes they have harvested to deliver their maximum potential for expressing their origins. In this, they regard themselves as essentially passive players, only intervening when absolutely necessary.

Others take the view that, like chefs, their job is to create a wine – to use the means at their disposal to transform the grapes into a style of their own choosing. They do not deny the importance of *terroir*, but argue that fine wine is perfectly compatible with several different expressions of the same origin. Theirs is an active role, intervening here and there to produce their own style of wine. Although each would probably contest the validity of the other's philosophy, neither is obviously wrong, and both are capable of producing superlative wine.

Shortcomings of the system

Whilst these and other Domaines will continue as producers of excellence, there is much that the regulatory authorities could do to raise the lowest common quality factor in Burgundy and to prevent some of the appalling abuses of the system which they are supposed to control. Some of these are discussed in the text. But, in the hope that this might provoke some action, it is worth restating the most urgently needed reforms.

Firstly, there should be an AC-specific register of permitted clones and rootstocks for use in Côte d'Or vineyards; this would prevent the planting of maladapted or indifferent material which inexorably leads to inferior wine. Secondly, greater efforts should be made to police the existing yield restrictions and to limit permitted yields to healthy vineyards; allowing a grower to harvest a maximum yield from a diseased vineyard where a proportion of the vines are dead or missing is a manifest absurdity. Thirdly, fractional *chaptalisation* should be legalised forthwith – it is recognised by growers and independent oenologists alike as indispensable to quality. Finally, and most importantly, the existing controls should be rigorously enforced to ensure that mediocre wine submitted for tasting, for appellation approval, is declassified or rejected altogether if it fails to meet high standards, and that tasting juries are as independent as practicably possible of the local market and its vested interests.

For all its fragmentation and idiosyncrasy, or perhaps because of it, the Côte d'Or is a magical place; small, intimate and determinedly individual. At its best it produces sensational, sensuous wines, which leave one marvelling, almost in disbelief, that the contents of a glass are no more than the transformation of bunches of grapes.

The growers are as interesting a range of personalities as can be found anywhere – warm, friendly, abundantly welcoming and hard-working, for whom the bonhomie and joie de vivre which invariably accompany good wine conceal a profound dedication to the unique land with which they have been entrusted. This book brings some of these vignerons and their Domaines into more public relief. I hope that they, and the Côte d'Or, will benefit from that process.

MARSANNAY-LA-CÔTE

Leaving the traffic clot which is central Dijon, the visitor, if he manages to fathom the eccentricities of French sign-posting and locates the correct artery, will soon find himself on Napoléon III's RN 74 – la Voie Royale – travelling down the Côte de Nuits towards Nuits-St.-Georges and Beaune.

Although most of the vineyards on the outskirts of Dijon – La Côte Dijonnaise – have long been swallowed up by urban sprawl, a few remain, notably the 'Montre-Cul' so named because women working on the steeply inclined slope involuntarily showed off their ample bottoms.

The first wine commune of any significance one encounters is Marsannay, a rather pedestrian village of 6,000 inhabitants which keeps alive on a modest tourist trade, encouraged by a developing wine industry. In 1783, probably fearful of being gobbled up by its larger neighbour, it tacked 'La Côte' on to its designation, to remind predatory officials in Dijon of where its real allegiance lay.

Marsannay has a long connection with viticulture: wine was being produced here under religious aegis in the middle of the seventh century, and Charlemagne is said to have stopped in the village under a tree next to a fountain in La Charme. Despite this recommendation, however, the advent of the railway in the middle of the nineteenth century engineered the replacement of the Gamays of Marsannay with the more robust,

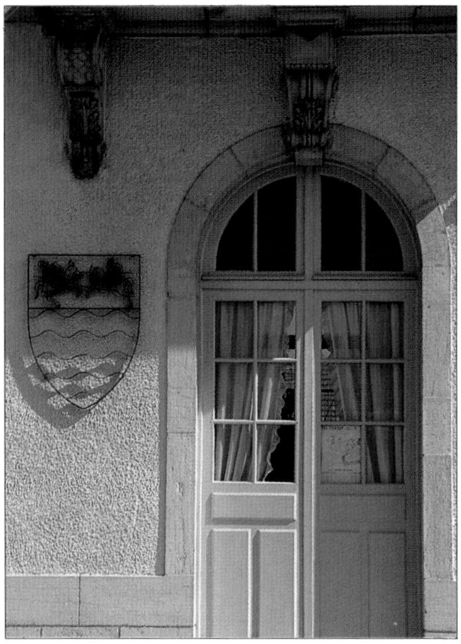

The Mairie

alcoholic beverages of the Midi.

The commune saw its fortunes steadily decline until, by the beginning of this century, matters had become so serious that the village was reduced to within a hair's breadth of financial ruin. Then, in what amounted to a stroke of marketing genius, a local grower, Joseph Clair, decided that the impetus of a new product was needed. Accordingly, 'on 22nd September 1919' to quote Anthony Hanson, he invented Marsannay Rosé. This wine, made by light pressing of Pinot Noir and vinification 'à gris', rapidly became the fashionable drink of Dijon café society of the day and its popularity restored the fortunes of the growers and put the village back on the wine map.

However, things got worse when the appellations were delimited in the 1930s, because the commune was given neither its own AC nor the right to the catch-all designation of Côte de Nuits-Villages. It seemed to have been forgotten in the rush, ending up with mere Bourgogne, or Côte Dijonnaise, which no one wanted anyway. Decline set in again: by 1962 the area of land under vine amounted to 29 ha. and during the 20 years which followed it sank to virtual extinction at a mere 19 ha.

The vignerons decided that they were entitled to their own AC and set about a legal battle to convince the *INAO* of their case. Some 20 years later, in 1987, Marsannay – together with northerly neighbour Chenove and southerly Couchey – was granted the appellation Marsannay for red, white and rosé wines.

Fortunes restored, growers set about capitalising on their hard-won appellation which presently covers some 512 ha. of land. Much of the 300 ha. currently in production had to be reclaimed from scrub before it could be replanted. Whilst most of the lower lying land bordering the RN 74 is designated for rosé alone, the more steeply sloping vineyards behind the village are considered finer and zoned for red, white or rosé.

Since the grant of AC status, there has been a strong revival of interest in the commune. Land continues to be reclaimed and replanted at a fierce rate, and anything available is easily sold, for high prices.

The heart of the appellation is some 65 *climats* stretching from Chenove to just south of Couchey. These vineyards, exposed marginally south of east, exhibit a mixture of soils of which the principal constituent is limestone. Patches of richer clay soil are restricted to regional appellations, such as Bourgogne Grande Ordinaire. Some, on higher, better drained ground, are prone to suffer from drought in particularly hot and dry years such as 1989 and 1990.

There has been much debate over the question of whether some favoured sites merit Premier Cru status. Henri Cannard lists over 20 individual vineyards which he considers produce finer wine than the rest. However, there seems to be no imminent move towards a reclassification.

Marsannay has around 40 growers producing some 22,000 cases of white, 120,000 cases of red and between 13,000 and 33,000 cases of rosé annually. In particularly abundant years, such as 1982, the proportion of rosé increases as vignerons *saignent* their red cuves.

The white, made principally from Chardonnay, although there is still some Pinot Beurot and Aligoté in the vineyards, can be good, somewhat rustic, sappy stuff. It will age, but is best drunk young.

The rosé, though no longer fashionable, has a small faithful following. It is a sound, firm, dry wine which can stand up to a variety of food, especially the rather rich reconstituted offerings which pass for the gastronomic end of charcuterie in the area. It is, however, much better as an aperitif or with a piece of cold fish – Bruno Clair, grandson of the inventor, makes by far the best version.

The future will undoubtedly bring more recognition to Marsannay; the acquisition in 1985 by Louis Jadot of the village's greatest Domaine, Clair Dau, is certain to raise its profile significantly and the collective efforts of the commune to establish an identity for itself seem to be bearing fruit.

Behind the church

Domaine Bruno Clair

MARSANNAY

Bruno Clair's excellent Domaine has grown out of a certain amount of Burgundian misfortune. His grandfather Joseph Clair married a Mlle. Däu in 1910, a union which gave birth to three children – Bernard, Monique and Nöelle – Marsannay Rosé and the Domaine Clair Däu. This Domaine, formed in 1950 to run the family vineyards, which had by then been divided between them, was regarded by many as one of the finest in the Côte, with Grand and Premier Cru land in Gevrey-Chambertin and Chambolle-Musigny.

This worked well until the late 1970s when family dissension broke out, principally over whether to distribute profits or to re-invest them in the Domaine. As usual, one of the children wanted to take out as much as possible – her husband's business was not doing too well – whilst the others wanted to plough the profits back.

Matters came to a head in 1980 when Bernard, exasperated by increasingly bitter family warfare and damaging restrictions – for example, he was not allowed to buy essentials, such as new casks – left to start up on his own. His sister Noëlle took over the management but did not succeed in quelling the dissension. In 1985 she sold her vines – Etournelles St.-Jacques, Clos St.-Jacques, Chambertin Clos de Bèze, Chambolle-Musigny Les Amoureuses and the Clos Vougeot – to Maison Louis Jadot in Beaune. So was a great Domaine split up.

Bernard's son Bruno was thus left without the Domaine which he might otherwise have expected to run. In 1978, after working with his father for a short while, he started to replant a parcel of his own in Marsannay, rented some vineyards in nearby Fixin and bought some scrub land for planting in Morey-St.-Denis. During the 1980s he built up his Domaine to its present size of 17.90 ha. – all *en fermage* except for 0.5 ha. of Marsannay.

During 1985–86 his mother and father, together with 4 brothers and a sister, formed a company with Bruno to farm their own vineyards, which are all now marketed under the label Domaine Bruno Clair.

Shortly after all this upheaval, Bruno Clair recruited Philippe Brun, a talented wine-maker who had worked for both Domaine Couvreur and Louis Jadot. Philippe is engagingly enthusiastic about his wines – realising perhaps that, unlike wine-makers at Domaines with only a handful of wines from their own locality, he has the opportunity to make and taste wines from throughout Burgundy. 'Let's make a little tour round the Côte,' he invites, waving his pipette at a bank of barrels.

Bruno Clair at work with his secateurs

Bruno Clair is an enthusiastic, fast-talking man, with a deep knowledge of the Côte in general and of Marsannay in particular. His expertise is by no means just theoretical, but extends to vineyard and cellar work, of which he has considerable experience.

He believes that good viticulture comes from knowing your vines – their personalities and characteristics – and from the minimum interference with their environment. Thus, his vineyards are treated as organically as possible; only humus and organic fertilisers are used, with adjustments for potassium, nitrogen and phosphorus deficiencies. Magnesium is also carefully monitored and adjusted, both to counteract the excess of potassium put on the soil after the last war and also because 'it is as essential for plants as for humans.'

Most replanting is by individual replacement from a *sélection massale,* although Bruno is now using a variety of clones for larger parcels. Clones, he believes, are beneficial provided one learns to master them. The older vines, especially in vineyards such as the 70–80-year-old plot in Savigny Les Dominodes, are, of course, products of a turn of the century *sélection massale.* Learning to work with this kind of plant material is a matter of getting a feel for each vine; 'one ends up by knowing the vines', so pruning, for example, is a question of individual judgement and adaptation, rather than rigid rules.

Bruno Clair and Philippe Brun produce an extensive range of Côte d'Or wines. However, Bruno's signature wine is indubitably his

Marsannay Rosé. Its creation by Joseph, in 1919, was a brilliant stroke of marketing genius at a time of almost insuperable economic difficulty. The wine is designed to give a mouthful of true Pinot Noir character with some underlying richness – rather than to use Pinot Noir to make a tinted white wine with plenty of freshness.

This result is achieved by an *assemblage* of 25–33% 'vin gris' from direct pressing of the black grapes and juice from a 2–4-day cold *macération pelliculaire*, followed by *écoulage* and then pressing. Both these elements contribute to the final product: the 'press direct' gives the wine its finer, more subtle aromatic aspect, whilst the maceration contributes the pure Pinot flavours which are its hallmark. The juice is invariably vinified in bulk, without new wood, by slow fermentation at low temperature, to ensure an even development. The result is a wine which is fresh without being lively, with a marked Pinot Noir character.

Bruno's pair of distinctly individual white wines are a Marsannay Blanc – about 2,500 bottles annually, from equal proportions of Chardonnay and Pinot Gris – and a Morey-St.-Denis Blanc – from 100% Chardonnay – of which he is one of only a handful of producers. The Morey vines are a series of about 15 scattered plots in the *climat* En la Rue de Vergy, just above the Clos de Tart, which Bruno reclaimed from scrub in the late 1970s.

Both wines are vinified along the same lines: pressing, *débourbage*, and then immediate passage to casks, to achieve a long, slow fermentation which, being less tumultuous, Bruno considers better for extraction of glycerols and finesse. In vintages such as 1989 or 1990, where the natural yeasts are particularly active, cooling the juice to 15–20° C ensures that fermentation proceeds without risking excessive temperatures.

The major part is vinified in second- and third-year oak, with just a touch of new wood (15% in 1990). Although it is easier to control the temperature when fermenting in bulk, Bruno Clair believes that wood adds depth and elegance.

For his red wines, Bruno also seeks a slow fermentation and a long *cuvaison*. The bunches are 40–80% destalked, vatted and macerated at 15° C for 4–5 days, in open wooden *cuves*. Natural yeasts are used with about 20% of whole bunches in each vat to retard fermentation and to extract more finesse and fruit into the wines. Frequent and regular *pigéage* – 'about 5–6 times a day if we can manage it' – keeps the solids in maximum contact with the juice and further aids extraction. Pumping-over is discontinued after fermentation has started, otherwise the yeasts multiply too quickly and risk putting the temperature above the desired 30–32° C.

'We don't hesitate to let the wine and skins macerate after fermentation,' Bruno argues, even though this extracts tannins which make the wines a little hard for the first few months in bottle. In 1990, *cuvaisons* lasted a total of 17-22 days, which is not apparently exceptional, although Bruno stresses the need for vigilance as open vats can easily spoil.

Once the press-wine has been added and the wine allowed to settle for 3 days, part of each *cuve* is decanted into large 13–14 hectolitre oak vats and the rest – about 33% – put into new wood. Charmingly, each appellation has the luxury of its own particular *foudre*, perhaps to make it feel more at home. The wines in small oak are racked cask-to-cask – the more important appellations being rotated from old to new wood. The Marsannay Rouge is put into second- and third-year casks already used by the Grands Vins, and has only a touch of new oak.

The amount of time spent in cask is a function of the vintage and of the wine's structure, 6–12 months in cask before fining – with fresh egg-whites – being the average. However, not all the wines are fined: the 1988s were, but Bruno does not expect to fine all the 1989s or 1990s. He and Philippe Brun regard fining as much an expedient for reducing aggressive tannins as a means of clarification. Wines that they do fine remain a month *sur col* before being bottled in the late spring of the second year, before the great heat of a Burgundian summer. Otherwise, the reds are kieselguhr filtered to polish them up without removing too much of their innards.

Bruno's perspective on his work is that wine is 'l'expression d'un *terroir* et d'un homme'. Tasting wines from the different vineyards of Marsannay, one is left in no doubt of his commitment to this philosophy. Although his wines are regularly analysed during their vinification and *élevage*, Bruno exudes a healthy scepticism about technical advice, knowing his vineyards and their wine characteristics so well that he does not leap to adjust here and there if there is an imbalance. He cites the 1959 vintage, which analytically was hopelessly deficient in acidity – almost dead – yet which has lasted magnificently and will continue to do so, probably well into the twenty-first century.

The Domaine's style is for red wines which have high tannins and marked acidity, but which are designed to age well: 'tannin is good for you,' according to Bruno. The Marsannays are excellent, particularly in the 1988, 1989 and 1990 vintages, with no lack of depth or finesse. The Gevreys are more complex, with good structure and attractive elegance – the best being the Premiers Crus Cazetiers (which only produced 20 hl./ha. in 1988) and the Clos St.-Jacques, which has more finesse and less rusticity than the Cazetiers.

The Grands Crus have even more length and complexity but need years of cellaring to give of their best. Fortunately, something of the fine old Clair Däu tradition seems to have rubbed off on Bruno. The Marsannay Rosé is delicious – a beautifully thought out wine, which should be enough to convert anyone who professes undying disdain of rosé, whatever its provenance.

The two whites are also excellent, especially the Marsannay Blanc, whose combination of Chardonnay for finesse and Pinot Gris (here, Pinot Beurot) for fat results in a gorgeous, ripe mouthful.

Bruno is philosophical about the difference between Burgundy and, for example, Bordeaux: 'there, when you choose the wine, you also choose the vigneron,' the equation being manifestly false in Burgundy. This is one amiable vigneron in whom you are unlikely to be disappointed.

VINEYARD HOLDINGS

Commune	Level	Lieu-dit/Climat	Area	Vine Age	Status
Marsannay	V	(Blanc – various)	0.80	12	F
Marsannay	V	(Rosé – various)	2.45	25	F
Marsannay	V	(Rouge – various)	2.84	30	F
Marsannay	V	Les Vaudenelles (R)	1.96	25	F
Marsannay	V	Les Longeroies (R)	1.36	50/85	F
Savigny	PC	La Dominode	1.67	6 (0.35) 80 (1.32)	F
Morey	V	En la Rue de Vergy (R)	0.64	13	F
Morey	V	En la Rue de Vergy (W)	0.51	12	F
Gevrey	PC	Bel Air	0.22	20	F
Gevrey	PC	Cazetiers	0.87	35	F
Gevrey	PC	Clos du Fonteny	0.67	30	F
Gevrey	PC	Clos St.-Jacques	1.00	19/40	F
Gevrey	GC	Clos de Bèze	0.98	22 (0.32) 75 (0.66)	F F
Vosne	V	Les Champs Perdrix	0.92	55	F
Chambolle	V	Les Veroilles	0.71	2	F
Regionales	_	(Various)	1.30	4/15/25	F
		Total	**18.90 ha.**		

Domaine Philippe Charlopin-Parizot

MARSANNAY

Philippe Charlopin, who looks rather like a French version of the English King Charles II, with a mass of frizzy dark hair and a friendly chubby face, is a rising star in the vinous firmament. Having started in 1976 with 1.8 ha. from his father, he has gradually increased his Domaine to its present 11 ha. Up to 1986 he vinified in Gevrey, but he moved the cuverie and cellars to Marsannay for the 1987 vintage.

His wines are carefully thought out, on the principle that the precise qualities of the grapes determine the details of vinification.

Old vines play a particularly important part in Philippe's thinking and this is reflected in his vineyard management, which is designed to interfere as little as possible with nature, while yet encouraging the vine to produce small yields of highly concentrated fruit. Vines are left until they cease producing altogether – they are never grubbed up.

Maximum life expectancy is achieved by only working the soil, except for spot weed-killing to get rid of deep-rooted Iseron grass, using sulphur and copper-based products as much as possible. He gives his plants a yellow-oil treatment before budburst, when the temperature has risen above 15° C, to protect them from infestation and to 'clean the vines'.

Philippe puts particular stress on *évasivage* to remove any double or excess shoots, but will not countenance green-pruning. In his view, this is a waste of time, since it has apparently been proved to his satisfaction that if you eliminate 50% of the bunches, the others yield more in compensation, so you are effectively back where you started. In addition, bunches remaining afterwards tend to have thinner skins than normal and 'you can't make Grand Vin with thin skins'.

Since 1990 the crop has been totally destalked. In earlier years most of the stalks were left in the vats, but after consultation with Henri Jayer, Philippe was persuaded that they only brought astringency and no benefits. So, the policy was changed. There is also a heavy elimination of unripe or rotten grapes, and a *saignée de cuve* in years such as 1982 which threaten to be unusually dilute.

There is no recipe for a Charlopin vinification – everything depends on the particular qualities of the fruit being handled. Philippe generally prefers to have as long a pre-fermentive maceration as possible to extract colour, fat and the aromas of ripe fruits. In 1990 this maceration lasted 4–5 days, in 1989 up to twice as long.

During fermentation, there is no pumping-over because Philippe believes that the oxygenation involved dissipates important aromas which cannot be recaptured; 'go into any cellar during *remontage*, you can smell the aromas escaping from the *cuves*'. Rather there is a frequent and lengthy *pigéage*, up to 10 times per day, to extract maximum colour and matter into the wine.

The amount of *cuvaison* depends on the state of the grapes at harvest: in 1990, for example, the skins were quite thick and the volume of juice quite small, therefore *cuvaison* was reduced to 10–12 days in total to avoid excessive tannin extraction; by contrast, in 1989 maceration was allowed to continue for 25 days in view of the relatively fine skins and the dilution of the juice – although Philippe admits that he might have overdone it somewhat. *Chaptalisation*, when it is needed, is performed in several small doses, as late as possible, in order to prolong fermentation.

Another point of quality is that only press-wine extracted from the lightest of pressings – 200 grams – is added; it is almost free-run wine, claims Philippe. There is no *débourbage*, because after such long *cuvaison*, the amount of fine lees left is small and the chances of the *malo* starting spontaneously would be much diminished by removing yet more lees.

From there 30% of the wines pass into new casks which have been very heavily charred to avoid the extraction of harsh tannins and to maximise the aromas of coffee and vanilla, whilst the remaining 70% sees no wood but is kept in large stainless-steel tanks.

In 1990 the new casks were a mixture of Chatillon and Jura wood : 'that's all my cask-maker could give me – the Bordelais had taken all the Tronçais and Allier,' confessed Philippe, rather ruefully.

To minimise loss of fruit aromas, there is, unusually, no racking, and the wines remain on their lees for just under a year before a light kieselguhr filtration and bottling.

Aroma and freshness can also be conserved by keeping as much as possible of the natural carbon-dioxide gas (a normal by-product of fermentation) dissolved in the wine. Philippe has worked out that, at bottling, the CO_2 should titrate at 400–500 mg/litre and since the wine in tank has double the concentration of gas of the wine in cask, there is some juggling to be done to arrive at the desired level. If necessary, Philippe will either pump some CO_2 in to top up or else use a sparge of nitrogen gas to reduce the level. In these low concentrations, it is undetectable on the palate.

On the palate the wines are distinctly on the meaty side but are well made and invariably need keeping, even in 'lesser' vintages. There is an attractive Marsannay Blanc, made from Chardonnay vines planted in patches of limestone soil, and excellent Village Vosne and Morey.

The cream of the cellar are the Gevrey-Chambertin, Clos St.-Denis and Charmes-Chambertin. The produce of less than 40-year-old Gevrey vines are vinified and sold to local négociants, leaving that of the 40–70-year-old plants for the Domaine. This is good wine – with a fine concentration of old-vine fruit and real depth. Something to keep for 5–10 years, or more in better vintages.

Of the two Grands Crus, the Mazoyères-Chambertin which is sold as Charmes-Chambertin, as it is entitled to be, from 40-year-old vines, is usually somewhat meaty for a Charmes, but has a finesse and underlying richness which keep it from becoming lumpen. The Clos St.-Denis is also a big wine – but with a touch more suppleness than the Charmes. Both merit their Grand Cru status, and are worth looking out for.

Philippe Charlopin has made great strides both in quality and reputation over the last few years. There is still an air of 'feeling the way' a little, but this is a reliable and interesting source of good wine which seems to be improving year-by-year.

VINEYARD HOLDINGS

Commune	*Level*	*Lieu-dit/Climat*	*Area*	*Vine Age*	*Status*
Gevrey	GC	Mazoyères-Chambertin	0.20	40	P
Morey	GC	Clos St.-Denis	0.20	40	P
Gevrey	V	(Various)	4.00	7/70	P/F
Morey	V	Clos Solon/Les Crais	1.00	50	P
Vosne	V	Les Ormes	0.15	40	P
Fixin	V	Les Germets	0.30	7/40	M
Marsannay	V	(Rouge/Blanc/Rosé)	4.00	20	P/F
Bourgogne	R	(Rouge)	1.00	15	P
		Total	**10.85 ha.**		

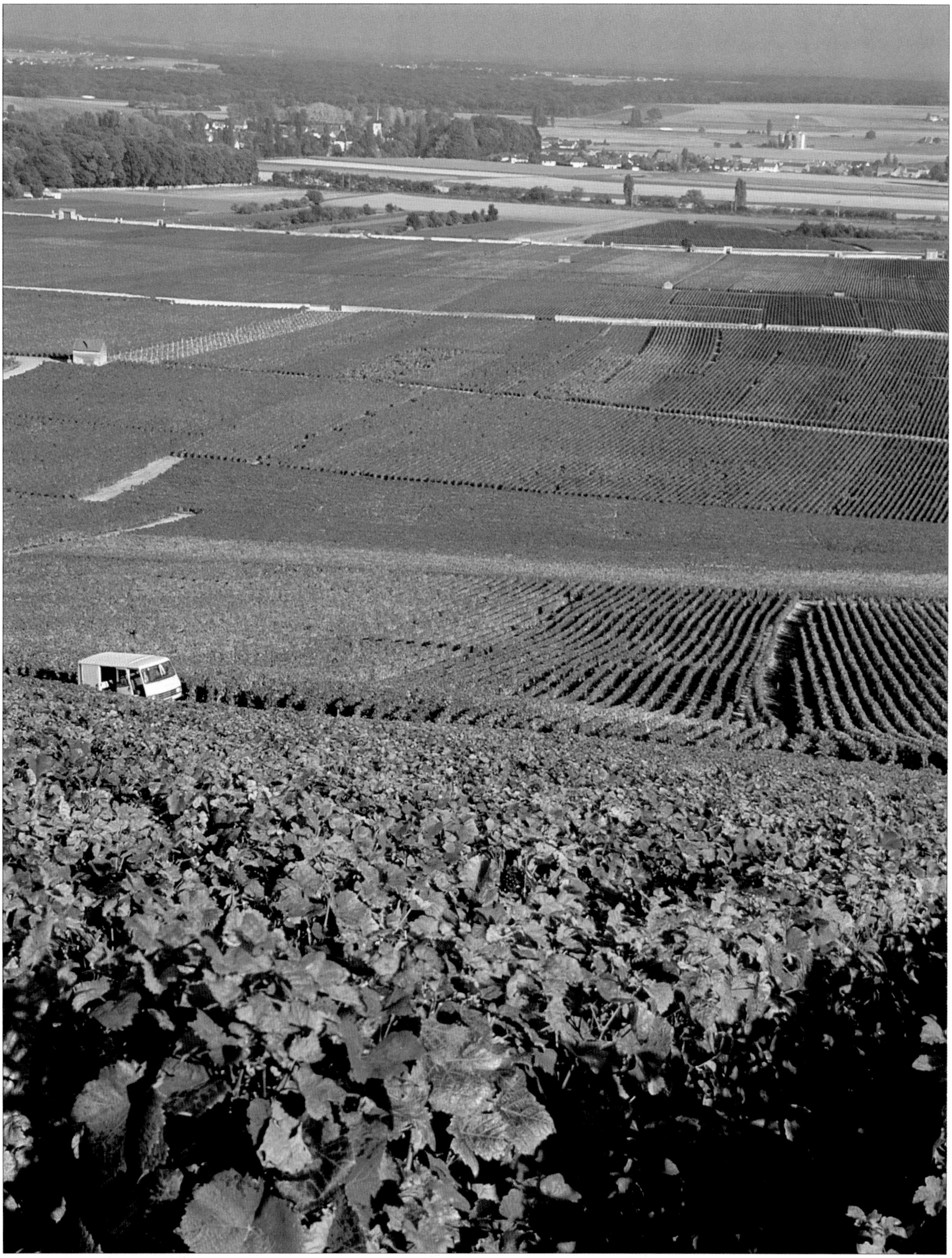

Vineyards of the Côte de Nuits

Fixin

Fixin is an attractive little village of some 1,000 inhabitants, sitting on a slight incline to the immediate south of Couchey. An underrated commune, suffering perhaps in the shadow of its illustrious neighbour Gevrey, it is pleasantly encircled by vineyards with an enchanting mainly fourteenth- century lizard-roofed church which stares out over the vines.

Fixin is in fact the fusion of two ancient hamlets – Fixin and Fixey – each of which used to boast its own silk-worm nursery. However, these are long gone and wine and its attendant tourism have taken over. The village is well worth a detour. There is a splendid nineteenth-century wash-house which still functions, although the red soils which colour the water cast doubt on its cleansing properties.

The main attraction is the 15 ha. Parc Noisot at the top of the village, surrounding a house built by Claude Noisot, one of Napoléon Bonaparte's Imperial Guard Commanders, as a replica of that on St. Helena where Napoléon died. A rather over-fed bronze statue of the Emperor, sculpted by François Rude, looks down on the scene and a museum of Napoleonic memorabilia

The other place of interest is La Résidence de la Perrière, named after the nearby quarry from which stone was extracted to build the church. Originally the summer retreat of the Dukes of Burgundy it became a rest-house for monks when it was ceded to the Abbey of Cîteaux in 1192. It offers a fine panorama of the surrounding countryside. The church in the hamlet of Fixey is also interesting; a mélange of romanesque and renaissance.

When you have finally exhausted the history and yourself, there is always 'Chez Jeanette', a friendly little restaurant which keeps travellers well victualled with simple local fare, washed down with a decent bottle of Fixin – or Gevrey if you are feeling flush.

The vines are on mainly gentle slopes rising 270–360 m. in height and exposed due

Autumn vine colours mirrored in Fixin's church roof

east. Although they cover some 326 ha. in all, only 107 have the appellation Fixin and 22 Fixin Premier Cru, the remaining 197 ha. being Côte de Nuits-Villages.

Due to an administrative anomaly, the appellation Fixin Premier Cru extends for 1.62 ha. into Brochon which has a fine Château – now part of the local Lycée Viticole – but no appellation of its own and is forced to borrow from neighbouring Gevrey and Fixin.

The 6 Premiers Crus are all situated at the top of the village. The largest, the 5.36 ha. Clos de la Perrière, sits at the westerly extremity of the appellation, on a 12–14% slope surrounding La Résidence with the 4.78 ha. Clos du Chapître just below it. The soils in both these vineyards are predominantly limestone with an overlay of stones.

Les Hervelets (3.83 ha.) and Les Arvelets (3.36 ha.) to the north, are separated by the smallest Premier Cru, Le Meix Bas (1.38 ha.). The Clos Napoléon, which was originally Aux Cheusots before Claude Noisot married its owner and changed both their names, is almost flat, gazing across a small road at the Clos du Chapître opposite.

Fixin is devoted exclusively to the Pinot Noir for its AC wines, which tend to be masculine, with plenty of robust, muscular fruit and can be delicious after a decade or so.

Apart from Pierre Gelin and Philippe Charlopin, it is worth seeking out the Clos de la Perrière, the only wine of Domaine Philippe Joliet who owns the vineyard and the house. Outside the commune, both Bruno Clair and Faiveley produce good examples.

Like its neighbour Marsannay, Fixin deserves a better press. The best of its wines are excellent, especially if given time to develop; they are also incredibly good value.

Domaine Pierre Gelin

FIXIN

Here is a splendid smallish Domaine, making wines which, with the welcome renaissance of Fixin and Marsannay, are destined to become more widely known and appreciated.

The history of the Domaine is briefly told: Pierre Gelin, a native of Fixin, bought some vines in the commune between 1925 and 1930. His son Stephen, who came to work with him in 1959, at the age of 21, took over the running of the Domaine in 1978 on the death of his father, at the same time giving it its present name. Working with him was André Molin, a long-time employee of Pierre's, who is now a partner in the firm.

The vineyards are a mouthwatering selection of the best of Fixin, together with some Village, Premier Cru and Grand Cru Gevreys. They have the Monopoly of the 1.80 ha. Clos Napoléon and of the 4.78 ha. Clos du Chapître, as well as 0.57 ha. in a third Premier Cru, Les Hervelets and 2.50 ha. of Fixin 'tout court'. In Gevrey, there is the 1.80 ha. Monopole of the Clos de Meixvelles – a Village vineyard, plus 23 ares of Premier Cru Clos Prieur. There are two Grands Crus: 37 ares of Mazy-Chambertin and 60 ares of Chambertin Clos de Bèze.

The majority of the vines are 20–35 years old, except for the Clos de Bèze which has seen some 60 vintages. All are owned outright by the Domaine, except the Clos du Chapître which is worked on a *fermage* basis for the owners.

Low yields are a priority for the Domaine. Stephen Gelin prefers to spring prune, when the sap has started to rise, and to prune very short if he can without breaking the fragile fruiting cane. Once the shoots appear, there is a severe *ébrossage* to remove excess buds. What counts is not the average yield, but the yield per vine : 'a vine which has too many bunches is like a woman who has too many children – she has difficulty feeding them.' It is essential to realise that the produce of 1,000 vines yielding 10 bunches apiece, is not qualitatively identical to 500 vines each producing 20 bunches – although the quantity is the same.

A further problem for the Fixin grape-grower is that this part of the Cote is the 'secteur tardif'. Being more northerly, with much of its vineyard area exposed north or north-east, ripening is late and thus prone to the risks of the autumn wind and rains. Gelin tries to counteract this by planting his vines on to early-ripening SO4 roots; whilst this can help, the increased risk of *coulure* – the loss of flowers – can result in badly reduced crops. However, he refuses to green-prune: 'from principle, I never go against nature' – believing perhaps that one fine day, nature will turn round and take some unspoken revenge.

The vinification is what might best be described as 'modified traditional' – 100% destalking, and long, slow fermentation in open wooden *cuves*, without any pre-fermentive *maceration*, at up to 36° C with 7–8 *pigéages* interspersed with *remontage*.

The modification, introduced with the 1988 vintage, comes at the end of the 15 or 20-day *cuvaison*; when all the sugar has been fermented out, the *cuves* are heated to 35–45° C and left overnight before being decanted at about 20° C. This brief heating helps extract colour and flavour components from the grapes, but requires that the last milligram of sugar has been fermented first.

The wines then pass into cask. Fixins are reared partly in *foudre* and partly in older casks – depending on space available and on the characteristics of the wine. Stephen Gelin finds that they evolve 'more gently' in large cooperage, giving a touch of softness to the final blend. Their high natural tannins would certainly not benefit further from new oak. However the Grands Crus are permitted the luxury of some 70% new wood before fining and passing into the hands of the contract bottler some 16–18 months later.

Stephen Gelin and André Molin are not growers who are prepared to adapt their style to the whims of their customers. The *terroir* at Fixin, in particular, gives naturally tannic, long-lived wines, which they happen to prefer. 'The customers adapt to us, not we to the customers,' he explains, so if the style is not to your taste, then you go elsewhere.

Whilst the Gevreys are generally well-made and interesting wines – the 1989 Grands Crus are particularly successful – it is the Fixins which provide the identity of this fine Domaine. Of the three Premiers Crus, Les Hervelets tends to be the one with the greatest finesse. It has more expressive fruit aromas than either the Clos Napoléon or the Clos du Chapître, which show the more animal, musky, spicy peppery side of the Pinot Noir.

The 1989 Hervelets was very deep purple in colour with the *fruits rouges* nose and a soft, rounded layer of tannins underneath plenty of ripe succulent fruit. The Hervelets vineyard has soil with a significantly higher iron content than the others, and more stones in the topsoil.

In contrast, both the Clos Napoléon and the Clos du Chapître contain more pink clay, which endows their wines with a broader, more muscular structure; distinctly more 'sauvage' both on the nose and on the palate. In the 1989 vintage, the Chapître was the richer of the pair, soft and fleshy, with a distinct note of *surmaturité,* whereas the Napoléon was more structured, with the spice and pepper notes which seem to characterise these vignobles. Stephen's policy of very late harvesting would explain the extraordinary richness one finds in these wines.

For many years the wines of Fixin have been unfairly regarded as the 'little wines' of the Côte. Consequently merchants don't buy them and collectors won't give them cellar space. This is a great pity – and an injustice. Fixins are capable of making fine old bottles, given half the chance. A 1961 Clos du Chapître tasted at the end of 1990 was magnificent – a fine deep colour, plenty of richness and complexity both on the nose and palate, and a very long, warm finish. Not a Gevrey Grand Cru by any means, but infinitely preferable to many wines of greater pretension at several times the price.

It is about time that people took the wine of this part of the Côte more seriously – Stephen Gelin has more than enough ammunition to make them sit up and think.

VINEYARD HOLDINGS

Commune	*Level*	*Lieu-dit/Climat*	*Area*	*Vine Age*	*Status*
Fixin	PC	Clos Napoléon	1.80	35	P
Fixin	PC	Clos du Chapître	4.78	25/30	F
Fixin	PC	Les Hervelets	0.57	20	P
Fixin	V	(Various)	2.50	15/20	P
Gevrey	V	Clos de Meixvelles	1.80	25	P
Gevrey	PC	Clos Prieur	0.23	23	P
Gevrey	GC	Mazy-Chambertin	0.37	35	P
Gevrey	GC	Clos de Bèze	0.60	60	P
		Total	**12.65 ha.**		

GEVREY-CHAMBERTIN

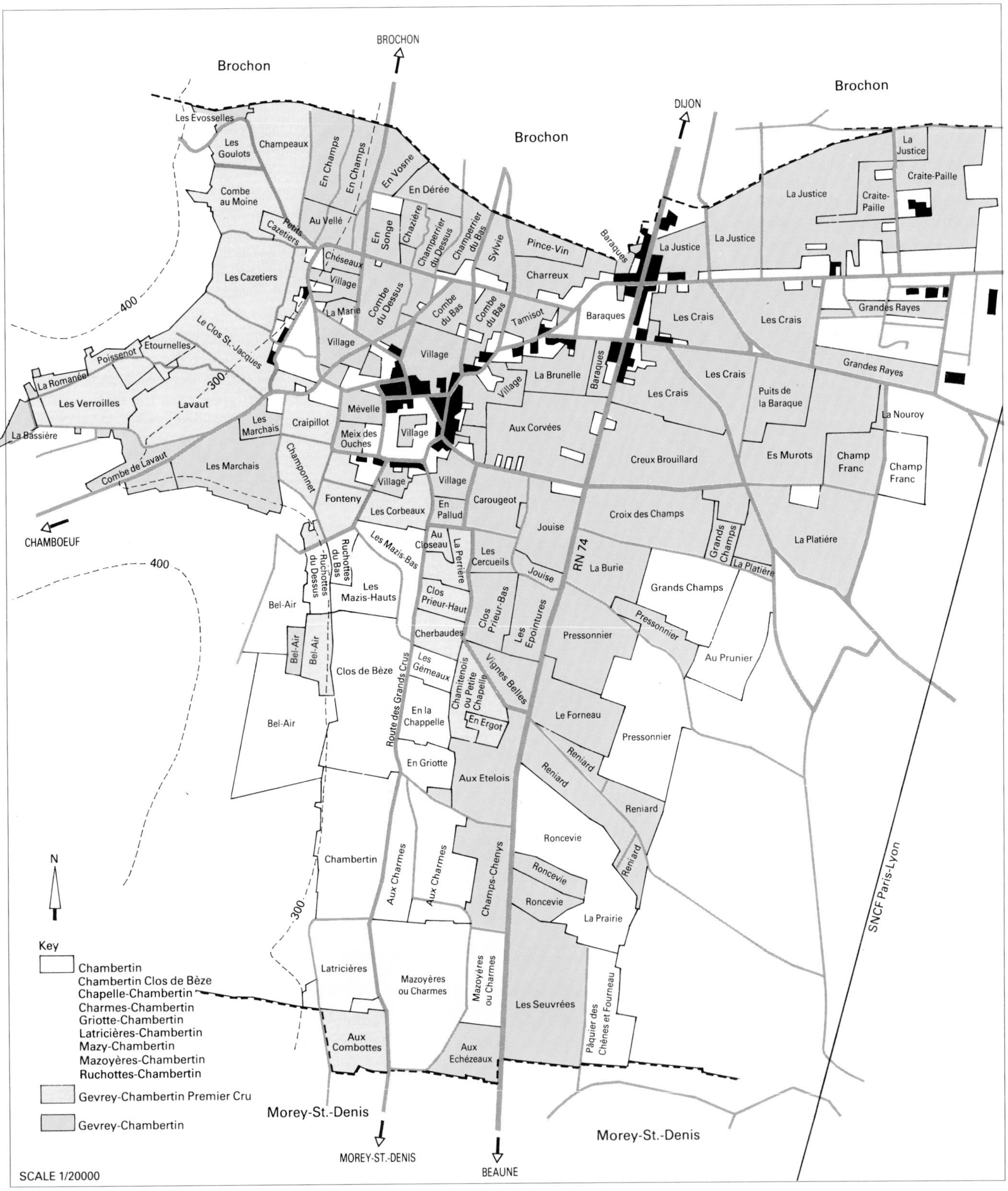

For many, Gevrey-Chambertin marks the real northern limit of the Côte d'Or. By far the largest commune in the Côte de Nuits, with 9 Grands Crus it is very much the flagship of the northern Côte.

The village, recorded as Gabriacus in 640, belonged to the Abbots of Bèze and monks from this Abbey were largely responsible for clearing the ground and pioneering the original vine plantations. In 1257, the Abbot of Cluny decided that fortifications were desirable and started constructing a château, the remains of which can still be seen.

Nothing of significance happened thereafter until 1553–1558 when the plague struck with devastating effect. Massive infestations of insects laid waste the vines for over a century, too. In 1847 a Royal decree granted the village the right to add the name of its most renowned Grand Cru to its designation; thus was Gevrey-Chambertin born.

The village itself is really a small town. Its 2,600 inhabitants benefit from shops, a wine bar, an hotel and a couple of prestigious restaurants. Building has expanded the place, especially on the eastern side of the RN 74.

The vineyards extend to 532 ha., 87 are spread over 9 Grands Crus, 86 ha. over 26 Premiers Crus and some 359 ha. of Village appellation, including 11 *climats* from Brochon which are entitled to call their wine Gevrey-Chambertin.

The Village vines extend on both sides of the Dijon-Beaune road, mostly to the east and north of the village centre. The Premiers Crus lie in two bands, one to the south and the other, larger, section to the west towards the Combe de Lavaux. This latter includes Les Cazetiers, La Combe aux Moines , Le Clos St.-Jacques, Lavaux St.-Jacques and Etournelles St.-Jacques, and is regarded as the first division of the Premiers Crus.

The Grands Crus are sited to the south of the village on an east-facing gently sloping hillside at a height of 260–320 metres, protected from wind-chill by the forest above. The commune has recently taken the unusually extrovert step – for Burgundy – of putting up signs in the vineyards giving details of each Grand Cru for the tourist.

Micro-climates are particularly important here, since the Combe de Lavaux, a steep-sided valley behind the village, acts as a funnel for bad weather, especially for hail. Fortunately the higher ground is inimical to frost, which like water runs off to the flatter land near the main road. In 1985, whilst more than 80 ha. of Village vineyards were destroyed by frost, the Premiers and Grands Crus escaped virtually unscathed. The relative coolness of the top of the slopes slows down the ripening process; these vineyards are less successful in marginal vintages or when weather necessitates an early harvest.

For centuries the richness and finesse of Chambertin has moved writers to exotic descriptions of its glory. Writing between the wars, Gaston Roupnel described it as combining 'grace and vigour, firmness and strength, finesse and delicacy... it is the summit of Burgundy's potential.' Chambertin, together with its neighbour Clos de Bèze, is now considered as *primus inter pares* of the Grands Crus. Owing to some administrative idiosyncrasy, wine from Clos de Bèze may be labelled Chambertin, but not vice versa.

The soils of Gevrey exhibit wide diversity. The Grands Crus are planted on a base of compacted limestone – the substratum of which is visible at the site of a disused quarry on the left of the Route des Grands Crus coming into Gevrey from Morey-St.-Denis. Topsoils are more or less rich in clay particles – less in Griotte-Chambertin and Chapelle-Chambertin, more in Mazoyères, which is altogether more fecund arable soil, with a 30–35 cm. outcrop of well-drained gravel. Another oddity permits wine from Mazoyères-Chambertin to be called Charmes-Chambertin, but not vice versa.

Latricières-Chambertin and Ruchottes-Chambertin are on higher ground, with a topsoil of white marl; a highish limestone content tends to give the wines a dimension of hardness and tannin not so marked in the other Grands Crus.

Griotte-Chambertin, the smallest of the Grands Crus, takes its name not from any cherry-tree planted there, nor from the supposed whiff of cherry in its wine, but rather from its shape, a concave bowl which trapped the sun so much in summer that it was like a little grill or 'grillotte'.

Elsewhere in the commune, soil depths vary; topsoils are frequently thin with clearly visible rock outcrops. The flat land on either side of the road, where Village and Regional appellations are concentrated, have more clay in their composition, giving breadth and body but less finesse.

Such a large commune – Poupon and Pitiot list 110 growers in Gevrey itself – is inevitably home to a diversity of quality and styles. A Chambertin from Jean Trapet, emphasising delicacy, will have little in common with Charles Rousseau's denser, more structured version. Whilst Gevreys are broadly characterised by power and muscle, they are often compact and need time to unpack. Premiers and Grands Crus can develop well over 30 years or more – a 1957 Clos de la Roche from Armand Rousseau was still immensely fine in 1991.

A vigneron's house in Gevrey-Chambertin; grand houses are the exception in the Côte d'Or

Unfortunately, some Domaines are significantly under-performing. Recent vintages from Henri Rebourseau, Hubert Camus, Gabriel Tortochot and Remy are distinctly patchy. In many instances yields are too high, vinification ignores vintage differences and the wine spends too long in cask. What is referred to as traditional wine-making frequently conceals sheer laziness, sloppy *élevage* and evisceratingly harsh filtration. Such Domaines are well aware that their wines are poor.

However, several less grand enterprises make excellent wines. In particular, René Leclerc, brother of Philippe, Jean-Philippe Marchand, Lucien Boillot and Philippe Rossignol are all capable of top-quality, though lacking the overall consistency of the best. It would be interesting to see what one or two of the younger vignerons would make of some of the under-exploited vineyards owned by the less able Domaines. The shortage of land might just tempt someone to a charitable experiment!

THE GRANDS CRUS OF GEVREY-CHAMBERTIN

Lieu-dit	*Area*	*Props.*	*Av. Prod.*
Chambertin	12.90.31	25	4000 C/S
Chambertin Clos de Bèze	15.38.87	18	5200 C/S
Chapelle-Chambertin	5.48.53	9	2000 C/S
Charmes-Chambertin + Mazoyères-Chambertin	30.83.24	67	10500 C/S
Griotte-Chambertin	2.69.18	9	800 C/S
Latricière-Chambertin	7.35.44	12	2500 C/S
Mazy-Chambertin	9.10.34	28	3000 C/S
Ruchottes-Chambertin	3.30.37	8	1000 C/S
Totals	**87.06.28 ha.**		**29000 C/S**

Domaine Bachelet

GEVREY-CHAMBERTIN

Denis Bachelet is a modern 27-year-old with a centuries-old traditional Domaine with which, despite the serious disparity in their ages, he gets on remarkably well. Perched on a couple of plastic wine boxes in the *cuverie*; he passionately discusses his charge, his slim figure, outsize brown eyes and large ears giving the appearance of a lively gallic version of E.T.

The family house was originally the post-house for Gevrey. The original Bachelet, Victor, was a tonnelier in the area, but Denis was uncertain precisely where – 'perhaps grandmother . . .' He has a clearer memory of his grandparents who 'bought vineyards right and left' – an expression meant to convey quantity rather than orientation. Included in these whirling purchases was a parcel of Grand Cru Charmes-Chambertin, which remains the pride of the Domaine.

On his demise in 1984, grandfather bequeathed 5 ha. of vines which were divided between Denis' father, Bernard and his aunt, Michelle who cared for the estate until Denis completed his studies in 1983.

The vineyards are presently owned by his father, who went to Belgium in the 1960s to pursue his career as an electromecanicien. Although Denis' young wife has recently become involved he admits that the full 'équipe technique' currently consists of himself, his father and grandmother.

Denis' Domaine may be short on hectares, but neither on quality nor commitment. He is concerned to maintain, and where necessary improve, the traditions he has inherited. In the vineyards the aim is the highest average vine age; only organic fertilisers are used, which, with low herbicide doses and hand working of the soil, help retain these ancient plants – some in Charmes-Chambertin having already seen their century.

Each year some 300 vines per ha. need replacing – victims of disease, natural death or tractor accidents. This is done by digging a hole, disinfecting the soil and then covering it up for the winter. In the spring the new vine is planted – one of 3 or 4 chosen clones – and carefully nurtured until it is 4 years old. Young vines planted between 2 old vines often give particularly good fruit – the old plants take much of the light and spread their foliage, so the relatively impoverished newcomer is obliged to struggle for nourishment. Further, after its initial clean soil period once roots are established, it becomes infected with nematodes from its neighbours; these restrict youthful vigour and give the fruit a depth and concentration which are compatible with Grand Vin.

Low yields just seem to happen. Denis has never had to green-prune to remove excess bunches and dislikes that practice. The 1988 and 1990 figures indicate the small *rendements* achieved: Charmes-Chambertin 25/30 hl./ha. and 37+ hl./ha. respectively; in Gevrey-Chambertin corresponding yields were 35 and 45 hl./ha.– about 17% higher.

Great care is taken to eliminate rot. Pickers are trained to make 2 separate cuts on each bunch – first to remove rot, second to cut the bunch itself. In particularly difficult vintages – 1983 for example – a further *trie* is made at the *cuverie. Pourriture sec* is the worse form of rot; it imparts an ineradicable flavour to the wine. *Pourriture humide* taints less, if present in small quantities.

About all this Denis is philosophical: 'costly, but the price to pay for Grand Vin ... we can't afford to get it wrong; every drop of wine counts.' He is acutely aware of the financial consequences of even minor spoilage, and equally mindful of the vulnerability of a fragile reputation: 'when you're at the top of the quality scale, it's so easy to slip' – a reflection more on the volatility of critical acclaim than on his ability as a wine-maker.

What happens in the cellar is often constrained by money. 'I can't afford to cool or heat the *must* – I haven't got the equipment.' All he can do is extract 300 litres from one overheating *cuve* at a time, cool and return it, hoping that this will moderate the temperature. Sulphur is affordable and knocks out the feebler yeasts which produce least alcohol, so it is systematically used.

Denis' and grandmother's philosophy is that the grapes contain everything necessary for making good wine. Thus, 7–11 days of fermentation is preceded by 3–4 days of pre-fermentive maceration, to maximise extraction. One hundred per cent of the press-wine is added to the free-run wine – 'we can't afford to leave any aside' – before the wine is put into casks, 100% new for the Grand Cru and 50% for the Premier Cru. These casks are left in a specially cold part of the *cuverie* for the winter, to ensure that the malolactic fermentation starts as late as possible. 'My grandfather had no means of heating to start his *malos*, but made good wine all the same. After the *malo* the lees are dead, so it is better to keep the wine on the lees as long as possible before.' In early summer the wines are racked off their lees and returned to cask, thence to a deeper, cooler cellar before the high summer temperatures set in.

Each cask is fined with fresh egg-white and rested for one month before being hand-bottled without filtration. If Denis manages 4 casks in a day his supper is well earned.

Bachelet wines are expressly *vins de garde*; but they are also supple and attractively *tendre* in their youth. Denis admits that he prefers these qualities; he is not interested in extracting concentrations of raw tannins which render wines unapproachable for several years.

The all-powerful triumvirate of Bernard, Denis and grandmother decides how long a *cuvaison* is appropriate for each wine. In 1990, fearing that they might have another 1976 on their hands, they deliberately shortened *cuvaison* to amortise tannin extraction.

Denis believes some of his best wines were made in 1988. The Charmes-Chambertin – 'all sold', he admits wistfully – was his single greatest achievement. If the 1989 vintage is anything to go by, it must be very fine. Even in cask, the 1989 Charmes had a perfume both aristocratic and seductive. Underneath, it had a soft, ripe structure with thoroughly rounded tannins. The comment that it was redolent of a Musigny delighted Denis, who has a great love of Chambolle-Musignys and to some extent looks for their elegance and finesse in his own *cuvées* .

This is a fine, small Domaine. The wines are conscientiously thought out and expertly put together. The amalgam of youth and tradition is completely successful.

VINEYARD HOLDINGS

Commune	*Level*	*Lieu-dit/Climat*	*Area*	*Vine Age*	*Status*
Gevrey	GC	Charmes-Chambertin	0.44	80/100	P
Gevrey	PC	Les Corbeaux	0.28	70	P
Gevrey	V	(Several parcels)	0.94	55	P
—	R	Côte de Nuits-Villages	0.28	25/30	P
—	R	Bourgogne Rouge	0.59	5/13	P
—	R	Bourgogne Aligoté	0.19	5	P
		Total	**2.75 ha.**		

Domaine Pierre Bourée et Fils

GEVREY-CHAMBERTIN

Pierre Bourée is among the most old-fashioned Domaines in the Côte. Its present director, Louis Vallet, great-nephew of the eponymous founder of the House, is a slim, quiet man in his sixties, of old-fashioned values and courtesy. Sitting behind his large, old-fashioned desk in the Domaine's large, old-fashioned headquarters he happily expatiates on the desirability of sticking to tradition and fashioning late twentieth-century wines in the old way.

The small business that Pierre Bourée bought in 1864 had no vines of its own, so he splashed out in 1874 and acquired the entire 2.04.35 ha. Clos de la Justice – a Village vineyard which remains the firm's flagship. More land followed, the most recent addition being 1.22 ha. of Beaune Epenottes.

In the vineyards, old fashion is modified: clones have crept in since 1985 and some synthetic treatments are countenanced. However, only natural manure, sheep-droppings, has been used for the last 40 years which has apparently encouraged wild asparagus to grow among the vines. Unfortunately its moment is short-lived, since it coincides with sulphur spraying which kills it.

Harvesting is, of course, manual; a couple of mechanical harvesters have been spotted in vineyards but, as Louis Vallet wryly points out, 'they suck up dust, dead leaves and insects, which are not neutral if you crush them and involve much pumping which induces premature oxidation.' In addition, since they only harvest berries, not stalks, and split them in the process, *cuvaison* must perforce be shorter than with traditional bunch harvesting.

Blind tastings show a significant preference for wines vinified with stalks. Destalked wines start with more colour which rapidly degenerates after 2–3 years in bottle. Many claim 'traditional' vinification, but, as Louis cynically observes, one has often only to look behind the *cuverie* to discover 'a mountain of stalks' awaiting removal. He is equally sceptical about those who claim to eliminate rotten grapes at the *cuverie*; in 1971 they employed 15 people to sort grapes but had to stop after a few hours: 'it's impossible, imagine 300 kilos of grapes . . . we're not in Sauternes here.'

Eschewing modern aids makes tradition difficult: the first 10 cm. of each old wooden Bourée *cuve* are filled with grapes which are then crushed by foot; the remainder is filled with whole bunches, and fermentation starts naturally after 2–3 days. No artificial yeasts are used: 'Yeasts have personalities; those in Charmes-Chambertin are not the same as those in Clos de la Justice or in Beaune.' Thereafter, 3 or 4 times daily, the pulp is trodden by foot 'until you are up to your waist, or frequently further – in fact, sometimes immersed completely.'

Tradition does not permit cooling; if the *must* rises to the heretical temperature of 39° C, Louis just shrugs his shoulders, adds some yeasts and gets the vat going again.

The Domaine possesses no cooling apparatus, just an endearing faith in nature's abilities : 'la nature est bien faite', he declares, presumably with crossed fingers in 1985 and 1989 as temperatures in 3 *cuves* rocketed to 40° C – without apparently sticking!

The argument from nature is graphically analogised: 'People in the Congo don't suffer from heat; they don't need to wear hats on their heads. If they ate a European diet they would be very ill.' One wonders how Louis Vallet deals with a headache, or indigestion.

A 15–22 day *cuvaison* precedes decanting into cask : 'We don't use a mustimeter – this is a tool of the laboratory, not of the professional.' When the cap sinks to the bottom of the vat, then is the moment to decant. Between 20–30% well-charred new Cognac oak is used: 'charring is more important than the provenance of the wood.'

After 15–20 months the wine is racked, unified and given a light gelatine fining : 'A unified *cuve* is always better than the best of the original casks.' Some 3–6 months later the wines are re-racked and fined.

The decision to use gelatine is no whim: they tried but stopped fish fining, because they could no longer be certain of its purity and provenance; Louis Vallet will not countenance fresh egg-whites, believing that commercial fresh eggs lack sufficient concentration of albumen to do the job.

The Bourée wines are not filtered but simply checked by candlelight for colour-purity then hand bottled – cask by cask. All are given the same exacting treatment. Casks appear to be bottled over a 6-month period, as and when bottles are needed. Louis is unequivocal about the style of wine he wants: 'Burgundy must not be fruity – this is no good for great wine. If you want fruit aromas, why pay 100 francs when you can have the same for 20 francs.' Short cask ageing and early bottling are the denaturing of real Burgundy – only a long period in wood followed by a long bottle-ageing will produce finesse, breed and elegance.

His wines bear him out: still in cask 25 months after the vintage, the 1988s show every sign of longevity, with pronounced crushed fruit, beginning to give way to more complex secondary aromas, quite well-structured and underpinned with some tight, harmonious tannins. The Clos de la Justice – 'This must be the worst vineyard in the entire Côte,' declares Vallet, 'it faces north and east' – smells of violets and crushed strawberries, with some attractive Pinot fruit and fair length. The Charmes-Chambertin was beginning to develop a fine, complex nose, although its tannins were tight and a little dry, giving the structure for longevity.

The Bourée wines are well crafted, thoughtful, creations. Although older vintages seemed a trifle rustic, what is being produced now is of sound, interesting quality. Vallet is proud of the fact that his yields are invariably below the *rendement de base* for each appellation, a factor he considers indispensable for quality.

He is mistrustful of the younger generation who don't vinify traditionally, because technology has bred security at the expense of quality. Why take risks when one can harvest early, cool a vat to avoid a stuck fermentation, use chemical controls in the vineyards and so on. The modern vigneron has technically clean wines which he can sell early, at attractively high prices. However, this is not all good news for the consumer; wines are not like shoes – you cannot rely on an examination before you buy!

Pierre Bourée and its twin Vallet Frères (identical wines under a different label), are traditional because Louis Vallet is a man cast solidly in the nineteenth century and his sons seem to be following in his footsteps. Perhaps occasionally, they might allow themselves the dream of a cooling machine . . . ?

VINEYARD HOLDINGS

Commune	*Level*	*Lieu-dit/Climat*	*Area*	*Vine Age*	*Status*
Gevrey	V	Clos de la Justice	2.00	30	P
Gevrey	GC	Charmes-Chambertin	0.70	70	P
Beaune	PC	Les Epenottes	1.22	40	P
		Total	**3.92 ha.**		

Domaine Alain Burguet

GEVREY-CHAMBERTIN

This small, new Domaine has made a disproportionate impact in recent years. Alain Burguet, its founder and proprietor, is a gruff, solid individual, highly suspicious of questions, which he regards as undisguised attempts to extract classified information, with an evident dislike of having to explain his methods, but who enjoys the minor renown which success has brought.

A visit here is among the least intellectually rewarding in the Côte. Most of Burguet's comments are prefaced by the remark that 'I am not a technician', leaving one unsure whether his *modus operandi* is largely haphazard or whether he just cannot be bothered to explain.

Like their maker, the wines are distinctly unforthcoming. Old vines and rigorous pruning keep yields low and concentration high. Burguet takes care over the health of his vines, with up to 3 separate annual treatments for grape-worm and 2 for red spider. Bordeaux mixture is also used, with 6 treatments for mildew and 5 for *oïdium*.

No herbicides are used, Burguet preferring to hoe his vineyards several times a year. In the winter, soil is ploughed up round the vine roots both as direct frost-protection and to aerate the earth because 'the softer the terre the less the frost penetrates', he claims.

Burguet is a man of determination with a clear – and perhaps somewhat inflexible – idea of how things should be done. He started his career as a vigneron working with his father from 1964 to 1972. He then worked for 2 years with Domaine Tortochot in Gevrey before leaving to create his own estate.

In 1974 he acquired 2.10 ha. of Gevrey on a share-cropping basis from an elderly farmer, the contract requiring him to deliver one-third of the crop, as grapes, to his landlord and to pay all the costs of exploitation. In 1976 he bought a house in Gevrey and set about constructing a *cuverie* next door.

From the beginning, Burguet was interested in nothing less than top quality. A sojourn in Oregon gave him a fascination for America and, in particular, a profound respect for *terroir*. His first vintages brought little profit, as he watched his neighbours making fortunes from excessive yields and indifferent wine. However, he was encouraged to continue his policy of quality by friends who tasted his 1978s and were impressed.

Burguet's Domaine now extends to 5.35 ha., 1.5 ha. owned outright, the rest share-cropped Gevrey-Chambertin Village vineyard, much of it 50 years old, or more. There is a minuscule patch – 4 ouvrées (0.16 ha.) – of Gevrey-Chambertin Premier Cru planted with young vines which will not be declared separately until it is at least 10 years old.

Alain Burguet clearly enjoys tending his vineyards; from 1985 to 1988 he even undertook the skilled task of making each graft by hand from his own *sélection massale*. Unusually, he prefers to harvest early to retain a good acid : sugar balance.

The grapes are lightly crushed and destemmed: 'nearly 100% – it depends on the vintage'; in riper years including a few stalks helps maintain an acceptable level of acidity.

Only indigenous yeasts are used, although there may be a *pied de cuve* should things appear sluggish, as Burguet prefers fermentation to start as soon as possible. No sulphur is added to the crushed grapes to delay fermentation artificially, but no one minds if a natural delay means that skins and juice macerate together for a few extra days.

The policy is to ferment at the riskier high end of the temperature scale – about 35° C. For this, uncharacteristically, Burguet explains: 'you see, it's like washing clothes, the higher the temperature the more you extract.' The risks are that fermentation will stick and be difficult to restart, causing spoilage, or that excessive temperatures will lead to jammy flavours.

After 15–20 days in the sultry habitat of a Burguet cement fermenting vat, only disturbed by the occasional *pigéage* (no pumping over here) the wine is decanted and amalgamated with the press-wine. It is then removed, with or without lees (depending on their quality), to mature in oak casks.

About 5% of the casks are new Allier oak. Having tried Limousin – 'too strong' – Vosges and Charente, Burguet decided that Allier gave the best structure and finest tannins.

He prefers to have a rapid *malolactic* fermentation followed by a long period of maturation on the fine lees, provided they are healthy. If not, then the wine is racked earlier. Normally, racking occurs about one year after the *malolactic* fermentation, the various casks being equalised, and the wine subjected to 2 separate filtrations – first, a kieselguhr earth filtration at low pressure followed by a light, polishing, plate filtration.

Burguet does not fine his wines because: wines contain dissolved CO_2; if you want to fine them you have to de-gassify them first and this perforce removes some freshness; QED: no fining. Incidentally, he points out, 'degassifying a wine may add an element of suppleness but I want to make a wine which will keep for 15 years, so I am not looking for it to be flattering at the start.'

Despite this, his 1989s, especially the *cuvée* of Gevrey-Chambertin Village, was remarkably approachable in cask a year later, with a deepish colour, an almost sweet undertone and a dimension of concentration derived partly from old vines.

In comparison, the Gevrey Cuvée Vieilles Vignes was marginally more open on the nose and palate – with fine concentration corseted by a layer of harmonious ripe tannins and a distinctly spicy flavour. He believes that it will start to become drinkable in the early 1990s, but the concentration of tannins would suggest the later 1990s.

The 1988 Vieilles Vignes Gevrey seemed to be at an awkward stage in its evolution – a lightish colour and rather nervous acidity sat on top of a powerful bed of tannins. Underneath there was length and fruit, but this is a wine for longer keeping than the 1989.

The 1987 Vieilles Vignes was quite light in colour, giving little on the nose beyond a slender aroma of raspberries. Decidedly of lesser complexity than the 1988, it did not lack stuffing and had a firm dollop of ripe fruit under a slightly tight exterior.

It may be that wines, like dogs, mirror their owners. If so, chez Burguet, they are aggressive to start with but Alain is confident they will blossom into something more charming on further acquaintance.

VINEYARD HOLDINGS

Commune	*Level*	*Lieu-dit/Climat*	*Area*	*Vine Age*	*Status*
Gevrey	V	Pince-Vin	1.20	50	P/F
Gevrey	V	Aux Corvées	0.50	40	P/F
Gevrey	V	Jouise	0.42	50	P/F
Gevrey	V	Creux Brouillard	0.90	50	P/F
Gevrey	V	La Justice	0.30	60	P/F
Gevrey	V	Reniard	1.26	35	P/F
Gevrey	R	Pince-Vin/Genevrière (Bourgogne)	0.77	35	P/F
		Total	**5.35 ha.**		

Domaine Philippe Leclerc

GEVREY-CHAMBERTIN

This is an unusual Domaine in that it has tradition, but no past. When Philippe Leclerc received 4.3 ha. as his share of the family vines in 1974, at the age of 23, he was already steeped in wine, having left school at 13 to work with his father. Time spent talking to older vignerons in Gevrey taught him to appreciate traditional practice helped, no doubt, by some traditional tasting.

Nonetheless, Philippe is something of an iconoclast in his desire to make big, uncompromisingly tannic wines, which take years to evolve. The results are often stunning – wines of great depth and hefty structure, but not without matching finesse.

Low yields from carefully husbanded old vines provide his raw material. He usually harvests 8 days after everyone else – in 1990 this meant 4 October, when most had finished by 25 September. He likes his grapes to arrive at the *cuverie* as cool as possible – he doesn't pick when it is very hot – but with the added ripeness of a late harvest.

He used to leave 50% of stalks in his vats but reduced this to 20%, having discovered that stalk tannins rarely harmonise, whilst oak tannins usually do. The crushed grapes are encouraged, by cooling and sulphur, to macerate for as long as possible before natural yeasts start fermenting the sugars. Over 8 days or so, tannins and colour are extracted, which also gives Philippe time to finish the harvest: 'you can't concentrate on picking and deal with a problem *cuve* at the same time.'

Once fermentation has started, it is persuaded to proceed as slowly as possible – a long gentle extraction. Temperatures rarely exceed 30° C., which allows *cuvaison* to last for up to a month. As soon as all the sugar has been transformed the wine is run off and the *marc* lightly pressed. For Philippe an excess of tannin does not exist, since his aim is uncompromisingly old-fashioned *vin de garde.*

What happens next is less than traditional: having cooled the *cuverie* and sulphured his wines, Philippe then blankets them with liquid paraffin. This effectively blocks the *malo* until the last but one vintage has been bottled in January/February and there is then space to transfer the new wine to casks. Philippe insists that having the *malo* in cask extracts noticeably rounder and more harmonious tannins.

The two Premiers Crus find their way into 100% new Nevers oak – except in lighter years when Allier is preferred – the Village Gevrey getting 10–20%. Here the *malo* passes off, at its own unhurried pace, since the wine will not be racked until the following November. The period under paraffin helps rid the wine of all but its fine lees – reducing the need for racking and helping clarification. Philippe prefers to have *malos* on the lees, provided these are healthy, believing that this adds a further dimension of richness.

The wines spend 2 years or more in cask before bottling: 'two summers for the *malos* and three winters for clarification', is how he sees it. This extended *élevage* enables him to bottle with neither fining nor filtration, thereby retaining the maximum of each wine's natural stuffing.

This is a highly individual and unusual vinification – yet entirely logical. 'I don't pretend always to be right,' admits Philippe, with rare modesty; 'I like to try this and that, analyse the results, then adjust here and there. One must always question things, that is the only way to the summit of quality.'

Philippe's wines are intense and fine. The Bourgogne Rouge – his largest appellation – is a big, sappy wine, with dryish tannins and plenty of sound, firm fruit. Not a wine for early drinking, but lovely after half a decade in bottle.

The Gevrey Village wine comes from La Platière – a vineyard 150 m. from the main railway line on the opposite side of the RN 74. Its richer soil gives the wine a characteristically broad, meaty structure – evident in both the 1988 and 1987 – helped out by extra concentration from 35-year-old vines.

The pair of Gevrey Premiers Crus, Les Cazetiers and La Combe aux Moines, are next door to each other in the north-west corner of the commune, in that band of superb land which includes Lavaux St.-Jacques and the Clos St.-Jacques. Philippe's 1989s had not finished their *malos* in December 1990, and this, together with his instruction to his barrel-maker for heavy char in 1989, made them difficult to taste. However, there could be no possible equivocation about their structure – powerful, tannic wines, both, with masses of succulent, concentrated, ripe fruit. The Combe aux Moines was a shade more open and delicate than the Cazetiers, but was constantly changing.

The 1988 Premiers Crus had only just begun to evolve. Here the Combe aux Moines was more closed than the Cazetiers, which was starting to show attractive animal overtones, with aromas of wild fruits and violet and a touch of *volatile acidity* – possibly from a gram or two of residual sugar remaining during the *malo* which were subsequently broken down into acetic acid. This will probably be assimilated as the wine develops. Both were characteristically big wines, with plenty of depth and potential.

It is often the lesser vintages which put wine-makers to the severest test. In 1986 and 1987 Philippe passed with flying colours. The 1987 Premiers Crus were deeply coloured wines, with the Cazetiers developing attractive aromas of *fruits noirs* and the Combe aux Moines those of a more savage, tarry style. Both had sound, firm, ripe fruit, a good balance and plenty of depth. Not as complex or profound as the 1988s, but fine wines to enjoy during the mid 1990s.

The 1986 Combe aux Moines is a triumph. A gorgeous, complex nose of ripe strawberries, with a finely judged layer of tannins supporting ripe, stylish, almost sweet fruit. Not a wine of hallmark Leclerc density, but one of seductive opulence, and a great success for the vintage.

Philippe Leclerc will tell you that he has difficulty in finding inner serenity. He is a restless man who appears to be always questing for something elusive – a loner. It is not unknown for him to disappear for a few days, when he feels he needs to escape. His wines obviously give him both pleasure and pain – there is always something that might have been done differently. However, the results are invariably excellent, and for most growers that would be ample compensation for the occasional imperfection!

VINEYARD HOLDINGS

Commune	*Level*	*Lieu-dit/Climat*	*Area*	*Vine Age*	*Status*
Gevrey	V	La Platière	2.00	35	P
Gevrey	PC	Les Cazetiers	0.67	45	P
Gevrey	PC	La Combe aux Moines	0.67	45	P
Chambolle	V	—	0.50	40	P
—	R	(Bourgogne Rouge)	4.00	35	P
		Total	**7.84 ha.**		

Domaine Maume

GEVREY-CHAMBERTIN

Whilst the 1970s and 1980s have brought considerable prosperity to the Côte d'Or, there are a few Domaines which appear stuck in a previous age and give the impression that they have no intention of being updated.

Bernard Maume and his son Bertrand run such an estate. The visitor to number 56, Route de Beaune, can consider himself as leaving the present decade for an epoch which has more to do with the 1920s than the 1990s. There is nothing as ostentatious as a sign to indicate the Domaine nor the contents of the various cellars which underpin – and undermine – the house.

Bernard Maume, a charmingly courteous man in his mid-fifties, exudes a quiet passion for his work and a scholarly thoughtful manner in discussing it. The Domaine was started by his great-uncle – Louis Mariller – whose father had vineyard land at Gevrey during the nineteenth century. Bernard was brought up in Dijon, but spent all his holidays with Louis Mariller at Gevrey, first playing around the casks and *cuverie*, and later helping wherever needed during the harvest. At Dijon University he distinguished himself as a bio-chemist, met his future wife and, fortuitously, added a National Diploma in Oenology and a Certificate in Viticulture to his qualifications.

In 1956, while Bernard was still a student, great-uncle Louis died, childless, prematurely pitching him into running the estate. He vinified his first wine in 1957, and thereafter managed to continue both his work at the Domaine and his research at the University which lasted until he had a 2 year break to take up a research post in Houston, Texas. This, and other important work, led to his being offered the Chair of Oenology at Dijon. He declined, and returned with his wife to run his Domaine.

His academic interests remain, though to a lesser extent, with some lecturing and supervision of research students, and his own research into yeasts and sterols. His various absorptions are evident from his study, a friendly clutter of acadaemia interspersed with bills 'in' and invoices 'out' and an air of a great variety of 'work in progress'.

The Domaine has grown piece by piece to its present size of 4 ha. To the original holding, Louis added the parcel of Mazy-Chambertin, which came from the estate of Thomas Collignon – one-third of which went to the Hospices de Beaune, for the Cuvée which bears his wife's name. Although Bernard did not acquire Charmes-Chambertin until shortly after taking over in 1957, he admits that many of the significant changes in land ownership on the Côte came from the financial difficulties of négociant houses after the 1929 crash.

Bernard's intellectual background exacts a thorough and considered approach to everything he does. The core of his philosophy lies in his belief that much of what is now considered innovative in fact derives from traditional practices. 'Intellectually,' he says, 'there is very little new to discover' (about wine-making). There is no point tinkering with a tradition which produces excellent wine without some convincing justification.

In the vineyards, average age of the vine is kept as high as possible by *repiquage* with plant material selected by Bernard from his own land. Until 1988 he grafted the wood himself, but abandoned this when his only vigneron finally retired. Now he gives the wood to a nursery he trusts, to be grafted onto rootstocks 161/49 and 3309 (a low-yielding Riparia-Rupestris cross).

The soil is subjected to a light biodegradable organic herbicide and is hoed every three or so years. Any obstinate grasses are dealt with by hand, with a pick. Bernard does his best to prevent rot with an organic anti-rot fungicide spray followed by a traditional Bordeaux mixture. His insecticides are, as far as possible, also biodegradable.

During the harvest three separate *tries* ensure that any rotten fruit is removed before it reaches the fermentation vats. This, and the high proportion of old vines, mean pitifully small yields which must be among the lowest in Gevrey. In Mazy-Chambertin, for example, recorded yields were (in hl./ha.): 1984 – 13.5; 1985 – 23.0; 1986 32.0; 1987 – 23.0; 1988 – 36.0 and 1989 – 33.0. In Charmes-Chambertin, the average figure is hardly more generous – 26 – 30 hl./ha. Set against an authorised yield of 37 hl./ha. plus any permitted increase in abundant vintages, these seem positively niggardly. Would that a few others followed suit!

Bernard Maume

Once past the selection process, a bunch of Maume grapes may expect to be 100% destemmed and lightly crushed. 3 or 4 days pre-fermentive maceration at ambient cellar temperature precede a long, slow alcoholic fermentation in large old oak *foudres* which line the wall of the ground-floor *cuverie*.

A peculiarity of Louis Mariller's vinification was the use of a liquid, cultured yeast bought annually from a specialist in Dijon. Bernard continues the practice, his researches having convinced him that these produce a better result than natural yeasts, which are a mixture of more and less desirable strains.

On the question of *chaptalisation* Bernard is circumspect. Until recently, the rules allowed just one single dose of sugar; however, since 'this is not very satisfactory from an oenological point of view' he prefers to *chaptalise* in several small doses, to prolong fermentation.

Cuvaison lasts up to 4 weeks, including a short period of post-fermentive maceration after which the new wine is run off into one of a remarkable battery of underground glass-tiled *cuves*, built by great-uncle Louis. The remaining pulp is taken out of the *cuves* by hand and fed into a horizontal plate press. This article is a museum piece, constructed in 1929 and although 'un peu particulier' continues to work well, giving a gentle, slow pressing which extracts good quality press-wine. As well as pressing, this device also rotates, driven by an ancient lorry engine mounted on a wooden table, complete with 5-speed gear-box harnessed up to a distinctly do-it-yourself system of belts and wheels. When reverse gear is required, this is achieved by the simple expedient of changing round the polarity on the lorry-motor contacts.

Whilst this remarkable contrivance normally functions perfectly, it occasionally breaks down. Then a back-up, a monstrous wooden nineteenth-century square screw-press, mounted on wooden legs, is, so to speak, pressed into service. In view of the fact that it takes 3 strong men some time to

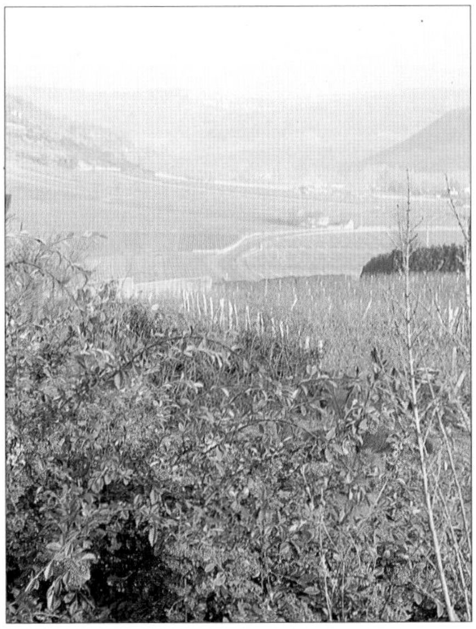

Late autumn landscape in the Côte d'Or

remove the large blocks of wood which weight down the pressure plate, much effort is expended by Bernard's son to keep the 1929 press running sweetly .

By whatever means it is extracted, the press-wine is added to the free-run wine. Whilst for the Grands Crus, only the first pressing is added, for the Premiers Crus and Village wines both first and second pressings are used. Each *cuve* is then allowed a few days to homogenise in underground vats before being decanted into casks.

The Grands Crus arrive in some 40% new wood whilst for other wines the proportion is about 20–25%. Experiments have resulted in the Mazy-Chambertin and Village en Pallud Gevrey going into Nevers oak, whilst the other Gevrey Villages and Charmes-Chambertin are lodged in Vosges. For the Lavaux St.-Jacques the new wood is 50/50 Vosges and Nevers. The Vosges imparts a softer tannin, with hints of vanillin, whilst the Nevers gives the wine a stronger foundation of tannin and considerable body.

The casks are then put into a small cob-webby cellar underneath the house, which is heated to about 17° C to start the *malolactic* fermentation. The Village Gevreys invariably start, just followed by Lavaux St.-Jacques and Charmes-Chambertin. The Village en Pallud and the Mazy-Chambertin are the last to go.

Since Bernard reduces racking to the bare minimum, often casks remain untouched until the time comes for bottling. Should a racking be needed after the *malo* then the wine is returned to its original cask; this enables him to follow the evolution of each wine and to assess the effects of different types of oak.

In April or May of the second year, after about 20 months in wood, the wines are fined with fresh egg-whites. The larger lots are then assembled by amalgamating 4 barrels – 3 old to 1 new. Each 4-barrel lot is bottled separately. The smaller lots – for example the Charmes-Chambertin, of which there are only 2 barrels – are bottled barrel by barrel. All Bernard Maume's wines are unfiltered.

Tasting chez Maume is an unforgettable experience. The expansion of the Domaine has meant that to make room for others, casks have found their way into all sorts of obscure corners. The young wines, reposing in Uncle Louis's glass-lined apartments are got at by lifting a species of iron drain-cover interposed with a sheet of thick plastic. An elegant nineteenth-century silver Tastevin – won by Louis at skittles – is then dipped into the liquid and carefully extracted, along with a goodly population of resident flies, for considered appraisal.

Although the cellar is a delightfully eccentric muddle, Bernard Maume's wines are superbly crafted and unquestionably among the best in Gevrey. Their style is dominated by a concentration derived from a deliberately late harvest, low yields and old vine fruit. The care with which the oak is chosen and used results in a harmonious balance of wood and grape tannins – enough to bolster the natural structure but not enough to dominate it.

The Gevrey en Pallud(1989), from a *lieu-dit* just below the Route des Grands Crus, has characteristic succulence and power with an overlying finesse and cask aromas of red fruits and blackcurrant, whilst the Gevrey Village *cuvée* is softer and rounder with ripe, well-integrated tannins and aromas of vanilla and cocoa beans.

By contrast, the Lavaux St.-Jacques has more finesse, with a foundation of restrained power and ripe tannins. In cask the 1989 was developing an attractive spectrum of aromas, which according to Bernard characteristically combine the secondary and tertiary derivatives of *sous-bois* and mushroom with a noticeably floral element. The wines from this vineyard tend to long retain the structure of their youth

The Gevrey-Chambertin Premier Cru – a blend of wines from the Perrière and Cherbaudes vineyards showed distinctly more nervous acidity than the Lavaux St.-Jacques with noticeably less class and finesse – though not without interest and ageing potential.

Of the two Grands Crus, the 1989 Charmes evinced considerable finesse with an attractive, deep, limpid mid-red colour. It had, at that particular moment in cask, a seductive spectrum of complex aromas which promised to evolve well over the next 5–10 years.

The Mazy is undoubtedly the best of the Maume wines. Tasting the 1989 from both new Vosges and Nevers oak as well as from a second-year cask, showed the common denominator to be a concentration of old vine fruit and a complexity more than meriting its Grand Cru status. Whilst the wine in Nevers oak had more obvious structure, the Vosges *cuvée* outshone it with considerable complexity and finesse. The same wine in older wood was relatively soft but lacked the balancing structure of the new oak.

Underneath the house, a small part of the cellar is allocated to a few stone bins of older vintages. Bernard consulted some mouldy cards on top of several of these bins, before removing a bottle and extending an invitation upstairs. Installed underneath the remarkable flagstone staircase leading to the first floor from the main hall he uncorked the bottle and poured the contents into large Burgundian ballons. The wine – chosen to show what a Maume wine becomes after a dozen or so years of ageing – had a refulgent, limpid, deep cherry-red colour and an extraordinarily complex aroma of *sous-bois* and forest-fruits. In the mouth it was a magnificent, complete envelope of ripe, almost sweet fruit, with a well-nigh impeccable balance and great finesse and length. It was a pleasure to share this 1978 Gevrey-Chambertin Lavaux St.-Jacques with its kind and thoughtful progenitor.

Bernard Maume is one of the best sources of wine in Gevrey-Chambertin. You may just as soon find him up an Alp cross-country skiing or climbing as in the cellars, but seek out his wines and you are unlikely to be disappointed.

VINEYARD HOLDINGS

Commune	*Level*	*Lieu-dit/Climat*	*Area*	*Vine Age*	*Status*
Gevrey	GC	Mazy-Chambertin	0.67	60	P
Gevrey	GC	Charmes-Chambertin	0.17	36	P
Gevrey	PC	Lavaux St.-Jacques	0.29	40	P
Gevrey	PC	Champeaux	0.28	7	P
Gevrey	PC	Cherbaudes/Perrière	0.18	30	P
Gevrey	V	En Pallud	0.66	35	F
Gevrey	V	La Justice + Etelois + Combes du Dessus + Les Fourneaux + Clos Prieur Bas =	1.47	25	P
—	R	Bourgogne/PTG/BGO	0.52	15	P
		Total	**4.24 ha**		

Domaine Charles Mortet

GEVREY-CHAMBERTIN

Denis Mortet is a talented young vigneron, custodian of more than 30 different plots, developed from an original hectare entailed by his grandfather to his father, Charles, in the 1950s.

The quality of wines is remarkable. From the first skirmish with the Bourgogne Rouge, it is clear that Denis knows the technical skills of wine-making and has its art at his fingertips. The fact that he works his 8 ha. mostly alone makes the achievement the more extraordinary. His guiding principle is to keep culture and vinification as natural as possible to make wines of concentration which are supple yet capable of long ageing.

The soils are hoed to deepen the root system and weeds controlled with organic products, preferably vegetal based, whilst pests are dealt with by standard sprays applied as long as possible before the harvest so that no trace finds its way into the wine. Denis admits to particular difficulty with the proliferous red spider, where effective control is only possible if everyone treats conscientiously. Soil viruses are also troublesome since hoeing can easily lead to re-infection.

To reduce yields, Denis uses low-yielding clones and low-vigour root-stocks in addition to maintaining a high average vine age, on which he places especial emphasis. In 1988 experiments with 'green pruning' of young vines in Chambolle and Gevrey led to 'superb results' which encouraged him to continue the practice whenever there appear to be an excess of bunches.

The Mortet harvest is unusually early. There is no point in delaying after the harvest declaration when the grapes are already fully ripe, although in less favourable seasons, Denis is happy to wait for a hot spell of autumn sunshine to add a degree or so of ripeness and a touch more concentration.

Picking is scrupulously careful. The pickers, 'gens très serieux', have been drilled to take only healthy grapes and to excise anything that appears substandard. Not content with their efforts, Denis also scans each small harvesting box as it is emptied at the *cuverie*. One is left feeling that a rotten Mortet grape would be pretty well friendless.

Vinification is fairly orthodox and stalks are completely taboo. There is a long fermentation at 29–32° C; a touch of pumping-over to begin with and 2–3 regular, firm, *pigéages* each day. Yeasting is beyond the pale; when the fermentation won't start, a *pied de cuve* is used to get things going. In general, *cuvaison* lasts 13–15 days, including a short period of pre-fermentive maceration.

Once the press-wine has been added, the Village Gevreys and the Bourgogne Rouge *cuvées* are assembled from the various lots at Denis' disposal, weeding out the poorer vats which are destined for the local négociants – a pity some grander Domaines don't follow this example – before transferring the wines to casks in the cellars below the *cuverie*.

By careful experiment, Denis has found that a mixture of Allier, Nevers and Vosges oak is preferable for the Gevreys (33% new), whereas the Premiers and Grands Crus, and wine from very old vines, fare best in Vosges oak, which although it takes longer to marry with wine, in the end gives something better.

In late April the wines are racked, where possible exchanging new and old wood. For the Village wines this means that some wine remains in older wood, whereas for the Premiers Crus (50–60% new wood) there is a simple exchange of new casks with old. The Grands Crus, being in 75% or more new wood, remain in the same cooperage.

Bottling takes place after 17 months in cask, without fining to avoid a further racking which tires the wine. The various lots are unified, given a light kieselguhr filtration and then bottled by a visiting bottler whose competence Denis trusts. The lots of Clos Vougeot and Chambertin are hand-bottled by Denis.

Although he started working with his father in 1976 it was not until 1984 that they exported their first bottles. Now they produce 3,000 – 4,000 cases, much of which finds its way out of France. The wines are characterised by suppleness and succulent ripe fruit, with great depth and complexity. The least of the Mortet wines, their Bourgogne Rouge, which comes from family vineyards at Daix, in the Côte Dijonnaise, is particularly precious. The 1989 is a tender, quite fat wine, with plenty of attractive ripe fruit, a firm backbone and a distinct *goût de terroir*. For its appellation it is exceptionally good.

The Gevreys differ markedly one from another: the 1989 Village wine had a deep red-cherry colour and a soft plummy nose – on the palate soft, well-structured with length and roundness, lacking perhaps a little acidity but hardly enough to mar a good future.

The Clos Prieur – an *assemblage* from two parcels, one touching Mazy-Chambertin and the other nearer the village – had notably more liveliness and complexity, with lashings of ripe fruit and an attractive fleshy softness.

The Premier Cru Les Champeaux – situated high up beyond Les Cazetiers – showed a stronger character with greater delicacy and significantly more acidity; altogether a delightful and promising trio.

The 1989 Chambolle-Musigny, matured in 50% new Vosges oak, is typical of its origin, with attractive finesse and length; a complete wine with perhaps a touch less than ideal acidity. By contrast, the Clos Vougeot, from vines situated near the Château de la Tour, was deep in colour, giving nothing on the nose, but with a fat *charpenté* structure, supporting a layer of powerful, ripe fruit.

These wines were eclipsed by the 1989 Chambertin, from a tiny parcel of 35-year-old vines, whose class came shining through. Mid red-cherry in hue, relatively closed up on the nose, but with length, depth and beautifully rounded tannins impeccably balanced by attendant acidity and marked, at this young stage, by a varied spectrum of fine complex flavours – a knockout in the making!

The white Aligoté and Chardonnay, also from the homeland of the Côte Dijonnaise, are less successful, both being dominated by a curious and aggressive *goût de terroir* and lacking somewhat in freshness.

However, this should not diminish the remarkable achievement of the young Denis Mortet's reds. These wines are among the best in the commune and would easily earn their place in a cellar of fine red Burgundy.

VINEYARD HOLDINGS

Commune	*Level*	*Lieu dit/Climat*	*Area*	*Vintage*	*Status*
Gevrey	GC	Chambertin	0.15	35	F
Gevrey	PC	Les Champeaux	0.21	70	F
Gevrey	V	Clos Prieur	0.32	50	P
Gevrey	V	(30 difft. plots)	4.00	40/70	3P/1F
Vougeot	GC	Clos Vougeot	0.27	18	F
Chambolle	PC	Les Beaux-Bruns	0.44	6	P
Daix	R	Bourgogne Rouge	1.37	18	P
Daix	R	Bourgogne Blanc Chard.	0.31	14	P
Daix	R	Bourgogne Aligoté	0.60	8	P
		Total	**7.67 ha.**		

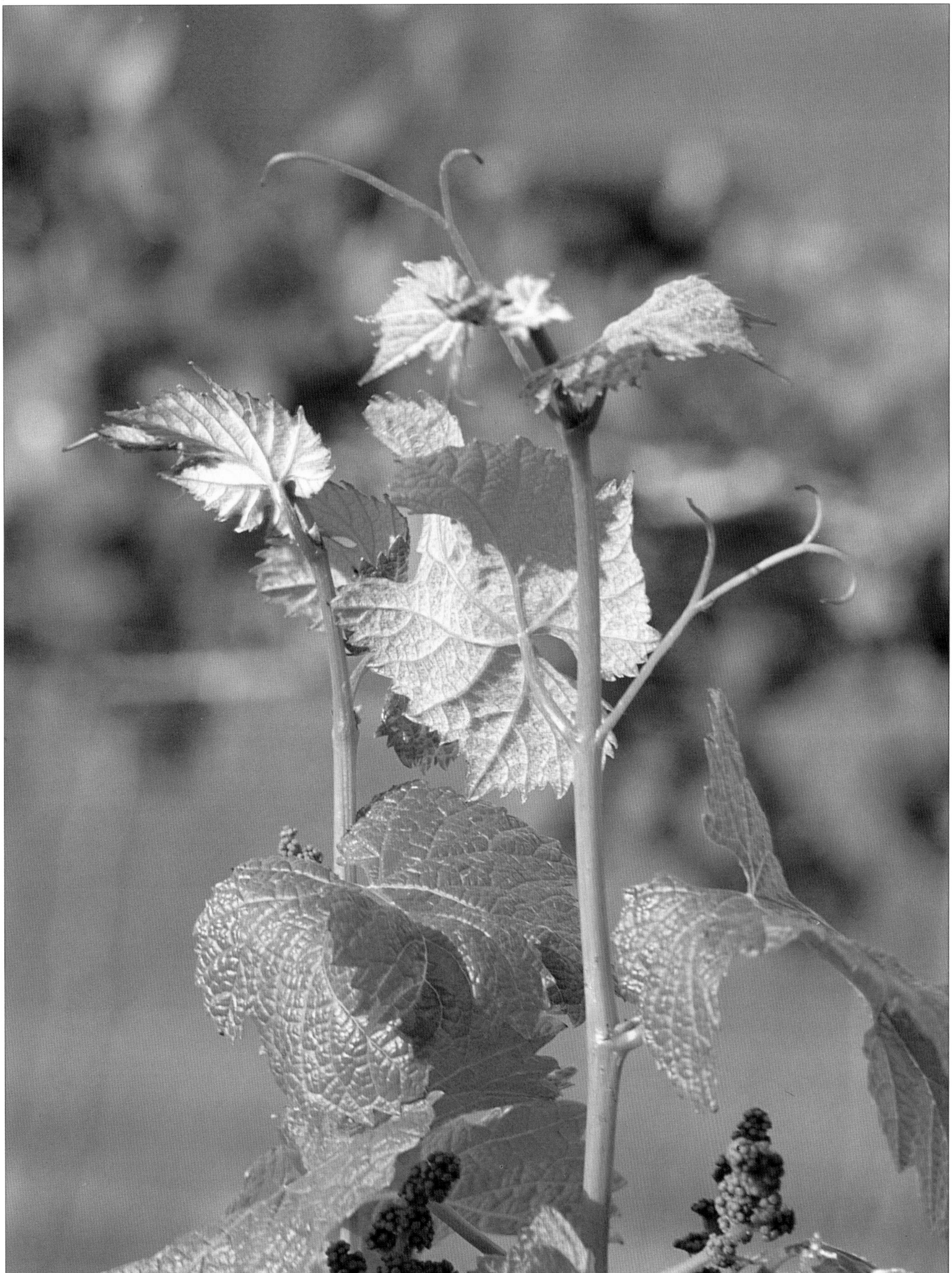

Domaine Joseph Roty

GEVREY-CHAMBERTIN

Among Burgundian viticulteurs – a decidedly heterogeneous collection of distinct individualists – Joseph Roty stands out . If his weathered complexion, copious whiskers and quotidien overalls, all vigorously animated by a wickedly disarming grin, were not enough to set him apart, his strength of purpose and sometimes iconoclastic ideas would serve in their stead. Here is a forceful character with a hearty distaste for pretension and pomposity, combined with a mischievous sense of humour.

Roty's philosophy rests on foundations as solid as his shoes: firstly, he considers wine to be the equal product of *terroir*, climate and vigneron; and secondly, a proposition instilled by his grandfather, who brought him up: 'the work of the vigneron is only the result of observation'.

From these principles, much follows: observation conditions every stage of wine-making. When you buy land, don't just look at a plan, instead prostrate yourself in the vineyard, touch soil, look at exposition, slope and surroundings, then decide. One vineyard Roty was offered was within a few metres of the water-table – he saw a well, and declined the offer. Equally, when the grapes arrive at the *cuverie*, look at them, taste them, try to find out how best to treat them. He spends a lot of his time observing – he likes to understand to the utmost, whatever it is he is dealing with. When he married, his son was conceived in the first week : 'I wanted to find out what it was all about – how it all worked,' he confessed with a broad grin.

The original Roty arrived around 1710 and his descendants have remained, tilling the land and making Gevrey-Chambertin. Joseph is the tenth generation and the Domaine as it is now owes much to his thriftiness and skill. When his father died, it took 7 years of profits to pay the death duties, and as much as possible thereafter has been reinvested in purchase of good vineyard land.

Jo Roty refuses to disclose what acreage he has – 'no one but me knows the age of my wife or the extent of my vineyards... my importers will think that I am a millionaire and will want to know why there isn't more wine,' he muses, so one is left to guess.

He started in 1968 with a legacy from his grandfather, Joseph Antoine, which, apart from the important maxim, included Charmes, Mazy, Griotte-Chambertin, Gevrey Premier Cru and Village land. He learned the trade by working vineyards for other proprietors; his prices being reasonable and his work careful, he was much in demand.

Now his goal is to pass on enough fine land to his 22-year-old son Philippe, his daughter Patricia (18) and his young son Pierre (9). Jo's father died at the age of 35, when he was 7, so he is determined to give his children the best possible start.

The Rotys appear to live modestly – a pleasant house on the northern side of the village, with cellars everywhere: 'I can never be found that way,' explains Jo with a grin.

His way of working is ruthlessly logical and highly individual. He is scathing of those who work by formulae and fail to think through what they are doing. As one might expect the Roty vineyards are looked at and looked after with great care. The vines are trained to 'the true taille of Dr. Guyot' – a maximum of 6 eyes on the *baguette* and 2 on the *courson* – and there is vigorous removal of redundant growth.

Fertilisers are limited to an occasional dose of 'guano', an organic manure, with frequent workings of the soil to cut surface lateral roots. 'Those who use chemical fertilisers and don't work the soil are not vignerons – they are jokers,' laughs Jo – meaning that fertilisers merely encourage the proliferation of surface roots, the opposite of what is wanted. He makes sure that any Roty laterals have a short life by hoeing round the root of each vine; with some 10–12,000 vines per hectare, this is no inconsiderable labour.

'Vineyards are like horses, one must be in tune with them and drive them' – more a question of coaxing from a vineyard what one wants by good husbandry and empathy than by letting fertiliser and treatment salesmen loose. This is delightfully illustrated by Jo's views on dealing with pests. No insecticides are permitted – even the rapacious grape-worm is allowed to munch away at the grapes to its heart's content. 'In the Middle Ages they would have simply excommunicated them,' reflects Jo. Now he considers, with an air of mock gravity, that by far the best treatment is ... a hammer; just squash them. Green-pruning is disdained – not because it is ineffective but because, if you have pruned and tended the vines properly and not planted over-productive clones and vigorous root-stocks, it is unnecessary.

An average vine age of a healthy 3 score, with some 60–80% on original roots, and deliberately late harvesting, reduces yields and concentrates the wines. The pickers are trained to remove any rotten or unripe grapes, and not to harvest the *verjus*.

Each batch of grapes harvested is looked at and tasted by Jo. This – a practice also gleaned from his grandfather – tells him the ripeness of the pips, the thickness of the skins, the quality of the tannins and the levels of acidity and sugar. The stalks are removed, more or less depending on the vintage (1990 100%) and the temperature lowered to 14–15° C for a cold *maceration* of about a week. Unusually, unless there are problems, no sulphur is added to the pulp: 'why take aspirin if you are perfectly well' is the argument here.

He prefers to extract colour by cold maceration rather than by allowing the fermentation temperature to rise excessively. Colour extracted by heat does not last and such a process risks *volatile acidity*.

Jo's process for cooling his pulp is somewhat unorthodox: one mustn't shock but cool gently, bit by bit. This is achieved with a piece of hand-made homeopathic apparatus which Jo designed himself. The details are obscure, but the process allows a small part of the pulp to be slowly cooled each day and returned to the bulk.

This same contrivance permits the fermenting *must* to be kept below 30° C – preferably at 28° C. This is unusually low, conventional wisdom being that, within reason, the higher the temperature the better and more complete the extraction of aroma and flavour. Temperature control is effected by one of three separate expedients: firstly, frequent *pigéage*, to break up the cap of skins etc. and distribute it with the juice. Chez Roty this means 4 people employed doing virtually nothing else day and night; the frequency rising with temperature; secondly, cooling the *must* homeopathically, with the special apparatus without aeration, at the sluggish rate of 1 centigrade degree per hour. This also helps to conserve aromas; thirdly, in years with a healthy population of strong yeasts, 'all you need to do is to de-gassify' the *must*. This is done by immersing 4 or 5 special plungers (another Roty invention) each with a flat, perforated stainless-steel cone at the end, into the *must*; the gas leaves immediately, and the vat cools. It is important that CO_2 can escape easily during fermentation – otherwise you have an undesirable Burgundian version of the Beaujolais' *carbonic maceration*.

The wines are fermented in open wooden *cuves*, since wood is considered far better than cement, which takes several days to heat or cool. The goal is a slow, gentle maceration 'like tea', declares Jo (he obviously doesn't drink French tea very often). A little initial pumping over homogenises the *cuve* and also gives a sounder idea of its ambient temperature. The shape of the *cuve* is no accident – 'The Romans knew how to build cathedrals and casks.'

Cuvaison lasts up to 3 weeks, during which each vat is analysed daily by Jo in his private laboratory. In addition each *cuve* is tasted regularly during fermentation and Jo reckons that he is able to tell within about half a gram per litre, the amount of sugar left to ferment. In addition to the pleasure of seeing how it works, this saves both time and money and enables Jo to react more quickly if there is something amiss. His equipment includes a sophisticated gas chromatograph – 'that analysis takes a little longer.'

Deciding when to decant the wine off its gross lees is precise and not simply a question of waiting until all the sugar has been converted; in fact Roty decants when there is just under 1.5 grams per litre of sugar remaining. The temperature is also critical – the *débourbage* which follows must be at the same temperature as that of the *cuve* from which the wine has come.

The small amount of sugar remaining has an important role to play in what follows. The press-wine, extracted with a motor-driven vertical press, is added to the free-run wine at the moment of pressing – i.e. as soon as practicable. It is only added according to the vintage – found to be too harsh, or unbalanced, it is sent for distillation.

At this point the various *cuves* of wine are assembled and each is left for 7–15 days for the lees to settle (compared with a norm elsewhere of about 12–48 hours). During the early part of this *débourbage*, the small amount of sugar is fermented by the remaining yeasts. The process releases CO_2 gas; the *cuve* by now being closed, this remains on the top of the wine to protect it from air ingress and thus from oxidation.

After all this care, the wine now passes, by gravity, into casks for *malolactic* fermentation and maturation. As one might expect, the choice of cask-maker and wood is undertaken with the usual Roty thoroughness. He has used the same firm for many years – deeming them trustworthy to air-dry the wood for 3 years before fashioning it into his precious casks. Thus, the only heat the wood sees is when the staves are heated to bend them. The Cîteaux monks used to air-dry their wood for 6–8 years but this, Roty admits, is no longer a commercial proposition.

Up to 1968 Jo Roty made all his own casks, but no longer has the time. However, this experience makes him a fine judge of the finished article and only too ready to reject anything substandard. Each year's intake is subjected to a meticulous personal scrutiny which consists of selecting a cask at random and inserting an inspection lamp through the bung-hole. If there is any doubt about its quality, it is opened up and inspected further. 'Given the size of the cheque I pay the tonnelier each year, he will only cheat me once,' Jo observes, adding 'I am not buying a piece of furniture, I am buying a cask.'

The tonnelier has instructions that each cask be well charred, using only heat from a wood fire. This high toast of the Burgundy and Chatillonais oak gives a very slow release of tannins into the wine.

The proportion of each wine that goes into these carefully scrutinised casks depends on the vintage and on the particular *cuvée* concerned. 'It can be 0–100%' of new wood; there are no rules. The remainder of the wine goes into older wood.' Casks have a maximum Roty life of 5 years before they are replaced. The *malo* preferably takes place in wood, although if there is no cask space left it happens in a tank, under a blanket of liquid paraffin. It is worth noting that the wine is not simply pumped into each cask, but filled from the bottom, which means that the wine rises in level rather than spraying down with consequent aeration.

Racking is not part of Roty's vinification. Jo is clear that the purpose of racking a red wine is not to get it off its lees – that has been done by a long *débourbage* after fermentation – but to aerate it. So, unless racking is absolutely necessary, the wines are kept on their fine lees as long as possible – even until bottling.

During their *élevage*, the wines are periodically roused to distribute the lees evenly through the mass. In Burgundy, most white wines are *batonnés* but not the reds. It is felt that whites gain in fat and richness from this extra lees contact, but reds do not. However, Jo Roty believes that as long as the lees are genuinely fine – both in size and quality – there is no risk of a *goût de lie*, a yeasty, cardboardy taste which can easily render a wine flat and disagreeable.

After all this consummate care, Jo will not compromise his wines in preparation for bottling. There is thus no filtration and no fining. The various casks of each wine are assembled in bulk a quarter of an hour before bottling. When is the right time to bottle? There are no rules. However, the humblest of the Roty wines, the Passe-Tout-Grains, generally spends some 12–14 months in cask.

Cleared for take-off; an early dose of fertiliser

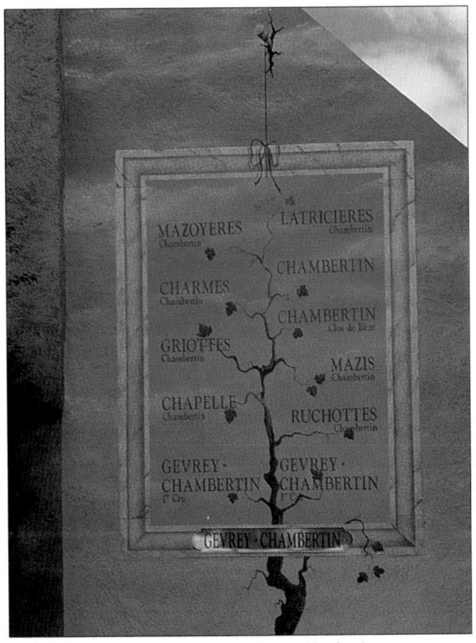

A splendid trompe l'oeil on the wall of a house in Gevrey

The grander *cuvées* spend longer – the 1969s were finally bottled in March 1972, some 30 months after harvest.

Jo Roty makes exceptional Burgundies. The high proportion of very old vines, even in the Village and Regional appellations, give low yields which, with long *maceration*, produce wines which are, atypically for the Pinot Noir, virtually black in their youth with a remarkable depth of fruit and a structure to keep them going for decades.

The range starts with a pair of Bourgogne Grands Ordinaires – one from Gamay grapes from Marsannay and the other from Pinot Noir from Brochon/Gevrey. The BGO Gamay is deeply coloured with a warm, long flavour. The vinification of these basic wines is not skimped – *élévage* in cask with as much care as if they were Grands Crus. Such was the depth of the 1988, that it did not finish its *malo* until the summer of 1990 – just short of 2 years after the harvest. The young Pinot Noir is yet more closed, with a highish natural acidity and plenty of 'matière'.

The Bourgogne Pressonniers comes from both AC Bourgogne and AC Gevrey parts of this large vineyard, and is sold with the lower appellation. It is usually deep black-cherry in hue, with a structure and depth well above its official classification; a wine to buy and keep for at least 5 years in good vintages.

Jo Roty is justifiably proud of his Marsannay Rouge – from a recently acquired parcel of well-sited 55–60-year-old vines. The wine is deeply coloured and harmoniously structured, with plenty of old-vine concentration and some attractive complexity. The 1988 and 1989 versions need at least 5 years in bottle before being ready to drink.

The range of Gevreys starts with a Champs-Chenys – a vineyard bordered by Charmes-Chambertin and Mazoyères. The soil is a mixture of pebbles, flat rocks and limestone, with a significant proportion of iron-pyrites in the subsoil, which together with 25% of pre-1914 vines, contributes to the density and style of the wine. Although Jo calls this his 'petit Charmes-Chambertin', there is nothing little about it – dense black-cherry in colour, with an excellent concentration of fruit, but noticeably more delicacy and complexity than the Pressoniers. With age it takes on a rather caramellised, vanilla and liquorice aspect which is most attractive. Again a wine to keep for many years in a good vintage and a few less in other years. For a Village wine, this is of exceptional quality.

Next is the Gevrey Brunelle – a vineyard adjoining Jo's house in the village. This wine is produced from grapes grown in the Brunelle and the Clos de la Brunelle vineyards, vinified as a single *cuvée*. The soils here differ from Champs-Chenys, being principally Marne clay, with 'têtes de loup' rock outcrops, and well-drained, more fertile soils. Not quite as dark or dense as the Champ-Chenys, it is often marginally more forward. Given that Roty's wines start life at double the density of everyone else's – except possibly Alain Burguet's – this Brunelle is still a big item. On the palate it shows some delicacy even in extreme youth, which promises well. In 1988 and 1989 a wine to hold on to for at least 5 years before drinking.

The third Village wine is the Clos Prieur – the superior part being a Premier Cru and the lower section AC Gevrey. The soils are richer here – no stones but rather 'têtes de loup' and a deep bed of clay. Difficult to assess when young, being very closed and concentrated, the general structure of the 1988 and 1989 versions leaves no doubt of a long and splendid future.

Jo Roty's sole Premier Cru is Les Fontenys – a vineyard adjoining the strip of Grands Crus between Gevrey and Morey. 'Fontenys' is a corruption of old French for 'little fountains' – a reference to wells some 30 m. below the vineyards. The soils vary significantly: at the top, layers of clay and sandy marls tend to reflect Ruchottes-Chambertin, which borders this part of the vineyard; lower down, the soils more resemble Mazy-Chambertin, just below. This blend of characteristics, together with vines which are so old that no-one has a record of their planting, gives a massively dense concentration with a strong, firm structure which takes years to open out into a wine of great power and finesse, showing a nose of 'fruits sauvages' and a somewhat spicy, tarry aspect – very long and concentrated. In good vintages, this is unquestionably a wine of Grand Cru quality.

The Grands Crus in this stable are truly remarkable; made, like all Roty wines, from old vines, they are deep, impenetrable, black-cherry in colour when young with a vast structure of tannins and acidity supporting an equally massive concentration of fruit; all of which, in vintages such as 1988, 1989 and 1990 will take decades to soften out and unpack.

Despite their daunting structure, the wines are not lacking in charm. On the contrary, delving below the corsets, as it were, one comes to sweet ripe flesh and a magnificent complexity with considerable finesse.

The Mazy-Chambertin and the Griottes-Chambertin are mouthfilling wines of great depth and complexity – vinified for longevity and seeming fit to last a century. Arriving at the end of a long tasting it is almost inconceivable that there should be something greater to tempt the palate. Yet in the Charmes-Chambertin one finds a virtually black wine – the colours of a young Syrah and seemingly little to do with the Côte d'Or – with a staggering concentration of pure fruit and massive extract. These wines are multi-dimensional mouthfuls, with a life expectancy far beyond the mortal three score and ten. The Charmes derives its depth from vines planted in 1881 and its length and complexity from careful and painstaking vinification.

It matters little to Joseph Roty that he makes wines of a different style from those around him. Those he produces are individuals of exceptional quality at every level and this alone entitles him to be classed among the topmost ranks of the Côte d'Or.

VINEYARD HOLDINGS

Commune	*Level*	*Lieu-dit/Climat*	*Area*	*Vine Age*	*Status*
Gevrey	GC	Griottes-Chambertin	N/A	N/A	N/A
Gevrey	GC	Mazy-Chambertin	N/A	N/A	N/A
Gevrey	GC	Charmes-Chambertin	N/A	N/A	N/A
Gevrey	PC	Les Fontenys	N/A	N/A	N/A
Gevrey	V	Champs-Chenys	N/A	N/A	N/A
Gevrey	V	La Brunelle	N/A	N/A	N/A
Gevrey	V	Clos Prieur	N/A	N/A	N/A
Gevrey	V	Les Crais/Charreux	N/A	N/A	N/A
Gevrey	R	(Bourgogne Blanc)	N/A	N/A	N/A
Gevrey	R	Les Pressoniers	N/A	N/A	N/A
Gevrey	R	BGO – Les Marcellys	N/A	N/A	N/A
Marsannay	R	(R/W/Rosé)	N/A	N/A	N/A

Domaine Serafin Père et Fils

GEVREY-CHAMBERTIN

Domaine Serafin is a young establishment, founded by Serafin Père with the acquisition of a patch of Gevrey-Chambertin in 1947. He continued to add good land until his Domaine reached its present extent of 4.39 ha. When Père died in the late 1960s, his son Christian took over; the vineyards now belong to him and his sister, who lives nearby. Overseeing all their activity is 'Madame Serafin Mère', who lives above the cellars.

Christian is quiet and dedicated to quality. His viticulture is as organic as possible, aiming at low yields and old vines. In particular, shortish pruning, rigorous *évasivage* and green-pruning in abundant vintages reduces yields, and scrupulous removal of *verjus* bunches which sap strength from the vine maintains concentration.

Treatments are copper-based and relatively traditional. Christian's cynicism about the effect of anti-rot sprays on the market limits their use to a minimum. 'In 1983 even though I treated three times, we had as much rot as if I hadn't treated at all.' He is particularly assiduous in treating the grape-worm, a major cause of rot; 3 applications, before grape-set, in early July and again in early August usually suffice.

At vintage, a double *trie* – once in the vineyards and again at the *cuverie* – removes any rotten or unripe grapes; this is because it is difficult to find good pickers.

Serafin's vinification is still evolving. After 70% destalking the pulp is left to macerate for 3–5 days with one pumping-over every other day. Once fermentation has started, *remontage* stops and twice daily hand-*pigéage* takes over to break up the cap. Artificial yeasts are not favoured, rather a *pied de cuve* is used should fermentation not start naturally, in the cold Serafin cellar.

Christian is somewhat dubious about his tradition of leaving 30% of the stalks with the fermenting pulp. 'The oenologue tells me to do it,' he moans, 'but I don't like it.' The justification is that stalks add tannin and acidity, make the pulp easier to work with and extract more colour, although 'they absorb as much as they put in, so where are you?' His Bourgogne Rouge, however, is 100% destalked, for suppleness and early drinking.

Fermentation, at up to 35°C, is followed by a long period of post-fermentive *maceration*. In 1990 Christian experimented with a *cuvaison* of 3 weeks, though, as he hastens to point out, it is normally 15–18 days. The wine

Christian Serafin – skilled hands

loses a touch of colour by long *cuvaison*, but since his aim is to make *vins de garde*, he believes he has no alternative.

The *marc* is then lightly pressed. 2–3 days *débourbage* precedes the passage of the wine into casks. There is noticeable hesitancy here: 'I was rather against new wood, but my American importer pushed me into trying some new oak for the first time in 1987. I think it gives something to the wine, especially in years like 1984 when the new wood hides some of the acidity.'

Now the policy is for an average of 70% new wood – the Bourgogne Rouge having none and the Charmes-Chambertin perhaps 90–100%. The excellent Gevrey-Chambertin from the Vieilles Vignes sees about 90% new oak, with the other 10% in second or third year casks. Christian claims to be convinced by the results – but his look contradicts him.

In 1990 he decided to delay the first racking until after the following harvest. The wines thus spent 15 months in cask before racking and fining around November, were left *sur col* for 2–3 months and then bottled. He remains unsure what this achieves but is content to follow the practice of such an illustrious Domaine as Romanée-Conti.

In contrast to his father, Christian regards filtration as an unacceptable interference, and considers a little deposit essential to the longevity of a wine. Whilst samples of Gevrey Le Fonteny which were neither fined nor filtered were kept to monitor their progress, he seems wedded to eliminating both processes if he can.

Two *cuvées* of Gevrey-Chambertin form the majority of the annual 2,200-case production; one from 12-year-old vines, for which he hopes to get back the original status of Premier Cru Les Corbeaux, and a Vieilles Vignes from 1.67 ha. from 8 different *lieu-dits* planted in 1920 and 1960.

Christian Serafin's wines have considerable style and finesse, together with the weight derived from a long *cuvaison*. The basic Gevrey is almost Chambolle-Musigny in its delicacy, without any lack of fruit or underlying power. The Vieilles Vignes, assembled early from the various lots, has an altogether more concentrated and firm structure, the old vine fruit imparting a most attractive dimension of depth and complexity; the 1989 and 1988 versions are indubitably better than many other Premiers Crus and probably a few Grands Crus into the bargain.

The Premier Cru Les Cazetiers comes from poor soil, with visible limestone outcrops giving the wine a different structure from the Gevreys – more *charpente*, more obvious acidity and a touch of bitter cherry flavour. Underneath, plenty of ripe fruit waits to open out and give the wine character and breed. Christian reckons 'Les Cazetiers is for men, Les Charmes for the ladies.'

The Gevrey Premier Cru Le Fonteny has a greater immediate appeal. The 1988, neither fined nor filtered, showed excellent length and a good balance, whilst being in a temporarily reduced state on the nose.

There are at most 2½ barrels of Grand Cru Charmes-Chambertin – the Domaine's top wine – and Christian manages to extract something special from his 0.12 ha. The colour matures to a limpid red-velvet and the nose opens to reveal a complexity of aromas dominated by griotte cherry and raspberry with overtones of violets. Further ageing brings a more spicy, damp vegetation aspect to the nose, whilst succulent flavours evolve on the palate. The wine makes a fine summit to a conscientious and attractive range.

VINEYARD HOLDINGS

Commune	Level	Lieu-dit/Climat	Area	Vine Age	Status
Gevrey	GC	Charmes-Chambertin	0.12	1948	P
Gevrey	PC	Les Cazetiers	0.24	1961	P
Gevrey	PC	Le Fonteny	0.33	30	P
Gevrey	V	(Vieilles Vignes)	1.67	1920/1960	P
Gevrey	V	(Basic Cuvée)	1.52	10	P
—	R	(Bourgogne Pinot/Chard.)	0.49	1967/68	P
		Total	**4.37 ha.**		

Domaine Armand Rousseau

GEVREY-CHAMBERTIN

There are two distinct types of great Domaine in the Côte d'Or. The one evinces constant experimentation and innovation. The other gives a feeling of tradition honed down to a fine art. Domaine Rousseau is definitely of the latter style.

Charles Rousseau, who has run this superb estate since the premature death of his father in a car accident in 1959, is one of the kindliest and most genuine people one might wish to meet. Eager to expound his own philosophy, he is quietly confident of the quality of his wines, which are unquestionably among the finest in the Côte.

A glance at Rousseau's land-holdings alone is enough to make one rush for a bottle: nearly 8 ha. of Grands Crus, nearly 4 ha. of Premiers Crus and 2.25 ha. of Gevrey Village land. Charles inherited some 7 ha. and has added several vineyards to the estate since 1959: Clos St.-Jacques, Clos des Ruchottes, Chambertin Clos de Bèze and Chambertin.

However, whilst quality land may be a desirable prerequisite, it does not by itself guarantee fine wine. Charles Rousseau's policy is clear: fine land plus old vines plus low yields are essential. He keeps his vines as long as they are remotely productive.

Meticulous care is taken to ensure that only the best fruit reaches the *cuverie*. As little fertilisation as possible is used, but all organic, horse and sheep droppings and some humus. Every 20–25 years each parcel of vines is treated in this way; the vines on the poorer soils of the Côteaux are treated slightly more often – and given a dose of compost superadded to the fertilisers.

Rousseau has reason to be particularly careful about soil management. After the last war, his father was persuaded, along with other viticulteurs, that the soil needed massive doses of potassium to enrich the soil and promote extra vigour in the vines and thus to increase sugar levels. Charles vividly remembers the lorry-loads of potassium turning up at the *cuverie*. This turned out to be a signal error: the potassium infiltrated the soil at the rate of 1 cm. per year and the vine roots were effectively saturated. Being chemically 'basic', the opposite of acidic, it combined with the increased vigour and ripeness of the vines to lower the natural acidity of the grapes and thus of the wine.

The problem was first noticed about 20 years later and became yearly more acute. But the first indications came, when wines were reported apparently re-fermenting in bottle. It was thought that bacteria from imperfectly washed bottles was to blame, but when this didn't solve the problem they sought elsewhere for a solution. The wines left the winery in an exemplary state, yet were found by customers to be out of condition.

Rousseau tried everything he could think of – heating the bottles to 30° C, cooling them to –15° C – before the answer was found. It appeared that bacteria normally dormant were being activated by the reduced acidity levels caused by the increased potassium. Bacteria flourish when the pH (the measure of acidity at which zero is highly acidic, 7 neutral and 10 highly alkaline) reaches about 4.5. Wine is usually bottled at 3.2 – 3.8, at which levels there is no significant risk. Since all malic acid had been removed by the normal process of *malolactic* fermentation, what was refermenting?

Further investigation revealed that the re-activated bacteria were in fact breaking down the tartaric acid usually found to some degree in both red and white wines. The problem for Rousseau became, therefore, how to reduce the pH in his wines. Removing the potassium already in the soil was impossible, so the only alternative was to acidify the wines to an acceptable level. This was done and the problem satisfactorily solved. Each year now, as a precaution, acidity levels are carefully checked at fermentation, again after *malolactic* fermentation and once more just before bottling, and any deficiencies adjusted with a dose of tartaric acid. In 1981, 1982, 1983, 1984 and 1989 small doses were needed; however, in 1985, 1986, 1987 and 1988 no acidification was made. It appears, thankfully, that the mistake made in 1945 is finally being rectified – naturally.

The vines are tended with particular care: an initial organo-cupric treatment at the beginning of the summer is followed by a dose of sulphur against *oïdium* and then as few sprayings with Bordeaux mixture as are comfortably needed. Apart from a second sulphur treatment no other chemical sprays are countenanced. For the soil between and around the vines, a light herbicide followed by 2 or 3 hoeings makes sure that most of the wild grasses and weeds are kept at bay.

Harvesting is equally careful: Rousseau reckons that if he watches over his pickers like a hawk on the first day then things go smoothly thereafter, averring that 'unlike most vignerons, my place is in the vineyards, not in the *cuverie*'. At harvest, 'I let any visitors look around but they have none of my time.' So strict is he about excising rotten fruit that in 1986 there was a carpet of grapes in his vineyards. For as long as he can remember, the small hods or boxes of grapes were required to be emptied slowly – to avoid unnecessary crushing – into the crusher, which enabled the pickers to make a final check for rotten fruit which could, even at this late stage, be kept out of the *cuves*.

Charles Rousseau in his cellar – nothing great was ever achieved without enthusiasm!

A stemmer-crusher removes 80–90% of the stalks and the crush, accompanied by 1 litre of SO_2 solution per 1,000 kg. of grapes, goes into a battery of stainless-steel tanks for fermentation. Rousseau prefers to keep some stalks with the pulp to give a better distribution of heat throughout each *cuve*. Fermentation is never induced with cultured yeasts but starts normally: 'Once the first *cuve* goes then the others all go ...woooof' – with a grin and a broad wave of his hand. So, a few days' delay in starting fermentation amounts to a pre-fermentive *maceration* (now used by many as a matter of policy). However, he is not much in favour of the deliberate heavy sulphuring of the pulp to allow an extended *maceration* before fermentation – the practice of Guy Accad and his adherents.

Rousseau has never seen the need to bleed or *saigner* his *cuves* – a normal practice among conscientious growers in relatively dilute years such as 1982; 'with old vines and low yields, there is never a problem of poor concentration.' Alcoholic fermentation proceeds at 31–33° C ('I am not in the business of making jam') and lasts about 15 days. An old balloon-shaped contrivance serves to cool the *must* if things look as though they will get out of hand and *chaptalisation*, if needed, occurs at the end.

The free-run wine is settled for 24 hours before being run into casks. A new Vaslin press extracts the press-wine, which is then added to the free-run wine. This enables Rousseau to get the same yield from the press, with significantly lower pressure, thus avoiding the harsh stalk and pip tannins.

The Chambertin and Chambertin Clos de Bèze go into 100% new Allier oak; the Clos St.-Jacques into 70% new oak; the Ruchottes Chambertin, Clos des Ruchottes into 20–30% new oak and the Charmes-Chambertin, Mazy-Chambertin, Clos de la Roche, the Premiers Crus and the Village Gevrey-Chambertin are put into 100% of second-year casks employed for the Grands Crus in the previous vintage. Rousseau believes that the essential femininity of the Charmes-Chambertin, Mazy etc. would be destroyed by any contact with new oak. He is clearly in a minority here – but the sublime elegance of these wines makes argument difficult. About new wood he holds a strong conviction: 'you can't put a little wine into new wood and expect to have a Grand Vin.'

A Rousseau wine will spend 18–24 months in cask with 2 rackings. The second racking is preceded by an egg-white fining. The 'equalising' of the various casks of the same wine is an unusual procedure: 'I unify the wine and I don't unify the wine' is Charles Rousseau's cryptic description: the casks are lined up on a pair of wooden railways tracks, 4–6 at a time; taps are inserted into each and connected up to a system of pipes ending in a common feeder pipe. Turning the taps simultaneously runs the wines from each cask together into the feeder which delivers them to the most delicate of filtration plates and thence to the bottling machine.

A tradition of excellence, backed by sound intuition, pervades the Domaine. The Rousseaus evince a mastery of everything from first vine shoot to bottling.

Descending into the cellars beneath the *cuverie* and passing through several galleries brought forth an assessment of vintages at the Domaine since 1970. Apart from excellent and generally underrated 1972s, that decade was not remarkable. The 1970s themselves are holding up, but the 1971s 'had too much over-ripeness'. 1973 was a large crop of good but not great wines, and the 1974s rather light. 1975 was for most in the Côtes de Nuits 'an unmitigated disaster' as a result of extensive hailstorms which had their epicentre round Vosne and Chambolle. However, Rousseau's stringent harvesting methods yielded a small but good crop and he reports much praise for his 1975s. The 1976s, particularly in the Grands Crus, are rated a great success – just coming to drinkability for those with the patience to wait. 1977 turned out worthy wines despite being badly affected by the bacterial problem. 1978 was a good but not great vintage for Rousseau; whilst not obviously faulty, the wines seem to lack precision and depth.

1979 was an unfortunate year, in which there were special problems. Rousseau took his laboratory's advice and called in a contract bottler to flash pasteurise half the crop; this worthy correctly passed the wine over a flame to deactivate all known microbes, but omitted to cool it afterwards. The bottles were so hot that Rousseau could hardly hold them. The 'unactinised' wines are probably sound, but dull, the rest are distinctly problematical.

The 1980s, however, have been an excellent decade: 1980 was 'one of the best vintages I have ever made'. Having tasted most of the Grands Crus it is easy to see why. Although generally decried as a mediocre vintage, these wines whilst quite light in colour have a superb silky elegance and lack nothing in attractive, complex Pinot flavours. 1981 and 1982 are good sound vintages whilst 1983 will be excellent, without any traces of the rot which tainted so many otherwise fine *cuvées*. 1984 is light, but elegant, 1985 a very fine, ripe, succulent success and 1986 good, but not spectacular quality. The 1987s are very promising – Rousseau rates them very highly – but they need a good while longer (in 1991) to show their paces. The 1988s are for keeping – austere but with remarkable depth and balance needing years to unpack, and the 1989s and 1990s seem set for a classic maturation.

Tasting the 1989s is not only a striking proof of the superb quality of Charles Rousseau's wines, but an opportunity to compare the characteristics of the different *climats*. He does not claim to direct his efforts at producing any particular style of wine, his intention being to preserve as much as possible of the delicate Pinot Noir fruit and to retain as much elegance as he can. His Gevrey-Chambertin shows well what great wine-making and old vines can do with a simple Village appellation: soft, plump succulent fruit, attractively *framboisé*, supported by a firm structure, balanced acidity, ripe tannins and good length.

Of the Premiers Crus the Cazetiers is the most closed and the Clos St.-Jacques the most muscular and rustic – although still very fine. The Charmes and Mazy-Chambertin are characterised by the length one would expect from Grands Crus, with considerable finesse and elegance. Even in their first year in cask, there was no doubt of their intrinsic qualities. The Charmes shows more delicacy, but with time both will be rich, long thoroughbreds.

In Morey-St.-Denis, Rousseau's Clos de la Roche seems to take on something of the Gevrey tone of its neighbours in the cellar, with definite youthful mineral flavours and muscularity. With age it develops the majestically complex *sous-bois*, vegetal, secondary aromas of old Pinot Noir and in good vintages has great longevity. For example, the 1957 Clos de la Roche provided a firm, sublime glassful of great concentration and complexity in 1990 with no signs of imminent decline.

In contrast, the Ruchotte Chambertin, Clos des Ruchottes, a Monopole of Domaine Rousseau, is much softer and more tender in its youth. The 1989 showed a somewhat bitter chocolate nose with rather soft, ripe, well integrated tannins. Of all Rousseau's wines this tends to retain its youthful characteristics longest.

The 1989 Chambertin Clos de Bèze showed, as expected, strongish oak influence from the 100% new wood. Although Clos de Bèze tends to support rather less oak than Chambertin, the dominance of wood-derived aromas and flavours will disappear once the wine begins to mature. A further difference is that the Clos de Bèze has less soil depth than the Chambertin, endowing it with more obvious power. Both have considerable length and great elegance, the hallmarks of Rousseau's winemaking skills.

Charles Rousseau is a modest man, one of those rare people who exudes quality in everything he touches. The joy and depth he manages to extract from a life he so obviously enjoys, is amply reflected in his wines. His struggle with the bacteria demonstrates his determination to succeed. Fortunately that problem is behind him; no doubt there will be others – nothing is stable or certain in a vigneron's life. He and his son, Eric seem intellectually equipped to face whatever the future may bring. It is to be hoped that this will include an abundance of Rousseau wines.

VINEYARD HOLDINGS

Commune	*Level*	*Lieu-dit/Climat*	*Area*	*Vine Age*	*Status*
Gevrey	V	(Various climats)	2.25		P
Gevrey	GC	Mazy-Chambertin	0.50	1937/60	P
Gevrey	GC	Charmes/Mazoyères	1.50	35	P
Gevrey	GC	Clos de Bèze	1.33	40	P
Gevrey	GC	Chambertin	2.00	44+	P
Gevrey	GC	Ruchottes Chambertin	1.10	35/65	P
Gevrey	PC	Lavaux St.-Jacques	0.50	1941	P
Gevrey	PC	Les Cazetiers	0.75	1942	P
Gevrey	PC	Clos St.-Jacques	2.50	1924/54	P
Morey	GC	Clos de la Roche	1.50	30	
		Total	**14.43 ha.**		

Domaine Louis Trapet

GEVREY-CHAMBERTIN

Domaine Trapet is one of those engaging establishments where it is difficult to decide whether you are in the last century or the next. There is a strong feeling of 'esprit familial' which, together with the accumulated intellectual baggage of six generations, respectfully referred to as 'tradition', remains quietly in the background as the ultimate justification either for doing something or not doing it, as the case may be.

To visit the cellars and offices is to be transported back to the earlier part of the twentieth century. One can imagine ancient frock-coated, top-hatted Trapets holding their counsels and their celebrations in these small, formal rooms – deciding whether to buy this or that parcel of land, or welcoming a younger member of the family into the deliberations of the house.

Celebrations there must have been, for it is almost a Trapet tradition for each generation to add its 'stone to the edifice' in the form of a parcel of vines. The original Louis Trapet, from distant Chambolle-Musigny, started it all by marrying an orphan from Gevrey and moving there.

Around 1870 , Louis' son Arthur – great-grandfather of the present head of the house, Jean Trapet – realising that it was possible to rehabilitate *phylloxera*-infested vineyards by grafting on to resistant rootstocks, began to acquire Village land in Gevrey – the Grands Crus Chambertin and Latricières-Chambertin were added around 1904. He was in fact among the earlier converts to this way of working and his success gave a strong impetus to the Domaine to produce better wine than their competitors.

In common with many Domaines, the Trapets suffered during the 1920s and 1930s from insufficient labour and a weak market and up to the end of the 1940s Louis Trapet (II) sold most of his production in barrel to the local négociant trade. The early 1950s saw the gradual introduction of Domaine bottling which by 1975 had spread to the entire annual production of some 4,000 cases – about half of which is exported.

Tradition imbues the Trapet spirit. Louis (II), who retired in 1965, is still there to add his wisdom to deliberations and to help preserve the sense of oral tradition which so clearly matters to the family. A quarter of a century later, Jean Trapet – a short, kindly man, with an air of honest and old-fashioned courtesy, now in his late fifties – is slowly handing over the reins to his own son, Jean-Louis, who joined the firm in 1987 to understudy the vinification, and has been in sole charge of this since 1990.

One suspects that the traditional methods of working have been entrenched here longer than might have been entirely desirable. The wines have been generally in the upper-middle part of the quality spectrum with some occasional remarkably fine bottles and some occasional lapses. Criticism has focused on high yields and the emphasis on finesse at the expense of real depth.

Jean-Louis is an earnest, self-confident young man, in his mid-twenties. He has inherited his father's courteous disposition and is deeply thoughtful about everything that the Domaine does.

He is presently reviewing all the Domaine's practices, starting in the vineyards: here, the aim is to preserve the maximum natural humus and fauna in the clay-limestone soils of Gevrey. To this end Jean-Louis uses minimum fertiliser and much hoeing to replace the more usual herbicides. Strong chemicals, which remain in the soils for many years and are slow to degrade, denature the soil and destroy its fragile balance; they also kill useful predators on, for example, red spider, a notable enemy of the vine. He is also trying more precise insecticides to deal with grape-worm and red spider and only uses herbicides on particularly stubborn patches of deep-rooted weeds – such as Iseron.

The Domaine suffered – as did many others in the Côte de Nuits – from excessive enrichment of the soil with potassium, just after the last war. This is gradually working its way out of the land; but meanwhile, small deficiencies in other minerals such as magnesium are corrected only after extensive expert soil analyses.

Although the Trapets were among the earlier users of clones in the 1950s, Jean-Louis is considering reintroducing the traditional *sélection massale* for some of his plant material. He does, however, believe that it is essential to have several different clones in a single vineyard, both to guard against a clone-specific malady, and also to add complexity to the wines. He is cultivating both his own vineyard policies and his nurseryman to find out which rootstocks are best adapted to the calcareous Gevrey soils.

The problem of rot is part of life in the Côte de Nuits, where the autumns can be wet, where summer hail can split the grapes and where the destructive grape caterpillar is endemic. Jean-Louis is concerned that too rich a soil, especially in nitrogen and sodium, encourages *botrytis*. He is therefore investigating clones of Pinot Noir which have phenotypically thicker skins and give less tight, more regular bunches, to help combat the incidence of rot.

Jean Trapet – with his hand firmly on technology, keeping it at the service of the vigneron but never dictating to him

Strenuous efforts are now being made to limit the production of each vine to add concentration to the wines. Together with low fertilisation and the use of low-vigour rootstocks, Trapet believes in a very severe *ébourgonnage*, to cut off excess buds early on in the growing season. This has the additional benefit of spreading out the vine's vegetation and thus encouraging more efficient photosynthesis. In addition they restrain vigour by planting vines at relatively high densities – 12,000 vines per ha., compared with the more usual 9 or 10,000. Appellation rules limit the number of buds per ha. to 80,000, so one is at liberty to achieve this by longer pruning on a lower density, or by short pruning on a high density, which is the Trapet policy.

For the first time, in 1990, a green-pruning was performed, to excise some 30% of the bunches. Jean-Louis believes that this is an optimum, because above this level the vines compensate, leaving the vigneron with the same quantity but with thinner skins and more dilute juice.

As one might expect, harvesting is entirely manual. Jean Trapet and his son recoil in horror from the thought of harvesting machines in the Côte. They aim to harvest at maximum maturity, and are encouraged by their recent experiments with a form of high wire culture to expand the height of the Pinot Noir foliage; this increases both grape sugar content and the concentration of polyphenols – which help to fix colour in young wine and add to its structure.

Since 1990, the grapes are hand-sorted as they arrive at the *cuverie* and there are plans to add a further sorting in the vineyard from 1991. It is these small details which Jean and Jean-Louis agree make the difference between good and really fine wine.

Once any substandard or rotten grapes have been eliminated, they are destemmed – up to 95% depending on the vintage – and lightly crushed. The policy is to have a longer *cuvaison* to extract tannins rather than to add stems. With the 1990 vintage, a pre-fermentive *maceration* was introduced: the grapes are sulphured at the rate of 1 litre per tonne, cooled to 16–18° C and then left to macerate for 5 days. According to Jean-Louis, this extracts both glycerols which give a certain fleshiness and fatness to the wines, and anthocyanins which are valuable colour compounds.

Jean-Louis is also interested by the work of Guy Accad, whom he met in 1990. He has already made some experiments with different levels of pre-fermentive sulphuring, to see how the wines react and, whilst it is too early to evaluate the results, seems inclined to pursue this line of thought further.

The first *cuvées* are yeasted to get fermentation going – 'we have good yeasts at Gevrey' – and the rest soon follow naturally. Alcoholic fermentation is carried out in open, temperature-controlled, cement *cuves* and *cuvaison* lasts for up to 19 days. Pumping over of the juice at strategic moments to ensure that the temperature in the vats remains in equilibrium is interspersed with the use of a piston device, suspended above the *cuves*, to break up the cap.

Tasting rather than analysis is used to determine when the tannin extraction is at its optimum and the new wine is then decanted off its lees, given 12 hours *débourbage* and run into casks. The lees are gently pressed and the resulting press-wine is added only if it is needed. Jean-Louis believes that tasting is of primary importance in all the choices he and his father make. The technical analyses are only regarded as background information to be used in conjunction with whatever the palate reports.

The Trapets make sure that any wood which comes into their cellars is air-dried, and not force-dried in kilns. They would like, ideally, to use a little more new wood, but do not regard this as a means of imparting more structure to their wines, rather as a means of providing young wines with an environment

Short pruning on a high density of vines

of controlled oxidation. At present, the Grands Crus see 30–40% of new wood and the Premiers Crus about 20%. Vosges, Allier and Tronçais wood are all employed, and a proportion of each used in each *cuvée*.

The following February, after the *malolactic* fermentation, each lot of wine is tasted, racked and unified before returning to barrels. Altogether, the wines spend 11–18 months in cask – least for Village Gevreys and most for the Grands Crus.

In June or July of the second year, wines still in cask are racked and assembled in tanks before being fined with albumen. Then, and only if necessary, they are lightly plate-filtered before being bottled. The Chambertin Vieilles Vignes *Cuvée* is never filtered, but given a slightly higher dose of albumen fining.

The aim of all this is to produce wines which respect the characteristics of *terroir* and vintage: 'le plus naturel possible'. The Trapets feel that one should work with nature and not try to force it to produce a certain style of wine every year.

Do not expect massive, blockbusting wines from this Domaine. Their style tends towards elegance and finesse, with a hallmark backbone of succulent old vine fruit and a gentle lace-like delicacy. Despite this apparent lack of overt muscle, the wines age extremely well. They have power and structure, no doubt derived from the high proportion of old vines, which seem to sustain and nurture, without making them in any way burly or clumsy.

Whilst the Gevrey-Chambertin Premier Cru tends to an attractive nose of redcurrants and raspberries, more pronounced in riper years, it is the Grands Crus Chapelle-Chambertin, Latricières-Chambertin and Le Chambertin which have made this Domaine's reputation for superb wine-making.

Part of the special quality of the Grands Crus is due to the way that they react to rainfall: the vine needs a short period of dryness just at *veraison* – the moment when the grapes change colour from green to black – so that they can derive maximum benefit from soil nutrients. The Grands Crus, being on slopes, tend to drain off water better than the Gevrey Village vineyards lower down on flatter slopes.

The Grand Cru wines have uniformly deeper colours than their Village or Premier Cru brethren and a noticeably greater depth of concentration and complexity. This is, of course, as it should be. There is no hurrying a Trapet wine; in youth they are closed up and difficult to taste for a year or so, and then begin to show perceptible signs of opening out. They tend to be complete, but without any of the lumpiness that one so often finds in this commune.

The Chambertin Vieilles Vignes *cuvée* – introduced for the first time in 1976 – comes from the parcels of vines in the Chambertin vineyard which are 60–80 years old. This wine only makes an appearance in particularly good vintages – 1976, 1978, 1983, 1985, 1988, 1989 and 1990 to date. It is a remarkable achievement – an immensely concentrated, powerful wine, yet having an extraordinary delicacy and finesse – a gentle giant, which opens out with age into a glorious, opulent mouthful of considerable complexity and unmistakable class.

It is to be hoped that the Trapets are uncompromisingly committed to reducing yields, since some of their wines have been justly criticised for lacking concentration. If so, there is nothing to prevent their Domaine becoming one of the finest in the Côte. What is needed is a much greater consistency than was evident in the 1970s and early 1980s. They seem to be a family dedicated to quality and to the maxim that, as for wine-maker so for drinker, 'a pleasure implies an effort'. Progress will be watched with interest.

VINEYARD HOLDINGS

Commune	*Level*	*Lieu-dit/Climat*	*Area*	*Vine Age*	*Status*
Gevrey	GC	Chambertin	1.80	35/80	P
Gevrey	GC	Chapelle-Chambertin	0.60	40	P
Gevrey	GC	Latricières-Chambertin	0.80	40	P
Gevrey	PC	Petite-Chapelle + Clos Prieur	1.50	15/35	P
Gevrey	V	Derée + Petite Jouise + Champerrier + Vigne Belle	5.00	10	P
Marsannay	V	Le Foirier	1.00	20	P
	R	(PTG/Bourgogne R/W)	1.00	5/15	P
		Total	**11.70 ha.**		

MOREY-ST.-DENIS

Morey-St.-Denis is the rather somnolent filling in the sandwich of which the outside pieces are Gevrey-Chambertin and Chambolle-Musigny. A compact little village of some 800 inhabitants, it has long suffered from lack of exposure and from the renown of its more illustrious neighbours, with the result that its wines are among the least well-known in the Côte de Nuits.

There is no obvious reason for this. Although the commune is small – some 150 ha. compared with 180 in Chambolle and a massive 532 in Gevrey – it has its fair share of excellent growers, and 4 fine Grands Crus, plus a patch of Bonnes-Mares curiously left over from Chambolle-Musigny when the appellation maps were drawn up in 1936.

Even now, many of the 20 Premiers Crus are relatively unknown, being frequently sold as a blend of several under the designation Morey-St.-Denis Premier Cru without the name of the individual *climat*, which cannot but compound the problem.

However, with the efforts of the commune's 65 growers, Morey is gradually establishing its own identity. Fine wines from Domaines Dujac, Clos de Tart, Groffier, Clos des Lambrays, Hubert and Georges Lignier, Ponsot and others in the village, together with those from Roumier, Pernin-Rossin, Rousseau and others outside it, are giving Morey the much higher profile it has long merited.

This pleasant little commune has had a mixed history. Known as Moriacum, or Muriacum, its origins have been incontrovertibly established by archaeologists as Gallo-Roman. First mentioned in 1120, it has been something of a shuttlecock, belonging variously to the Abbeys of Cîteaux, La Bussières-sur-Ouche and St. Germain-des-Prés, near Paris. In 1636, during the 30 Years War, it was completely destroyed by fire. Perhaps all this has led to an ineradicable sense of collective insecurity and to parochial introversion.

The village itself seems, like so many others along the Côte, to be permanently asleep. Apart from the occasional passage of a straddle-tractor along the Route des Grands Crus, which bisects it, nothing much stirs. The road in from the RN 74 leads to the church and a small 'rond-point' illuminated by a painted scroll announcing that you have arrived at the Centre des Grands Crus and a signpost telling you to turn left for Chambolle and right for Gevrey.

Obeying the first injunction will take you smartly out of the commune passing below Les Bonnes-Mares, whilst a right turn leads upwards to the top of the village. There you will find a large municipal concrete space with a bench, another roundabout and a cluttered one-eyed shop, selling everything from beetroot to batteries, generally presided over by a lady who gives the distinct impression that customers are an inconvenience she could well do without.

Here the road forks – right for Gevrey and left, up the hill to the newer part of Morey – a festival of modern brick and dubious architectural taste which seems to have bypassed whatever minimal planning regulations exist in this part of France.

The vineyards cluster tightly round the village. The Grands Crus continue the band of hard Bathonian limestone from Gevrey, although with markedly more gradient. A vein of marlstone traverses Bonnes-Mares and the Clos de Tart, both of which have a topsoil of thickish scree. This peters out in the upper sections of the Clos des Lambrays which has more sand-sized particles in its topsoil. The Clos St.-Denis and the Clos de la Roche, to the north of the village, both of which are predominantly at the base of the hillside, have soils richer in brown limestone and also benefit from a particularly sheltered micro-climate.

At the northernmost edge of the village, just under the wood, is the Monts Luisants vineyard. This is something of a double curiosity: in the first place, it is the source of the minuscule production of Morey-St.-Denis Blanc, and secondly it is zoned across all 3 quality designations: the topmost section (2.19 ha.) is AC Morey Villages, the strip below (5.39 ha.) is Premier Cru Monts Luisants and the lowest section contributes

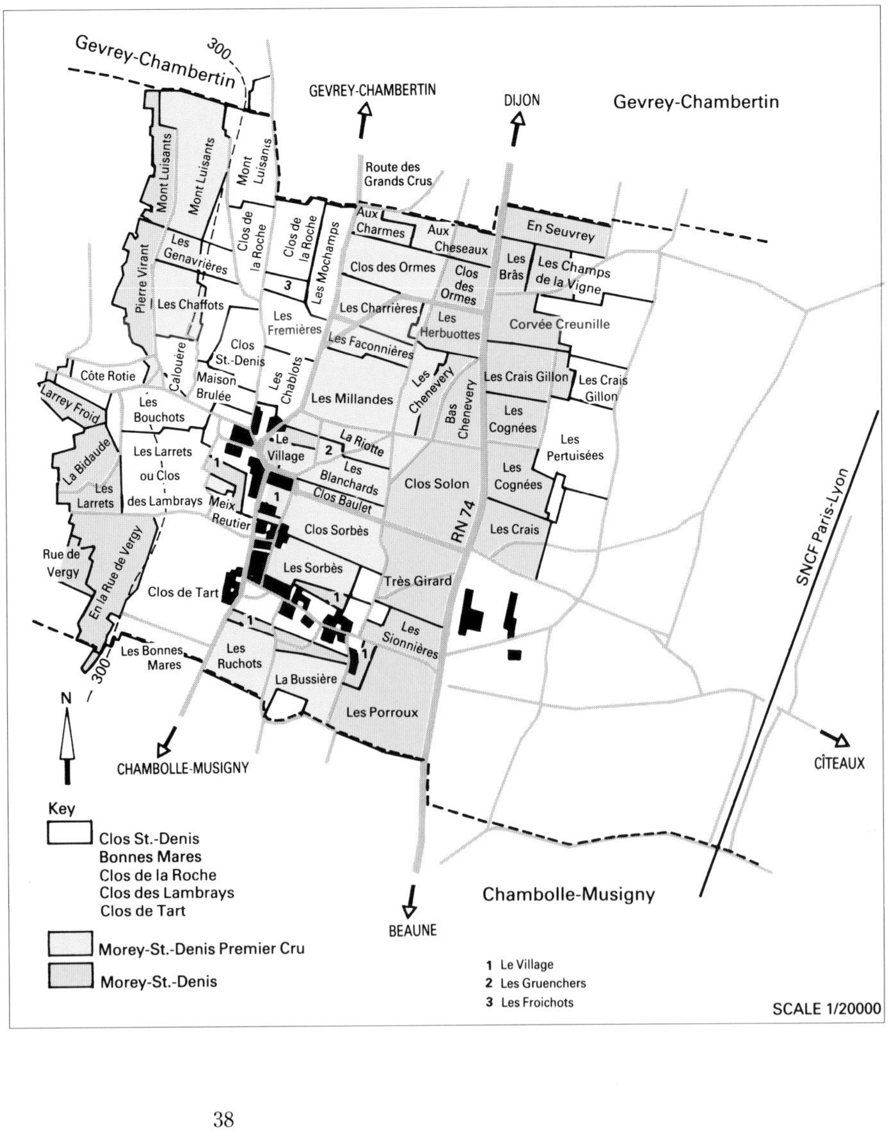

Morey-St.-Denis from the La Bussière vineyard

3.74 ha. to the Grand Cru Clos de la Roche.

The white wine is unusual and rare – only 200–300 casks are made annually. Although the appellation rules allow any Village or Premier Cru Morey to produce white wine, it is in fact confined to the Monts Luisants and the En la Rue de Vergy vineyards, because their relatlvely poor soil – high in gravel and iron, with virtually no clay – is considered ideal for Chardonnay. The exception is Jacques Seysses' plot of Chardonnay between his house and the main road, which is on rather richer, more fertile soil.

Seysses apart, there are two other principal producers of Morey Blanc – Bruno Clair from Marsannay, who reclaimed much of his land from scrub, and the Ponsot family from Morey. Clair uses 100% Chardonnay for his wine, but Ponsot, who has some 1.5 ha. of Monts Luisants, vinifies a mixture of Aligoté vines, Chardonnay and 'le vrai Pinot Blanc'.

Morey-St.-Denis Blanc is a gustatory oddity – broad in flavour, with plenty of guts but rarely much delicacy. It can support quite highly sauced dishes, and ages moderately well. As with Musigny Blanc, it has nothing to do with mainstream white Burgundy.

The red wines of Morey have been characterised as combining the firmness and muscle of Gevrey with the finesse and elegance of Chambolle. The wide stylistic differences between growers far outweigh any common factors, so generalisations are meaningless. The pure fruit elegance of Jacques Seysses' wines, or the velvet silkiness of the Clos de Tart, when it is on form, share little with the masculine style of the Ligniers, Robert Groffier or the Ponsots; in between is Jean Taupenot who makes stylish, opulent wines of medium weight.

There are not as many thoroughly disappointing Domaines in Morey as there are in Gevrey. However some, such as Ponsot, Pierre Amiot, Clos de Tart and the Clos de Lambrays, lack consistency, producing some excellent wines and then for no obvious reason lapsing into mediocrity.

However, the wines are well worth searching out and the village worth a visit – if not to wander in the Grands Crus, then to dine by the fire at the Castel Très Girard where, if your pocket was deep enough, you could enjoy a bottle of 1945 Clos de Lambrays whilst contemplating in all wisdom the prospect of the Clos Solon beyond.

THE GRANDS CRUS OF MOREY-ST.-DENIS

Lieu-dit	*Area*	*Props.*	*Av. Prod.*
Clos St. Denis	6.62.60	20	1900 C/S
Clos de la Roche	16.90.27	40	4850 C/S
Clos des Lamrays	8.83.94	4	2300 C/S
Clos de Tart	7.53.28	1	2100 C/S
Bonnes Mares	1.51.55	2 or 3	500 C/S
Totals	**41.41.64 ha.**		**11650 C/S**

Domaine Dujac

MOREY-ST.-DENIS

Jacques Seysses is a rare species – a cross between the young, knowledgeable and passionate for quality and those great wine-makers of the old tradition whose influence still suffuses the Côte. In his 23 years in Burgundy he has built up not only a fine Domaine but a reputation for wine-making which has helped many who have passed through his hands on their own path to success.

Arriving in Burgundy in 1966 with the inestimable benefits of maturity and money and the doubtful benefit of inexperience, Jacques spent two vintages at the Domaine de la Pousse d'Or in Volnay before buying the 4.5 ha. Domaine Graillet in Morey-St.-Denis in May 1968. He continued working with the family biscuit business in Paris for 5 years until he felt that wine sales might support him and his American wife, Rosalind, whom he met in 1971 when she came to help with the vintage.

Meanwhile, the original 4.5 Graillet ha. were growing – with the addition in 1969 of 69 ares of Echézeaux. Since then land has been added piecemeal to bring the Domaine up to its present 11.21 ha. Jacques calculated that, when he finally moved to Burgundy in the mid 1970s, the sale price of his Paris flat would have bought enough good vineyard land to support a small family. Unfortunately, this is no longer the case since the price of his plot of Echézeaux has risen by a multiple of 50–60.

Jacques was particularly fortunate in that his father's love of good food and fine wine enabled him to taste old vintages and thereby experience great wine. The awareness that marvellous wines were produced before the last war, when there was minimal technological support and vinification was little understood, and a diploma in oenology from Dijon, gave him the foundation of his wine-making philosophy which remains steadfast: 'use knowledge and technology to counter accidents – for example, bad weather – but if all is going well, don't interfere.'

This principle – although not entirely the 'laissez-faire' precept it might sound – governs much of what goes on in the Dujac vineyards and cellars. Whilst Jacques Seysses vinifies the wines, care of his vineyards is entrusted to Christophe Morin, a native of the Loire, who has worked at Calera in California, Domaine de La Folie in Chagny and in Bordeaux; he is also consultant to Jean-Pierre de Smet at the Domaine de l'Arlot, one of Jacques' erstwhile apprentices.

Christophe has the task of producing the healthiest and ripest possible fruit for Jacques to vinify. Much experimentation has gone on to achieve this. Earlier plantings on SO4 – a precocious rootstock, ill-adapted to the limestone hillside soils of the Côte, had to be replaced. Trials with 10–12 different clones on 4–5 different rootstocks in the same vineyard suggested that 161/49 and 101/14 were best. Having several rows of each clone also enabled Jacques to test the hypothesis that the more clones in a given vineyard, the greater the complexity of the resulting wine – a theory still widely held along the Côte. Tasting 'clone' wine against that from old vines from *sélection massale*, it was clear that the theory was false. Both within a single vineyard and between vineyards of different classifications, complexity is not dependent on the number of clones contributing to the final wine. It must, since other variables were equated, come from *terroir*. Although entrenched in the collective psyche of generations of Burgundians, the concept of *terroir* has yet to be accepted by many who spray vines indiscriminately around the hills and plains of the New World.

Jacques Seysses in his cellar

The choice between working or hoeing the vineyards to deal with grasses and weeds, and using defoliants or herbicides (one burns, the other destroys the roots) was also studied. Hoeing breaks up the soil which is good for aeration and for retaining a balanced population of micro-flora, including yeasts. However, the more friable the soil the more prone it is to erosion, especially on hillsides; carrying it up again is both time-consuming and expensive.

Herbicides, whilst not contributing to soil erosion, have the benefit of keeping surface stones in place, to store up summer heat for the vines; being chemical products they can alter the ecology of the soil and, containing water, tend to encourage the proliferation of undesirable surface lateral roots which discourages the main tap root from seeking nourishment deeper down. Jacques' regime is a compromise: 1–2 years herbicide followed by a similar period of hoeing. This was not easy for the field-workers to accept, since it tended to leave vineyards less neat than otherwise. The look of an English garden is not what Morin is trying to achieve.

Jacques used to fertilise with significant amounts of guano – a natural, nutrient-rich, manure. Mindful of the excess of potassium widely employed in the 1950s and 1960s, he now uses minimal doses – none since 1986.

Producing the best possible fruit at harvest entails much hard work during the 6–7 months growing season. It also means low yields, which in turn demand short pruning – a maximum of 6 eyes on each cane, not what is generally stated to be 6, which on scrutiny turns out to be 7 or 8. In addition, a strict *évasivage* each spring is followed by a green-pruning just before *veraison*, usually in mid-July.

It is essential to choose the right moment, for this to work. Experiments have convinced Jacques that if you prune too early – in May or June – the vines compensate and produce larger berries – the reverse of what you want. If, however, you prune at *veraison* this does not happen and yields diminish.

Illustrating the practice in action, he cites 1988, 1989 and 1990: most growers produced more in 1989 than in 1988 and again more in 1990. Christophe actually reduced the Dujac yields by 10% between 1988 and 1989 and kept the 1990 yield at the 1988 levels.

The Domaine encourages the vine foliage to higher levels, both at base and apex, to increase the 'factory floor' area for sugar production. Experiments have shown that this augments potential alcohol by up to 2 degrees. Useful by-products are an improvement in the micro-climate within the vine – more air circulation which reduces humidity, a major factor in the development of rot – and better penetration of sprays, thus less frequency and concentration of treatments.

In years where an early flowering indicates an early harvest, Seysses may take the risk of discarding all anti-rot treatments, since the rot-risk is much lower in September. A further tangential anti-rot measure is to spray any insecticides and fungicides separately, rather than in one large cocktail. By directing these sprays at the part of the vine where they are needed – at the level of the berries for the insecticides, and all over the vine for the fungicides – the total volume of spray, and thus the humidity, are significantly reduced.

The Domaine's greatest investment in recent years has been in the unlikely area of the harvest; in fact outlay has doubled. Jacques considers it makes no more sense to ask a wine-maker to make wine with inferior raw material than to expect a great chef to create a Coq au Vin with a battery-reared chicken. So there are more pickers taking more time over each bunch, carefully removing any green, pink or red berries, leaving only those which are black and thus fully ripe. Attention to such details marks out the great Domaines from the merely good.

By what alchemy does Jacques Seysses transform this cosseted ripe fruit into such fine wine? He will cheerfully tell you, with a rather mischievous yet genuinely surprised look, that there are no tricks. Whatever he knows has been gleaned from here and there, watching what goes on in their *cuveries* and chatting to old wine-makers, encrusted in local tradition.

The two harvests he spent in Volnay appear to have been a seminal influence on everything he has done since. Whilst appreciating the value of tradition, he was deeply impressed by the modern equipment and hygiene at Pousse d'Or. 'Potel used three times more water than wine, so I started like that.'

The most important traditions which have stuck are the absence of cooling of the *must* (none, except for 1985) and an unwillingness to destalk. In order to avoid cooling, it is essential to ensure impeccable hygiene to promote a long, slow fermentation. This is also why Seysses does not destalk his grapes; if he destalked, the grapes would be split and crushed which would give the hungry yeasts more juice to work on and thus an earlier start to fermentation. 'If I could find a way of destemming without crushing I would do so,' he confesses. It is perhaps superfluous to add that if there were any conceivable way, Jacques would by now certainly have discovered it.

This 'no-destemming' is not just a bow to tradition, but a conviction buttressed by experiments made between 1981 and 1986 with first small then larger lots of grapes from the same vineyard either left whole or destemmed. Whilst Jacques admits that the stalks absorb colour from the wine – his wines are generally lighter than darker – the enforced 3–5 days of intra-cellular fermentation which whole bunches undergo adds an element of finesse which destemming would probably sacrifice.

As well as slowing down fermentation, the stalks help maintain an even exchange of heat throughout the *cuve*. For the remainder of the 16–21 days of *cuvaison*, the policy is to interfere as little as possible. Hence, no cooling, save in extreme circumstances, but plenty of *pigéage* to increase extraction. In the natural course of events, the temperature rarely rises above 31–32° C. Enzymes are added to each *cuve* – at maximum temperature for best results – to give better clarification and thus to help avoid filtration.

For a wine to be great, according to Seysses, it needs 11.5–12.0 degrees of alcohol to put it in equilibrium. In the marginal climate of Burgundy it is rare to harvest a Grand Cru at above 12 degrees potential alcohol so *chaptalisation* is a concomitant of almost every vintage; moreover, even with a natural 12 degrees, some is inevitably lost during vinification. Believing that the best quality of extraction occurs towards the end, he prefers to add the sugar in several small doses during the final phase of fermentation. This prolongs the process, which without *chaptalisation* would probably only last 10–12 days.

Once the free-run wine has been decanted, the pulp is pressed very lightly in a pneumatic press. Normal practice is to add the press-wine immediately; Seysses prefers to vinify it separately, deferring its suitability for incorporation into the final wine until later: 'work at it first, then see'.

The wine then passes into cask. Wood is a subject on which Jacques is especially knowledgeable, having served in 1976 on a commission for research into *élevage* in wood. Finding that he invariably gave higher marks to wines which had been kept in new wood, he didn't wait for the results of the research but started to put all his Grands and Premiers Crus into 100% new oak irrespective of the vintage. This practice remains unchanged – the Crus have new oak, the Village wines only second year or older wood.

Certainty about the quantity was not matched by certainty about the quality. Doubts led Jacques to buy his own Allier oak and have it air-dried for 3 years before use. New barrels he believes are doubly beneficial – they add to the structure and flavour of a wine and also are easier to keep clean, thus reducing SO_2 levels. However, he is careful to specify that they should be only lightly charred since too much gives the wine a woody taste.

The wines spend up to 16 months in cask and are racked once, in April or May, after the *malo* (which tends to happen sooner in new casks than in old). There they remain until after fining – with powdered egg-white – when they are racked and unified in 8 cask lots. Since it is physically impossible to equalise, for example, 40–50 casks of Morey-St.-Denis, the lots are chosen by tasting to ensure maximum uniformity. Exceptionally, there was no fining for the 1989s.

The red wines are bottled as they are, unfiltered. Seysses argues that if one uses enzymes and presses gently for a clearer juice, the wine will fall bright naturally, so filtration is unnecessary.

The result of such patience and thought is a remarkable galaxy of wines. An obsession with detail makes vintages matter less than they otherwise might. If a Dujac wine is bottled, one can be sure that it will be not just acceptable but complex and interesting. In fact, some of the lesser vintages have been among Jacques' notable successes – for instance 1980, 1982 and 1987. Nowhere is the absurdity of an inflexible belief in vintages more apparent than in Domaines such as this.

Dujac wines have a highly individual style which threads through the range. They tend to be lightish in colour – rather a limpid sort of crushed strawberry hue of varying depth – with a fine, almost succulent nose of ripe Pinot Noir; in great vintages such as 1985 and 1989 this sometimes comes as near as one can get to quintessential Pinot. The flavours are equally seductive – sometimes lighter, sometimes richer, yet always complex, fine and often marvellously silky; wines of great depth and elegance.

As Jacques is constructively critical of his own wines, it is perhaps worth contrasting the last two vintages of the 1980s. The 1988s have a base of hard tannins; giving the impression of being wines which will need at least a decade to start becoming drinkable – wines for connoisseurs – is Jacques' summary, not a vintage for those who can't wait. By comparison, the 1989s are classic Dujacs – low yields giving an extraordinary concentration and finesse which will unpack relatively early. Jacques recalls the mocking laughter when his neighbours saw him green-pruning the vines that July. There was almost open disbelief when he announced that he had not sent any wine to distillation – some even accusing him of hiding wine and falsifying his declarations to cover up over-production. The wines are delicious, with a balance and depth of extract right through the range, from the Morey Villages to the majestic twins, Clos St.-Denis and Clos de la Roche.

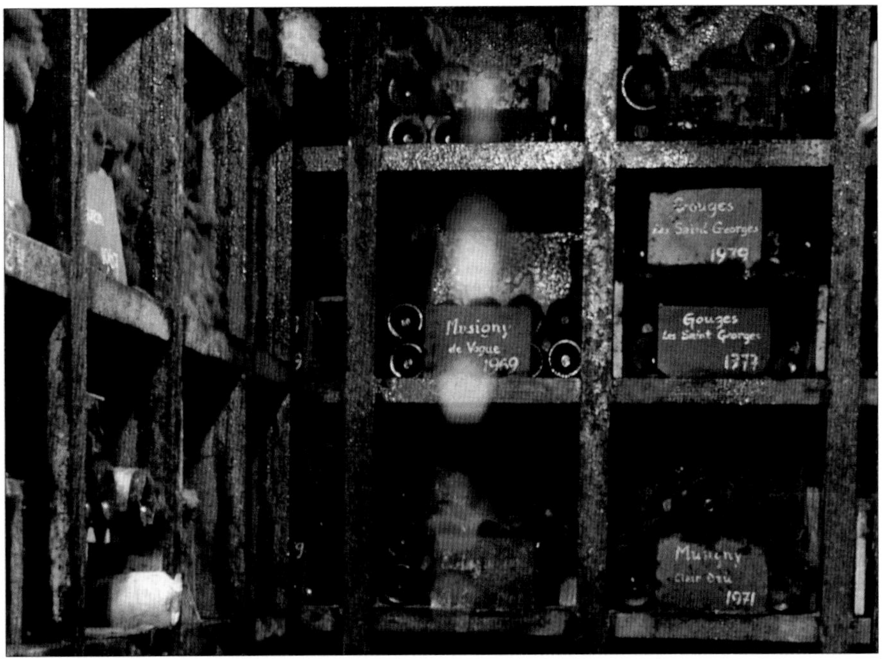

A corner of Jacques' private cellar

Content with his 1988s, Jacques is even happier with his 1989s and 1990s. The 1990s are especially fine, having the structure of the 1988s with the gorgeous fruit of the 1989s.

The situation of his vineyards often contributes to their quality; for example, the Gevrey-Chambertin, aux Combottes, a fine Premier Cru, is entirely surrounded by Grands Crus. In years such as 1989 it could convincingly be taken for a Grand Cru. In most vintages there is little to choose between the Clos de la Roche and the Clos St.-Denis; perhaps the Clos St.-Denis is a shade more masculine and firmer.

The Charmes-Chambertin is generally a wine of great delicacy and class – packed with almost creamy soft fruit and underpinned with harmonious tannins.

The Echézeaux and Bonnes Mares complete the list of Grands Crus. The Echézeaux tends to have a lively acidity to start with, which helps its balance in the long run. The quality of the wine vindicates the decision to plant with selected clones; even though the vines are only 13 now, the depth and concentration of this wine is remarkable.

The Bonnes Mares, from vines of similar age, from the Morey end of this extended vineyard, tends to have more obvious power than the Echézeaux, with the Seysses hallmark of almost creamy old-vine fruit and considerable length. Jacques avers that at least part of the complexity of his wines derives from the short period of whole-bunch *carbonic maceration*, which delivers extract into the juice without adding tannin.

There is also a little white wine: a few barrels of Meursault, from grapes bought from his parents-in-law, which is not sold in Europe, and an equally small quantity (10–15 barrels) of a delicious Morey-St.-Denis Blanc, made from Chardonnay vines planted on a patch of moderately rich soil between his house and the main road.

Dujac claims to be the first Domaine in Burgundy to use a *macération pelliculaire* for its whites. This process consists of a few hours *maceration* on the skins – too much and you risk a predominance of exotic-fruit flavours – which gives added 'gras' and structure to the wine. The juice is fermented in cask –75% new wood – with plenty of *batonnage*. After 8–9 months on its lees the wine is racked, retaining some of the fine lees to further enhance complexity. Bottling is deliberately early – after 10–11 months – to preserve maximum freshness and fruitiness. 'I make white wine the way I like it,' explains Jacques, adding, 'when they are young you should feel that you are cracking berries.'

If the 1989 Morey Blanc is anything to go by, the result is triumphant. A wine with a ripe, open nose, moderately powerful and concentrated with excellent length and attractive complexity – in style, a Corton-Charlemagne rather than a Puligny but in reality neither – just *sui generis*.

Jacques Seysses lives far from the parochial optic plane of many vignerons on the Côte. Apart from spending as much time as he can with his 3 teenage sons, he manages to cycle some 3–4,000 miles each year. These jamborees are not rudderless pedallings but carefully planned circuits, usually studded with gastronomic stops at the restaurants of chefs whom he admires. The most notable of these 'randonnées', he recalls, was in 1989 when he organised an excursion from Venice to Fredy Girardet's restaurant in Switzerland. Girardet also happens to be potty on cycling.

Manifestly unable to sit still, the Seysses have just acquired, with Aubert de Villaine, co-owner of the Domaine de la Romanée-Conti, and another friend, a 46 ha. vineyard, the Domaine de Triennes, in Provence. After much T-budding of the existing roots on to Syrah and Cabernet Sauvignon, the first harvest was picked in 1990. Sitting in a corner of the *cuverie*, exhausted, Jacques remembers saying to himself: 'you are very stupid to come 'ere.' As wine and vineyards mature, he will undoubtedly relish this new challenge.

Domaine Dujac is a remarkable synthesis of talent and opportunity. Jacques' private cellar is a testimony to his father's early influence on his taste for fine wine. A litany of the greatest of France's non-Burgundian wine-producing Domaines, each represented by a small or not-so-small pile of mycelium-covered bottles annotated in chalk on a piece of slate, attests the breadth of his taste and, no doubt, the willingness of Domaine owners elsewhere to exchange some of their precious wine for some of his.

Although thankful for the past, Jacques Seysses is not nostalgic. His optimism for the future of Burgundy is boundless – 'the younger generation have patience,' he says, 'whereas the older generation had to make a living; kids can study now, which gives them the chance to meet and talk to each other.' If this optimism is justified, the future of Burgundy is indeed in good hands.

VINEYARD HOLDINGS

Commune	*Level*	*Lieu-dit/Climat*	*Area*	*Vine Age*	*Status*
Morey	GC	Clos de la Roche	1.95	Old + Young	P
Morey	GC	Clos-St.-Denis	1.43	40+	P
Morey	PC	(Various climats)	0.54	1/2 Repl'nt	P
Morey	V	(Various climats)	1.60	60+	P
Morey	V	(Chardonnay)	1.60	7	P
Chambolle	GC	Bonnes Mares	0.44	12	P
Chambolle	PC	Les Gruenchers	0.33	60+ (Most)	P
Chambolle	V	—	0.53	10–60	P
Gevrey	GC	Charmes-Chambertin	0.70	15	P
Gevrey	PC	Aux Combottes	1.15	2/3 60+	P
Flagey	GC	Echézeaux	0.69	13	P
Vosne	PC	Les Beaumonts	0.25	5	F
		Total	**11.21 ha.**		

Domaine Robert Groffier

MOREY-ST.-DENIS

Robert Groffier is, like his wines, a man of considerable depth and charm. A kindly, reflective Pickwickian person, he lives in a substantial post-war house in the Route des Grands Crus on the Chambolle-Musigny side of Morey-St.-Denis, at the southern edge of the village.

His establishment frames 3 sides of a large courtyard, the other 2 being the *cuverie* and cellars. This is clearly a family business, with his son Serge working with him and a small grandson dashing everywhere and contriving to fall over everything.

In contrast to her relaxed husband, Mme. Groffier, whose role in the family business seems to be to manage the office and who is most likely to answer the telephone if you ring, appears to be in a permanent state of the utmost confusion which renders even the slightest request 'impossible'. Despite a long-standing appointment, carefully re-confirmed the day before, one was met with 'impossible, Monsieur, my husband is far too busy bottling to receive you.' Fortunately, at that moment Robert turned up and the crisis was resolved; but the Groffiers' customers must find this 'front of house' technique bizarre, to say the least.

Whatever the reception, the wines are very fine. Robert Groffier is one of the best wine-makers in the Côte. His efforts are naturally helped by 7 ha. of fine vineyards, including nearly 1 ha. of Bonnes Mares, some Chambertin Clos de Bèze and 1.5 ha. of 15–30 year old vines situated just below the Clos de Vougeot, which supplies his excellent Bourgogne Rouge.

Robert's father, Jules, put the Domaine together in the 1950s having inherited some vineyards from his father. In 1960, Jules split the land between Robert, his brother and sister, upon which his brother went into fruit and vegetables giving Robert the chance to buy him out. This added Les Amoureuses, the Gevrey vineyards and the Premier Cru Chambolle Les Hauts Doix to the Bonnes Mares and Bourgogne he owned already.

Having started to work with his father directly after leaving school at the age of 14, Robert had a good basic understanding of how things were done but no formal training. In time, his son Serge joined him straight from school in the late 1960s, presumably undergoing a similar osmotic apprenticeship.

The Groffier vines are conscientiously tended. Young vines – up to 18 years – are ploughed up round the roots each winter and unploughed in the spring. A light herbicide is applied to treat weeds and grasses in February or March and from May onwards the soils are hoed. The young vines are given large doses of humus for about 4 years after planting, otherwise a small amount of organic fertiliser is used as needed

Following the frosts of 1985, new plant material is a *sélection clonale* rather than the more traditional *sélection massale* always planted on to 161/49 rootstock: 'more finesse, less yield, better quality', reckons Robert. Treatment for *cryptogamic* diseases – *oïdium*, mildew, *botrytis* etc. – is with Bordeaux mixture, and pests are dealt with by modern insecticide sprays.

Although they prune quite long – 7 eyes on each fruiting cane – Robert is very severe in removing any excess vegetation and wood: a debudding just before flowering to remove any double shoots, and a green-pruning in August before *veraison* to remove bunches from overcharged vines, both reduce yields and increase concentration. He is clear about the importance of these measures: 'it's not the pruning which counts, it's the debudding.' In addition to all this, *verjus* bunches are removed during trimming in the summer.

As at any top-class Domaine, there is nothing inflexible about the vinification. Whether to leave stalks in the fermenting vats, and if so what proportion, is an annual decision. In 1990, none were left 'because of the volume of pulp'; in 1984 all the stalks remained; in 1987 and 1988 50% were removed – and so on. Stalks give tannins, which can often be green and aggressive if the wood isn't fully ripe, and add a certain substance to the wine. However, they physically absorb colour, which is undesirable.

In common with most other growers, Robert needs to *chaptalise* his wines in less sugar-rich vintages. He would infinitely prefer to do so in several stages 'if it were permitted'. In this way he would get a long, slow fermentation: 'it is necessary to feed the *cuve* from time to time,' he says, adding ruefully, 'but it is not permitted.' The authorities who man their regulatory desks in Beaune and Dijon would do well to note what Robert and many other vignerons are telling them. Permitting only one dosing may help them to control over-*chaptalisation*, but no one interested in top-quality much doubts that the process gives far better results when performed in stages. They are thinking of changing the rules – or probably, more Burgundian, of turning a couple of blind eyes – but nothing is certain.

Once in the *cuves*, the pulp is sulphured and left to macerate for 5–6 days 'à froid', that is to say 20–25° C. During the first stages of fermentation, the cap is broken up at least 3 or 4 times a day. Even the nights are not sacrosanct: Robert and Serge may have to get out of bed 3 a.m. to do this if necessary, as in 1988 and 1989. Mme. G. must be severely discomposed when this is in progress!

An inoculation of good dried yeasts is then used to get fermentation going; according to Robert, these give an additional aromatic dimension to the wines. There is a little pumping-over to begin with, but the Groffiers prefer *pigéage* to ensure that there is as much fine tannin and colour extraction from the skins as possible, even if it means sleepless nights.

Yet greater vigilance is demanded during the active phase of fermentation, since Robert and Serge prefer to allow the *cuves* to rise to the risky temperature of 35° C. Robert believes, vehemently, that 'you need a good heat to dislodge flesh and matter', adding dismissively, 'those who *cuve* at 30° C have no colour ... no colour'. In other words, the higher the temperature of the pot, the more you extract.

After reaching the giddy heights of 35° C the *cuves* are allowed to cool to about 30° C for the remainder of their fermentation which is followed by a longish further *maceration* of about 5 days. Robert insists that all through this period one must 'crush, crush, crush' to macerate the juice properly with the solid matter.

When the temperature finally arrives at 20–25° C, they start to decant the wine off the skins. The pulp which remains is then pressed more or less (which means nudged rather than squeezed dry), and the wine extracted amalgamated with the free-run wine. This press-wine is of course harsher and more tannic, but 'one must, it's necessary,' says Robert cheerfully.

A further 48 hours pass in tank under an hermetically sealed cover before the wine is transferred by gravity to cask. For the Clos de Bèze, the Bonnes Mares and the Amoureuses (which Robert considers, with justification, as Grand Cru quality), there is 100% new Vosges oak every year, although he is openly sceptical about the origin: 'my tonnelier tells me that it's Vosges, and the bill says it's Vosges, but . . .' His other wines are put into one-year-old wood. Some of the new casks come from Drouhin, in Beaune, to whom the Groffiers sell about 20% of each year's crop –

'a few barrels of each *cuvée*'. The Drouhin barrels are distinctively varnished, Robert's are not. 'They look nicer,' says Robert, 'but I don't know why else they do it.'

After their *malos* the wines are racked cask-to-cask, although not completely off their fine lees. Then, any time between the following October and the second year spring – determined by tasting – the wines are again racked, this time clear. They are returned to casks and fined with albumen or egg-white.

In the month or two following, the wines are racked off their fining, assembled in *cuves*, then bottled. Kieselguhr filtration sometimes replaces fining, if tests show that a wine is unlikely to clarify properly without it. Bottling thus takes place 12–18 months after the harvest – the wines in new wood, unusually, being bottled earliest as Robert and Serge believe that new casks, being more porous, contain significantly more oxygen which develops the wine faster.

The Groffiers have their own bottling machine. 'Assisted' by Robert's grandson, who sits contentedly with his feet in a pallet full of new bottles, enveloped in shrink-wrap, sticking 4 little fingers in the tops of 4 bottles before handing them over to be filled, the bottling line whirrs into action. Occasionally it breaks down, issuing a small fountain of precious, elegant, Chambolle-Musigny Les Amoureuses all over itself and the concrete floor. 'On a quelque fois des petits problèmes,' muses Robert phlegmatically. Mercifully, Mme. Groffier does not see all this, as she hurries off across the courtyard to dispense a bit more 'front-of-house'.

Robert is in no doubt of the style he is aiming at: 'good structure, powerful, with plenty of colour and tannin, for long keeping, real Burgundy'. Of these desirable qualities, he particularly stresses colour; looking at his wines in the glass, one is sure they are meant to last – high colours, deep and vivid in youth, but holding their hue well in bottle.

The 1989 Amoureuses, direct from the flooded bottling line, is already delicious – full of supple, ripe, succulent fruit, with impressive finesse and well-rounded and harmonious tannins. It would be sheer infanticide, though, to broach it yet. Five, ten years hence the wine will be sublime, with a firm structure underneath to sustain and develop it.

The Bonnes Mares is deeper and richer still – less finesse at present perhaps, more masculinity and burly muscle, but with an extraordinary depth of fruit and *charpente* which will give it years of life. The 100% new oak barely breaks the surface, submerged as its contribution is under this impressive weight of ripe, structured fruit. As for the 1990, 'oh là là là là!' chirps Robert. It must be something sensational.

By contrast the Clos de Bèze is more closed up, with a zing of rather nervous acidity beneath a covering of more evident delicacy and femininity. It exudes class and finesse – a wine of restrained, thoroughbred power.

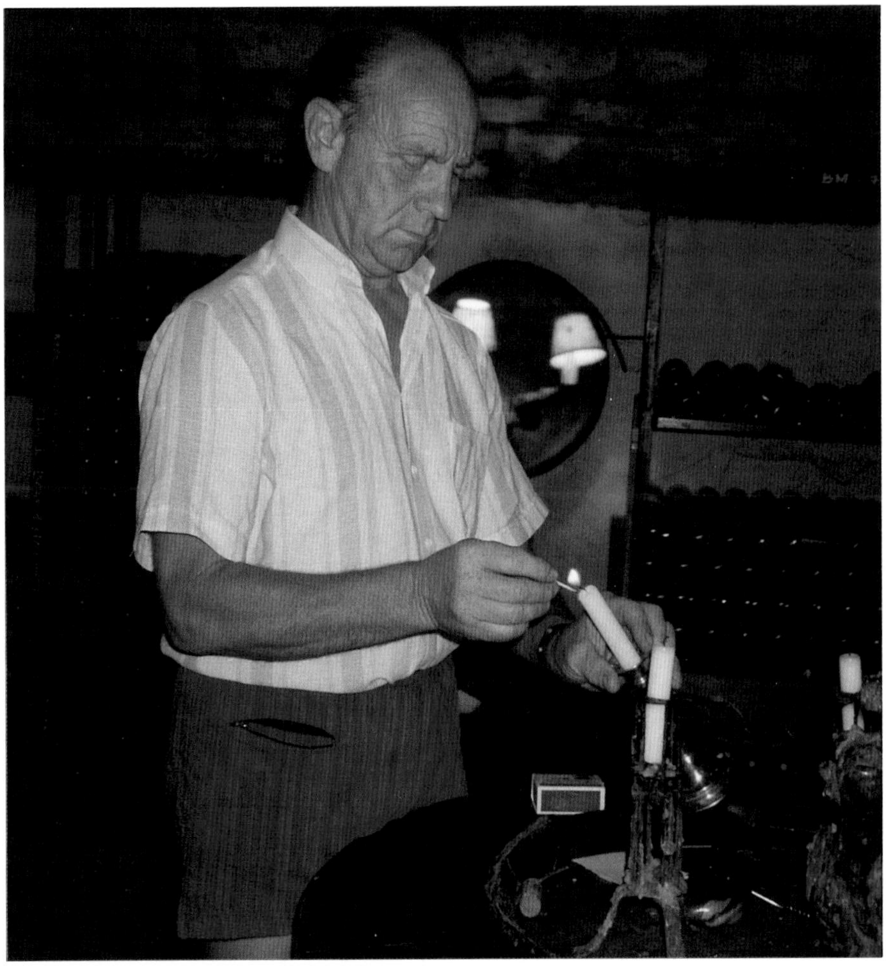

Robert Groffier preparing for an assault on Mme. G's vinous bottom drawer

The 1990s seem yet more complex and concentrated than the 1989s – similar profiles but even tighter and firmer, with a remarkable balance of constituents set to keep them into the next century. And the Bonnes Mares is indeed sensational!

A maze of cellars underneath the house leads into a large open room fitted out with leather seats around a few small tables. The walls are covered in bins full of older vintages – some 1972 Bonnes Mares here, a pile of 1978 Bèze there. 'My wife insists that I keep some bottles back every year,' explains Robert, gesticulating at the walls. 'I would have sold everything, but she makes me do it. I'm not meant to open them, they're hers.'

A bottle is fetched from somewhere else to assist in the contemplation of Mme. Groffier's vinous bottom-drawer – a Bonnes Mares 1986. The wine is just as Robert would have his Burgundy – deeply coloured, very little sign of any age, with a seductively complex mixture of *sous-bois*, game and cinnamon aromas beginning to poke their collective heads above their rather tannic parapet. On the palate: lovely old-style Burgundy, ripe, long and mouthfilling with a magnificent balance. A really excellent bottle, which gives the lie to much of the adverse publicity surrounding the vintage – as do so many of the wines from growers of the quality of the Groffiers.

VINEYARD HOLDINGS

Commune	*Level*	*Lieu-dit/Climat*	*Area*	*Vine Age*	*Status*
Gevrey	GC	Chambertin Clos de Bèze	0.42	40	P
Gevrey	V	Les Seuvrées	0.95	5 & 50	P
Chambolle	GC	Bonnes Mares	0.98	30	P
Chambolle	PC	Les Amoureuses	1.15	30	P
Chambolle	PC	Les Hauts Doix	1.00	25	P
Chambolle	PC	Les Sentiers	1.07	35	P
—	R	(Bourgogne)	1.50	15–30	P
		Total	**7.07 ha.**		

Domaine Hubert Lignier

MOREY-ST.-DENIS

Hubert Lignier, like his cousin Georges who lives next door, is not a self-publicist. However, in their own understated ways, they both make excellent wine – not perhaps up to the standard of Jacques Seysses at Domaine Dujac, but definitely towards the top end of the scale.

Hubert is an amiable, self-effacing, modest man – someone who is content to do the best he can and make a living from it, without the need for ego-boosting headlines. Unlike his cousin, however, he does not seem interested in building up his sales in bottle, being content to sell more than half his total production to the négociant market, whatever the quality of the vintage.

This policy does not appear to rebound on the care with which the wines are made, or the vineyards tended. Hubert goes for sensible yields from old vines, with as much *repiquage* and as few chemicals as he can manage. One idiosyncrasy of his viticulture is a machine designed to cut any small roots which appear above the level of the graft – known as 'racines à collé' – in the varietal part of the plant, which should they get as far as the soil would effectively by-pass the rootstock and become easy prey for soil infections in general, and *phylloxera* in particular.

Once he has overseen the harvest, Hubert returns to his *cuverie*, 'has a good shower' and gets into the *cuves* himself, with 4 friends to ensure adequate *pigéage*; 'un travail amicale', as he calls it! Vinification is classical, with no frills: 100% destalking, and fermentation in cement *cuves* – 'better for temperature insulation' – and a minimum of 15 days *cuvaison*, with the temperature peaking at 33–34° C.

Only natural yeasts are used – if the fermentation won't start itself within a few days of vatting, Hubert simply warms the *cuverie* and pumps over again to help the yeasts to work. He is certain that the best extraction occurs during the principal phase of fermentation, rather than with *maceration* before or afterwards.

Most, but not invariably all, of the press-wine is added to the free-run wine before being left to its *malo*. Hubert admits that there are no rules, just a matter of expediency. If he has the time and space the wine goes into cask; if not, it stays in bulk, either under a floating platform seal or else under a protective blanket of liquid paraffin.

Considerations of expediency also govern the cooperage: the Grands and Premiers Crus normally have up to 50% new oak; the Morey, Gevrey and Chambolle being treated to an amount which seems to depend on how many sound casks he has left over from the previous vintage.

Morey St.-Denis from the Clos de Tart

Hubert is an avowed sceptic when it comes to a preference for the provenance of his wood: 'there is no appellation contrôlée for wood,' he remarks quizzically, 'perhaps an "Allier" cask may be ten percent of Allier and the rest from elsewhere.' He does however believe that the quality of the wood is of greater importance than its precise provenance – making a virtue out of necessity?

Although he hardly ever filters his wines, he does fine them. He is willing to bend to the request of one American importer for unfined wine (one can understand not wanting filtration, but to specify no fining seems absurd – what is there to be gained?). So after some 18–24 months in cask, the wines are bottled – by Hubert.

Sadly, the excellent Chambolle and Gevrey Village wines are usually all sold in bulk; half the Morey Village leaves the cellar in cask, as does the same proportion of Premiers and Grands Crus, with the exception of the Morey Premier Cru of which two-thirds are bottled and sold at the Domaine. With such excellent wines, it seems a great pity that such a high proportion are sold 'en négoce'.

Hubert Lignier's wines look distinctly more towards the finesse and elegance of Chambolle rather than to their more muscular brethren from Gevrey. Despite the depredations of the 'négoce', there is still a good spread left to choose from: Clos de la Roche and Charmes-Chambertin in Grand Cru, a Morey Premier Cru, Chambolle-Musigny les Baudes and Gevrey-Chambertin les Combottes in Premier Cru plus an excellent Morey Village.

Of the Premiers Crus, the Chambolle les Baudes, from 32-year-old vines next to Bonnes Mares, is probably the most elegant. The 1989, still in cask, had a lightish, crushed strawberry colour, an open, ripe-fruit nose, and a powerful, concentrated multi-faceted spicy flavour with good acidity, harmony, length and finesse. All in all, an excellent wine which will develop well.

The Morey Premier Cru is an *assemblage* of several different *climats* and is usually excellent. In 1989 the *cuvée* from vines 33-55 years old showed a good deep, limpid colour, a hint of chocolate on the nose and a most attractive structure of concentrated old vine fruit balanced with a firm tannic backbone. A wine of considerable length and complexity – one to buy and keep for at least 5 years.

There is not a great deal to choose between the two Lignier Grands Crus. The Clos de la Roche is usually the more closed and structured of the two, the Charmes-Chambertin showing more finesse in youth with perhaps a shade less concentration and complexity. There is no significant difference in vine age to account for this impression. Both wines more than live up to their classification, and are worthy summits of Hubert's vinous pyramid. It would be pleasant to think that greater international recognition might tempt Hubert Lignier to bottle more of his production at source.

VINEYARD HOLDINGS

Commune	*Level*	*Lieu-dit/Climat*	*Area*	*Vine Age*	*Status*
Morey	GC	Clos de la Roche	0.79	25–35	M/P
Morey	PC	(Several climats)	0.98	22–50	P
Morey	V	(Several climats)	2.06	4–40	M/P
Gevrey	GC	Charmes-Chambertin	0.09	30	P
Gevrey	PC	Les Combottes	0.14	28	M
Gevrey	V	—	1.03	25–35	P
Chambolle	PC	Les Baudes	0.17	31	P
Chambolle	V	—	0.50	35	P
—	R	(Bourg./BGO/Aligoté)	1.74	10–35	P
		Total	**7.50 ha.**		

Domaine Georges Lignier et Fils

MOREY-ST.-DENIS

The Domaine Georges Lignier, hidden behind a pair of unostentatious solid iron gates in the main street, is one of the foremost Domaines of Morey-St.-Denis.

The present Georges Lignier, who does not seem entirely sure whether he is the great-great-grandson or simply the great-grandson of the original Georges, is a quiet, softly spoken and mild-mannered man in his forties. With his wife, 13-year-old daughter and rather corrugated old grandfather, he inhabits the house which has been the family home since Ligniers first appeared in Morey in the 1870s.

This edifice, an architectural fruit-salad of various ages of construction, gives on to the Clos des Sorbes vineyard at the back of the house from which, on a clear day, one can enjoy a magnificent view of the Grands Crus behind the village. The place has the air of being thoroughly lived in – odd accumulations of bits and pieces of viticultural equipment from bygone days jostle with some abandoned rubber tyres at the back of the cellar, whilst the family ginger cat hops around making imaginative use of these haphazard playthings.

The Domaine's vineyards, built up piece by piece since the coalescence of the 'family of my grandfather, from Morey', with 'the family of my grandmother, from Gevrey' at some undisclosed date in the 1870s, comprise a goodly spread of the Grands Crus of Morey-St.-Denis with some useful parcels of Chambolle-Musigny, Gevrey-Chambertin (both Village and Premier Cru) together with a touch of Pommard, some Aligoté and Passe-Tout-Grains. The process of acquisition was helped along by the abandonment of vineyards by wealthy families who found wine-making uneconomic after the *phylloxera*. Among these illustrious people was the Poupon family who, if they didn't invent it, scooped a fortune out of Dijon mustard.

Reconstituting the vineyards after years of disease and relative neglect took time, patience and money. By the time grandfather Georges was installed in the late 1920s, this was complete and the Domaine became set on course for the future.

Georges (III) exemplifies a family tradition of starting early in the cellars – he came to work there in 1967 when he was only 15. This, in fact, was rather late in life by Lignier standards – his father, Bernard, started in 1940 when he was 14 and grandfather (Georges I) in 1914 at the tender age of 13. As for training, Georges avers that he was privately taught – 'the same training as I would have received at the Lycée Viticole, but with the family' – and learned all he needed to know about viticulture and vinification.

His quiet manner hides a wealth of thoughtful knowledge and practical experience. For instance, he continues to produce his own grafts from material selected each year from the Domaine's vineyards. He is reponsible for the vinification and oversees the 9 others who make up the permanent staff including 'myself and my wife' but presumably not grandfather, who is now 90 but can no doubt be relied upon for a decision should there be some matter of traditional practice in contention.

For this is a thoroughly traditional Domaine in everything it does: 'we try to make the vineyards so that vinification can be the most traditional possible.' Clones are eschewed in favour of an eyeball selection just before the harvest of suitably healthy and productive plants from which to take graft material for *repiquage* and for the 10–15 ares which are replanted each year. The fact that even healthy plants are neither virus-free nor necessarily virus resistant is dismissed lightly: 'you can't work on the principle that everyone is ill, otherwise all work would stop' – so, on with the *sélection massale*. Only organic fertilisers are used, 'well fermented, well balanced and easy to use – we can add any individual elements as they are needed.'

Rootstocks are chosen with care – 161/49 for more limestone-based soils; 5BB for 'hauts coteaux' where the soils are more strongly acidic and 3309 for flatter land where the soils are specially humid and where their greater fertility promotes less development of the all-important tap-root system.

All the Domaine's vines are subjected to a light herbicide treatment in February or March and a hoeing in mid-spring when there is reduced risk of frost. Thereafter, grasses are spot-treated by hand. Standard chemical treatments are applied for the major virus and pest infestations, after bud break. In addition, small doses of oil-based products in April help to destroy noxious pests which have misguidedly over-wintered in Lignier vines.

Georges is adamant that viticulture is not an exact science, however much the text-books would have us believe that it is. As far as pests and diseases go, one can try and prevent infestation in the first place by sound vineyard practices and treatments; one can certainly eradicate many of the symptoms once they are manifest; but the possibility of effecting a cure is remote.

There is a great awareness that, in an area where each vineyard has several owners, it is essential to foster co-operation. It is no use, for instance, splashing out on expensive sprays for your vines to eradicate red spider, if the man with the rows next door has a raging plague of them and can't afford or can't be bothered to treat it.

Georges is also aware of the need to use as specific treatments as possible, in order not to

Georges Lignier's cellar – chaos often breeds life where order breeds habit!

disrupt the balance of nature. Yeasts, beneficial predators, soil-worms and the rest all need to be protected if this fragile eco-system is not to be irreversibly damaged.

Many believe that excessive use of phosphates after the war resulted in higher pHs and consequent difficulties with low natural acidities in the wines throughout much of the Côte de Nuits. Georges Lignier has a more interesting sociological explanation for this: today the tendency is to harvest as late as possible to achieve maximum ripeness. Thirty years ago, he claims, the harvest was generally earlier. The extra days on the vines significantly diminish acidity which may then have to be replaced. If these facts are correct then the explanation might be plausible, but there is scant supporting evidence. It is true that it was only during the 1960s that the acidity problems really came into focus, and it may well be that the modern trend to later harvesting has contributed to the problem, but no more. Certainly, knowing that you can correct an acid deficiency might have led growers to take the risk of exchanging higher maturity for less natural acidity.

Surprisingly, Georges Lignier does not expressly seek low yields. What he does want, however, is the best from each vineyard, and this may depend as much on other factors as on yield. For example, the moment of harvest is equally important for quality as any raw measure of crop size. Equal yields from the same vineyard, harvested at different times, are unlikely to match in quality. In 1990 the vintage lasted a month, in 1977 just a few days.

Once gathered, the grapes are crushed and totally destemmed. Sulphur is added and the temperature is lowered to 15° C to give a cool, slow start to fermentation. Late harvesting often helps this process naturally, since the weather is likely to be cooler. This is, according to Georges, no more than the tradition of leaving grapes on the vines in less ripe years and harvesting them in cooler weather, and he adds that 'in cooler years, 1980 for example, we made very good wines because fermentation started very slowly.'

The wines are fermented in enamelled-steel *cuves*, custom-built to sizes corresponding roughly to an average harvest from each of the Lignier vineyards. *Cuvaison* usually lasts about 15 days (1990) or less (13 days,1989) – about 4 days at each stage, pre-fermentive *maceration*, fermentation and post fermentive *maceration*. Only natural yeasts are used, and the fermentation is allowed to proceed naturally – rarely exceeding 32° C.

Georges Lignier prefers to pump-over his wines with a powerful pump which breaks up the cap and keeps it moist, rather than the more traditional practice of breaking it up manually. His reasoning is closely argued: *pigéage* tends to precipitate a lot of grape pips to the bottom of the fermentation vat which diminishes the extraction of pip tannins; pumping-over, however, keeps more pips in the cap where, apparently, they are more stable. As a result there is better pip tannin extraction – a wholly desirable result.

It is, Georges admits in a rare concession, necessary to have thoroughly modern materials to achieve this properly.

The press-wine is extracted by a Vaslin press and assembled with the free-run wine. The Grands Crus then pass directly into 50% new oak casks and 50% second year casks, while the Premiers Crus go into second year casks from the previous year's Grands Crus and the Village wines are put into third year oak. It is interesting to note that the new wood is from the Chatillon forest, in Burgundy itself. Lignier has now decided to buy his own cask wood, and this is stacked together with a few old vine stumps and other miscellaneous bric-à-brac, in a great pile along one side of the *cuverie.*

A first racking during the winter is followed by an *assemblage* during the next summer. The wines are only fined in years which are too marked by tannins – 1976 and 1983 – but are invariably subject to a light plate filtration before being bottled after 17–19 months in cask. Lignier believes that it is important for his wines to spend two winters and a summer in cask to give them a good balance and a gentle oxidation. It is also part of his policy that they should spend a year in cask after being assembled – for better harmony.

The wines themselves are very fine, especially the Grands Crus. From one's first sniff there is no doubt that Georges Lignier, without any diplomas or degrees, knows as well as anyone how to make great wine. He is philosophical about his intentions: 'I try to guide the vines to give wines of tradition which are homogeneous and which are well marked by the spirit of the vintage'.

The Morey-St.-Denis wines have a distinct family resemblance: most attractive mid-deep limpid appearance, with a hue of black cherry.

This cherry-like aspect continues on the nose which, in all the 1989s, was opulent and delightfully seductive – the sort of aromas which make it difficult, if not beyond reasonable human endurance, to stop there without taking a mouthful. The flavours are above all round and complete – characterised by a touch of over-ripeness which, added to the concentration from old vine fruit, gives these wines an extra depth and complexity.

The Grands Crus – Clos St.-Denis and Clos de la Roche – show less marked difference from each other than they do from their Premier Cru cousin – Clos des Ormes. As one might reasonably expect, this latter has a little less ripeness and complexity – a wine to enjoy whilst waiting for the Grands Crus to mature.

If there is a difference between the two Grands Crus, then it lies in their micro-climates: the Clos St.-Denis suffers less in particularly dry years, whilst the Clos de la Roche is generally better in more humid vintages. These vineyards have a common boundary – so one is not surprised by their similarity.

Talking to Georges at the back of one of his many subterranean cellars, which seem entirely to circumnavigate the house, the 1986 vintage of the Clos St.-Denis and Clos de la Roche are produced for comparison. Both are beginning to open out, the former more so than the latter, and a ripe concentrated old-Pinot nose starts to emerge. Both wines are powerful and very long in the mouth, with a velvety envelope of soft, ripe, almost sweet flavours which are hopelessly seductive. The Clos St.-Denis has a notch more obvious acidity than the Clos de la Roche but both are supremely elegant and clearly set for a fine future over the next 5–15 years.

One suspects that the Domaine Georges Lignier will flourish equally – provided that Georges does not come to grief in his single-engined Robin-DDR400 aircraft. He contends that the Côte looks even better from the air on a bright October morning than it does from the ground. Perhaps to the visitor it might seem better still viewed from the Lignier cellars.

VINEYARD HOLDINGS

Commune	Level	Lieu-dit/Climat	Area	Vine Age	Status
Chambolle	GC	Bonnes Mares	0.29	N/A	P
Chambolle	V	(3 difft. climats)	0.82	N/A	P
Gevrey	GC	Charmes-Chambertin	0.09	N/A	P
Gevrey	PC	Les Combottes	0.42	N/A	P
Gevrey	V	(4 difft. climats)	1.53	N/A	P
Morey	GC	Clos St.-Denis	1.49	N/A	P
Morey	GC	Clos de la Roche	0.94	N/A	P
Morey	PC	(9 difft. climats)	1.53	N/A	P
Morey	PC	Clos des Ormes	1.53	N/A	P
Morey	V	(6 difft. climats)	1.69	N/A	P
Pommard	V	Le Poisot	0.13	N/A	P
—	R	(PTG/Bourg./Aligoté)	3.39	N/A	P
		Total	**13.72 ha**		

Domaine des Lambrays

(DOMAINE SAIER)

MOREY-ST.-DENIS

This estate has had a sorely chequered recent history, and the decision to include it in this book was not an easy one. The *terroir* is undoubtedly capable of producing Grand Cru quality but for many years seems to have been jinxed into producing wine which, although often fine, really didn't provide the frisson one expects from a Côte de Nuits Grand Cru. You had to search for the class, for the depth and breed, which is the antithesis of what Grands Crus are all about.

The Clos is documented as existing in 1365 and as belonging to the Abbé at Cîteaux, a substantial local landowner. Its recorded history thus post-dates that of its neighbour the Clos de Tart, by some two centuries. Passing the Middle Ages, the Renaissance and le Grand Siècle without major incident, the great Revolution of 1789 came to shatter its calm. Its precious 8.84 ha. were subdivided among 74 different owners, an arrangement which continued until 1836 when they were all somehow bought out – a major achievement, given French peasant farmers' capacity for obstinacy – and the Clos reverted to a single piece, owned by a single family, the Jolys, négociants of Nuits-St.-Georges.

The modern history of this important Domaine is the history of several notable families who followed Joly. In 1865 it was bought by M. Albert Rodier, a sub-inspector of Domaines from Dijon. In 1938 the Clos des Lambrays again changed hands, coming into possession of the Cosson family. M. Cosson was a Parisian banker His wife was a sculptress who had managed both to win the Prix de Rome and to have a lengthy affair with Camille Rodier, Albert's grandson.

Sadly, the Cossons did not look after their great Domaine; the latter part of their 42-year custodianship saw it crumble bit by bit, into severe disrepair. The vines were neglected and the vinification became haphazard and sloppy – at one time much of the wine spent 6 years in cask before they got round to bottling it.

In 1979 the wheel turned once again, with the acquisition of the Domaine by the wealthy Saier brothers – Fabien and Lucien – together with a M. Rolland Pelletier. The Saiers, Algerian by extraction, made their money from property in France and elsewhere. In addition to the Clos, they have a large wine Domaine (Domaine des Quatre Vents) in Algeria, and important land holdings in Mercurey, as well as about 3.6 ha. of other vineyards in Aloxe-Corton and Morey-St.-Denis.

The Saiers expended considerable effort and resources in reconstructing the buildings and installations of the Domaine as well as putting the vineyard back into good order. Those who have criticised recent vintages, particularly for lack of concentration, have all too often relied on a supposed complete replanting as a convenient scapegoat. This belief is mistaken. In fact, whilst the vineyards were generally tidied up and dead or hopelessly old vines individually replaced, replanting only accounted for 2.44 ha. – less than a third of the total surface. The majority of the old vines were left intact, and it was only the northernmost part of the vineyard – that abutting the Clos St.-Denis – which, in 1981, was grubbed up and replaced.

Two further matters of fact are worth noting: firstly, the Clos is not a Monopole – there are 3 other owners of small parcels, 2 of whom have courtyard or gardens which are classified but not planted, whilst the other, Jean Taupenot, has only 430 sq. m. at the bottom of the slope next to his house.

Secondly, when the Saiers bought the Domaine, the vineyard was only classified Morey-St.-Denis Premier Cru. In 1981, this was upgraded to Grand Cru. It may seem extraordinary that after a period of appalling neglect, with the vineyard in a dishevelled state, the authorities should have chosen to reclassify the Clos upwards. However, it must be remembered that what is classified in Burgundy is neither the wine, nor the vineyard, but the potential quality of which that specific plot of land is capable. The fine bottles of the earlier Cosson period and the considerable reputation built up during the Rodier era were clearly enough to convince the inspectors. If the vineyard had been planted to Brussels sprouts it probably would have received the same treatment – such is the way of appellations in the Côte d'Or! To an impartial observer, it might perhaps have been more prudent to have granted a 20-year probation – presenting the Saiers with a bill rather than a receipt.

Realising that vineyards are useless without skilled personnel, Lucien and Fabien Saier engaged a distinguished young oenological graduate from Dijon, Thierry Brouin, to run the Domaine and its sister

The Domaine from the Clos des Ormes

establishment in Mercurey. They were clearly determined to restore the Clos, and its reputation, to its former level and fortunately possessed the will and the means to do so.

Thierry Brouin is something of a poacher turned gamekeeper, since he was for a time employed by the 'repression des fraudes', searching out those whose vinification practices were not always what they should be. He has now been with the Domaine for 10 years and been given more than a fair chance to show what he, and his vineyard, are capable of. What are the results?

The practices which Brouin has introduced, both for vineyard management and in the cellars, include nothing that is not found in the best Domaines elsewhere on the Côte. He is aware of the risks of over-fertilising, and of the profligate use of chemicals to treat the vines. Treatments are kept to a safe minimum with an emphasis on organic products and on working the soil in preference to using herbicides. Yields are deliberately low – from 25 hl./ha. in 1987 to 38 hl./ha. in the relatively abundant 1989 – and maintained at these levels with the use of low-vigour clones and rootstock, strict ***évasivage*** and a green-pruning whenever necessary, especially in the younger vines. In addition, a sorting table at the ***cuverie*** enables the removal of any rotten or unripe grapes as the small harvesting boxes are emptied out.

Once sorted, the grapes are partially destalked before being lightly crushed, sulphured and put into the fermentation vats. Thierry has definite ideas about grape stalks. They have, he says, many advantages: they help keep fermentation temperature down and aerate the ***must***; they promote a gentle lowering of temperature at the end of fermentation and a slow, even rise in temperature during its active phase; they provide natural juice ducts so that the juice runs freely off the skins when the time comes and they help promote an even pressing of the pulp which remains. Moreover, wines from non-destalked grapes are less sensitive to oxidation. However, he admits that stalks have compensatory disadvantages: they provide generally poor quality tannins and moreover absorb colour which would otherwise find its way into the wine. All-in-all this seems a perfectly fair rationale for his policy of variable destemming – 1983: 100% – 1985: 20%.

There is nothing curious or iconoclastic about the vinification either: fermentation at 30–32° C in one of an impressive battery of stainless-steel ***cuves***, about 21 days of ***cuvaison***, 5 being spent in pre-fermentive ***maceration***, 5 or more in fermentation itself and the rest in post-fermentive ***maceration*** – the latter with the ***cuve*** covered. A ***saignée de cuve***, to increase the juice:skins ratio is implemented in dilute vintages, as it should be at all conscientious Domaines. The press-wine is extracted gently with a Bucher press and added more or less, according to the vintage, at the moment the free-run wine is decanted. Only natural yeasts are used for fermentation, and ***chaptalisation*** performed in several stages to keep fermentation going as long as possible for maximum extraction.

Maturation is perfectly traditional: the Clos des Lambrays goes into 50% new Nevers oak plus about 5% Vosges – this after trials with the 1986 and 1987 vintages proved the suitability of this wood. Thierry Brouin looks for an early end to the ***malolactic fermentation*** 'so that I can bottle the previous year's crop'. Thus, in February or so, the young wine is racked off its fine lees into another cask and then left for a further year. It is never fined nor is it filtered, unless the lees are fat and unhealthy in which case kieselguhr is used. This is helped by the use of pectolytic enzymes, added during fermentation to help remove excess proteins which otherwise would need to be fined out.

This is then careful, no-expense-spared, traditional wine-making – nothing fancy, except the plethora of stainless-steel and perhaps the somewhat luxuriously spaced-out and back-lit casks. Some experiments have been tried with a rotating fermenting tank but without particular success, so this will certainly not be used for the Grand Vin. Thierry Brouin may lament the lack of space in the ***cuverie*** for his machines and tanks but he is unquestionably better off than most vignerons who often have plenty of space but lack the machinery their dreams would buy to fill it.

The wines themselves are invariably correct – with the prominent exception of a disgraceful 1983 – with good colour and a firm structure of acidity and tannins; but are they of sufficient depth and complexity to justify their current Grand Cru status?

Tasting recent vintages, the answer has to be in the balance. The problem seems to lie in the depth of fruit. The concentration one expects from a Grand Cru just isn't there – and the flavours simply tail off.

The 1987 was all in finesse – a gentle, soft wine from a small harvest of healthy grapes. However, it has an element of dilution beneath the ripe, succulent fruit, which leaves a note of doubt about its future.

Thierry Brouin

The 1988 is altogether better: ripe, quite sweet fruit, good acidity and tannins and a fair measure of length. Whether, with evolution, the tannins will come to dominate the somewhat delicate and ephemeral fruit is a question only time can answer.

In 1989 perfectly ripened grapes produced a deep-hued Clos des Lambrays with plenty of round tannins and adequate acidity. However, underneath this envelope, the wine lacks concentration. There is enough fruit for balance, but not the depth and complexity commensurate with Grand Cru classification.

Indicating the symptoms of the Domaine's problems does not suggest an obvious solution. Care, cash and expertise are not in question; the Domaine has these in abundance, together with the will to produce top-class wine. There is equally no doubt that the land is capable of producing Grand Cru quality and yields are kept low enough for this to be achieved. It may be that too rapid a replanting programme – even though it is less than a third of the Clos – has contributed to the poor concentration; if so, much greater rigour is needed in selecting only the finest casks for the Grand Vin.

Thierry Brouin, and his masters, will be acutely aware of what is being produced elsewhere in Morey and of how their wines have withstood comparative tastings. They have a Domaine which is potentially fine, but there is still some way to go to the top.

VINEYARD HOLDINGS

Commune	*Level*	*Lieu-dit/Climat*	*Area*	*Vine Age*	*Status*
Morey	GC	Clos des Lambrays	8.70	40	P
Morey	PC	Le Village/La Riotte	0.34	1/2:50	
				1/2:	P
Morey	V	La Bidaude	0.90	12	P
Aloxe	GC	Corton Clos des Marechaudes	0.50	45	P
Aloxe	PC	Corton Clos des Marechaudes	1.50	3/4:50	
				1/4:1988	P
Aloxe	V	Les Citernes	0.50	35+	P
		Total	**12.44 ha.**		

Domaine Ponsot

MOREY-ST.-DENIS

Jean-Marie Ponsot is a bluff, gruff, inflexible man of unequivocal views, which, as is so often the case, are restated rather more than is absolutely necessary for their portent to be fully appreciated and in a didactic manner which gives the impression that they are less secure than their author would like you to believe. In addition, an arrogant, mocking, manner makes any real dialogue with Jean-Marie very difficult indeed.

He is also a minor politician, being Mayor of Morey-St.-Denis and therefore much 'pris à la Mairie', a dull yellow corner building opposite the village well. However, if one has the patience to listen to him and is prepared to face out an overt and undisguised dislike of outside scrutiny, there is much to be learned from this man – the proprietor of one of the Côte's finest estates.

The Domaine is an old one – established by some great Ponsot ancestor in 1772 after the Prussian war. However, it was not until the end of the last century that today's estate began to take shape with Jean-Marie's great-uncle who had the indubitable blessing of 3 ha. of vineyards and the less certain one of no children. His nephew, Jean-Marie's father, therefore took over in 1922 by which time, as far as it could be gathered from M. Ponsot, who was still smarting from having to tell this to anyone at all, the estate had dwindled to 1 solitary hectare.

Jean-Marie's father bought land to the extent of several hectares, so that by the time Jean-Marie started working there in 1949, it had grown to 6 ha. In 1957 he took over the running of the Domaine and added 2.6 ha. of share-cropping in Morey, Gevrey and Chambolle. Now Jean-Marie's son, Laurent, is in charge of vinification, although a recent accident seems to have restricted his involvement.

The vineyard holdings are a mixture of Village wines and a mouthwatering selection of Grands Crus in Gevrey and Morey. The most important parcel is 2.5 ha. of the Grand Cru Clos de la Roche, which includes a substantial plot of older vines, planted in the 1950s, from which a Cuvée Vieilles Vignes is produced.

The Ponsots were among the very first in Burgundy to recognise the value of, and to use, clones. In addition, the Ponsot vineyards have provided the mother vines from which most of today's finest Pinot Noir clones were propagated. Among these are clones 113, 114, 115 and 177, 178 originated by Professor Raymond Bernard and a friend of the Ponsots, Bernard Clair of Domaine Clair Däu.

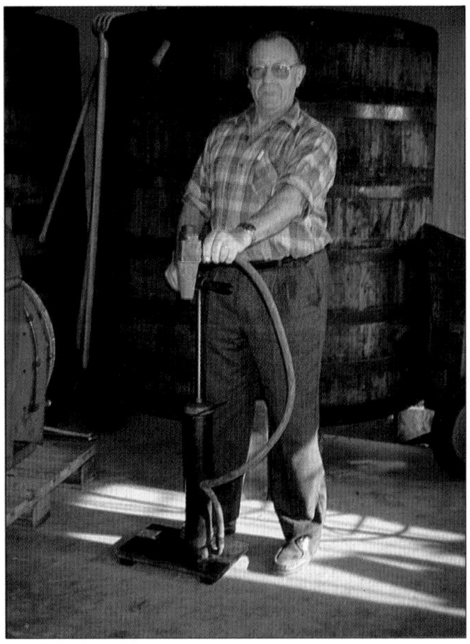

Jean-Marie Ponsot – preparing to inflate something.

To develop a single clone takes many years of propagating, selecting and virus-indexing each batch of plant material. The original Ponsot *sélection massale* aimed to have nothing more than clean, healthy plants, which is still the most important factor in the selection of plant material. Their part in the development of clones is something of which the Ponsot family can justifiably be proud.

M. Ponsot insists that it is important to work the soil mechanically to ensure that the lateral root system of the vines is not allowed to proliferate. By cutting these surface roots, the main tap-root is forced to penetrate deeper into the soil to pick up nutrients and water, thereby adding greatly to the quality and complexity of the wines, and particularly to their typicity.

Herbicides are therefore used as little as possible. M. Ponsot has, however, nothing against the process itself, provided one uses products which are biodegradable, so that the soil does not become infected or resistant. In fact, he has a patch of vines which he has systematically treated with herbicides since 1965 and which 'is still good'. In general, he likes to resist the blandishments of product salesmen and continues to do his own thing which, after all, has worked perfectly well for several decades.

M. Ponsot, as one might expect, holds definite views on the subject of root-stocks: 161/49, which he generally uses, is best for the clay-limestone soils on which most of his vineyards lie. Teleki 5C is finer than 5BB and SO4 is 'trop factice' and does not hold the maturity of grapes ripened on it.

Beyond these avowals and the asseverations that none of his treatments are 'systematic' – which seems to mean 'invariable' – that it was better to use copper-based products rather than synthetic treatments and that grey rot has provided the most difficult technical challenge ever, since 1936 — it was difficult to extract much more from him on the subject of matters viticultural.

He is clearly aware of the need to keep the soil and vine environment as natural as possible, and is distinctly cynical about the new breed of people who appear to have just discovered ecology: 'the true ecologists are people of the soil, like me, who have never abused the equilibriums of nature, not the people who ring me up at the Mairie and ask to plant trees in the commune.'

The Ponsot hand-picked, rot-excised grapes are passed through a Demoisy crusher-stemmer. This marvel of modernity also removes any berries affected by rot – but only dry rot. M. Ponsot admits to trying what he colourfully describes as 'all sorts of fantasies'. These consist of experiments with a variety of percentages of destemming his grapes, to determine what effect various quantities of stems have on fermentation and on the quality of the final wine. His conclusions, after trying everything from 0 – 100% destemming, are that 'stems bring nothing to the quality (of the wine)' and that 'whole bunches will help bring down the temperature of fermentation and provide a reserve of yeasts which are liberated at a late stage in fermentation', thus prolonging it.

Nowadays, therefore, Ponsot grapes are destemmed 'for the most part . . . according to . . .' 'According to . . .' means that a small proportion of stems may be left if M. Ponsot deems fit.

Fermentation is carried out in a new *cuverie*, built in 1989, in a battery of old wooden *foudres*. He has a policy on yeasts: 'I never yeast . . . never' – and while he's 'nevering', he 'never wants to stop the onset of fermentation'. This means that fermentation proceeds with the population of natural yeasts and there is no attempt to delay its onset with massive doses of sulphur. There is, therefore, no deliberate pre-fermentive *maceration*, and *cuvaison* lasts 8 – 15 days. Temperatures are allowed to rise to 30° C with a *pigéage à pied*, says M. Ponsot,

The little house at the top of Monts-Luisants

demonstrating with his foot.

For both red and white grapes a marvellous 50-year-old vertical screw press sits on a contemporary trolley to be rolled around to where it is needed next. A system of cogs and wheels, worked from a small motor, turns the screw to drive the press and incorporates a cut-off mechanism which comes into play when the pressure becomes too great. After the pressing 'au maximum', whatever that means, is over for the year, this picturesque antique is left to dry naturally, not washed, because this apparently keeps the wood from drying out and splitting.

After a short period of *débourbage* to settle the gross lees, the wines are put into cask. M. Ponsot has, as one might expect, some definite views on new oak: '20%', a figure which depends entirely upon the number of older casks that need replacing.

It seems curious for a Domaine such as this to be so laid-back about the amount of new wood it uses and difficult to see what possible relationship there can be between the number of casks that have given up and the number that are appropriate to the *élévage* of a fine wine.

By this time, M. Ponsot was evincing even more recalcitrance at having to explain his thinking, so what follows is the barest outline: a first racking clear of the lees, at a time after the *malolactic fermentation* which is determined by tasting; a further period in cask followed by fining with egg-whites, 'no filtration', and bottling about 2 years after the vintage.

In addition to a clutch of excellent red wines, the Domaine also makes a rare white Morey-St.-Denis from the Monts-Luisants vineyard. This consists mostly of Chardonnay, with a touch of old Aligoté and 'Pinot vrai blanc' which came originally from Domaine Gouges in Nuits-St.-Georges. This wine is fined with either casein or fish fining and, if it has not finished its *malolactic fermentation* at bottling, is then filtered.

Ponsot's wines are, fortunately, neither as direct nor as abrupt as his manner. They are among some of the finest in the Côte. The style is above all for finesse and elegance, with a structure of old vine fruit and a dimension of opulence and concentration, which will keep them going, in most vintages, for a very long time. The Cuvée Vieilles Vignes, from the Clos de la Roche vineyard, is usually the best of the bunch, with a marvellous depth of flavour and the length and persistence one would expect from a Grand Cru.

The 1989s in cask showed a variety of profiles, all with ripe, harmonious tannins and delicious succulence. The Chambolle-Musigny Les Charmes had an attractive softness, with a pronounced 'cherry- stone' flavour and good length. The Chapelle-Chambertin was especially interesting since M. Ponsot had hitherto sold the grapes from this vineyard, having no space in the cellar to keep the wine. However, with his new cellar he has the space, and the 1989 is his first vintage from these, his wife's, vines. The result is a wine of great roundness with a griottes-cherry and spice flavour and a marked acidity to ensure longevity.

The Griotte-Chambertin was distinctly more structured, with yet more complexity and finesse than the Chapelle-Chambertin. This is a very fine wine which will develop superbly over many years.

The 1989 Clos de la Roche was equally fine – with a deep red limpid colour and a tight, but very promising nose. It is not a rich, overpowering wine, but its qualities are all in finesse with a reserve of power and sinew which will give it a relatively long life.

The Clos de la Roche, Cuvée Vieilles Vignes, is yet a quantum further in depth, concentration and power. It is multi-dimensional in flavour yet 'flatteur' and very stylish. This wine will live well into the twenty-first century.

Fine as are Ponsot's 1989s, the Domaine is not as reliable as some, frequently wavering in quality in more difficult vintages. Inconsistencies in the 1980s include the 1982s and 1986s which generally lacked concentration and grip. This may reflect an inadequate *saignée de cuve* or a reluctance to discard inferior casks in the face of an eager market, hungry for every bottle of Ponsot Burgundy.

Against the occasional trough must be set the undoubted peaks. The Domaine produced some glorious 1985s, exceptionally fine – although somewhat lighter-framed – 1980s and some remarkable 1983s. The Clos de la Roche Vieilles Vignes from that year shows every sign of developing into a magnificently complex and opulent bottle, given sufficient time.

However Jean-Marie Ponsot reacts to outsiders, there is no doubt of his ability to produce great wine. Whether his son, Laurent, has inherited the parental flair will become apparent as time passes. Meanwhile, the best advice to potential buyers is to humour Jean-Marie, and to be selective – if you get the chance.

VINEYARD HOLDINGS

Commune	*Level*	*Lieu-dit/Climat*	*Area*	*Vine Age*	*Status*
Gevrey	GC	Griotte-Chambertin	0.89	1947/1982	M
Gevrey	GC	Chambertin	0.14	1961	M
Gevrey	GC	Latricières-Chambertin	0.32	1961/71/81	M
Gevrey	GC	Chapelle-Chambertin	0.47	1955/72/87	P
Gevrey	V	—	0.51	1960	P
Morey	GC	Clos de la Roche	3.03	1950–1987	P
Morey	GC	Clos St.-Denis	0.38	1938	M
Morey	V	—	1.14	1966/69	P
Morey	PC	Monts-Luisants (Blanc)	1.51	1939–1980	P
Chambolle	PC	Les Charmes	0.58	1947/1980	M
		Total	**8.97 ha.**		

Domaine Taupenot-Merme

MOREY-ST.-DENIS

This is a prime example of a Domaine churning out a mixture of good and very good wines, year after year, but which could, with a few minor modifications, propel itself into the top flight.

Denise Taupenot (née Merme) was born in the magnificent house in the Route des Grands Crus in Morey in which she lives with her husband Jean. He is from the Côte de Beaune, but moved north in 1973 on her taking over after buying out her three sisters. Jean is a quiet pensive man, who enjoys his work in the vineyards and cellars, and, like many of his fellow vignerons, is content to leave marketing operations to his vivacious, dark-haired, wife. In his spare time he sculpts and paints, as well as penning a little poetry.

Denise's creative faculties turn in a more practical direction. When they started in 1973, selling wine was difficult, but, undaunted, she drove up and down the Côte persuading shops and restaurants to stock her bottles. Success enabled her to pay off the family purchase and thereby to keep the Domaine intact.

The Taupenots' vineyards, spread over Morey, Gevrey and Chambolle, cover some 9 ha., including a mere 4.30 ares of the Grand Cru Clos des Lambrays. This minuscule plot effectively denies the Saier brothers the right to the designation 'Monopole'; they would like to buy, but Jean Taupenot and his wife have no intention of selling.

Much of Jean's philosophy originates from his 83-year-old father, a vigneron in St. Romain, who apparently continues to cause considerable parochial anxiety by insisting on driving his tractor round the village. His traditional upbringing is still apparent: he does not use herbicides, hoeing instead, and dislikes clones, preferring to replace individual plants with his own hand-made grafts. Only copper-based products are employed against mildew and *botrytis*, rather than the modern insecticides, which he distrusts. However, there is little risk with yields: vines are pruned to 7 eyes, which produced 45 hl./ha. in 1989 and more in 1990. There would be a dramatic improvement in quality if these were reduced by at least 10%.

In the cellar, there have been beneficial changes: where his father used to leave all the stalks in the vats, Jean removes all but 10% or so. There is now a short period of cold *maceration* before fermentation starts, although, where *cuvaison* is concerned, Jean agrees with his parent – 15–21 days is desirable to extract as much noble tannin and colouring matter as possible.

Once the press-wine has been assembled with the free-run wine the *cuves* are closed and left for 1–3 weeks – a '*débourbage* serieux'- to precipitate out any gross lees . Unusually, the *malo* generally takes place in *cuve* rather than in cask, since Jean feels that it is more uniform this way. Perhaps he is too cautious – *malos* in cask, particularly where new wood is involved, give a much more harmonious uptake of tannins. A change here might also prove beneficial. Only at first racking, the following spring, does the wine pass into oak, where it remains for a further year before fining in tank, a light plate filtration, and bottling.

For Jean Taupenot achieving the best equilibrium in his wines 'c'est le problème'. This said, he tries to produce *vins de garde* in the best traditions of fine Burgundy. The results are impressive; these are wines which emphasise finesse and harmony, although sometimes at the expense of concentration.

The 1989s are skilfully made showing well the quality of this Domaine. Both the Morey and Chambolle Village *cuvées* are deep in colour, with a fine aromatic development becoming evident. The Morey is full of ripe succulent fruit with enough tannin to keep it going for several years.

Curiously, for one would expect the reverse, the Chambolle is the deeper and richer of the two wines, with a long structured flavour, based on that delicious 'crushed raspberry' tone, which so often characterises fine Côte de Nuits Pinot.

The Gevrey-Chambertin Premier Cru Bel Air, planted in 1975 from reclaimed land just above Le Chambertin, is distinctly more muscular, with enough good fruit, but as yet a raw edge which needs time to soften. Whether it will approach the Chambolle or Morey in quality is debatable.

The Charmes-Chambertin, from 1.45 ha. of 25-year old vines in Mazoyères, is the Taupenots' standard-bearer. The 1989 was distinctly promising – with aromas of '*fruits sauvages*' and touches of liquorice and spice on the palate. An elegant, but powerful wine in the making. The 1972 Charmes showed how well wines from this Domaine age – no hint of disintegration, rather a complex, well-integrated wine, retaining the essential components of youth, but showing flashes of the wisdom of age – touches of *sous-bois* and those delicious vegetal nuances which add so much to a mature wine.

Jean and Denise Taupenot's wines are elegant and structured – but not quite in the top class. Several small changes might tip the balance: firstly a later harvest – Jean prefers to harvest early, to retain acidity; however, wines more often than not survive perfectly well with low acidities, but nothing will help a lack of ripeness and concentration. People asked to pay high prices expect the vigneron to risk harvesting late to ensure proper maturity. A second change might be to go over to *malo* in cask, rather than in bulk; a third shorter pruning – 6 eyes rather than 7 – again a risk, but one which would significantly decrease the charge per vine with a commensurate increase in concentration. Green-pruning at *veraison* rather than beforehand as at present might also be worth trying: the available evidence suggests that removing bunches in advance of *veraison* results in compensation, greater dilution and thinner skins. Finally the Taupenots could use more new wood. Tasting the wines suggests that they would profit from more than the 20 – 30% new oak they presently enjoy.

Notwithstanding these suggestions, Jean and Denise Taupenot are an excellent and conscientious source of fine Burgundy. They deserve greater recognition.

VINEYARD HOLDINGS

Commune	*Level*	*Lieu-dit/Climat*	*Area*	*Vine Age*	*Status*
Gevrey	GC	Charmes-Chambertin	1.45	25	P
Gevrey	GC	Clos des Lambrays	0.04	15	P
Gevrey	PC	Bel Air	0.45	15	P
Gevrey	V	—	1.70	20	P
Morey	PC	La Riotte	0.50	30+	P
Morey	V	—	1.00	25	P
Chambolle	PC	Combe d'Orvaux	0.47	20	P
Chambolle	V	—	0.86	25	P
—	R	(PTG/Aligoté)	2.50	15/20	P
		Total	**8.97 ha.**		

Le Clos de Tart

MOREY-ST.-DENIS

This is one of the rare examples in the Côte d'Or of a Grand Cru which has remained intact since its creation. In the mid twelfth century the Benedictine monks of the Abbey of Tart-le-Haut bought the site then known as the Climat-des-Forges, and in 1184 changed this to Clos de Tart. It was classified Grand Cru in 1939, shortly after the main decree delimiting the vineyards of Morey was promulgated in 1936. In 1932 it was acquired from descendants of the Marey family – of Marey-Monge lineage – by the Mommessins of Charnay-les-Macon and remains in their ownership.

Since 1969 the vinification and running of the Clos has been in the hands of M.Henri Perraud - a charming and informative man who has lost none of his enthusiasm for what he regards as his personal Grand Cru. He believes in what he refers to as 'méthodes traditionelles', although these appear to include putting all the stalks into the fermentation vats – a very untraditional proceeding.

His Clos is a superbly sited 7.53 ha. plot just above the southern extremity of the village, being the filling in the sandwich of which Bonnes Mares and the Clos des Lambrays represent the outsides. A peculiarity of the Clos de Tart is that it originally contained 27.80 ares of Bonnes Mares and a 7-are parcel of Village Morey-St.-Denis. However these were obligingly re-classified as part of the Clos in 1956.

The oldest part of the vineyard was planted in 1918 and the average vine age is about 35 years. Every 3 years about a third of a hectare plot is grubbed up in a single piece and replanted. Otherwise, vines are replaced individually as they expire. As for clones, the 'méthodes traditionelles' do not appear to care much for them. Henri is conducting some tests with them on 60 ares (the last two triennial replantings) but says that he will have to wait at least 12 years to assess their effects on his wine – by which time he will have retired and this novelty will be someone else's responsibility!

The soil being argilo-calcaire, much of the planting is onto rootstock 161-49, which is better adapted to this soil, especially on slopes. Interestingly, the vines are planted transversely, across the fall-line of the vineyard. This helps to contain soil erosion and, more importantly, to maximise insolation – the morning sun reaching one side of each row, the evening sun the other.

Most of the vineyard work is truly 'méthode ancienne', with no concessions to modern materials. Henri does permit a certain judicious amount of preventive spraying, for *court noué*, grape-worm, *oïdium*, mildew etc., but is careful to use as small a dose as he effectively can.

Herbicides, on the other hand, are not admitted, so the soil is ploughed regularly by Henri and his two colleagues.

The vines are pruned each spring and trained in *Guyot simple*. Even the oldest plants are somehow coaxed into this form; Henri did point to a vine or two which they had allowed to grow straight and then tied up with straw. The most determined traditionalist can't force a frail old lady to bend over backwards – even to please Mommessin! Selection at harvest ensures that only healthy bunches reach the *cuverie*. There they receive a light crushing but no destemming – 'except sometimes 20% maximum when the grapes are very tannic'. There is no *maceration* as the aim is to start fermentation quickly. If it remains unobliging, Henri heats the *cuverie* to 20° C to give the yeasts a 'kick in the backside'.

Fermentation in ancient cement *cuves* lasts for about 15 days, including 9 days of *cuvaison* after the active phase. The temperature is not allowed to exceed 33° C – 'the yeasts stop working at about 35° C and then you have problems with *volatile* (acidity) and getting it started again.' Henri puts a proportion of grapes from the 2 ha. of younger vines into each *cuve* to keep a balance – a sort of pre-*assemblage*. The press-wine is extracted by a modern Vaslin press and assembled with the free-run-wine. This is put into 100% new oak – 80% Allier and 20% Tronçais – and taken down to the first level cellar.

All subsequent cellar operations are carried out, as Henri stresses, without pumps. This includes the first racking – after the *malolactic fermentation* in December/January – and the second racking in June/July following the vintage.

The casks are fined with egg-white and bottled after a final *assemblage* in a large cylindrical plastic-lined tank. After being racked off its fining the wine is returned to casks which are then moved to the lower cellar for bottling.

Henri's wine has received mixed reviews. It has been deemed pleasant and correct, but not the stuff of which Grands Crus are made. Clos de Tart is certainly not a blockbuster; it is not designed to be. Neither the *terroir* of Morey nor Henri Perraud is capable of producing wines of this kind. Their style is demonstrably 'en finesse'.

The comment that the wines perhaps lack stuffing is, however, justified. Notwithstanding, this fault is slight when set against their complexity and refined elegance. It is surely infinitely preferable to have a wine of delicacy and finesse which could do with a touch more flesh than a clodhopping artisan.

Henri does not go for broke in his vineyards – yields of 30 hl./ha are the average, with another 5 hl./ha or so in abundant vintages such as 1973, 1982 or 1990, so over-production does not seem a credible criticism. Any touch of dilution might be easily corrected could Henri bring himself to contemplate a pre-fermentive *maceration* and a more traditional level of *égrappage*.

Tasting recent vintages, it would seem that whatever criticisms might have been merited, any deficiencies are now being corrected. The wines are powerful, but still supremely elegant, with no disequilibrium from the massive dose of new wood, or from fermentation with 100% stalks. The aromas of black cherry, griottes, sometimes pepper and often 'petits *fruits rouges*' suffuse the wines, which have characteristic length and an impeccable balance. In 1991 Mommessin decided to confide a part of their crop – already reduced by hail and rot – to the vinification of Guy Accad; so maybe there is an important change in direction in the wind.

Nonetheless the 1978 sipped on a warm October morning under the stone wall at the top of the Clos was as opulent and complete a wine as one could wish for.

The critics might cavil that the last few vintages of the 1980s are exceptional, and that it needs another 1984 to put the question fully to the test. If so, the 1978, 1986, 1988, 1989 and 1990 will provide enough ammunition to confound them whilst Henri Perraud gazes out of his window at his vineyard and waits for the weather to turn.

VINEYARD HOLDINGS

Commune	*Level*	*Lieu-dit/Climat*	*Area*	*Vine Age*	*Status*
Morey	GC	Clos de Tart	7.53	35	P
		Total	**7.53 ha.**		

CHAMBOLLE-MUSIGNY

Chambolle-Musigny is one of the most delightful and unspoilt villages of the entire Côte. Driving south along the RN 74, just before the road bends east to bypass Vougeot, a great sign proclaiming 'Chambolle-Musigny . . . Son site . . . Ses vins' attracts the visitor's eye to the right. There, in the mid distance, with its ecclesiastical head just above its parochial vines, is Chambolle-Musigny, a gently elevated village with its medieval bell tower clearly visible against the back-drop of the limestone escarpments of the Combe d'Ambin.

The settlement is of no great antiquity, compared with others along the Côte. It appears in records as Cambolla in 1110, when the monks of Cîteaux took up residence. By 1302 the name had changed to Chambolle – thought to be a corruption of champ bouillant, meaning a boiling field, which refers to the frequent storms which caused the little river Grone to overflow into the fields (1965 was the last time this happened).

Thereafter, until 1500 when permission was granted to build a church, the hamlet was in the fief of nearby Gilly-les-Cîteaux. In 1878 the commune annexed the name of its most illustrious vineyard and became Chambolle-Musigny and in 1960 it decided to widen its viticultural horizons and twinned itself with Sonoma, USA.

It is often said that the wines of Chambolle epitomise the finesse of which Burgundy is capable. Gaston Roupnel wrote of 'silk and lace' and of 'supreme delicacy', and others emphasised the stylistic differences between it and its neighbours – Vougeot to the south and Morey-St.-Denis to the north.

Although these are generalisations, which inevitably mask a diversity of styles, there is geological support for the view that the wines of Chambolle emphasise finesse at the expense of weight or muscle. Erosion of the limestone escarpments of the Combe d'Ambin has deposited a layer of fine, gravelly scree on to the land, as far down as the regionale vineyard sites on the opposite side of the RN 4. This, combined with substantial top-soil erosion in the more sloping Grands and Premiers Crus, has left a meagre base for viticulture. With the exception of the northerly section of Bonnes Mares towards Morey, there is little clay found in the soils.

This limestone-dominated geology is completely different from that of Morey and Gevrey, which tends to endow Chambolle wines with a high initial acidity, developing into a supreme elegance which particularly expresses itself in aromatic purity and finesse, without the breadth and power of its neighbours. Fine young Chambolle often smells of crushed strawberries.

There are some 180 ha. of vines in the commune of which Village appellation land accounts for 94.46.54 ha. There are 22 Premiers Crus spread over 60.78.20 ha., and two Grands Crus, Bonnes Mares towards Morey and Musigny towards Vougeot, which occupy a further 24.24.40 ha.

The Premiers Crus are a mixed bag in quality. Les Amoureuses, which is very similar in soil to Musigny, is the finest and most prestigious and moreover, the most plausible candidate for elevation to Grand Cru, in the unlikely event of a re-classification. Les Charmes is also excellent, followed closely by Les Beaux-Bruns, Les Cras and Les Fuées. Whilst Les Charmes and Les Amoureuses are close in style to Musigny, Les Cras and Les Fuées are nearer to Bonnes Mares, of which they form an extension.

Many of the smaller, lesser-known Premiers Crus are sold simply as Chambolle-Musigny, Premier Cru, an *assemblage* of more than one named vineyard. These wines, whilst often fine, rarely reach the heights of an Amoureuses or a Charmes.

The two Grands Crus mark the northerly

and southerly boundaries of the commune. Bonnes Mares, which abuts the Clos de Tart of Morey and which is possibly named after the sisters, Les Bonnes Mères, of the Abbey of Tart-le-Haut, is composed of a mixture of soils. There is a gradation from the relatively clay-limestone of Morey, with a deepish top-soil of marl, towards the redder clay and iron-bearing soils of Chambolle, which are generally thinner and finer in texture. So a Bonnes Mares from the Clair Däu (Jadot) section – in the commune of Morey – is likely to have more tannin and power, but less rondeur and finesse, than the same wine from the Chambolle end of the vineyard.

Musigny, at the opposite end of the village and at a lower elevation than Bonnes Mares, is divided into Les (Grands) Musigny and Les Petits Musigny. The first, oriented to the south-east with a 10–14% slope, is predominantly limestone with a high proportion of pebbles and some ferruginous clay. The second, exposed almost due south, has a deeper soil with a higher proportion of clay with surface rock outcrops. Since the Domaine Comte Georges de Vogüé owns 71% of the entire Musigny vineyard, the wine usually represents a blend of the two parcels.

The Petits Musigny also contains half a hectare of Chardonnay from which comes 1,000–2,000 bottles of the rare and expensive Musigny Blanc produced by the Domaine de Vogüé. The wine is '*sui generis*', quite heavy and rich, and ages well.

A fine Musigny is a magnificent wine. It seems to combine seductive power with unrepentant aristocracy with an extraordinary spectrum of aromas – crushed strawberries when young, *sous-bois* and liquorice later on. Fully mature after 10–20 years, it is often the quintessence of finesse and from a great vintage, an unforgettable experience.

At any season the village is a place of quiet and serenity. There is no commerce here – apart from a solitary restaurant – and only 49 growers, making it an attractive alternative to the main tourist circuit.

Whether under snow in winter, in the fragrance of a still summer evening, or glowing in the warm russets of an autumn afternoon, it is a delight to wander through the little streets redolent of the past, musing perhaps on some of the great wines which have left here to give pleasure on many a less tranquil shore.

Apart from the three estates profiled here, a number of other outside growers produce Chambolle Grands Crus of excellence: Drouhin, Dujac, Robert Groffier, and Georges Lignier have Bonnes Mares and Drouhin, Faiveley, Leroy and Jadot offer Musigny.

Nothing momentous seems to happen in Chambolle, although, in the early 1950s, there was a gripping dispute between the Mugniers and the Grivelets about who had the right to use the designation Château de Chambolle-Musigny for their wines. The Mugniers and Grivelets both live in the village, the Mugniers in the Château and the Grivelets in another substantial, eighteenth-century building round the corner. It appears that, many years ago, the Mugniers ceded the 'brand' designation 'Château de Chambolle-Musigny' to the Grivelets for their wine. Latterly, the Grivelets became unhappy with the Mugniers' continued use of it, even as their address, on their labels. The matter rumbled along in the courts, but, according to Henri Cannard, was never finally adjudicated, having been amicably settled in favour of the Mugniers in 1956.

The 'vrai' Château is an attractive mid nineteenth-century building with an imposing carriage-sweep, surrounded by a pleasant wooded park. A circuit from the church through the village will take you past its gates, perhaps on the way to lunch at the friendly little 'Le Chambolle-Musigny' where meat and fish are grilled on a large open fire, and the prices are remarkably reasonable.

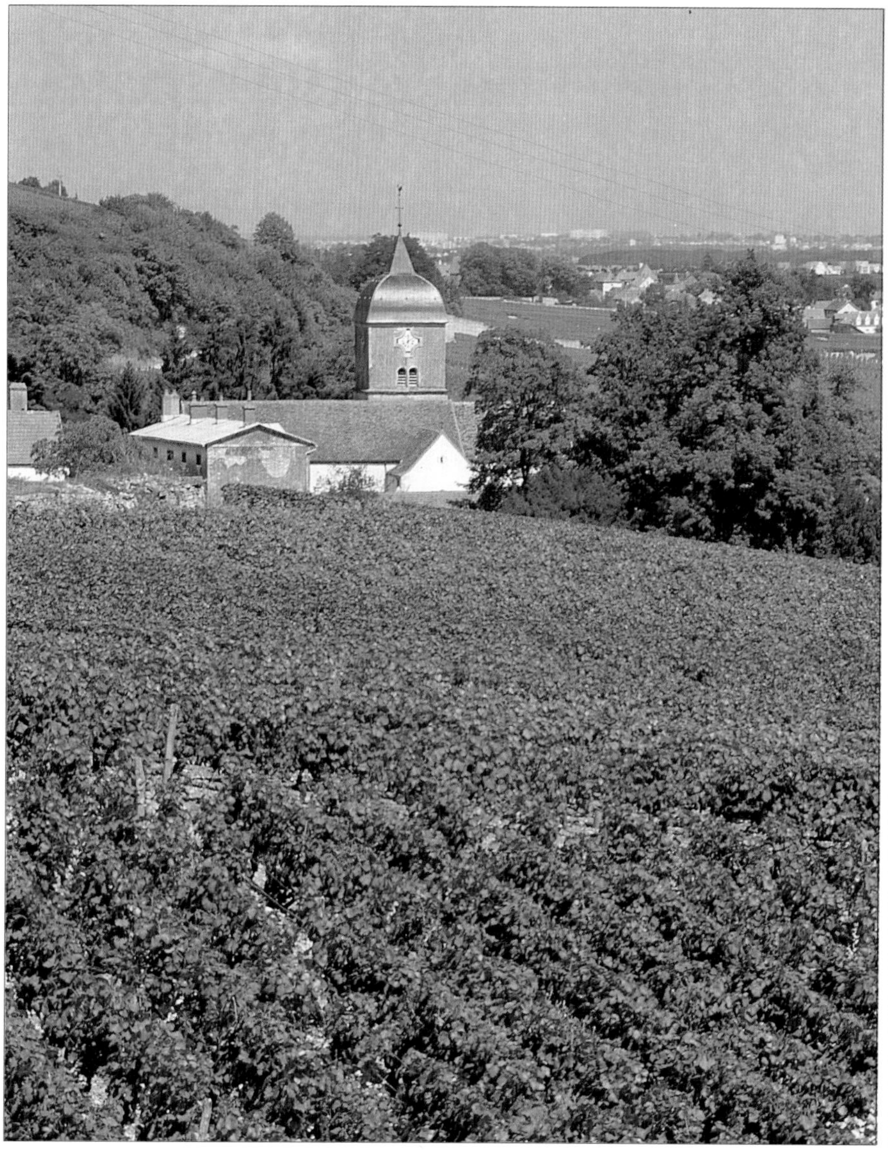

Jean Moisson's and Chambolle's restored church looking towards distant Morey-St.-Denis

CHAMBOLLE-MUSIGNY GRANDS CRUS

Lieu-dit	*Area*	*Props*	*Av. Prod.*
Musigny	10.70.23	17	3000 C/S (red) 80 C/S (white)
Bonnes-Mares	13.54.17+ 1.51.55 (Morey)	35	4500 C/S
Totals	**25.75.95 ha.**	**52**	**7580 C/S**

Domaine Barthod-Noëllat

CHAMBOLLE-MUSIGNY

Whilst the popularity of Domaines in Burgundy waxes and wanes with the quality of the wine they are producing, it is a pleasure to highlight some less exalted establishments which have been steadily turning out fine quality for some considerable time.

Ghislaine Barthod and her courteous father run one such small enterprise from a substantial turn of the century building on the edge of Chambolle-Musigny. Although the Domaine has existed from the late 1920s, they only recently acquired these premises from the Savigny négociants Henri de Villamont, who in turn bought them from Bernard Grivelet's mother. It is only in the last few years that the Barthods' wines have attracted any serious attention.

The Domaine is not extensive – just under 5 ha. in all – worked by Ghislaine and one labourer, plus occasional help from her mother in the vineyards and her father in the cellars.

This is not a Domaine where one should expect to fnd pioneering theoretical advances – trials with clones, experiments with wood, deep pondering over vine maintenance regimes or 'biodynamie' – but sound, careful wine-making from relatively old, well-tended vines; more perhaps, excellent provincial fare rather than studied grande cuisine.

The Barthods tend to harvest early. The distillation of Ghislaine's father's 30 years' experience is that better wines are made from earlier picking, which of course reduces the considerable risks from waiting too long in the capricious Burgundian autumn. Moreover, they are not in favour of green-pruning, preferring to remove any potential excess earlier on in the growing season.

A maximum of one-third of the stalks are left in the vats to help maintain the fermentation temperature at no higher than 32°C and only natural yeasts are used. Whole bunches are deliberately put into the middle of the mass in each vat to encourage a long, slow extraction of colour, aromas and tannins. Alcoholic fermentation is preceded by 2–5 days of *maceration* – depending on the temperature at which the grapes reach the *cuverie*.

Except for the Regional wines, the rest see about 25% new wood for about 20 months. Ghislaine complains gently, with a broad affectionate smile, that her father racks sooner than she does, but this apart, she and M. Barthod seem in general agreement as to how their wines should be treated.

Chambolle's village pump – one way of watering the flowers

Up to 1985 they bottled the wines themselves; now a contract bottler does the job for them. Curiously, some wines are just fined – if the customer wishes it this way; for those who do not, their wines are given a light 'white kieselguhr' filtration.

Perhaps the Barthods' past obscurity owes something to their strong home sales base. Of the 100–110 barrels they produce, the lesser appellations are virtually all sold in France, although there is a growing export following for their excellent Bourgogne Rouge. Many of their private clients have, after 30 years or more of loyal custom, become family friends, and account for a significant proportion of their annual sales. Most of the Premiers Crus and Village Chambolle find their way into foreign hands.

The Domaine is clearly in the international ascendant. Ghislaine, a charming 32-year-old, with 2 years at the Lycée Viticole in Beaune behind her, is working hard to consolidate and improve on what has already been established. Her husband, Louis Boillot from Gevrey, helps with the vinification when he can spare the time from his own *cuverie*, and will no doubt exercise an increasingly important influence over the Domaine's future, since he married into it in 1991.

The wines are already attracting considerable plaudits. They range from a beautifully balanced, ripe Aligoté – well above its class in style and quality – through a delicious, long, Chambolle Villages to a quartet of fine Premiers Crus: Les Beaux Bruns, a vineyard which is part Premier Cru and part Village, which has a base of ripe, concentrated fruit, and an underlying structure more reminiscent of masculine Morey than of feminine Chambolle; Les Cras – an extension of the Grand Cru Bonnes Mares towards the village of Chambolle-Musigny which contrasts yet firmer depth of fruit with the Beaux Bruns; and Les Veroilles, only a Premier Cru since 1987, which was largely replanted from scrub land; this has a markedly more 'sauvage' character with a deep colour and relatively high tannin and acidity in youth and an attractive amplitude on the palate.

The pick of the Barthod cellar is undoubtedly the Premier Cru Les Charmes. Its hallmark is concentration and considerable length, with an attractively promising youthful complexity on the nose which cries out to be kept for several years to show its paces.

There are two other small plots of Chambolle Premier Cru – Les Baudes and Les Châtelots. From the 1991 vintage, these were declared as Premiers Crus rather than being amalgamated with the Chambolle Village *cuvée*.

This is a very fine stable of conscientious wine-making. One gets the impression of youth and age combining their experience wisely to great effect. This is not a Domaine of theory, but one of practical experience and a sound nose for quality. There may be ups and downs, but there is no doubt that this is an estate which is capable of fine wine-making. Ghislaine and her parents are people of immense quality and charm and their wines run them a close race in this regard.

VINEYARD HOLDINGS

Commune	*Level*	*Lieu-dit/Climat*	*Area*	*Vine Age*	*Status*
Chambolle	PC	Les Charmes	0.25	31	P/M
Chambolle	PC	Les Cras	0.43	28	P/M
Chambolle	PC	Les Beaux Bruns	0.39	16	P/M
Chambolle	PC	Les Veroilles	0.37	23	P/M
Chambolle	PC	Les Baudès	0.19	19	P/M
Chambolle	PC	Les Châtelots	0.23	11	P/M
—	R	(Bourg. R. + Aligoté)	1.54	16/21	P/M
		Total	**4.75 ha.**		

Domaine Georges Roumier

CHAMBOLLE-MUSIGNY

The Domaine Georges Roumier is one of the many beneficiaries of a new perception that the reputation of an estate, especially such small enterprises as those of the Côte d'Or, rests largely on that of its wine-maker. Until quite recently, people talked of Domaine X or Domaine Y as if they turned out bottles in some mysterious manner which did not involve human intervention. Now, a change of wine-maker at an important estate triggers a re-assessment of its standing.

This willingness to evaluate each vintage from each property afresh is beneficial for the Domaine as well as for the consumer. It diminishes the ability to rely on past reputation – and equally, gives a Domaine which has been through a rough period the chance to wipe clean the slate.

Up to 1982 Jean-Marie Roumier had been producing good but not headline-making wines. The arrival of his son Christophe, however, soon rocketed the Domaine into the cult league, as people began to realise that this articulate, intelligent young man had an exceptional wine-making talent. Subsequent vintages have done nothing to diminish that impression.

Christophe's Domaine consists of 14.2 ha. of vines, the nucleus of which is a dowry of land in Chambolle brought by a local girl to her wedding to his grandfather, Georges, in 1924 : Les Amoureuses, Les Fuées and some Bonnes Mares. A further parcel of Bonnes Mares – next to the Clair Däu vines – was added in 1952, together with some Clos de Vougeot, when Georges bought a third share of the Domaine Belorger. In 1953 he acquired the whole of the Morey St.-Denis Clos de la Bussière. The final additions were made by Christophe's parents: in 1969 his mother bought 0.2 ha. of Corton-Charlemagne, in the colder, westerly, section of the vineyard towards Pernand-Vergelesses, and his father 0.1 ha. of Musigny, already *en fermage*, in 1978.

On his retirement in 1961 Georges divided his vines between his 7 children and formed a company to keep the Domaine intact. After his death in 1965 this arrangement continued, with Christophe's father, Jean-Marie, running the Domaine and making the wine.

In the early 1980s Jean-Marie and two of his brothers – Alain (ex- manager of the de Vogüé estate) and Paul – formed a limited company for their own vineyard holdings, which, together with those of the rest of the family, remained rented to the Domaine. The last major change came in 1990, when Christophe bought out his two uncles. Thus he and his father now own the Domaine, although some of its vineyards belong to other members of the family.

Christophe, now in his late twenties, gives the impression of quiet confidence. Trained at the Faculty of Oenology at Dijon University, he started work with his father in 1981 and took full charge of technical matters the following year. He thinks deeply about everything he does and has made a considerable impact, not only on the Domaine's affairs and standing but also upon other young wine-makers in the Côte, amongst whom he is much respected.

Nothing he does is systematic, that is to say determined in advance, since he believes that each season and thus each crop of grapes is different. This may appear trivial, but, in a region where growers are only too ready to tell you that they do X or Y 'tous les ans', it has greater portent than one might imagine.

His over-riding principle, that the vine must be allowed to express itself through the soil, is coupled with a strong desire to respect the natural balances between and within the plant and its environment. This brings a definite emphasis on organic treatments and products. However, where these are manifestly inappropriate or simply not available – for example for yellow spider, which seems to have taken over from its red cousin as a major pest around Chambolle-Musigny – standard treatments are used.

The vineyard policy is directed to maintaining as diverse and healthy a population of natural yeasts as possible. This means using Bordeaux mixture to protect against *cryptogamic* diseases – *botrytis, oïdium*, mildew, etc. – rather than strong, synthetic products which would effectively sterilise the soils, destroying valuable yeasts as well as the undesirable *cryptogams*. 'Yeasts are a mushroom – there are lots of different

Gardening is not the Domaine's strong point

species; we must respect this.'

For this reason, herbicide treatment is only used once every 3 years. Otherwise, the soils are hoed which both aerates them, encouraging the development of micro-flora, and cuts surface vine-roots, forcing the vine to put down a deeper root-system. This is important since it protects the plant against deficiencies in surface water and nutrients and maximises the extraction of the elements which provide the typicity of each commune and vineyard which Christophe strives so hard to protect.

When a patch of vines reaches the age of 50 or so, individual replacement ceases in favour of larger replanting. Christophe's aim here is to try to mimic the qualities of the traditional *sélection massale* by using the maximum diversity of clones in each vineyard. This is achieved by dividing each parcel to be replanted into 7 sub-areas in each of which a clone is planted. Trials with selected clones have proved highly successful. Most of those used – 113/114/115/167/777 and 778 – come from mother vines on the Ponsot estate in Morey and are planted onto classic rootstocks 161/49 with a touch of SO4 on hillsides with colder micro-climates or high limestone content.

The young Roumier vines are trained *en gobelet* for their first seven years and then mostly *Guyot simple*. A few over-productive vines are reined in by training *cordon de Royat*, but this is rare. The *guyot* vines are pruned long – since fruit production tends to be concentrated in the eyes at the end of each cane. This works provided it is accompanied by strict measures to limit production.

Yields are deliberately small and controlled both by a high average vine age, and also by careful *évasivage* and green-pruning. *Évasivage*, about which Christophe confesses himself 'trés rigoreux là dessus', consists of removing excess buds and spurs from each vine between bud-burst and flowering in early June. Green-pruning (*vendange verte*) which only happens in particularly prolific years – such as 1986 – consists of removing excess bunches from overloaded vines during the summer. Christophe is contemptuous of those vignerons who admit to a regular *vendange verte* – it reveals that their vineyards are too productive in the first place. Chez Roumier they never get near to the maximum yields authorised whereas, according to Christophe, most vignerons complain that these aren't generous enough!

The foliage of the vines is looked after with exemplary care. Experiments have convinced Christophe that the quality of the fruit is better if the height of the foliage is increased, and if summer pruning reduces the foliage width at the top of the vine. Part of the benefit comes from a reduction in *verjus* – small, unripe bunches near the tip of the vine – which adds to the concentration of the important bunches lower down.

Not only are the pickers trained to excise rot as they cut, but they learn to recognise these second-crop bunches and not to harvest them. A further control is exercised as the harvesting boxes are emptied into specially designed flat bins to be taken off to the *cuverie*.

Here, the first job is to reject any juice that may have been liberated during transport. The bunches are then partially destalked – 'we keep at least 20% of stalks as a minimum except in special vintages like 1983 where none are left.' There is no pre-determined level of destalking – in 1985 none of the stalks were removed, whilst in 1990 only 30% were left, since there was much *millerandange* at flowering and the stems were much larger.

Pre-fermentive *maceration* lasts for between 2 and 8 days, and extracts 'practically all the colour' into the juice; however this colouring matter consists of unstable anthocyanins which need to be 'fixed' by tannins which are progressively leached out by alcohol during fermentation. The enzymatic process which mediates this important colour extraction also delivers much of the future aroma compounds into the juice.

During this time, the natural yeast population gradually multiplies, generating a slow and spontaneous start to fermentation. Christophe is in no doubt that these days of pre-fermentive *maceration* add significantly to the structure, harmony, richness and aroma of his wines.

Whilst the chemical intricacies of fermentation are not yet fully understood, it is known that a diversity of yeast species seems to provoke not just one, but a series of separate reactions which are generally believed to impart significantly more complexity to a wine than fermentation with a single species of cultured yeast. For this reason, Christophe never resorts to cultured yeasts.

In the *cuverie*, his principal thought is to extract the maximum from the grapes: 'you must get everything out of the grape into the wine.' Fermentation is thus 'as long as possible, as intense as possible; for me this is fundamental.'

Cuvaison lasts for 17–21 days at as near to 30° C as practicable. Christophe confesses that he would like to reduce the temperature of fermentation a degree or two to maximise what he calls the discreet aromas – the indiscreet ones are the more obvious fruit aromas such as those of crushed strawberries – and to keep the fermentation going as long and as slowly as possible. He also admits that 'it's an error on my part if it goes to 32° C; that means I haven't intervened quickly enough'.

Pigéage is also important, occurring twice a day during the active phase and once a day during pre-fermentive *maceration*. *Remontage* with aeration during fermentation extracts glycerol and richness into the wine, although it is made without aeration after the active

Christophe and Jean-Marie Roumier

phase starts to wane. When *chaptalisation* is needed it is carried out in at least 4 stages to further prolong fermentation.

Christophe prefers to extract before and during fermentation for the greatest 'delicatesse et typicité' and believes, conversely, that extracts obtained after fermentation are not by and large of positive benefit to the wine. His aim is therefore to make the *cuvaison* coterminus with fermentation so there is consequently a strong emphasis on pre-fermentive *maceration*. In 1990 the charts plotting the progress of fermentation showed 1 *cuve* which macerated for 8 days before fermentation started – which suggests heavier than normal doses of SO_2 – perhaps he is beginning to 'Accadise' just a little?

The press-wine is vinified separately – a rare occurrence in Burgundy, though more common in Bordeaux – because the quality of extract obtained is inferior. Christophe uses it for topping up casks but only 'as a function of its taste qualities'. 'After all,' as he points out, 'it only accounts for 5% of each *cuve*, so that is hardly a great sacrifice.'

He is equally decisive about his wood: 'the provenance of the wood is less important than having wood which is dried properly and naturally.' New casks bought by the Domaine each year thus come from a tonnelier who guarantees that his wood – usually Allier – is dried slowly rather than in a kiln. It is also essential that the amount of wood used enhances rather than destroys the typicity of each wine, so he only uses up to 30% of new wood, 'according to the year; never more . . . whatever happens'.

How much new oak any given wine gets is estimated on the principle that the greater its natural grape tannin structure and concentration, the more it can support new wood. 'New wood is the best mask for wine faults; when I taste a wine in a new cask, I want to taste the wine before the cask.' With wines from Chambolle-Musigny, whose hallmark is supreme delicacy, the over- riding need is for just a discreet touch of oak, rather than a massive wooden pie-crust.

Racking is left as long as possible after the *malo* to extract the maximum from the lees. Tasting determines the precise moment of racking, when wine in a new cask is transferred to an old cask and vice versa by gravity, of course, without contact with the air. Provided they are healthy, some fine lees are left in each cask until the following September when the wine is racked clear of its lees.

In preparation for bottling, the wines are fined with egg-whites. This is intended to stabilise their colour by eliminating any unstable colours rather than fixing those which are already there. A careful fining also eliminates gross lees and refines the aromatic components of the wine.

Filtration is avoided, unless a wine has not clarified sufficiently in cask; there was no filtration in 1983, 1985, 1988, 1989 and 1990 but there was in 1984, 1986 and 1987. As to the bottling date: 'it's the wine which makes the rules.' The 1989s, for example, were bottled relatively early, in January 1991, to preserve their fresh, succulent fruit, whereas the 1988s were bottled between April and June 1990 – nothing is immutable!

Christophe Roumier gives one the impression, with characteristic modesty, that he regards his role as that of an intermediary between '*terroir*, nature, the grape and the wine'. Along this chain of transformation he is required to intervene from time to time as a sort of vinous midwife, to help extract the pure expression of the soil through the medium of the grape. His philosophy is both articulate and persuasive: 'we don't make Pinot Noir, we make wines from *terroir* which expresses itself through Pinot Noir.'

His own wines are designed – or at least intended – to give prominence to the structure and typicity of each *terroir*, not to emphasise the fruit. Wines which are 'fruité' Christophe regards as 'simple and therefore, not Grand Vin'; the expression of fruit alone is fugitive, impermanent. Some vintages – for example 1987 – are characterised by a dominance of fruit and are not, to Christophe's way of thinking really the expression of 'terroir véritable' but of the grape variety instead. His aim therefore is to ensure that his wines are dominated by the *terroir* and not by the grape.

He has travelled and tasted widely outside France and seems genuinely appalled by wine-makers, especially in the New World, who seem to regard the vine as of secondary importance to the wine-making process – some sort of utility which is there to produce the grapes they vinify. To make great wine one must go beyond the simple expression of fruit, to the expression of *terroir*. Unfortunately, in the USA and elsewhere, people are not attached to *terroirs* in the way in which Europeans are – indeed, on the whole, they have yet to find them.

His own wines express his philosophy admirably. Whilst their balance and harmony are impeccably tuned, they differ markedly one from another in underlying character. The 1989s well illustrate this: the Chambolle-Musigny has a gentle softness underneath attractive young fruit aromas, and a good length. The Clos de la Bussière, however, shows its predominantly clay soil in a much tighter, firmer profile, with more *charpente* and a notch more vinosity, whilst the Chambolle-Musigny Les Amoureuses combines the elegance of the Village wine with a more complex and powerful base. This is already a complete wine with a marvellous balance and a structure which will keep it alive and interesting in bottle for a considerable number of years.

Of the two Grands Crus, the Bonnes Mares had a solid, firm and more muscled structure – there is more soil here – than the Musigny which combines great power with an exceptional elegance. Whilst they are very different, both have the Roumier softness and length, and will make very fine bottles for the medium to long term.

The 1988s show similar differences between the vineyards according to Christophe, but with less obvious softness and more obvious tannins. The 1988 Corton-Charlemagne is presently somewhat austere, only hinting at its eventual development. It needs at least 5 years before being considered for drinking and gives the impression of lasting for a long time.

This then is a Domaine of great quality, as reliable and authentic in lesser vintages as in greater. Because he is passionate about what he is doing, and firm in his belief that 'the essentials of a good wine are made in the vineyard', as well as being a fine wine-maker, Christophe Roumier will continue to succeed. 'Wine-making is not an art, it is a craft – nature is like a dog on a lead, you have to be led around by it. You must let nature make the choices, and occasionally point it in the right direction.' Those high-tech wine-makers elsewhere, who believe in total control, would do well to heed his advice.

VINEYARD HOLDINGS

Commune	*Level*	*Lieu-dit/Climat*	*Area*	*Vine Age*	*Status*
Chambolle	GC	Bonnes Mares	1.80	1920–89	F
Chambolle	GC	Musigny	0.10	60	F
Chambolle	PC	Les Amoureuses	0.50	26	F
Chambolle	PC	Les Fuées	1.00	30	F
Chambolle	V	Les Cras +Les Veroilles + Les Pas de Chat + Les Combottes	5.80	4-65	F
Vougeot	GC	Clos de Vougeot	0.30	1/4:4 3/4:60	F
Pernand	GC	Corton-Charlemagne	0.20	1971	F
Morey	PC	Clos de la Bussière	2.50	30	F
Chambolle	R	(Bourgogne Rouge)	2.00	20	F
		Total	**14.20 ha.**		

Domaine Jacques-Frédéric Mugnier

CHAMBOLLE-MUSIGNY

Frédéric Mugnier came late to wine-making. When his father died in 1980 he was pursuing a successful career as an off-shore oil engineer, travelling the world from Africa to Aberdeen in what he confesses was by no means a culture-rich life, and one which left much to be desired in personal relationships.

His father, a Parisian banker, being no wine-maker himself, delegated the management of his Domaine in the hands of Bernard Clair (Bruno Clair's father), co-owner and manager of the Domaine Clair Däu in Marsannay. Between 1978 and 1985 Clair was responsible for the estate's wines, most of which were sold in cask to négociants.

In 1985 Frédéric decided to take a sabbatical and return to Chambolle-Musigny to see the family Domaine; he became so attached to the way of life that 1985 was the last the oil industry saw of him. To gain expertise he enrolled at the Lycée Viticole for a 6-month crash course. Not only did this enable him to manage his Domaine, but also supplied him with many useful contacts throughout the Côte.

Not content to be in charge of one of Burgundy's finest estates, Frédéric also wanted passionately to pursue his other interest, flying, obtaining his commercial pilot's licence in 1988. He now flies Fokkers 3 days each week for the French airline TAT, spending the rest of his time at Chambolle.

His flying is not entirely self-indulgence; it gives him a measure of financial independence from the Domaine, owned jointly by him and his family, which enables him to take a slightly more risky line with his wine-making. For example, he prefers to harvest late and to ferment at relatively high temperatures, both of which would entail an unacceptable level of risk for vignerons for whom wine was their sole source of income. Tangentially, having what he pleasantly refers to as 'pocket money' from the airline, allows him to hold back some of his best bottles to mature at the Château.

This enviable position grew out of a prescient great-great-grandfather, also Frédéric Mugnier, who established himself in the last 30 years of the nineteenth century as a manufacturer of liqueurs and a négociant in Cognac and wine in Dijon. This enterprise financed the purchase of some 9 ha. of vines in Chambolle, Clos Vougeot and Nuits-St.-Georges, and the magnificent Château de Chambolle-Musigny, bought from the Marey-Monge family in 1889. In 1945 the vines were divided between different members of the family, and rented on a long-term contract to the large house of Faiveley in Nuits.

In 1977 Frédéric's father decided to take back the family vineyards into his own management. However, French laws being designed to protect farmers and Guy Faiveley, being a skilled laywer, this was not achieved without difficulty and compromise. The deal that was finally struck ceded the Clos Vougeot land absolutely to Faiveley and the Nuits-St.-Georges Premier Cru Clos de la Maréchale to them on a long-term contract. In 2003 this vineyard will revert to the Mugnier family. Whether the principles of French law intended such consequences is not clear.

Frédéric's own principles are both clear and direct: 'everything is contained in the grape; what you include and what you exclude is a matter of your own choosing.'

In the 7 years since taking over the Domaine, he has come to several important conclusions. Firstly, one must use fertilisers as sparingly as possible. Apart from a small plot of Amoureuses which, curiously for this part of Burgundy, lacked potassium, no fertilisers whatsoever have been used for the past 3 years. Secondly, insecticides are only valuable if employed to the minimum extent compatible with keeping infestations at bay. Frédéric is content to tolerate a slight outbreak of yellow spider, for example, rather than to treat his vines to the maximum to protect them from pests. The grape-worm, a major cause of rot, can be eradicated by repeated strong treatments; this is attained only at the expense of killing the insects which naturally predate on red spiders.

The vines are deliberately pruned to a reasonable length because Frédéric believes that conventional short pruning, to restrict yields, is misguided: 'if you prune too short, you augment the vigour of what remains and therefore increase the area of foliage in a smaller space'. Instead, a longish *baguette* is left on each vine and unwanted growth and shoots excised during a rigorous *évasivage* each May.

He also dislikes green-pruning; this, like *saigner,* is 'only a means of dealing with mistakes elsewhere'. Far better to use appropriate clones and well-adapted root-stocks, together with foliage control and severe *triage* to obtain a low yield of concentrated fruit. Rootstocks, clones and no fertilisation are the three best control mechanisms, which Frédéric uses to the full.

His yields bear out his words: over a 10 year period the yield averaged 34 hl./ha. – 1 hl./ha. below the *rendement de base* for Grands Crus, and 6 hl./ha. below that for Village wines. Frédéric believes that to make real Grand Cru, yields should not exceed 30 hl./ha. It would be difficult to find many Domaines who would content themselves with this level of production, even for their Grands Crus.

So severe is Frédéric over *triage* that his mother complained that during the 1990 vintage he had as many members of the family as he could muster sitting up until midnight in the *cuverie* sorting grapes before these were allowed anywhere near the *Cuves*. 'It took me three weeks to get my hands back to their proper colour,' groaned Mme. Mugnier, waving the palms of her elegant hands in the air with a disarming smile.

In the cellar, matters proceed with the same attention to detail as elsewhere. Stalks, being either good or bad according to their ripeness, are added to the pulp, up to a maximum of 40%. 'People who talk about selection are usually concerned with the

Frédéric Mugnier – vigneron and commercial pilot

quality of the grapes and not with the quality of the stalks,' argues Frederic. 'The qualities that they bring to the wine depend upon the type selected.' He is therefore as careful in his selection of stalks as in his selection of grapes. Some parcels of vines yield riper and better constituted stalks than others.

Pre-fermentive *maceration* lasts for about 4 days: 'if you want to prolong this you have a problem without massive doses of sulphur.' So fermentation starts naturally, with no need of cultured yeasts. Frédéric seeks to prolong fermentation but without closed vats – his are splendidly ancient and open – and an inert gas blanket, is powerless. The temperature is allowed to rise to 36–37° C before a system of heat-exchangers lowers it.

Frequent *pigéage* – as much as 5 times per day – ensures the maximum contact between liquid and solids. *Cuvaison* lasts for a total of 15–17 days before the wine is passed into cask for its *malo*.

The press-wine is vinified separately and blended, or not, with the free-run wine just before bottling. This gives Frédéric another chance to add a further element to the composition of the final wine, which would have been denied him had he followed the usual Burgundian policy of assembling both before decanting into cask.

One quarter of each harvest goes into new Allier wood, with the Grands Crus having 5% or so more than the rest. The tonnelier, François Frères, known for a rather heavy toast on their casks, is instructed to give Mugnier's only a light charring. Frédéric abhors excessively grilled aromas and rinses each cask with steam and hot water to leach out some of the more aggressive tannins before they impregnate his wine.

Élévage follows no pre-determined timetable. There will be a first racking, from cask-to-cask, in about May, but thereafter tasting determines the sequence. If a wine is unduly reduced in aroma and flavour, it is likely to be racked again any time between the following August and November. In general, the wines remain about 18 months in cask before fining with fresh egg-white a month before bottling. Frédéric does not like filtration, but has found that recent vintages have been too turbid to avoid it, a circumstance he attributes to his deliberately not using pectolytic enzymes to aid clarification – something which he has come to regret. The various casks of each wine are finally unified in a splendid rank of 2,700-litre *foudres* before being bottled by the Domaine.

Frédy Mugnier's wines are characterised by both elegance and power, often represented as hallmarks of Chambolle, but so often lacking. These are not wines which can, despite their distinctive finesse, be hurried; they take time to undress and to reveal their hidden charms. The Village wine, and indeed the Premiers Crus, can start life noticeably ungainly and discomposed, being difficult to taste and unforthcoming, particularly on the nose. However, left alone, they blossom into wines of considerable delicacy and charm, underpinned by a restrained but powerful structure.

Not surprisingly, the Chambolle Les Amoureuses is generally the best of the two Premiers Crus. Les Fuées, with a higher clay content in the soil, gives a broader more fleshy style of wine – definitely Mahler rather than Wagner. This is not to belittle one at the expense of the other – both are fine.

Frédy admits an admiration for the techniques and wines of his neighbour, Christophe Roumier, and there is more than a passing resemblance in style between the two Domaines. Frédy's wines tend to be less approachable to start with but share the same underlying balance, depth of fruit and delicacy. He evaluates his own wines in terms of their structure rather than of their aromas, reasoning that in an infant Burgundy – as elsewhere – this is the only immutable anchor. Whilst the aromas may change in type and intensity week by week, the scaffolding of the buildings remains, by and large, constant.

Of the two Grands Crus, the Bonnes Mares is usually the chunkier – the more overtly muscular and masculine. The 1989 has a deep almost creamy nose, still in bud but seductively promising, with good length and soft, ripe tannins.

Frédy replanted half of his holding in Bonnes Mares recently because the 30-year old vines were clones which were proving erratic in yield and quality. The 1988 is the first vintage which he believes has truly regained typicity. The wine is sturdy and long, but the reduction in vine age shows in a more open-knit texture and lack of real Grand Cru concentration.

The Musigny has no such problems. In good vintages, there are two *cuvées* offered – a 'standard' and a Cuvée Vieilles Vignes. Both are of high quality with all the power and concentration expected from a Grand Cru, and all the finesse and silkiness expected from a Musigny. The 1989 vintage was vinified with 30% of stalks in the vats. The 'standard' wine has a deep young velvet-purple colour and a soft almost creamy nose which is a most promising complex bud, hinting at this and that, but not revealing very much in detail. The palate has a tight, complete structure, supported by ripe, harmonious tannins; above all, however, its superb length and persistence mark it out as true Grand Cru.

The 1989 Vieilles Vignes, which Frédéric intends to bottle a few months later than normal, is yet deeper, both in colour and in concentration. It has a firm, quite broad frame, with an almost *surmature* old-vine fruit and remarkable length. The vines from which this great wine is produced are more than 45 years old (the 'standard' *cuvée* being from relatively youthful 28-year-olds), and are harvested as late as possible.

The 1988 'standard' *cuvée* is a shade more forthcoming on the palate, showing a spectrum of flavours – cocoa, violets, cachous and *'fruits noirs'* – with dryish tannins and excellent length. By contrast the 1988 Musigny Vieilles Vignes is, as yet completely closed up – one can discern a fine, densely packed structure, with an overlay of very ripe, almost over-ripe, late harvested fruit. The wine is superbly long and complete – no gaps or imbalances – but needs many years before one should contemplate drawing a cork.

These 1988s are generally more accessible than the 1989s – the converse of what most growers will tell you. The Mugnier 1989s are more muscular than the 1988s, but then Frédy admits that he made an expressly soft vinification in 1988 because the quality of the fruit was so fine that he wanted to preserve it at all costs and not to swamp it with tannins. In 1989, by contrast he went for a more developed structure.

The 1990s eclipse both the 1988s and 1989s. Throughout the range they are characterised by a fine concentration and great depth – giving an impression of marvellous quality in the making.

Frédéric Mugnier a fine wine-maker. He thinks each vintage through with care and invariably turns out wine of great elegance and typicity. It will be fascinating to see what a decade's maturity brings both to him, and to his wines.

VINEYARD HOLDINGS

Commune	*Level*	*Lieu-dit/Climat*	*Area*	*Vine Age*	*Status*
Chambolle	GC	Bonnes Mares	0.36	1/3:30 1/4:10 5/12:new	 P
Chambolle	GC	Musigny	1.13	32	P
Chambolle	PC	Les Combottes + les Plantes + La Combe d'Orveaux	1.30	30	P
Chambolle	PC	Les Fuées	0.71	30	P
Chambolle	PC	Les Amoureuses	0.53	35	P
		Total	**4.03 ha**		

Domaine Comte Georges de Vogüé

CHAMBOLLE-MUSIGNY

This Domaine is, as Charles Dickens put it in another context, 'as old as the hills and infinitely more respectable'. The Musigny family, who gave their name to the famous vineyard in the fourteenth century before vanishing into obscurity, lived in the small hamlet later to become Chambolle. About 1450, a Jean Moisson constructed there a small chapel which subsequently under the protection of Cardinal Rollin, son of the Burgundian Chancellor Nicolas Rollin, became its parish church.

It was not, however, until 1766, that de Vogüé first appears in the records, when the last direct female descendant of the Moissons, Catherine Bouhier, married Cerice François Melchior de Vogüé. Since then, five generations of de Vogüés have taken charge of the Domaine, each adding, by acquisition or exchange, something to the estates.

In recent years it was Comte Georges de Vogüé whose name was inextricably linked with the Domaine. By all accounts a lively, old-fashioned aristocrat of great charm, he came often to Chambolle from his home in Paris to discuss and oversee the work of a closely-knit team led by the forthright and irrepressible Alain Roumier. Sadly, Comte Georges died in 1986, the same year that Roumier retired after 30 years' service.

George's wife took over as owner, but left the day-to-day management of the Domaine to her daughter, Elizabeth de Ladoucette. During 1985/86 a new, young team was installed, consisting of oenologue François Millet, who bottled the 1985 vintage and vinified the 1986, and Gerard Gaudeau who arrived as Chef de Culture in April 1986. To this duo was added the amiable and urbane Jean-Luc Pepin who was appointed 'commercial attaché' in 1989, to take charge of the Domaine's sales and marketing operations.

There was much to be done. Since the late 1970s there had been disquiet in expert circles about the Domaine's wines which were widely felt to be less concentrated and consistent than before; even years such as 1978 seemed to have none of the extraordinary quality of such legendary vintages as 1945, 1947, 1959, 1969 and 1972.

It is difficult to discover whether there really was a problem. The Domaine itself kept virtually no stocks of older vintages for comparative tasting. It may also be commented that Musigny – the core of the estate's production – is often misjudged, being a wine of naturally lightish colour, predominantly characterised by finesse and elegance. Those expecting the colour or style of neighbouring Morey-St.-Denis or of Vougeot may erroneously be led to the conclusion that the wine is unduly light in fruit. With Pinot Noir in general, and with Chambolle-Musigny in particular, colour is often an unreliable indicator of flavour. A pale rosé hue often disguises considerable power and depth. Even so, the critics are unlikely to have all been wide of the mark.

Precisely what happened during the 70s and early 80s is unclear; some speculated on overproduction, others on excessive filtration. The first is verifiable, and false, the second plausible but unlikely given Comte Georges de Vogüé's undoubted commitment to quality. The absence of a really fine vintage, except 1978, between 1973 and 1985 is a more tenable explanation.

The new team is now firmly in place and it is by their output that the Domaine must be judged. François Millet comes with excellent credentials: after extensive studies he spent 12 years as a consultant oenologist to various houses 'from Mâcon to Montelimar'. He distrusts rigid formulae and stresses the importance of approaching each vintage with an open mind. What may be good for one particular lot of grapes may not necessarily suit the next.

The result of this vintage by vintage, *cuvée* by *cuvée* policy is that it is senseless to speak of a system of vinification. François is adamant that it will take many more than the few years he has been at the Domaine to establish a real rapport between him and his wines for him to grow into the de Vogüé mould. However, he is careful to avoid isolation in his nineteenth-century cellars from what is going on elsewhere; tasting widely, not just Burgundies, and making regular visits to vineyards elsewhere, he regards as an integral part of his job. So François Millet travels and tastes.

In the vineyards, his colleague Gerard Gaudeau pursues a traditional line. He believes that working the soil is more important than using sprays to deal with excess herbaceous growth; however, whilst it is impossible to be efficient without herbicide sprays, it is undesirable to use these alone. So, at the end of each winter a light herbicide is followed by a series of gentle hoeings. Pests are dealt with by spraying, varying the product from year to year to minimise the risk of resistance.

The average age of the Domaine's vines is

François Millet and Jean-Luc Pepin – looking into the future

deliberately kept high. Individual replacements are preferred to major replanting, although this would be entirely feasible with the relatively large surfaces in each particular *climat*. The new team is taking its time to see how the vines perform before embarking on any substantial replanting, although there is an inherited programme of gradual replacement a few ares at a time, every few years to avoid reducing average vine age.

Clones and rootstocks are chosen with great care. Clonal selection depends on the soil, it is not merely a matter of seeing which vines perform best in which vineyards – the clone as well as the rootstock must adapt to its climatic and soil environment. There is nothing revolutionary in this, but the team's desire to take things slowly is an encouraging sign of its determination to get them right.

Even allowing for the 'no-formulae' approach, trying to discover how the Domaine sets about vinifying its impeccably nurtured fruit is met with curious evasiveness. Replies to questions are so defensive and entangled in qualifications that one suspects that there may be something that one is not supposed to know.

What is clear is that the aim is to try and adapt the vinfication sequence to the year and to the particular vineyard or lot of grapes concerned. Even given equally healthy grapes, there may be significant differences in the way each vineyard's produce is dealt with. Getting to know the peculiarities and idiosyncrasies of each patch of vines and each patch of *terroir* is, in François' view, a cornerstone of his work.

This willingness to remain flexible, to take decisions as individual circumstances dictate, does not mean that there are no preferences. The grapes are usually destemmed 30-100% – depending on vintage, appellation and the individual parcel of vines. 'Stems,' according to François Millet, 'are difficult to evaluate; tannins vary in quality, and soil is an important factor.' Equally, some parts of a vineyard tend to give more natural grape tannin than others, so lessening the need for the addition of stem tannin. Furthermore, tannin has several sources, so he may extract better tannins from a longer *cuvaison* than from a greater proportion of stems in the vats.

In all but the worst of rot-infected years, a short period of *maceration* usually precedes fermentation in large open wooden vats. François likes 'to work with nature – the sun and the earth' and therefore is less than enthusiastic about modern methods which start by dosing the crushed grapes with massive amounts of sulphur to force a long cool pre-fermentive *maceration*. As he picturesquely puts it: 'this is not natural – not a way to thank God for his work.'

Yeasting, with dried Burgundy yeasts, may be used on vats which are sluggish in starting to ferment. Once fermenting, temperature is controlled at a maximum of 32–33° C with a length of *cuvaison* adapted to the parcel being vinified. In general, the longer the *cuvaison* the better, although it has been noted that some vineyards produce better results with 15 days, others with a month.

François believes that the length of *maceration* after fermentation is of greater importance than the length of fermentation itself. The pulp left after the wine has been run off is gently pressed and the wine extracted kept apart. Although this will generally all be added to the free-run wine, this only happens after several tastings and when the time is deemed right. 'The wines of Chambolle,' François points out, 'are characteristically feminine and it is therefore rare not to include 100% of the *vin de presse*, even in riper years, to add an element of backbone and structure.'

The Domaine's policy on casks appears to be still evolving. There is presently 40–70% of new wood. Efforts are being made to determine which forest provides the most suitable wood for each particular wine. So far François has tentatively decided that Nevers adapts well to Bonnes Mares – or is it the other way round? The only firm conclusion is the negative statement that they do not want to simply use new casks of several different provenances as a cautious averaging.

A further complication is that wood from the same forest can differ from year to year. So the Domaine is trying to educate its barrel-maker by inviting him to taste and to become more involved in their thinking.

Whether a wine is racked at all – except, of course for bottling – and if it is racked, when and how often – is a matter for individual decision. What is certain is that if a cask is racked, then gravity not pumping is used. There is a general tendency to rack after the *malo*, but this decision is tempered by the desire 'to keep enough lees in the barrel.'

The moment of *assemblage* is equally fluid. The later the *assemblage* the more precise it can be: 'it is like a painting, there are more colours to use.'

Fining is not an unvarying piece of the de Vogüé vinification jigsaw. 'Fining undresses a wine,' chorus both François Millet and Jean-Luc Pepin. So a separate decision is taken on each cask. If fining is deemed necessary then samples are analysed to determine the best fining agent. Fresh egg-whites are generally preferred, but gelatine may sometimes be more efficient. Neither is filtration a cornerstone: 'it is ridiculous to filter a wine if it is brilliant.' When necessary, either kieselguhr or plate filters are used or, in extremity, both.

The most exigent decision facing a winemaker is when to bottle. Here, at least, there seems to be a policy: 'we are looking for a wine that is beginning to open out. This is not easy to figure out, but we do not want a wine which is too open.' Cask maturation has both a good and a bad side – whereas too much cask age can dry out a wine and destroy its delicate Pinot Noir fruit, the right amount can greatly enhance a wine's quality and life expectancy. 'One is taking a wine out of his house and putting it into a bottle.'

Trying to assess the quality of the de Vogüé 1990s is thus difficult. Flexibility is fine, but there is a point when it comes perilously near to indecisiveness. A great Domaine should be able to define a style and set out the broad lines of policy for effecting it. At de Vogüé there is a definite aura of casting around, heavily disguised as the need to treat each vintage differently.

Since taking over in 1985, the team have produced wines of excellent but not top-class quality. The wines are still rather young for definitive judgements; however, it would seem that the frisson, the indefinable thrill, of great Bonnes Mares, great Les Amoureuses and, above all, of great silken, opulent Musigny, has yet to be recaptured.

The Domaine produces about 4,000 cases a year comprised of 5 wines: Musigny Blanc: a minuscule output of some 100 cases of a most sought-after and unusual wine from Chardonnay grown on Grand Cru Côte de Nuits soil. This curious cross-fertilisation produces a wine of striking power and considerable presence, without much of the finesse of a great Puligny. For some it is the ultimate in dry white wine, for others just an interesting curiosity. Apart from the recently acquired 1.8 ha. of Chambolle Village vines, the range begins with the Chambolle-Musigny Premier Cru Les Amoureuses. The soil in this particular vineyard has a high limestone content which characteristically gives a wine of great delicacy, with a lightish colour and a soft, mouthfilling flavour. The wines of Chambolle-Musigny tend to have a good natural balance of tannin and acidity and the Amoureuses beautifully exemplifies this. François will tell you that he never acidifies his wines – which leaves one marvelling even more at the quality of the soils of Chambolle-Musigny!

The part of the Grand Cru Bonnes Mares owned by the Domaine is towards the southern end. The wine invariably has a much denser and darker appearance than the Amoureuses, and ages into a fine spectrum of aromas. It is much wilder than its brother Musigny, with a little less raw power, but with a more masculine tone.

The Musigny, of which there is one single blend, *Cuvée* Vieilles Vignes, is capable of divine sublimity. It can disarm one with its limpid light colour, with a hue of red silk taffeta, which belies the enormous concentration and depth of fruit underneath. The nose develops into a harmonious amalgam of discreet but seductive aromas of great class, each sniff offering a different facet and a new perspective. On the palate, a superb concentration of ripe fruit with generally well rounded tannins is offset by a fine balance of acidity. The length passes right down one's throat, whilst the persistence allows the flavours to remain on the palate long after it is swallowed.

This is one of the Côte d'Or's greatest and noblest estates, of whose potential for making some of the finest and most remarkable wine in Burgundy no one is in serious doubt. However, although current offerings are good, sometimes even excellent, they fall well short of the excitement they used to generate: the Domaine' unwillingness to disclose yields suggests that they have still failed to grasp that overproduction inexorably leads to diminished reputation.

The new team appears to have the skills and the commitment to revitalise the Domaine's fortunes. How they measure up to the challenge remains to be seen. One thing is certain: lovers of fine Burgundy will be watching them with keen interest.

VINEYARD HOLDINGS

Commune	*Level*	*Lieu-dit/Climat*	*Area*	*Vine Age*	*Status*
Chambolle	GC	Musigny	6.70	N/A	P
Chambolle	GC	Bonnes Mares	2.60	N/A	P
Chambolle	GC	Musigny (Blanc)	0.50	N/A	P
Chambolle	PC	Les Amoureuses	0.60	N/A	P
Chambolle	V	—	1.80	N/A	P
		Total	**12.20 ha.**		

VOUGEOT

With only 67.08 ha. of vines, Vougeot is the smallest commune in the Côte d'Or. Yet through the work of the Confrérie des Chevaliers du Tastevin, based at the Château du Clos de Vougeot, its name is known throughout the wine-loving world.

Outside the activities of the Confrérie, the village's reputation principally rests on the vines from the magnificent 50.59 ha. of walled vineyard known as the Clos de Vougeot – the largest Clos in the Côte d'Or. The red and white wines from the remaining 16.59 ha., which are only entitled to the appellation Vougeot, or Vougeot Premier Cru, remain for most Burgundy lovers an obscure curiosity.

Vougeot is a small village of some 200 inhabitants, reached from a short spur off the RN 74, which now by passes it. In the spring, summer and autumn months a seemingly constant river of tourists is to be seen visiting the Château and buying wines from one or other of the large cellars which act as shrimping nets. There is a half-hearted general store, a few predictably expensive restaurants and, for the hot weather, an excellent municipal swimming-pool. If you feel like staying, Domaine Bertagna has an attractive small hotel in the vineyards or there is the luxuriously restored Château de Gilly, a blissfully peaceful Relais et Châteaux with a tennis court and an excellent restaurant, a kilometre away on the opposite side of the RN 74.

The village takes its name from the little river Vouge which has its source near Chambolle-Musigny. In the twelfth century it was in fact called Vooget, although its existence was already known three centuries earlier, thanks to a toll established at the river.

Before the monks of Cîteaux arrived at the beginning of the twefth century, the land which is now the Clos was either forest or fallow. Gifts of land to the Abbey of Cîteaux encouraged the clearing of scrub and the plantation of vines . However, unable to complete the Clos from donations, the brothers were obliged to spend lavishly to do so . Between 1227 and 1370 plots of land were acquired at elevated prices and by the fifteenth century a great wall had been constructed round some 50 ha. to form the Clos as it is today.

According to Henri Cannard's excellent concise history, the Clos and the Château de Gilly were ransacked during the wars of religion. Although Gilly was rebuilt, the Clos was left with no more than a few utilitarian buildings for the making and storage of wine and remained so until 1551 when the present Château, designed as a fortress, was constructed . Cannard also notes that, apart from a small Oratory, the Château contains no chapel, confirming that it was indeed a dependency of the Abbey of Cîteaux.

Meanwhile illustrious visitors appeared: Louis XIV came to the Abbey in the course of a cure, consisting chiefly of Nuits wines, prescribed by his doctor, Fagon, and it is reported that 'auberges reputées' sprang up in the village to cater for visitors who generally preferred to stay in Vougeot rather than in Nuits.

In 1860 a group of English tried to buy the Château, but the owners refused, selling instead to the Thenard family in 1869. Thereafter the estate remained in single ownership until 1889 when the vines were divided between some 15 different proprietors. Among those, Léonce Bocquet, who spent much effort and money on the buildings, is particularly remembered, being buried – presumably upright – in the entrance gate.

However, the buildings gradually fell into disrepair, until finally coming into the hands of Etienne Camuzet whose legatees sold them to the Chevaliers de Tastevin on 29 November 1944. The Château now belongs to a company called Les Amis du Château du Clos Vougeot and remains the headquarters of the Chevaliers du Tastevin.

This Confrérie, founded 10 years earlier in 1934, was designed as a promotional organisation at a time when sales were particularly difficult. Today lavish banquets, noted more for their length than anything else, are accompanied by 'Intronisations' at Vougeot and elsewhere, of luminaries and others who are esteemed valuable to the reputation of Burgundy around the world.

Over the years, however, becoming a Chevalier du Tastevin has come to be regarded as evidence of expertise. As Anthony Hanson remarks: 'certainly the idea is widely held that membership of the order is some sort of qualification.' If so, this is entirely without justification; but as a marketing gimmick it is masterly!

There are some 4.82 ha. of appellation Vougeot land and three Premiers Crus which account for a further 11.68 ha. These latter – Les Cras, La Vigne Blanche and Les Petits Vougeots (part of which is Bertagna's Clos de

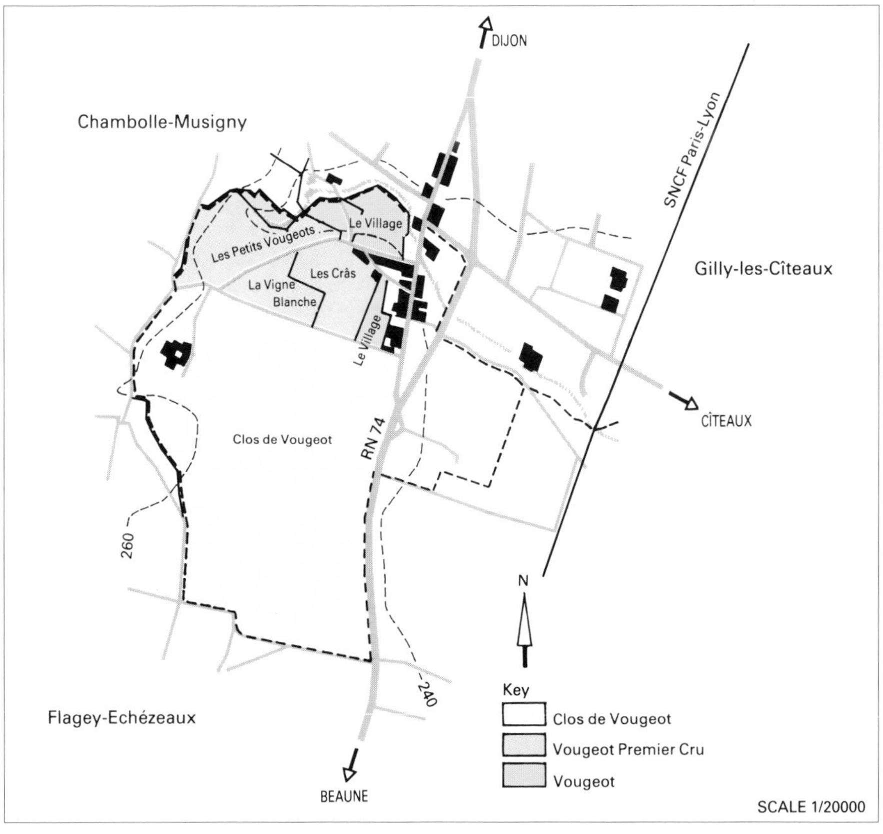

The Château and the upper part of the Clos de Vougeot – the most subdivided vineyard in the Côte d'Or, with 82 owners

la Perrière) – are not widely known, probably by virtue of their size. The wines tend to solidity and tannicity, but can with age sometimes develop finesse. In addition, some 5–600 cases of white wine are made annually; this can be delicious or dull, depending on the grower and the vintage.

The Clos itself is now in the hands of some 82 different owners – companies, individuals, domaines large and small, with a corner belonging to the French department of roads and bridges – so there is considerable variation in quality.

The Clos de Vougeot is one of the few Grands Crus where the location of vines within the vineyard matters. The monks of Cîteaux, having gratefully accepted everything they were offered, found themselves with a great diversity of land. Mme. Rolande Gadille (1957) has described no less than 6 different soil types within the Clos, and honest growers themselves recognise the better drained top section, nearest to the Château, as superior to that next to the RN 74, which has a higher humidity and thus increased risk of mildew and frost. Moreover, since the turn of the century successive local authorities have contrived to raise the road level by about 2 m., further increasing moisture retention in the lower part of the Clos.

Although it appears quite flat from the road, the Clos is in fact on gentle 3–4 degree slope, with a vertical displacement of some 30 m. towards the Château. Soils at the top are mainly limestone based and of fossil origin, whereas those by the road are considerably deeper, with an increased proportion of clay, and closer to the water-table. The middle section has a significant clay content, with soils of some 40–50 cm. in depth which are stony and well drained.

Jean Grivot used to claim that the best wines came from a mixture of grapes from both top and bottom sections – a generously frank sentiment given that some of his own large plot is right next to the road, marked by an ornate wrought-iron gate. In truth, the skill of the vigneron is probably more important than the location of the vines, although this may play a negative role in particularly wet or dry years. However, so ingrained is this idea that one is at pains to find a grower who admits to having vines at the bottom of the Clos. Most tell you that their patch is 'at the top', usually adding 'up near the Château' for good measure.

Wines from the Clos can range in quality from thin, acidic and dreadful to superb, with the majority being lumpen and tannic without the promise of ever blossoming. Invariably expensive, they often score highly on the price/disappointment scale.

Among the best producers are: Alain Hudelot-Noëllat, Louis Jadot, Méo-Camuset, Daniel Chopin-Groffier, Jean Gros, Gros (Frère et Soeur), Dom. Georges Mugneret, Jean Grivot, Christophe Roumier and Jacky Confuron-Cotétidot.

There is a strong case for re-examining the vineyard with a view to re-classification of some of the less good land. This, together with a much more stringent tasting assessment, would do much to restore the rather tarnished image of this noble Grand Cru.

THE GRAND CRU OF VOUGEOT

Lieu-dit	*Area*	*Props.*	*Av. Prod.*
Clos de Vougeot	50.19.10	82	16,500 C/S

Domaine Bertagna

VOUGEOT

Although originally created by M. Bertagna, an Algerian businessman, in the late 1940s, the Domaine Bertagna has recently passed into the young hands of 25-year-old Eva Reh and her English husband Mark Siddle. Eva's business and marketing training and Mark's work experience with Robert Mondavi in the Napa are bringing strenuous efforts to bear to re-establish the Domaine whose reputation slipped badly during the 1970s.

The enterprise is part of an unusual family group of businesses, each of which is run by one of Karl Reh's 5 children. The system is simple: the managing member of the family holds the majority interest in his or her particular enterprise, the other members of the family owning the balance. The other holdings in the group include a large Sekt house, the fine Reichsrat von Kesselstadt estate in Trier and substantial hotel interests.

Since taking over in 1982, Eva and Mark have worked hard with their wine-maker, Roland Masse, to bring the cellars up to date and to replant where it was considered necessary. Massive investments have included an impressive battery of computer-controlled fermentation tanks. These provide temperature control, an automatic *pigéage* through an internal paddle and an ingenious system for extracting the lees without decanting the wine.

The tanks are filled brim-full of completely destalked grapes so there is little need for SO_2; *cuvaison*, including a pre-fermentive *maceration* of 5–8 days at 20° C, generally lasts 3 weeks, the grapes being fermented for preference at below 30° C.

The vineyards are harvested several times over to pick only the ripest fruit; a green-pruning is preferred to a *saignée de cuve* – although there is not much to suggest that these are genuine alternatives. The number of different individual lots of grapes presents important handling problems, which provide an additional motive for restricting yields.

All the Domaine's wines are matured in 30% new Vosges oak. Concern about the quality of wood used by barrel-makers has persuaded them to buy their own trees in the Vosges, so that from 1991 they exercised complete control over the quality of their casks.

Bottling takes place about 18 months after the vintage, and is preceded by 3 rackings and an egg-white fining, carried out after *assemblage* in tanks. Roland Masse is currently experimenting with different bottling intervals, and there were also small trials with machine-harvesting of a plot of Nuits-St.-Georges in 1985.

The vinification is deliberately designed to return to what Mark calls 'traditional Burgundy' – that is to say the extraction of concentrated, obvious Pinot Noir flavours and aromas. 'Burgundy is unique soil, so it is not just a question of making good wine, but of making good Burgundy,' he explains.

If their Vougeot Blanc is fair evidence of what they are capable, then the signs are indeed promising. This wine comes from half a hectare of Chardonnay planted in Les Cras in 1985 following the widespread frost damage throughout the Côte. 1988 was the first vintage – yielding about 1,000 bottles. The wine has a light yellow-gold colour with a positive floral aroma and a powerful, mouth filling flavour. The 1989 is even better, much riper and more opulent, characterised by exotic-fruit aromas and a solid, firm, frame. The wine is quite broad in profile with a lively acidity and good length. In style something between a Premier Cru Meursault and a more masculine Corton-Charlemagne, it needs a few years yet to round out and show of its best.

Tasting a vertical run of the Domaine's Monopole Vougeot, Clos de la Perrière, a 2.2 ha. Premier Cru vineyard situated in the Les Petits Vougeots *climat* just opposite the main entrance to the Château de Clos Vougeot, provided an interesting opportunity to see how the Domaine's wine evolves with age and also to see the change of style which came with the introduction of the Amos fermentation tanks for the 1986 vintage.

The 1988 and 1987 are still closed up, as one would expect, but both have a firm, masculine structure, underpinned by dry tannins. The 1986 Clos de la Perrière is starting to show positive aromas of *fruits noirs* with hints of the vegetal side of the Pinot Noir. On the palate the wine has a dry attack, opening out onto some attractive soft fruit.

Despite the rather sturdy skeleton, which runs through all the wines of the mid 1980s, the Clos de la Perrière has underlying warmth and charm. It represents its origins well, and has a concentration and complexity in better vintages which become most attractive, given time to evolve. Whilst the 1984 and 1983 were, for different reasons, less successful, the 1985, the last vintage of the old vinification, is delicious and just starting to be drinkable, with an array of ripe, warm supple flavours and good concentrated fruit. Unlike their neighbours in Chambolle-Musigny, Vougeot wines are rarely feminine, generally sporting instead a firm masculine charm.

This Domaine needs to look carefully at how it vinifies its wines; in particular, there is a real danger that too much *maceration* will over-balance the tannins and stifle the fruit. There may also be a case for keeping out some of the press-wine, especially in less ripe years. However, the efforts of Eva and Mark Siddle are to be applauded and encouraged. This is definitely a Domaine to watch.

The cellars, Vougeot

VINEYARD HOLDINGS

Commune	*Level*	*Lieu-dit/Climat*	*Area*	*Vine Age*	*Status*
Vougeot	GC	Clos de Vougeot	0.30	70%:50+	P
Vougeot	PC	Clos de la Perrière	2.20	70%:30+	P
Vougeot	PC	Les Petits Vougeots	2.30	100%40	P
Vougeot	V	—	0.80	100%:18	P
Vougeot	PC	Les Cras (Chard.)	0.50	Pl.1985	P
Chambolle	PC	Les Plantes	0.20	Replant.	P
Chambolle	V	—	0.40	100%:35	P
Morey	GC	Clos St.-Denis	0.53	1975/40	P
Gevrey	GC	Chambertin	0.20	100%:25	P
		Total	**7.43 ha.**		

Domaine Georges Clerget

VOUGEOT

Georges Clerget, now well into his sixties, presides over a Domaine of some 3.54 ha. of land situated in Morey-St.-Denis, Vougeot, Chambolle-Musigny and Vosne-Romanée. The Domaine was created by Georges' maternal grandmother and grandfather, the one from Flagey, the other from Chambolle, who each contributed vines to the family property. What remained after the obligatory division between him and his brother, together with vineyards bought by his mother, provided Georges with the nucleus of what he has today.

He is a charming, friendly man, rooted firmly in the traditional mould of working, who, whilst he is prepared to follow the advice of his oenologist, has healthily sceptical views on modern technology.

His father died when Georges was a boy of 9; his mother thereupon took up the reins of their 6 ha. Domaine and roped in her two sons – Georges and his brother Michel – to help her with the work and to learn the trade at the same time. Georges remembers being given 'a vine or two to keep me interested' – which stratagem obviously succeeded, since he has never left the job.

In 1978 the vineyards were divided, Georges receiving about 3 ha. and his brother the same. Since then his son Christian, now 28, who worked with him, has taken Michel's vines as well as half a hectare of Grand Cru Echézeaux, which Georges let him have *en fermage*. Christian's studies at the Lycée Viticole in Beaune will keep both Domaines in tune with modern developments.

Whilst the vineyards are now tended by hand and by tractor, Georges remembers vividly the days of horse-power. Then, he will tell you, the vines were planted deeper than today, which meant that one had to be very careful, after ploughing down the soil which had been ploughed up to protect the roots for the winter, to ensure that any lateral roots put out by the French scion were cut off, to avoid infection. With modern shallower planting, the risk is minimised, but the Clergets are no less careful in their spring *évasivage*.

This traditional ploughing up, *buttage*, continues. As well as covering the roots and thereby lowering the frost-risk, Georges argues that when he ploughs back the soil level the following spring, he has the chance to mix in any small allowance of fertiliser he may have administered, so it is well integrated with the top-soil.

Efforts are made to keep yields as low as economically sensible. Georges' team of regular pickers are well trained to spot any unripe or rotten fruit, and are fully aware of what constitutes acceptable Clerget grapes.

The wines are vinified in cement, enamelled-steel or old wooden *foudres*, and kept in a plethora of garages and small underground cellars near Georges' house just off the RN 74 at the northern end of Vougeot. Whilst the intention is to destalk the bunches completely, such is the age of the Clerget destalking machine that some 10–15% of stalks usually remain after it has done its work.

Good as Clerget's wines undoubtedly are, they would benefit immeasurably from a modest capital investment. Unfortunately George is in the same position as many other vignerons, with millions of francs tied up in land but walking a cash-flow tight-rope.

For instance, lack of resources means that there is no equipment for cooling the pulp. In consequence, the important phase of pre-fermentive *maceration* is excluded if the grapes arrive at the *cuverie* warm, since the yeasts multiply rapidly and begin to ferment the sugars immediately.

The wine is decanted within a day or two of finishing fermentation and the *marc* given 'two gentle pressings,' explains Georges, turning an imaginary knob in the air in front of him. The wine from both pressings is then added to the free-run wine.

Barrels, new and old, present a further financial problem. Up till 1990, they had virtually no new oak, even for the Grand Cru Echézeaux. Now, fortunately, a friendly négociant has lent them some new casks in return for an allocation of the wine – and Georges appears to be well-pleased with the results.

Yet another cash crisis seems to have been precipitated by the new policy of bottling after 22 months – before the second harvest. Keeping the wine much longer than before has inevitably led to a lack of cask space. Since they couldn't afford any more barrels, much of the 1989 crop was stored in tank until August 1990 before being transferred to casks liberated by the bottling of the 1988s.

Georges and a client

Trying as all this may be, Georges somehow manages to turn out excellent wines. These have two broadly distinct styles: the Village appellations tend to an elegant, lighter frame, with the pure crushed strawberry aromas and red fruit flavours of young Pinot Noir. Usually quite succulent and slightly peppery, they have a delicate balance of tannin, but are not of massive structure.

In contrast, the wines which have the benefit of new wood are much richer, with a firmer backbone and naturally greater power. The new casks suit the Echézeaux and would, in moderation, benefit the Vougeot and Chambolle-Musigny Les Charmes.

There are some very fine wines in the Clergets' cellar; it is to be hoped that somehow or other they can find the money for a few more new casks which, together perhaps with a slightly longer *cuvaison*, might make the difference between good to very good and Grand Vin. When Georges is next sitting on his customary Spanish beach, on his annual summer holiday, he might give this idea some serious thought!

VINEYARD HOLDINGS

Commune	*Level*	*Lieu-dit/Climat*	*Area*	*Vine Age*	*Status*
Flagey	GC	Echézeaux	1.00	1945	P
Chambolle	PC	Les Charmes	0.30	20	P
Chambolle	V	Les Babillières + Les Condemennes	0.50	5-30	P
Vougeot	PC	Les Petits Vougeots	0.46	4 & 21	P
Morey	V	Les Crays	0.40	5 & 25	P
Vosne	V	Les Violettes	0.38	1946/49	P
—	R	(Bourgogne)	0.50	4/20/35	P
		Total	**3.54 ha.**		

Domaine Alain Hudelot-Noëllat

VOUGEOT

Alain Hudelot-Noëllat's wines have been among the best in the Côte for many years – full of charm and exuberance, but with considerable depths for those who care to look for them. Alain mirrors his wines: a solid, hard-working man, with short-cropped hair and a broad friendly face, exuding passion for his work and an abundant enjoyment of wine and the people that go with it. Talking to him in front of a roaring November fire of vine prunings blazing away in a massive chimney-piece, one is aware of a mischievous grin which, when coupled with a brief, but totally deliberate, wink of his left eye, rapidly divorces his real meaning from whatever he happens to be saying.

He receives his visitors in what appears to be a large converted garage with a set of curiously ornate wood-framed doors squeezed incongruously onto the front. One wall is binned with stock, whilst another is occupied with a variety of ancient viticultural tools – brightly polished copper hand-sprays, disinfecting syringes and so on. On top of the mantel a couple of boxes of cartridges, being gently warmed by the fire below, betray Alain's interest in hunting, whilst suspended above the fire a double cattle-yoke betokens the indissoluble harmony of Hudelot and Noëllat, their names inscribed one on either side.

The history of the Domaine is no greater than the history of Alain and his wife. Leaving school young, he started working in the vineyards of Drouhin and Champy – négociant houses of Beaune. In 1960 – his twenty-first year – he was given 2 small plots of vines by his father Noël in Chambolle-Musigny Les Charmes and in Chambolle-Musigny itself.

At that time, much of the vineyard work was done by horse-power, so Alain saved up enough to buy a tractor and rented out himself and his équipage in the locality. With the money he earned, he bought more vineyard land to add to his Domaine. In 1977, the addition of 42 ares of Clos Vougeot, *en fermage* from his father, brought the Domaine up to 5 ha.

In 1960 the young Alain Hudelot married the young grand-daughter of Charles Noëllat from Vosne-Romanée, bringing with her entitlement to several choice parcels of vineyards from that commune. Unfortunately, one of her relatives refused to release these to her and she and Alain were obliged to fight a legal battle to regain possession. This took 15 years and substantially drained their resources; however they won and the land finally became theirs in 1977.

The Domaine now stands at nearly 10 ha. – including over one hectare of Clos Vougeot and just under half a hectare of Romanée St.-Vivant together with a small parcel of Richebourg and a chunk of 3 ha. of Chambolle-Musigny.

The vine age is kept deliberately high by a systematic grubbing up and replanting schedule. However, the vines in the Romanée St.-Vivant plot are so old that Alain prefers to replace them individually rather than to completely grub up such a small area. He has further difficulties, of a more emotional nature, with his plot of Vosne-Romanée Les Suchots; he wanted to grub it up and replant, but the ancient vines continued to produce such marvellous grapes that he couldn't bring himself to do it; thus they remain in situ, getting gradually more venerable, and no doubt less productive, as the years go by.

Alain's way of working in his vineyards follows broadly traditional lines. One peculiarity is his choice of SO4, which is known for its precocious growth and abundant foliage, as one of his root-stocks. Alain is not unduly worried: 'the more the foliage, the better the grapes are nourished!' He tries to keep a rotation of treatments, to avoid the build-up of resistance, and ploughs up the soils regularly.

Despite a relatively standard viticultural regime, Alain does have some preferences and dislikes. For example, he abhors green-pruning to remove excess bunches of grapes, preferring to *saigner* his *cuves* in particularly abundant years. 'Never refuse what the good Lord gives you.' In any case 'green-pruning changes the balance of the vine,' he barks, adding, 'I don't like going against nature' – throwing up his hands in the air, and winking.

His scepticism was reinforced when he went into one famous vineyard nearby during the summer of 1990 and saw some much-photographed workers green-pruning the vines. 'C'était la folklore, c'était de la grande musique' (meaning roughly, 'all show and no real effect'). Apparently they were much more interested in being photographed than attending to the job they were supposed to be doing. Alain was horrified to see them cutting off heaven knows what and, worse still, handling the young bunches of grapes which affects their natural bloom.

He considers that many who chose to green-prune in 1990 did not make a success of the vintage since, when the much-needed rain came later at the beginning of September, the vines blotted up the water so rapidly that many of the berries on the less-charged

Alain Hudelot proudly sporting his Irish cap

vines swelled up and burst, which gave rise to rot. 'Pure theatre, la musique, nothing to do with Grand Vin.'

On yields, Alain is less than conventional, declaring that it is perfectly possible to make excellent Grand Cru with healthy yields. This comes from the time when the powerful Alexis Lichine awarded the unknown 26-year-old Alain Hudelot a silver cup for his 1964 Clos de Vougeot. 'The best wine of the Côte,' chuckles Alain, 'it beat all the Richebourgs and Romanée St.-Vivants – everyone else was furious, hopping mad. I made one barrel per *ouvrée* (55 hl./ha.). There was lots of publicity; all these grand people came to wander through my vineyard to see how the vines were pruned, planted, trained,' adding, with a wink, 'truly, de la grande musique!'

In the cellar, fermentation proceeds with natural yeasts and is allowed to reach 32° C before the *must* is cooled to 25° C. Alain dislikes stalks, but generally leaves up to 25% in the vats, for no particular reason – his father and grandfather worked like that, so why change – after all, it keeps the customers happy! In 1990 however, fearing a repetition of the excessively hard and unyielding tannins of 1976, he decided to remove all the stalks. The total *cuvaison* generally lasts 15–18 days, although Alain firmly believes that *maceration* before fermentation extracts more finesse and complexity into his wines than *maceration* after fermentation.

When it comes to the question of wood, Alain grows particularly animated. He seems to have tried every forest in France for his casks, and yet to have found nothing completely satisfactory. His usual tonnelier provides new barrels each year from Nevers, Allier and even Limousin into which Alain puts 100% of his Grands Crus. He has recently started working with a small barrel maker who supplies him with some local wood – Cîteaux and Chatillon. Alain likes the results from Cîteaux and will probably increase the proportion of these in future.

In general he is thoroughly disbelieving of the nuances, or lack of them, from different types of wood: 'c'est de la musique, de la grande, grande, grande musique; moi, j'estime que c'est de la grande musique!' However, he took the matter seriously enough in 1990 to put some of his Vosne-Romanée Les Suchots into new wood – from where he couldn't quite remember.

The wines are racked cask-to-cask in March following the vintage: 'my grandfather did it this way, my father did it this way, so I do it this way.' A second racking around the following September precedes fining, with egg-whites, a plate filtration and bottling in May of the second year, or 'when I have the time to do it'.

The Domaine used to bottle its own wines; then Alain felt that it might be better done by a contract bottler, and gave one a try. However this worthy, being remunerated on a piece-work basis, bottled the wines so rapidly – which is not good for them – that Alain decided to take bottling back into his own hands. His 3 workers are at full stretch in the vineyards during the early summer so bottling just has to be fitted in with whatever else is going on.

Alain Hudelot is at a loss to explain why his wines are so much finer and better constructed than those of many of his neighbours. Talking to him, it is clear that he finds it difficult to believe in the quality of what he is producing: 'I don't think I really have any good wines' and, when pressed, 'there is nothing particularly special about my wines'. This crisis of confidence sits oddly on a man of such international renown, but his doubt is genuine.

A group of French customers turn up at the door in search of some of his 1988 Richebourg – they had read about this wine in the respected *Guide Hachette Des Vins*. 'I'm not really in there, am I?' asks Alain, grabbing the book. Then, finding the reference: 'that's very kind of them'. Sadly there is no Richebourg left; he had only 2 casks and it is all sold. In vain he suggests the 1988 Romanée St.-Vivant as a suitable alternative – 'I have about twice as much,' he tells them. To no avail, they make some feeble enquiry about the 1989 Richebourg, which they are informed is still in cask, and leave. Such is the power of the press!

The Domaine's style tends to supple, aromatic wines, of great elegance. They are not designed for early drinking but to be kept a long time to show their full potential. Alain's avowed aim is to make wines which combine power and finesse and which typify their origins. It is this ineffable combination of qualities with a remarkable depth of ripe fruit which makes his wines so sought after.

Although his Chambolle-Musigny and his Nuits, Les Murgers are usually very successful, it is his Vosne-Romanées for which he is best known. The Vosne Village *cuvée* is invariably beautifully balanced and quite delicate. The 1989 was almost sweet in tone, with flavours of crushed strawberry and spice. Not a big wine, but one with moderate length and supple fruit.

The Vosne-Romanée, Les Suchots, from Alain's precious 70-year-old vines, has characteristic fat and depth. The 1989 showed plenty of sweet, ripe fruit, with a well judged underpin of oak, and good length – a really lovely wine, which shouldn't be touched for 7–10 years.

Alain's Clos Vougeot is one of the best from that frequently disappointing Grand Cru. The 1989 is a wine of plump, stylish ripe fruit, rich and concentrated, with none of the burly rusticity which so often appears in other growers' wines. It has real depth and length – a wine to start drinking a little time after the Suchots.

The Richebourg and Romanée St.-Vivant represent the summit of Alain's considerable achievements. Both the 1989s were compact and closed up in the autumn of 1990; however, it was possible to see their structures of ripe, round tannins, amply covered with succulent, seductive fruit. Although the 60-year-old vines in Romanée St.-Vivant give it an extra dimension of depth neither wine is over balanced by clumsy fruit which might threaten their underlying finesse. The Richebourg is a bigger wine than the Romanée St.-Vivant, with great power and majestic depth, a bass compared with a tenor. The RomanéeSt.-Vivant, in contrast, has more obvious refinement and elegance – yet with fine, restrained power. Both these magnificent 1989s are glorious tributes to Alain's wine-making skills.

Searching for a clue as to why his wines are so much finer than many of his neighbours with equally good vineyards, Alain suggests that too long a *cuvaison* is often a cause of loss of finesse. Delaying decanting the wines off their solids after fermentation can, he believes, lead to a certain dryness and coldness which closes up the aromas in such a way that they never fully develop. Beyond that, he shrugs his shoulders and chucks more logs onto the blazing fire – presumably 'c'est la grande musique' as well.

VINEYARD HOLDINGS

Commune	*Level*	*Lieu-dit/Climat*	*Area*	*Vine Age*	*Status*
Chambolle	V	(Various climats)	3.00	1–20	P
Vougeot	PC	Les Petits Vougeots	0.50	30	F
Vougeot	GC	Clos de Vougeot	1.08	30	P/F
Vosne	V	—	0.68	12	P
Vosne	GC	Romanée St.-Vivant	0.48	60	P
Vosne	GC	Richebourg	0.28	40	P
Vosne	PC	Les Suchots	0.45	70	P
Vosne	PC	Les Malconsorts	0.20	35	P
Vosne	PC	Les Beaumonts	0.32	35	P
Nuits	PC	Les Murgers	0.80	35	P
Chambolle + Gilly	R	(Bourgogne Rouge)	2.00	25	P
		Total	**9.79 ha.**		

Domaine Château de la Tour

VOUGEOT

The situation of this Domaine must be among the most unusual in the Côte d'Or. In a gaping breach in the northernmost wall of the Clos de Vougeot, facing out the Château itself, stands a curious pointed edifice glued to a conical tower which gives the appearance of a sort of gothic rocket, set to ignite and depart for somewhere else, as though it were dissatisfied with its present surroundings. This is the Château de la Tour, a Domaine consisting of a single, enviable, 5.5 ha. slab of Clos de Vougeot.

The 'rocket' was built in 1890 to house the wines of the Beaudet family, négociants in Beaune, following the inconvenient sale of the Château de Clos Vougeot where, by arrangement, they had bottled and stored their wine. Faced with the urgent need for space, they decided to sacrifice part of their vineyard to build a cuverie and cellars and selected the northern wall because this was the widest point of their land.

When the great-grandfather of the present manager, François Labet, lost a lung in the First World War, he was advised to live abroad in a hotter climate and sold his négociant company – the Clos de Chapître, in Beaune – to a M. Morin in 1921. Between 1921 and 1925 Morin ran the business – which therefore technically passed out of the family succession. However, it came swiftly back into it when Morin married François' grandmother. A 'donation partage', made before Morin died, brought the Château and vineyards into the family of the present owners, Mme. Jacqueline Labet and Nicole d'Echelette – François Labet's mother and aunt respectively.

The Rocket – next to the north wall of the Clos

Following business school and a brief apprenticeship at the estate from 1984, François took over from his father, Pierre, in 1986. His subsequent travels in the USA and Australia convinced him that the Domaine was not fulfilling its potential, either in quantity or in quality. Advances in vinification, in particular, seemed to him to point to a different style of wine-making. The work of Emile Peynaud at Château Margaux in the late 1970s, particularly in the rigorous cask selection for the Grand Vin and in the use of wood, had a marked influence on François. He is now 37, and is determined on making his Clos de Vougeot the best there is.

Soon after taking over, François was introduced to the Lebanese Guy Accad, who was beginning to gain converts in Burgundy for his revolutionary system of vinification. Accad's method was characterised by a substantial period of pre-fermentive maceration at low temperature, under a massive blanket of sulphur.

Talking and tasting convinced François Labet that he should try this on an experimental basis, with the result that the Domaine converted to Accad from the 1987 vintage. A few years on, both François and his father are convinced that their wines have more colour, a deeper aromatic concentration and structure and more mellow tannins.

François encapsulates his viewpoint thus: 'Making Grand Vin is like making Grande Cuisine – you must sometimes forget your books and put a hint of something in . . . to get a new dish, something new; what is important is to have the skeleton of a wine – that is sugars, acids etc.; it is up to the vinifier to build the body. You can't change the basic skeleton, but you build the wine with your guts.'

The Labets consider that the quality of their raw material is of prime importance. The vineyards of the Domaine are kept in pristine condition by Henri Legros – the third and sadly the last in a line of Legros who have worked as vignerons at Château de la Tour.

A light herbicide is followed by regular ploughing with as little fertiliser as possible. Soil analyses are monitored closely to determine any adjustments for *trace element* deficiencies. Neither humus nor manure is used because they can bring disease – but a spray of guano is employed from time to time.

Bordeaux mixture is used for *botrytis* and other *cryptogams* and vigorous war is waged against spider, cochylis and grape-worm with whatever products the local 'Service de Protection des Végétaux' advise – the Domaine is one of their test sites in the Côte de Nuits.

Replanting is normally by annual *repiquage*; however, the extensive frosts of 1985 meant that larger surfaces needed grubbing up and it was decided to replant from material selected from the vineyards and grafted by the Domaine onto rootstock 161/49. During 1990/1991 they also replaced 50% of a substantial replanting carried out in 1980, since it was found to be infected with *eutypiose* – an insidious and potentally disastrous form of 'dead-arm'. François believes that this infection – which takes several years to manifest itself – came from the clones and is currently 'having discussions' with the nursery involved.

'It is better to prune short and have small grapes, than to summer-prune,' argues François; 'green pruning is the worst thing you can do.' In support, he cites experiments demonstrating that removing 50% of bunches only results in a 25% reduction in yield, so the effect is largely illusory. This misses the point: summer pruning is not intended to reduce the yield in strict proportion to the number of bunches removed, but to concentrate the limited vigour of each vine, so that it can bring to full and concentrated ripeness a smaller number of bunches, thus increasing the overall quality. Moreover, short winter pruning and summer pruning are not alternatives, as François seems to suggest, since even a strict pruning does not automatically exclude the need to summer-prune if growth is particularly vigorous.

François also argues strongly against any *saignée de cuve* – the practice of bleeding off juice from a vat before fermentation to increase the ratio of juice:solids and thus, hopefully, the concentration – because he believes that this unbalances the wine. This also misses the point, since in a year when the proportion of juice to solids is too high there is ipso facto already a disequilibrium, so bleeding off some juice helps restore the ratio to a more normal level. Of course, if the skins are thin, no amount of maceration will give the wine more guts, because the colour and tannins simply aren't there; what a careful *saignée* can do is to better balance out whatever tannins and flavour compounds there are – no more than that.

The major part of the Domaine's 5.5 ha. is ideally placed in the central 'kidney' of the Clos. This is an important quality factor since it is generally considered that the soils near to the Abbey are too dry and those near to the RN 74 too humid for Grand Vin.

François prefers to harvest as late as possible: 'wait, wait, wait, until the maturity is there' – more difficult in years like 1984,1986 and 1987 than in ripe years such as 1988, 1989 and 1990. This avoids the need for *chaptalisation*, without apparently creating problems with low acidity levels. François claims that he never even contemplates acidification because his wines show no signs of deficiency in that direction.

Destalking is not systematic, depending rather on the quality of the vintage – 100% intact bunches in 1987, whilst in 1988,1989 and 1990 50–75% of the stalks were removed. The whole bunches that form part of each vat-load are put at the bottom of the vat so that they gradually degrade by inter-cellular fermentation to extract as much colour as possible – in effect a part *carbonic maceration*.

An automatic sulphuring, at a rate of 1.5–3.0 litres of 5% sulphur solution per tonne of harvest, is followed by one week of cold maceration at 5° C. This exaggerated dose of sulphur is intended to destroy less virile yeasts which only ferment weakly to about 4–5% alcohol and to delay the onset of fermentation.

When it reaches about 10° C the top part of the vat starts to ferment normally; there seems to be no clear explanation for yeasts working at this extraordinarily low temperature – under 'traditional' conditions, they tend to remain inactive until reaching about 15° C.

Fermentation is allowed to proceed normally, but not to exceed 25° C – a low level by usual standards – cooling the *must* if necessary to achieve this. Pumping-over without aeration is used to keep the cap moist, with just two *pigéages* during the entire fermentation cycle, to avoid too much tannin

Francois and Jeanine Labet – Bermudas in the Côte

extraction. *Cuvaison* normally lasts 2–2½ weeks.

As soon as all the sugar has been converted, the wine is run off and the remaining pulp lightly pressed once to yield as soft a press-wine as possible. This is added to the free-run wine which then spends a further week in vat to ferment out any sugar extracted from the press-wine. Pectolytic enzymes are added to help clarification, which in turn means one less racking than would otherwise have been needed. The wine is then racked completely clear of its muddy lees and put into casks.

The argument is that the cold maceration extracts significantly more of the water-soluble anthocyanins, which though inherently unstable are subsequently 'fixed' by the tannins in solution; further, the policy of fermentation at a relatively low temperature retains important volatile trace-aromas which would otherwise escape at higher temperatures.

The wood used by François is 15–50% new oak – the wine from the oldest vines in the middle of the Clos have 50%, the younger vines 15%. The *malos* are allowed to proceed at their own pace – 'let nature work – don't force it' – before a first racking in the June or July following the vintage. At this point , following his mentors at Château Margaux, a rigorous selection is made from the 100 or so casks of Clos Vougeot. Any that are unacceptable are put aside to be sold to négociants.

The remainder are then assembled in 15–16 cask lots, corresponding to each original fermentation vat, before being returned to cask to await a further racking the following spring.

The final *assemblage* of the Clos Vougeot *cuvée* is made between July and September, 21–24 months following the harvest. Except in rare circumstances, François Labet neither fines nor filters his wines.

This method of vinification is certainly iconoclastic – large doses of sulphur, cooling to low temperatures, a long pre-fermentive maceration and a practically non-existent post-fermentive maceration. What are the benefits? The effects are clear: much deeper colour; much less obvious Pinot Noir fruit aromas and flavours; debatably more mellow tannins and a distinct maceration aroma and flavour when tasted young in cask. In short, more concentration and power.

To assess whether these are genuine improvements one has to taste the wines at a much later stage of their evolution. Judging by recent vintages, there is no doubt that, whilst they have considerable depth and concentration, the spectrum of flavours and aromas is different from that one would expect from a traditional vinification. The red fruits, which so characterise fine young Pinot Noir, have given place to the darker fruits – black cherries and blackberries – with mildly tarry undertones. In addition, the wines are much less approachable in cask than their traditional counterparts and consequently more difficult to assess.

With age, they unpack very slowly indeed. The oldest of the Domaine's new vinification, the 1987 vintage, was barely starting to show signs of maturation on the nose and palate in October 1990. The 1985, however – vinified 'à l'ancienne' – showed a positive and attractive aroma of *fraises des bois*, and a lovely soft spectrum of ripe flavours, with a touch of *sous-bois* underpinned with harmonious tannins – a wine of real breed and undoubted Grand Cru quality.

François Labet's wines show considerable promise. There is little doubt that they are worthy of their origin but only time will tell how they will develop. The love-affair with 'la méthode Accad' may not last, but the reputation of the Domaine and the quality of what François is doing augur well for the future. However, as François is well aware: 'there is only one judge – it is the customer . . . the one who opens the bottle.'

VINEYARD HOLDINGS

Commune	Level	Lieu-dit/Climat	Area	Vine Age	Status
Vougeot	GC	Clos de Vougeot	5.50	3.5 ha.:35 2.0 ha.:60	P

VOSNE-ROMANÉE AND FLAGEY-ECHÉZEAUX

There can be little doubt that, in the firmament of the Côte de Nuits, Vosne-Romanée is the brightest star. Turning off the RN 74 into the village never fails to evoke the mystery of pilgrimage, a sense that this unpretentious little village and its backdrop of magnificent vineyards are something special and that those who own this precious land must be among the most fortunate souls on earth.

The pilgrim needs no other reason to visit Vosne than to wander through its streets and up to the slopes behind, perhaps to visit a grower and taste, or just to take a picnic and sit among the vines on a warm afternoon, inwardly marvelling that from this ordinary-looking land come some of the world's most legendary and sumptuous wines.

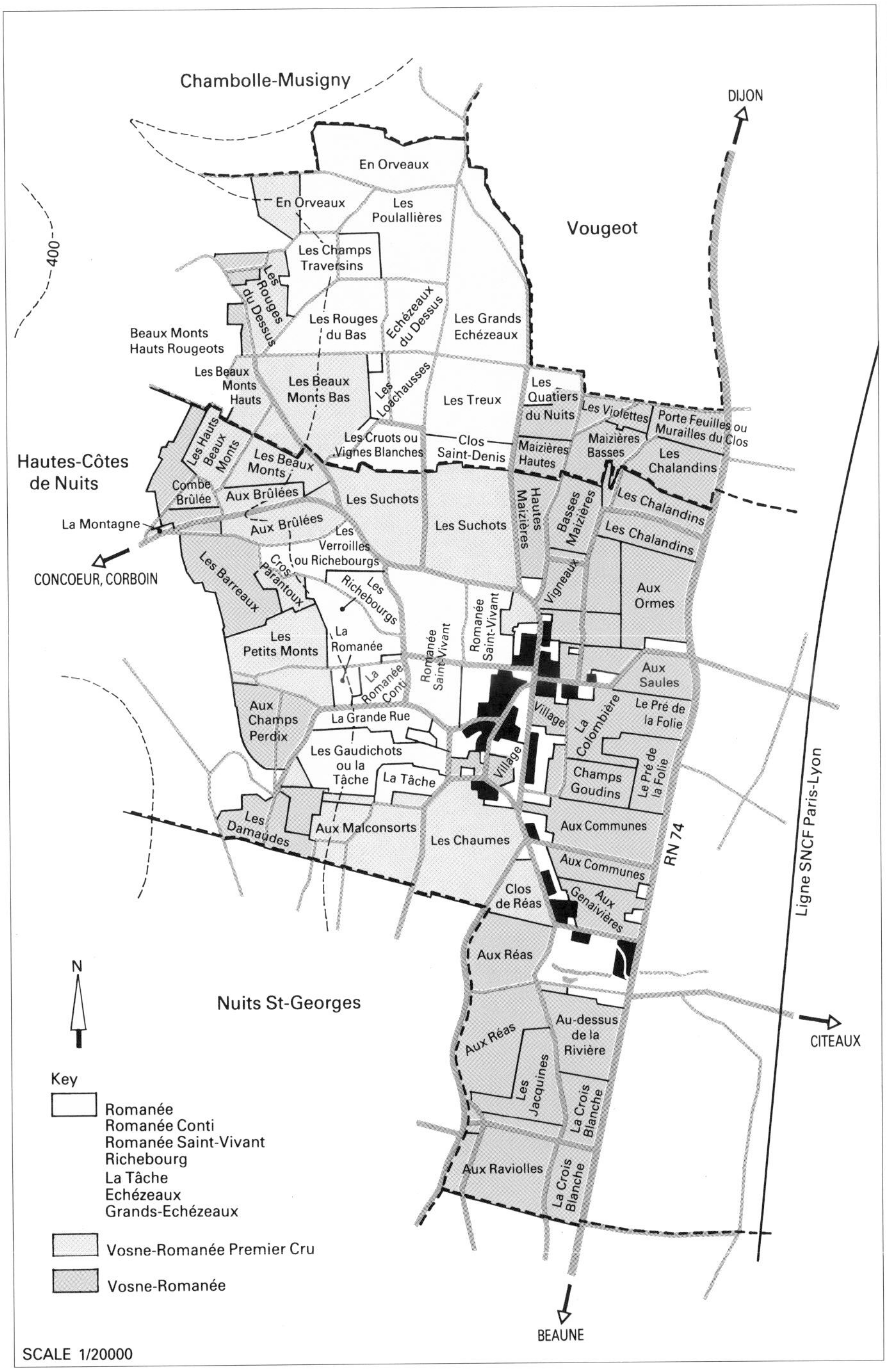

By comparison with the other villages of the Côte, Vosne is not large – just 182 ha. of vines, but vines of a quality that almost brings one to one's knees. To the east and south-east of the Post Office lies the lion's share of the Village appellation – some 98.57 ha., mainly of thin but well-drained clay-limestone soils, with a top layer of pebbles and limestone scree. From here come wines which balance depth and richness with elegance and breed; often described as silky, they are usually marked by a finesse and perfume which, together with their natural power, ages beautifully.

Scattered round both sides and to the west are Vosne's 16 Premiers Crus. These occupy some 57.19 ha., often on slopes of up to 15%, and are mainly exposed to the east or south-east. The soils tend to have less depth and to contain a higher proportion of limestone than those in the Village and the topsoil is mainly scree, which makes for excellent drainage. Although there is no marked quality distinction between them, Les Suchots (13.07 ha.), Les Beaux Monts (11.39 ha.), Aux Malconsorts (5.86 ha.) and Les Chaumes (6.46 ha.) are probably better known, being the largest.

The associated commune of Flagey-Echézeaux is something of a curiosity: this perfunctory hamlet of some 450 souls, erstwhile an annex of Vosne, lies not along the main flank of the Côte but on the eastern side of the RN 74 beyond the railway tracks. It apparently derives the first part of its name from the 'flagellation' the peasants used to harvest the corn in the sixth century; the 'Echézeaux' was glued on in 1886. Having no appellation of its own for Village and Premiers Crus, the handful of vineyards falling into these categories are treated to the relevant Vosne-Romanée appellation. Were it not for its two Grands Crus – Les Echézeaux and Les Grands Echézeaux – which are generally considered part of Vosne-Romanée, Flagey would not merit notice. However, the village now has an excellent small restaurant owned and run by Robert Losset, an ex-chef from the liner 'France', which for some mysterious reason is only open at lunchtime and closes altogether on Wednesdays.

Vosne's Grands Crus are capable of producing quintessential Burgundy – wines of such opulence, depth and refinement that it is difficult to believe that they are solely the product of bunches of grapes.

Of these, Les Echézeaux is both the largest and the most variable in quality. Many believe that most of its 11 different *climats* are unworthy of Grand Cru status and should not have been included when the original 1936 delimitation – which only included the 3.57 ha. Les Echézeaux-Dessus was subsequently revised.

The Echézeaux vines extend to the dizzy height of 360 m. above sea level on slopes of up to 15%. The soils vary within the vineyard, but are relatively deep, even in the top sections, being composed chiefly of fine siltstone, clay and pebbles, on the hard limestone base on which most of Vosne-Romanée rests. It is this depth and finesse which gives the potential for quality.

Les Grands Echézeaux, a 9.14 ha. slab of moderately flat land bordering the western edge of the Clos de Vougeot, is undisputed Grand Cru – with soil of similar content and structure to Les Echézeaux. Of the 8 Vosne Grands Crus, it is the only one which comes anywhere near to a sensible quality-price ratio. In good vintages, from Domaines such as Clos Frantin, Drouhin, Jean Mongeard, Philippe Engel and the Domaine de la Romanée-Conti, it is superb wine.

La Romanée, at 0.85 ha. the smallest Grand Cru in the Côte d'Or, is sandwiched on a 16% slope, between La Romanée-Conti to the east and Premier Cru Aux Raignots to the west, with Les Richebourgs to the north and La Grande Rue to the south. Originally joined to the Romanée-Conti vineyard, it was split into two in 1760 when the Prince de Conti bought the lower part. Owned since 1815 by the Liger-Belair family, its annual production of some 300 cases is sold by the négociants Bouchard Père et Fils.

By contrast, Romanée St.-Vivant is situated on virtually flat ground to the north and west of the village. The soil is unusually deep, dominated by limestone with a high clay content. More than half of the 9.43.74 ha. are owned by the Domaine de la Romanée-Conti, who acquired them from the Marey-Monge family in 1988. The wine can be excellent, but is often overshadowed by the other Grands Crus. Louis Latour and Alain Hudelot-Noëllat also make reliable examples.

Les Richebourgs, which Camille Rodier described as 'one of the most sumptuous Crus of Burgundy', is an amalgam of 5.05 ha. of genuine Richebourgs and 2.98 ha. of Vosne-Romanée Premier Cru Les Verroilles which was tacked on later. Oriented eastwards, the vineyard is mainly on limestone deposits, with some clay, which gives the wines plenty of robustness and *charpente* and thus a long life expectancy. The finest examples generally come from the Domaine de la Romanée-Conti, Méo-Camuzet, Henri Jayer, Alain Hudelot-Noëllat, Jean Gros, Jean Grivot and Jean Mongeard.

Vosne's next generation of vignerons enjoying the hospitality of a rather famous wall

The 1.42 ha. strip of La Grande Rue was, until 1991, one of those anomalies of classification one sometimes encounters in the Côte d'Or – a Premier Cru sandwiched between two Grands Crus – in this case La Tâche and Romanée-Conti. It has belonged to the Domaine Lamarche (qv) ever since Henri Lamarche was given it as a wedding present in the 1920s. The present generation, François and Marie-France Lamarche, finally succeeded – after a long and persistent campaign – in persuading the authorities to re-classify it as Grand Cru, chiefly on the ground that it shares the same soil band as its neighbours.

The last two Grands Crus represent the summit of which Burgundy and Pinot Noir are capable. La Tâche (6.06.20 ha.) and Romanée-Conti (1.80.50 ha.) are both *Monopoles* of the Domaine de la Romanée-Conti. The one lies on mainly flat land to the west of the Post Office, whilst the other sits majestically in the heart of the Grands Crus, marked by a simple stone cross.

The wines from these precious plots are supremely elegant and aristocratic; at once silky, opulent and fine, with mature aromas of spice and violets and multi-faceted flavours of glorious richness and length. Attempts at describing them easily degenerate into senseless pretension. Words – even if suitable ones could be found, which is doubtful – are woefully inadequate when faced with such superlative examples of the wine-maker's art. These are the wines of which vignerons throughout the Côte and well beyond, whether or not they admit it, stand in awe; these are the bottles they will hoard in their own cellars and bring out to crown some special occasion. Vosne-Romanée is the apotheosis of Burgundy.

THE GRANDS CRUS OF VOSNE-ROMANÉE AND FLAGEY-ECHÉZEAUX

Lieu-dit	*Area*	*Props.*	*Av. Prod.*
La Grande Rue	1.42.00	1	550 C/S
Echézeaux	37.69.22	84	10,500 C/S
Grands-Echézeaux	9.13.45	21	2,750 C/S
Romanée St.-Vivant	9.43.74	6	2,600 C/S
Richebourg	8.03.45	10	2,500 C/S
La Tâche	6.06.20	1	1,870 C/S
Romanée	0.84.52	1	300 C/S
Romanée-Conti	1.80.50	1	500 C/S
Totals	**74.42,08 ha.**		**21,570 C/S**

Domaine Confuron-Cotétidot

VOSNE-ROMANÉE

Jacky Confuron is an individual – a person who, once met, is difficult to forget. Physically striking, with short hair sometimes swept back, sometimes standing up on end, he is short and stocky with slightly bowed legs. His personality matches his mien – rather rugged, determined and not to be gainsaid or swayed – he is someone for whom the world is either black or white, with few shades permitted in between.

He lives with his wife in a large, pleasant house in one of the feeder roads into Vosne from the RN 74. From here, they run their 6.89 ha. Domaine with the help of agronomist and oenologist Guy Accad.

The Confurons – of which those at Premeaux are another branch – have been in Vosne for a long time: 'my great, great grandfather, at least, started the Domaine.' Generations later, when 'Le Père', as Jacky refers to his father, decided to divide up his 18 ha. in 1964, Jacky received 2.5 ha. as his share – 'Le Père' having resolved to keep the largest slice for himself. Gradually more land was bought – Chambolle-Musigny, Gevrey-Chambertin, Nuits-St.-Georges and Bourgogne – to turn it into an enterprise which would comfortably support a wife and two children.

It takes only a few minutes conversation to realise that Jacky Confuron is not someone who acts on impulse, but who weighs every decision with the utmost care and precision. For him there is no short cut to quality.

He originally sought the advice of Guy Accad in 1977 to help bring back an equilibrium to his soils, but Accad's influence soon extended into the cellars. However, it would be a mistake to think that Jacky has abrogated his reponsibilities there to Accad – as long as the advice is good he will take it, otherwise he is perfectly capable of making up his own mind. 'It takes 25 years to get a client and it is so easy to lose them,' Jacky adds reflectively. His wines are rapidly sold out, so for the moment the clientèle seems totally faithful.

Part of his philosophy is a hearty dislike of anything of which he is not completely sure. Clones fall into this category. He did try them but was dissatisfied with the quality: 'the vine perished in 15 years'. 'No clones – I make my own plant selection.' There is no compromising on quality – the 'plant selection' is grafted by Jacky himself on to Riparia rootstock – a traditional root which is returning to favour in the Côte for its low yield and berry quality – 'good on to good'.

Generally the vines are pruned in the customary *Guyot simple* mode, limited further by Jacky to 5 or 6 'eyes' on each cane. If an individual plant is becoming feeble, then it is trained *en gobelet* to encourage it to produce.

This is expert work for which he enlists the skills of his wife: 'it is like making love,' he explains, 'you must concentrate.'

As one might expect, Jacky Confuron likes yields to be small and does everything he can to limit them. In this he is helped by the vines themselves, many of which are a venerable 60 – 70 years old. A young vine for Jacky would be an old one for most other growers.

The yields tell their own story – in 1988 and 1989 average Confuron yields were 30 hl./ha. – against an authorised base for Vosne- Romanée village and Premier Cru of 40 hl./ha. and 35 hl./ha. for Grand Cru. In 1990 they climbed to 40 hl./ha. for his village wines and to 35 hl./ha. for the Premiers and Grands Crus.

All this is achieved by meticulous attention to detail – plenty of *repiquage*, the barest minimum, if any, fertilisation, rigorous *évasivage*, the minimum of treatments and certainly no anti-rot sprays. In addition, the foliage is summer-pruned 'much higher than normal', to encourage photosynthesis and thus maximum sugar levels, and any second-generation bunches are scrupulously removed each August.

The right moment to harvest is one of the most important decisions a conscientious vigneron has to make. In Jacky's case there is no difficulty – 'We harvest late to have the maximum degrees,' he remarks, as if this were a self-evident truth, adding, 'you must take risks.' He cites some tests carried out recently by the French wine-writer, Michel Bettane, in which samples of grapes were taken from a number of vineyards which were being harvested – many were found to be far short of proper maturity.

Jacky Confuron stamping out his grafts – most vignerons buy them in

In the cellars beneath the house the work continues: 'I operate on the ancient method,' says Jacky, referring no doubt to his old wooden *cuves* and to the 150-year-old press, originally used by his great-grandfather.

The grapes are not destalked, but put whole into the *cuves* where they receive a 1.5–2.0 litre per tonne dose of SO_2. Selection in the vineyard is so rigorous that 'there are never any rotten grapes here', so the sulphur simply serves to knock out the yeasts and, together with cooling to 8–10° C, to delay the onset of fermentation for about 8 days.

At the end of this cold maceration, yeasts are added to get fermentation started. The average length of *cuvaison* is 3 weeks, during which time the temperature is permitted to rise to no more than 28° C: 'above that you get evaporation and the risk of *volatile acidity.*'

The 'méthode ancienne' extends to the '3 good *pigéages*' to which each *cuve* is subjected daily. This involves Jacky, completely naked, immersing all but his head in the *cuve* and using his feet to break up and submerge the cap of skins and stalks.

Chaptalisation is kept to the minimum and performed in one fell swoop. In 1989, for example, only 1–2 kilos of sugar per cask were needed – an adjustment of about one tenth of a degree of alcohol. Once most of the sugar has been fermented out the free-run wine is drawn off and the remaining pulp forked into the 150-year-old which is then galvanised into action with the aid of a hand-pump. A single pressing is enough – for the pulp and, one suspects, for Jacky as well.

The press-wine is then tasted and, if up to scratch, added to the original wine which is allowed to settle further for 2–8 days, depending on the state of the lees, before transfer to casks to begin its *élevage*.

Because he considers that not destalking gives his wines enough tannin, Jacky sees no reason to add any more in the form of new oak. Only 10% of his casks are renewed annually, and they last him for 5–10 years.

The *élevage* here is highly individual: the

The Confurons' house on the edge of Vosne

wines spend some 24–30 months in wood, more a Bordelais than a Burgundian time-scale. Each February/March and each August the casks are racked, the final racking being into bulk to unify the different lots of each wine. The wine is then returned to cask, the sulphur adjusted, and then it is carefully bottled by hand, straight from cask.

Jacky's 'méthode ancienne' tolerates neither fining nor filtration. 'Wine,' he remarks dryly, 'is living, and should be treated like a person. Filtration takes the trousers off a wine – it removes everything.' In his view careful racking achieves better results without destroying the stuffing and balance of the wine.

Whatever the rationale, Jacky's wines are remarkably good. Unfortunately, some commentators have sought to heap opprobrium on him for producing what they refer to as 'méthode Accad' wines. Such blanket criticisms are offensive to those who retain Guy Accad, and frequently conceal a limited understanding of what he and his clients are trying to achieve.

What cannot be denied is that his long, cold maceration produces wines which start life with deep colours – this is not, be it said, unique to this system of vinification. They also tend to have somewhat exuberant aromas – which are extracted, and fixed, by a relatively low fermentation temperature.

Tasting a range of 1989s there could be no argument about the individuality of each wine. The Vosne village *cuvée* – completely closed up, no nose, but heaps of concentrated fruit with deep, round tannins and considerable length – was thoroughly different from the Nuits-St.-Georges which was showing much more structure and fatness. In contrast to the Vosne, it was very perfumed, with an opulent nose of *fruits sauvages* and liquorice, with a dimension of old-vine fruit which was particularly appealing. The vineyard is situated on the Vosne side of Nuits, which would tend to emphasise similarities rather than differences.

The *cuvée* of 1989 Gevrey-Chambertin was different again – 75-year-old vines contributing an open, exotic nose and a massive layer of ripe, almost silky fruit. The wine shows that marvellous combination of power and finesse which makes one's heart miss a beat.

The Chambolle-Musigny was less typical than the others – with a fine, deep consistent robe, right to the edge of the glass, and a seductive array of complex aromas – violets and griottes in particular. On the palate, plenty of concentration and tannins, but almost too much depth for a really copybook Chambolle. This is not an argument about the quality of the wine, rather about its typicity.

The Nuits-St.-Georges Premier Cru – an *assemblage* of fruit from 70-year-old vines in Les Murgers and Les Vignesrondes – was altogether different from the rest – much more 'sauvage' on the nose, and with considerable acidity and *mache* – less typical perhaps of 1989 than of Nuits. This wine will take a long time to integrate .

The 1989 Vosne-Romanée Les Suchots was going through a difficult phase, or so it seemed – reduced on the nose and without much charm, although underneath there was plenty of flesh and depth.

The Echézeaux, however, was clearly on form – a mid-garnet colour, with a tantalising embryonic nose and a beautiful balance of finesse and structure underneath. This will be a wine of fine complexity, with great vinosity and nuance. The overall impression was of length, ripeness and almost flawless balance.

The Clos-Vougeot, from 60-year-old vines, had an impenetrable appearance of deep, limpid black-cherry hue. The nose was either beginning to open out or just closing up – again griottes and violets with a touch of 'greenness'. This latter also appeared on the palate which was dominated by a heavy-weight, muscular scaffold of tannins and power. The size of the wine suggests that it will need at least a decade before it might be willing to reveal itself.

Among those more interested in sterile analysis than in pleasure, the debate about the typicity of 'cold-maceration' wines will no doubt rumble on. This should not blind people who seek only to enjoy their wines, to trying some of the very fine bottles to be had from such as Jacky Confuron – wines as carefully crafted as it is possible to make them, which have great richness of fruit and, in vintages such as 1989, immense charm.

Jacky and Bernadette Confuron can sell every drop they produce – a position of which many lesser wine-makers might be thoroughly envious. Perhaps those who denigrate should pause to reflect on this before rushing into print.

VINEYARD HOLDINGS

Commune	*Level*	*Lieu-dit/Climat*	*Area*	*Vine Age*	*Status*
Flagey	GC	Echézeaux	0.22	40	P
Vougeot	GC	Clos de Vougeot	0.26	60	P
Vosne	PC	Les Suchots	1.34		
Vosne	V	Porte Feuilles du Clos + Jacquines	1.45	5–35	M/P
Nuits	PC	Murgers + Vignesrondes	1.00	70	M
Nuits	V	Bas de Combes + Lavières	0.55	70	P
Gevrey	V	Les Champs Chenys	0.40	75	P
Chambolle	V	(Various climats)	0.71	45	P
—	R	(Bourg. /Aligoté)	0.98	35	P
		Total	**6.91 ha.**		

Domaine René Engel

VOSNE-ROMANÉE

René Engel was one of the great personalities of post-war Burgundy and of Vosne-Romanée in particular. One of the founders of the Confrérie des Chevaliers de Tastevin, Professor of Oenology at Dijon University for 35 years and a respected writer on Burgundy and its wines (*Vade Mecum pour Viticulteurs* and *Vosne-Romanée, l'Histoire du Village* are perhaps the best known), he was dedicated to the Côte d'Or and to encouraging the production of better quality wines.

He lived to the age of 94, dying in 1986. His son Pierre, who had taken over the running of the family Domaine, had sadly died at the age of 53, five years earlier, after a long illness. Unfortunately, as Pierre had neither the will nor the strength to carry on in the late 1970s, and his son Philippe was not yet capable of taking charge, standards had inevitably slipped. When Philippe finally took over, in 1981, much needed to be done to remedy the neglect evident in the vineyards and in the cellars; vines had died and not been replaced, posts and wires were rotten, and the soil contained too much nitrogen and potassium. In the cellars, casks and *foudres* were in poor repair .

Gradually Philippe put things right and began to stamp his own personality upon the Domaine and its wines. Standards have improved considerably over the last decade as the wines become annually more consistent and more impressive. In addition to implementing the physical improvements referred to, it has taken the passage of time for Philippe to shake off the legacy of his father and his grandfather and to begin to think through each wine for himself.

Unlike his father, he did not study at Dijon, but at the Lycée Viticole in Beaune – an altogether more practically oriented training which seems to have served him well. He is happy to discuss his wine-making openly, and to take counsel when he feels it is needed.

Philippe is in no doubt about the style of wine he prefers and the exponents of that style whom he most admires. Not for him the lacy finesse and feminine elegance of some of his contemporaries' wine; rather wines which are richly structured in their youth, with plenty of *charpente* and concentrated meaty fruit, which need years of cellaring to develop their potential. Philippe Charlopin in Marsannay and Alain Burguet in Gevrey are his friends, occasional dining companions and informal consultants.

Having been so long tied to the methods of an illustrious parent and an even more illustrious grandparent, it is not surprising that Philippe is slow to find his self-confidence. He now indulges in experiments when he feels that there is something to be learned thereby. For example, a *cuvée* of 1985 Clos

In the cellars

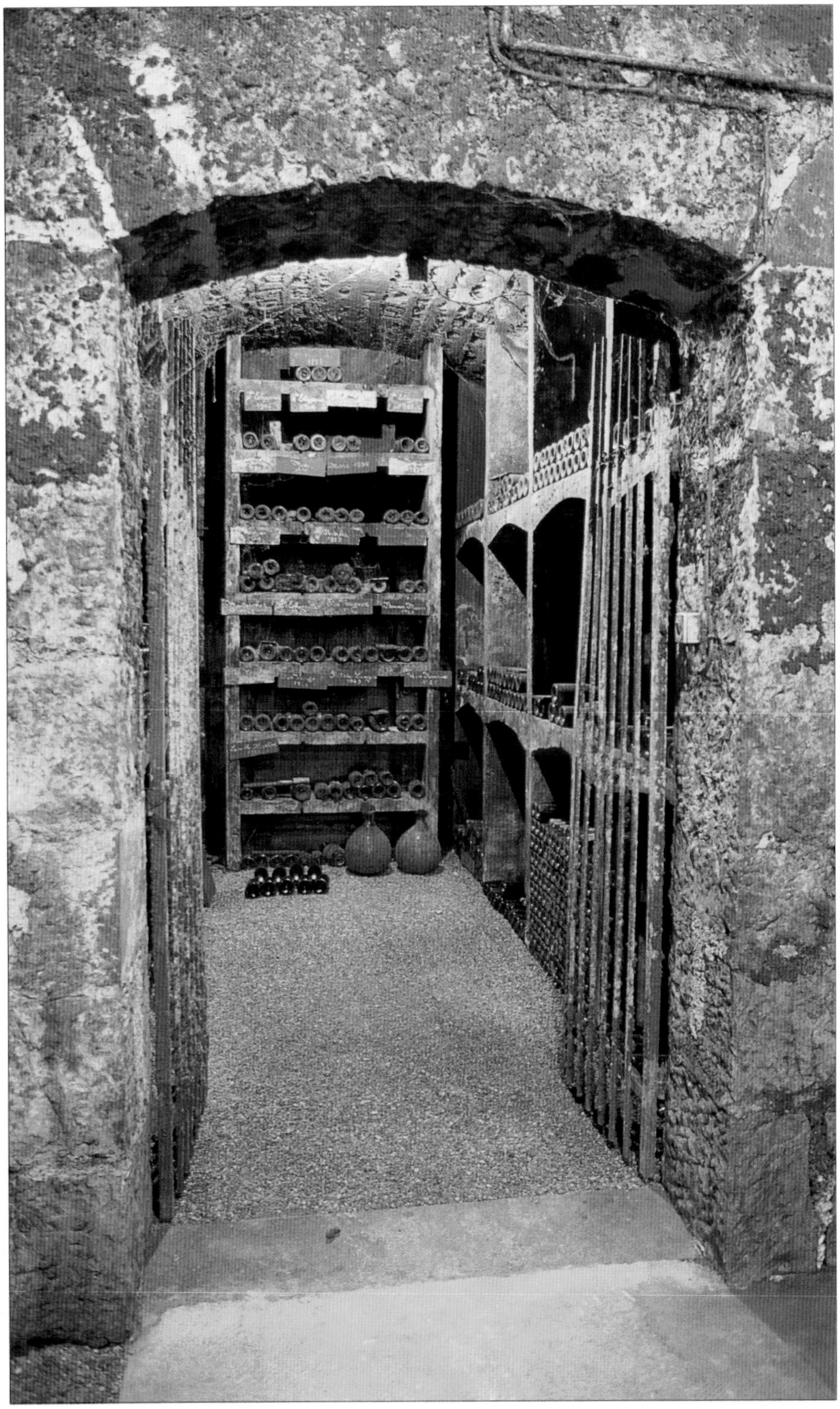

de Vougeot resisted all attempts at cooling and continued fermenting up to the dizzy heights of 36° C. Being consulted on what to do next, René's advice was along the broad lines of 'leave it alone'. Philippe did, the wine was superb and generally admired. As a result, he is happy to let his *cuves* rise to 35° C to render the wine 'bien gras'.

Much of the family wine-making tradition is retained. Up to 21 days *cuvaison,* total destalking, no pumps and twice daily *pigéage* during fermentation. Sulphur, at the normal rate of 1 litre of 5% solution per tonne of harvest, is added as each *cuve* is filled with grapes. Surprisingly, in some years this results in the need to use cultured yeasts to start fermentation; perhaps more of a panic measure than a necessity. Hopefully this practice will soon discontinue.

Philippe has a wide choice of *cuves*: metal tanks, glass-lined tanks, 3 old wooden open *cuves* and stainless-steel. Perversely, he much prefers cement *cuves*, but hasn't, as yet, got any, although he does admit that *must* in the wooden *cuves* rises to a higher temperature and stays there longer, which is a distinct benefit for his style of wine.

René Engel liked to add only the wine from the first, gentler pressing. Philippe, having experimented with a Premier Cru without press-wine, and with first press-wine, continues in this way. However, in years when the harvest is small, there is a second press-wine which is vinified apart and then either added or not at *assemblage*, just before bottling, or 'kept for a vintage which has less structure'!

Although the wines see 30% new wood, Philippe would prefer more. He cites the cost of new casks, the poor image of new wood (hard to believe) as present deterrents, but admits that those of his wines which see most new oak are universally preferred by his customers. He also cites the excellent wines of Jean-Nicolas Méo, which are vinified in 100% new oak and among his personal favourites.

The casks are generally racked 'à l'air' with a push of nitrogen to avoid pumping, following the *malo* in March or April of the first year. However, in 1988 Philippe left the wines on their lees until bottling 18 months after the harvest: 'vins solides' can, he believes, safely be left without racking, which helps to retain their freshness. Equally, pumping adds a grassy dimension to a wine and detracts from its freshness. Hence, minimum racking and no pumping.

In 1989, by contrast, the wines were racked in the spring. His laboratory advised a strong dose of sulphur, since they predicted a high risk of *volatile acidity* in the wines. Philippe, to his credit, ignored this advice for most of his wines, which have turned out entirely unproblematical. It is true that many growers panicked needlessly over levels of *volatile acidity* in 1989 and over-sulphured. It takes courage to gainsay the advice of the technicians, but conscientious growers rely less on this than one might suppose, tending to regard analysis as only part of the equation. Laboratories must perforce err on the side of caution.

René Engel apparently studied the question of when to bottle in some detail and discovered that after a certain time in cask a wine does not further evolve – at least not beneficially. Whilst some viticulteurs in Gevrey, for example, bottle their wines after only 9 months in cask, in a misguided attempt to mimic the freshness and delicacy of a Vosne-Romanée, Philippe Engel leaves his wines for 18 months before bottling, generally with an albumen fining in bulk and a kieselguhr and/or plate filtration. In his view, fining rounds out a wine and endows it with a brilliance which filtered wine lacks. Filtration, however careful, tends to remove some of the stuffing of a wine, and is less and less used.

Philippe recently made an interesting experiment to test the relative importance of vinification and vineyard on the character of a wine. He exchanged a tonne of Vosne-Romanée grapes with Burguet and Charlopin and they delivered Gevrey grapes to him. Not surprisingly, Philippe made rather Vosne-like wine with his Gevrey grapes whereas Burguet and Charlopin made somewhat structured and Gevrey-ish Vosne-Romanées. There seems to be considerable scope for imaginative experimentation along these lines – how about Leflaive grapes vinified at Bonneau de Martray or some Monthelie grapes vinified in Chambolle-Musigny?

Like many of his contemporaries, Philippe Engel is not completely glued to his cellars – although large chunks of free time are scarce. However, he manages to indulge his passion for motor-cycling, probably making a great deal of noise around the locality and to sail quietly on nearby lakes.

He follows in his father's and grandfather's footsteps at the Château de Clos Vougeot, where he takes his duties as a member of the 'Grand Conseil' very seriously. This exacts his attendance at some twenty 'Chapters' a year, and his knowledge of the history of the Château and of the Confrérie lets him in for conducting visitors round the building.

The headquarters of the Domaine Engel is an imposing mid-nineteenth-century brick house on the eastern side of the Place de la Mairie in Vosne. This is where the wine is made and bottled. One-third of the production is sold to the local négoce and the remainder – some 20–30,000 bottles – goes largely to export, the USA, UK, Switzerland and Belgium being principal markets.

Consonant with his preferred style, Engel wines are darkly coloured, brooding animals in their youth, with a firm structure of tannins and acidity beneath which lurks considerable substance. The density of the wines is accentuated by a *saignée de cuve* when it is deemed necessary – in 1990, for instance, Philippe *saignéed* many of his *cuves*, once again against the advice of his oenologist. In 1989, although there was no *saignée*, Philippe's wines were true to type and, unlike many, tough, muscled and unflattering in cask. Despite their character the wines are the product of a relatively prolific harvest – even a green-pruning failed to bring Engel's yields below the PLC for the vintage.

Of the range, the Clos Vougeot is the tightest at birth, with something of the structure of Burguet's Gevrey-Chambertin Vieilles Vignes. The Vosne-Romanée, Les Brulées, is distinctly better than its Village sibling, with more breed and complexity. The Echézeaux with its deep, limpid, black-cherry hue and nose of griottes, liquorice and *fruits noirs* was somewhat too burly for its own good and the Grands-Echézeaux a distinctly masculine interpretation of that Cru.

With time and patience, however, these wines slowly emerge from their iron cage to reveal considerable finesse and a most attractive richness. What presents itself as raw meatiness in cask reveals itself as a ripe layer of old vine fruit supported by what some might regard as an overkill of tannin. These judgements must be a matter of personal taste, but the wines would benefit enormously from slightly less scaffolding so that one can more easily appreciate the building underneath.

There is no doubt, however, that Philippe Engel's wines are very fine, and with his burgeoning self-confidence, seem set fair to continue improving.

VINEYARD HOLDINGS

Commune	*Level*	*Lieu-dit/Climat*	*Area*	*Vine Age*	*Status*
Flagey	GC	Echézeaux	0.55	15 & 70	P
Flagey	GC	Grands-Echézeaux	0.50	65	P
Vougeot	GC	Clos de Vougeot	1.37	45	P
Vosne	PC	Les Brûlées	1.05	35	P
Vosne	V	—	2.54	40	P
		Total	**6.01 ha.**		

Domaine François Gerbet

VOSNE-ROMANÉE

This is one of those elegant miniature Domaines, of a scale that seems almost homespun – a small office, with a computer and a log-fire, a small bottling-labelling-and-packing room and a neat, but modest, cask cellar. This is definitely the artisan rather than the factory – the sort of enterprise for which a 200-case order spells panic. However, Domaine Gerbet is a source of well-made, consistently interesting wines, with plenty of depth and character – good and sometimes very good indeed.

Since a significant proportion of the Domaine's sales are to private customers, to ensure that they miss no one, there are well-signed premises on the RN 74, opposite Robert Arnoux's establishment, and a much more substantial building, telling you to visit the first when the other is closed, in the Place de la Mairie in the centre of Vosne.

The founder, François Gerbet, who came from his native Haute Pyrenées to marry a girl from Vosne-Romanée in 1947, has now retired. In his stead, 2 of his 3 daughters have taken over the operation and although both are married, the wines are marketed under their maiden names: Marie-Andrée and Chantale Gerbet.

They are a veritable Côte-Rotie of sisters: Marie-Andrée, La Blonde, is an extrovert with a diploma in oenology from Dijon, which enables her to take responsibility for vinification; Chantale, La Brune, is short, elfin and dark-haired. Her role seems to be the administration of the Domaine.

Of the Domaine's 15 ha., only 4 ha. are in the Côte d'Or. Of these, 2 ha. are in the Vosne-Romanée Premier Cru, Aux Réas, with a patch in Les Petits Monts, with a touch of Grands Crus Clos de Vougeot and Echézeaux.

The vines have a high average age – most were planted just after François arrived in 1947 and have been individually replaced ever since. This and a severe *ébourgonnage* have kept yields low, without the need for any green-pruning.

The wine-making is careful, with the result that the overall quality is well above average. By far the largest volume is the Hautes-Côtes de Nuits from 11 ha. of land bought and planted in 1965. The wine is mechanically harvested, but traditionally made, although there are some experiments under way with a Rototank; it is usually a wine of some depth and personality which needs to be kept for several years to be at its best, especially in riper vintages.

The Côte d'Or wines are given some 15 days *cuvaison* withm 2 *pigéages* per day; the temperature is allowed to rise to 32° C and encouraged to remain there for as long as possible. The crop is generally destalked, although up to one-third of the stalks may be left in the Vosne-Romanée *cuvée*, since this is felt to need a touch of added *mâche*.

Interestingly, in the mid 1980s the girls used to work with the controversial oenologist Guy Accad; however, as Marie-Andrée quickly explains, this was only because his laboratory produced test results more rapidly than the oenologist they inherited from their father.

Once the press-wine has been added, the various lots are tasted and a selection made to separate the wine for sale to the négociants, which is put into enamelled vats, from that for Domaine bottling, which goes into casks in the small cellar underneath the office. About half the Domaine's Vosne-Romanée is sold in bulk, so this selection is critical.

All the wine destined for Domaine bottling is kept in oak, of which approximately 75% is new each year. The Vosne-Romanée spends only 9–10 months in wood and is effectively bottled without racking. The two Grands Crus, however, are kept for a full two years, since Chantale and Marie-Andrée feel that they are naturally more structured and thus able to support a longer period in cask.

The wines are well made and stylish. The Vosne-Romanée and the Premiers Crus are quite soft expressions of their kind, with enough, but never too much, new oak to add a touch of support and firmness. In both 1989 and 1988 the Premiers Crus had noticeably more concentration and real depth of fruit than the Village wine, with the Petits Monts being the better of the two.

The Gerbet Clos Vougeot is equally on the delicate side of the spectrum, with plenty of substance and fruit overlaid with an attractive perfume; a Vosne Clos Vougeot rather than the more usual muscle-bound version.

Blonde et brune: Marie-Andrée and Chantale Gerbet

In terms of raw power there is not much to choose between the Clos Vougeot and the Echézeaux. The latter seems to have more scaffolding in its youth, to support a considerable concentration of tannin and fruit. More obviously sauvage in character than the Clos Vougeot, the Echézeaux is built to be cellared for many years before it is remotely ready to drink. The 1988 and 1989 examples of both Grands Crus are well worth laying down – the 1989s being a shade or two more forward than the 1988s.

Marie-Andrée and Chantale's wines age impeccably. A 1978 Vosne Premier Cru (a blend of two) tasted in 1991 was just beginning to take on the mantle of an older Pinot Noir – a touch of brown at the edge of the glass and a soft, attractive *sous-bois* aroma developing on the nose. Plenty of fruit, ripe, long and very stylish, with flavours of *fruits sauvages*, touches of spice and an enticing complexity made this a most attractive bottle – worth keeping for a few years yet.

This is a Domaine which deserves to be better known. Unfortunately, much of its small production tends to be mopped up by eager Swiss and French private customers. However, a good share of the grander wines manage to find their way on to the export market, so bottles should not be too difficult to come by.

VINEYARD HOLDINGS

Commune	*Level*	*Lieu-dit/Climat*	*Area*	*Vine Age*	*Status*
Vosne	PC	Aux Réas	1.99	40	P
Vosne	PC	Les Petits Monts	0.40	40	P
Vosne	V	—	1.35	40	P
Flagey	GC	Echézeaux	0.19	50–60	P
Vougeot	GC	Clos de Vougeot	0.31	20	P
—	R	(PTG/Aligoté/Bourg. Blanc)	0.90	8–40	P
		Total	**5.14 ha.**		

Domaine Jean Grivot

VOSNE-ROMANÉE

The Domaine Jean Grivot is generally regarded as one of the finest in the Côte d'Or. An old Domaine, its origins date back to the French Revolution at the end of the eighteenth century, when Grivots from the Jura first appeared in Vosne. Whilst the maternal branch came from Italy's Val d'Aosta, the paternal roots were local farmers, barrel-makers and blacksmiths. Gradually, viticulture superseded the agricultural and forging activities until, by the end of the nineteenth century, Gaston Grivot had built up a Domaine of considerable quality.

Gaston had foresight – selling several disparate parcels of vines, including those in the Hautes Côtes at Chaux, replacing them with 1.68 ha. of Clos Vougeot, a single strip from the RN 74 to abeam the Château de la Tour at the upper end of the Clos which remains one of the Domaine's most important holdings.

His planning extended to marriage – to Madeleine Grivot (no relation), who had good vines in Nuits; so the Domaine grew yet again. He also earned a diploma in oenology from Dijon University, as one of the earliest students of that now famous faculty. The sound understanding of the technical complexities of viticulture and vinification thus acquired led, in 1919/20, to bottling his own wines and selling in bottle. Together with Henri Gouges and the Marquis d'Angerville, Gaston Grivot was among the first in the Côte to Domaine bottle, both as a guarantee of authenticity and as a measure of protection against adulteration.

Jean Grivot took over on his father's death in 1955 with, as his son Etienne puts it, 'all the oenological baggage'. Since 1959 all the Domaine's wine was sold in bottle, except in lesser vintages when it proved financially more interesting to sell in bulk. Now, it is claimed, everything is sold in bottle.

Under Jean's hand the Domaine flourished and achieved a high reputation for the typicity and quality of its wines. Bottles from the Gaston and early Jean Grivot era are a remarkable tribute to the skill and quality of two great vignerons.

However, recent years have seen significant changes which demand a re-appraisal of this great estate. In 1982, Etienne – fresh from the Lycée Viticole in Beaune with a diploma in oenology and viticulture and solid work experience in France and California – joined his father.

Gradually Jean handed over responsibility for the technical aspects of the Domaine to

Etienne and Jean Grivot

Etienne, who is now in full charge of vineyards and wine-making. His father, meanwhile, looks after sales and sees most of the clients who visit the Domaine – a self-imposed task he clearly enjoys.

The change has brought controversy. To put this into proper perspective it is necessary to underline that Etienne is both intelligent and of the utmost integrity. The radical changes he has made since 1987 are not the fruit of youthful rebellion, but of deep conviction and considerable heart-searching. Whatever may be thought of the results the sincerity of the motives behind them is beyond question.

Tasting his own and others' wines over many vintages, Etienne found himself dissatisfied with what the Domaine was producing; in his opinion, the wines generally lacked colour, structure and longevity. He desperately wanted to improve on what he regarded as a disparity between actual and potential quality and believed that he had the ability to do so.

The core question was: why are recent wines so elegant yet lacking in guts, whilst those of earlier times are so rich and such long keepers? Preliminary conclusions were that the relatively feeble fertilisation in previous decades gave a much higher level of grape maturity, and further that if one did not crush the grapes deliberately, then the fermentation temperature rarely exceeded 32° C, so it lasted longer and produced a greater extraction of colour and tannins.

These thoughts led further: Etienne considered that the most important factor in the production of fine wine was the health of the grapes which could only be maximised by a soil in as near perfect equilibrium as possible. Furthermore, since the maximum quality potential is in the grapes it can be destroyed or maintained, but never surpassed. These two tenets, together with that relating the uniqueness of each soil to each wine type, triggered a re-appraisal of his viticulture in the quest for perfect soils and fruit.

Given that this happened at a time when Domaine Jean Grivot was regarded as among the finest in the Côte, to question the fundamentals of its quality was an act of great courage. Further, handing over the Domaine's magnificent vineyards to Etienne to pursue his goals was an act of equal courage and considerable faith on the part of Jean Grivot.

Since taking over in 1982, Etienne's priority has been to re-establish a true equilibrium of soil constituents. Here he was influenced and helped by an oenologist, Guy Accad, whose views he shares. They set about adjusting the excesses of nitrogen, potassium and phosphorus which were seen as a serious threat to soil balance. The nitrogen was especially worrying since it blocked the natural magnesium essential for photosynthesis and thus for the production of chlorophyll. Chlorophyll is effectively the vine's factory, so any deficiency retards production, affecting grape-sugar levels and thus maturity.

The legacy of years of over-fertilising was a severe soil disequilibrium which Etienne was not alone in seeking to rectify. The principles upon which he and Accad worked were that: i) any element is acceptable up to a certain level of concentration – above which it becomes toxic; ii) the soil mechanism should be regarded as an integrated whole – break one link in the chain and that integrity is destroyed and iii) it is all too easy to add an element to the soil, but less simple to reduce an excess.

Once the soil balance was in hand, attention was turned to the plant material being used and, in particular, to clonal selection. Clones, Etienne judged, were generally good, but risked excessive production. It is essential to have the competence to adjust fertilisers and pruning to each clone and to its soil, rather than just planting them out and trusting to nature.

In 1985 the Domaine instituted trials using the maximum available number of quality clones and planting them in 2–3-row stands on different rootstocks. These will be evaluated for several more years.

The manner and length of the *taille* and the density of planting are no less important. Etienne has concluded that for optimal fruit quality it is essential both to prune the vines *en cordon* and to increase the number per ha. from the present 10–12,000 to 15,000 – against the current trend of reducing density.

These improvements will result in higher and more consistent yields. Furthermore, the better condition of the soil and the nourishment of the vines should provide increased protection against infestation, reinforcing Etienne's policy of using as few treatments as possible, and then only in minimum dose. His guiding philosophy is that one should regard a vineyard as a complex, integrated biological mechanism and avoid tinkering with individual bits without having careful regard to the effects upon the whole. All this holistic viticulture is designed to optimise the functioning of the vegetal machine – that is the production of sugar and the ripening of skins and wood, and the production of pips – the next generation.

It might be thought that such careful husbandry would only increase yields with a consequent drop in quality – since there is generally held to be an inverse relationship between the two. Etienne addresses this question by suggesting that the only sensible way to reduce yields is to harvest late, and that one can only do this effectively if the vines are thoroughly healthy.

To those who claim that beyond a certain level of maturity there is no further beneficial development, so no point in waiting to pick, Grivot counters that one has only to watch the *verjus* – the second crop of grapes – mature perfectly well, even when the vine has shed all its leaves in late October, to demonstrate that this argument is false. Moreover, he argues, if customers are asked to pay high prices for Burgundy they have the right to expect vignerons to accept the risks in harvesting late to ensure that the wine is of top quality – which rather begs the question.

In 1990, to test his theories, he left a plot of Vosne-Romanée until 16 October when it was harvested with a potential alcohol (that is to say, the alcohol level if all the natural sugar were fermented out) of 13.7 degrees; the resulting two *cuvées* were, in his view, far above Village quality.

Grand Cru vegetables maturing in the Grivot cellar

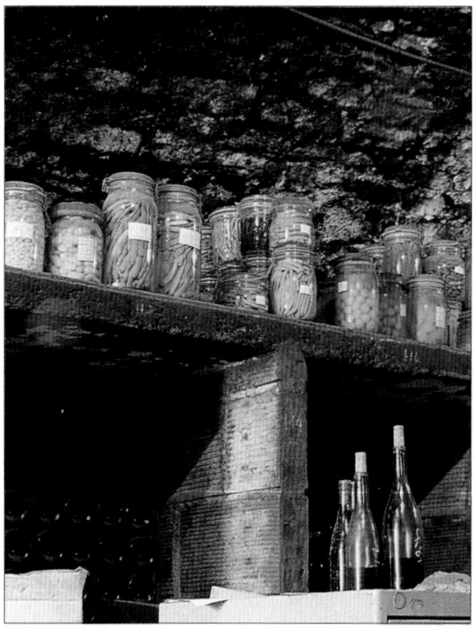

Feeling increasingly in tune with what Guy Accad was trying to achieve, in 1987, Etienne persuaded his father to extend Accad's consultancy to the Grivot vinification. This decision brought them both considerable criticism. It was said that Accad's methods had nothing to do with proper Burgundy and effectively amounted to cheating by adding colour, acidity and tannins to the wines. Others who sought Accad's services came in for similar opprobrium.

This is not the place to attempt to settle these arguments, but those seeking to make a fair assessment of what Grivot, Accad and others are trying to achieve should appreciate that Accad's methods are the consequence of a clearly thought out philosophy, rather than a haphazard vinification recipe. The cornerstone of that philosophy is that much of what passes for traditional vinification in the Côte d'Or is a crystallisation of bad habits resulting from starting off with poor quality raw material – hence the stress on careful viticulture and the best possible grapes.

However, this, by itself, will not do: there are examples aplenty of superbly made Burgundies, young and old, which have been vinified without recourse to Accad. One may, without inconsistency, agree with the viticultural principles but not accept the modifications in vinification. One does not follow from the other.

There is a certain tone of arrogance in his principles of vinification as Etienne Grivot states them, starting with the patently false assertion that, with other wines, it is impossible to distinguish in blind tasting the origins of each – in other words the similarities outweigh and mask the important differences between communes, and typicity suffers. With 'Accad' wines, however, these distinctions are apparently restored. There is no evidence whatsoever to support this view and it is an unwarranted slur on growers who strive, with considerable success, to preserve the unique individuality of their vineyards as expressed in their wines – not least Jean Grivot and Gaston Grivot before him. If this is what was being said in the early 1980s, it is hardly surprising that others retaliated.

The keys to Etienne's vinification are twofold: i) one must have the maximum potential quality in the grapes one harvests; ii) they must be vinified in such a way as to extract the maximum of that potential. In order to achieve this, it is necessary to vinify to augment those elements – chiefly solidity and tannins – which protect the wine through a long, slow evolution in cask and in bottle, and to minimise those unfavourable elements which gradually degrade a wine – namely, the oxidases – an excess of which induce browning and premature ageing.

Etienne asks himself why the 1964s, for example, are still delicious, but the 1980s have mostly fallen apart. The staying power of some of the older vintages, led him to reflect on their longevity – concluding that the natural accident of supremely healthy, ripe fruit in certain years, maximised the elements favourable for ageing at the expense of the unfavourable ones. So if one can remove the uncertainty by producing healthy fruit and by controlled, properly directed vinification, it should be possible to replicate this phenomenon regularly.

Added to these fundamental beliefs is one which might, in some quarters, be considered heretical: namely that the Pinot Noir, far from being the fragile grape it is generally considered, is robust and sturdy. If vinified properly it has both power and subtlety and considerable potential for long ageing.

The specific key to making long-lasting wine, according to Etienne, is its underlying structure. That means, in essence, its level of tannins and extract – the stuffing extracted from the skins of the grapes. Tannins – the most effective natural protection of the wine against oxidation – are extracted by long maceration, which in turn is achieved by cooling the pulp to around 5° C and dosing it with enough sulphur to kill any natural bacteria and to protect the juice from initial oxidation until the tannins take over. These tannins, along with important colour, aroma and flavour compounds, are thus slowly extracted before fermentation begins. It is important to understand that the Grivots, and Accad, consider that a much finer extraction occurs in aqueous solution – i.e. before fermentation – and that alcohol is regarded as far too powerful a solvent for the extraction of subtle aroma and flavour compounds. Hence the long pre-fermentive maceration.

After whatever length of maceration is considered desirable, usually about 4–5 days, cultured yeasts are added to the *cuves* and fermentation started. As this progresses, further tannins are leached out into solution reducing the natural exuberance of the yeasts and slowing down fermentation. This conveniently keeps the fermentation temperature within desired limits – allowing a long *cuvaison* of 15–21 days for further extraction of tannins, aroma and flavour. The tannins also act to stabilise colour extracted before fermentation. All this effort results in the cleanest possible wine being put into casks for maturation. Etienne believes that the wine's best protection against oxidation is a healthy, tannic structure.

Very little new wood is used – about 15–20 new casks, some 10% of the total, are bought each year to replace those that are no longer considered serviceable. Etienne is against new wood for his own wines, although he readily accepts that there are other perfectly good methods of making fine wine, including the use of 100% new oak. He believes that new wood accelerates ageing, producing wines which are ready to drink sooner and which evolve faster in bottle. Above all, he feels that new oak masks the individuality of a wine and tends to standardise – something which runs counter to his most basic beliefs.

However, before nearing a cask, Grivot's wines spend their first winter in tanks, under a blanket of liquid paraffin. The following February, even if *malos* have not finished, they are racked into cask. All his rackings – there are 3 (one more than usual in the Côte) – are performed with deliberate aeration. Etienne considers that his vinification augments the naturally reduced state of the wines and that they therefore need oxygen to re-establish their proper qualities.

The time each wine spends in cask is determined by the vintage – the better the wine the longer the *élévage* it needs. Grivot disagrees with those who believe that Pinot Noir should be bottled early to retain its freshness and fruit. His wines are robust, not delicate, and need no such precaution. There are no formulae – just tasting; for example the 1984s were bottled after some 16 months, whilst others remain in cask for nearly 2 years.

Etienne's somewhat informal argument is that 'if a wine is destined for 20 years in bottle, it should be capable of holding out for two years in cask.' This is hardly the point. What matters is that a wine should be bottled when it has derived maximum benefit from staying in cask and not allowed to linger to the detriment of its balance and overall structure.

What are the results of this vinification? Grivot's wines tend to be deeply coloured and to retain considerable time. Both in cask and in bottle they begin life noticeably reduced in aromas and flavours – an initially disagreeable side which takes some time to disappear. Their generally big structures tend initially to mask the taste and aroma qualities which mark their typicities – so they are as a rule more difficult to taste young than the wines of other producers.

This new vinification has only been in place since 1987, so it is too early for detailed evaluation. The chief criticisms of this style of wine are that: i) they do not represent true Burgundy (whatever that is supposed to be), and ii) they will not age. It is impossible to assess either of these questions sensibly until the wines of 1987, 1988, 1989 and 1990 have had at least a decade in bottle.

Tasting all these vintages in 1990 there is no doubt that Etienne's wines have considerable intensity. The Clos de Vougeot has distinctly more muscle and seemingly less finesse than the Vosne-Romanée, but it is too early to judge typicity.

It is now time for the critics of what Jean and Etienne Grivot, and others, have done to recognise that their motives are of the highest – they want, as much as anyone, to get the very best from their soils and from their vines and have gone to considerable lengths to achieve that end. Their vinification may comprise some unusual features, but it is absurd to brand it as cheating or artificial – large doses of sulphur are no worse, or better, than sterile filtration or excessive cask ageing. The Grivots have given much careful thought to what they are doing and this should be respected.

As to typicity and ageing, there is only one test – time – and that cannot be hurried. Tasting these rather burly but promising young wines, one has the feeling that what finally emerges might shame many into regretting their premature, hasty and often bitter judgements.

VINEYARD HOLDINGS

Commune	*Level*	*Lieu-dit/Climat*	*Area*	*Vine Age*	*Status*
Flagey	GC	Echézeaux	0.62	45	P
Vougeot	GC	Clos de Vougeot	1.86	32	P
Vosne	GC	Richebourg	0.32	50	P
Vosne	PC	Les Beaumonts	0.78	38	P
Vosne	PC	Les Brûlées	0.15	28	P
Vosne	PC	Les Chaumes	0.15	35	P
Vosne	PC	Les Suchots	0.20	45	P
Vosne	PC	Les Reignots	0.07	50	P
Vosne	PC	Les Rouges	0.34	25	P
Chambolle	V	La Combe d'Orvaux	0.62	30	P
Nuits	PC	Les Boudots	0.84	60	P
Nuits	PC	Les Pruliers	0.76	55	P
Nuits	PC	Les Roncières	0.50	45	P
Nuits	V	Les Lavières	0.62	30	P
Nuits	V	Les Charmois	0.52	25	P
—	R	(Bourg/PTG/BGO)	1.75	35	P
		Total	**10.10 ha.**		

Domaine Jean Gros

VOSNE-ROMANÉE

There are a score or so of Domaines along the length of the Côte which simply sing quality. There is no doubt about their ability to make wine at the finest level, almost irrespective of vintage. When you come across them, it is merely a matter of the first whiff or two – even the young wines, chilled as they are in their winter casks, reek of quality – and you can relax and enjoy the fruits of the master's art. No need to delve and grope beneath a miserably diluted or searingly brutal exterior in the vain prospect of something unbelievably fine which one somehow happens to have overlooked.

Mme. Jean Gros personifies the elegance of her Domaine. A dignified and charming lady, some 20 years Mayoress of Vosne, she presents a mien of unmistakable class. This extends to the family house in a quiet back-street, near enough to her Mairie, from which she administers the affairs of 8 or so fine hectares scattered between Nuits and Chambolle. This attractive pre-Revolution residence – divided between the Domaine Gros and the Domaine Mugneret-Gibourg – is full of elegant period furniture and stylishly combines grace with cosy family comfort.

The fragmentation of the original Louis Gros Domaine between each of his four children spawned at least three separate 'Gros' enterprises. Jean's vineyards are now run by Mme. Gros and the wine made by her son, Michel Gros – who has also created his own Domaine principally from purchases in the Hautes Côtes and Vosne. The vines of two other of Louis' children – Gustave, now dead, and Colette, a somewhat feeble old person, still living – were amalgamated and are vinified by Michel's brother Bernard under the Domaine 'Gros, Frère et Soeur'. The fourth of Louis' children, François, exploits his share of the vines with his daughter Anne, under the Domaine 'Anne et François Gros'.

The final complication comes from Jean's daughter, Anne-Françoise Gros, who married François Parent, from the Pommard Parents, and has her own Domaine called 'Anne-Françoise Gros'.

Jean Gros seems not to take a great interest in his Domaine – preferring to shoot game. His brother, François, also takes life leisurely, adding resting to hunting as his preferred recreations. The senior members of the Gros family appear gradually to be divesting themselves of their vineyards in favour of their children. Anne-Françoise, for example, has taken her 20 ares of Richebourg out of the Jean Gros ambit – the remaining 40 will in time be divided between her two brothers, Michel and Bernard. With such a plethora of legatees, this important Domaine is constantly in flux.

Michel Gros – an amiable, short-cropped man in his early forties – is the Domaine's wine-maker and technician. Immensely able and conscientious, he clearly enjoys his job and relishes the opportunity to think carefully about his responsibilities. Though a traditionalist by conviction, he is happy to experiment with anything in the vineyard or in the cellar which might lead to an improvement.

However, it is among his vines that Michel is found at his most interesting and articulate. He has evidently thought deeply about the ways of the vine and takes pride in the nurture of those entrusted to his care.

The aim of the viticultural year is to produce both optimum quality and a yield which makes commercial sense, without forcing the vines. Michel has observed that up to a certain level, increased yield is not detrimental to quality. However, the point on an imaginary curve at which quality starts to decline varies from year to year. Thus in 1990 one could harvest 50 hl./ha. from one plot of vines and make top quality wine, whereas the following year, in the same vines quality may start to fall off at two-thirds of that figure. The conclusion is that one must adjust one's expectations year by year and not aspire to some preconceived fixed annual yield.

To achieve the optimum, Michel believes that it is necessary to replace individual vines, wherever possible. Once a Gros vine fails to produce half the permitted maximum yield, its days are numbered. He admits, however, that he is sometimes forced to replant whole parcels when successive interbreeding results in virus infection and degeneration. Fortunately, however, most of his vines are young – replanted in the 1960s and 1970s, presumably because of the progressive degeneration of post-war plants and root-stocks – so this is not a frequent occurrence.

Vignerons such as Michel Gros generally combine their technical expertise with a feel for their vines. This empathy enables them to treat each plot as an individual, adapting pruning, treatments, planting and harvesting to its idiosyncrasies, rather than coaxing them all into one common viticultural mould.

Experiments with bilateral *cordon* training and wide spacing in his vineyards in the Hautes Côtes and in the Bourgogne Rouge parcels in Vosne have given Michel further insight into the way vines behave and provided valuable economies in labour and materials.

In his quest for the mastery of yields, Michel considers that it is preferable to remove any potential excess of buds or of shoots as early as possible in the growing season. Realising that an advance knowledge of the likely fecundity of the vines would be a distinct advantage in this endeavour, he has developed a technique for early estimation of a vine's likely output. This relies on the fact that a vine will form the bud material for one year during the previous June. By taking a cutting from the wood and soaking it in hot water, he can count the number of embryo buds and extrapolate from that. So far this information has enabled him to avoid removing fully developed bunches in August – a practice he abhors. One must realise, he will tell you, that the vine is an irregular producer. One year you may get 15 bunches, the next year only 5.

Michel's intimate knowledge of his vines also helps him plan his harvest. In general, the Domaine has two separate pickings: the first, at the normal time, takes place in the vineyards on the Côte; the second, a late harvest in the Hautes Côtes, starts once the crush from the Côtes has finished fermenting and there is space in the *cuves*. The order of harvesting in each area tends to be the same from year to year – some plots of vines just happen to ripen earlier or later, and Michel knows which they are.

As for vinification, nothing is systematic. Grapes arriving at the *cuverie* will probably have 66–75% of their stalks removed, or the lot, in years where there is much *millerandage* (undeveloped bunches, high in sugar and extract, low in water). Michel keeps some stalks if he can because they both help aerate the pulp and thereby ensure a gentle, regular start to the fermentation, and also for their tannin contribution, which strengthens a wine's resistance to ageing.

The Domaine's *cuves* are variously cement, wood and glass-fibre. According to Michel Gros, however, the insulation of a *cuve* is of greater significance than its precise composition. He personally prefers cement to wood because the latter is so time-consuming to maintain – it takes one man, working full-time, a week to prepare and clean the Domaine's four wooden *cuves* for use, and even then, there is a risk of damage if they are hydrated or dried too quickly.

Since the process of fermentation adds an

almost invariant 15 centigrade degrees to the temperature of the pulp, Michel starts his vats off at about 16–18° C aiming to arrive at a maximum of 35° C. Too many vignerons, he complains, don't worry about the temperature of their vats until it is too late; so he prefers to be cautious. The action of the screw-pump taking the grapes to the vats crushes about half of them – but only lightly, just to liberate the juice and give access to the yeasts. This, together with the ensuing foot-*pigéage*, helps to ensure as long and slow a fermentation as possible.

With all this tradition, it is curious to find that Michel is against the use of natural yeasts for fermentation. Instead, he uses a starter culture of selected, rehydrated dried yeasts to inoculate each *cuve*. This is no whim: cultured yeasts, he claims, are a cleaner strain and thus give better results, in particular producing alcohol levels nearer to theoretical expectations than natural yeasts. Moreover, by eliminating the bad elements of the natural population, one avoids the bad by-products. Thirdly, by choosing when to inoculate, he can ferment when it suits him – and the rest of the harvesting programme.

So, following just 24 hours of maceration, the *cuves* are inoculated and fermentation starts within 12 hours. Then 4–5 days later, the *cuves* are covered with plastic lids, to minimise oxidation and the loss of alcohol and aromas, and left for a further 3–4 days of maceration – on average a total *cuvaison* of 10–12 days.

A light pressing of the pulp gives a rich press-wine which is added to the free-run wine and allowed to settle for 24 hours before being transferred to cask.

The Grands Crus, plus the Vosne-Romanée Premier Cru Clos des Réas, are lodged in 100% new wood, the Village Vosne, Nuits and Chambolle having about one third depending on the style of the vintage. The wines are only racked once – just after their *malos*. Thereafter they remain in cask until the following spring when the different lots of each wine are unified by pumping, with moderate aeration, into tanks. Here they are fined with albumen, left for 1–2 months, finely filtered through a mixture of kieselguhr, earth and cellulose, and bottled. Before 1987 the wines were plate-filtered, but this was dropped in favour of the kieselguhr, which was found to give a finer wine.

Michel's methods are deliberately conservative – he seeks to stray as little as possible from traditional wine-making chiefly because he realises that the Domaine's customers are used to its style and he sees no reason to change something that is obviously successful.

The point de départ for his entire philosophy is the observation that Vosne-Romanées are by nature 'tendres et parfumés'. Since the taste of a wine is also the consequence of the method of making it, he is able to use his influence to give some extra muscle to the wine's natural qualities, thereby adding structure and longevity. The instruments he chooses to exert this influence are a combination of longish *cuvaison*, fermentation at a high temperature, plenty of new wood, low yields, and the use of new clones which also add tannin, force and structure to the wines.

Madame Gros in her office

There is no doubt that the results justify the theories. Tasting a range of Gros wines is invariably a delightful and rewarding experience. In the curious way that these things happen, the wines seem to know their masters and to mirror their qualities – the muscle of Michel combines perfectly with the elegance and charm of Mme. Gros – sinew and style working harmoniously together.

The Gros wines do not have the exuberant silkiness of Jean-Nicolas Méo's, nor do they flex muscles to the same extent as those of Michel's cousin Bernard Gros. Somewhere in between there is a firm, rich charm which never fails to seduce.

A range of Vosne-Romanée Village vintages, tasted in the Gros cellars in late 1990, demonstrated Michel's wine-making skills. A really gorgeous 1987 – beginning to show most attractive aromas of *sous-bois* and spice, quite complex and ripe with finesse, balance and plenty of fruit – was followed by a different but no less good 1986 – more of the vegetal Pinot qualities, still ripe and complex with marked 'puissance' and equally fine length.

The 1984 was something of a revelation – rather more vibrant and lighter in colour than the others, with, as one might expect, a more open, evolved nose; yet good fruit, no hint of unbalancing dilution, and plenty of charm to make up for its light structure; marred only by a touch of dry tannins on the finish – 'it hasn't said its last word yet,' remarked Mme. Gros with a delightful smile.

Of the 1989s, the Clos des Réas and the Richebourg stand out. The former, a Monopole from 20-year-old vines, started life with a deep, limpid colour of crushed strawberry hue, an almost musky, ripe, smoky nose, with flavours of cherry and liquorice, a touch of toastiness and a long, soft finish. A meaty wine, without being coarse in any way, which will be excellent from the mid 1990s.

The Richebourg, from 40-year-old vines, is yet more complex and concentrated. Very much in the same style as the Clos des Réas, its over-riding characteristics are those of great breed and distinction. The slightly charred, toasted undertone is there, supporting a rich layer of ripe, classy fruit. In short, the epitome of restraint and finesse.

Age brings out the elegance in these superb wines. They need time, above all, and cannot be hurried. Unfortunately, too many are drunk long before they can begin to show the true craftsmanship which has gone into their making. As with all Domaines, there are occasional lapses – a 1983 Richebourg tasted at the Domaine had an irremediable touch of rot, not enough to render it undrinkable but enough to jar a sensitive palate. However, Michel would be the first to admit to imperfection. What matters is that this fine Domaine is in careful and conscientious hands and is constantly striving to improve on its already undoubted excellence.

VINEYARD HOLDINGS

Commune	*Level*	*Lieu-dit/Climat*	*Area*	*Vine Age*	*Status*
Vosne	GC	Richebourg	0.40	40	P
Vosne	PC	Clos des Réas	2.12	20	P
Vosne	V	Les Réas	2.30	15	P
Vougeot	GC	Clos de Vougeot	0.20	3	P
Nuits	PC	La Perrière Noblot	0.17	15	P
Nuits	V	Les Athées	0.20	20	P
Chambolle	V	(5 difft. climats)	0.35	10	P
Vosne	R	(Bourg. Glapigny)	3.00	20	P
		Total	**8.74 ha.**		

Domaine Henri Jayer

VOSNE-ROMANÉE

The fragmentation of viticultural Burgundy has limited the means of growers and thus the scope for the emergence of gurus. In Bordeaux, where estates are large and cash-rich, Peynaud and his like have flourished. This is no accident, reflecting perhaps the greater international outlook of the Bordelais, driven by the need for volume sales. In Burgundy where holdings are small, perceptions seems to be introspective, conditioned more by family tradition, and village café chatter.

However, if any one person can be said to have influenced the skill and morale of younger growers in the Côte over the last two decades, it must surely be Henri Jayer. This modest, kindly man, just reaching retirement, has counselled and befriended several of those now running their own Domaines and producing some of the best that Burgundy can offer.

Meeting him, in his unostentatious modern house on the way out of Vosne towards the main road, one is aware of a man of great, quiet wisdom and almost self-effacing modesty. It has been frequently noted that he does not suffer fools; maybe, but his over-riding concern is with the reputation of the region he has worked in for the past 60 years and with the new generation now taking over for the next half-century.

Henri Jayer's own reputation is founded securely on an almost unbroken succession of superlative wines from his small Domaine – some 6.30 ha. concentrated in and around Vosne-Romanée and comprising everything from Passe-Tout-Grains to Echézeaux. Although he continues to work in his own cellar, and is still much in demand from vignerons of all ages wondering where they have gone wrong, he has handed over the day-to-day running of his Domaine to his rather gruff and somewhat overbearing nephew, Emmanuel Rouget, whom he rescued when there was no work for him at his chosen trade of tractor mechanic.

Henri has recently, and not without some regret one imagines, handed back to his protégé, Jean-Nicolas Méo, the vineyards which he has share-cropped since the early 1940s. In his turn, Emmanuel Rouget now share-crops some of Jayer's vines – so there will be less appearing under the Jayer label as the years go by.

Jayer is a man who clearly thinks deeply about what he does and about what really determines the quality of a wine. For him the *terroir* is paramount – a Gevrey-Chambertin can never be as fine as a Vosne-Romanée because it lacks the individual elements in the soil and in the atmosphere which give Vosne its characteristic finesse. He is also firmly convinced that each vigneron has his personal optic – his view of what, for example, a fine Chambolle-Musigny or a fine Corton should be.

This perspective cannot but influence how a vigneron sets about making wine, explaining perhaps in part the result of a recent trial in which Philippe Engel in Vosne exchanged a tonne of Vosne grapes with Alain Burguet in Gevrey and Philippe Charlopin in Marsannay for a tonne of their grapes. Tasting the wines later, it was agreed that Vosne-vinified 'Gevrey' appeared to be more typically Vosne and *mutatis mutandis* for the other appellations. Of course yeasts and bacteria may have played their role, but Jayer's 'optique' is a powerful force which should not be discounted.

His own vinification comports nothing particularly unusual. Wine, he reminds you, is for pleasure, so 'one seeks as perfect an equilibrium as possible'. His personal philosophy begins with the observation that 'wine must not be brought up in cotton-wool' – 'let nature go'. He hopes that the analytical secrets of fermentation, now so minutely studied, will continue to elude researchers and is adamant, moreover, that one cannot successfully replace artificially elements in a wine which are absent at the start. Tinkering with *musts* and wine to adjust the results of inadequate fruit is not the way to achieve quality.

Like so many great vignerons, Henri Jayer believes in expending whatever skill and effort is necessary to produce top-class grapes to vinify. Most of his vines are more than 50 years old – an age by which many less quality-minded colleagues would have grubbed up and replanted in order to achieve higher yields. He harvests neither late nor early, hoping to achieve maximum quality, which he defines as '90% of potential maximum'. If you wait longer you may indeed gain in some respects, but you will, in all probability, lose in others.

If fruit quality can be quantified, it means, generally, a ratio of two-thirds liquid to one-third solids. A corollary of this is that stalks must be eliminated. Apart from destroying this equilibrium, Jayer is convinced that they bring nothing except astringency to a wine. He tells the story of a young Côte d'Or

Henri Jayer setting out on his tractor

vigneron, lauded by all his friends, who consulted him and was dismayed to be told that he must destalk if he really wanted to improve his wines. The following year he removed 15% of the stalks and, glowing with more friendly approbation and pride, invited Jayer to taste. To his chagrin, the advice was the same – good but not great, remove more stalks. This charade continued for three years, pruning away at more stalks each year, until the grower was finally persuaded to destalk completely. He is now making very fine wine and has his own band of admiring disciples.

Jayer is convinced of the value of a period of pre-fermentive maceration: 'the wines with the most bouquet and the finest robe have 5–7 days of maceration – this releases extraordinary aromas and colours.' In this, he agrees with Guy Accad; however, whilst Accad delays fermentation by chemical means – a heavy dose of SO_2 – Jayer achieves the same result by cooling his pulp to 15° C – a mechanical operation. As the pulp warms, so the natural yeasts start to work, helped by one or two *remontages* each day. Once fermentation is well under way and any necessary *chaptalisation* has been carried out, *pigéage* takes over from *remontage*.

Great weight is placed on using only indigenous yeasts: 'everything is in the yeast' says Jayer, remembering a half-bottle of Pinot Noir he bought in the USA which tasted just like Cabernet Sauvignon. 'They had yeasted it with 80% Cabernet yeasts and 10% Pinot yeasts,' he recalled with a mournful groan which evinced the unvoiced: 'what do they expect?'

His dislike of tinkering extends to the widespread practice of *saignée de cuve*, which he regards as a palliative for those whose juice is too dilute because their *évasivage* was inadequate. 'No one is prepared to take risks these days – they all want insurance'.

Jayer makes his wines in cement *cuves*, arguing that these give less risk of atypical or off flavours and also that they hold the heat less than traditional wooden vats, so reducing the maximum temperature. He allows this to rise to 34° C – but thereafter is 'très vigilant'. *Cuvaison* lasts 15–20 days – until the cap of skins and pips starts to descend in the vat, indicating that there is no more carbon-dioxide to keep it afloat, and thus no more fermenting sugar.

After the press-wine – extracted by a 1958 Vaslin – has been added, the new wine is put into 100% new oak (except for the regional wines) for about 18 months. This policy is invariant since Jayer believes that a wine with proper balance can support this regime, even in less naturally ripe vintages: 'it is a question of concentration,' he affirms.

The *malolactic fermentation* is allowed to proceed at its own pace. Jayer is not in favour of heating his cellars to provoke the lactic bacteria into action: 'it's no use being in a hurry.' If wines with a low pH (i.e. high acidity) take longer to ferment than those with a high pH, so be it, don't interfere. Each *cuvée* is an individual and should be allowed to work in its own way.

The wines are racked twice – once after the *malo* and again just before fining. Only fresh egg-whites are used because they appear to produce better results than dried egg albumen. The wines are bottled directly from cask, without racking off the fining, at the prodigious rate of 5 casks per day.

The results of Henri Jayer's skill and care need little description here; their quality has been well-enough extolled. Anyone wanting to see how a great wine-maker works should try perhaps his Bourgogne Rouge, progressing through the range of Vosne-Romanées from the rich, stylish Village *cuvée*, to the deeper, silkier and more complex Premier Cru Les Beaumonts, from an 'argilo-calcaire' vineyard, with a notably poor soil of rock and stones, to the magnificent Cros Parantoux, from a higher, cooler site with a significant proportion of fine sand-like particles in the shallow soil where they sometimes have to use explosives to blast holes in the bedrock to plant new vines. The vines here are a good 40 years old, giving an extraordinary depth of fruit and an almost black concentration to the young wine. This is quintessential Vosne-Romanée – raw power but with marvellous distinction and class.

The sole Grand Cru in Jayer's quiver is a 2 ha. chunk of Echézeaux. This is in 2 separate plots – Les Treux, with a deepish brown soil of limestone and clay, and Les Cruots with yet more depth and clay. The issue is a brooding wine of marked depth and structure, but without the youthful finesse and nascent complexity of the Cros Parantoux. It tends to need many years in bottle to emerge from its shell. Whether, finally, it is a greater wine than the Premier Cru, is debatable. They are just different.

If Jayer, by word and by deed, endows the wine-making process with such thoughtful simplicity, where do so many go wrong? The 'wound' of Burgundy, in his view, is that some 80% of its wines are good, if tasted before their *malos*, considerably fewer after the *malos*, subsequent incompetence leaving about 20% which are worth considering in bottle – a gradual bleeding to neutrality, or worse.

Specifically, Jayer believes that too much SO_2 and too many manipulations contribute significantly to poor quality. Conversely, vignerons frequently fail to top up their casks regularly, and to taste the wine each time they do so. Cellar hygiene – especially with older casks which need much time and care to maintain in a proper state – is often skimped. Infection from dirty bungs and their hemp surrounds are a frequent source of spoilage.

All these details matter. However, even when you have got this right, it is so easy to eviscerate a fine wine by over-fining or too severe filtration. Henri Jayer sees no need to filter his own wines but gives them just the purest of finings. Harsh manipulations may provide bright, sterile wines, and thus peace of mind, but there is no doubt that this is achieved at the expense of balance and complexity.

Jayer is convinced that only the customer is capable of dramatically influencing standards in Burgundy. 'It is up to the client not to buy bad wine; he has more power than he realises.' He tells his own customers to be sceptical of cellars – the cellar ambience, animated by a lyrical vigneron skilfully vaunting his wares, is not the atmosphere in which to make a dispassionate buying decision.

Of his own achievements he is dismissively modest: 'Perhaps I have helped some younger vignerons not to make mistakes,' is as far as he will go. As for the future, he is optimistic: 'The young have both the finance and the technical means to make fine wine – borrowing was unthinkable 50 years ago. They don't work in the same way as the older vignerons – by "pif", by instinct. They have much more curiosity; they get out more, and taste more, so can see if they are incompetent. Vignerons were individuals before, they are more communicative now; the better ones are models for the rest – there are no secrets now.'

If anyone is in a position to make such judgements it is Henri Jayer. Burgundy and its young generation owe much to his wisdom and to his generosity of spirit. When he finally retires, he will be hard to replace.

VINEYARD HOLDINGS

Commune	*Level*	*Lieu-dit/Climat*	*Area*	*Vine Age*	*Status*
Flagey	GC	Echézeaux	2.00	60	P
Vosne	PC	Cros Parantoux	1.00	50	P
Vosne	PC	Les Beaumonts	0.30	50	P
Vosne	V	—	1.00	50	P
Nuits	V	—	0.40	50	P
—	R	(Bourg./PTG/Aligoté)	1.46	Various	P
		Total	**6.16 ha.**		

Domaine Lamarche

VOSNE-ROMANÉE

Sandwiched myopically between the Domaines Mugneret-Gibourg and François Gros, in a long unassuming back-street known as the rue des Communes, at the back of the equally unassuming little village of Vosne-Romanée, is the Domaine Lamarche. François Lamarche, a short, quiet and thoughtful man, runs the estate with his pleasant but forceful wife, Marie-France, from Metz, whom he married in 1975. At that time he was already working with his father, Henri, who sadly died on 4 October 1985 – a date François remembers vividly.

The Domaine, which belongs jointly to François and his sister Geneviève, is the result of careful acquisition by 3 generations of Lamarches, preceded by 2 generations of viticulteurs on the female side of the family. The vineyards are almost a model compound of an impressive 4.17 ha. of Grands Crus, a 1.36 ha. trio of Vosne-Romanée Premiers Crus – Suchots, Malconsorts and Chaumes – and 1 ha. of Vosne Village. There are a further 1.58 ha. of Bourgogne and Passe-Tout-Grain.

The jewel in the Lamarche crown is undoubtedly the 1.42 ha. strip of land running east-west down the fall-line of the Côte between La Tâche and Romanée-Conti, La Grande Rue. This was originally a wedding present to Henri Lamarche in the 1920s. Lying between such prestigious Grands Crus, one might be forgiven for wondering why, until 1991, it was only classified Premier Cru. The explanation is that when the official classification was drawn up in the 1930s, Henri believed that there was nothing to be gained – except perhaps increased taxes – from Grand Cru status; vignerons were not prosperous then, and the price differential between Grand Cru and Premier Cru wine was insufficient justification for a more exalted designation. So La Grande Rue became a Premier Cru.

However, things have changed since those difficult days. An application for re-classification was finally approved in 1991. François is thus one of the few single proprietors of an Côte d'Or Grand Cru. His Grande Rue is the second smallest of these fabled patches of land, the smallest being La Romanée (0.84.52 ha.), just above Romanée-Conti.

François is an excellent wine-maker in no doubt as to what he is trying to achieve. He believes that a fine wine, particularly from Vosne-Romanée, should maximise finesse rather than matière; that tannins and stuffing should take second place to charm and elegance. Alcohol is rarely an abundant ingredient – in 1989 and 1990 only two *cuves* passed 13 degrees – La Grande Rue in 1989 and Grands-Echézeaux in 1990.

Vinification is a matter of adjusting to what comes in from the carefully picked vineyards. If the grapes lack acidity, an appropriate amount of separately harvested *verjus* is added to correct the deficiency. If, on the other hand, *chaptalisation* is required, it is done little by little to avoid raising the temperature of fermentation too high and to 'better adapt the sugar to the *cuve*'. François adds a modest dose of sulphur to the crush and lets the fermentation rise to 33° C, before settling down to an ideal 27–28° C.

Cuvaison and fermentation take place in open wooden *cuves* and last some 12–15 days. Four *pigéages* daily at first and 3 later on ensure that the cap remains moist and maximise extraction. There are 3 pressings – the first 2 being added in total to the free-run wine after it has been decanted off at a density of 1,000-1,005. Wine from the third pressing goes into the Passe-Tout-Grain casks, an interesting way of adding muscle and depth and perhaps a little finesse.

A maximum of 40% of new Allier and Tronçais oak is used, the rest being wood which has only seen one or two wines. The *malo* is not provoked by heat but allowed to happen naturally; once it is fully finished, each cask is racked and the wine left for a further year in wood. A second racking, with air to eliminate any dissolved CO_2, precedes an egg-white fining. François does not hold with filtration, which removes much essential stuffing, and therefore limits it to vintages which fail to fall bright naturally. The Domaine bottles its wines after about 15 days *sur col*.

There is, then, nothing exceptional about François Lamarche's vinification. He clearly believes that with healthy, ripe grapes from fine land planted with old vines, giving low yields, the minimum interference is necessary for good results. Fruit quality is favoured by an *évasivage* to reduce the extent of the foliage and thus to improve the microclimate of each vine. This occurs in two stages – firstly just after the shoots have appeared and later, when the canes are being gathered by raising two wires above the *baguette*. A green-pruning to reduce production further is undertaken before *veraison*.

All this tends to yields which rarely rise above the *rendement de base* for each appellation. 8.35 ha. produces an average of 350 hl. (4,500 cases) or 44 hl./ha.; bearing in mind that this figure includes the larger production of 'ordinaires' which distort the picture, these yields are by no means excessive.

Wandering around in the maze of cellars beneath the house – one end of which abuts onto those of Jean Gros, the other onto those of François Gros, François detaches a pipette from a 4-pronged meat hook in the ceiling and taps away at casks drawing off samples. Old bottles are stacked in corners, wherever there is some room, and one is sometimes momentarily taken in by what appears to be a solid wall turning out to be a floor-to-ceiling stack of mould-covered bottles, waiting presumably for an order or perhaps being kept to mature for sale later.

Lamarche is not a man much given to casual chat, but will admit to making wines in the elegant style which he prefers rather than being swayed by any reflections of his world-wide clientèle.

He more than achieves his goals: his wines show, above all, finesse, having in the Village and Premier Cru Vosne-Romanées mid–deep colours, always bright and invariably limpid, with that alluring robe of brushed velvet so typical of fine Pinot Noir.

The Vosne-Romanée Village wine develops an attractive, smoky, crushed strawberry nose and followed this up with a fine, elegant swathe of flavours, backed by firm tannin and enough balancing acidity to keep it alive for years.

Of the 3 Vosne Premiers Crus, Les Suchots is the most typically 'Vosne' – coming from a vineyard situated at the

Henri with his wife Marie-France

northern end of the village with Grand Cru Romanée St.-Vivant to the south side and Grand Cru Echézeaux to the north. The soil contains more silica, giving great finesse; the wine generally has a mid black-cherry hue and a nose of griotte cherries, red fruits and violet. In the mouth it is ripe and stylish, with plenty of concentration – from the 43+-year-old vines – and a finely-tuned balance. This is quintessential Vosne-Romanée.

Les Chaumes, situated south of La Tâche, has more clay in the soil which gives a firmer, full structure. It generally takes longer to show its underlying qualities, being less forthcoming at first than either Les Suchots or Malconsorts. By contrast, Malconsorts – right in the 'kidney' of the hill, along the band of Grands Crus – has a much richer soil than Les Suchots, giving its wine a more 'rustic' edge, with distinct tones of neighbouring Nuits-St.-Georges. The wine seems to have more red in its colour and a discernible touch of chocolate on the nose, mixed with an attractive aroma of *fruits noirs*. In the mouth it is fuller and more structured than either Suchots or Chaumes when young, opening out with age to reveal a fine spectrum of old Pinot Noir smells, typically *sous-bois* and vegetal in character.

The Grands Crus are, not unexpectedly, slower to develop; in cask they show their breed and style, in depth of flavour, length and overall structure. The Clos Vougeot – divided into two parcels: two-thirds at the top of the Clos, near the Château, the remaining one-third lower down, near to the RN 74 – is by far the meatiest of the quartet. François Lamarche believes that one has to wait at least 15 years for a good vintage to become truly drinkable; given the muscle and weight of the 1989, this would seem to be no exaggeration.

The other three Grands Crus – Echézeaux, Grands-Echézeaux and La Grande Rue – are finer yet. The Echézeaux is characterised by a marked acidity in good years, which gradually melts into the wine as it ages. Underneath, roundness, finesse and puissance wait to emerge into a most attractive and finely structured whole. The Grands-Echézeaux is still more closed until it chooses to reveal itself and should not be considered before 5–7 years old in a good vintage. The La Grand Rue is probably the finest of the Lamarche wines. Broadly similar in soil composition to the Grands Crus which surround it, when young it shows a promising nose of 'petits *fruits rouges*' (redcurrants and raspberries) and also hints of blackcurrants. These positive, complex aromas overlay a wine of complexity and substance, with length and finesse; it is generally complete, without being in any way heavy. La Grande Rue has more in common perhaps with La Tâche and Richebourg than with Romanée-Conti.

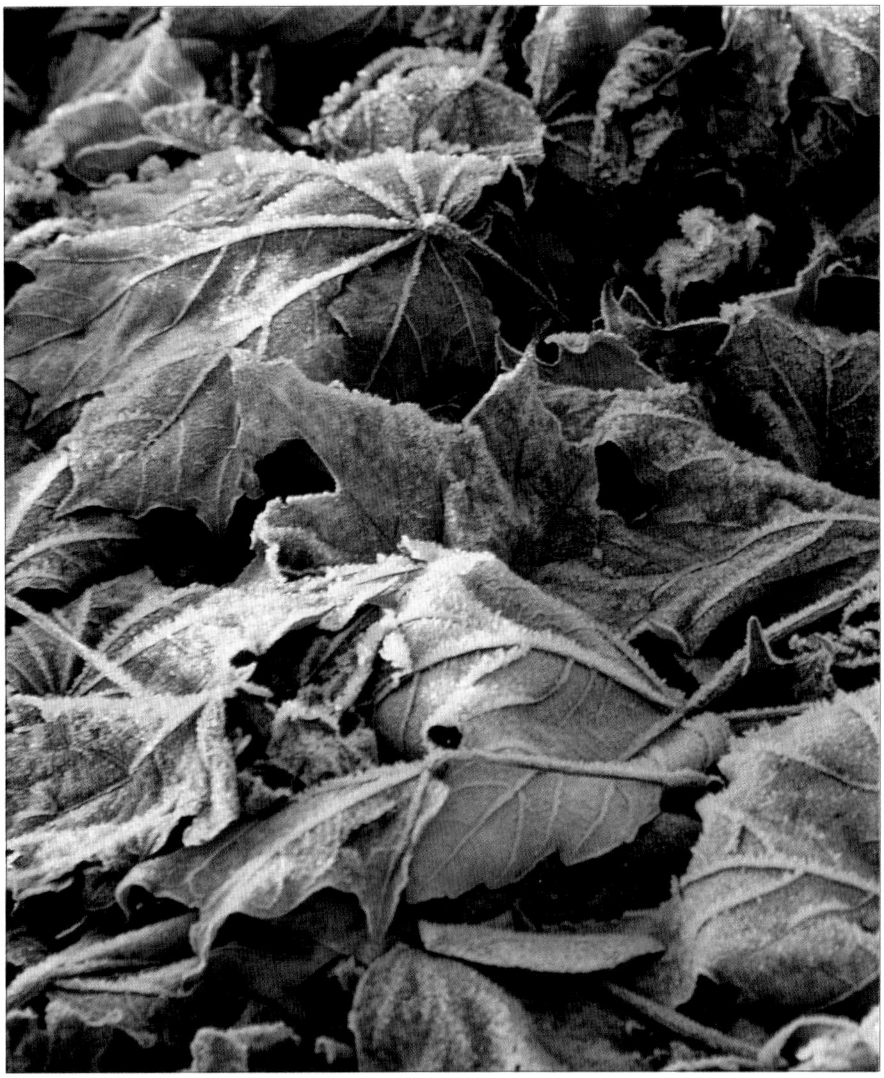

Harsh frosts in winter hurt nothing but the vine leaves

Lamarche Grands Crus need several years before they begin to give of their best. Even in less ripe vintages, there should be no hurry to open these bottles. François is sometimes berated for his prices, which tend to be painfully above what is being asked elsewhere in the village. This probably reflects the hard-nosed economics of Marie-France who obviously keeps properly tight control of the family finances.

Whether the wines are worth their price must be a matter for individual judgement. However they are by and large fine. François' determination to achieve low yields, and his willingness to *saigner* in dilute years means that vintages matter less here than one might imagine. Whilst fine years, when everything goes smoothly and the grapes are perfectly ripe and concentrated, are justifiably sought after, those who neglect second-rank vintages such as 1987 and 1982 miss much that is worthwhile and thoroughly enjoyable.

VINEYARD HOLDINGS

Commune	*Level*	*Lieu-dit/Climat*	*Area*	*Vine Age*	*Status*
Flagey	GC	Grands-Echézeaux	0.30	1961	P
Flagey	GC	Echézeaux	1.10	1961	P
Vougeot	GC	Clos de Vougeot	1.35	1960/71/76	P
Vosne	GC	La Grande Rue	1.42	1955–1988	P
Vosne	PC	Les Chaumes	0.50	1960	P
Vosne	PC	Les Malconsorts	0.50	1934	P
Vosne	PC	Les Suchots	0.36	1947	P
Vosne	V	—	1.00	25	P
		Total	**6.53 ha**		

Domaine Méo-Camuzet

VOSNE-ROMANÉE

The appreciation of Burgundy is often as much one of style as of quality. Even at the highest level, styles vary considerably as growers tend to make wine to match their own specifications and perceptions rather than trying to adapt to the whims of their customers.

However, some Domaines seem to hit a universal style and yet make wine of uncompromising excellence. One such is the Domaine Méo-Camuzet in Vosne. The first whiff of their Bourgogne Rouge is enough to convince you that you are dealing with a level of quality attained by few others in the Côte.

The Domaine underwent a significant upheaval in the late 1980s. Henri Jayer, who had made the Domaine's wines since 1945, retired after the 1988 vintage. At the same time, though not in compensation, the vineyards he farmed *en métayage* from the Méo family reverted back to them.

The reason for Henri Jayer's regency was that Jean Méo, a career petroleum engineer who inherited the Domaine from his uncle, Etienne Camuzet, in 1959, had neither inclination nor time to run his inheritance, preferring to pursue his career, at one time being a member of General de Gaulle's cabinet, and more recently President of l'Institut de Pétrole, in Paris.

Although Henri remains as an advisor, the Domaine is now in the hands of a younger generation.

Christian Faurois, the son of one of M. Camuzet's vignerons, joined the Domaine in 1973 from the Lycée Viticole in Beaune, first working in the vineyards and then in the cellars. Jean Méo's son, Jean-Nicolas, arrived a few years later with a diploma from Dijon University and a year working at Domaine Chandon and elsewhere in the USA under his belt. Christian and Jean-Nicolas are now jointly responsible for running the Domaine – Christian being concerned more with technical matters and Jean-Nicolas with sales.

A visitor to the Méo establishment, a modest, attractive house towards the top of Vosne-Romanée, is more than likely to encounter the oldest member of the Méo household – Mme. Méo. This delightful relict is Jean-Nicolas' grandmother; at the age of 85 she still takes a lively, if somewhat forgetful, interest in what goes on, and on bright days is to be found in her slippers and dressing-gown standing on the threshold gazing out into the street beyond, carefully scrutinising anyone who happens to be passing. If you find her inside, she will probably be shuffling around in an exaggerated pair of fluffy slippers, busying herself at heaven knows what, and chatting away to herself in a perfectly pleasant and contented fashion. A most personable and affecting living reminder of a bygone generation.

Etienne Camuzet left his nephew a magnificent legacy: nearly 7 ha. of excellent land in the communes of Nuits, Vosne, Vougeot and Corton, with 2.3 ha. of Grands Crus. Many of the vines are now over 60 years old, adding an extra dimension of concentration and depth to the wines. Much of the land was rented *en métayage* to Henri Jayer, Jean Tardy, Jean Faurois and Jacques Faurois; however, as these tenants retire and their agreements expire the vineyards are reverting to the Domaine.

Christian and Jean-Nicolas are striving to be as organic as is compatible with keeping the vines healthy. Only organic fertiliser is used, in minimum dose, with an adjusting touch of magnesium. Efforts are also made to encourage natural predators of spiders and grape-worms, but Christian admits that this is difficult in parcelled vineyards when your neighbour insists on using insecticides. Where possible vine diseases are treated preventively with copper-based products to harden the grape skins and thus provide a measure of resistance to the rot-inducing grape-worm.

Individual plant replacement is considered better than grubbing up entire parcels of vines – the Domaine loses about 1% of its vines each year. It is hoped to reintroduce a *sélection massale* for plant material – a policy which had been discontinued. Vines are replanted onto 161/49 rootstock, generally regarded as best adapted to the soils and vines in this sector of the Côte.

An integral part of the viticulture policy is to remove excess production before it has had the chance to sap strength from the vine. A great deal of effort is put in, just before the flowering, to select the material to be excised, especially among the young vines in the Vosne-Romanée and Richebourg vineyards.

When the grapes are finally harvested, strict control is exercised both in the vineyard and with a sorting table at the cuverie, to

Jean-Nicolas Méo and Christian Faurois – the new generation running the Domaine

ensure that only the ripest and healthiest fruit goes into the fermenting vats. Because summer pruning is deliberately at as high a level as possible, to encourage greater development of vegetation and thus of sugar, a particularly sharp eye is kept to ensure that the bare minimum of *verjus* is cut. (Most *verjus* appears at the top of the vine and would normally be removed during the 2 or 3 routine summer prunings.)

At the cuverie all the stalks are removed and the grapes sulphured with a minimum dose, to kill any promenading bacteria. They are then cooled, without crushing, to 17–18° C and put into wood or cement *cuves* where they are left for 5–6 days. During this time an intracellular extraction removes colour and aroma compounds from the grape-skins.

Only the indigenous yeasts are used for the fermentation – 'there are enough on the grapes,' says Christian, 'to avoid the need for cultured yeasts.' If necessary the *cuves* are bled in years where the juice is too dilute, and the *saignée* used to make sparkling wine for the family. Fermentation is allowed to rise to 32–33° C with *cuvaison* lasting 15–18 days. The cap is broken up twice a day by hand.

They aim to *chaptalise* as little as possible. Fortunately Jean-Nicolas's first two vintages, 1989 and 1990, have been exceptionally ripe so the question has not yet arisen. Presumably when it does, they will decide to add sugar in small doses, preferably at the end of fermentation to prolong it and to avoid any temperature-shock to the *must*.

The pulp is then lightly pressed and the press-wine assembled with the free-run wine. After only 3–5 hours settling, the new wine is run into casks where it spends some 18 months – more or less, depending on the vintage. The Méo policy is for 100% new oak for all its wines, except for the Bourgogne Rouge which gets 50% and the Passe-Tout-Grain which goes into second-year oak. This indicates serious dedication to quality – most growers who are content to use high proportions of new wood for their Premiers and Grands Crus would not stomach this expense for their Régionales. Jean-Nicolas and Christian prefer Nevers, Tronçais and Allier oak and now have their casks less heavily charred than was normal with Henri Jayer. This will give the wines a less obvious toasted contribution from the oak.

The *malos* are left to take place naturally, without any heating. Some finish early, others late, but generally by the following spring the wines are ready to be racked cask-to-cask. The following November – the timetable can vary by up to 2 or 3 months – the wines are again racked off their lees and unified in tank. Eight days later they are returned to casks, given a fining of fresh egg-white, remaining *sur col* for 2–3 months before being bottled by hand, direct from cask without filtration. In 1988 the Domaine's 100 casks took some 25 days to bottle.

The style of wine is unlikely to change significantly from that made under Henri Jayer's watchful eye. The over-riding hallmarks are a profound concentration, combined with exquisite delicacy; wines which are both ample and fat, but with a firm grip and immense charm. 1988 and 1989 are classic vintages for this elegant, round style of wine-making.

Tasting the 1989s in cask provides an opportunity to compare the individual *climats*: the basic Pinot Noir, with 6 months in new wood followed by a further year in older oak, betrays its Vosne-Romanée origins. Attractively perfumed, it has a good concentration of fruit and a sound structure which will develop and soften over the next few years; an excellent wine for its class.

The Vosne-Romanée Village *cuvée*, from the Barreaux *climat* just above Richebourg towards the Combe de Concoeur, is most attractive – well perfumed, with its larding of new wood showing through. On the palate it is both long and powerful with plenty of almost sweet, ripe fruit. A wine of some distinction, needing a few years to integrate and show at its best.

The two *cuvées* of Premier Cru Nuits St.-Georges have considerably more of Vosne finesse than normally expected from Nuits. For Les Boudots, this is not entirely surprising, since it is on the Vosne side of the appellation and has a finer soil. The wine has a soft, concentrated but delicate profile, and is altogether classy and harmonious. The second Premier Cru, Les Murgers, is yet richer, with a lively acidity and notable finesse, perhaps more typically Nuits than the Boudots, but these are fine distinctions. Nonetheless wines which promise well for the future.

There are 3 separate Vosne-Romanée Premiers Crus. Les Chaumes, with similar soil to adjoining Nuits-St.-Georges, has a mixture of aromas – liquorice, red fruits, violets and new wood – a deep, round, quite complex structure and well-integrated tannins; a most harmonious wine. The Les Brûlées is similar in style, with perhaps a touch more acidity and softer tannins. The Cros Parentoux, with a north/north-east exposition, has a slightly higher acidity than the other Vosnes, but balances this with considerable power and mouthfilling fruit; perhaps the best of the 1989 Premiers Crus.

At the top of the Méo pyramid sit a superb trio of Grands Crus. The Corton, made from 60-year-old vines, exudes richness and concentration; more *charpente* than the Vosnes but none the less immensely stylish – a fine, deep, complete wine. The Clos Vougeot – from vines at the top of the Clos – has a deep, almost Victoria plum hue, with a bud of very ripe fruit on the nose – some 60-year-old vines again – and a powerful, muscular structure. The fruit tends to amortise the effect of the tannins, giving the feeling of opulence rather than brute strength. This is very much a Vosne interpretation of Clos Vougeot – and probably the better for it! The Richebourg has a concentration and profundity to which mere description is inadequate. From these 25-year-old vines comes a wine of complexity, length and balance with a myriad of nuances and immense charm, which is rather like sipping liquid silk.

If the Méo 1989s are wines which are above all seductive, with a long-lasting charm; the 1990s add a further dimension of concentration. Provided that nothing goes awry between late 1990 and bottling in 1992, these will be exceptional wines – bottles to lay down and forget for at least a decade.

Taking the ensemble of Méo wines it would be difficult to find fault with what they are producing. Above all, the wines have great harmony and richness and invariably unmistakable class. They are rarely heavy-framed, but fine, more delicate expressions of their individual origins. This is a first-rate Domaine.

VINEYARD HOLDINGS

Commune	*Level*	*Lieu-dit/Climat*	*Area*	*Vine Age*	*Status*
Vosne	GC	Richebourg	0.35	25	P
Vosne	PC	Les Brûlées	0.70	60	P
Vosne	PC	Les Chaumes	2.01	15 & 30	P/F
Vosne	PC	Cros Parentoux	1.03	30	P
Vosne	V	(Various climats)	1.09	14	P/F
Vougeot	GC	Clos de Vougeot	1.40	17–60	P/F
Ladoix	GC	Corton	0.45	60	P
Nuits	PC	Les Boudots	1.04	40	P/F
Nuits	PC	Les Murgers	0.75	20	P
Nuits	V	(Various climats)	0.57	35	P
Vosne	R	(BGO/PTG/Bourg. R)	1.15	6–20	P/F
		Total	**10.54 ha.**		

Domaine Mongeard-Mugneret

VOSNE-ROMANÉE

Jean Mongeard is a man with his feet firmly on the ground. In fact, so long is the lineage of Mongeards in the region that he is more 'in' the ground than on it. They came to Flagey at the end of the eighteenth century and have been either there, or in Vosne, ever since. The earliest recorded viticultural Mongeard worked as a vigneron for the Domaine de la Romanée-Conti in 1786.

The present custodian of the family reputation is Jean, a large, bluff and hearty no-nonsense sort of individual and proud of his ancestry. His mother, he tells you, was a Mugneret, hence the connection with the various branches of that family scattered around Vosne and elsewhere on the Côte. Since his father and uncle arrived there at the same time, he was brought up with his cousin, the late Dr. Georges Mugneret. They were at school and in military service together; so should the indomitable Mme. Mugneret have problems with her wine, she knows where to turn for willing assistance.

If Jean was of the soil, then he was certainly pitched into it neck and crop when, in 1945, at the age of 16, he was required to make his first wine. His father had died 5 years before, and there was simply no one else to do the job. Having grappled as best he could with that task, he was put under yet more pressure by the appearance at the cellar one day of the Director of the École Viticole in Beaune, Philippe Trinquet ('un bon vigneron et un bon homme'), accompanied by a trio of the most illustrious personages in French viticulture: Baron le Roy, the owner of Château Fortia in Châteauneuf-du-Pape and one of the the fathers of the Appellation Contrôlée system, the Marquis d'Angerville from Volnay, and a great friend of his father's, Henri Gouges, these last being two of the pioneers of Domaine bottling in Burgundy.

They asked to taste Jean's wines. Having done so they astonished him by asking his price for the entire 1945 crop. Although a sound vigneron, Jean knew little of commerce and stumbled out a figure which seemed sensible to him. After some reflection his visitors told him that they would only take the wine if he doubled the price. When he had got over this shock, they told him that, instead of the normal practice of delivering the wine in barrel, he would have to bottle it personally, by hand.

Gouges was to be a great help to Jean in the years that followed. He introduced him to the Haas family who have been the Domaine's exclusive US importers ever since. As Jean proudly proclaims: 'we have no signed contract – but we have not sold a single bottle to the US except through Haas.' With Gouge's help the Domaine's fortunes grew, to the extent that from 1959 they were able to sell their complete harvest in bottle, a practice which, apart presumably from the odd few substandard casks, has not changed.

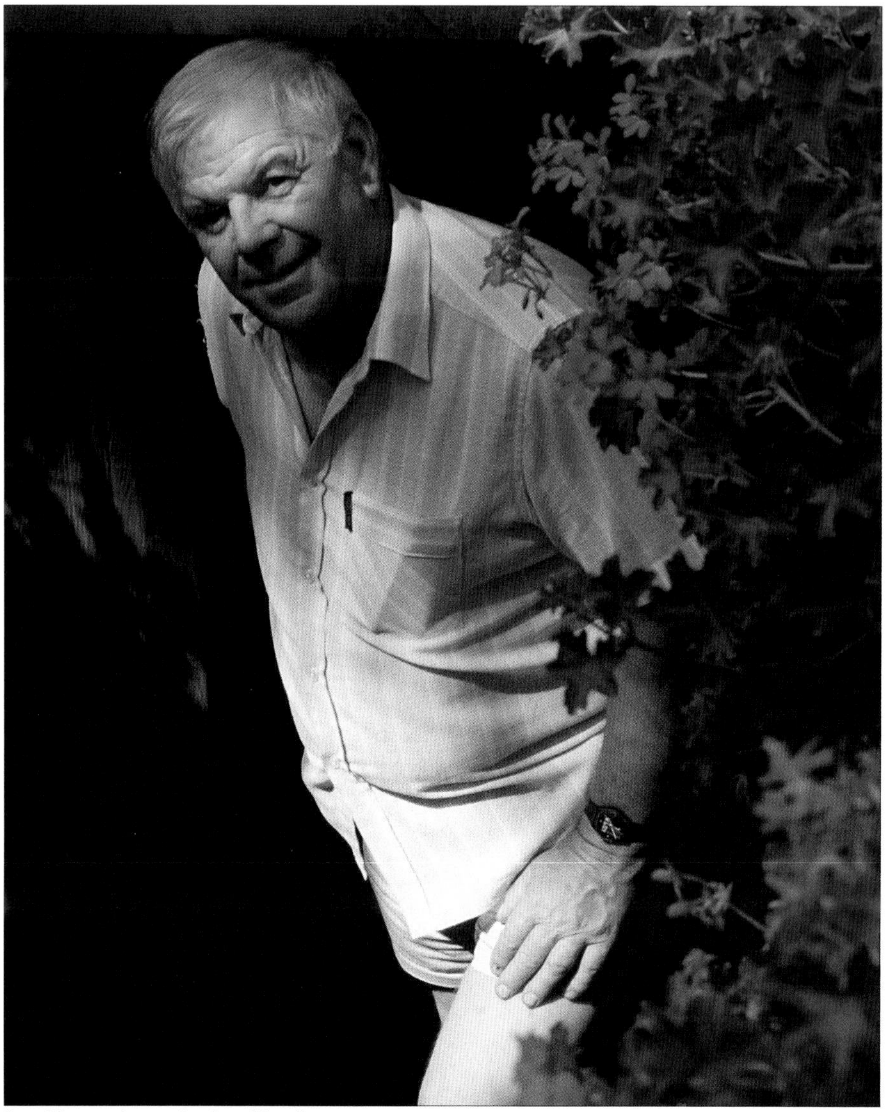

Jean Mongeard emerging from his cellar

Jean Mongeard admits that he has made mistakes. For example he was one of the many vignerons to succumb to the fertiliser salesmen in the 1960s, which resulted in a veritable mine of potassium being put onto the vineyards throughout the Côte. For the last decade he has been trying to pedal backwards – using the results of frequent soil analyses to gradually readjust magnesium levels to counteract the acidity-munching effects of the potassium. He was also 'badly advised' to use rootstock SO4 which gave problems of *chlorosis* and was maladapted to the dry, limestone based soils of the Coteaux.

All this is slowly being rectified. Jean Mongeard is a man who gives the impression of being in full empathy with his vines and is not to be put off by the occasional reverse. A traditionalist by conviction, he is however happy to try anything which he feels will benefit quality. Thus, he is now replanting on 161/49 and 3309 and respacing his vines to enable him to train them *en cordon*. This practice is becoming more popular along the

Côte, as vignerons discover the control it gives them over the spread of bunches and foliage; this is important now that clones are such prodigious and reliable producers. Some of Jean's older vines, in contrast, are highly capricious – yielding in some years and not in others.

His traditional roots, and probably the experiences with the fertiliser salesmen, have endowed him with a healthy distrust of new products and treatments. The rot problems which SO4 and the excess potassium brought in their wake are now resolved, so he is happy to stick to traditional remedies for mildew and *oïdium* and to use the smallest doses of insecticide to deal with the grape-worm.

The financial success of the Domaine is evident in every corner of the cellar. Here, a very sophisticated apparatus controls a pre-fermentive maceration at 12° C. There, a computer controls the fermentation in each of a battery of open stainless-steel and enamelled vats – the first in Burgundy, according to Jean. Then there is the pair of expensive, high-tech '*cuves* rotatives'. These were first used to vinify the Bourgogne Rouge, but have now been impressed into service for the Hautes Côtes reds, and have even been tried out on the Village Vosne, apparently requiring a day or two less *cuvaison*.

Jean Mongeard uses all this technology to procure as long a fermentation for his wines as possible: 'the temperature control can maintain the temperature at 32 degrees right to the end,' he boasts. He also uses enzymes on a regular basis to help clarify the wines. 'The more brilliant, deeper and cleaner the wine the better it takes its fining,' he announces, adding that he finds pectin specially useful in this respect.

He has also tried the latest piece of state-of-the-art vinification hardware – a machine which removes water from pulp by heat-induced evaporation. Tested on a *cuve* of Passe-Tout-Grains in 1990, it managed, in 2½ hours, to extract some 200 litres of water from 1,500 litres of pulp. Jean pronounced himself highly satisfied with the results with a technique which seems to be causing the nearest thing to collective excitement of which the phlegmatic vignerons of the Côte are capable.

Jean likes new wood for his wines and is content to rely on his tonnelier for the origin and charring of the casks he uses. The Premiers and Grands Crus find their way into 60% of new oak, the Village wines getting 40–50%; however, in weaker vintages, with less natural structure, the proportions are reduced to avoid giving the wines a dominantly dry taste from too much wood tannin.

The Mongeard wines used to spend 2½ years in cask before bottling – it was felt that this was somehow good for them, although no one really knew quite why. Nowadays, in common with most vignerons, the interval has been reduced to around 18 months, although in exceptional vintages the 'Grands Appellations' might be left for 2 years.

On the subject of filtration Jean Mongeard is somewhat cynical, an attitude which extends to colleagues and customers alike. On the one hand, he is sceptical of his colleagues who claim that they never filter – 'you only have to look round to find a filter machine in the corner of their cellars,' he smiles – on the other he berates those of his customers who simply follow fashion – 'the clients who want their wine unfiltered now are the same clients who wanted clear wines 20 years ago.'

What now happens in the Mongeard cellars is that all the wines are lightly filtered – 'only 9–10 hectos per hour,' he stresses – whether or not they are fined. In 1988 the wines were fined, in 1989 not.

Mongeard interests himself in what goes on outside Vosne-Romanée and has his fingers in several wine-political pies. He is currently President of the 'Syndicat Locale de Vosne-Romanée' and the 'Commission Technique of the Bureau Interprofessionel dęs Vins de Bourgogne' (the main technical organisation in Burgundy), also of the 'Association des Viticulteurs de la Côte d'Or'. Despite this he still finds time to do his own grafting, something which he thoroughly enjoys – perhaps because it gets him out of the office.

Of his own wines he is quietly proud, enjoining his customers to 'consider the vigneron, not the vintage', when provisioning their cellars. However, Mongeard's wines are a mixed bag. They can be sensationally good, as with the 1985 Echézeaux and Grands-Echézeaux, or just plain dull – for example, the 1983s from these same two vineyards which are broad-framed, farmyardy wines with leaden feet. In fine vintages, Mongeard manages to coax plenty of style and ripeness into his wines, and it is the absence of these which often renders the lesser years uninspiring.

The 1990s, however, although still infants in cask, give every appearance of turning out in the finer camp. The Richebourg 1990, in particular – from a vineyard of very old vines bought in 1984 from Charles Vienot which needed much *repiquage* to put it back into good order – has all the depth and structure for greatness; at once tender and tough, it seems to have great finesse and style in the making – a very big wine, in the monunental Mongeard mould.

The cellars which run under the Mongeard's house, on the southern extremity of Vosne, are as neat as one would expect. Having worked one's way through the casks, the visitor is taken into a small room, off the main cellar, where there are a few crooked stools and a table. Ranged round three walls are the family reserves of old wine – a magnificent library of maturing vintages going back half a century or more.

Jean Mongeard tastes widely, as evidenced by a corner of the cellar devoted to wines from a variety of provenances – Alsace, Jura, Bordeaux, the Loire and a few odd bottles of vintage port – probably presents from satisfied customers.

He has just bought a substantial vineyard and house for his daughter and son-in-law in the South of France, near Rivesaltes. Unfortunately his taste in wine does not extend to the local speciality – Muscat – so he has planted 6 ha. of Syrah – 'on schist and iron, on hillsides,' he adds excitedly – plus 3 ha. of Mourvèdre. There are 2 ha. of Muscat, he admits, but he can probably manage to visit his daughter without getting too close to their produce.

Jean Mongeard is evidently a contented man. His cellar is a good source of wine, but not one from which to buy blind, as it were.

VINEYARD HOLDINGS

Commune	*Level*	*Lieu-dit/Climat*	*Area*	*Vine Age*	*Status*
Vosne	GC	Richebourg	0.32	50+	P
Vosne	PC	Les Orveaux	1.10	45	P
Vosne	PC	Les Suchots	0.51	50+	P
Vosne	PC	Les Petits Monts	0.30	45	P
Vosne	V	(Various climats)	2.08	50	P
Flagey	GC	Grands-Echézeaux	1.70	50	P
Flagey	GC	Echézeaux	3.38	45	P
Vougeot	GC	Clos de Vougeot	0.80	45	P
Vougeot	PC	Les Petits Vougeots	0.54	25	P
Nuits	PC	Les Boudots	0.40	18	P
Nuits	V	—	0.20	15	P
Savigny	PC	Les Narbantons	1.40	60	P
Savigny	V	—	0.60	30	P
Fixin	V	—	1.30	50	P
—	R	(Hte. Cte. Nuits)	0.70	20	P
—	R	(Bourgogne Rouge)	1.70	35	P
—	R	(Bourgogne Blanc)	0.60	20	P
		Total	**17.63 ha.**		

Domaine Mugneret-Gibourg

VOSNE-ROMANÉE

It is refreshing, in this era of equality, to find Domaines of excellence throughout the Côte run by women. This, not from merely anti-sexist sentiments, but for the less hard-headed feelings of pleasure at being received, now and then, by a fragrant, well-groomed woman instead of a hoary aromatic old man of the soil, usually with much of it on his boots. At the Domaine Mugneret-Gibourg, that pleasure is likely to be doubled, since following the death in 1988 of Dr. Georges Mugneret the estate is run by his charming widow Jacqueline and her daughter, Marie-Christine.

Georges Mugneret, apart from being one of France's finest ophthalmologists, was a man 'passioné du vin'. In 1930, at the height of the Depression, he materialised this passion by purchasing a substantial house in Vosne together with parcels of Bourgogne, Vosne-Romanée and Echézeaux. With his career to provide income the ship stayed afloat at a time when a full cask sold for little more than an empty one.

The Domaine today is, in reality, two separate exploitations: the original Mugneret-Gibourg vines bought in the 1930s and still marketed under that name, and the land added subsequently by Georges himself, sold as Domaine Georges Mugneret. But these divisions are no more than Chinese walls, since the ensemble of vineyards are tended and the grapes vinified under the care of mother and daughter.

In 1982, when it was clear that George was seriously ill, Marie-Christine began to take time off from her work as a pharmacist to understudy her father. She and her mother took more and more on their shoulders so, when he died, 'we just had to get on with it'. As Marie-Christine explains, it was like one's first solo in a car – you can do it perfectly well, but the reassurance has gone. She still finds herself asking: 'Would he have done this?', and generally erring on the side of caution.

Georges was clearly a man of shrewd judgement, building up a small Domaine spread across 5 communes at all quality levels. In addition, the vines are all 20-40 years old – so there is no need for concern about serious replanting for some time yet.

Whilst Mme. Mugneret occupies herself with the Domaine's clients and administration, it is to Marie-Christine that the task of vinification falls. Her pharmaceutical training and a diploma in oenology have equipped her with a natural inquisitiveness which fortunately banishes inflexibility. Although the spirit of her father still guides her, there is nothing routine in her approach. She is well aware of the chemistry of wine and willing to question whatever is being contemplated with an independent thoroughness.

However, since the wines George produced were fine, and the customers liked them, she sees no reason to change their style. Receiving the children, grandchildren and even great-grandchildren of Georges' original clients – he started selling direct in bottle just after the Second World War – maintains a pleasant continuity and is proof of customer satisfaction.

Of the 8.70 ha. of vineyards, all but the Clos Vougeot and the Ruchottes-Chambertin are cultivated on a share-cropping basis. However Domaines of this quality in this situation, work closely with their *métayeurs* to ensure the vineyards are maintained as they would wish.

Over the years it has been a rare vintage in which the Grands Crus did not need *chaptalisation*. This may seem surprising, but it must be remembered that their unique qualities derive not from high alcohol but from a particular site, soil and micro-climate . Often these vineyards are on poor soil, poorly exposed, which make ripening difficult. In addition, Grand Cru wines tend to need more alcohol to balance out their natural power and structure and thus more sugar. If the requisite natural grape-sugar is absent, it must be added at fermentation, bearing in mind that to end up with say 12.8% actual alcohol in a wine, you must probably start with a potential – in sugar – of 13.5%, to compensate for anticipated loss.

To minimise *chaptalisation*, the Domaine and their vignerons have worked hard to increase natural sugar levels. In the summer excess foliage is regularly trimmed off to expose as much of the canopy as possible to sunlight. High pruning of this sort has been found to add a degree or more to potential alcohol levels. The Mugnerets consult with their vignerons on the date of the harvest, in order to maximise ripeness, without risking over-ripeness which can detract from the purity of a wine's flavour.

In hot years such as 1989 and 1990, there is often a second crop of bunches, usually at the top of each vine. If not excised before turning black (*veraison*), they take energy from the vine. When this 'second sortie' (*verjus* or conscrits) is almost as large as the original crop as in parts of the Côte in 1990 it seriously threatens the quality of the vintage. It is therefore essential to remove it before the beginning of September in advance of its maximum damage-potential. Since the *verjus* consists largely of unripe grapes, it is equally essential to ensure that none gets into the fermenting vats – so a strict watch is kept on pickers to see that *verjus* is left on the vine.

Another useful expedient for maximising sugar concentration in the grapes is to remove part of the harvest in August. The theory is that this green-pruning concentrates the vine's energies into the remaining bunches. Experiments during 1990 showed that vines which were green-pruned – compared with rows in the same vineyard which were not – gave a significant 1.5-2.0 degrees higher potential alcohol. Moreover, they also ripened sooner and, although having a touch of *surmaturité* in that exceptionally hot summer, gave a distinctly more concentrated juice. At the Domaine this operation is confined to the younger vines, generally the culprits at over- producing. In 1990 the older vines, flowering later than the rest, were caught by rain which destroyed some of the flowers and thus irrevocably reduced the crop.

If sufficiently ripe and healthy fruit is one side of the vineyard equation, limiting yields is the other. *Répiquage* to maintain a high average vine-age and low fertilisation has helped keep the Domaine's yields below 35 hl./ha. over the years. Between 1988 and 1990 they needed to replace only 500 individual plants, although the severe frosts of 1985 destroyed larger parcels of their Vosne-Romanée. Unexpectedly and, perhaps, unwisely, they replant systematically on the rootstock SO4 . This promotes early ripening, but has a relatively short life and needs an ultra-clean vineyard environment to thrive. The wines that Marie-Christine and her mother produce are above all stylish, but with fine concentration. The vineyards may supply fruit of great potential, but, as vignerons know that can so easily be destroyed in the cellar. There is nothing radical about the Mugneret vinification except for a firm belief that natural yeasts are not the best. Thus, each year, selected yeasts are added to the *cuves* because they tolerate higher alcohol levels and thus give a longer fermentation, both of which add up to more alcohol and glycerols in the final wine.

Long fermentation is important, since it is felt to give better extraction and greater complexity to the wine. To this end

Marie-Christine and Mme. Jacqueline Mugneret

chaptalisation, when necessary, is done in several stages, towards the end of fermentation. Grape sugars – glucose and fructose – are fermented quite rapidly, so a late addition of cane sugar (sucrose) can be propitious.

The extent to which the bunches of grapes are destalked is a serious decision depending on the character of the vintage. Generally, the riper the wood the more stalks can be safely left in the vats, up to a maximum of 20%. Ripe wood can add beneficial tannin but unripe wood will only impart a 'green' herbaceous taste and unwanted water, often with a twist of residual bitterness. Interestingly, older vines have less wood than younger, greener, plants, so a higher proportion of old vine stalks can be considered in riper vintages. Expert thinking on this subject changed radically during the 1980s; the tendency to leave the majority of the stalks shifted to the present practice of removing most of them.

Otherwise, vinfiication is relatively straightforward: a 24–36 hour pre-fermentive maceration at 16–18° C with the addition of enzymes to help eventual clarification, is followed by fermentation, in either cement *cuves* for larger lots or wood vats for smaller lots, at up to 34° C for about 18 days.

Fermentation is a sequential process – unstable colour is leached out first, in aqueous solution, to be 'fixed' later by the tannins only extracted in the presence of alcohol. The important middle phase of *cuvaison* extracts aroma compounds – if you lift the cover of the vats, you will notice a different odour from each *cuve* each day.

Gentle pressing, even when low yields might tempt some to press harder to extract a few francs more juice, gives 'an honest quantity of softish press-wine which is amalgamated with the free-run wine before being run off into cask.

For new barrels, the Mugnerets are attached more to their tonnelier than the precise provenance of the wood. Marie-Christine thinks their oak comes from the Tronçais, but is unsure. Whatever, the Grands Crus see some 80% new wood, the Premiers Crus up to 70% and the Village wines 40–50%. Even the Bourgogne has 'a touch' of new oak.

The time the wines spend in cask before first racking depends on when the *malos* finish. In years such as 1989, when fermentation temperatures tended to soar, the wines have a higher risk of *volatile acidity* which is unpleasant in both aroma and flavour above a certain concentration, so they are racked cask-to-cask as soon as their *malos* have finished, with a shot of sulphur to neutralise bacteria which might attack any residual sugar.

After a second racking some 6–8 months later, the wines return to cask until the following February, when they are assembled in tanks, fined with dried albumen and bottled 2 months later – a total *élevage* of some 18 months. Of the annual production of around 90 *pièces* of 300 bottles each, half goes to export and half to French and passing trade, much of it Swiss.

In the cellars, built around 1750, there is an air of tradition, of quiet dedication to quality. Nothing seems hurried or forced – the wines work at their own pace. The 1989s were just starting to emerge from their shells in January 1991 – and the 1990s, of course, still thoroughly reticent.

The range starts with an excellent fruity Bourgogne Rouge, worth keeping for a few years to soften out. The Village Vosne has usually all the elegance and depth one would expect – again a wine to cellar for several years, especially in the better vintages.

The Nuits Premier Cru, Les Chaignots – a vineyard on the Vosne side of Nuits with thin, stony, topsoil – produces a wine of highish natural acidity which has both the elegance of Vosne and a touch of the rusticity of Nuits. The 1989 had aromas of red fruits and a good, long, complex flavour.

The Chambolle-Musigny Premier Cru Les Feusselottes – of which the Mugnerets normally have 4 casks, 3 new wood – is quite different; the 1989 has a deep colour with a ripe, expansive nose of *fruits sauvages* with hints of spice, tar and liquorice. The deepish, rich high clay soils in this relatively flat vineyard, give a broad wine, with plenty of Chambolle finesse and style.

The Mugneret Clos de Vougeot – from a one-third ha. plot in the Vosne section at the top of the Clos, is distinctly more 'sauvage' than the Nuits-St.-Georges. Both the 1989 and 1990 are big, spicy wines, with more than a touch of elegant rusticity and plenty of richness and depth. The younger wine had slightly more muscle, though neither lacked for structure.

The Echézeaux is generally, with the Clos de Vougeot, the most backward of the Domaine's wines, needing a long time to express itself, but worth the wait. The 1987 is a fine example of what can be done in a less opulent vintage – deep mid-red in colour, an attractive nose of *sous-bois* and *fruits-noirs* and a deliciously long, ripe, complex flavour. Still young, but most appealing.

The Ruchottes-Chambertin is probably the Mugnerets' finest wine. Invariably long and attractive, it seems to have that inspiring combination of great richness and great complexity. Not a wine, in top vintages, to touch for 5–10 years, but to put away patiently, to await its maturity. The 1983, tasted at the Domaine, was just starting to lose some of its austere envelope of tannins and to exhibit flashes of charm and quality. There is a touch of dryness at the edges which is unlikely to go, but it is perfectly healthy and will be at its prime in the mid-1990s.

This is a Domaine of great quality and style. Mme. Mugneret and Marie-Christine make a formidable team of which Dr. Georges Mugneret would be proud.

VINEYARD HOLDINGS

Commune	*Level*	*Lieu-dit/Climat*	*Area*	*Vine Age*	*Status*
Vougeot	GC	Clos de Vougeot	0.34	35	P
Gevrey	GC	Ruchottes-Chambertin	0.64	35	P
Vosne	GC	Echézeaux	1.05	35	P
Vosne	V	(Various climats)	3.64	40	P
Chambolle	PC	Les Feusselottes	0.46	30	P
Nuits	PC	Les Chaignots	1.27	35	P
Nuits	PC	Les Vignes-Rondes	0.26	20	F
—	R	(Bourgogne Rouge)	0.85	25	P
		Total	**8.51 ha.**		

Domaine Pernin-Rossin

VOSNE-ROMANÉE

André Pernin-Rossin is unusual in that he is one of the few, perhaps, who has taken and then dispensed with the services of Guy Accad in the search for higher quality. He is a mild-mannered, quiet man who lives in a modern house on the eastern side of the RN 74 in Vosne.

The creation of the Domaine started in 1970. André's father worked as a piece-worker for Gaston and later Jean Grivot in their Clos Vougeot vines. André succeeded him – working 14 years for Jean Grivot, before leaving for another 14 years working for the Hospices de Nuits. In 1964, after a further 2 years working 'à la tâche', he was given a parcel of Nuits Premier Cru La Richemoine by his father, and thereby started off on his own account.

Capitalising on his good fortune, André soon built up his Domaine to its present size of 7.67 ha., some vines share-cropped, the others owned outright. The geographical spread is wide, encompassing Vosne, Morey, Nuits, Chambolle-Musigny – as far south as Auxey-Duresses, where there is a parcel of Village red. Apart from 10% of his Vosne-Romanée Chante Perdrix, which is sold to Olivier Leflaive, he makes about 100 barrels annually, 90% of which is bottled at the Domaine and sold direct.

In the vineyards, André eschews *repiquage*, preferring to replant completely parcels which become uneconomic or diseased. For the last 4–5 years he has used a mix of clones, planted on rootstock 161/49, with which he is happy. Any anxieties are perhaps eased by the knowledge that his nurseryman is the father of Laurence Jobard, Drouhin's talented oenologist.

For the last 15 years he has used nothing but fish mulch to fertilise his vines; there have been no anti-rot treatments since 1987, but plenty of copper-based products to harden the Pinot skins as a measure of protection against grape-worm and thus against rot.

Although the vines are severely pruned to remove excessive buds and double shoots, there is no green-pruning later on in the growing season. André considers that those who green-prune don't gain a single degree more of potential alcohol. No doubt many would disagree with him.

Guy Accad was consultant to the Domaine between 1980 and 1989. However disagreements over his manner and attendance led to his dismissal in 1990 – leaving the 1988 and 1989 vintages still in cask.

The theoretical base of the 'vinification Accad' is the affirmation that one can control the progress of fermentation better with cool *must*. In practice, this means a dose of 2 litres of SO_2 in 5% solution per tonne of harvest, plus cooling to 5–8° C (in contrast to the more usual 1 litre of SO_2 and cooling to 16–18° C). After 8–10 days pre-fermentive maceration at this low temperature fermentation proceeds normally for a total *cuvaison* of around 18 days with at least one *pigéage* and one *remontage* each day.

The aim of this long, slow, cool vinification is to extract as much colour – in the pre-fermentive phase – and tannin – in the post-fermentive phase – as possible. This is intended to give the wine maximum richness, structure and eventual longevity.

The *malos* take place in bulk – in large resin or fibre-glass *foudres* – after which the wine is put into cask for further ageing. Chez Pernin-Rossin, there is only 10–15% of new wood, the rest being up to 10 years old. In August, following the vintage, the wines are racked, and then left for 12–13 months in cask before being unified in bulk, fined with albumen and bottled without filtration.

André is a careful and conscientious winemaker. He contends that, in general, people try to vinify their wines too quickly, losing depth and complexity in the process. His own philosophy is to delay the harvest for as long as possible – in 1990, for example, he harvested a week or so after everyone else – and to vinify slowly; in culinary terms, the difference perhaps between a quick seal and grill and a long slow simmer.

How successfully André's own wines stand up remains to be seen. What is apparent now is that everything he makes is carefully and skilfully put together. His wines tend to be dark in colour and muscular, perhaps more than one would consider totally typical for a Vosne-Romanée or a Morey-St.-Denis. Nonetheless they are fine and it would be blind prejudice to deny them that accolade.

Of the various parcels of Vosne-Romanée, that on the higher ground, in fact within 20 m. of the Grand Cru La Romanée vineyard, produces the finest wine, with an opulent nose, redolent of blackcurrants and ripe *fruits noirs* (1989 vintage) and beautifully balanced acidity and tannins. The vines from lower down, on the flatter land nearer the village, produce a good wine of greater muscle and strength, but without the same finesse.

The Vosne-Romanée, Premier Cru Les Beaumonts, from 30–80 year-old-vines, produce wines of a different style – much more raspberries and liquorice on the nose, spicier, with greater finesse and length. The 1989 is a gorgeous, opulent mouthful, which will be at its elegant best in the late 1990s.

The Nuits Premier Cru La Richemoine is also a remarkably fine wine. A high proportion of very old vines contributes a depth of fruit and concentration of flavour which are mouthwatering. The aromas are typically more 'sauvage', animal rather than fruit, with a decidedly mineral element in the taste which well sets off the tannins. The richness of dark, crushed fruit gives the Richemoine 1989 superb profundity and softness which put it almost into the top class.

A curiosity of the Pernin-Rossin stable is an Aligoté, made in pitifully small quantities, from 50-year-old vines in Vosne itself. To show its best, it needs keeping for 3 years in a good vintage, when it will give out a magnificent rich aroma of pine-honey, almost resinous, with a delicious long, warm flavour, rather reminiscent of honeyed sweets.

André Pernin-Rossin is a skilled winemaker, dedicated to quality. No-one's prejudices about Accad should preclude a trial of his excellent wines.

VINEYARD HOLDINGS

Commune	*Level*	*Lieu-dit/Climat*	*Area*	*Vine Age*	*Status*
Vosne	PC	Les Beaumonts	0.45	30-80	M
Vosne	PC	Les Reignots	0.05	35	P
Vosne	V	Chante Perdrix	0.12	12	M
Vosne	V	(Various Climats)	0.74	30-40	M
Nuits	PC	La Richemoine	1.45	45	P/M
Morey	GC	Clos de la Roche	0.04	70+	M
Morey	PC	Monts Luisants (R)	2.34	1968	M
Morey	V	—	1.07	1968	M
Chambolle	PC	Les Baudes	0.04	25	M
Chambolle	PC	Les Charmes	0.10	40	M
Auxey	V	(Rouge)	0.88	10	M
Vosne	R	(BGO/Aligoté)	0.39	30-60	P/M
		Total	**7.67 ha.**		

Domaine Jean Tardy

VOSNE-ROMANÉE

A short, slim man, with close-cropped grey hair, Jean Tardy exudes assiduity and passion for his job and will argue a point with gallic animation. When something of particular importance arises his voice jumps a couple of octaves and he repeats the phrase for further emphasis.

Jean Tardy's father, from whom he took over in 1970, did not own a single vine but share-cropped on a 'half-fruit' rental. Starting in 1972, Jean bought 2.5 ha. mainly in *Régionales* and some Nuits Village. He would like to add to his Domaine, since he now has more customers than wine to sell, but current prices make buying or renting uneconomic.

At present, the Domaine – some 5 ha., spread over Vosne-Romanée, Nuits-St.-Georges and Chambolle-Musigny – comprises two parcels of good Premiers Crus – Nuits-St.-Georges Les Boudots (a steep vineyard with a very thin topsoil onto rock) and Vosne-Romanée, Les Chaumes – with a little Clos Vougeot and some Chambolle and Nuits Village vineyards. The remainder is Passe-Tout-Grains, BGO and Aligoté.

Jean is meticulous about everything he does and scathing of those who have fine land yet produce sloppy, indifferent wine. He enjoys being out-of-doors – whether replacing earth washed down Les Boudots, or dealing with an outbreak of grape-worm or red spider – seems to relish hard work.

Careful *repiquage* to ensure that no vines are missing is coupled with a complete replanting programme at the stately rate of 10 rows per year. So, at its present size, the entire Domaine will be replaced every 28 years. Otherwise, a fairly orthodox viticultural cycle – organic fertilisers and treatments in minimum doses, no anti-rot sprays, and a very strict *évasivage* – all help to keep the plants healthy.

The oldest vines are picked first, since their smaller crop tends to ripen sooner; in the Tardy Domaine this generally means the 40-year-old Nuits Les Boudots and Clos Vougeot. Bunches are always completely destalked and vatted without cooling so that fermentation can start as and when it is ready. In 1990, at the request of Jean Méo (owner of the Boudots which he share-crops) Jean cooled the pulp before fermentation. The results were apparently highly unsatisfactory, so he won't try that again: 'you must let things go themselves,' he moans.

Thereafter what is sought is the longest, slowest possible fermentation. Though each year is different, Jean normally achieves a *cuvaison* of 15–20 days; in 1982 the average was 23 days, but that was exceptional.

One practice, however, is invariant: every year the *cuves* are *saignées*, to concentrate the wine further. Surprisingly, even the old vines of Les Boudots, which naturally produce very little, were *saignées* in 1990. Such sacrifices show in the depth of Tardy's wines.

Another peculiarity concerns his use of new oak. Up to 1985 the proportion was 50% but, convinced that the extra expense and trouble were justified, he decided to use 100% for all the Village, Premiers and Grands Crus from the 1986 vintage. The mere thought of colleagues who 'use 25-year-old casks, badly filled' makes him decidedly animated. His new casks are never prepared or treated in any way – 'no rinsing, never a drop, never a drop' he trills, an octave higher

The idea of 100% new oak, which must to some seem heresy, is not just a whim. 'The *élevage* of wine is very important; one must be obsessive,' he argues, adding that with his small yields, long *cuvaison* and 'grosses *saignées*', even a vintage like 1984 can support 100% new wood.

The wines spend some 16–18 months in cask. Following a first racking after the *malo*, they are left until the start of the second year before being lightly filtered, assembled and bottled. Jean vehemently opposes any kind of fining and most types of filtration. He reckons that fining takes too much out of a wine and has no time for the kieselguhr filtration used by many of his colleagues.

If making the wine to his satisfaction is difficult enough, the business of dealing with his customers is even more problematical. His low yields give him about 2,000 cases a year, which simply won't go round. Having to refuse a constant stream of hopeful suitors leaves him near desperation: 'I have refused the Japanese three times; a German who wanted 1,200 bottles was allocated 300 – that was really very generous, very generous.' Fortunately, he can see the mild humour in his situation: 'Oh, là là, oh, là là,' he shrills, 'the clients want the wine and I haven't got it!'

Whilst all this may be a minor trial, Jean Tardy clearly enjoys being something of a celebrity. Nothing gives him more pleasure than having top Swiss restaurateurs and their sommeliers, tasting in his cellar.

There is no doubt that his manic obsession with detail pays off; though by no means all the wines are great, the overall standard is high with some spectacular successes among the selection. However, despite having the oldest vines of all, Jean's Nuits Les Boudots is sometimes rather dull; not badly made, nor uninteresting, just lacking in nuance.

This cannot, however, be said of the Chambolle Villages, Vosne-Romanée Les Chaumes or Clos Vougeot. Jean admits that such a long *cuvaison* may unbalance the delicacy of Chambolle-Musigny, but seems determined to stick to his methods. The 1989 Chambolle is a fine wine – full of *fruits noirs sauvages* on the nose, and plenty of depth of flavour. The extra maceration shows up in a heavier structure – more Morey-St.-Denis than Chambolle-Musigny perhaps?

The 1989 Vosne-Romanée Les Chaumes is an entirely delicious wine – elegant, almost musky on the nose, quite firm on the palate, but complete and most attractive, with great finesse, derived from the poor, predominantly limestone soil.

The Clos Vougeot is even richer and more complex, with added power and vinosity. Jean's vines, located in the sector 'Aux Grands Maupertuis', adjacent to Les Grands Echézeaux, seem to give the expected depth and power of a Grand Cru, without the rustic earthiness which so often characterises wines from the Clos. The balance in 1989 is finely-tuned; it seems deceptively straightforward, but should be magnificent in the late 1990s.

Jean Tardy's style is for well-structured, long-lived wines. If you can lay hands on a case or two, they are well worth having. Let's hope that somehow he manages to find some more vineyards , otherwise the Swiss restaurateurs may collar the lot !

VINEYARD HOLDINGS

Commune	*Level*	*Lieu-dit/Climat*	*Area*	*Vine Age*	*Status*
Vosne	PC	Les Chaumes	1.55	15	M
Nuits	V	Les Bas de Combes	0.45	35	P
Nuits	PC	Les Boudots	1.04	40/60	M
Vougeot	GC	Clos de Vougeot	0.23	40	M
Chambolle	V	Les Athets	0.32	12	P
	R	(BGO/PTG/Bourg.)	1.20	20-40	P
		Total	**4.79 ha.**		

Domaine de la Romanée-Conti

VOSNE-ROMANÉE

The status of the Domaine de la Romanée-Conti as the leading producer of red Burgundy – the white Crown is perhaps more controversial – should be questioned by no one. There may be arguments over this or that wine from this or that vintage, but year on year the Domaine has turned out wines of supreme excellence with that balance of power and finesse which both seduces and excites the senses.

Much has been written about the history of the Domaine – the ownership of the Prince de Conti – and the long-time renown of the Romanée vineyard as a site of special viticultural significance.

What, surprisingly however, has not yet been fully expounded is the way in which the Domaine works to extract the maximum possible from its magnificent vineyards – the traditions of management and vinification which contribute ineluctably to the quality of wines, so highly prized and so much discussed throughout the wine-loving world.

There is no doubt whatever that the present owners, Aubert de Villaine and Mme. Bize-Leroy, share with their predecessors the conviction that quality begins in the vineyards. Fine wine is not, as some seem to think, a matter of the wine-maker's art alone; the skills required to look after the vines and the soil in which they are planted is of equal – if not greater – importance. It is the individuality of these small plots of land which find unique expression in the grapes grown there, and thereby in the wine made from those grapes.

Thus the potential of quality is determined by the quality of the fruit which reaches the *cuverie* and not by the wizardry of the wine-maker who then takes charge of it. As one wine-grower put it: 'the vineyard gives the maximum potential of quality – one can either diminish or equal this in the cellar; but, one cannot augment it.'

Apart from the infrequent occasions when the topsoil in the Romanée-Conti vineyard is renewed, fertiliser is rarely added. Annual soil analyses provide the Domaine and the 'chef de culture', Gerard Marlot, with continuous monitoring of the state of the soil and the equilibrium of its constituents. Apart from small re-adjustments of magnesium in the lower part of La Tâche and in Les Grands Echézeaux, nothing more than occasional applications of organic fertilisers have been needed in recent years. In 1990, there was no fertilisation at all.

Some parts of the Domaine suffer particularly from soil erosion – especially the southern section of La Tâche, and also the land between Richebourg and Romanée-Conti. Here the topsoil which has been washed down has to be put back again. It is hoped that the provision of special open cement drainage will mitigate the incidence of erosion over the coming years.

Romanée-Conti itself, despite a slope of only 3%, has suffered erosion and occasionally needed soil replacement. In 1786/7 Grimelin, the régisseur of the Prince de Conti, ordered 800 cartloads of 'terre de montagne' from the 'arrières Côtes' to be brought down to fill in depressions in parts of the Romanée-Conti vineyard which had suffered more than elsewhere from erosion.

More recently, in 1980, an unfortunate mistake led to the in-filling of some depressions in Romanée-St.-Vivant with 'terre blanche', an earth which is wholly out of keeping with the existing topsoil. At the request of the INAO, the Domaine swiftly removed it and replaced it with more appropriate soil from hillsides near Gevrey.

The perspective of the Domaine's vineyard policy is to retain the micro-climate of the soil and vines. It is not an expressly organic policy, but rather oriented towards the minimum use of synthetic products and towards traditional viticulture.

The soils – particularly for the young vines – are worked with a tractor-mounted hoe, to aerate the earth. This provides a better environment for natural micro-flora to flourish and helps drainage. The vines are ploughed up round the roots each winter and ploughed down in the spring. For the younger vines this provides an element of frost protection which is valuable in minimising losses, especially in years of severe frost such as 1985.

Pests and diseases are treated as traditionally as possible – Bordeaux mixture and sulphur for the *cryptogams* (*botrytis, oïdium* and mildew) preceded by the protective copper-based 'Cuivrol' early in the growing season. The sulphur treatments also discourage red and yellow spiders which are particularly virulent on the Côte. The menace of grape-worm is dealt with by specific protective sprays, but a conscious effort is made to avoid any systemic products, unless there is really no alternative.

Apart from dealing with the grape-worm and using copper-based products which harden the skin and thus make penetration more difficult, no specific anti-rot treatments have been used since 1986. The Domaine considers it better to let the grapes ripen naturally and then to excise any rotten material at harvest than to spray needlessly. In 1988, 1989 and 1990 weather conditions were dry, so neither dry nor damp rot were a problem.

A rigorous policy of low yields brings a dimension of extract and concentration to the Domaine's wines which is truly remarkable and indeed, one of its hallmarks. Average yields are generally well below the *rendement de base* for Grands Crus of 35 hl./ha., or 1,848 bottles per acre. A 10-year average shows yields of 25 hl./ha., with a planting density of 10,000 vines per ha.; in other words it takes the grapes from 3 vines to make a single bottle of Domaine wine.

Such low yields are achieved by a combination of factors of which short pruning and a deliberately high vine age are the most significant. An old vine produces less, but of better quality and better natural equilibrium, especially in acidity. This is important for ageing a wine, particularly in very ripe years such as 1989 when natural acidity levels throughout the Côte tended to be low.

Pruning is undertaken with scrupulous care by dividing the vineyards (notionally, that is) into individual plots and then allocating to each pruner a plot. Tending the same plot each year engenders a feeling for each vine and its growing characteristics, so pruning can be adapted accordingly. Generally the Domaine's vines are trained *Guyot simple* with some older vines *en crochet*.

For many years the pruning of Romanée-Conti itself was the personal undertaking of Mme. Andre Noblet, the wife of the then cellar-master.

Much work is done whilst the vine is growing to help it yield the best and most concentrated fruit. Apart from a very strict *evasivage* and *dédoublage*, there is a passage through the vines , normally in June after the flowering, to remove either excess embryo grape clusters or sometimes excess wood, which might sap valuable energy from the principal bunches.

In some years, when it is considered that there are still too many bunches, there is a further green-pruning. In 1990, for example, a team was sent through the vineyards to remove some 7–8 bunches per vine. It is essential that this operation is performed relatively late in the growing season to ensure that the sugar levels remain high and that the plants do not compensate for their loss.

In addition to this, several leaf prunings are carried out during the summer – the first by hand – to increase foliage exposure . There is a tendency to prune higher now, since this has been found to increase photosynthetic efficiency and thus ripeness.

The cost of all this pruning work is considerable: some 5–6 extra passages through the vines by skilled workers, otherwise the effort is pointless.

One of the hardest decisions for the Domaine was taken in 1945 when Romanée-Conti needed replanting because production from its ancient vines, still on their original roots, had become uneconomic. Before grubbing it up, however, plant material was taken to reconstitute La Tâche, 5% of which are now based on Romanée-Conti grafts. No one quite knows what rootstock was used in 1946, but Aubert de Villaine believes that it was probably riparia.

Nowadays, vines are replaced individually if they are younger than 30–40 years old, otherwise they are replanted as part of the Domaine's programme – one 'journal' (= one-third ha.) per year. Plant material comes from a population of 50 vines from the Romanée-Conti vineyard, selected for small berry size. Cuttings are treated like clones and sent to the research station at Colmar for virus-indexing, before being grafted on to either 161/49 or riparia.

Riparia is an excellent rootstock but especially sensitive to an excess of lime in the soil, which yellows the leaves and affects the photosynthetic mechanism of the plant. Great care is therefore taken to ensure maximal adaptation of young vines to its soil.

The attention to detail does not diminish at harvest time: *prélèvements* – 'très, très sérieux' – at the rate of one per week per vineyard, start 3 weeks before the anticipated vintage date. The results of these will determine the order of harvesting. Once a vineyard has been started it will be finished before the team moves on to the next. The date of starting the harvest is regarded as of greater significance than the order in which the vineyards are picked. Generally, it takes no more than 8 days to complete the harvest, so there is less urgency to start early.

In fact, the Domaine prefers to harvest late, to maximise concentration and ripeness. With a high proportion of older vines this brings little risk of unacceptably low acidities. However, they do not want grapes which are so concentrated and over-ripe that they impart a 'figgy' taste to the wine. Late harvesting is a distinct risk, but one which the Domaine believes any conscientious vigneron should be prepared to take. If an occasional loss due to adverse weather is the price of quality, then so be it.

The pickers are skilled, and well supervised. No effort is spared to ensure that only the very ripest, intact fruit reaches the *cuverie*. In fact, so great was the concern in 1983 after the June hailstorms that a small team was despatched early into Romanée-Conti, La Tâche and part of Richebourg, armed with typesetter's tweezers to remove one by one any hailed berries which had dried out and failed to detach themselves from the bunches. This saved the wine from an ineradicable taste of hail. Whatever the circumstances, damaged berries easily spread the oxidising enzyme laccase to healthy fruit, increasing the extent of premature oxidation. So the earlier they are removed the better.

Once cut, bunches are put into straw baskets which are emptied onto a table where a further scan is made for ripeness. When they reach the *cuverie*, in Vosne, they pass into the hands of Bernard Noblet – the successor to his father André – and his team in the cellars.

For a short period after André Noblet's retirement, the Domaine enlisted the services of a professional oenologist. However, this arrangement soon foundered – oenologists tend to work by the book rather than vinifying in sympathy with each vineyard. No doubt, the imposing presence of Aubert de Villaine (a skilled wine-maker in his own right) and a few hundred years of history breathing down your collar may have proved too intimidating. Ruining a vat of Romanée-Conti is no short-cut to enhancing one's

Romanée-Conti with Romanée-St.-Vivant and the village of Vosne-Romanée beyond

personal standing, certainly not in the close-knit circles of Burgundian oenology.

The philosophy behind the Domaine's wine-making is to achieve 'l'expression le plus pur du terroir'. The vigneron is no more than an intermediary between the soil and the wine and should interfere as little as possible. As Aubert de Villaine somewhat cryptically puts it: 'nothing is more difficult than to act simply; the ideal is to do nothing,' adding, 'but that is impossible.' Trying to reduce a Grand Cru to a certain number of 'savoir-faires' is like attempting to define the music of Mozart by describing his technique.

Translated into more tangible terms, vinification is 'ultra-traditionelle' – no destalking, even in the leanest years, a smallish dose of SO_2 which varies with the vintage and a light crushing by foot.

Thereafter, the wines come to life in a series of old open wooden *cuves* of various shapes and sizes which line the walls of the neat *cuverie*, in a side street a short walk from the Domaine's offices. No two *cuves* are the same shape – one is oval, another tall, some conical and at least one straight on one side and tapering on the other. Collectively, they give the appearance of a pot-bellied, overfed and decidedly misshapen wooden chorus. Romanée-Conti itself is invariably fermented in *cuve* number 17, a splendid receptacle made in 1862.

There have been trials with stainless-steel *cuves* for at least 20 years, but since they give no appreciable difference in final quality there are no plans to demolish the 'ultra-traditionelles' wooden *cuves* – 'plus ça change . . . .'

In rare instances where the precautions taken in the vineyards fail to prevent an excessively dilute harvest, a *saignée de cuve* precedes alcoholic fermentation. However, this is considered only as a last resort – not even, for example, in 1982 was there the need to *saigner*.

Under ideal conditions, the pulp would come into the *cuves* at 15° C – the temperature at which Burgundian grape yeasts begin to ferment grape sugar. In years like 1989 when the grapes are picked in great heat attempts will be made to cool the pulp by natural means – e.g. mixing cooler morning harvest with the warmer afternoon crop. As Aubert de Villaine points out, pulp is far less easy to cool than juice. However, the *cuves* are fortunately equipped with internal heat-exchangers which can be used for cooling if all else fails.

Only natural yeasts are used for fermentation, with a *remontage* at the beginning to get them working. Two or three times each day, the cap is broken up by compressed-air pistons, which are more effective than the traditional expedient of human feet. Their power means that they can be used earlier, further maximising extraction and minimising the risk of acetification from a dry cap.

The temperature is allowed to rise to 33–34° C., with cooling where necessary. Since the aim is to have the longest *cuvaison* possible – on average 18–21 days – any necessary *chaptalisation* is performed in several small doses towards the end of fermentation. This must be done with care, since the added sugar must be fully fermented out to alcohol – it is not wanted in the wine.

The *vin de goutte* is run off as soon as the cap in the *cuve* starts to fall, indicating that there is no more CO_2, and thus no more fermentation. The remaining pulp is pressed in a new pneumatic Bucher press, tasted and generally added to the free-run wine. The pressing is very light, yielding about 5–10% in volume of the total.

No *débourbage* is considered necessary before running the new wine into casks, since the care taken to excise any unripe or rotten material leaves the wine with only fine, healthy lees. These will nourish the wine and help the *malolactic fermentation* to proceed smoothly.

The casks in which these precious wines spend the rest of their upbringing are completely renewed each year, a policy of long standing. It is felt that the advantage of eliminating any possible problems from older casks, which might impart a bad taste, justifies the considerable expense. Since 1979, when the surge in demand for French oak caused widespread doubts about the authenticity and quality of casks, the Domaine has secured its own supply of wood from the forest of Tronçais which is delivered to its coopers to be air-dried.

This is a massive investment – 300 new casks are needed each year and the Domaine has 2 harvests in cask at any one time. Since the wood takes 3 years to dry, provision has to be made for 5 years supply. In other words, this ties up the cost of 1,500 casks at around £230 sterling each.

Although there is no fixed policy on racking, Aubert de Villaine does admit that bottling without racking incurs risks which are best avoided. However, provided the lees are clean, there is little chance of *goût de lie*, 'goût de reduit' or unpleasant hydrogen-sulphide appearing in the wines. At present, they are 'playing with the possibilities' and examining the variables which determine the best moment to rack. Neither the 1979s, 1980s nor 1981s were racked – except of course to be unified and bottled.

In any event, there is never more than one racking which, tradition dictates, occurs in early spring, after the *malos* are complete. However, clean lees allow the Domaine to delay this to give the wine more 'fat' and complexity. At present the wines are racked

Aubert de Villaine

cask-to-cask, by gravity (all cellar movements following fermentation are by gravity), some 2–3 months before bottling. This is not a fixed interval, but something which is under constant discussion.

The Domaine's red wines are fined, but not 'since a long time' filtered. Although not completely excluded, Aubert de Villaine is strongly disinclined to filter. In advance of fining, which is carried out with customary care, Bernard Noblet is despatched to a local farm to order 900–1,200 fresh, free-range eggs – the fresher the eggs, the better the fining. The chickens having delivered, the whites are added 3–4 per cask and allowed to settle for 1–4 weeks.

The Domaine used to bottle cask-by-cask – the 'ultra-traditionelle' method. However, they concluded that the variation between different casks of the 'same' wine and even between first and last bottles from the same cask was great enough to be unacceptable. Since 1982 the wines have been unified in 5-cask lots – by gravity, as always, but with access to air – and assembled in stainless-steel vats before being bottled.

The Domaine's only white wine, a meagre 3,000 bottles from old vines on a precious 0.67.59 ha. of Le Montrachet – is vinified with exemplary care. According to Aubert de Villaine, 'the fruit from this vineyard is of very high quality', to which, no doubt, vine age and a deliberately late harvest both contribute. The Domaine generally harvests the Montrachet after its other vines, and is often the last to pick in that fabled vineyard.

The Chardonnay grapes are brought directly to the *cuverie* at Vosne-Romanée, pressed, and the juice immediately sulphured to prevent oxidation. After the lightest possible overnight *débourbage*, the juice is put into new Tronçais oak casks to start its fermentation (never, as has been widely reported, in stainless-steel).

There is no attempt to intervene to control the fermentation temperature – which rarely rises beyond 21–23° C. The wine is 'roused' 2 or 3 times each week, to keep the lees evenly distributed – a practice which adds richness and flavour.

Following the *malo*, the wine remains on its fine lees for about 9 months or until the time is deemed right for racking. This is performed by gravity, cask-to-cask. It is then fined with fresh, unpasteurised skimmed milk – Bernard Noblet being again despatched to a nearby farm to choose and collect this – 'almost direct from the cow'. After 3–4 weeks *sur col* – 'not too long on milk, it isn't good,' says Aubert de Villaine – the wine is racked clear and unified before being bottled. If necessary, it is first lightly plate-filtered.

The Domaine de la Romanée-Conti is surrounded by much myth and some absurd speculation. The intense, almost quintessential Pinot-extract of its wines has led some to the malicious and groundless conclusion that the fermentation is somehow stopped – it was even rumoured, with vintage port. The rarity and price of these wines has made them collectibles – Romanée-Conti and Montrachet above all. Recently there has even been fraud. One unsuspecting Japanese collector apparently paid $5,000 a case for 5 cases of Montrachet, only to find that it was counterfeit. His wine merchant refunded him, but the Domaine had the headache of tracing the source. Curiously, the alarm would not have been raised were it not for a simple mistake on the labels. Instead of 'Appellation Montrachet Contrôlée', the ignorant tricksters had put 'Appellation Romanée-Conti Contrôlée' – nonsense of course.

Few would contest the claim that the Domaine's wines are among the finest one can find. Their hallmark is an extraordinary finesse and complexity allied to a great concentration of and magnificent length. The care that goes into their making invariably results in virtually impeccable balance, and in fabulously seductive richness.

Each Cru has its own characteristics. The Montrachet is among the finest from that appellation with an old-vine concentration and a magnificent complexity which takes ages to develop. When fully mature, the depth and completeness of flavour are stupendous. As with so many really great wines, what leaves such a lasting impression is its combination of mighty power and thoroughbred class. If in 'lesser' vintages, the wine needs time to evolve, in great vintages it seems to need as long as its red stable-mates. For example, the 1978 Montrachet tasted in 1989 was still in its infancy – just beginning to show the honey and grilled almonds stamp of its origin, but in reality far from full throttle.

The 200 cases of the Domaine's Montrachet made in each normal year are fiercely fought over at ever-soaring prices. As with any rarity, price bears no automatic relationship to quality – a Chevalier Montrachet from Leflaive or a Montrachet from Ramonet would probably give DRC's Montrachet a good run in a blind tasting, at a fraction of the price.

For the Domaine's red wines, however, there is less contest. The Echézeaux and Grands Echézeaux might find peers worthy of comparison, but in great vintages the Richebourg, La Tâche and Romanée-Conti stand above all others. Their individuality is difficult to characterise – especially in youth when they can range from the depth and pepperiness of a young syrah to deceptively lean-framed liquids with mouth-puckering acidity. It may not always be easy to foresee what will emerge after a decade or more in bottle but one is rarely disappointed. In particular, in lesser vintages the wines often provide some most rewarding and enjoyable drinking.

It happens, however, but rarely, that the Domaine is castigated for one or other of its wines. Many, for example, considered that the 1975 vintage should never have appeared under the Domaine's label. Mme. Bize-Leroy countered that the wines were fine but needed time to show at their best. Those still waiting perhaps feel that in this case, at least, faith has been trounced by experience.

The Domaine's wines are generally characterised by individual aromas and flavours of spice – especially cinnamon – violets, sometimes liquorice, and often by almost, but not quite, over-ripe sweetness. This great concentration results in wines which take a long time to develop. After many years, often 20 or more, they lose their youthful awkwardness and transform into seductively ripe, silky mouthfuls – with the texture of slightly worn velvet. A 1953 La Tâche drunk in 1988 was a yardstick example of what fine Burgundy is all about – a deep, limpid, slightly singed black cherry colour, with a massive, yet understated, complex nose of *sous-bois* and over-ripe wild fruits and a complete flavour from front to back of the mouth which simply went on and on, ending in the famous Romanée-Conti marker – a peacock's tail.

Romanée-Conti itself takes this 'expression le plus pur du terroir' a stage further. Perhaps – although trying to describe these wines brings one perilously close to pretentious verbosity – a touch more elegant than La Tâche, but always with that supreme aristocracy. There is nothing obvious or showy about these wines – just essence of quality. Comparing the different Crus is futile – they are fine but distinct individuals, each with its own personality, each with its different origin.

Their fame and scarcity makes the Domaine's wines more tasted than drunk for pleasure as they were intended to be. The care that goes into them provides a yardstick and an object lesson to vignerons along the Côte who may be tempted to think that it is enough to have Grand Cru land, some old vines and a competent hand in the cellars. The Domaine's policy and its lesson is that there are no short cuts to quality.

For Aubert de Villaine, the monks who 'invented' the Côte, and who planted a mosaic of vines on its precious soil, rather like a window of stained-glass, are his inspiration. Those who try to imitate come in for some mild mirth – 'the gimmicks of wine-makers' who believe, as did the unfortunate frog in the Fable de la Fontaine, that they can mimic something greater. Putting 'Montrachet' yeasts to ferment a new world Chardonnay will not turn it into a Montrachet.

Aubert de Villaine and Mme.Bize-Leroy would be the first to admit that their wines fall short of the perfection that is their constant goal. Their own contribution is 'the most attentive, but also the most humble and invisible', to ensure that their wines are sound and free from faults and that this matchless 'terroir' expresses itself with the utmost purity. The intrinsic qualities and personalities of their wines rest, not on them, but on the mysterious fusion of soil, micro-climate and 'that génie of terroir' of which they are merely 'the modest and obliging servants'. If anyone is in a position to defend the primacy of 'terroir' in the production of great wine, it is the Domaine de la Romanée-Conti.

VINEYARD HOLDINGS

Commune	*Level*	*Lieu-dit/Climat*	*Area*	*Status*	*Av. Prod.*
Vosne	GC	Romanée-Conti	1.80.50	P	450 C/S
Vosne	GC	La Tâche	6.06.20	P	1500 C/S
Vosne	GC	Richebourg	3.51.10	P	1000 C/S
Vosne	GC	Romanée St.-Vivant	5.28.58	P	1500 C/S
Vosne	GC	Grands-Echézeaux	3.52.63	P/F	1000 C/S
Vosne	GC	Echézeaux	4.67.03	P/F	1340 C/S
Chassagne	GC	Montrachet	0.67.59	P	250 C/S
		Total	**25.53.63 ha.**		**7460 C/S**

NUITS-ST.-GEORGES AND PRÉMEAUX-PRISSEY

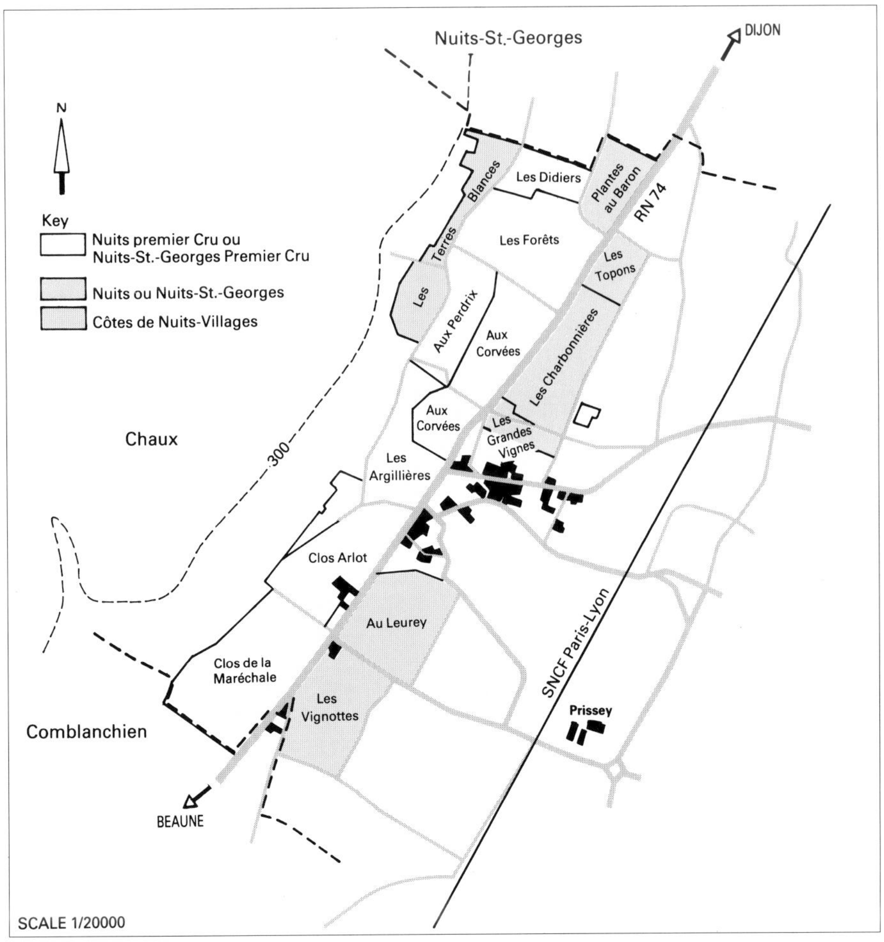

Nuits-St.-Georges is not the largest commune in the Côte d'Or but it is the longest. Extending for some 5 km. it joins Vosne Romanée to the north and finally peters out at the Clos de la Maréchale in Prémeaux, which marks the southern extremity of important vineyards in the Côte de Nuits.

Together – for Prémeaux has only the appellation Nuits-St.-Georges or Nuits-St.-Georges Premier Cru – there are some 175.32 ha. of Village land and 144.79 ha. of Premiers Crus. Nuits itself has no less than 28 different Premiers Crus and Prémeaux contributes 12, of which 9 are Clos. In 1987, following strong lobbying by growers, the Terre Blanche vineyard was upgraded from a *Régionale* AC to a full Premier Cru – although they had only asked for Village classification!

Nuits is an ancient settlement – recent excavations have revealed the site of a Roman villa – which developed during the Middle Ages into a substantial fortified town. In 1366 Philippe-le-Hardi, Duc de Bourgogne,

Prémeaux-Prissey

established a wine-tax to help pay for the fortifications, but in 1576, these were destroyed by the Protestant Duc Casimir.

Like many small wine towns Nuits is built on a river. No raging torrent, the Meuzin, which still tumbles down from the hills and runs through the town centre, has been tamed since it managed to burst its banks in August 1747, repeated in January 1757, flooding the surrounding vineyards on both occasions and generally wreaking havoc. Perversely, in 1788 it, and all the local wells, dried up completely.

Today Nuits is the commercial entrepôt of the Côte de Nuits. Some refer to it as the 'kidney' of the Côte, since so much wine flows through it. The diligent tourist is not kept idle: here are the large négociant houses, many selling much ordinary wine at extra-ordinary prices; here is one of France's largest fruit-juice factories; here is the 'fons et origo' of the cassis and sirop trade; here are shops and offices, trading and dealing and much besides. Here is a noted restaurant, an excellent patissier and a sixteenth-century bell-tower covered in ivy.

Away from the tourist's gaze, the town also boasts an attractive older quarter, with some remarkable cellars hidden by unremarkable façades. The square opposite the Mairie has been renamed Place Apollo XV since the astronauts on that mission christened one of the Moon's craters 'St. Georges', apparently after Jules Verne's Captain Anders who chose to toast his moon-landing with a bottle of Nuits. There is a Rue Fagon, with a wine shop in it, named after Napoléon III's doctor who prescribed a cure consisting of seemingly limitless quantities of Nuits, and the usual run of Avenue Pasteur, Place République and Rue Egalité. So far the town council has restrained itself from adding General de Gaulle, Winston Churchill or President Kennedy to anything.

After much lobbying in the 1970s, the Nuitons managed to persuade the builders of the Lyon-Mulhouse autoroute to put in an interchange at Nuits; this keeps unnecessary traffic away and has enabled them to tack a sizable industrial zone onto the eastern edge of the town.

The mischievous river Meuzin bisects the vineyards. To the north, Côte Vosne, lie some 13 Premiers Crus and Village land, at altitudes of 240–340 m. Here the soils are close in type to those of Vosne-Romanée, dominated by limestone and pebbles, with varying but small amounts of clay. The wines tend to have less of the *charpente* and earthiness of the southerly Nuits, and more of the finesse and elegance of Vosne. None the less, they are well-structured wines needing plenty of bottle-ageing to give of their best.

On the Prémeaux side of the Meuzin valley lie a further 16 Premiers Crus, including those generally regarded as the cream – Les Cailles, Les Vaucrains and Les St.-Georges as well as the excellent Les Pruliers. These vineyards are also on hillsides, with soils which are generally deeper and browner than those nearer Vosne, with a more even mix of clay and limestone. Les Porrets St.-Georges, Les Cailles and Les St.-Georges are planted on deep brown limestone soils, on a band of rock and pebbles which is a continuation of the marble quarries of Comblanchien to the south. Les Vaucrains, however, just beneath the forest above Les St.-Georges, has a shallower soil, often red-brown with a proportion of fine sandy particles and white oolite limestone, which often outcrops as 'tête de mouton'.

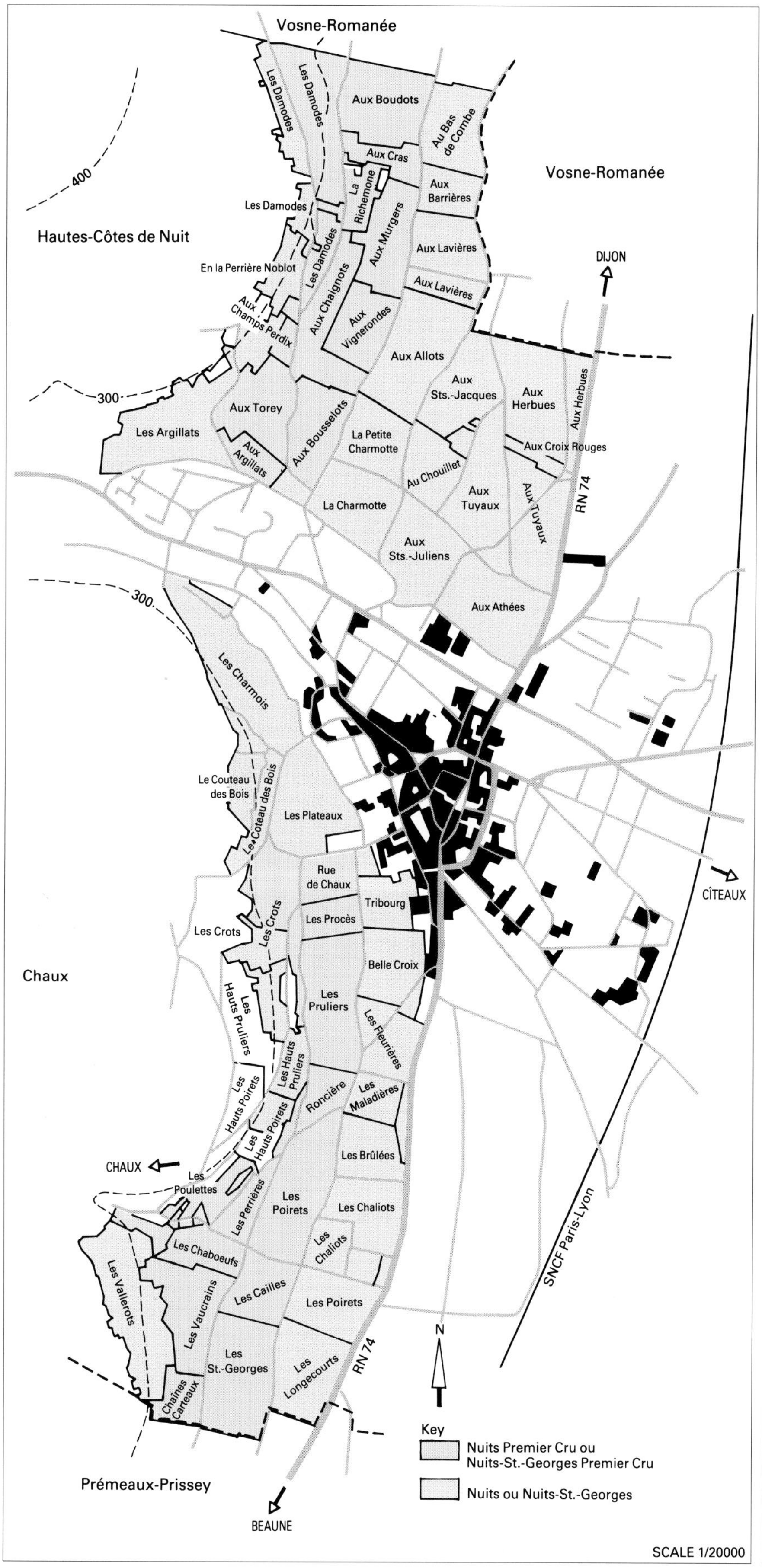

The 12 Prémeaux Premiers Crus occupy a narrow band of gently sloping ground between the RN 74 and the woods. Here are the Clos des Forêts St.-Georges, the Clos des Corvées, Clos de l'Arlot and the Clos de la Maréchale, all capable of producing superb wine. The soils vary with altitude, becoming particularly fine and thin between the Clos des Forêts and the Clos de l'Arlot with a limestone subsoil. Nearby Comblanchien is known for its marble – often given a pink tinge from veins of dolomite.

There is a trickle of Nuits-St.-Georges blanc mainly from 3 producers. Jean-Pierre de Smet makes a delicious wine from Chardonnay and a touch of Pinot Beurot from 1 ha. in the Clos de l'Arlot, Domaine Henri Gouges extracts an unusual example from a Pinot Noir blanc in Les Perrières. They are very different in style, the Clos de l'Arlot having greater finesse than the Perrières, which is sometimes rather flabby. Robert Chevillon also makes a delicious, mouthfilling wine from old Pinot Blanc vines.

The appellation seems to have caught the international imagination after the war – probably because it was large enough to supply a thirsty, wine-starved Europe. Much of what then passed for Nuits was deep-coloured, gutsy, hearty fluid cut with Rhône Grenache if you were lucky or with sunburnt Algerian if you weren't. The particularly privileged got a dollop of port superadded to give the British squirearchy a sort of gastronomic central heating.

Nowadays, although a disturbing quantity of dreadful 'Nuits-St.-Georges' still seems to find its way onto the market, the true quality of the commune's wines is emerging, thanks to the efforts of a coterie of excellent, conscientious growers. Anyone foolish enough to rely on the growers' maxim that 'a glass of night (Nuits) prepares yours', will at least be relieved to know that they are not tuning themselves up with the vintner's equivalent of 'electric soup'. A profusion of poor quality recipe-book wines has fostered the belief that quintessential Nuits.-St-Georges is elusive. Even the genuine article, with the usual wide variation between producers and the geographical spread of the commune, with concomitant variations in soil and micro-climate, has reinforced this impression. Many tasters, some pejoratively, characterise Nuits as 'earthy' or 'rustic'. There is indeed often a granular feel about fine young Nuits, beyond its adolescent tannins, which some consider detracts from its class, but these qualities rarely appear, at least in wines from the best Domaines, without a concomitant measure of complexity and finesse. Nuits may indeed have a touch of the maverick, but the robust charms of linen and denim are sometimes no less alluring than the soft elegance of silk and satin.

Domaine de l'Arlot

PRÉMEAUX-PRISSEY

The Domaine de l'Arlot was created in 1987 by the French insurance company Axa, with the purchase of the buildings and land from the Domaine Jules Belin – a decaying entity which had pottered along unhindered since it was put together by its founder, the son of a Burgundian 'Notaire', in 1891.

To oversee this, the first of their Burgundian interests, Axa appointed Jean-Pierre de Smet, an accountant by profession who had arrived in Burgundy in 1977, after 7 years running his own practice in New Caledonia, to help in Jacques Seysses' cellars in Morey. Jean-Pierre, an ex world-class downhill skier and a passionate yachtsman, had met Axa's Chairman Claude Bebéar, by chance at dinner, and discovering that Axa were searching for suitable vineyards, mediated the purchase of Domaine Belin.

The Domaine consists principally of two splendid *Monopoles*: the splendid 7 ha. Clos des Forêts St.-Georges, and the 4 ha. Clos de l'Arlot, a contoured block of vines bordering the RN 74 at Prémeaux, just outside Nuits-St.-Georges. In addition, a 2 ha. block of Côtes de Nuits–Villages – the Clos du Chapeau – and a recently acquired 0.25 ha. of Grand Cru Romanée St.-Vivant which produced its first wine in 1991. Three ha. of the Clos de l'Arlot are planted in Pinot Noir, the remaining ha. being Chardonnay, with 4% of Pinot Beurot.

The marriage of de Smet and l'Arlot has borne rich fruit; not however, without much effort. When he took over, the estate was in need of much internal and external restoration; in particular, extensive replanting among young and old vines alike and careful soil nutrient adjustments were necessary. Apart from the 1986 vintage still in cask, all that remained in the cellars were a few bottles of Belin's Marc de Bourgogne. Fortified, no doubt, by this meagre legacy, Jean-Pierre set about the vineyard restructuring, with the help of Christophe Morin, Jacques Seysses' talented 'chef de culture', while stonemasons set to work to uncover original brickwork in the *cuverie*.

The Domaine is run from a fine late seventeenth–early eighteenth century building on the RN 74 at Prémeaux, 3 km. south of Nuits-St.-Georges. The Clos de l'Arlot itself was created by Jean-Charles Vienot, a vigneron from Nuits, at the end of the eighteenth century, when he enclosed 4 ha. of vines with a wall. During the nineteenth century his son enlarged and reconstructed the buildings and laid out a splendid park,

Old vines in the Clos de l'Arlot and a glimpse of Prémeaux

complete with a maze, on land just behind the house.

Under its new ownership, a thoughtful thread ties vineyard to cellars – Jean-Pierre de Smet is a positive, careful and intelligent man who is firmly focused on quality. He is absolutely convinced that fine wine is made – or lost – in the vineyard. This means very low doses of organic fertilisers – the Belins dosed low from parsimony, Jean-Pierre from conviction – and investigations into the new 'biodynamie' – a sort of viticultural homoeopathy whereby any treatments necessary are in minimum dose, with preventive treatment being seen as less damaging to the vines than curative.

Much time is spent in pruning for low yields and in removing excess buds and shoots in the spring. In 1990, a bunch count was made in July and then pickers sent in to to remove any excess, just before the *veraison*. The vines did not compensate – as they tend to do if the operation is badly timed – but rewarded the Domaine with yields of some 32 hl./ha. – well below the average for this abundant vintage.

Great attention is paid to the harvesting process – Jean-Pierre oversees picking personally for the first day or two, making sure that any substandard fruit is excised. Rot, both 'sec' and 'humide', is the greatest problem; pickers prefer not to have the trouble of removing patches of rotten grapes from within a bunch, so they tend to get left to the vigilance of the Domaine's regular porters, who check each basket as it is emptied.

The quality of the raw material is matched by equal care in vinification. The foundation of Jean-Pierre de Smet's philosophy is that the more one knows the less one interferes. He wants a vinification which is 'le plus naturelle possible'. That is to say: virtually all the stalks left in the vats; minimum doses of SO_2 (as soon after harvest as possible); only natural yeasts; an ideal maximum temperature in the *cuve* of 32° C and a long *cuvaison* of 15–22 days.

Although fermentation does not in fact start for 2–5 days from vatting, no cold maceration is expressly sought. Cooling the harvest merely establishes the base point; the lower this is, the lower the maximum temperature during active fermentation. In general, one can calculate on a 15 centigrade degree differential, so it is important to start at a sensible level. Thus pre-fermentive maceration is considered as an aid to temperature control rather than a means of colour extraction. In his first three vinifications, including the abnormally hot 1989, Jean-Pierre has yet needed to cool an overheating vat; so the theory seems to work.

The high proportion of whole grapes encourages a species of intra-cellular fermentation, whereby the CO_2 gas in the vat starts to degrade the grape skins round it, extracting greater complexity colour and aroma compounds. Once fermentation is properly under way, the cap is trodden down regularly, by foot, to keep it moist and to dissipate any excess heat which might have built up.

After the new wine has been decanted and the wine from the first light pressing added, it is left to rest for 24 hours before being put into oak casks to age. In company with many enlightened Domaine managers, Jean-Pierre now buys the cask wood he needs 3 years in advance. It is inventoried, numbered and delivered to their barrel-maker so it can be dried in the open air before being used. Although Jean-Pierre prefers Allier wood, he contends that the manner and extent of charring each barrel is a more decisive determinant of quality than its provenance. A light, gentle, charring is his ideal.

Into these carefully crafted casks go 40–50% of the Premiers Crus and some 20% of the Côte de Nuits-Villages, where they remain for 15–18 months before bottling. They are racked twice, without pumping, cask-to-cask, and kept on their fine lees, provided these are clean, up till the second racking. The precise timing of each racking depends on how each wine is tasting. If a particular cask tastes *reduit* – a curious smell allied to a rather stale, flat taste – then it is summarily racked, by gravity, but with air, which restores the normal smell and flavour.

When each *cuvée* is ready for bottling it is fined, with egg-white or albumen – in 1991 Jean-Pierre hopes to use eggs from his own hens – and then unified and bottled direct from the *cuve*, without filtration. This is made possible by the addition of pectolytic enzymes during fermentation, which considerably aids clarification and obviates the need for filtration.

Jean-Pierre's approach is considered, but flexible – heuristic rather than didactic. There are no recipes, just as much care and as little interference as possible.

After just 3 vintages, the results are striking. The white Clos de l'Arlot is a remarkable effort – a 'vin blanc' grown on *terre à rouge* – classy, but with a touch of *terroir*, rather like an over-cosseted duchess who has taken a holiday in a mine and come out a bit dusty and with some of her refinement knocked off.

This transmogrified aristocrat is achieved by a broadly classic vinification – with the exception of a 4–6 day *débourbage* and the start of fermentation in *cuve*. As soon as it is heard to begin, the wine is racked off its lees and put into cask. A proportion of fine lees is then added and then the wine allowed to ferment naturally, with the help of 2 or 3 rousings a week up until around Christmas. The wine is bottled the following July or August, following a fining and a light plate filtration – this latter 'plus psychologique' than for any real effect it may have. Jean-Pierre has tried both fish fining and bentonite on small lots of his white wine, bottling and keeping the results. At present, he seems to prefer the former.

If the first trio of whites are any indication, then these will become highly sought after wines. Whilst each reflected its respective vintage – the 1988 being more structured and closed up in 1990 than either the quite powerful and concentrated 1987 or the more opulent and fat 1989, which had noticeably less acidity than its predecessors – they all evinced more or less open aromas of exotic fruits – especially of pineapple and banana – and excellent depth and complexity. One suspects that this part of the Clos has more limestone, since the wines seemed very well adjusted to their soil and not to have the rather tired, flabby structure of many whites which are grown, like some gardening curiosities, on inappropriate soils.

The soil upon which the Pinot Noir is planted in the Clos de l'Arlot is a mixture of limestone and clay. The vineyard is in fact just below a rock quarry in the park behind the house, and the earth is consequently quite shallow. The 1989 red showed a most attractive almost sweet strawberry nose in cask, and filled the mouth with succulent, ripe fruit. In common with many wines of that vintage, it is not a blockbuster, but has medium weight with plenty of power and finesse. A second cask was slightly more closed and *corsé*. All in all, a wine for 5–10 years time.

Jean-Pierre de Smet

In contrast, the Clos des Forêts St.-Georges was firmer and more structured – a bigger wine with more depth and density, and a layer of thoroughly integrated round tannins.

This general difference between the two wines carried over to the 1988 vintage. However, the comparisons ended there; the 1988s have much more muscle and tannic scaffolding to soften out before they should be approached. Both are long and stylish, with the Clos de l'Arlot having the greater delicacy at present. The building blocks are all there but they need time to fit together.

It is perhaps surprising to find wines of such finesse with virtually no destalking. It may be that Jean-Pierre considers that the act of destalking, twisting the vine wood to remove the berries, itself liberates 'greenness'; it certainly tends to rupture the individual berries and thus accelerate fermentation, making a long, slow *cuvaison* difficult.

Whatever the secrets, Jean-Pierre de Smet seems to be making a first-class Domaine of the Clos de l'Arlot. It will be interesting to see what another decade of maturity brings for the man and for his promising wines.

VINEYARD HOLDINGS

Commune	Level	Lieu-dit/Climat	Area	Vine Age	Status
Vosne	GC	Romanée St.-Vivant	0.25	18	P
Nuits	PC	Clos des Fôrets St.-Georges	7.00	25	P
Nuits	PC	Clos de l'Arlot	3.00	32	P
Nuits	PC	Clos de l'Arlot (Blanc)	1.00	25	P
—	V	Côte de Nuits-Villages	2.00	20	P
		Total	**13.25 ha.**		

Domaine Michel Chevillon

NUITS-ST.-GEORGES

There are two branches of the Chevillon family, both in Nuits. Michel, son of Georges, and his wife Pascale form one branch; his cousin Robert, son of George's brother Maurice, the other. Michel, a large, smiling generous-spirited man, runs his cheerful enterprise from a modern house in one of the many broad back-streets of the town. Some of his 8.2 ha. of vines, notably those in Nuits and Vosne, are *en fermage* from his father; the rest, all in Nuits, is either rented or share-cropped. He has recently bought some Hautes Côtes de Nuits which he has planted with Chardonnay, to have a little white wine in the cellar.

After attending the Lycée Viticole, Michel worked with his father from 1963 until he took full charge in 1987. One gets the impression that not much has changed here since the war – there may be a touch of modern technology to help out in difficult years, but the broad lines of vinification and style of wine have altered little. The old wooden *cuves* have given way to cement, although there is still a large oak vat in a corner in case of emergencies, and there is a machine to destalk the grapes, instead of having to do it by hand. A heat exchanger has been acquired, but 'we use it very little,' says Michel, smiling.

For his plants, Michel infinitely prefers his own *sélection massale* to modern clones, which he tried in the early 1980s in the Nuits Premiers Crus and rejected on the grounds that they yielded too generously.

The 1957 Vaslin press – 'the first Vaslin in Nuits' claims Michel, proudly – is still going strong. 'We can't press too hard,' he adds, 'because it has a circuit breaker which stops it going too far.' He himself is under pressure from the local salesmen to buy a new press but is determined to resist their blandishments: 'they tell me I can get 4–5 per cent more juice from a modern press, but – what juice!' he expostulates, screwing up his face and smiling.

The style of wine produced is deliberately old-fashioned, what Michel calls traditional: 'A bit hard to start with, but it ages well.' The vine age is not specially high because they had to replace many vines over the last 20 years which were planted on rootstock SO4 and which had degenerated. Short pruning and careful husbandry keep yields moderate and a *cuvaison* of up to 3 weeks, with 50–70% of the stalks and plenty of *pigéage,* ensures the wines have a firm enough structure to keep them going for several decades.

A Côte d'Or village well

The wine is put into cask for up to 22 months. Michel is not a partisan of new oak – so there is virtually none in the cellar. 'I like casks, but not new casks' is his dictum on the subject. Rackings are done in the traditional manner, a sulphur candle being burned in each cask to drive out any air before the wine is returned to it.

In years when it is deemed necessary the wines are given a fining – the 1987s were fined, the 1988s not. In case of fining, the wines are afterwards racked, kiesleguhr filtered and then returned to bulk for 2 weeks before bottling. Otherwise, the wines are simply filtered and bottled directly.

Michel and Georges used to bottle by hand, from the cask. Modernity has crept in with the acquisition in 1987 of a small bottling line, which speeds the process up no end.

This is a cellar where it is necessary to be selective; some wines are very much better than others. Tasting a range of 1989s and 1990s in November 1990, it was clear that whilst all the wines had a good solid structure, some lacked depth or finesse. Yields can be high – the 1990 crop averaged 50–52 hl./ha. – but Michel claims that he is quite prepared to *saigner* in vintages such as 1990 where the overall balance would benefit.

In general the 1990s seemed markedly better than the 1989s, as far as could be seen at such an early stage in their life. The Nuits Premier Cru Les Porets stood out for its complexity and depth of structured ripe fruit.

However, Chevillon wines are not really fit to judge properly until they have had several years in bottle. This was very clear from tasting the 1987s – a good Nuits Villages which will continue to develop well into the mid 1990s, and a rather better Premier Cru Les Porets which, although tempered by rather dry tannins, had some elegance and style. Those who so prematurely wrote down the 1987 vintage made an error of judgement.

Michel Chevillon does not have the range of his cousin Robert. There is no doubt that his wines would benefit enormously from a judicious ration of new wood and rather less time in cask. These measures would help preserve fruit and suppleness, the absence of which most often mars these otherwise good wines.

A Nuits Premier Cru 1983 demonstrated the quality of wine-making of which this small Domaine is capable. Starting to show some of the brown tints of age, the wine had a positive complex of ripe old *sous-bois* Pinot aromas, with a fine ample depth of mouthfilling fruit, peppery with hints of *fruits noirs* and spice, and a good long finish. A stylish wine, which if it can be repeated in the more recent vintages, makes Michel Chevillon a man worth following.

VINEYARD HOLDINGS

Commune	*Level*	*Lieu-dit/Climat*	*Area*	*Vine Age*	*Status*
Nuits	PC	Les Saint Georges	0.45	42	F
Nuits	PC	Les Porets	0.59	34	M
Nuits	PC	Champs Perdrix	0.34	18	F
Nuits	PC	(Crots/Bousselots+)	0.78	8–70	P
Nuits	V	St.-Julien	0.98	15–35	P/M
Nuits	V	(6 difft. climats)	2.37	18–50	F
Vosne	V	Croix Blanches	0.30	15–45	F
—	R	(Bourg.P.N./PTG)	1.81	7–32	P
—	R	(Hte.Cte.Nuits Chard.)	0.65	2	P
		Total	**8.27 ha.**		

Domaine Chopin-Groffier

COMBLANCHIEN

Daniel Chopin presides over one of those odd consequences of the fragmentation of Burgundy – an excellent Domaine that hardly ever appears on the international market. For years, 32 in fact, this friendly, reticent man has been beavering away in his modest cellars at the end of a nondescript back alley in Comblanchien producing superb wines to satisfy the appetites of a band of faithful customers, mostly private individuals from Paris and elsewhere. Yet it is only now, in the early 1990s, that the fine quality of his wines is becoming more widely appreciated.

When he took over the family holdings from his father in 1959 there were both vines and cereal crops, a true Burgundian post-war polyculture which produced enough to keep a family and, through diversity ensured they were not totally at the mercy of the weather.

With Daniel's marriage in 1957 to a Mlle. Groffier from Vougeot came some Chambolle-Musigny and Village Vougeot, and in 1964 he added the Nuits-St.-Georges and the Clos de Vougeot, bringing the estate up to its present size of 9.40 ha. Now approaching retirement, Daniel is gradually handing over the harder work to his son-in-law, Hubert Chauvenet – who runs a small Domaine on his own account, in Nuits.

There is nothing iconoclastic, nothing revolutionary about Daniel's methods – just a determination to produce the best he can. He is a Tartar for fruit quality: securing the quantity and quality of the vintage – 'c'est primordiale, ça,' he declares. The key is a rigorous *évasivage* and an uncompromising selection at harvest time.

It has taken time to persuade Daniel that there might be some benefit in clones. Although he largely changed over in the early 1980s, he is still clinging on to his splendid *sélection massale* by constant *repiquage*, at least until the vines reach the age of 40 .

He is not a deliberately late harvester: 'We don't throw ourselves in at the Ban de Vendanges, but pick when the degrees are there.' Daniel dislikes *surmaturité* and is never the last – nor the first – to harvest.

In the cellar, vinification proceeds along simple, broadly standard lines. 'A large part' (circa 70%) of the crop is destalked. The exact proportion depends on the state of the grapes and the style of wine Daniel is trying to make. The alcoholic fermentation lasts some 15 days in total – including 3–4 days maceration beforehand. The temperature of the *cuves* rarely exceeds 31° C and *chaptalisation*, when necessary, is carried out after it has peaked to ensure a long and even cycle. Like most vignerons, 1988, 1989 and 1990 were generally rich enough in natural sugar to need only the barest minimum of addition. Of 1990 Daniel was moved to remark: 'I would sign a contract to have a vintage like this to end my days.'

As soon as fermentation is over the wine is run off the *marc*. All but the final press-juice is added and the cuves are left for a couple of days to settle before the wine passes into cask. Everything of Village quality and above goes into barrel, whilst the *régionales* are vinified in large volume up to their *malo*, after which they are put into old oak.

Daniel Chopin has strong views on wood, the chief of these being that a wine must be already naturally well-structured to benefit from the addition of further *charpente* from new oak. Even then he allows no more than 40–50%, with a decided preference for Allier and Cîteaux, adding cynically, 'but the barrel-maker puts in whatever wood he wants.' He also regards it as bad practice to try to beef-up a weak wine by keeping it in new wood.

The wines are reared in cask for 15–18 months, being bottled no later than a year after their *malo*. The timing of rackings and bottling depends as much on tasting as on intuition or habit. Since most *malos* are finished by February, the usual sequence is a second racking in November or December followed by fining either in bulk or in cask (for smaller lots). Two–three months later the wines are racked and polished with a plate filtration before being bottled. Daniel is experimenting with no filtration – the magnificent Clos Vougeot 1989 was bottled direct; perhaps this will signal a cautious change of policy?

As one might expect with deliberately low yields and some patches of venerable old vines, the wines lack nothing in concentration and depth of fruit. In 1989 the Côte de Nuits Villages was a gorgeous mouthful of ripe, plummy fruit – nothing raw, but plenty of class and guts which will give immense pleasure if it is allowed the privilege of a few years cellaring.

Daniel's small production of Vougeot – as distinct from Clos de Vougeot – comes from the Petits Vougeots vineyard, just next to the Chambolle-Musigny Les Amoureuses of his distant cousin Robert Groffier. Here, 40-year-old vines give a wine of good concentration – from somewhat meagre soils with a predominance of limestone and pebbles. The 1989 is a deeply coloured wine, very soft and rich on the palate with plenty of attractive succulent fruit – a real mouthfiller; most promising.

Whilst the Nuits and the Chambolle-Musigny are both excellent examples of their origins, the Clos Vougeot is very special. The 1989, tasted just before bottling, was an extraordinary wine, very deep Victoria-plum in colour, a nose which just hinted at the array of aromas to come, and a mouthfilling mass of beautifully structured ripe fruit. What made this wine so exciting was its sheer density of flavour – one of those which has real 'fond'. It will need 5–10 years at least before it gets anywhere near approachability. Sadly it is all sold – the UK allocation being a mere 12 bottles.

If Daniel's classic vintages are superb, the others are no less remarkable. The 1987s are beautifully crafted – the Chambolle-Musigny and the Clos Vougeot were just beginning to show their paces in 1991 – both wines of real depth and genuine complexity. A 1981 Nuits Premier Cru Les Chaignots, tasted in Daniel's cellar in early 1991, was just beginning to replace its fruit aromas with *sous-bois* and a touch of muskiness; very rich and soft on the palate with plenty of interest and complexity. Daniel's Paris doctors and notaires are indeed people of good taste – and good fortune!

VINEYARD HOLDINGS

Commune	*Level*	*Lieu-dit/Climat*	*Area*	*Vine Age*	*Status*
Vougeot	GC	Clos de Vougeot	0.35	50	P
Vougeot	V	Les Petits Vougeots	0.40	25	P
Nuits	PC	Les Chaignots	0.40	35	P
Nuits	V	Les Plateaux	2.00	30	P
Chambolle	V	—	0.45	12 & 50	P
Comblanchien + Corgoloin + Prémeaux	R	Côte de Nuits	4.50	35	P
—	R	(Bourgogne R)	1.30	30	P
		Total	**9.40 ha.**		

Domaine Robert Chevillon

NUITS-ST.-GEORGES

Robert Chevillon is one of the most succesful wine-makers in the entire Côte d'Or. The succession of Nuits-St.-Georges which emerge from his cellar are among the finest in the commune; not the dark, lumpy, rustic concoctions which often appear under this much vaunted appellation, but wines of real depth and complexity, classy and stylish.

A tall, grey-haired and dignified man, Robert has the aloof air of someone completely secure in his own convictions about how things should be accomplished. 'A job well done' is what he likes to see. He is not someone who appears to court publicity – but seems to attract it despite himself – with an impatient manner which gives the impression that visitors in general, and those who might want to buy something in particular, are a diversion he could well do without.

Robert lives with his somewhat over-protective wife and one of his sons in an ordinary house in one of the many back-streets of Nuits. They rarely leave, certainly not for anything as frivolous as a holiday, content rather for the world to come to them.

There is plenty of evidence that this happens, in the form of a miscellany of press cuttings, in various stages of disintegration, fixed to a piece of pegboard on the wall of the packing room. Wherever the family name appears, it is carefully highlighted, although the import of much of the comment probably escapes them, being mostly in English, Swedish, Dutch or German, none of which languages they understand.

Although Robert stoutly claims that there is no history to his Domaine, he has produced an excellent pamphlet setting out what there is. This document consists of a map on one side, showing the *climats* in Nuits in which they have vines and, on the inside, a list of the various medals obtained since 1976 at the annual Paris wine fair. The middle page contains some Burgundian proverbs relating to the vine ('With good wine, good bread and good flesh one can pack off the doctor on his travels'; 'Hailed vine, smoky wine'; 'If there are more apples than pears, drink your wine, if more pears than apples, keep it' etc.) together with a delightful résumé of traditional Burgundian measures of surface and volume. The final page is the Chevillon history.

The atmosphere of 'no change' which pervades the length of the Côte is probably attributable, at least in part, to the fact that it is virtually impossible to find a vigneron whose ancestors have been resident in it for less than a couple of centuries. If by chance one does stumble across someone without this crust of antiquity, then there is bound to be an elaborate 'histoire' prominently featuring an in-law or other respectable relative to supply the requisite ancestry.

As far as it can be understood, it would appear that the current branch of Chevillons materialised from a largely undocumented mist of Chevillons, all vignerons somewhere along the Côte, in the late nineteenth century. From this primordial plasma there emerged Symphorien Chevillon who exploited vines for himself, whilst working as a vigneron and caviste for a local négociant. His land consisted of 30 ares comprising AOC wine, vin de table and 'a little cassis'.

Symphorien died at Nuits in 1926. His only son, Eugène-François, born in 1887, worked mostly part-time for local vigneron-proprietors up to 1912 before 2 years of military service, marriage in 1914 then 5 years of war as a bandsman. Returning in 1919 he took over the family Domaine, such as it was, and started buying small parcels of Nuits Premier Cru and share-cropping others.

Up until 1940 sales of wine were poor; so, being a competent musician, Eugène-François formed his own orchestra which played at local functions to supplement the income of the family, which by then consisted of his wife, Marthe, and 5 children.

Upon his sudden death in 1943, Marthe and the children were forced to carry on making wine and looking after the vines. In 1946 the vineyards were divided between the 2 sons of the house, Maurice and Georges (the father of Michel, Robert's cousin). Following his marriage in 1937, Maurice continued to add to his share of the vineyards – principally in Premiers Crus – acquiring along the way a couple of mobile stills to augment his income.

Robert was born in 1938 and married Christine in 1961. The history comes up to date with their 2 sons – Denis and Bertrand – both of whom help Robert with the Domaine. The two stills continue to function during the winter for the production of Marc de Bourgogne and Eaux de Vie.

The Domaine presently extends to 13.04 ha., all in Nuits, apart from some *régionales* and 10 ares of Aligoté. The list includes 8 Premiers Crus, 3.25 ha. of Nuits *tout court* and 17.50 ares of white Nuits. The vines belong principally to the family, but some are worked on a half-fruit share-cropping basis.

Whilst much of the vignoble is between 20 and 35 years old, probably reflecting the degeneration from poor rootstock and low disease resistance of post-war plantings, there are three magnificently old plots still in production: 1.18 ha. of Les Cailles of 71 years average age; 1.55 ha. of Les Vaucrains averaging 73 years (of which 0.25 ha. is over a century old) and 0.63 ha. of Les St.-Georges 71 years old.

It is an integral part of Robert's scheme to let vines go on producing as long as possible, replacing individual plants as they give in. With 10,000 plants per ha. and 13 ha. in production, there are some 600 individual vines which need replacing annually.

New plantings are on a mixture of standard clones, with young vines being trained *en gobelet* for the first 7 years or so. This enables their natural vigour to be restrained. A strict *évasivage* and green-pruning, when necessary, both before and at *veraison,* help keep yields down.

Robert sets great store by an intimate knowledge of his vines. He will tell you that the Roncières and the Pruliers always ripen first and that those vineyards nearest to Vosne have a tendency to rot, particularly lower down the hillsides, so that they must be picked first.

When one grower in a commune makes markedly better wine than most of his neighbours with comparable land, it is natural to ask, 'Why, how does he manage it?'. Intriguing as may be the question Robert Chevillon can think of no obvious answer – no gross differences in viticulture or vinification to which he can point in explanation.

There is, nonetheless, one practice which does set him apart from most of his Nuits colleagues – a markedly longer and slower fermentation. Believing that the extracts obtained in alcoholic solution – in other words towards the end of fermentation – are better than those obtained in aqueous solution – at the start of fermentation – he allows his *cuves* to macerate for 3–4 weeks, or longer, as in 1990. Pre-fermentive maceration he regards as no more than a passing fashion – rather like nouvelle cuisine.

There is not much restraint on temperature either – it is allowed to rise to 35° C before his serpentine heat-exchangers are put into action to cool things down. Undoubtedly the removal of up to 70% of the stalks contributes to higher temperatures; however Robert likes to leave some stalks in the vats: 'they are there for something,' he muses.

Chevillon Père et Fils –waiting for the flag to drop?

The wines remain on their fine lees until a second racking, without air, just before the next vintage. They are then fined, in cask, left a further 4–6 weeks *sur col* before being reunified in bulk, lightly filtered and bottled – a total *élevage* of some 18 months. Robert has a horror of contract bottlers – 'when I see the froth on a Chambertin . . . .'

Asking Robert Chevillon to account for the great finesse he manages to achieve in his wines merely provokes a verbal shrug of the shoulders. Perhaps it comes from the long *cuvaison*, perhaps from the slow, natural *malos*; there again, it may be the relatively small proportion of new wood (about 33% in rich vintages, less or none at all in others) or the policy of leaving a proportion of fine lees to nourish the wine throughout its *élevage*. Equally, the contribution from the sprinkling of white vines in each vineyard cannot be discounted – about 0.80% by volume. However, whatever the explanation for the exceptional Chevillon quality – there it is, year after year.

Before 1984 all the produce of the white vines went into the red *cuvées*. However, Robert now makes about 1,000 bottles of an excellent Nuits-St.-Georges Blanc from 20–30-year-old Pinot Blanc vines. The *must* is fermented in cask – no more than 33% new wood – and bottled without filtration after 14–15 months. The result is a wine of attractive golden colour, with a nose of honey and almonds and a firm, tightish structure; delicious after a few years in bottle, it seems to have the capacity to age. No doubt Robert has kept back a few bottles of the first few vintages to see how they evolve.

The Nuits-St.-Georges *cuvée* comes from vineyards on both sides of the village. The wine from the Prémeaux quarter has slightly less finesse but a touch more richness than that from the Vosne quarter; however, the two well complement each other, producing an harmonious blend with a finely judged balance of fruit, acidity and tannins.

The Les Roncières is a wine which develops slowly from a base of rich fruit, with moderate levels of round, ripe, tannins. The soils here are quite light and high in limestone, in a semi-sloping setting. Les Perrières, just above Les Roncières on the southerly Prémeaux side of the village, gives a wine which is always marked by its finesse with marginally more structure than its neighbour.

Les Cailles, which adjoins Prémeaux, has a deep, clay-limestone soil, which gives long-lived, solid wines. From Robert's 70-year-old vines, the elements of structure are accentuated – producing a wine of considerable depth and richness, with a buttress of firm, but not aggressive, tannin.

Just above Les Cailles is Les Vaucrains, which has a similarly deep soil; however, its high ironstone content seems to impart a hardness to the wine in the form of pronounced tannin and a big, angular structure. A good Vaucrains is relatively austere in its youth, without the round charm of Les Cailles or the finesse of Les Perrières. However, a decade or so in bottle moulds the wine into a less awkward, more polished item, which is well worth waiting for, especially in good vintages. A quarter of a hectare of Robert's holding is planted with century-old vines, which give his Vaucrains a magnificent, craggy depth.

The finest of the Nuits Premiers Crus, Les St.-Georges, adjoins Les Cailles, at its northerly boundary. Although broadly similar in soil type to Les Vaucrains, the wine has a much more soft, fleshy character, with plenty of plump fruit from 70-year-old vines. Robert's Les St.-Georges is usually as good a Nuits as you can hope to find – a big, fleshy wine, with bags of fruit and great concentration. It has nothing to do with the rustic offerings of less competent growers, but is a wine of finesse and class. Not perhaps the unbridled aristocracy of a Vosne-Romanée Premier Cru, but rather a well-covered courtesan who has gone in for a little body-building – and is all the more attractive for it !

Robert Chevillon produces yardstick Nuits-St.-Georges, with care and devotion. Not a man given to hyperbole or self-aggrandisement, but an industrious vigneron who thoroughly merits his exalted reputation. Perhaps, one day, he will allow himself the luxury of a short holiday; meanwhile he is busy re-tiling his cellar – to replace those worn out by 4 generations of Chevillons, not to mention all those unwanted visitors.

VINEYARD HOLDINGS

Commune	*Level*	*Lieu-dit/Climat*	*Area*	*Vine Age*	*Status*
Nuits	PC	Les Roncières	1.09	25–40	P
Nuits	PC	Les Perrières	0.53	20	P
Nuits	PC	Les Cailles	1.18	72	M
Nuits	PC	Les Vaucrains	1.55	70–100	M
Nuits	PC	Les St.-Georges	0.63	70	M
Nuits	PC	Les Chaignots	1.53	25–30	P
Nuits	PC	Les Pruliers	0.61	25	P
Nuits	PC	Les Bousselots	0.64	30	P
Nuits	V	(Various climats)	3.27	20–40	P/M
Nuits	V	(Blanc)	0.18	20–30	P
—	R	(BGO/PTG/Bourg.R)	1.57	12–35	P
—	R	Aligoté	0.10	30	P
		Total	**12.88 ha.**		

Domaine Faiveley

NUITS-ST.-GEORGES

The Domaine Faiveley, with 115 ha. split between an estate of 75 ha. in Mercurey and 40 ha. in the Côte d'Or, claims to be the largest vineyard owner in Burgundy. Until recently, it was not a House whose wines were widely known outside France; however, critical acclaim, especially for the 1985 vintage, has brought it into the forefront of that select handful of top-quality land-owning négociants who dominate Burgundy's export market.

François Faiveley, who took over from his father Guy in 1976 as head of the house, is the sixth generation to follow Joseph Faiveley who laid the foundation stone in 1825. Successive generations have each added 'leur pierre à l'édifice', literally and figuratively, to make the Domaine what it is today.

The firm is also related to Faiveley Industries, an engineering enterprise responsible, among other things, for manufacturing rolling-stock for France's high-speed train, the TGV, a connection of which François is justly proud.

He is an urbane man of enquiring mind, who brings careful deliberation to everything he does. Despite ruling an estate where size might drive others back into the comfort of their padded offices, he takes an active interest in the vineyards as much as in the cellars.

A fundamental tenet of the Faiveley philosophy is that the material planted is of critical importance to the quality of the wine it will produce: 'if you completely bungle a vintage, it's not dramatic, but if you bungle the choice of rootstock you're stuck with it for 50 years.' Thus everything starts with rigorous soil analyses; samples from different levels in each vineyard, down to 1m. deep, are sent to 2 or 3 different laboratories. The results determine any small adjustments in base minerals which may be necessary (they have used nothing other than organic fertilisers for the past 8 years) and also the rootstock best adapted to each vineyard.

Each year, 3.3% of the total vineyard surface is replanted. François is a strong defender of clonal selection, his somewhat picturesque argument being that if it is acceptable to try by selective breeding to combine the flanks of a horse which won the Arc with the heels of another which won the Derby, why not for vines which combine resistance to disease with proven quality of fruit and low yields? Having struck his position, he will then admit that he continues to use two-thirds *sélection massale*, the remaining one-third being a mixture of several different clones.

François Faiveley – head of this top-flight Domaine and Négociant House

In order for the vine to give of its best, it must have adequate nourishment. Like most educated vignerons, François Faiveley tries hard to strike a balance between famine and excess. There is no gain in stressing a vine to the limit at which it ceases to work and expires; nor is there any sense in overfeeding it to the point at which it becomes lazy. The fulcrum is not easy to find, especially in the marginal climate and among the multiplicity of unique *terroirs* of the Côte d'Or.

In the mid 1980s, François consulted Guy Accad on the management of the Domaine's vineyards. Extensive soil analyses then carried out resulted in the complete cessation of fertilisation in some *climats* which were found to be too rich in nutrients. Although excessive amounts of manure were used, without proper analyses, in the 1960s and 1970s, François believes it is also possible for water to transport elements from a fertilised to an unfertilised vineyard. The programme of soil analyses continues and Accad remains viticultural consultant to the Domaine.

Low yields are another obsession: important as are the rootstock and age of the plant, there is much to be done during the growing season to keep production in check. Even with short-pruned vines, a vintage like 1990 can still produce 60 hl./ha. – a third more than desirable. So further measures are taken in the form of a green-pruning, carried out with exemplary care as near to *veraison* as possible: first the number of bunches on each vine is counted, then the average number of berries per bunch. This tells the pruners not only how many bunches to cut, but which ones. The ideal is to remove the bunches least well exposed, generally those furthest from the trunk, leaving 6–8 bunches per vine. The result of these efforts in a naturally abundant vintage, such as 1990, is yields near or below the *rendement de base.*

The harvest is no less precise an exercise: 3 weeks before the expected picking date, grape samples are taken to measure sugar, pH and total acidity. This continues, with increased frequency, up to harvest. At one time, sub-standard fruit was eliminated in the vineyards; however, experience proved that this was of limited value, since pickers were less than thorough in poor weather, when most care was needed. So now, the cases of grapes are covered and taken to the cuverie to be sorted on a table. Up to 12 sorters, often including François, pick over each batch for rotten or unripe material as it comes past on a conveyor. He has also installed an impressive drying tunnel to remove excess surface moisture – only a step away from concentrating the juice!

François' natural anxiety at harvest time is augmented by the practical problems of looking after 200 pickers. In the evenings they are fed and watered, before retiring to mixed dormitories: 'I feel as though I am populating France,' he groans, 'c'est l'horreur'!

In the cuverie it is François' obsession with aromas which determines the vinification sequence. He would cheerfully have been a career perfumier if the family Domaine had not got in the way. As a well-travelled experienced taster, he claims that Burgundy is capable of the most aromatic diversity in the world and it is essential to preserve this uniqueness. As an afterthought, he adds Emile Peynaud's dictum, 'if it smells good in the cuverie, that's a great misfortune; you make a wine for the nose of the drinker, not for the nose of the person who ferments it.'

To extract and preserve aromas, the bunches are first destalked and the pulp moderately sulphured. The *cuves* are then left to a long, slow fermentation, with the mediation of their indigenous yeasts, without pumping-over. Regular *pigéage* helps to increase extraction, but otherwise the juice is touched as little as possible.

The over-riding principle on which red fermentations are conducted is that it is better to simmer gently for longer than, as it were, to microwave. If temperatures rise above about 26° C then cooling is applied to the enamelled *cuves* through a splendid system of external sprays, rather like a vertical garden hose. Fortunately, the cuverie was originally used for making cider, so the old cider vats are put to good use as water-reservoirs, in case of shortage.

Cuvaison is deliberately long – the aim being 3 weeks and the reality often longer, although the average is about 15 days – and *débourbage* short. Thereafter, the wine is passed into cask. The Domaine needs plenty of new wood: its Grands Crus have 50-66%, the Premiers Crus 33%. However, François entertains a healthy cynicism about the putative provenance of wood: 'if everyone who claims they use Tronçais actually used it, the forest would stretch from Lille to Bordeaux.' To minimise the uncertainties, he buys his Vosges oak at auction and has it carefully dried so he can be sure that it is properly treated – cut when the sap is receding and dried in the air rather than in kilns.

The wines are first racked and the SO_2 adjusted, just after their *malos*. Candelight is still used in the Faiveley cellars, as the wines are racked cask-to-cask – new casks to old to ensure an evenness in the final wine. After about 16 months the contents of each cask is tasted and any gross disparities corrected by racking the casks and unifying them in bulk – all by gravity. The wines are then egg-white fined and left *sur col* for up to 2 months before bottling.

The Domaine's Grands and Premiers Crus are invariably bottled direct from the cask by hand, without filtration, at the stupendous rate of 900 bottles a day; in a good vintage, more than 60,000 bottles may be filled in this way. Lesser wines are cartridge-filtered at a very high porosity.

François' concern with aroma – his favourite book is one on perfumes – is no less scrupulous for the Domaine's whites than for its reds. Vinification in both new (Vosges and Allier) oak and in stainless-steel precedes blending of the two components just before bottling. In 1990 3 casks of Bourgogne Blanc were vinified in new acacia-wood casks to see what style of wine they gave – a revival of a traditional practice of using Acacia for *élevage*.

Clearly François regards the production of wine as an amalgam of hundreds of details, small and large, each contributing to quality. 'The trick is that there are no tricks – just well-tended vines, small yields, cool vinification and not destroying the wine with filtration. What matters is the wine in the glass.' He greatly admires Henri Jayer, generally regarded as one of the most important influences on Burgundian wine-making in the latter half of the twentieth century.

Once in bottle, the wines are stored in the magnificent network of cool, ancient galleries beneath the firm's modern-fronted offices in the Rue de Tribourg. Everywhere there are piles of this and that, stacked in bins of various sizes, awaiting the moment of release. When the time comes, the selected bottles are loaded onto a splendidly Dickensian system of individual buckets on an overhead tramway and conveyed to the floor above for dressing and packing.

The Domaine owns some 35 different appellations in the Côte d'Or. Its sole white wine of significance, a Corton-Charlemagne from a parcel of vines at the very top of the hill in Aloxe-Corton, is vinified in new Vosges oak, with a single racking before bottling. Since François dislikes the practice of *batonnage* – 'a fundamental error – it oxidises the wine' – the lees are roused instead by giving each cask a periodic rolling. The wine tends to be well coloured from the new oak, with plenty of extract and a highish initial acidity. Rich in fruit, powerful and firmly structured but austerely masculine, it needs years to integrate and open out. This Charlemagne is usually among the best in the appellation. The 1989 in particular was a masterpiece, outclassing all the Domaine's earlier Charlemagnes. However, yields of 18.4–26.0 hl./ha. are pitifully small, resulting in 125–200 cases per year – hardly a glut!

Faiveley's red wines are a consistent and stylish range. François' love of 'parfum' shines through, occasionally perhaps at the expense of structure and length, expressing itself in elegant, seductive, complex aromas of great distinction. Of the Domaine's 7 red Grands Crus the Mazy-Chambertin, Corton, Clos des Cortons and Chambertin Clos de Bèze stand out – wines in vintages such as 1971 and 1978, of masterly build, extra-ordinary concentration and immense style.

In addition to the wines from the Domaine, which account for some 70–80% of their requirements, grapes are bought and vinified to augment the range. Whilst perhaps a shade less exalted in quality than the Domaine wines, these *cuvées* are usually sound examples of their various appellations.

François is working hard to take his excellent Domaine to the top and has made powerful strides in that direction. Faiveley now represents one of the best and most consistent sources of fine Burgundy one which should continue to set standards for both négociants and growers into the next century.

VINEYARD HOLDINGS

Commune	*Level*	*Lieu-dit/Climat*	*Area*	*Vine Age*	*Status*
Gevrey	GC	Chambertin, Clos de Bèze	1.29	30	P
Gevrey	GC	Mazy-Chambertin	1.20	35	P
Gevrey	GC	Latricières-Chambertin	1.21	20	P
Gevrey	PC	La Combe aux Moines	1.20	25	P
Gevrey	PC	Les Cazetiers	2.05	20	P
Gevrey	PC	—	0.55	12	P
Gevrey	V	Les Marchais	1.08	28	P
Chambolle	GC	Musigny	0.03	46	P
Chambolle	PC	La Combe d'Orveau	0.26	33	P
Chambolle	PC	Les Fuées	0.19	45	P
Vougeot	GC	Clos de Vougeot	1.29	18–25	P/F
Flagey	GC	Echézeaux	0.87	36	P
Nuits	PC	Clos de la Maréchale	9.55	25	F
Nuits	PC	Les St.-Georges	0.30	25	P
Nuits	PC	Les Poret St.-Georges	1.70	30	P
Nuits	PC	Aux Chaignots	0.73	30	P
Nuits	PC	Les Vignerondes	0.46	32	P
Nuits	PC	Aux Athées	0.50	22	P
Nuits	PC	Les Lavières	1.07	38	P
Nuits	PC	Les Damodes	0.82	12	F
Nuits	V	Les Argillats	0.53	10	F
Nuits	V	Les Damodes	0.70	17	F
Nuits	V	—	1.22	20–30	P/F
Ladoix	GC	Rognet et Corton	2.97	30	P
Aloxe	GC	Corton-Charlemagne	0.62	22	P
—	R	(BGO/PTG/etc.)	14.13		P/F
—	R	(Aligoté)	0.77	35	P
		Total	**37.89 ha.**		

Domaine Henri Gouges

NUITS-ST.-GEORGES

Henri Gouges is one of the seminal figures in twentieth-century Burgundian history. It was he who, with a small coterie of dissatisfied growers, decided to challenge the monopoly of the mighty négociants by bottling his wine at the Domaine and selling it direct to his customers. The first bottles were sold in 1933 and the stir that this caused brought a measure of enduring fame which seems to have done the Domaine's reputation no noticeable harm.

The Gouges make very fine wine. Their 9 ha. of vines are those which the present generation's grandfather, the original Henri, cultivated when he created the Domaine around 1925. Profiting from the financial slump of the 1920s, he bought parcels of vines which came on the market at advantageous prices.

Henri was a shrewd buyer. Confined entirely to the commune of Nuits-St.-Georges, his vineyard holdings were spread over 6 well-sited Premiers Crus plus 1.3 ha. of Village appellation land. Apart from a touch of Nuits-St.-Georges which has been bought since, the Domaine is now as it was when Henri stopped spending. Its kernel is the 1.08 ha. of Les St.-Georges, generally regarded as the *primus inter pares* of the Premiers Crus, closely followed by the 3.5 ha. Monopole Clos des Porrets St. Georges.

The supremacy of Les St.-Georges was recognised at the end of the nineteenth century when the village of Nuits – seeking no doubt to emulate the rest of the Côte and having but Premiers Crus, tacked on the name of its most illustrious vineyard to maintain its standing among its famous neighbours.

Although their supremacy among Nuits growers is not without challenge, Gouges continues as one of the best known names in the Côte. An unfortunate dip in the quality of their wines in the late 1970s badly dented their reputation, but this seems to have been no more than an extended aberration, and the Domaine is now restored to form.

When Henri died, his two sons, Michel and Marcel, took over ownership and running of the Domaine. Now, their respective fathers remaining in the background, the third generation are in control. Michel's son Christian and Marcel's son Pierre have been working together since 1970 and although they take joint responsibility for whatever is produced, Pierre is in charge of the vineyards whilst Christian looks after the vinification and commercial aspects of the Domaine.

Pierre has a deep feeling for his vines, and a strong interest in the geology of the commune. He is currently undertaking a study on the soils of each of the 30 or so Premiers Crus of this extended and heterogenous appellation, publishing the results in the form of a small booklet.

He will tell you that one of the most significant difficulties faced by Nuits vignerons is the constant erosion of the soil in the steeper vineyards on either side of the village. When it rains, the water tends to wash down the more friable topsoil which must then be taken back up again. Because the replacement is, perforce, somewhat arbitrary, the construction and composition of these vineyards is gradually changing.

In an effort to combat this, Pierre started experimenting in 1977 with a special grass. Planted between the vine rows, this Ray-Grass is designed to hold the soil together and provide a physical barrier to soil movement in wet weather. Apart from limiting erosion in this way, Pierre found that there were other advantages: such a grass-covering stifles other undesirable weeds and grasses, virtually eliminating the need for herbicides; it controls the vigour of the vines, especially young ones, probably by competing with their proliferous lateral surface roots for soil nutrient, forcing the important tap-roots to dig deeper for their nourishment, and also removes excess humidity, thereby reducing the incidence of rot.

However, there is a disadvantage in that, being perennial, its presence in the vineyard in spring brings an increased risk of frost damage, since the grass tends to hold the frost longer than bare earth. On balance, however, the Gouges consider that the advantages outweigh the disadvantages, and Ray-Grass is now a permanent fixture in a large part of their steeper Premiers Crus.

Pierre clearly enjoys finding new ways to tackle old problems. Studying the treatments normally applied to their vines, and being ecologically inclined, he found that by determining precisely the right moment to spray or treat any given malady, he could significantly reduce the number and dose of each type of treatment. In 1990 he needed 4 fewer treatments – advantages both to the environment and no doubt to the Domaine's bank balance.

The proximity of some of the Gouges vines to woodland enabled Pierre to try another experiment: using predators to deal with red and yellow spiders – a major vineyard pest. He distributed predators' eggs around the vineyards and measured the reduction in spider populations compared with untreated vines. This experiment only started in 1990, but results seem encouraging. The woodland was important since it eliminated the possibility that the demise of the predators resulted from neighbours' pesticides.

Pierre uses a mixture of clones and plant material from their own vineyards to replant – approximately 50/50 – since he is uncertain how clones planted now will develop over the next generation. Although concerted efforts are made to limit yields by pruning short – to 6 eyes – there are fears of both over-production and possible premature degeneration.

Much is done whilst the vine is growing to further limit yields. A strict *évasivage* within a fortnight of budburst removes any unwanted growth – shoots and buds – above and below the graft. Later on there is a 'taille en verte', the removal of unwanted vine wood all round the ripening bunches. This operation clears space around the bunches for air circulation and sunlight, concentrates the vigour of the vine where it is most needed and fortifies the wood which remains for the following year. As the branches trailing near the ground are also removed, it helps to reduce humidity and thus the risk of *botrytis*. It also acts as a sort of pre-pruning, saving a great deal of time the following winter.

Once the fruit is picked, Christian takes over. To start with he is very particular that the bunches are completely destalked, believing strongly that stalks in the fermenting vats bring more bad than good qualities

Christian and Pierre Gouges sharing a bottle – and, it appears, a glass

to the wine. The machine which destalks the bunches also removes unripe and rotten grapes before they are crushed. This is important especially in years with a high proportion of rot or unripeness, since crushing such material before removing it would contaminate the juice. So the distinction between a 'crusher-destemmer' and a 'destemmer-crusher' is not an idle one.

Fermentation, chez Gouges, is a somewhat individual process. Henri considered that more subtlety, finesse and fruit resulted from starting fermentation with his cement vats closed and thus full of natural carbon dioxide. He tried this in 1947 and the practice has remained. This is not a full-blown *carbonic maceration* as all the grapes have been crushed before vatting, but rather a species of semi-*carbonic maceration*, which lasts for a couple of days and is designed to extract colour. Thereafter, following a pumping-over with air to get the indigenous yeasts working, fermentation proceeds normally, rising to a maximum of 28–30° C, with one pneumatic *pigéage* and one *remontage* daily. Then the *must* macerates for 10–12 days at 20–25° C, to fix the colours and extract tannins.

Interestingly, one side-effect of the Ray-Grass regime is that the acidity levels have improved. Perhaps the grass roots are munching up some of the potassium excess which resulted from over-fertilisation in the 1960s and dramatically reduced acidities?

When necessary, the vats of younger vines, particularly in Les Chaignots and in parts of the Clos des Porrets, are *saignéed* between 10–20%; the older vines produce a more concentrated juice, so it is unnecessary to *saigner* them.

Once fermentation is over, Christian Gouges tastes the free-run wine and then tailors the strength of his pressing of the pulp to its tannin level. After adding the press-wine and after 2–3 days *débourbage*, the wine is put into cask where it remains until 3 months or so after its *malo* has finished.

The Domaine does not attach great importance to new wood for its *élevage*. Only 10% of the casks are renewed each year – one of the smallest proportions in the Côte de Nuits. Neither is the provenance of the wood of particular interest to Christian: 'People pay more attention nowadays to the origin of the wood than to the grape variety.' Fortunately, their barrel-maker is a member of the family, whose firm has been supplying them since grandfather Henri started, so they seem content to take whatever he delivers.

The first racking is cask-to-cask, leaving some fine lees to continue nourishing the wine. The following December, half a dose of egg-white fining is added to each cask and the wine left for 2–3 months *sur col*. Each cask is then racked – by candlelight – into a tank, to unify the different casks of each wine, and then bottled following a 'half-filtration' through a plate filter.

The Domaine also makes a minuscule quantity of white Nuits-St.-Georges from 39 ares of vines in the Premier Cru La Perrière. This is a rarity as well as a scarcity, since it is made not from Chardonnay, Pinot Blanc or Pinot Beurot as one might expect, but from a white mutant of Pinot Noir. One has to imagine Henri Gouges wandering through Les Perrières admiring his grapes – perhaps one warm summer evening in the late 1940s – when he comes across a few vines on which both red and white grapes are growing. Being curious, he decided to cut a single branch and try to propagate from it – perhaps this is the source of the experimental zeal of the third generation. The result is an unusual and delicious white wine.

Christian vinifies the La Perrière Blanc traditionally: fermentation is started in *cuve*, then the wine is put into casks – 20% new oak – with its fine lees, where it ferments at 18–20° C. It is roused once a week until Christmas and then left to evolve until racking the following June. After fining with a mixture of bentonite and casein, it is assembled in bulk in July or August and bottled following a light, polishing filtration.

Tasting a young La Perrière is a delight; it tends to have a moderately deep yellow-green colour, even from cask, and aromas variously of dried orange-peel and rather subdued exotic fruits. On the palate it is noticeably structured, in fact quite tannic, for a white wine, with plenty of old vine fruit (the vines are 40 years old), complexity and length. In particularly ripe vintages, however, it can become somewhat flabby and lacking in nerve. With age it often develops flavours more typical of a red wine, difficult as this is to imagine. However, finding the wine to taste, be it young or old, is difficult since each vintage produces no more than 120 cases.

The Gouges reds are fortunately more plentiful, around 3,000 cases per year. The Village wine is usually good sound well-made Nuits – much better than what generally passes for this appellation. The Premiers Crus, whilst retaining their Nuits characteristics, show up the wide differences between the soils and expositions of the various *climats*.

The Chaignots, from young vines on the northern, Vosne-Romanée, side of the village, tends to have a distinctly Vosne touch about it – more 'tendresse' and finesse with somewhat less tannin than the more quintessential Nuits vineyards. The 1989 in cask had a deep reddish colour, with touches of purple, a very fine perfumed nose – cherries, violets – with highish acidity and a touch of final bitterness, though good ripe fruit on the palate; well made, but rather four-square.

The Clos des Porrets, a *Monopole* situated in the southern end of the appellation, well outside the village, produces wines of a more 'animale, sauvage' character – quite spicy and high in acidity and tannins when young, evolving *sous-bois* and wild fruit aromas after half a decade in bottle. It seems to start all in fruit, but finishes with a more typically Nuits rusticity – in good vintages a wine to buy and keep for at least 7 years.

The Les Pruliers, from 35-year-old vines, is characterised by very mineral flavours: *corsé*, full, with sweet fruit and fine, long, beautifully balanced flavours – as with most Gouges wines, long keepers in the best vintages.

The Vaucrains, right in the heart of the Premiers Crus, just above Les St.-Georges, is the most typically Nuits of all Gouges wines – small yields from 45-year-old vines generally giving a deeply coloured wine, dense and limpid in the glass. The 1989 was closed up on the nose, but more forthcoming on the palate – ripe sweet fruit, good acidity and tannins, a beautiful balance,with no rough edges and considerable length. The concentration of old-vine fruit gives a dimension of complexity which puts it several notches ahead of the rest – except for the Les St.-Georges.

This is the finest of all Nuits vineyards, producing a wine of yet more completeness than the Vaucrains. Tannic, plenty of *charpente* and muscle to start with, developing ripe complexity as it ages in bottle. If there were ever to be a Grand Cru Nuits-St.-Georges, it would come from this vineyard.

Pierre and Christian seem to have responded to the justified criticisms of their efforts of the late 1970s and early 1980s: weak-kneed, dilute and thoroughly uninspiring wines, lacking in depth and concentration – probably the result of over-cropping. If one can extrapolate the trend of the late 1980s, this fine Domaine is returning to the top.

VINEYARD HOLDINGS

Commune	*Level*	*Lieu-dit/Climat*	*Area*	*Vine Age*	*Status*
Nuits	PC	Les St.-Georges	1.08	35	P
Nuits	PC	Les Vaucrains	0.77	45	P
Nuits	PC	La Perrière (Blanc)	0.39	40	P
Nuits	PC	Clos des Porrets St.-Georges	3.50	25	P
Nuits	PC	Les Pruliers	1.63	40	P
Nuits	PC	Les Chaignots	0.43	13	P
Nuits	V	—	1.30	30	P
		Total	**9.10 ha.**		

Domaine Machard de Gramont

PRÉMEAUX-PRISSEY

This, the larger of two similarly-named Domaines, is the product of a rather turbulent recent history which consists chiefly of 2 brothers and a quantity of pressure-cookers. The brothers, Arnaud and Bertrand Machard de Gramont, are sons of a career civil servant who, returning to Paris from Morocco in 1952, decided to set up a négociant business with his father-in-law, M. Dufouleur. His wife ran the firm until 1964 when she sold her shares in Maison Dufouleur to her nephews.

The proceeds of this sale enabled her and her husband to buy vineyards and to establish a Domaine in their own name. This grew until 1970 when the two sons took over the running of the Domaine. However, in 1973 the petrol crisis intervened and threatened to ruin them – prices plummeted to the point at which a cask of Nuits St.-Georges barely made 800 francs.

Fortune then intervened, figuratively and literally, in the form of Bertrand's new wife, Mme. Lescure, a lady who arrived munified with considerable capital, founded entirely upon the sale of 'cocottes minute', a species of home pressure-cooker without which no worthy French housewife appears capable of surviving.

Capital was injected into the Domaine, and some very advantageous land purchases made – especially just before the disastrous 1975 vintage. In 1983 however, Bertrand divorced the pressure-cookers, whereupon his wife extracted her large share of the Domaine and departed.

This left the brothers with some vines but no buildings. Bertrand took off with his 2.5 ha., which he still farms in Nuits, and Arnaud took his older brother, Xavier, into partnership and embarked on the work of reconstruction. Cellars, in the form of what seems to be a dilapidated set of farm buildings in Prémeaux, were bought from the négociant Charles Vienot, and a cellar-master, M. Louis Poignant, installed. Gradually vineyards were acquired; these, owned by Arnaud, his wife (née Bichot) and Xavier, now extend to some 20 ha., and at last things seem to be comparatively settled.

Despite these vicissitudes, Arnaud is a cheerful, optimistic and talkative man. His disarming bonhomie conceals, however, a determined search for quality; he is well aware of what fine wine is about and will settle for nothing less. Rooted firmly in his own tradition – 'I made my first vintage in 1963 and haven't stopped since' – he is critical of those who compromise, deploring, for example, those market-driven colleagues who make a Nuits-St.-Georges which is ready to drink in 3 years.

His own wines reek of tradition – wines made with muscle, to be kept for the future: 'We want to keep what is traditional and what is proven.' For example, the old wooden *cuves* are still in use – although Arnaud laughingly admits that if he had limitless resources he would buy a 5,000 litre circular stainless-steel *cuve*, with a double jacket for cooling – 'the Rolls-Royce of *cuves*', he explains, smiling.

For all that, his wines are lovingly tended. The grapes are more or less destalked – a recent and the only concession towards less tannin – and then given 'a fair dose of SO_2' – about twice the usual level. The pulp is not cooled, but the SO_2 serves instead to anaesthetise the yeasts and delays fermentation for a few days. During this period, colour and aroma are extracted into the juice.

The practice of heavy sulphuring was introduced at the Domaine between 1973 and 1975, when their oenologist was Michel Bouchard, who coincidentally manufactured and sold some 90% of the SO_2 used in Burgundy. At that time, he used up to 3 litres of SO_2 per tonne of grapes – 3 times the usual dose. This was well before Guy Accad appeared in the Côte.

Cuvaison lasts some 17–21 days, with temperatures rising to 34° C, and yeasts are added towards the end to prolong fermentation and ensure that all traces of sugar have been fermented out. There is plenty of '*pigéage* à la main' to maximise extraction from the skins and enzymes are added to help clarification – a process with which Arnaud is highly satisfied since it produces wines which are 'très brillant'.

The 18–24 months of maturation in cask are designed to minimise later interference with the wines. Fining is rare – 'you can kill a tender vintage with fining' – and only the lightest of polishing filtrations is considered, when it cannot be avoided.

Depending on the Cru and the vintage, up to 50% of new oak, from a variety of local and other forests, is used; the balance is composed of third- and fifth-year wood. Arnaud does not care unduly for barrel-makers – 'You must first mistrust your tonnelier' – and reproaches them for taking the convenient short-cut of kiln-drying their wood. Fortunately, however, Louis Poignant is himself an ex-barrel-maker, so the Domaine's cooper can hardly argue if a cask or two are rejected.

Although there is a common stylistic thread of opulent silkiness running through the range, the wines are individual and their quality uniformly high. Arnaud de Gramont is a vociferous partisan of late harvesting: 'when I pick my Nuits-St.-Georges, many of my colleagues have already made their wine,' he grumbles. This, and the extent to which each *cuve* is destalked, will contribute to its final character. For example, in 1989 the Chambolle-Musigny was completely

VINEYARD HOLDINGS

Commune	*Level*	*Lieu-dit/Climat*	*Area*	*Vine Age*	*Status*
Chambolle	V	Les Nazoires	0.30	1966	P
Nuits	PC	Vollerots	0.78	1969	P
Nuits	PC	Les Damodes	1.00	1955/60/66	P
Nuits	V	Les Damodes	0.65	1973	P
Nuits	V	En la Perrière Noblot	0.76	1974	P
Nuits	V	Les Hauts Poirets	0.64	1980	P
Nuits	V	Argillats + Fleurière	0.25	1981	P
Aloxe	V	Les Morais	0.76	1964	P
Chorey	V	Les Beaumonts	2.00	1945/58	P
Savigny	PC	Les Guettes	1.00	1945/74	F
Savigny	PC	Les Vergelesses (Blanc)	0.25	1983	P
Savigny	V	Les Roichottes	0.45	1974	F
Savigny	V	Vermots + Picotins + Planchots	0.75	1955/79/80	F/P
Beaune	PC	Les Chouacheux	1.00	1935/76	F
Beaune	PC	Les Coucherais	0.42	1957	F
Beaune	V	Les Epenottes	0.40	1950	P
Pommard	PC	Le Clos Blanc	1.80	1914/82	P
Pommard	V	Vaumuriens	0.35	1955	F
Puligny	V	Houilleres (Blanc)	1.00	1964/68	P
—	R	(Bourg. Rouge + Blanc)	5.00	1955–1985	P
		Total	**19.56 ha.**		

destalked whereas the Aloxe-Corton had only half the stems removed. Whilst the former was long with great finesse, with a nose of crushed strawberries and spring flowers, the latter was more tannic with great natural power and depth. It is admittedly difficult, with two such different communes, to isolate the contribution of differences in vinification. In 1990 all the reds were 100% destalked, so the comparison will carry more weight.

There are 3 principal *cuvées* of white – a Savigny Premier Cru Les Vergelesses – made from a mix of Chardonnay with 3% Pinot Beurot on marls which strongly resemble the soils of Corton-Charlemagne – a Puligny-Montrachet and a straight Bourgogne. Together, these account for some 10% of the Domaine's production.

Arnaud Machard de Gramont makes wines which are well worth seeking out. They need keeping, but are thankfully somewhat less massive than one might have found 20 years ago. It is to be hoped that the Domaine is now out of its period of flux and on unshakeable foundations. In Arnaud de Gramont's hands it has a deservedly promising future.

Downtown Nuits-St.-Georges – the vignerons' source of necessities and nightlife

Domaine Alain Michelot

NUITS-ST.-GEORGES

There are few growers who make Nuits-St.-Georges as well as Alain Michelot. Apart from a touch of Morey-St.-Denis and a patch of Bourgogne in Prémeaux, his Domaine consists entirely of Nuits, with no fewer than 7 different Premiers Crus and almost 2 ha. of Village vineyards.

By Burgundian standards the Domaine is distinctly young, having been built up by Alain's father between 1920 and 1939, especially just after the 1929 Depression, when good land was relatively cheap.

Sadly Michelot senior died in an accident in 1966, leaving the young Alain – fresh from military service and viticultural school – in charge. The Domaine, of course, had to be divided between him and his many sisters. Being the only brother, he was the natural choice to keep things going and fortunately, his sisters allowed him to work their vines *en métayage*, so the Domaine remained intact. He has since added 0.50 ha. of Morey-St.-Denis, 22.5 ares of Premier Cru Les Charrières and 28 ares of Nuits Village land.

The Michelot cellars, along with the Michelot 'esprit', are in the heart of Nuits-St.-Georges. An impressive arch, next door to the grand Mairie, gives on to a spacious courtyard, off which lead various offices and cellars. Nothing except 'Les Toilettes' is signposted, so pressing bells at random you might get either Alain's cheerful old mother, still in her dressing-gown at mid-morning, Alain, or what seems to be a firm of painters and decorators ensconced in one corner. The Domaine clearly has enough customers without wasting money on signs, which might encourage even more.

Sitting in Alain's orderly little office, one is aware of a man who is tuned-in to fine detail and is convinced that this is the only reliable route to quality. Although getting an appointment with him is one of the more taxing tasks in Burgundy, once obtained he gives generously of his time and expertise. A large, bear-like man, he clearly enjoys talking about his own philosophy in particular, and about the wisdom and folly of the region in general.

Once warmed to his discourse, Alain's mildly scholarly manner occasionally cracks and gives way to a gently cynical impishness. However, his intelligence and depth of knowledge make him one of the most articulate and well-informed sources of comparative information on vinous Burgundy.

As one would expect, Alain's vines are tended with loving care. He believes, to a

The Pinot Noir grape

limited extent, in individual vine replacement – as the state of each vineyard permits – but undertakes a systematic programme of annual replanting, trying to divide each parcel into 3 notional pieces to avoid undue dilution of the average vine age. He also admits that some older vines have been replanted in order to facilitate working.

When it comes to the subject of yields, Alain becomes positively voluble. He readily acknowledges that in recent vintages – 1988, 1989 and 1990 – his vines have produced an average of 50–55 hl./ha. and he has been obliged to send good wine to the distillery. He is happy to bring out colour photographs to show you how many green bunches he pruned in 1990, but is adamant that figures by themselves are misleading indicators of yield. In the 1930s, when authorised yields were laid down, only a proportion of the vines in any vineyard produced in any given year. Now, with clones producing almost predictable annual quantities, yields per hectare have perforce risen.

What really matters, according to Alain, is the yield per vine. If each of 11,000 vines per ha. produces 8 bunches, one has a total yield of 54.72 hl./ha. Whilst by no means excessive, this is well above both the permitted *rendement de base* of 40 hl./ha. and the additional *PLC* which brings the authorisation up to 48 hl./ha. in particularly productive years.

In short, Alain believes that in evaluating yields it is essential to take account of how and with what the vineyard is planted. In a growing season free of *botrytis, coulure, millerandage* and other quantity-reducers, fine, concentrated and complex wines can be produced from what might at first seem excessive yields.

Whatever the quantity of grapes harvested, meticulous care is taken in turning them into wine. An impeccably tidy cellar, generally a good sign – although the converse is not always the case – betokens an obsession with hygiene.

The bunches are 90–95% destalked – the stalks that remain help drain the juice through the cap – given a normal dose of SO_2, cooled if necessary, and then put into cement *cuves* for 2–3 days of pre-fermentive maceration. Alain invariably adds enzymes which help both colour extraction and later clarification, but does everything he can to favourise the work of the natural yeast population. If fermentation is slow to start, he uses a heating apparatus to generate 3 or 4 hot points in the *cuve*, which usually provokes the desired result.

His aim is to have a long, slow fermentation, with no obvious *coup de feu*. To achieve this it is necessary for the temperature to rise slowly to about 30° C. Thus, if you have to *chaptalise*, then it is best done in several small doses, both for completeness and to avoid a sudden leap in temperature. As he eloquently puts it: 'When you are cooking you don't put some ingredients in at the hottest moment.'

Each of Alain's 15 *cuves* are *saignéed* if needed, otherwise the pulp is left for 18–21 days of *cuvaison*, to extract the maximum matter from the skins into the wine. When there is no sugar left, the wine is run off, the pulp pressed and the resulting press-wine assembled with it. There then follows a '*débourbage* assez importante' for 'a good week', which is probably accurately interpreted as nearer 10 days than 7. If the *cuve* has a mobile ceiling it is put in place; if not, a layer of protective liquid paraffin is poured onto the surface of the wine.

This long period of settling is not so much a matter of improving quality but of buying time. Alain has only one worker to help him, and has neither time nor space to deal with all 15 *cuves* at once.

Sooner or later, the new wines are transferred into cask. The preference is for a mixture of wood from several provenances – in 1989 the cocktail was Allier, Nevers and Limousin; in 1990 the Nevers was eliminated – 'too rustic' – leaving Allier and Limousin, plus a touch of Tronçais. Alain tried Vosges, but abandoned it as making rather too discrete a contribution to the *cuvée* – he intends, however, to use some Vosges for the Chardonnay he planted in 1991 in the Perrière Noblot vineyard.

Alain Michelot – bon viveur and vigneron

The precise proportion of new wood depends upon the vintage. Generally it turns around 30–40%, although for some of the Premiers Crus, where there may be only one or two casks in total, the level may rise to 50%.

The wines spend about 20 months in wood. The first racking – 'never before September' – sees the unification of the various casks of each wine. Alain adjusts the SO_2 level after *malo*, but is content to leave the wine so long in cask before racking because it extracts more tannin. The CO_2 gas dissolved in the wine will keep it fresh and prevent premature drying out, and the long *débourbage* means that there are no large lees to impart off-flavours.

Once back in cask, the wines remain there until they are racked and re-unified in June or July of the second year. Alain dislikes fining – 'I am not looking to excoriate my wines' – and submits them to a simple polishing filtration before bottling.

As well as his passion for his wines, Alain is dedicated to good food, and much of the simile which seasons his conversation is taken from the kitchen. As his figure suggests, he is not a willing customer of 'la nouvelle cuisine' – thankfully now on the decline in France – but values the return to clearly stated, primary flavours. Thus it is with his wines – unmistakably Pinot, but with a rich aromatic panoply and plenty of guts.

Central to understanding Alain's wine-making is his view of what constitutes Grand Vin: in the first place Le Grand Vin can be very good drunk young, very good at 10 years of age and still going at 30 years. Youth, of itself, is not a defect. Secondly, it should be possible to see that a wine is Grand Vin although you may agree that it is too young to drink – for example, Alain enjoys drinking his, and some colleagues' 1985s, but admits that they are not really ready. Thirdly, there is little hope that a wine which is poorly constituted in youth will turn into Grand Vin simply by keeping it – Mozart was clearly a genius at the age of 7, and the 1977 Burgundies will never be fine.

When wine and cooking are under the microscope, women are never far away. Alain firmly believes that they, like the Pinot Noir, have their individual charms in youth and age. However, he is forced to admit that he prefers to enjoy the firmer beauty of youth lying on his holiday beach, with all its inexperience, than to contemplate the more mature pleasures of sagging sagacity.

Tasting, chez Michelot, is a veritable 'tour de force' of the commune of Nuits-St.-Georges. The individual characteristics of the various Premier Cru *climats* are very marked, and a striking education for anyone who dares to doubt the importance of *terroir*.

The vineyards on the northerly, Vosne-Romanée, side of the village, Aux Chaignots, La Richemone and the Premier Cru section of La Perrière Noblot have a highish proportion of clay in their soils. The Richemone, whilst by no means lacking in depth and structure, has more finesse and precision of flavour than the Chaignots which is below it, and has a higher clay content in its soil which gives more densely-packed wine, with more *charpente*. Perhaps the difference is to be accounted for, in part, by the higher gravel content and elevation of La Richemone. Both these wines have a Vosne-ish elegance in common; this, combined with an underlying Nuits richness, gives them a schizophrenic, but most attractive balance of characteristics.

On the southerly, Prémeaux, side of the town lie Les Vaucrains, Les Poirets, Les Cailles and Les St.-Georges. These have more ferruginous soils and produce wines which are distinctly more typically Nuits. Often a touch rustic, with plenty of tannic muscle and youthful power, they go supremely well with highly flavoured game and red-meat dishes and develop well over 10–20 years. Whilst the Les St.-Georges is probably the finest of all the Nuits Premiers Crus in Alain Michelot's hands, the Poirets, Vaucrains and Cailles are masterly wines. Les Poirets, between Les Cailles and Les Roncières, just below Les Perrières, has a relatively deep bed of clay soil, giving wine which is tannic and powerful to begin with and rather less harmonious than its 'Côté Vosne' brethren. It needs plenty of time to integrate and give of its best.

Alain's Vaucrains has plenty of depth and really warming concentration in a good vintage. The 1989 was just beginning in 1991 to develop a fine somewhat 'sauvage' nose and had bags of stuffing and concentrated fruit underneath its youthful tannins. The soil is predominantly stony with red clay but with a low iron content.

With such a fine range of wines it is hardly surprising that Alain Michelot has more customers than stock. Sadly, prevailing vineyard prices seem unlikely to alter that state of affairs, so suppliants will continue to be disappointed.

This small inconvenience does nothing to diminish Alain's 'joie de vivre'. He eats and drinks well and often, and occasionally hunts for the pot. One sphere, however, in which he has had no influence is on the eventual succession: he has 3 daughters ranging in age from 14 to 20. Apparently there is a Michelot gene which favours girls – his cousin Bernard Michelot has 3 daughters and he himself was the only boy among several sisters.

If you do feel like jumping the Michelot queue, it is worth noting that he tastes widely, and has a particular weakness for Sauternes and syrah – alternatively, you could wait and marry one of the daughters!

VINEYARD HOLDINGS

Commune	*Level*	*Lieu-dit/Climat*	*Area*	*Vine Age*	*Status*
Nuits	PC	Les St.-Georges	0.20	1978	M
Nuits	PC	Les Vaucrains	0.68	1971/83/88	P
Nuits	PC	Les Cailles	0.88	1938/1968	M
Nuits	PC	Les Poirets	0.55	1935/1983	M
Nuits	PC	Les Chaignots	0.38	1960/1980	P
Nuits	PC	La Richemone	0.56	1930/72/80	M
Nuits	PC & V	Aux Champs Perdrix	0.53	1936	P
Nuits	PC & V	En la Perrière Noblot	0.50	1991	P
Nuits	V	(Various climats)	1.35	1957–1989	P/M
Nuits	V	Les Belles Croix	0.46	1944–1978	P/M
Morey	PC	Les Charrières	0.22	1982	P
Morey	V	Les Cognées	0.28	1964	P
Nuits/ Prémeaux	R	—	0.90	1968/71/83	P/M
		Total	**6.59 ha.**		

Domaine Thomas-Moillard

NUITS-ST.-GEORGES

Looking at the vineyards owned by this family Domaine, one is struck both by the breadth of the estate and the size of some of the individual plots. For example, there are no fewer than 7 Grands Crus, nearly 3 ha. of Vosne-Romanée Premier Cru Les Malconsorts, over 4 ha. of Nuits Premier Cru Clos de Thorey and more than 2 ha. of arguably the best Beaune Premier Cru – Les Grèves.

The current head of the house is Yves Thomas. For a man approaching the age when most people would be contemplating retirement, he is forthright and determined with a lively mind and a distinct enthusiasm for inventing things.

In parallel with the Domaine, which produces some 17,000 cases annually, there is a substantial négociant business producing 7–8 million bottles. Although all the Domaine's wines are vinified by the same team, *élevage* and bottling for Domaine and négoce are, as French law requires, kept physically separate.

The Domaine is unusual in that most of its vineyards are cultivated on a share-cropping basis. Yves Thomas is convinced that they are much better looked after in this way than if tended by directly employed vignerons, since the *métayer* has a financial interest in the crop. Since the Moillard vineyards are so fine, there is no difficulty in attracting the finest vignerons along the Côte to take contracts. The Domaine has a policy of regular consultation with its vignerons, and although major disagreements seem rare, has the last word in case of dispute.

Although in theory each vigneron is entitled to half the crop, Moillard invariably buys out his share – at top prices – thus retaining 100% of the production. 'The vignerons of Burgundy,' Yves will tell you, 'are usually excellent vignerons but not always very good wine-makers.'

Apart from their recently acquired 2.5 ha. of Bourgogne Blanc at Villars-Fontaine, the Domaine's only white wine is a Corton-Charlemagne from 23 ares of 45-year-old vines. It is fermented in cask, of which 30% are new, at 18–21°C with plenty of *batonnage* up to about Christmas to give 'gras' and resistance to oxidation. The wine used to spend 2 years in wood, but this has now been shortened to 1 year.

The moment of bottling does not, surprisingly for a Domaine which professes itself dedicated to quality, depend on how the wine is tasting. 'Good heavens, no,' exclaims Yves, 'we don't have the time,' adding cynically that 'people want a wine with a young taste and an old vintage on the label.'

With such a range and volume of red wines, Yves is in his element as an experimenter and inventor. Although the wines are in the charge of Moillard's resident oenologist, he likes to know why things happen as they do, particularly if they catch his imagination. He has recently taken an interest in stalks and instituted experiments to evaluate their contribution to red wine. After exhaustive tests, he has concluded that they add nothing whatsoever 'except greenness'. So the Domaine's red grapes are now thoroughly destemmed before vatting.

As well as his experiments, Yves claims to be the inventor of the revolving *cuve*, which is used for any of the Domaine's wines where there is less than 3,500/4,000 litres of juice – not just the *régionales*. This device, as distinct from the *cuves* which actually turn during fermentation – 'they are no good,' says Yves – remains still but rotating arms which turn constantly at 2–3 turns per minute, uninfluenced by the volume of pulp in the *cuve*. Two turns per day give wines with maximum extraction without loss of alcohol.

The wines that are vinified in the classical manner have a *cuvaison* of 10–11 days, whereas the 'roto' wines need only one-third of that time – which leads Yves to surmise that, in red vinification, it is not the total duration of *cuvaison* which counts but the number of *pigéages*. Although the Domaine has had 'roto' wines rejected for their respective appellations, Yves seems enthusiastically happy with his invention.

The Domaine's red wines are reared in cask, of which about 30% are new – 'you mustn't exaggerate,' cautions Yves. Once casks are mentioned he becomes highly animated: 'they are a waste – casks,' he exclaims. What concerns him is the amount of precious forest needed to make a Burgundian barrel – one cubic metre of wood for 3 casks – which is generally thrown out after a few years' use. Putting his ever agile mind to the problem he has come up with a solution to this profligacy – the square cask.

However vinified, the Moillard Domaine reds spend some 18 months in wood before bottling. The *élevage* is however somewhat unusual in that at the second racking in June or July of the first year, the wines are assembled in tank and fined. Yves puts all his reds through 2 separate and long finings. The agent used is also unusual for reds, a fish fining made from the swim-bladders of sturgeons chosen because it takes out any particles in suspension, without removing too much tannin.

Yves does not seem clear why his wines need 6 months fining – all he says is that it has traditionally been this way, and he does not like experiments!

The Moillard reds are good, stylish wines – generally on the masculine side of their respective appellations. They might be improved by eliminating routine kieselguhr filtration and by taking back bottling from an outside contractor. Nonetheless, this is a reliable source of fine Burgundy, and one which deserves greater recognition.

VINEYARD HOLDINGS

Commune	*Level*	*Lieu-dit/Climat*	*Area*	*Vine Age*	*Status*
Vosne	GC	Romanée St.-Vivant	0.17	30	P
Vosne	PC	Les Beaumonts	0.94	50	P
Vosne	PC	Les Malconsorts	2.94	40	P
Gevrey	GC	Chambertin	0.05	30	P
Gevrey	GC	Chambertin Clos de Bèze	0.24	20	P
Vougeot	GC	Clos de Vougeot	0.60	25	P
Aloxe	GC	Corton, Clos du Roi	0.84	20	P
Aloxe	GC	Corton-Charlemagne	0.23	45	P
Chambolle	GC	Bonnes Mares	0.15	30	P
Beaune	PC	Les Grèves	2.20	20	P
Nuits	PC	Clos de Thorey	4.12	40	P
Nuits	PC	Clos des Grandes Vignes	2.12	30	P
Nuits	PC	Les Porrets St.-Georges	0.54	35	P
Nuits	PC	La Richemone	0.91	25	P
Nuits	PC	Les Murgers	0.17	15	P
Nuits	V	St.-Julien	0.58	30	P
Nuits	V	Les Charmottes	0.75	30	P
Concoeur	R	(Hte.Cte. de Nuits, R)	14.45	5	P/F
Villars	R	(Hte.Cte. de Nuits, W)	2.50	5	F
		Total	**34.50 ha.**		

Domaine Daniel Rion

PRÉMEAUX-PRISSEY

The international profile of this Domaine is high, largely due to Patrice Rion, son of the founder Daniel, who has made the wines since 1979. As one of the 'bande' of what is increasingly seen as the new generation of Côte d'Or vignerons, he seems to exemplify a sort of Platonic 'Universal' of a Burgundian wine-maker.

Traditional *sélection massale* from his grandfather's Les Chaumes vines gives Patrice excellent plant material for the *repiquage* he prefers. There has been no major replanting for 16 years except for 2.5 ha. of Chardonnay in the Hautes Côtes, planted in 1991 with a mixture of 5 different clones to see what quality they give.

Down on the Côtes, vine foliage is spread as high as possible to give maximum exposure to the summer sun; they even put larger wheels on their tractor to raise the height of the summer prunings, when top and side leaves are trimmed off. In years of drought this is most important; in wetter years, they can trim tighter.

Knowing the vines enables Patrice to determine when each parcel will be at optimum ripeness and thus plan his harvest. Though seeking maximum sugar levels, he regards over-maturity as undesirable as under-ripeness.

Whilst vinification is relatively straight-forward, it does include one or two idiosyncrasies. For example, in order to achieve a period of cool pre-fermentive maceration, to extract colour and aromas, the pulp is not expressly cooled; rather Patrice keeps all the vats etc. as clean as possible in the belief that this, of itself, will delay the onset of fermentation if the grapes arrive too hot at the cuverie.

Secondly, the vats are yeasted, but only towards the end of fermentation. Patrice reasons that the indigenous yeasts are fine for the initial phases, but lack the power to control the fermentation to the end. So after 4 or 5 days, cultured yeasts are added.

Fermentation is kept within a narrow temperature band – 31.5–32.5 °C. Above this, according to Patrice, the wines become vulgar and lack finesse; below 31.5° C they gain in finesse at the expense of body and structure.

On average, 80% of the harvest is destalked in healthy years – 1988, 1989 and 1990 – and 100% when rot is present – 1983, 1984 and 1986. Stalks are left not for their tannin contribution, but as anti-oxidants, green wood tannin fixing the oxidases naturally present in grape pulp.

Patrice Rion's house

Patrice and his father give considerable thought to the duration of *cuvaison*. An important factor in that decision is the ratio of solids to juice in the *cuves*. The ideal is about 25% solids to 75% liquid; this can support a longer *cuvaison* (about 18 days) whereas less favourable proportions (e.g. the 40 : 60 solids : liquid achieved in 1990) perform better with only 11 or so days in *cuve*.

After 2–3 days *débourbage* Rion's wines are put into casks – 20% new wood for the Villages, 30% for the Vosne Premiers Crus, 40% for the Nuits Premiers Crus and 50% for the Domaine's only Grand Cru, Clos de Vougeot. These proportions vary little with the vintage since Patrice believes that they are somehow absolutely right for each category of wine.

After the *malos* have finished, the wines are generally left on their lees for 2–3 months; although this brings an attendant risk of increased *volatile acidity*, Patrice is certain that it adds complexity. If a *cuve* should go above an acceptable level of VA there is a simple expedient to put it right: filter straight after the *malo*. One doubtful of 1983 was treated in this way and pronounced to be one of the best of the vintage.

Following the first racking in April or May after the vintage the wines are left a further 10–12 months in cask before fining with fresh egg-white. They remain 1–3 months *sur col* before unification in bulk and bottling without filtration.

Tasting both old and young wines, one is aware of a wide variation in quality – some excellent successes and some good, but rather dull wines which just fail to sing. There is a general tendency towards wines which are austere and dry, lacking in obvious charm, and uncompromisingly masculine. This is not just a matter of one or two vineyards which under-perform, or of mediocrity in a less good vintage – there is no pattern. Some notable 1985s were followed by some frankly rather disappointing 1986s and 1987s.

That said, there are some fine 1989s and 1990s in the pipe-line: the Nuits Vignesrondes 1989 from mostly 45-year-old vines on the Vosne-Romanée side of the commune has good depth and plenty of guts which need 3–5 years to integrate.

The 1989 Vosne-Romanée Les Chaumes is also promising; the vines, planted in 1930, give a wine of ripe concentration, silkier than the Nuits, with perhaps a note more class.

Of the 1990s, the Nuits Les Argillières stands out – a wine of great concentration with a firm bed of tannins which will take time to round out. Patrice considers this is the finest Argillières he has ever made.

This is an estate whose wines although conscientiously made are something of an acquired taste. A Domaine to taste carefully and to follow, if the style appeals.

VINEYARD HOLDINGS

Commune	*Level*	*Lieu-dit/Climat*	*Area*	*Vine Age*	*Status*
Vougeot	GC	Clos de Vougeot	0.73	1945	M
Chambolle	V	Les Beaux Bruns	0.33	1975/78	P
Vosne	PC	Les Chaumes	0.42	1930	P
Vosne	PC	Les Beaux Monts	1.08	1970	P
Vosne	V	Les Hauts Beaux Monts	1.16	1972	P
Vosne	V	Les Ravioles	0.70	1956	P
Nuits	PC	Les Vignes Rondes	0.46	1945/1972	P
Nuits	PC	Clos des Argillières	0.72	1955	P
Nuits	PC	Les Hauts Pruliers	0.42	1962	P
Nuits	PC	Terres Blanches	0.56	1959	P
Nuits	V	(Various climats)	2.50	1940/45/65	P
Nuits	R	Côte de Nuits-Villages	1.51	1950/1966	P
Nuits	R	(Bourg.Pinot PTG)	3.09	1955-1980	P
Nuits	R	(Bourg.Chard./Aligoté)	0.88	1901-1985	P
		Total	**14.56 ha.**		

Magny-Les-Villers
MAGNY-LES-VILLERS
DIJON
CORGOLOIN
CÎTEAUX
CHOREY-LÈS-BEAUNE
BEAUNE
Pernand-Vergelesses
Pernand-Vergelesses
Chorey-lès-Beaune
Chorey-lès-Beaune
Hautes-Côtes de Beaune
SNCF Paris-Lyon
RN 74
Le Corton
Les Renardes
Le Clos du Roi
Les Bressandes
Le Charlemagne
Les Pougets
Les Languettes
Les Perrières
Les Grèves
Les Chaumes
Les Chaumes et la Voierosse
La Vigne au Saint
Les Fiètres
Les Fournières
Les Chaillots
Les Valozières
Les Paulands
Les Maréchaudes
Le Clos des Maréchaudes
Les Vergennes
La Toppe au Vert
La Coutière
Les Grandes Lolières
Les Petites Lolières
Les Mourottes
Le Rognet et Corton
Le Village
Les Meix
Les Combes
Les Guérets
Les Vercots
Les Petits Vercots
La Toppe Marteneau
Les Citernes
Les Genevrières et le Suchot
Les Brunettes et Planchots
Les Cras
La Boulotte
Boulmeau
Les Caillettes
Les Bruyères
Les Morais
Les Crapousnets
Les Boutières
Ladoix
Clos Royer
Les Champs Rammes
Clos de Chagnots
Les Chagnots
Les Combottes
Sur les Forêts
La Butte
Les Forêts
Les Toppes Coiffées
Le Seuriat
Buisson
Les Issards
Les Barres
Les Ranches
Champ Pussuet
La Micaude
Les Madonnes
La Mort
Vigne Adaim
La Corvée
La Corvée Basse
La Toppe d'Abignon
Le Clou d'Orge
Les Buis
La Combe
Le Clou
Les Chaillots
Bois Roussot
Les Joyeuses
La Rangie
Les Marnées
Les Lièvrières
La Blancharde
Les Vris
Sur les Vris
Les Briquottes
Bois des Toppes
Le Bois d'Herbues
Bois de Gréchon
Les Gréchons et Foutrières
Sur les Gréchons
En Naget
Bas de Naget
Bois de Naget
Hautes Mourottes
Basses Mourottes
Les Carrières
300
Key
Corton (red wines)
Corton Blanc (white wines)
Corton-Charlemagne (white wines)
Corton (red wines)
Aloxe-Corton Premier Cru
Ladoix Premier Cru
Ladoix
Aloxe-Corton
SCALE 1/20000
N

Aloxe-Corton and Ladoix-Serrigny

The quiet village of Aloxe-Corton (population 250) has a reputation far outstripping its size. Nestling beneath the magnificent Corton hillside, it boasts the largest swathe of Grand Cru land in the Côte d'Or. From 160.19 ha. come the sole red Grand Cru of the Côte de Beaune, Corton, and white Corton-Charlemagne, plus a little Corton Blanc and the usual gamut of Premiers Crus and Village wines.

Aloxe has a long history: in 858 as Aulociacum, which evolved into Alossia, then Alussa until in 1577 it became Alouxe, finally Aloxe. Corton – apparently a corruption of Curtis d'Orthon after an Emperor of the same name – was added in 1862.

Roman artefacts attest to Aloxe's importance as a strategic outpost on the third century Roman road from Marseilles to Autun. Wine from these vineyards, known and respected from an early date, took on legendary status when Charlemagne acquired the land which, in 775, he ceded to the Abbey of Saulieu in compensation for its destruction by the Saracens.

The commune has no fewer than 3 Châteaux within its boundaries: the magnificent eighteenth-century Château Corton-Grancey, belonging to Domaine Louis Latour the nineteenth-century Château de Corton-André, showpiece of La Reine Pedauque, and the Château d'Aloxe-Corton. Their green, yellow and russet enamelled tiles give the village the appearance of having poked its head up above the vines one day to see what was going on, and having got stuck there.

The vineyards pack tightly round the village, precluding any expansion beyond perhaps a telephone box. Their division into *climats* and appellations has evolved in a haphazard and complicated fashion, producing much confusion. Part of the problem is that the neighbouring communes of Pernand-Vergelesses and Ladoix-Serrigny both have vineyards entitled to some of Aloxe's appellations, including Corton and Corton-Charlemagne. These administrative contortions are further complicated by rules entitling both red and white wines to be made from certain specified vineyards, but according them different appellations. So there are 15 *climats* in Aloxe, totalling 71.94 ha., and 6 in Ladoix, totalling 16.37 ha., which are designated Corton for both reds and whites. In addition to the Grands Crus, there are 89.71 ha. Village land, and 14 Premiers Crus, of which 9 (29.13 ha.) are in Aloxe and 6 (8.46 ha.) in Ladoix.

It should be stressed that red wine produced from Corton-Charlemagne vineyards is not red Corton-Charlemagne but Corton En Charlemagne rouge, and that white wine from Corton vineyards is not Corton-Charlemagne but Corton (blanc) - the latter because the authorities are endeavouring to reduce the production of white wine from essentially red soils. Not only is the vineyard organisation complex, but the existence of more than 200 owners of these Grands Crus scattered throughout the Côte make Aloxe-Corton particularly hard to understand. Pitiot and Poupon list only 26 growers and 1 négociant in Aloxe itself, but detail nearly 3 pages of other Grand Cru owners from Dijon to Santenay.

This results in a wide diversity of style and quality of Cortons and Corton-Charlemagnes. The best Charlemagnes undoubtedly come from Bonneau du Martray, Louis Latour, Faiveley, Jadot, Coche-Dury, Tollot-Beaut, Rapet and Remoissenet, and the finest Cortons from Chandon de Briailles, Jadot, Tollot-Beaut, Philippe Senard and Faiveley. There are also good wines from Maurice Chapuis and Michel Voarick.

A few Domaines continue to produce poor wine from excellent vineyards: Bouchard Père et Fils (who own nearly 7 ha. of Le Corton) and La Reine Pedauque are notable examples. Even in great vintages their wines are frequently unbalanced and uninspiring. Added to these peaks and troughs is much wishy-washy, over-cropped, over-*chaptalised* fluid from other growers, which seems to find a gullible market at Grand Cru prices.

The hill of Corton is a magnificent saddle of land. Expositions through almost 270 degrees vary from east-facing Ladoix through due-south to west-facing Pernand, where part of the En Charlemagne vineyard faces north-west. Westerly sections tend to ripen later and produce wines of less obvious richness than those more favourably exposed.

Perhaps more than anywhere else on the Côte, permutations of heat, cold, sun and shadow exert a significant effect on vegetation and ripening. North-east facing vines receive early morning sun, but it is cold; to the south it is hot and sunny; to the south-west hot, but for much of the day in shadow, while the west is both cold and shaded.

Unsurprisingly in so large a vineyard, there is no simple soil-profile, instead a wide variation on both axes: from top to bottom of the hill and around it, to which millennia of erosion have contributed. Higher up limestone predominates, contrasting with more scree, iron, clay and ammonite fossil material lower down where much of the village land lies. Each *climat's* soil-characteristics are reflected in its wine.

However, it is no accident that Chardonnay (formerly Aligoté) is planted on the upper sections, just beneath the Bois de Corton, where the clay topsoil of lower down gives way to oolitic limestone – with more marl and pebbles. This ideal terrain produces wines of masculine elegance – entirely different from those of Meursault and Puligny – which, given time develop a magnificently austere, aristocratic quality.

Towards the middle of the slope, brown limestone emerges and the proportion of clay increases – excellent territory for Pinot Noir. Here are to be found the best *climats* of Corton – Clos du Roi, Bressandes, Perrières, Poujets and Le Corton. Soils vary between *climats* – Les Perrières has only 25 cm. of soil on top of hard rock and Bressandes is planted on an old quarry.

Attempting to characterise a typical Corton with anything but the broadest brush-strokes is futile. The best are powerful, tannic wines, capable of great longevity but with an overlay of finesse – a touch 'sauvage' perhaps, with rather less self-restraint than a Clos Vougeot. A half-bottle of Jadot's 1928 Pougets was still strong, almost spicy and rich in 1990.

Here, as everywhere on the Côte, quality depends more on the grower than the vineyard. Some, however, consider that this Grand Cru is too large and should be reclassified, with a view to eliminating vineyards on colder, less favoured sites. They may have a case, but meanwhile yields and the integrity of the grower continue to count.

THE GRANDS CRUS OF ALOXE-CORTON

Lieu-dit	*Area*	*Props.*	*Av. Prod.*
Corton	160.19.26	200	30,000 C/S Red 450 C/S White
Corton-Charlemagne	71.88.34	75	13,500 C/S White
Totals	**232.07.60 ha.**	**275**	**43,950 C/S**

Domaine Cornu

MAGNY-LES-VILLERS

The Cornu family have been wine-makers in the quiet little village of Magny for over a century. Claude, the latest head of House, has been at the helm since 1970 when his father ceded him 3 ha. of vines; he took over the remainder of the 12 ha. Domaine in 1977.

The Domaine's survival was by no means assured. Claude, an only son, had just finished his third year in the vineyards and cellars of the Domaine de la Romanée-Conti when the time came to choose. If he stayed, he reckoned that he would probably become cellar-master, but the family Domaine would suffer. So, with some reluctance – since he clearly learned much and has happy memories of his time at 'The Domaine' – he left Vosne-Romanée and returned to work the family estate.

The vineyards are tended with minimum fertilisers and treatments – periodic adjustments of soil *trace elements* after deep soil analyses, which Claude regards as of great importance – no anti-rot treatments, for example, for the last 6 years – and vines systematically replaced to keep the average age as high as possible. 'All our Villages and Crus are sold in bottle, so we can't afford to take risks; we must have the maximum quality,' he explains. However, when he is convinced that the vines are over-producing, he cuts a proportion of the bunches off – though 'that breaks my heart,' he confesses.

Wine-making methods closely followed those of 'The Domaine' until 1990 when, instead of his usual practice of not destalking his crop, Claude decided to remove 75% of the stalks. He justifies this change by pointing to the tendency of his customers to drink their wines sooner – the stalks add tannins which make the young wines harder.

As for the remainder of his vinification: 'Je suis un homme de tradition,' he smiles. Plenty of *pigéage à pied,* and a moderately long *cuvaison* of 10–12 days in his open cement *cuves* – the Corton is privileged with a day or two longer and a temperature which is never allowed to rise above 33° C. Only natural yeasts are allowed in the *cuverie.*

Like many vignerons on the Côte, Claude works closely with an oenologist: 'one may be a good vigneron but that does not necessarily make you a good wine-maker,' he reasons. He has scant time for modern notions – especially when it comes to cold pre-fermentive maceration to extract colour – 'the professionals tell us this is the thing to do – a few years ago it was the opposite.'

He also follows 'The Domaine' in his attachment to the value of new wood; all his Village wines – Ladoix, Pernand, Savigny – as well as the Corton are put into 100% new Allier oak where they remain until their first racking after the *malo.* The *régionales* and Hautes Côtes reds are kept in bulk until after their *malos* and put, when space is available, into casks previously broken in by one or two wines. Unified at racking and returned to cask, they are left there until fining and bottling. In general, the Cornu Village reds remain 15 months in wood, the Corton 20 months. They are lightly plate-filtered before bottling with equipment which Claude owns jointly with his neighbours.

Claude's father, René Cornu, is still going strong – despite having retired several years ago. He has his own personal hectare of vines – all he is allowed by French law without forfeiting his pension – the wine from which he sells under his own label. He and his wife are to be found, on a raw winter's day, well wrapped up next to a glowing stove in the cellar, chatting away whilst counting and capsuling René's stock into cartons, with the aid of an ancient frog-throated apparatus which crimps the capsules to the necks of the bottles.

In the old family cellars Cornu senior has his private cask or two, carefully chalked up with his name to avoid any mistakes. In 1990 he was still selling his personal clientèle a 1985 Bourgogne Rouge, whilst his son was on to the 1988s. Interruptions from all of them, including the dog, give the place the air of a harmonious family enterprise, which is just what it is.

Claude's wines mirror the man – charming and sturdily dependable. The white Hautes Côtes de Beaune, made from 50/50 old 'vrai' Pinot Blanc and Chardonnay, is particularly attractive and fresh – but needs keeping to show its best. The red Savigny has great finesse (1989), whilst the Hautes-Côtes, Côte de Nuits-Villages and Ladoix reds are excellent examples of their appellations, made to be kept for a few years in good vintages such as 1989 and 1990.

Prunings against the hill of Corton

The Corton, however, is the star of the Cornu cellar. This comes from 2 *climats* – Les Maréchaudes (above Aloxe) and Les Rognets (in the commune of Ladoix). The vines are over 50 years old and replaced individually to retain the wine's typicity and structure.

The 1988 is still closed up, with a good depth of attractive fat, ripe, fruit and well-integrated tannins – a wine for 10 years on. The 1989 has elegance and finesse – with a more open, suave layer of fruit. The 1990 seems to be the most promising of this excellent trio – with a great depth of old-vine fruit and a beautiful balance between the ripe tannins, fruit, acidity and alcohol.

VINEYARD HOLDINGS

Commune	*Level*	*Lieu-dit/Climat*	*Area*	*Vine Age*	*Status*
Aloxe Ladoix	GC	Corton	0.61	50	M
Savigny	V	—	0.24	12	F
Pernand	V	—	0.26	20	F
Ladoix	V	—	0.96	30	M
—	R	(Côte de Nuits-Villages)	0.23	50	F
—	R	(Hautes-Côtes de Nuits-Village R)	3.23	30	P/F
—	R	(Hautes-Côtes de Nuits-Beaune R)	0.80	25	P/F
—	R	(Hautes-Côtes de Nuits W)	0.53	10	F
—	R	(Hautes-Côtes de Nuits Beaune W)	0.46	20	P/F
—	R	(PTG)	2.73	20	P
—	R	(Aligoté)	1.37	25	P/F
		Total	**11.42 ha.**		

Domaine Jayer-Gilles

MAGNY-LES VILLERS

Life is definitely more leisurely up on the 'arrière Côte' – that peaceful, gently undulating stretch of land behind the Côte d'Or.

However, wine is made in these attractive little villages. Although much of this is sound modest stuff which finds its way out through the négociant market, a few of the more enlightened vignerons are making valiant attempts to build up a bottle trade of their own and thereby to establish a reputation for themselves and their wines.

Among the best of these pioneers is Robert Jayer-Gilles. A man of military mien, tall and broad, with a luxuriant handle-bar moustache and a gravelly voice, he exudes the confidence of a freshly-minted British Sergeant-Major as he stands surveying his private army of casks lined up in impeccable review order in his immaculate cellar.

Robert is a native of Vosne-Romanée and a cousin of the great Henri Jayer. He started his career in 1948 as an apprentice vigneron working for André Noblet, then cellar-master at the Domaine de la Romanée-Conti. In 1955 he left to marry Mlle. Gilles, daughter of a viticulteur whose family had owned and worked vines at Magny-Les-Villers for centuries. With her came vines which, together with his inheritance of Echézeaux and Nuits-St.-Georges Premier Cru Les Damodes, remain the kernel of the Jayer-Gilles Domaine.

Further parcels of Hautes-Côtes de Nuits and Hautes-Côtes de Beaune, both red and white, Côte de Nuits-Villages, plus some Aligoté and Passe-Tout-Grains were added later, giving a current total average production of some 5–6,000 cases.

The wines are made with infinite care and are much sought-after, sometimes even by other top growers who perhaps need some more Bourgogne to sell to their clients. Robert clearly enjoys the rewards which his efforts have brought and like his neighbour, Claude Cornu, the physical manifestation of his prosperity is a magnificent new push-button cellar which features, among other things, an illuminated well – to show his visitors how near to the water-table they are – and an equally opulent spittoon surmounted by a large stone gargoyle, which could perfectly well do duty as a font if ever there was something to be christened in a hurry.

The vineyards are a mixture of high-training and *gobelet*, whilst the 45-year-old Aligoté vines are trained *en cordon*: 'they ripen better this way,' Robert explains. Treatments are mostly traditional, except for the use of insecticide against the grape-worm. He distrusts the skin-hardening powers of copper-based products to protect his vines: 'the worm has good teeth,' he argues, and so merits something more destructive.

Despite all the modernity in the cellar, vinification is by and large updated traditional. Although destalking is frowned upon –'I only destalked my Echézeaux once, in 1983' – Robert does leave 7–8 harvesting boxes of uncrushed grapes in each *cuve*, to prolong the maceration before fermentation starts. In 1985, the wood was so ripe that he left all the stalks in the vats.

Pushing the button to start the water in the spittoon, he explains that he has no means of cooling the juice in his *cuves* – 'I don't like pressing buttons' – but relies on a moderate dose of SO_2 to delay the onset of fermentation long enough for a reasonable extraction of colour. When the temperature in a vat rises above about 36° C, the *must* is simply decanted from its own *cuve* to a cooler one. In the unlikely event of fermentation stopping altogether, then the *must* is run off, the pulp pressed and off it goes again . . . somehow!

About 24 hours before finally decanting the free-run wine, Robert levers his giant frame into the vat 'up to the neck' and proceeds to give the solids a thorough treading.

The red wines generally spend some 15–17 months in new Allier oak – the Echézeaux has a touch of Tronçais as well – in the luxurious surroundings of the new cellar. Robert started using new wood in 1977 for all except his Passe-Tout-Grains. However, his Romanée-Conti training has encouraged him to use 100% irrespective of vintage or appellation. This can easily overpower a less naturally structured regional wine or even a better appellation in a weaker vintage. He should perhaps review this policy. The red wines are normally bottled without fining, but with a light kieselguhr filtration.

The Hautes-Côtes red and white are excellent wines. The whites are fermented in 50% new wood and 50% stainless steel to provide a final blend of freshness and structure and bottled after the second winter – some 18 months old. Of these the Aligoté, from 45-year-old vines, and the Hautes-Côtes de Beaune white, made from Henri Gouges' famous white mutant of Pinot Noir, are particularly successful. The 1989 Hautes-Côte had a complex, rich nose, with a delicious layer of old vine fruit – altogether fine and stylish.

For the reds plenty of good sound fruit flavours and a firm structure come from a vinification with most of the stalks, that high fermentation temperature, a 5-day pre-fermentive maceration, about 15 days *cuvaison* and a slow *malo* which can last up to 14 months. These are red wines of military proportions, sometimes rather four-square – but definitely not for the faint- hearted looking for something to drink young.

With the Nuits-St.-Georges Les Damodes, one leaps a quantum or two and begins to see the foundations of Robert's reputation. This vineyard, on the Vosne side of Nuits, is planted with 45-year-old vines. The 1989 in cask is a deeply coloured wine, just beginning to show some Vosne-ish complexity, quite fine, with a hint of chocolate on the nose and a generous layer of succulent ripe fruit; underneath, a firm tannic support which needs a decade to soften out.

The Echézeaux 1989 is yet another quantum away – a deep, limpid wine of almost black-cherry hue; completely unforthcoming on the nose, but with a vast, mouthfilling panoply of sweet, ripe fruit; a wine of considerable depth and concentration of flavour and superb length. A gentle giant, from a gentle giant.

VINEYARD HOLDINGS

Commune	*Level*	*Lieu-dit/Climat*	*Area*	*Vine Age*	*Status*
Flagey	GC	Echézeaux	0.54	40	P
Nuits	PC	Les Damodes	0.11	45	P
Nuits	V	Les Hauts Poirets	0.29	40	P
Corgolion	R	Côte de Nuits-Villages	1.31	20	P
—	R	Hautes-Côtes de Beaune (R)	1.03	15	P
—	R	Hautes-Côtes de Nuits (R)	1.96	15	P
—	R	Hautes-Côtes de Beaune (W)	1.01	25	P
—	R	Hautes-Côtes de Nuits (W)	0.45	25	P
—	R	(PTG)	0.44	15	P
—	R	(Aligoté)	2.95	40	P
		Total	**10.09 ha**.		

Domaine Prince Florent de Mérode

LADOIX-SERRIGNY

One potentially great Domaine which is sadly failing to produce the top quality of which its vineyards are perfectly capable is that of the Prince de Mérode, a 64-year-old nobleman who lives in the splendid Château de Serrigny.

His Domaine has nearly 12 ha. of fine land, including almost 4 ha. of Grands Crus Cortons. Since 1953 the wine-making has been entrusted to Pierre Bitouzet, an amiable but rather defensive grower from Savigny who has his own 3.2 ha. Domaine which, apart from 0.5 ha. of Corton-Charlemagne and 0.3 ha. of Aloxe-Corton Premier Cru, consists entirely of red and white Savignys.

Why this Domaine is not fulfilling its potential is easily explained. This is an unusual case where indifferent wines are not, as is so often the case, the product of incompetence or carelessness, but rather the result of a deliberate policy of making wines which are ready to drink early. The Domaine's long-standing principal clients (Americans) apparently prefer light, easy-drinking Cortons which are virtually consumable as soon as they are shipped.

To produce such wines entails eliminating youthful elements which would make for unpalatability and concentrating on a vinification which favours fruit, *rondeur* and suppleness. Depriving wines of an integral part of their structure in this way cannot but destroy much of their interest and quality. It is just as absurd to assume that you can remove tannins and acidity and simply leave the remainder to go on by itself as to suppose that you can have the grin without the Cheshire cat. A fine wine is not an assemblage of individual parts which can be omitted or included at will, but an harmonious whole whose constituents are indissolubly interdependent.

Pierre Bitouzet is impatiently frank about what he is trying to achieve and how he sets about it. The grapes are 80% destalked - totally if there is any evidence of rot – given a normal dose of SO_2 and then put into the Domaine's open wooden *cuves*. There is no pre-fermentive maceration to extract colour and aroma, neither is there any maceration after fermentation. The vats are simply heated lightly to start the fermentation which then proceeds naturally, with little pumping-over but 3 or 4 manual *pigéages* each day to keep the solids moist and well distributed in the liquid.

The *cuvaison* lasts 10–12 days at a maximum temperature of 28–32° C. As soon

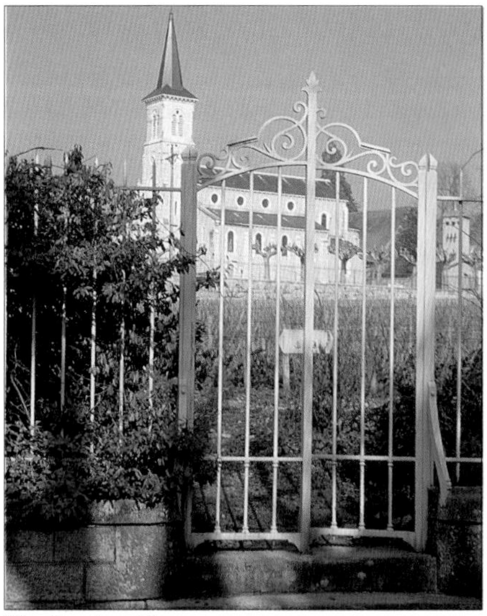

The church at Aloxe

as the specific gravity of the *must* goes below 1000 – indicating that nearly all the sugar has been transformed into alcohol – the wine is run off and the pulp pressed. This pressure is particularly light, presumably to avoid extracting any tannins which might give the wine backbone and thus longevity.

Once the press-wine has been added, the wine is put into casks for an *élevage* – which normally lasts 14–17 months. There are two rackings – the first after the *malo*, with aeration, and the second the following autumn, without aeration. The wines are generally fined with albumen, in cask, in November or December of the year following the vintage. After a minimum of 2 months *sur col* they are racked, unified in tank and then bottled – usually in January or February.

There is no filtration – the US client apparently specifies this – which is on balance a good thing, since to extract matter from a wine which has little enough to start with might leave it with charm, but probably little else.

Pierre Bitouzet hopes that by shortening the *cuvaison*, eliminating both pre- and post-fermentive maceration and using the minimum pressure to extract the press-wine, the fruit qualities will be retained without the unwanted tannins. 'Our American clientèle are mostly private buyers and restaurateurs who mainly consume the wines early. No one complained about our '77s – I suppose they have all been drunk – I fear so.'

The Domaine's sole white wine is a Ladoix Blanc, made from Chardonnay fermented in cask with *batonnage* for up to a year to give it fatness and bottled relatively early – after 10–12 months – to retain freshness. This can be pleasant and interesting – full, sappy and classily rustic, with a distinct *goût de terroir*, in fact a bit of a dark-haired gypsy.

Tasting a range of vintages gives an impression of great variability; even in good years the wines can be dilute and lacking in real spine and concentration – over-cropped and probably over-*chaptalised*. In the 1985 vintage, for example, most fine Domaines produced wines of richness and concentration, characterised by a striking depth of soft, open fruit. However, the Domaine's 1985 Corton, whilst correct and pleasant enough, lacked presence and 'fond' – a soft, drinkable mouthful of strawberry Pinot fruit, but with no real interest, and certainly not of Grand Cru quality.

M. Bitouzet seems more of a business man now than a serious wine-maker. He has recently acquired an important Domaine in the Midi, next to Château Vignelaure. As he taps his ruler abstractedly on his desk, perhaps his mind is on other things. The Prince de Mérode's land is capable of producing top-quality wine, yet this important Domaine appears to be stuck in a vein of mediocrity. In short, a disturbing example of squandering the potential of fine land to please what appears to be an undiscerning market-driven clientèle.

VINEYARD HOLDINGS

Commune	Level	Lieu-dit/Climat	Area	Vine Age	Status
Aloxe	GC	Corton Clos Du Roy	0.57	40	P
Aloxe	GC	Corton Bressandes	1.20	30	P
Aloxe	GC	Corton Renardes	0.51	30	P
Aloxe	GC	Corton Marechaudes	1.53	30	P
Aloxe	PC	Les Marechaudes	0.69	30	P
Pommard	PC	La Platière	3.73	15	P
Ladoix	PC	Hautes Mourottes	0.31	40	P
Ladoix	V	Les Chaillots	2.84	15	P
		Total	**11.38 ha.**		

Domaine Vigot-Battault

MESSANGES

This is a tiny, 4-year-old Domaine making impressively competent wine. Thierry Vigot, a large young man in his twenties, learnt his trade from his father and in 1982 had the good luck to take over the running of the small Vosne-Romanée Domaine belonging to Mme. Thomas where he had been working, first as apprentice, later as *tâcheron*. In 1987 she decided to let him have the vineyards on a share-cropping basis whereby they would divide the fruit equally. Thus he came to have his own small Domaine and to be his own master.

It is evident that this rather laid-back, somewhat unforthcoming vigneron knows his job. The wines emanating from the cramped cellars underneath his house in the village of Messanges, well off the beaten track in the Hautes-Côtes, are of a very high quality indeed. Helped by his wife, Thierry works hard to turn the wheels of this fledgling enterprise.

Unfortunately, there is not much of it – less than 3 ha. in total: 23.68 ares of Nuits-St.-Georges, 19.57 ares of Vosne-Romanée Premier Cru Les Gaudichots and 39.50 ares of Grand Cru Echézeaux form the heart of the exploitation. The rest of the Domaine comprises Bourgogne Grande Ordinaire, Aligoté and 1.32 ha. of Hautes-Côtes de Nuits, this last being land Thierry has bought himself. 'You can't really call it a Domaine,' he remarks laconically, shrugging his shoulders.

The vines in Nuits, Vosne and Echézeaux although not yet venerable, are distinctly old – 48–60 years. Thierry is well aware that the quality of their fruit contributes significantly to the intensity and concentration of his wines and tries to replace individual plants rather than replanting larger plots to keep the average vine age high. The overall vineyard policy is agreed with Mme. Thomas, although the day-to-day decisions are left to him.

To keep yields viable, only the bases of the older, less prolific vines are *évasivé*, neither is the process of removing double shoots systematic – it depends on the growing season. The effects can be dramatic: in 1989, for example, Thierry did not *dédoubler* his Aligoté vines – the fruit was picked at 9.5 degrees of potential alcohol; in 1990 he decided to *dédoubler* – and, with broadly similar weather conditions, the grapes came in at 12 degrees.

For matters of fertilisation and technical handling of his vines, he works with the local co-operative in Nuits-St.-Georges which advises on the details of suitable products and applications. Provided one doesn't accept blindly everything that is suggested, such organisations are of inestimable benefit to vignerons who may have little or no technical expertise of their own to call on.

The wines are still vinified at Vosne, but brought to Messanges for *élevage*. The only white wine in the Vigot stable is an Aligoté. At present this is vinified in bulk, since Thierry believes that this gives a better alcoholic fermentation. However, he has been experimenting with what he terms a Meursault vinification whereby the wines are fermented in second-year casks. Whilst the results are encouraging, it seems likely that until there are more resources for new wood and equipment, the bulk vinification will continue. The wine is generally bottled after a year or so to retain as much fruit and freshness as possible, as the Aligoté grape in particular tends to age rapidly.

Red vinification is more or less traditional. The grapes are destalked between 50% (1987) and 100% (1989) and fermented in open wooden *cuves* at 34°C for a minimum total *cuvaison* of 15 days with plenty of *pigéage* – and one *remontage* – each morning. Selected Burgundy yeasts are used rather than letting the natural yeast population loose, and enzymes added in the middle of the *cuvaison* to help later clarification.

The wines spend between 15 months (1989) and 17 months (1988) in cask and are normally bottled without fining but with a kieselguhr filtration. Thierry does not have his own bottling equipment, so a contract bottler is summoned to do the job. Hopefully, as soon as it is practicable, he will take this task back into his own hands.

Thierry likes to make wines which have plenty of tannins and *charpente*. Unfortunately his finances don't run to more than one or two new casks each year, so 3 *pigéages* per day, a long *cuvaison* and slow extended *malos* on the wine's fine lees help compensate for this deficiency. He professes a dislike of new wood – it unbalances the wine, but this may be no more than the old practice of making a virtue of necessity.

The lizard-enamelled roof stands out on Château Corton-André

The wines themselves are a pleasure to taste – especially in vintages such as 1988, 1989 and 1990. The Hautes-Côtes de Nuits is a vigorous, peppery wine, with more concentration and depth than would normally be envisaged from 3-year-old vines.

The Nuits-St.-Georges has more finesse than is typical from this commune – a Nuits with distinct Vosne overtones – the 1989 had lovely long, ripe flavours, predominantly of *fruits sauvages* and liquorice.

The Echézeaux 1989 was distinctly weak; Thierry admits that removing 100% of the stalks was a mistake in that vintage. The 1990 Echézeaux is a much better effort – firm, dense with plenty of 'fond' and promise.

The Vosne-Romanée Premier Cru Les Gaudichots, from a vineyard with thin granular calcaire soils situated just below La Tâche, is particularly fine. The 1989 has a silky elegance, no shortage of ripe, complex fruit and superb length. It is to be hoped that some wise importer will help Thierry to buy a few new casks – even the excellent Hautes-Côtes would benefit from a touch of new wood – and he deserves to be encouraged.

VINEYARD HOLDINGS

Commune	Level	Lieu-dit/Climat	Area	Vine Age	Status
Flagey	Gc	Echézeaux	0.40	30–58	M
Vosne	PC	Les Gaudichots	0.20	55	M
Nuits	V	Les Bas Combes	0.24	47	M
—	R	(Hautes-Côtes de Nuits)	0.30	4	P
—	R	(Hautes-Côtes de Nuits)	0.72	1991	P
—	R	(BGO)	0.26	23	M
—	R	(Aligoté)	0.37	7	M
		Total	**2.49 ha.**		

Domaine Daniel Senard

ALOXE-CORTON

In espousing the controversial methods of Lebanese oenologist Guy Accad, Philippe Senard has led his Domaine straight into the line of fire and, fortunately, straight up to the top level of quality. Travelling outside France, especially in Oregon, California and Spain, Philippe was persuaded that whilst other viticultural regions were making marked progress, Burgundy was under-performing and failing to emulate the really great wine-making of the past. His growing instinct that there was need for change was reinforced by his own 1982 and 1986 vintages, when he sensed that the grapes had 'Grand Vin' potential but felt himself incapable of extracting it. It was after the 1986 vintage that he came into Accad's ambit.

Much nonsense has been talked and written in recent years about the so-called 'méthode Accad'. He, and those who use his services, have been criticised both for destroying the unique typicity of Burgundy and for making wines which are unlikely to last. Whilst time is clearly needed to test these claims, there is far too much passion and prejudice which should be set aside whilst facts are laid out and put into sensible perspective.

Before taking over from his father's 'chef de cave' in 1971, Philippe spent 5 years as commercial director in the family factory in Beaune, making chips for casinos (only one of two in the world, apparently). Realising he knew little about making wine, he went to the Lycée Viticole in Beaune for some formal training, but after 16 years at the Domaine he confessed to becoming stale and de-motivated. The turning point came in 1986 when for the first time he tasted wines made by cold-maceration and was impressed with the results. Discussions with Accad led to his engagement as a consultant in 1987.

Philippe's Domaine is in fact an amalgam of two separate estates: the Domaine du Comte Senard, founded by his grandfather, Jules Senard, in the mid nineteenth century, comprises nearly 9 ha. of land in Aloxe, Chorey and Beaune, belonging to members of the Senard family. A further 6.34 ha. of Savigny, Beaune and Côte de Beaune constitute the Domaine des Terregelesses, created in 1984 by an anonymous 'lover of Burgundy'. Daniel Senard, Philippe's father, who did much to establish the identity of his family Domaine, has now retired, but still takes a keen interest in events.

Guy Accad's influence is not confined to wine-making. His principal concern is to establish the best possible soil equilibrium since he believes the soil's capacity to nourish the vine is limited by the extent to which it is in balance. The 'larder' is there, but you have to find the natural key to unlock its nourishment. Adding fertilisers merely encourages higher productivity. What are needed are regular, precise adjustments in the soil's *base elements* to promote a natural balance; this in turn helps fewer grapes to ripen earlier and to a better degree.

An integral part of Guy Accad's soil-care policy is the minimum use of strong, synthetic treatment products, which can easily unbalance the soil and destroy valuable micro-flora. Thus only Bordeaux mixture, sulphur and insecticides are used – 'we haven't much choice,' argues Philippe. His thinking is increasingly orienting to 'biodynamie' – a treatment system which works in precisely timed, homoeopathically dilute doses. However in Burgundy, with each vineyard subdivided among several owners, it would need an inconceivable consensus to introduce this on a large scale with any chance of success. Philippe does not view this prospect with unremitting gloom: 'this isn't altogether bad; if everyone did the same thing, it wouldn't be so interesting.'

Since starting work with Accad, Philippe admits that one of the most significant changes has been the date of harvest. 'I have put back my vintage by 3 weeks – it's obviously a risk; the drama of Burgundy now is that people unfortunately aren't prepared to wait for proper maturity – they won't take the risk to really ripen the grapes.' In this they are egged on by the officials who set the *ban de vendange*, the earliest permitted harvesting date. For 1990, for example, in Aloxe-Corton this was set at 15 September: 'Absolutely scandalous,' shouts Philippe, 'it should have been at least 10 days later.' He waited to start picking until 25 September and did not harvest his Cortons until 1 October.

The difference of ten days was striking: for example, his machine-harvested 3 ha. of Chorey-Lès-Beaune, on flatter land, showed 11.2 degrees potential alcohol on 2 October whereas the final batch, picked from the same vineyard on 12 October, came in at 13.2 degrees – a full 2 degree gain in ripeness in 10 days. 'We were entitled to harvest on 15 September – this is the whole problem!'

There are two main strands to Accad's and Senard's vinification: firstly 'the great principle' – to vinify as cool as is compatible with the extraction and (as important) the retention of maximum aroma and colour; secondly, to use only one single, large dose of SO_2, to delay the start of fermentation and to allow the vigneron to control its progress. The 'slow and cool' principle is described by Philippe as the difference between simmering and boiling a soup – one way you keep the aromas, the other you lose them. An 'Accad' cuverie has very little ambient aroma, whereas in a traditional cuverie there are fermentation smells everywhere.

The bunches are first destalked to a degree determined by the ripeness of the wood and the general state of the crop – 50% in 1988 and 75% in 1989 and 1990 – then given a calibrated dose of liquid SO_2 as the grapes emerge from the crusher. This contrasts with the traditional practice of waiting until a *cuve* is full, then adding the sulphur. The dose varies between 3.5 and 4 litres per tonne of harvest (the traditional dose being 1 litre per tonne) depending on the state of the crop, healthier grapes getting marginally less than others.

The crush is then cooled to 5–10° C and put into open *cuves*, where it macerates 5–6 days before the yeasts start to work. The heavy sulphur dose tends to neutralise the feebler yeasts, leaving the more resistant population to ferment the *must*. This is a bonus, since these yeasts are more likely to remain active as the alcohol level increases, thus ensuring complete conversion of the sugars.

During fermentation there are regular rapid *pigéages*, and heating is used if a vat seems sluggish. The temperature is allowed to rise no further than 25° C – although Philippe admits to becoming anxious at around 20° C, having once contentedly left a *cuve* fermenting at 19° C one evening and found it bubbling away at 30° C the following morning. As a matter of policy, the *cuves* are not *saignéed* – although a very dilute year might provoke a change of heart.

Cuvaison lasts some 20–25 days, after which the output of the first 2 pressings of the pulp is added and 2–3 days allowed to settle out the gross lees. The wines then pass into cask, the Cortons into a mixture of new and old wood – 25–30% new, 20% a year old and the rest older. The Premiers Crus and Village wines have somewhat less new wood. The taste of new oak is not one which Philippe likes – 'it's an artificial method, not a natural aroma,' he declares.

The wines spend some 2 years in wood –

Philippe Senard tasting with clients

about 6 months longer than traditional *élevage* – with 2 rackings, without any sulphur adjustments, to aerate the wine and unify the different casks of each Cru before bottling.

The addition of pectolytic enzymes early on enables Philippe to avoid both fining and filtration. He is scathing of some of his colleagues who 'bust their guts to make great wine and then filter it all out', and agrees with Accad that it is better to correct any faults a wine may have during the early stages of vinification, than to try making adjustments later. Thus enzymes are added to each vat to ensure perfect clarity later.

The results of Philippe's first collaboration with Accad – the 1988 vintage – are very impressive. Whilst not what one expects from traditionally vinified young Pinot – having rather a bigger, slightly more southerly feel to them, no doubt as a result of this long, slow maceration – there is no evidence of the standardisation or lack of individuality which this method is accused of producing.

Three 1988 Cortons tasted in 1991 showed every sign of considerable individuality and nothing more in common than any 3 wines from the same commune, made by the same hand, might be expected to have.

The Corton En Charlemagne – a red Corton and not, as one misinformed American commentator described it, a red Corton-Charlemagne – had a mid black-cherry colour, an attractive open nose of griottes and rich, soft, plummy, quite feminine flavours; a red wine from 'white' soil perhaps, but still very fine. The Corton *cuvée* from the Paulands vineyard, just below Les Bressandes, was altogether different – much meatier, more masculine, still closed up, but with an underlying 'sauvage' aspect and real Corton power and depth. The Bressandes was different again: aromas of almost over-ripe *fruits noirs*, warm and fleshy on the palate rather than massively powerful; above all, a seductive wine. The fourth member of the Corton quartet, the Clos du Roi, is, reputedly, even finer.

Tasting through the 1989s, differences between *climats* were equally evident, though perhaps to a lesser extent, as might be expected at a younger stage of evolution. These wines, like the even younger 1990s, were highly promising – plenty of real depth and complexity.

No honest and able taster could be in any doubt that Senard's wines differ one from another – the Cortons above are an excellent example – or that the differences increase with age. The wines may be bigger and richer than those produced elsewhere, but this alone is not sufficient reason for questioning their typicity. As for ageing, these wines – at least in 1988, 1989 and 1990 – have all the elements necessary for longevity: acidity, tannin, alcohol and fruit. How quickly and how they will develop is a matter of conjecture, but they are not set to fall apart in the next decade.

In addition to his excellent reds, Philippe makes about 900 bottles of white Aloxe-Corton – a rarity – from a plot of 65-year-old Pinot Beurot (Pinot Gris) grapes. This is sold almost entirely to the Domaine's privileged Michelin-starred restaurant customers.

Philippe has suffered much personal abuse and criticism for deciding to employ Accad. His critics conveniently ignore the fact that he is a highly intelligent and thoughtful man; hardly someone who would risk his Domaine and reputation on a mere whim. So far, his 'new' wines have enjoyed considerable success among his clientèle – proof that they are liked, though nothing more. In addition, he enjoys the acclaim and enthusiasm that his wines are generating among customers and the media.

The debate about authenticity and staying power will doubtless drone on until the 1988s and 1989s are mature and fit for proper assessment. Until then, it would help if much of the ill-informed mischief-making were to die down. What really matters is that this is a Domaine making fine wine with consummate care, a fact not lost on Philippe's fellow vignerons; or on his contented customers.

VINEYARD HOLDINGS

Commune	*Level*	*Lieu-dit/Climat*	*Area*	*Vine Age*	*Status*
Aloxe	GC	Corton Clos du Roi	0.44	45	P
Aloxe	GC	Corton Bressandes	0.63	50	P
Aloxe	GC	Les Paulands	0.83	50	P
Aloxe	GC	Corton Clos des Meix	2.12	40	P
Aloxe	PC	Les Valorières	0.70	20	P
Aloxe	V	—	2.39	27	P
Aloxe	V	(Blanc)	0.21	65	P
Pernand	GC	Corton En Charlemagne	0.40	18	M
Beaune	PC	Les Coucherias	0.29	25	M
Chorey	V	—	0.51	20	P
		Total	**8.52 ha.**		

PERNAND-VERGELESSES

The little village of Pernand – the Vergelesses was added in May 1922 – sits at the foot of the hill of Corton, about 3 km. from Aloxe-Corton itself. It is a friendly, attractive, peripheral place, largely bypassed by tourists who probably see no particular reason to go there, with a maze of narrow streets radiating from the church up and down the hillside. The fact that there is no hotel and only one small restaurant is an effective disincentive for casual travellers.

Pernand is architecturally most interesting, consisting principally of 6 large nineteenth-century mansions, distributed like sentinels around its periphery. Each has its own park – many planted with magnificent and important mature trees – and its particular Clos of vines. In the last century these maisons bourgeoises housed the grand employers for whom the rest of the village worked – de Grossets, Rameaux, Chansons, Copeaux, Ponnelles and Moreys. For the rest, rows of ancient village houses are huddled together cheek-by-jowl, no doubt befitting the scale and style of feudal dependants.

Time, however, has reversed roles and clipped the feudal wings of the great land-

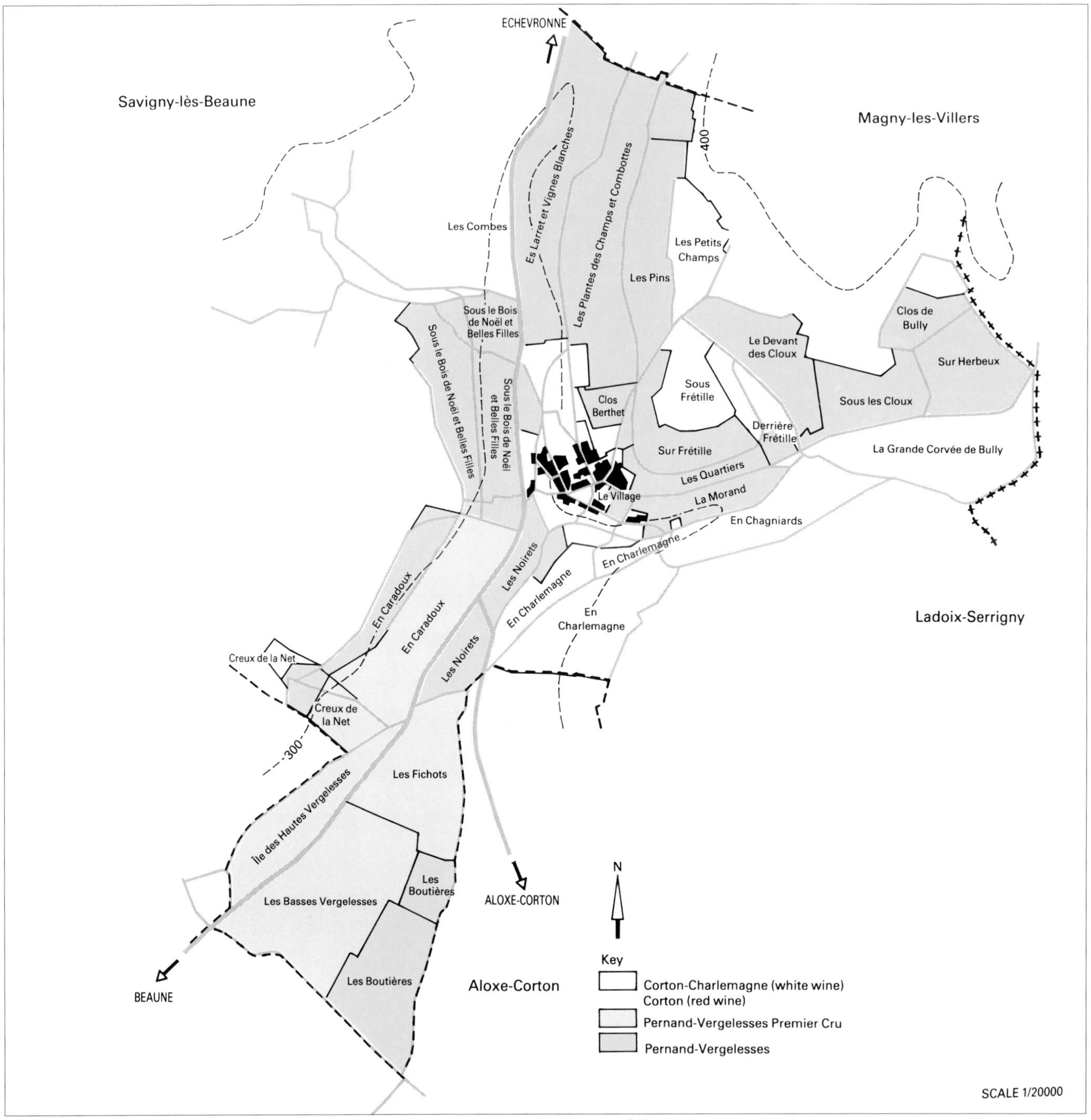

owners. No descendants of the original families remain in possession, each house now belonging to someone from the village, as if time had turned social history on its head and turned the village inside out.

There are about 35 growers in the commune, which has a population of under 350, making red and white wine from 137.63 ha. of village land and 56.51 ha. spread over 5 Premiers Crus. There are also 17.26 ha. – just over a quarter – of the Corton-Charlemagne appellation in a single swathe of land, known as 'En Charlemagne', which sits at the northern end of the Corton hill, on the outskirts of the village. It is believed that it forms much of the original land gifted by Charlemagne to the Abbey of Saulieu in 775 AD, although this attribution is by no means certain.

In 1978 the local growers' association successfully applied for several important changes to their 'vignoble'. Firstly, the area of Grand Cru was extended to incorporate several small parcels of land which were formerly within the appellation but had since lapsed; secondly, the Grand Cru designation was altered to allow production of Corton (red) as well as of Corton-Charlemagne (white), and thirdly, the right of growers to use the appellation Aloxe-Corton for red wines from certain of the commune's vineyards was rescinded.

The wines of Pernand-Vergelesses are among the least known of the Côte. This is largely because there are few growers who bother to market 'Pernand-Vergelesses', preferring instead to sell much of their red under the alternative appellation of Côte de Beaune-Villages. The problem might also be due, in part, to the awkwardness of the name – Pernand-Vergelesses is hardly the kind of snappy, punchy brand name likely to endear itself to modern marketing departments.

Nevertheless, low profile as the appellation may be, there is much to commend it, especially in good vintages, when the best wines are well worth buying and keeping for a few years. However, it is necessary to choose with care, since, although the growers are a conscientious bunch, there is much wine which is frankly meagre and uninspiring.

The difficulties faced by the vignerons of Pernand derive mostly from the poor exposition of their vineyards. Looking at the map, one can see that most of the vignoble is situated at the northern end of the valley, in the direction of Echevronne. This means that much is in shade for the greater part of each day, screened from direct sunlight by the hill of Corton. It is no accident that the best of the Premiers Crus – Les Basses Vergelesses and Ile des Hautes Vergelesses – are on the flatter, more open section of the valley floor, where they receive the most sunshine.

Pernand – one of the many unspoilt villages of Burgundy – nestles beneath the northerly end of the Corton hillside

Although some of the Village vineyards face south-east, much, including En Charlemagne, faces west or even north-west, which considerably delays ripening. Those who do harvest late risk grapes being destroyed by autumnal storms.

The soils, however, are good, especially for white grapes – which is curious since nearly 75% of the vineyards are planted with Pinot Noir. En Charlemagne is mainly of hard limestone composition – with significant outcropping in places; these 'têtes du loup' can destroy ploughs and hoes, so some of the Domaines concerned have recently brought in special machinery to excavate and pulverise them before returning the result to the vineyard as manageable ground-down topsoil. In addition, new walls in the lower end of the Pernand section of the Corton hill have been built to help retain topsoil washed down by rain.

Elsewhere, there is a diversity of soils, most being based on various forms of limestone. In Les Vergelesses, Les Bichots and the Ile de Vergelesses, significantly more clay is found, together with a high proportion of iron-bearing soil. Apart from reddening the earth, this provides ideal terrain for red grapes, giving breadth and structure to the wines.

The commune also produces a modest quantity of white Pernand-Vergelesses which may be made from either Chardonnay or Pinot Blanc; at present, this seems to be undergoing something of a revival. Bernard Dubreuil – with his excellent Village Monopole Clos Berthet – Roland Rapet and the de Nicolays at Chandon de Briailles in Savigny, make their white Pernand from 100% Chardonnay, although a few growers still retain a small proportion of Pinot Blanc in their blends.

In good vintages, such as 1983, 1985, 1988, 1989 and 1990, the Blanc has a green-gold appearance and is marked by an aroma of peach-kernels and a strong, flinty *goût de terroir*. They have the capacity to develop over several years, but are probably best drunk young for their uncomplicated, sappy fruit.s

The red wines are frequently criticised for a rusticity and lack of finesse. In many instances this is justified; however, the better Domaines have realised that destalking helps to remove an extra element of raw tannin which adds nothing to the wines, especially in unripe years which are naturally somewhat charmless. In good vintages, on the other hand, Pernand reds, especially from Les (Basses) Vergelesses and the Ile des (Hautes) Vergelesses, are wines of weight and structure, capable of ageing for 20 years or more. As usual, it depends on the grower. Apart from the 'hors classe' Domaine Bonneau du Martray for Corton-Charlemagne, the best wines come from the growers already mentioned. There is also a competent *cuvée* of Ile des Vergelesses from Louis Latour and a Village Clos de la Croix de Pierre, from Louis Jadot. All these wines are well worth seeking out, not only for their quality but also for their modest prices. If you taste carefully, Pernand-Vergelesses represents some of the best value in the Côte.

THE GRAND CRU OF PERNAND-VERGELESSES

Lieu-dit	*Area*	*Props.*	*Av. Prod.*
**En Charlemagne	17.25.89	35	6,600 C/S

** N.B. Wine from this vineyard is entitled to the Appellation Corton if red, Corton-Charlemagne or Charlemagne if white.

Domaine Bonneau du Martray

PERNAND-VERGELESSES

The white wines from Corton have a special place in the Burgundian mosaic. Local legend attributes the planting of white grapes on the hill of Corton to the desire of Liutgarde, Charlemagne's empress, to satisfy her bibulous lord's thirst for Corton with a white wine to avoid undignified red stains on his light-coloured beard. Whether or not you accept that, the production of a great white wine from this predominantly red hillside is an enduring curiosity, another expression of the Chardonnay grape to stimulate and tease the palate.

Although it has 2 ha. of red Corton, the Domaine Bonneau du Martray is best known for its great Charlemagne, produced from 9 ha. sited in the choicest parts of this magnificent hillside. Since 1969, when the Countess inherited it as chosen legatee of her godfather and uncle, René Bonneau du Martray, the Domaine has been owned and managed by the Count and Countess Jean le Bault de la Morinière.

On taking possession the de la Morinières found that 4.5 ha. of their vineyards had been leased out to an assortment of tenants; it took them 5 years to negotiate the re-purchase of the land and to put the totality back into proper order.

Although Jean le Bault administers the Domaine's commercial activity from an office in Paris, where he and his wife Alice live, he spends as much time as possible in their house in Pernand – particularly at weekends and during the vintage. This smallish 'maison de vigneron' is simply but beautifully furnished; one entire wall of the sitting-room is devoted to a superb Aubusson tapestry.

Jean le Bault is a meticulous man who is prepared to spare no expense to make the best possible wine from his magnificent land. He is often to be found walking through his vineyards, looking at the condition of the vines or examining the soil to see how it is reacting to whatever rainfall there has been. He knows each plot of vines intimately, how it behaves and what it needs.

All this information is duly discussed with his regisseur Henri Bruchon, who arrived at the Domaine from Volnay to work in the vineyards in 1963 in 'minus 20 and snow'. 'Monsieur Henri', as he is affectionately known, is a short, wiry-haired man, immensely (and justifiably) proud of the Domaine, who oversees everything that goes on both in the vineyards and in the cellars, where he has vinified the wines solo since 1975. Both his sons have now joined him, the start perhaps of a family tradition.

The vineyards in M. Henri's care are in a single piece – a rarity for such a large parcel in Burgundy. The 2 ha. of 45–50-year-old red Corton vines lie in the commune of Aloxe-Corton, at the base of the Corton hill, following the road from Aloxe to Pernand. Here the soil is moderately deep, ferruginous in character with hard limestone rock underneath. The 9 ha. of Charlemagne, although contiguous, are split equally between the communes of Aloxe-Corton and Pernand-Vergelesses but higher up the hillside, where the soil contains more clay and limestone and is distinctly more suitable for white wines.

Soil erosion is a constant problem in these vineyards. Rainstorms rapidly wash down the fine, valuable, topsoil to the lower part of the slopes, where M. Henri and his team regularly collect it and take it back up to the top again. Jean le Bault has recently taken this problem in hand, in characteristically thorough fashion: after much reflection, he has installed conduits for the water to ensure that such topsoil is readily collectible. Once recovered, it is restored to the vineyards by means of a mechanical harvester. As well as being the most efficient mothod of doing the work, he clearly enjoys the initial shock on people's faces when he tells them that he uses a harvesting machine.

Jean le Bault is a perfectionist. He enjoys doing things properly and, thanks to his factory making a significant proportion of the bottles used by the French perfume industry, has the necessary means to implement his ideas. 'Nothing is too fine, for Mon Seigneur the wine,' he avows, adding with a twinkling smile, 'It's a labour of love.'

He has now retired from the perfume-bottle business, and is thus able to devote more time to the Domaine and to give more thought to its future. His planning started in 1978 when the Domaine was officially handed over to his two sons – both international bankers, presently living outside France.

In 1990, following a long and unsuccessful quest for larger cellars, a magnificent new building with a splendid classical pediment – largely designed by Jean le Bault himself – was constructed on the outskirts of Pernand. This facility is capable of storing several vintages of the Domaine's production, of acting as a cuverie, and of being used as an entirely independent négociant premises, should the business expand in this direction in the future. Its top floor, lit by natural light during the day, is designed as a tasting and reception room.

In the search for perfection, it is necessary to be honest in recognising imperfection. Jean le Bault is the first to admit that, whilst his Corton-Charlemagne has gained wide critical acclaim, his red Corton falls far short of what others are achieving. Tasting a range of vintages, it is clear that the wines lack the depth of extract and concentration one expects in a Grand Cru, even in good years such as 1985.

It is not easy to pinpoint precisely what is going wrong. There is no material difference between the red and white vines – both are of roughly the same age (45–50 years) and tended by M. Henri with equal care. However, a similarity of yield would account in part for the relative dilution of the Corton. Experience throughout the Côte indicates that above about 35 hl./ha. the Pinot Noir loses concentration of flavour, whereas the Chardonnay can tolerate up to 45–50 hl./ha. without such consequences.

The vinification of the Corton also makes a contribution, since the Domaine's outside oenologist, who has dictated overall practice to M. Henri for many years, is unwilling to prolong *cuvaison* beyond 6–8 days; this is manifestly too short for proper extraction, particularly of aromas and tannins. With

Comtesse Jean le Bault framed by an Aubusson tapestry in the house at Pernand

reduced yields and another 4–6 days *cuvaison*, the Domaine's Corton would gain immeasurably in quality.

There are no such problems with the Corton-Charlemagne. This is a wine, in vintages both good and less good, of great presence and distinction. It is rarely a wine to be drunk young – although, sadly, most is – but one to be kept ten years or more to shed its youthful austerity and to develop into something of great breed and finesse.

The vinification for this aristocrat is a species of 'modified classical' – the principal modifications being firstly, that the fermentation is started in stainless steel to enable the temperature to be kept at a maximum of 18° C; then after 5–6 days when there is no longer a significant risk of the temperature rising, the *must* is passed into cask.

Then comes the second modification: the new casks, which form 33% of the total – the remainder being equally second- and third-year barrels – are made from Limousin oak – 'it's less strong,' says M. Henri, confidently, although virtually everyone else would affirm the opposite, namely that Limousin oak imparts such a strong measure of raw tannins to a wine that it is only suitable for cognac and for other base wines for distillation.

The Bonneau du Martray Charlemagne seems oblivious of this, generally absorbing its measure of oak without difficulty. Once in cask it remains there until after the second, *malolactic*, fermentation. M. Henri admits that this process is beyond his comprehension: '*malo*, it's very complicated, it's almost magic!' he adds.

Once all the casks have finished fermenting, the wine is racked off its lees and unified in stainless-steel tanks. It then returns to cask until just before the new vintage when it is re-racked into stainless-steel and left there to await bottling which usually takes place 15–18 months after harvesting. This operation, preceded by both a kieselguhr and a sterile plate filtration, is deliberately early in order to keep as much freshness and youthful fruit as possible in the bottled wine.

Whilst, according to Jean le Bault, you are the servant of your wine whilst it is being produced, the reverse is the case when the time comes to drink it. Then what is sought is nothing short of perfection.

It is to be regretted that the white wines from this, as from most other fine Domaines, are usually consumed long before they are mature. This seems to be a combination of the exigencies of holding stock, especially for restaurants, and of natural curiosity which encourages people to draw the cork far too soon. Young Corton-Charlemagne is by no means an unpleasant drink – on the contrary it is often thoroughly appealing given a year or two to overcome its *malade de mise* – but like the Grands Crus of Puligny, it gives its most satisfying performance after a decade or so in bottle.

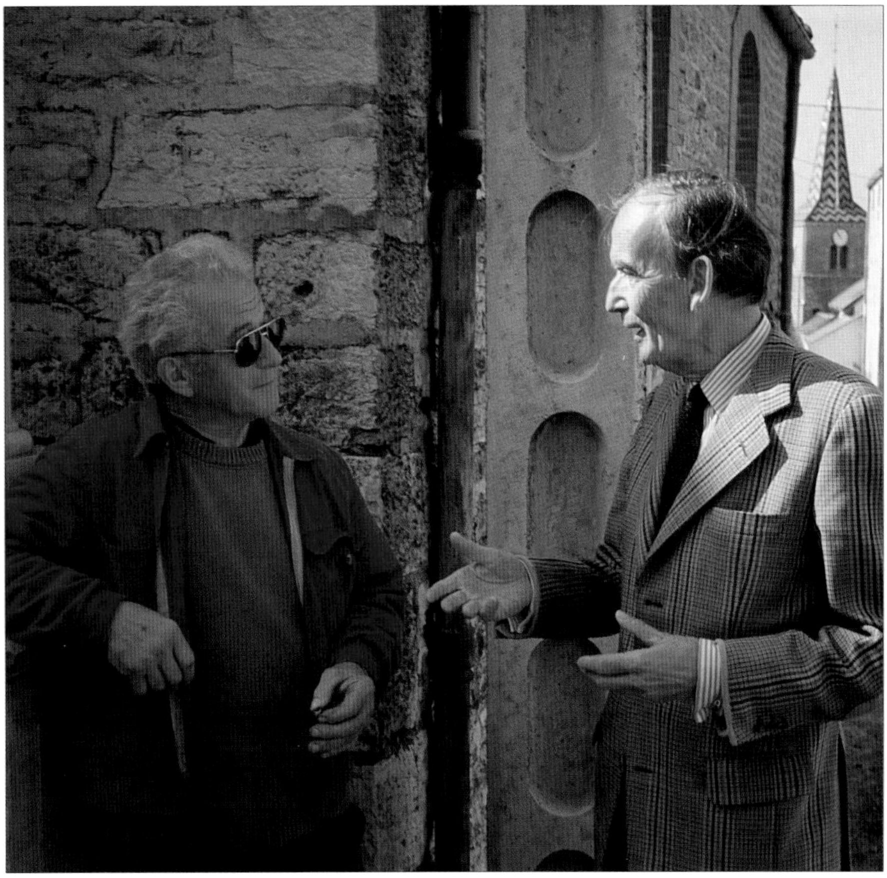

A wealth of experience: Comte Jean le Bault consulting with Monsieur Henri

The Bonneau du Martray wines are yardstick Corton-Charlemagnes: in early 1991, the 1990 tasted from several different casks was characteristically ripe, fat and masculine, a wine of exceptional promise, not dissimilar to the 1979 in style. The 1989 however, with just a few days of bottling was still showing an attractive peach kernel and dried apricot nose, rather reminiscent of a muted young Condrieu, but not surprisingly tasted distinctly flat; the wine clearly has length and a good firm structure, but needs a year at least before it can properly be re-assessed.

The 1987 was starting to emerge – quite a stony, steely, peachy sort of wine, with a fine nerve of 1987 acidity and yet plenty of depth and weight. There were flashes of the mature lime-blossom and hazelnut nose which so often characterises fine mature white Burgundy; but here is a wine which is by no means ready, yet much of the 4,000 or so cases produced have probably already been sunk by the importunate and the impatient.

To get a true line onto what a fine Bonneau du Martray Corton-Charlemagne tastes of in the early 1990s, one has to go back to the 1979, which is just reaching full power. Green-gold, a magnificent colour, with a burgeoning nose of steely, almost smoky, nuts and lime-blossom and a flavour which, although still tight, opens out into something of great richness and complexity. One should not expect the opulence and fatness of a Bâtard or a Pucelles, but rather a more intellectual sort of charm – wits rather than flesh.

The lesser vintages will stand up to plain fish and possibly light poultry dishes, whilst the grander bottles can take on something 'plus cuisiné', although anything too heavily spiced or sauced would destroy everything that Jean de la Morinière and M. Henri have striven so long to create.

VINEYARD HOLDINGS

Commune	*Level*	*Lieu-dit/Climat*	*Area*	*Vine Age*	*Status*
Aloxe/Pernand	GC	Charlemagne	9.0	45–50	P
Aloxe	GC	Charlemagne	2.0	45–50	P
		Total	**11.0 ha.**		

Domaine Roland Rapet Père et Fils

PERNAND-VERGELESSES

Roland Rapet is a reliable source of good wine in Pernand, where his ancestors have lived since 1792 – he has a 1792 Tastevin to prove it. Although there were inherited vineyards, it is he and his father, Robert, who have assembled the 16 ha. of vineyards which the Domaine exploits today. In 1975 the Rapets moved out of the centre of the village and built themselves a large house on the outskirts with adjoining cellars and cuverie.

There used to be two Rapet labels corresponding to the vines of father and son. However, when Robert died, it was decided to market all the Domaine's wines under the Roland Rapet label; although Roland's son, Vincent, plays an important role in the Domaine's workings, this is still the case.

Roland left school and came to work with his father at the age of 15. He cheerfully admits that his methods have not changed much for the last 20 years, although agreeing that some innovations have been wholly beneficial – such, for example, as the development of clones which make individual vine replacement feasible and thus prolong the useful life of a vineyard for 10–20 years.

Some years ago Roland bought a parcel of Corton-Charlemagne which had remained unplanted since the 1920s – when white wines were less popular than they are now – and planted it. However, so extensive has been the soil erosion in this vineyard that they were obliged to grub up the vines in 1990 and to reconstitute the walls before replanting. They took this opportunity to bring in special machines to extract and crush the many heavy limestone rock outcrops before returning the rubble back to the vineyard. Restoration of retaining walls has helped contain eroded soils and provided an element of aesthetic appeal to the hillside.

Evolution is slow chez Rapet; up to 15 years ago they made their own grafts and up to 10 years ago used only plant material from their own vineyards for replanting. Nowadays the time spent running a Domaine precludes home grafting – 'that's fine at Chorey, where they have black, rich fertile soils, suitable for grafting; here at Pernand the soil is poorer and grafting is more trouble.' Now, healthy clones are used to bolster their policy of keeping as high an average vine age as possible. Vines tend to be grubbed up a decade later now than they were a generation ago. Roland Rapet cites three reasons for this: firstly, there is better protection against soil erosion, so vines last longer; secondly, better quality grafts contribute to healthier and therefore longer-living plants; and thirdly, when vines eventually die, there are now machines which will excise more of the root and dig deeper than the sturdiest vigneron.

Increased average vine age avoids the necessity for anything so revolutionary as a green-pruning, although there is a very careful *évasivage* at the start of the growing season. Roland Rapet is somewhat scornful of green-pruning, remarking dryly that it it is easy to talk about but difficult to do properly. Removing bunches during the growing season to thin out the crop is indeed a skilled exercise. One suspects that the wines of many growers who have tried this have suffered in consequence.

When to harvest is perhaps a more difficult decision at Pernand than elsewhere, since the vineyards have a more westerly exposure which limits their insolation. Roland Rapet starts picking the lower vineyards which ripen first, proceeding up the hill to end with the Corton and Corton-Charlemagne.

Red vinification is more or less traditional – 75–100% destalking followed by a short *cuvaison* of 8 days and fermentation, with plenty of *pigéage*, at 30–33° C. The short *cuvaison* is a matter of expediency rather than policy – the *cuves* have to be used twice. So if the second load of grapes arrives before the first has finished fermenting, then Roland has to decant it. In 1988 one *cuve* was decanted at a specific gravity of 1005 – a more usual value being 995; in other words, before all the sugar had been transformed into alcohol. Conflicts of theory and practice are not as rare as vignerons would have us believe.

The cream of this Domaine are the two Grands Crus. The 1.5 ha. of Corton are in fact an *assemblage* of several *climats*: Chaume, Pougets, Perrières and Voierosse. These have more or less deep, red, ferruginous soils which impart power and substance to the wine. Rapet's Corton tends to be relatively light in colour in its first few years – a fact which Roland attributes to the action of sulphur dioxide in decolouring the wine. However he reckons that the colour returns with age to a mid-garnet. The 1978 showed well in 1990 with a very attractive, positive *sous-bois* nose allied to some almost over-ripe red fruits. On the palate the wine was long and puissant with a lovely finely-tuned balance of constituents. Roland Rapet reckons that his 1988s will end up resembling the 1978s, and the 1989s the 1979s.

The Corton is not matched in quality by its white sibling – from 1.5 ha. of vines in the cooler Pernand sector of the hill. Tasting the 1989, 1988 and 1986, there seems to be a want of matter in the wine which unbalances it. There is nothing unorthodox in the vinification to explain why this should be so. The wine would probably gain from rather more than the 10–15% of new oak it receives; it would definitely gain from being fermented in wood, rather than the present policy of starting the fermentation in bulk better to control the temperature and then putting the wine into cask. The wine is by no means poor, but just somewhat feeble for a Grand Cru. Tasting it against the Bonneau du Martray points up the differences.

Roland Rapet is perfectly capable of making fine wine. At present he produces sound quality – sometimes, but rarely, exciting. He seems to be losing interest. In short, a good but not always great Domaine, where it definitely pays to be selective.

VINEYARD HOLDINGS

Commune	*Level*	*Lieu-dit/Climat*	*Area*	*Vine Age*	*Status*
Aloxe	GC	Corton	1.50	25–30	P
Aloxe	V	—	2.00	25–30	P
Beaune	PC + V	—	1.00	25–30	P
Savigny	V	—	1.25	25–30	P
Pernand	PC	Ile des Vergelesses + Vergelesses	2.00	25–30	P
Pernand	GC	En Charlemagne	1.50	25–30	
Pernand	V	(Blanc)	1.50	5–25	P
Pernand	R	(Côte de Beaune Rouge)	1.00	25–30	P
—	R	(Côte de Beaune Vill.)	1.75	25–30	P
—	R	(Bourgogne Aligoté)	1.50	25–30	P
—	R	(Bourgogne Rouge)	1.00	25–30	P
		Total	**16.00 ha.**		

N.B. Roland Rapet was imprecise about the age of his individual *climats*, so these figures must be considered as approximations.

Domaine Dubreuil-Fontaine

PERNAND-VERGELESSES

Bernard Dubreuil runs one of the more substantial Domaines in Pernand. It was largely created by great-grand-father, a M. Arbinet, in the late 1860s, and continued by his son-in-law, Julien Dubreuil. Bernard, who started with his father in 1957, married a Mlle. Bidot from Pommard and made his own contribution to the estate – 0.75 ha. each of Corton-Bressandes and Clos du Roi in 1966, 0.16 ha. of Les Petits Epenots in 1969, the Monopole of Savigny Clos Berthet – 1 ha. of white and 0.5 ha. of red, just below the village – in 1971 and finally 0.25 ha. of Aloxe-Corton Village and a further 0.25 ha. of Corton Clos du Roi in 1985.

Bernard is a courteous, delightful and yet serious family man, perhaps a touch reserved at first, with a deep love of his vineyards and a sense of what makes a wine fine.

His method of working is unashamedly traditional. Up to 35 years old the vines are replaced individually, to maintain the average vine age as close to 50 as possible. Otherwise, 2% of the estate is replanted annually. *Sélection massale* ceased in 1983 – the inevitability of clones gaining what one suspects is grudging acceptance. For security, a mix of the best clones is used – Bernard having a sneaking preference for Pinot Clone 114 because it produces high sugars and low yields. These factors, along with short pruning – 'if we can't do a *baguette*, we do a bayonet to 2 eyes' – and a strict removal of any double buds early on, makes for small yields of good, balanced quality.

The young vines tend to ripen early and these are harvested sooner than later. Until recently, growers were allowed to make table wine from the produce of vines which were too young to be declared for their own appellation. However, in 1987 the rules were changed so that the produce of young vines had the right to its respective appellation a year earlier than before – after their third flowering. The *quid pro quo* for this was that vin de table may not now be made from these vines, so any young-vine production is either thrown out or sent for distillation.

Bernard destalks his grapes – up to 90% – preferring the tannins of new wood to those from stalks, should extra structure be needed. A peculiarity of the house is that neither red nor white juice is sulphured until first racking – a most unusual and curiously risky procedure, especially with white grapes, which demands supreme hygiene in the cellars, since the risk of oxidation before fermentation has started is notably high.

Deprived of their anaesthetic shot of sulphur, the yeasts start to ferment within 48 hours – Bernard begins to worry if the delay is longer. He is not entirely sure if his fermentations start rapidly because he does not sulphur, or he does not sulphur because he wants to avoid any maceration and to get fermentation going as soon as possible. One should perhaps not try to explain tradition.

The reds ferment at 28–32° C, with a *cuvaison* of 8–10 days. The absence of stalks and this short *cuvaison* result in wines which accentuate finesse rather than structure. Of the Domaine's Pernands, the Ile des Vergelesses, which has a markedly argilo-calcaire soil with a high iron content, has more structure though less finesse than the straight Pernand, and more potential for ageing. The Corton Bressandes, typically, starts life with a deepish colour and quite firm structure, taking several years, in good vintages, to show its real qualities.

Tasting the 1978 Bressandes and the 1969 Clos du Roi gave some indication of how well Bernard Dubreuil's wines age. The 1978 showed a distinctly visceral aroma, mingled with that gorgeous *sous-bois* which so often characterises mature Pinot Noir. The 1969 was surprisingly even more youthful – very different in style to the 1978, slightly *surmature* with quite firm almost tarry undertones, still a relatively immature wine.

The best of the whites are undoubtedly the Clos Berthet and the Corton-Charlemagne. The Clos Berthet – 100% Chardonnay – being better exposed than the Domaines Pernand Village vineyards has a notch more concentration added to the old vine fruit. In good vintages the Pernand whites tend to develop a hallmark *goût de silex* from the soil, which shows up as an earthy, slightly peachy flavour. The Corton-Charlemagne is usually a somewhat masculine example of that generally masculine wine – tight, almost austere in youth, developing with 5–10 years bottle-age a complex nose of charred almonds and lime-blossom.

Neither the whites nor the reds are marked unduly by new wood – the Grands Crus never see more than 30% – Vosges for the white and Allier or Nevers for the reds – the Village and Premiers Crus having much less. The whites start their fermentation in bulk at 20–22° C and are then decanted into cask with some sugar remaining to finish the transformation there.

As for the reds, no SO_2 is added until the first racking when the different casks of each wine are unified. The SO_2 levels are further adjusted at second racking and at bottling. All Dubreuil's wines are both fined – egg albumen for the reds and casein for the whites – and plate-filtered.

This is a serious house. Bernard Dubreuil – and his daughter, Christine, who speaks fluent Californian and is qualified in oenology and business studies – take great care with their vineyards and with their wine-making. If the wines lack anything, perhaps they could do with a touch more concentration. Bernard might do well to throw a little of his natural caution to the winds, especially in the matter of early, safe, harvesting and systematic, safe filtration – 'a client might return a bottle with a slight deposit'. While he's at it, a day or two longer *cuvaison* would give his reds a measure of more depth and interest. Nevertheless, for all its prudence, this is a high-quality Domaine, but one from which it is necessary to pick and choose.

VINEYARD HOLDINGS

Commune	*Level*	*Lieu-dit/Climat*	*Area*	*Vine Age*	*Status*
Aloxe	GC	Corton Bressandes	0.75	45	F
Aloxe	GC	Corton Perrières	0.60	40	F
Aloxe	GC	Corton Clos du Roi	1.00	30	F
Aloxe	V	Les Combes/Les Cras	0.50	35	F
Pernand	GC	Corton-Charlemagne	0.76	33	F
Pernand	PC	Ile des Vergelesses	0.73	36	F
Pernand	V	(Several – White)	1.90	35	F
Pernand	V	Clos Berthet (R & W)	1.50	20	F
Pernand	V	Les Fichots (R)	3.00	40	F
Savigny	PC	Les Vergelesses	3.72	40	F
Beaune	PC	Les Montrevenots	0.30	10	F
Volnay	V	(Several climats)	0.50	30	F
Pommard	PC	Les Epenots	0.40	50	F
Pommard	V	(Several climats)	0.59	25	F
—	R	(PTG/R/W/Aligoté)	5.44	5–35	F
		Total	**21.69 ha.**		

SAVIGNY-LÈS-BEAUNE

Anyone wanting to escape the waves of determined, eager summer tourists, whose loud and incessant babel fills the hotels and restaurants of Beaune, could do worse than make their way a few kilometres north to the pleasant green village of Savigny-lès-Beaune.

Sandwiched in the opening of a peaceful, wooded valley – La Combe de la Fontaine Froide – Savigny offers tranquil walks, a few small shops, a rather dismal café, 2 modest restaurants and a small hotel, in addition to a splendid seventeenth-century Château, a church with a remarkable clock-tower and a clutch of friendly growers.

The settlement of 'Villa Saviniaco' is Gallo-Roman in origin. By the twelfth century this had become Savigniaci – sounding like a cross between an exotic pasta dish and an Italian lyric-tenor – while further refinements led to Savigny-près-Beaune and Savigny-sous-Beaune before the place finally made up its municipal mind on Savigny-lès-Beaune in 1863.

Two Roman roads, parts of which are still visible, cross the village whilst the newer A6 autoroute provides superb, elevated views across the vineyards to the distant Bois de Corton from one of its most picturesque stopping-places which, according to a wall-plaque, marks the half-way point between Lille and Marseilles.

The Savigny Village AC covers both red and white wines, the former also being entitled to the AC Côte de Beaune-Villages. In fact, because Savigny is becoming much better known, the best producers seldom use this alternative. The AC Savigny vineyards cover some 238.58 ha., a further 144.02 ha. being divided between 22 Premiers Crus. Among Savigny's 1,500 inhabitants, Pitiot and Poupon list 91 growers in Savigny and 5 négociants, the largest and best known of this quintet being Henri de Villamont and Doudet Naudin.

The river Rhoin – a half-hearted, feeble water-course – neatly bisects the vineyards. On its northern side, beneath the Bois Nöel, lies most of the Village land and a narrow band of 13 Premiers Crus. These latter include: Les Guettes, marked by a distinctive castellated tower, built as an hunter's look-out by Leonce Bocquet who was ruined restoring the Château de Clos Vougeot; Les Lavières, so called because of the high proportion of 'laves' or shale in its soil; Les Serpentières – possibly so named because of the small water-runs which wriggle through the vineyard and Les Vergelesses (near to Vergy).

The soils vary markedly between *climats* – the flatter, lower slopes are deeper and richer, whilst the sloping hillsides have less generous but finer soils. The Bois Nöel vineyards' privileged southerly exposition, ripens grapes a week or more before those on the opposite side of the valley. There, under the Mont-Battois, lie a further 9 Premiers Crus – including Les Marconnets, Les Peuillets, Les Jarrons and Les Narbantons, marked by a functional workers' hut. Here, a less advantageous north-easterly exposure is compounded by some patches of heavy, wet soil, especially around the flatter Les Peuillets.

Savigny is unusual in having two small *Monopole* vineyards, each part of a larger Premier Cru: La Bataillère – a Clos until one wall collapsed – a 1.81 ha. plot of 28-45-year-old vines in Les Vergelesses and Champ Chevrey, 1.47 ha. of 35-year-old vines in the westerly corner of Les Fournaux, belonging to Domaine Tollot- Beaut of Chorey.

Savigny occupies an important place in Burgundian history, thanks chiefly to the innovative Count de la Loyère, who ran the Côte d'Or Viticultural Society from 1854 to1879. He is credited with planting vines in straight rows, rather than *en foule,* and with introducing the vineyard plough. He invented the grape-destalking machine, which can be seen on the ground floor of the Château, and presided over the prototype straddle-tractor and the first Burgundian vineyard map in 1862. He also entertained at Savigny Dr. Guyot, creator of the now famous pruning system.

The white wines of Savigny – on average 3.3% of Village and Premier Cru output – come mainly from Chardonnay vines on limestone and marl soils on the Bouilland side of the commune. Some growers consider that the marls at the top of the slopes resemble the soils of Corton-Charlemagne where Pinot Blanc is also allowed, but goes to make Bourgogne Blanc, most growers preferring Chardonnay for its finesse and staying power. Domaine Ecard, however, produces a *cuvée* of Savigny Blanc from 100% Pinot Blanc. However, whites made from grapes grown on *terre à rouge* are altogether less fine and more rustic.

Savigny Blanc is underrated. From a decent grower, it can be a delight – with a touch of *goût de terroir* and plenty of ripe, fat fruit. Better vintages repay a few years in bottle, emerging to a nutty, rather individual, middle age.

The reds need careful choosing. Whilst lean years can be harsh, charmless and rather angular, good vintages from the right Domaines can be plump, finely perfumed and seductive. Styles vary from Tollot-Beaut's pure crushed strawberry Champ-Chevrey and slightly more muscular Lavières, two of the best of the more delicate Savignys, to the thicker, slow-evolving 'méthode ancienne' of Doudet Naudin.

Between these 'book-ends' are finely-tuned, mid-weight offerings from Chandon de Briaille, especially attractive in riper vintages, and the excellent La Dominode from Bruno Clair (of Marsannay), made predominantly from 80-year-old vines. The Savignys, and everything else, of Henri de Villamont are overrated, although they have superb vineyards capable of producing fine wine; what a pity!

The best Savigny of all, however, is Françoise Choppin's Clos la Bataillère, a wine which ages wonderfully and has great class and style.

Anyone with time to wander through the village, should peer through the gates of Domaine Chandon de Briaille, in the Rue Soeur Goby. There you will find a marvellous example of a small eighteenth-century gentleman's manor, encrusted with the most unusual horticultural sculpture, and a small park laid out by Le Nôtre. Nearby is the Château, part thirteenth, but mainly seventeenth-century, sitting in its park flanked incongruously by a squadron of assorted war-planes.

In the early 1970s, it was acquired by an English company which instantly removed all its antiques, mostly museum pieces, to England without export licences, and auctioned them before the French could intervene. A thoroughly shameful episode. It has recently been bought by Japanese interests and is now completely restored.

When you have finished visiting, make for the Combe de la Fontaine Froide – either for a picnic in the water-meadows by the Rhoin, or else for a good meal and a fine bottle at the Vieux Moulin in Bouilland. If you have any surplus energy, you could always try scaling one of the vertical limestone overhangs opposite the restaurant.

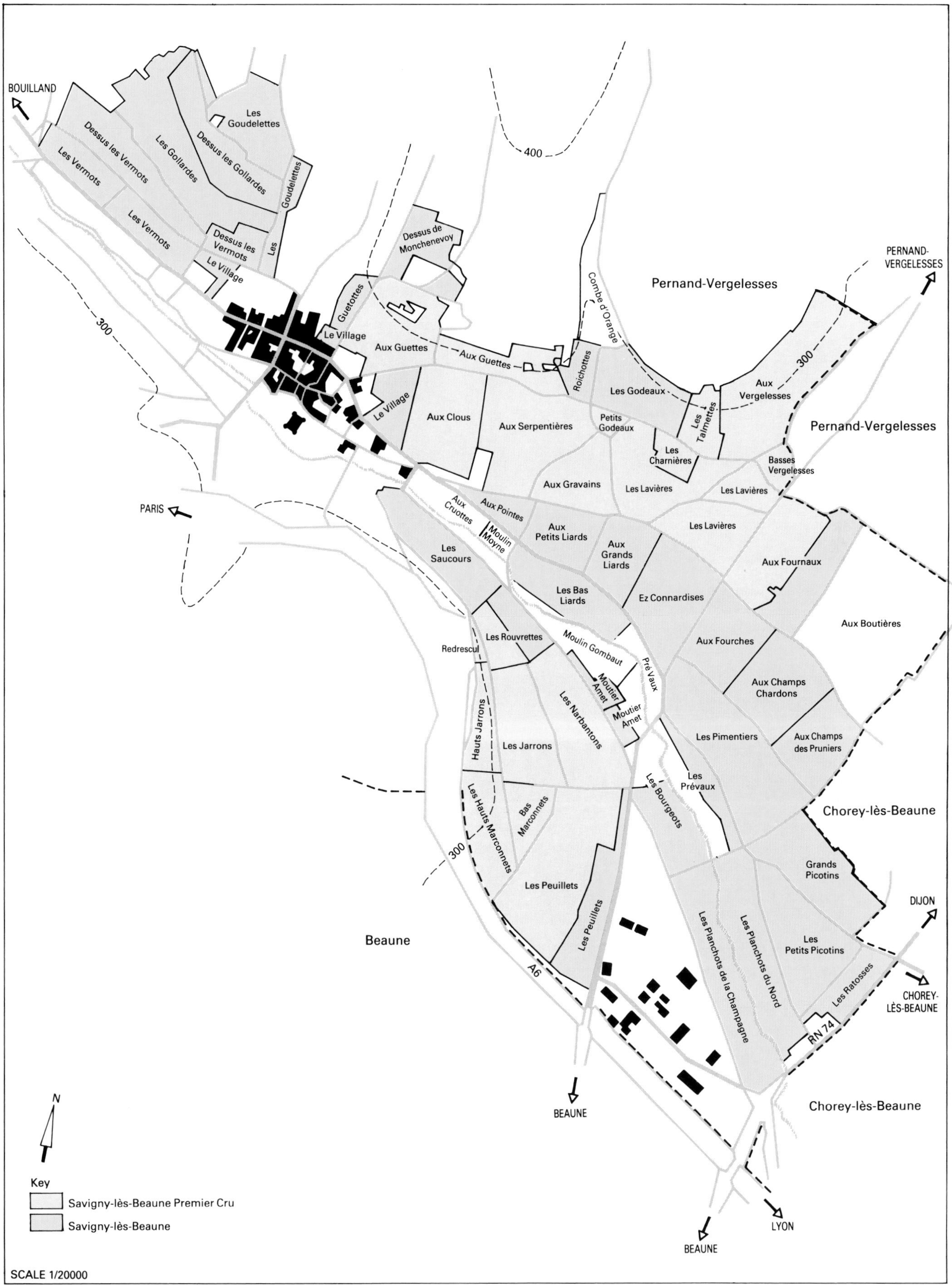
BOUILLAND
Les Goudelettes
Dessus les Vermots
Les Gollardes
Dessus les Gollardes
Les Goudelettes
Les Vermots
Les Vermots
Dessus les Vermots
Le Village
Dessus de Monchenevoy
Guetottes
Le Village
Aux Guettes
Aux Guettes
400
Combe d'Orange
Pernand-Vergelesses
PERNAND-VERGELESSES
300
Roichottes
Les Godeaux
Les Talmettes
Aux Vergelesses
Pernand-Vergelesses
Le Village
Aux Clous
Aux Serpentières
Petits Godeaux
Les Charnières
Basses Vergelesses
Aux Gravains
Les Lavières
Les Lavières
PARIS
Aux Cruottes
Aux Pointes
Aux Petits Liards
Moulin Moyne
Les Lavières
Aux Grands Liards
Les Saucours
Aux Fournaux
Les Bas Liards
Ez Connardises
Aux Boutières
Redrescul
Les Rouvrettes
Moulin Gombaut
Pré Vaux
Aux Fourches
Moutier Amet
Aux Champs Chardons
Moutier Amet
Hauts Jarrons
Les Jarrons
Les Narbantons
Les Pimentiers
Aux Champs des Pruniers
Les Prévaux
Les Bourgeots
Les Hauts Marconnets
Bas Marconnets
Chorey-lès-Beaune
300
Les Peuillets
Grands Picotins
Beaune
Les Peuillets
Les Planchots de la Champagne
Les Planchots du Nord
Les Petits Picotins
DIJON
A6
Les Ratosses
CHOREY-LÈS-BEAUNE
RN 74
N
BEAUNE
Chorey-lès-Beaune
Key
Savigny-lès-Beaune Premier Cru
Savigny-lès-Beaune
LYON
BEAUNE
SCALE 1/20000

Domaine Simon Bize et Fils

SAVIGNY-LÈS-BEAUNE

A quarter of a century ago, the status of a Burgundy Domaine would probably have depended more on the grandeur of its land than on its wine-making. Today, by contrast, the estates which excite most attention are often those making superlative wine from relatively modest vineyard holdings.

Among these is the Domaine Bize. Patrick Bize, a mildly serious man in his early thirties with a wry sense of humour and quietly forceful opinions, is a member of that emerging band of talented young wine-makers who are doing so much for the quality and image of Burgundy.

Savigny, with Beaune itself, has remained something of a Cinderella among the communes of the Côte de Beaune; buyers flock to Pommard and Volnay, but seem to bypass Savigny in the mistaken belief that it is somehow incapable of producing serious wine. Anyone who has enjoyed a mature bottle of Bize, Capron-Manieux or Girard-Vollot would happily set that record straight.

Patrick with his new van rouge

Patrick admits that he was a reluctant vigneron. Neither he nor his father had any formal training, and the only members of his immediate family who did – two uncles who spent some time at the Lycée Viticole in Beaune – gave it up after the war as a bad job.

Although there had been Bizes at Savigny for several generations, the Domaine really started with Patrick's grandfather who married into the local butcher's shop. Becoming a small proprietor of vines, he taught his son the trade who in turn passed it on to his son. Patrick admits that he 'had never worked in a vineyard nor in a cellar' and moreover, that he didn't like wine. However by degrees he came to like what he was doing – and almost 'changed without noticing it'.

The quality of Patrick's work is clear from his attitude to his vineyards: he insists that he knows the characteristics of each of his 5 Savigny Premiers Crus and his various Village plots intimately and seeks to adapt his viticulture to the way he can tell they will behave. He paints a strong contrast between his own attitude and that of wine-growers in the USA where the wine-maker is seen as the person who determines the quality of the bottle: 'it's nonsense, just publicity; it isn't Monsieur Gadget or Madame Machine who makes the wine, it's the appellation and the grape; one should never forget this.'

This 'esprit' suffuses everything he does – from the flexibility in the treatments for pests and diseases ('we treat as the vine demands, there are no formulae') to the way the vines are pruned and trained (for young vines – up to 20 years old (!) – *taille en Royat*; after that, the classic *Guyot simple*).

The twin aims are to keep the vines as healthy as possible and to keep yields down to 30–40 hl./ha. Patrick has come to know the productivity of each plot of vines, and can tailor his vineyard regime accordingly. This is not a question of simply reducing yields but of optimising the balance of constituents in the grapes.

There is a strict *évasivage* each spring, but no green-pruning. Patrick prefers to control production with his secateurs in March rather than removing grapes in July, or even performing a *saignée de cuve* at vinification. *Cordon* training the young vines also helps keep yields down.

The order of harvesting the various parcels of vines is critical. Patrick generally starts with the oldest vines which tend to be on the more precocious rootstocks (Aux Vergelesses) and works backwards – except in 1990 when the opposite was the case, the young Marconnets vines having matured more rapidly than the others.

In the cellars there is concern to retain the typicity of each vineyard and of each vintage. Each Premier Cru has its own style which it is Patrick's aim to express – he seeks to control and follow the characteristics of the vintage, but not to coerce it into any particular mould.

In the cuverie, the open wood or enamelled *cuves* receive grapes which are a mixture of whole bunches with stalks for the older vines and partially destemmed grapes for the younger vines. The aim is to have as long a *cuvaison* as possible with a prefermentive maceration of some 3–5 days with minimal sulphur (30cl. of 5% solution per barrel) and a maximum temperature of 32–33° C. A *cuvaison* lasting 18 days is not unusual here, in marked contrast with other growers in the commune. This doubtless accounts for the Domaine's style of wine.

The grapes are crushed by foot to liberate the juice, but very definitely not yeasted to start fermentation. Patrick believes firmly in the indigenous yeast population for the depth and complexity of his wines. When *chaptalisation* is necessary, it is performed at the end of fermentation in order to prolong it.

Patrick tastes each *cuve* to decide when to decant the free-run wine off the pulp. He is not wholly trustful of analysis to make decisions for him: 'numbers are interesting but . . . with numbers you would make a classic, stereotyped wine – straight from the oenology laboratory – but if you want class, you must taste.' In fact, he decants when there are about 5–6 grammes per litre of sugar remaining to lengthen fermentation further.

There is no *débourbage* – 'except in very rich years – for example 1983; it depends on the quality of the vintage.' Asked if he ever used pectolytic enzymes to help settle gross lees, he replied that he had kept some unused in the cupboard for 5 years, and finding them there decided to try them on the 1990 vintage. However, this was exceptional – they are only normally used when a high level of rot threatens the quality of clarification and thus the health of the lees.

The Domaine buys its own Nevers wood from 'the best grower in the forest' and dries it at Savigny. It is then delivered to 'the best tonnelier' to fashion into casks. These are made with a medium charring so as not to mark the wine excessively with toast flavours. Patrick's policy is to use the maximum new wood between decanting from the vats and the first racking. So 50–100% of the Premiers Crus start their *élevage* in new wood (100% in 1988) and the proportion is adjusted after tasting at first racking at any time between the March and September following the vintage, depending when the *malos* are finished.

Preparation for bottling follows no systematic routine – the 1988s were fined, the 1987s lightly filtered. It is a matter of tasting the wine and deciding what suits it best. In general, the wines are unified before fining or filtration, and bottled about 14–18 months after the vintage.

The excellent whites which Patrick produces are fermented in cask – 15% new wood – fined with either fish fining or a mixture of casein/bentonite and bottled after some 12–14 months to retain their freshness and aromas. His Bourgogne Blanc, from the Champlains vineyard, is a somewhat particular wine in that it comes from roughly equal proportions of Pinot Blanc, Chardonnay and Pinot Beurot, which are vinified separately. Approximately 20% new oak imparts a touch of butteriness and structure, whilst on the nose the Pinot Beurot and Pinot Blanc give a distinctly floral element to the aroma.

A second Bourgogne Blanc, Les Perrières, from older Chardonnay vines planted on stony ground, produces a wine of greater depth and matter than Les Champlains, although with somewhat less obvious elegance.

The Savigny Blanc *cuvée*, from the Les Pimentiers vineyard, is 100% Chardonnay. Its characteristic is an earthy *goût de silex* – a variety of silica – which is often found in white Savignys. Generally quite fresh and sappy, it is perhaps something of an (easily) acquired taste.

The Domaine produces a fine range of red Savignys – 5 Premiers Crus, one individual Village *lieu-dit*, Les Grands Liards, and a Village *cuvée*. In general the style is for quite meaty, structured wines which mature well over a decade or so in good vintages.

The Talmettes is probably the most forward of the range – soft, fruity and attractive. The Vergelesses (Savigny, not Pernand) comes from 7 different parcels spread over 2.20 ha. The vineyard is situated on poor soil on a band of rock which characteristically produces a wine with greater lightness and finesse than the other Premiers Crus. In lesser vintages it can lack depth. However, there is a useful contribution from a parcel of vines aged 40 years or more which adds *charpente* and weight to the ensemble. The 1989 vintage, tasted in late 1990, had a colour of deep, crushed red fruit and a very seductive elegant and complex aroma of violets, beetroot (yes!) and red fruits which continued onto the palate. A fine wine of flesh and guts, with enough tannin to hold it up for several years.

The Village Grands Liards *cuvée* is often deliciously soft and seductive with plenty of succulent, plump fruit and in good vintages an element of almost creamy richness, which is most attractive. A wine to lay down in magnums for 5–10 years!

The Savigny Marconnets vineyard lies just beneath the motorway lay-by (for the wine-loving motorist, probably one of the most appealing places to pause and picnic). Separated from the Beaune Marconnets by only these few metres of tarmac, it shares its geology. The result is a wine more redolent of the style and structure of Beaune than of Savigny – aromas of *fruits rouges*, quite fat and round on the palate with plenty of grip and length.

The Les Guettes – from the opposite end of the appellation – is different in character – more finesse, almost lacy in texture, though not lacking in fruit and depth. Its allocation of new wood gives it an harmonious scaffolding of creamy oak.

Patrick and his father have recently taken delivery of a magnificent new cellar which will give them more room to work. Although this has to be paid for, the Bizes' prices are usually more than reasonable, so anyone genuinely searching for quality, rather than grand appellations, would do worse than to visit this fine Domaine.

VINEYARD HOLDINGS

Commune	*Level*	*Lieu-dit/Climat*	*Area*	*Vine Age*	*Status*
Savigny	PC	Aux Vergelesses	2.20	35	P
Savigny	PC	Les Fournaux	1.00	30	P
Savigny	PC	Aux Guettes	0.48	25	P
Savigny	PC	Les Talmettes	0.80	18	P
Savigny	PC	Les Marconnets	0.60	18	P
Savigny	V	Grands Liards	1.00	30	P
Savigny	V	(Several climats)	5.20	20	P
Savigny	R	Les Perrières (Bourg.R.)	2.00	20	P
Savigny	R	Les Perrières (Bourg.W.)	1.00	25	P
Savigny	R	Les Champlains (Bourg.W.)	2.30	7	F
		Total	**16.58 ha.**		

Domaine Capron-Manieux

SAVIGNY-LÈS-BEAUNE

This is an exciting small Domaine of very high quality. It is also a young enterprise created by Jean-Marie Capron-Manieux and his attractive wife, Nicole, in 1974. After renting vines in Savigny, in 1977 they made their first purchase in the village of what was then pine forest. They cut down the trees and planted vines. Now, with some Aligoté from Nicole's father in nearby Bouze-lès-Beaune, the Domaine extends to 5.88 ha.

Jean-Marie admits he knew nothing about viticulture when he arrived in Burgundy : 'I hadn't touched a vine in my life.' Having no fixed idea about a career and liking the outdoor life, he enrolled at the Lycée Viticole in Beaune, emerging in 1965 with a diploma and a strong desire to start up on his own. Before embarking on such a serious undertaking he spent a year with Michel Pont in Volnay and 3 years with Michel Voarick in Aloxe-Corton, gaining practical experience. Jean-Marie's wines are yardstick Savignys – great delicacy in both colour and nose coupled with plenty of firm, ripe, almost mouthwatering fruit and considerable style.

Apart from refusing to use anti-rot treatments since 1982 – 'they don't work very well' – and a 50/50 organic/chemical fertiliser regime used only in years when the vine has been tired by high production, the vineyards are run on a mainly classical basis.

In the cellars proceedings are also broadly traditional: there is no destalking, rather the bunches are sulphured – in several stages if the *cuves* are large – and lightly crushed by foot. The stalks aerate the pulp and help to restrain the fermentation temperature, since the Domaine has no cooling apparatus to deal with *musts* threatening to exceed the desired 35° C maximum. For smaller parcels, the wooden *cuves* are designed to hold approximately the total expected volume – Jean-Marie prefers his *cuves* to be completely filled: 'they ferment better that way.'

The secret of the great elegance of Capron's wines lies partly in the short *cuvaison* – 8–10 days – including 2 days pre-fermentive *maceration*. When the *must* has reached about 28° C – no lower since any sugar extracted from the presses would then fail to ferment straight away – the wines are *débourbés* for 2–3 days and put into casks, 20% of which are new, with no special preference for origin of wood. They then spend a year in cask, on their lees, before racking with aeration to disperse any reduced or mercaptan aromas.

The colourful Caprons – Jean-Marie and Nicole – among their unpruned vines above Savigny

About 15–18 months after the harvest – this interval depending entirely on how quickly the *malos* start and finish – the wines are again racked and lightly plate-filtered before being bottled. It is worth remarking that those in new wood remain there only up to the first racking; this preserves freshness, and avoids marking the delicate fruit with excessive wood characteristics – and also releases casks for the new crop.

The white wines also see 20% new oak and spend 18 months in cask before a second racking and bottling. To keep the cash register revolving and to finance the two vintages always in the cellars, Jean-Marie sells most of his Aligoté and some Savigny and Pernand Blanc *sur pressoir* to négociants.

Of the Domaine's 1.63 ha. of Savigny Rouge, the grapes from hillsides and flatter vineyards are fermented separately before unification into a single *cuve*, whilst those from the *lieu-dit* Les Pimentiers, acquired in 1989, are vinified separately. Do not be fooled by the relatively light colours – the Pimentiers is a shade deeper than the straight Savigny – into thinking that the wines lack fruit; far from it. They have abundant, mouthwatering fruit and also great finesse, the Pimentiers with perhaps just a hint of 'Piments!'

The Premier Cru Les Peuillets – a vineyard in fact half Village AC and half Premier Cru – expresses its gravelly, sandy subsoil in a wine of firmer structure than the Pimentiers, with aromas of *fruits rouges* and wild berries – generally quite powerful and most attractive.

Les Lavières is generally considered among the best of the Savigny Premiers Crus – a wine from predominantly rocks (laves), hard at first but with greater longevity than the Peuillets which sets out with more obvious fruit.

These wines age beautifully – the 1985s are just beginning to show their real character with delicious layers of ripe, soft fruit setting off spicy, vegetal and chocolate flavours. The old vines add their dimension of concentration to the mixture, which typically has excellent balance and power.

Sadly, in 1985, February frosts wreaked disaster here, as elsewhere along the Côte, temperatures plummeting to minus 27° C for several days. Vineyards on the flatter land nearer the villages suffered most – for example, in Les Peuillets, Jean-Marie harvested only 600 out of 15,000 vines and had to grub up over half the vineyard.

Nicole and her husband work this small Domaine without help except at harvest time. Clearly completely dedicated to quality, they consequently spend little time away. The 8–10,000 bottles they produce are eagerly snapped up by a loyal following of importers and private customers who appreciate their quality. A pity they don't bottle more of their Aligoté and Savigny Blanc!

VINEYARD HOLDINGS

Commune	*Level*	*Lieu-dit/Climat*	*Area*	*Vine Age*	*Status*
Savigny	PC	Les Lavières	0.18	13	M
Savigny	PC	Les Peuillets	0.28	5 & 40	F
Savigny	V	Les Pimentiers	0.31	30	P
Savigny	V	(Various climats)	0.88	10–50	P/M/F
Savigny	V	(White)	0.44	10–50	M/F
Pernand	V	Les Belles Filles (W)	0.39	5 & 6	F
Pommard	V	—	0.11	1991	P
Savigny/ Bouze	R	(Aligoté)	2.58	30–40	P
—	R	(Hautes-Côtes Chard.)	0.26	1991	P
—	R	(Hautes-Côtes Rouge)	0.18	10	P
		Total	**5.61 ha.**		

Domaine Girard-Vollot

SAVIGNY-LÈS-BEAUNE

As with the other communes of the Côte d'Or, Savigny has a multiplicity of vignerons producing wines in a variety of styles. Of these, Domaine Girard-Vollot falls somewhere between the refined elegance of Capron-Manieux and the more structured and denser offerings of Jean-Marc Pavelot and Simon Bize.

This is a sizeable Domaine. From a total of some 16 ha. of vineyards, no fewer than 10 are dedicated to Savigny Rouge (Village); the remainder is spread among the Savigny Premiers Crus Les Peuillets, Les Rouvrettes and Les Narbantons, with a little Savigny Blanc, some Pernand Vergelesses Premier Cru and Aloxe-Corton, rounded off with some Aligoté and Bourgogne Rouge.

The Girards are one of the oldest families of vignerons in Savigny – tracing a founding Jean Girard back to 1529. Today, the Domaine is run by Georges Girard and his sons Philippe and Jean-Jacques – now both in their thirties. Girard Père is a charming man with infectious good-humour and short grey hair which stands on end as if he were permanently connected to a source of electricity of opposing polarity.

None the less, when it comes to business, he is forceful in stating his own point of view: the introduction in 1985 of clones into his vineyards he regards with some misgiving – 'they give too much *rendement,*' he says, adding, 'but they will probably make very good old vines.' To add concentration to his wines, in the face of these vigorous clones, Georges prefers to prune short – 3–5 eyes, which is very short indeed – and to make a strict *évasivage* rather than to *saigner* his *cuves*: 'that is the essential principle, take off the grapes at the beginning,' he affirms. There is definitely no green-pruning here, just careful husbandry. 'You mustn't force a vine too quickly – go slowly, and gently.'

The vinification is relatively classical – fermentation, with about 33% of the stalks, in cement *cuves* at up to 32–33° C. Georges is not entirely convinced that cement is progress but is prepared to go along with it. *Cuvaison* is shortish – 10–12 days in total – and for no articulated reason the *cuves* are yeasted to avoid any pre-fermentive maceration. According to George, long *cuvaison* produces more bad tastes than good, and moreover, 'we don't want wines which won't be drinkable for 30 years.'

However, the preferred style is for *vins de garde* which have a good firm structure to start with and which age well over 10–15 years. Long *cuvaison* is especially eschewed because it tends to extract too much from the grapes which masks the fruit underneath.

The wines spend some 18 months in cask – 25–33% new Allier or Nevers oak for the Premier Cru reds and Vosges for the white Savigny. Things are not specially precise here – the provision of new casks 'depends on what we have'. Clearly the economics of providing new casks for a wine which sells at a relatively modest price are different from those for Grands Crus. As Georges Girard sagely puts it, 'the casks for Chambertin are the same price as those for Savigny.'

The cold cellar means that the *malos* can take up to a year to complete – they are never forced: 'we let nature do its work', explains M. Girard. A low ambient cellar temperature also means that traditional fining is unlikely to work – 'then we have to filter again' – so the wines are just given a single kieselguhr filtration to clean them up before bottling.

There are two white wines – a good Savigny Blanc and a Bourgogne Aligoté. There is also a little Bourgogne Chardonnay made from young vines. These are fermented in bulk at low temperature (22° C) and spend about a year in cask before bottling. 20% of the wood is renewed annually.

The Savigny Premiers Crus, Rouvrettes, Peuillets and Narbantons vie for first place in the Girard cellar. The Peuillets tends to have more stuffing and finesse than the straight Savigny Villages, but is a shade less structured than the other two with a nose of coffee which blossoms out into a ripe open wine after 5–10 years of age.

The Rouvrettes, being on steeply sloping land – just beneath the motorway lay-by – and on poorer soil, tends to have at once more acidity when young, yet notably more finesse – perhaps more typically Savigny than the Peuillets. The Narbantons, just below the excellent Les Dominodes, is somewhere in between them in style – more *corsé* than the Peuillets, with a deeper colour and tighter structure, but with somewhat less finesse than the Rouvrettes.

The Mairie and town fountain at Savigny are guarded by a regiment of pollarded trees

The 1989s from this Domaine will probably mature more rapidly than either the 1988s or 1990s. The 1988s Premiers Crus will be excellent in 12–15 years from birth, probably resembling in style and character the 1978s.

These are wines of structure and interest. The Girards dislike large yields – their own averaging some 40–45 hl./ha. – arguing that 'Burgundy is not made for that'. However, even with moderate cropping, their 10 ha. of Village land produce far too much for them to handle in bottle, so half is sold to négociants. The Premier Crus are all bottled and marketed by the Domaine.

Contrary to general belief, there is no undue hurry to drink Savigny Rouge – or Blanc for that matter. If they are made à l'ancienne, as with Girard-Vollot, they will keep well for a decade or more. George Girard's wines are invariably sound and interesting – good but not great. They are often among the best in the commune.

VINEYARD HOLDINGS

Commune	*Level*	*Lieu-dit/Climats*	*Area*	*Vine Age*	*Status*
Savigny	PC	Les Peuillets	0.47	35	P
Savigny	PC	Les Rouvrettes	0.47	40	P
Savigny	PC	Les Narbantons	0.40	15	P
Savigny	V	(Several climats)	10.00	5–40	M/P
Savigny	V	(Blanc)	0.55	4–50	F
Savigny	R	(Bourg.R./Perrières)	0.87	15	P
Pernand	PC	—	0.45	60	P
Aloxe	V	—	0.39	30	P
Pernand	R	(Bourg. Aligoté)	1.00	10	P
—	R	(Bourgogne)	0.80	12	P
		Total	**15.40 ha.**		

Domaine Chandon de Briailles

SAVIGNY-LÈS-BEAUNE

Rarely in Burgundy can one honestly say of a Domaine that the beauty of its wines is matched by the beauty of its buildings. Chandon de Brialle is a notable, and welcome, exception.

By itself, the Rue Soeur Goby, tucked away at the back of the village, is not by any stretch of the imagination picturesque. However, a gap in the buildings half-way along makes room for a modest pair of stone pillars giving on to a splendid courtyard, at the far end of which is an imposing and beautifully proportioned Manor House. Built at the beginning of the eighteenth-century and now classified as an historical monument, this house is pure Louis XIVth. Classical in proportion, simple of line, it was once described as 'an eighteenth-century extravagance'. However, as it stands there looking at its visitors, it seems to be saying : 'Voilà, here is style, here is elegance, here "par excellence", is a fine Country Gentleman's residence.'

At the back of the house is a charming, small park, pleasantly wooded for shade in the summer and laid out by the famous landscape designer, Le Nôtre – the creator of Versailles and many other important French gardens. Low-cropped box-hedges, interspersed with narrow gravel paths, give an air of formality perfectly in keeping with the house itself. At the far end of the park, the family pony has a small allocation of paddock, enclosed presumably to prevent it further cropping the hedges and eating the family vegetables.

The only note of ill-proportion is struck by two tall asymmetrical brick chimneys grafted on to either side of the house. They seem like later additions, being far too large for their apparent purpose and more like an immense pair of distorted handles by which the entire building might be lifted up and turned round to face in another direction, for an occasional change of view.

The house, front pillars, the walls of the park and every conceivable parapet or lintel are decorated with a curious but most attractive species of stone embroidery. Consisting of assemblages of rather rustic stonework, it gives the appearance of very ancient sandstone statuary which has been haphazardly weathered away for several hundred years. This rather formless, rough-hewn decoration contrasts perfectly with the clean classicism of the house itself.

The family for whom all these delights are laid out are the de Nicolays who have owned the Domaine since 1834. Count Aymar-Claude de Nicolay, a Paris-based property dealer, inherited it from his grandmother, Countess Chandon de Briailles.

However, the Count, though proud of his Domaine, is not especially interested in wine. The passion that is currently driving the estate to new peaks of quality is that of his attractive wife Nadine, who left Paris to take charge in Savigny in 1984 when it became clear that the Domaine was badly in need of care and attention.

Nadine, who knew next to nothing about the technicalities of viticulture or vinification, applied herself assiduously to her new task. According to her daughter, Claude, her mother, having 'finished with the kids, needed something to occupy herself'. Vinifying her husband's wine and looking after their vineyards came as an ideal solution. She read extensively and worked very closely with their then *régisseur*, François Paquelin, to learn the basics.

Seven years later, the Domaine has been completely transformed from a good estate making mediocre wine to a top-class property with wine to match. Claude, having obtained an oenological and viticultural diploma at Dijon, is now working at the Domaine with her mother, and shows every sign of becoming a fine wine-maker in her own right. The day-to-day care of the wines and cellars is in the capable hands of Jean-Claude Bouveret, a short, completely bald man in his early forties known by everyone, including himself, as Kojak.

The Domaine's vineyards extend over 12.4 ha. – 4.71 ha. in Savigny, 4.56 ha. in Pernand-Vergelesses and 3.14 ha. in Aloxe-Corton.

The Domaine's impressive headquarters in the Rue Soeur Goby

The Savignys consist of Village and two Premiers Crus – Les Fournaux and Les Lavières. In Pernand, there is some Premier Cru Les Basses Vergelesses and the Ile des Vergelesses Blanc, and a superb 3.25 ha. chunk of the Ile des Vergelesses planted with Pinot Noir. The Aloxe vineyards, apart from Les Valozières, are Grands Crus: Corton Maréchaudes, Corton Bressandes, Corton Clos du Roi and some rare Corton Blanc. Altogether a fine medium-sized estate.

The vineyards are most carefully looked after. Nadine de Nicolay and Claude spend much of their time outside, and it is not remotely surprising to come across one or other wrapped up in old clothes, cheerfully pruning away at something or another on a freezing winter's morning.

Their regime includes hoeing all 12 ha. five times a year – they do not believe in herbicides. Neither are they particularly espoused to modern treatments, preferring to use traditional copper- and sulphur-based products as much as possible. Insecticides are used for spiders and grape-worm, and a preventive fungicide at the start of the growing season, all in the minimum possible dosage; and there is a rotation of any synthetic products to avoid habituation.

Since Nadine de Nicolay took charge much more care has been taken over replanting: greater emphasis on replacing individual vines, rather than larger replantation, to maintain a high average vine age, and a preference for *sélection massale* rather than clones. A parcel of Bressandes on 10 cm. of topsoil, replanted as recently as 1984, was found to have a disturbingly high incidence of *eutypiose* – an insidious degenerative virus infection which has caused some alarm in France, especially in Bordeaux and Cognac – and had to be grubbed up and replanted anew. This disease is virtually undetectable for 6 years or so, and once infected, vines rarely survive.

The vines are trained *en cordon* for their first few years, then *en Guyot*. The de Nicolays prefer to prune when it is humid, since the wood is easier to bend and there is thus less risk of breaking a shoot and losing a year's fruit.

During the spring and early summer the vines are stripped of any double shoots and excess buds. Just after *veraison*, usually in August, excess bunches themselves are removed to further limit production.

To complete the green work, the vineyards are summer-pruned 2 or 3 times to limit leaf production and to clear space round the ripening bunches. If the foliage is left to grow high, it improves sugar production and thus reduces the need for *chaptalisation.* In most years summer-pruning also helps remove the *verjus* – the second growth of grapes. In 1990 the quantity of *verjus* almost equalled that of the first sortie, so removal was essential to avoid the vine dissipating energy in useless grape-production.

A brochure produced by the de Nicolays tells you that the 'heart of the Domaine' is located in the 'fermenting rooms, wine-making plants and cellars'. These annexes flank the house, on both sides of the court-yard, and being of contemporary construction blend perfectly with the main building. The twelfth-century cask cellars are particularly fine, being of rare, low pillar-vaulted design. Here the wines pass their *élevage* in perfect tranquillity.

The vinification which precedes this is relatively straightforward with the one peculiarity of a 6-day intra-pellicular maceration at 18° C to maximise glycerol extraction before the main phase of fermentation starts. Although the grapes are not destalked, half the harvest is lightly crushed to liberate some juice. In prolific vintages, such as 1982/4 and 1986, the *cuves* are *saignéed.*

Thereafter, fermentation proceeds at 25–32° C for a total *cuvaison* of 15–20 days, with 2 pumpings-over and 2 human *pigéages* each day. Towards the end of fermentation, the *cuves* are blanketed with nitrogen and left for 2–3 days at 25° C to macerate and to ferment out any remaining sugar.

The pulp is pressed 4 times, as lightly as 'pressing in one's hand' for the first 2, which are generally added to the free-run wine; the addition of later pressings depends on tasting.

Since 1980 the totality of the Domaine's production is sold in bottle, so it has begun to establish its own style and identity. Moreover, recent years have seen a considerable improvement in the overall quality and consistency of its wines. Nadine de Nicolay intends her pre-fermentive maceration and low temperature fermentation to produce wines which emphasise elegance rather than tannic robustness. She argues that if you ferment at too high a temperature you extract harsh, herbaceous tannins, especially if you don't destalk.

In 1990 Claude decided to ferment a *cuvée* of Ile des Vergelesses at 25° C to see what a below-average temperature produced. The result was a wine of great finesse – light, stylish, but lacking in real depth and stuffing.

The reds spend 18–24 months in cask. Up to their first racking, the Premiers Crus have 20% new Allier and Nevers wood, the Grands Crus 50%. The cellars being particularly cold, the *malos* tend to happen slowly – 10–12 months is normal – and thus racking generally occurs just before the new vintage. The wines are then assembled by Cru, pumped from their casks with or without air, depending on their development, and returned immediately to older casks for a further 8–12 months. The Premiers Crus are normally kept for 18 months, the Grands Crus for 22–24 before bottling which takes place after egg-white fining and, if necessary, a kieselguhr filtration.

The Chandon de Brialle wines are never wines of heavy structure. However, it is all too easy to be deceived by their characteristically light colours, sometimes almost rosé, into concluding that they lack fruit. Nothing could be further from the truth.

The Savignys and Pernands are wines of considerable finesse. As one would expect, the Premiers Crus have more depth than the Village wines, although not necessarily more depth of colour. The Savigny Les Fournaux – from heavier, limestone soil – is usually more *corsé* than the Lavières from less profound soil with more rock and stones. On the palate, the Lavières has a distinctively mineral flavour with a good concentration of fruit from its 35-year-old vines.

The two red Pernands present a striking contrast: the Basses Vergelesses is a distinctively tannic wine – the de Nicolays refer to it as their 'petit Corton'; a wine to keep for several years in vintages such as 1988 and 1990. The Ile des Vergelesses is much more 'en finesse' – a wine of strong fruit aromas, sometimes almost floral; less of a keeper perhaps than the Basses Vergelesses, but according to the Domaine 'particularly appreciated by the female gender'. Generally, the Chandon Pernands evolve more slowly than the Savignys and age delightfully. A 1959 Ile des Vergelesses was gloriously ripe and generous in early 1991.

The Chandon de Briailles Corton vines are all relatively young, that is to say under 30. The wines they produce, however, rarely lack in concentration and depth of flavour. The Maréchaudes – from 11- and 16-year-old vines – tends to evolve more rapidly than the other Grands Crus. The 1989, in cask, although quite light in colour, had plenty of muscle, a firm tannic base with characteristic 1989 soft 'flatteur' fruit – typically Corton.

The Clos du Roi comes from much finer, more limestone soil, which is reflected in the wine – much more finesse and delicacy than one normally expects from a Corton; in fact, more typically Pernand than Corton. The 1989 had quite a ripe crushed *fruits rouges* tone with muscle and power underneath and good length; a fine wine which needs keeping for 10 years to show of its best.

The Bressandes is the most powerful of the Cortons – a wine of considerable depth and presence. Deeply coloured for a Chandon de Briailles wine, with a nose of *fruits sauvages* when young which slowly develops a marvellous complexity of truffle and *sous-bois* aromas. On the palate the wine tends to start off with a lean backbone of tannins and acidity which ensures its longevity.

There are only two white wines in this stable – Pernand Blanc, made from 6- and 7-year-old vines in Les Vergelesses, and a rare Corton Blanc, made from 3 parcels of 10- and 25-year old vines planted in the *climats* Chaumes and Bressandes. This latter is not to be confused with Corton-Charlemagne since it is made from Chardonnay planted on red wine soils. The wines are fermented in 20% new oak at 20° C for 10–15 days. An *élevage* of 12–15 months in cask is followed by a bentonite fining and bottling without filtration.

The Pernand Blanc is a ripe, fat wine, slightly rustic but with an attractive and marked *gout de terroir* and plenty of guts and style. It is the sort of wine which is best drunk young or else kept until after its fifth birthday.

The Corton Blanc is also a highly individual wine – more complexity on the nose which, although the 1989 was not showing it, tends to develop an exotic fruit quality. On the palate, it has similar richness and ripe fruit to the Pernand, but slightly better acidity and a touch more length. The Domaine has been taking its white wines more seriously since Nadine de Nicolay took over – there are only 2,000 bottles of each, but they are well worth looking out for.

This is a fine Domaine beginning to make top-class wines. It will be fascinating to watch its evolution over the next decade or so.

VINEYARD HOLDINGS

Commune	*Level*	*Lieu-dit/Climat*	*Area*	*Vine Age*	*Status*
Aloxe	GC	Corton Les Chaumes (W)	0.12	1980	P
Aloxe	GC	Corton-Clos du Roi	0.46	1961/86	P
Aloxe	GC	Corton-Bressandes (Pinot)	1.76	1962/75/84	P
Aloxe	GC	Bressandes (Chardonnay)	0.14	1980	P
Aloxe	Gc	Corton les Marechaudes	0.40	1975/80	P
Aloxe	PC	Les Valozières	0.29	1988/89	P
Pernand	PC	Ile des Vergelesses	3.33	1938–1986	P
Pernand	PC	Les Basses Vergelesses	1.27	1954	P
Savigny	PC/V	Les Fournaux	2.10	1956/61	P
Savigny	PC	Les Lavières	2.61	1955	P
		Total	**12.48 ha.**		

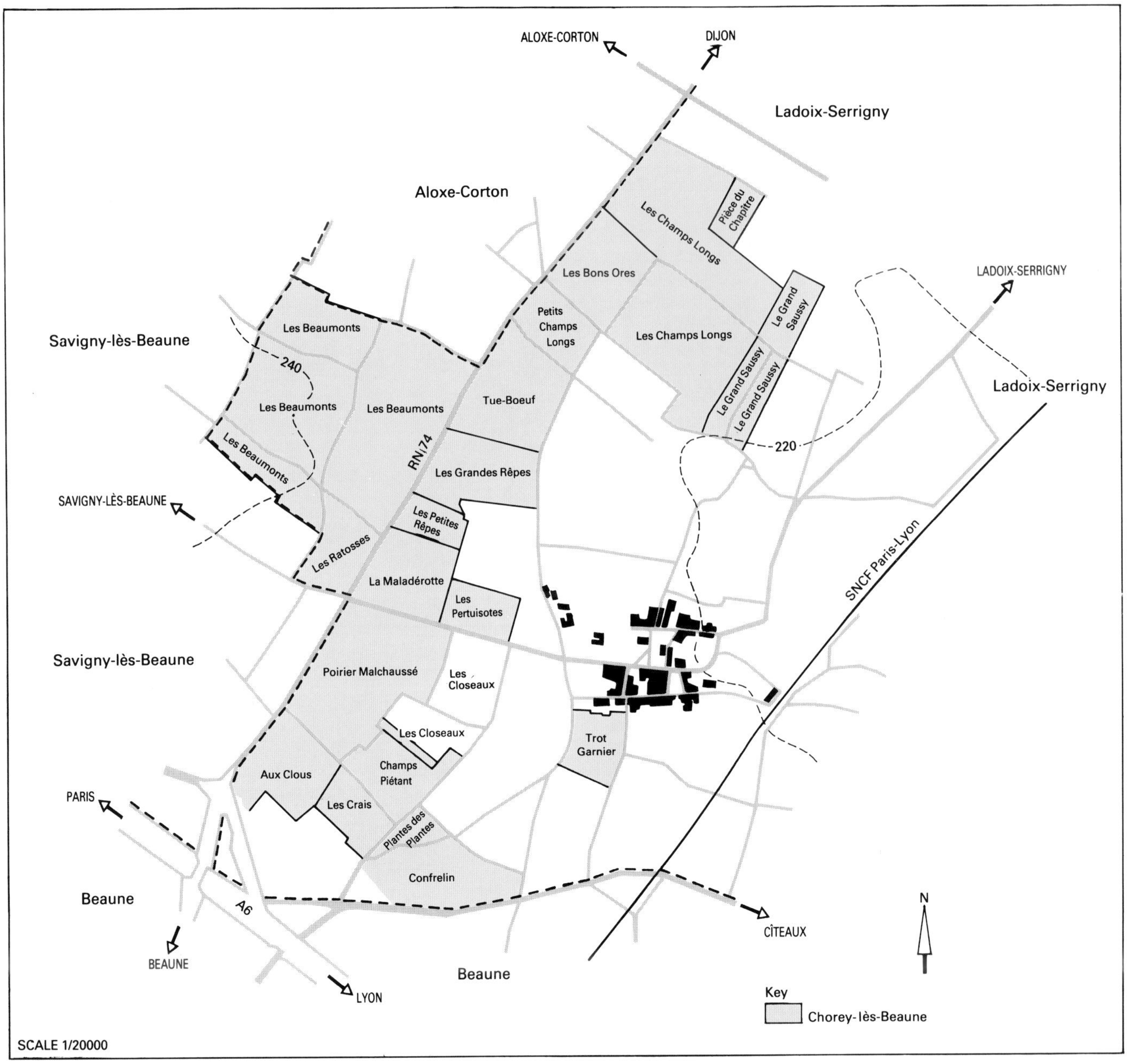

The vineyards in springtime

CHOREY-LÈS-BEAUNE

Chorey is a place which has got itself on to the wrong side of practically everything. Sandwiched between the main Paris-Lyon railway line and the RN 74, on the wrong side of the road, it is a dispirited little village, neat and tidy but perpetually aware of the fact that, unlike its neighbours on the right side of the road, it was ignored when the appellations were being dished out, and had to wait until 1974 before it was granted an appellation of its own. Even then, it ended up without a single Premier Cru.

Kept in the limelight by a handful of fine Domaines, it languishes somewhat forlorn, shaken periodically by a passing goods train, subsisting largely on its surrounding vines and bolstered by sporadic outbreaks of private-enterprise bed-and-breakfast.

The problem, which Chorey is quite powerless to solve, lies in the land, much of which is low-lying flat ground. Although parts of the commune sit on well-drained sandy soils, much consists of water-retentive clay. Moreover, some of the vineyards to the east of the RN 74 are renowned frost-pockets. There is a better section, on the western side of the road, which comprises two vineyards – Les Beaumonts and Les Ratosses – squeezed into 45.61 ha. between the adjoining communes of Aloxe-Corton and Savigny-lès-Beaune. These produce some good wine, particularly those sections farthest from the main road.

Fortunately the 40 or so growers of Chorey have several appellations to choose from for their red wines, so they are not stuck with a single denomination which may suffer from an indifferent press. They may be sold either as Chorey-lès-Beaune, Chorey-Côte de Beaune or Côte de Beaune-Villages. If a grower is really desperate, he can declassify to Bourgogne, Bourgogne Grand Ordinaire or Bourgogne Ordinaire. In theory, therefore, a vigneron with one red wine could market it under 6 different appellations, if he felt the need to give an impression of diversity.

The Château de Chorey – home to the Domaine Jacques Germain

The history of the village is, unfortunately, no more exciting than its wines. Like many other communes along the Côte, it took a few centuries to fix its present name: Hauriaco, in 667, became Cariacum in 1004; there followed Cherriacum in 1150 and Charrère in 1207. Thirty years later came Charrey, which gave way to Cherriey in 1304. Finally Chorrey (sic) arrived in 1437, which more or less settled it for the next five and a half centuries.

The only moment of fame came to Chorey in May 1658, when it was chosen by the burgers of Beaune as the site to welcome Louis XIV, who happened to be passing.

From then on, however, things deteriorated. In May 1681 Chorey was shaken by an earthquake, which recurred in 1783. Despite this, it was not until 1851 that the local firebrigade was finally formed. Moreover, in 1688, much of Chorey's crops were ravaged by wild boar which descended on the wretched village from the woods of Cîteaux.

Thereafter, Chorey enjoyed a period of calm and relative prosperity. Religious foundations owned about 16% of the vineyards, and it was renowned as an unusually healthy spot, perhaps helped by its proximity to the river Rhoin, which makes a muted, fitful appearance on the south side of the village. The Beaunois liked to use the village as a refuge from the plague and reciprocated by granting Chorey rights of access to the favoured markets of Beaune for their wines.

The principal architectural interest lies in the Château. Originally built as a 'maison fortifiée' in the thirteenth century, it was destroyed several times between then and its most recent reconstruction in the late 1660s. It is an impressive building, with an imposing pair of entrance gates, surrounded by a large, deep ditch which has been known to contain both water and fish. It is presently owned by François Germain and his family.

The wines of Chorey, which are nearly all red – there is a very little white made from Chardonnay – are generally sound but uninspiring. In good vintages they can be pleasant, well-balanced wines, for inexpensive drinking. The best come from Domaines Tollot-Beaut and Jacques Germain in Chorey itself and from Domaine Daniel Senard in Aloxe-Corton. They are reasonably priced and so when they are good, usually represent excellent value.

Domaine Tollot-Beaut et Fils

CHOREY-LÈS-BEAUNE

The Tollot family is unusual – 3 brothers each with 1 offspring, all working together, making and selling wine. Jacques and Alain each have a son in the business whilst François' daughter manages the office and helps receive the clients. The whole enterprise seems remarkably harmonious; the wine is excellent and the business, no doubt, successful.

The present trio of brothers are the fifth generation of Tollots to vinify at Chorey. The original Tollot was their great-great-grandfather who apparently successfully combined the heterogeneous callings of musician and vigneron. His son continued the exploitation and started buying vineyards on his own account, while working as a vigneron for the Prince de Mérode. The 'Beaut' arrived with the present older generation's grandmother, clearly something of a forceful lady. In the 1920s she started selling wine in bottle under her own label, which must have brought down not a little négociant wrath on her head – for the négoce then enjoyed a virtually uncontested monopoly of the market.

Careful acquisition has gradually enlarged the Domaine, which now comprises some 22 ha. spread over Beaune, Chorey, Savigny and Aloxe-Corton – good Village and Premier Cru sites in Beaune, Savigny and Aloxe; Village and *régionales* in Chorey and a trio of Grands Crus in Aloxe to top off the pyramid. The most recent additions have been plots of Savigny Lavières and Aloxe-Corton Villages in 1989. François admits that they would, collectively of course, like to add 'a few ares' more of Grand Cru, but 'you know what the prices are like,' he shrugs.

Somehow, the Tollots have managed to avoid the fragmentation of their vineyards which most other family Domaines have suffered by ensuring that whilst individual ownership might change through death and division, the land remained in the same 'exploitation'. This requires exceptional family cohesion – one wonders what the secret is. A sister who left to marry a few years ago was presumably bought out.

Looking at the Tollots collectively, one cannot help but be reminded of Dickens' Cheeryble brothers; kindly, warm-hearted models of courtesy, charm and charity, vying with each other to help the needy and brimming over with generosity of spirit.

Their wines mirror their progenitors – characterised by soft appealing flavours, with much finesse and charm. The reds are vinified to mature in the medium term, with a shortish *cuvaison* of 7–10 days to conserve the more evanescent aromatic elements. François believes that concentration and extract should properly come from old vines and low yields, rather than from prolonged maceration. Any pre-fermentive maceration is positively discouraged. So keen are the brothers not to delay the onset of fermentation a moment longer than necessary, that they pick a quantity of grapes 3 days before the main harvest and add selected yeasts to make a *pied de cuve*. When the main crop arrives each *cuve* is inoculated with 20–30 litres of this active potion so that it starts fermenting immediately.

Grape health and hygiene are matters on which the brothers lay great stress. For the former, they try to keep treatments to minimum dose, following the advice of the Service des Végétaux 'without exaggerating'. Precise soil analyses in each vineyard enable them to adjust any deficiencies in *base elements* – chiefly nitrogen, phosphorus, potassium or magnesium – to maintain an equilibrium of nutrients.

If they do have to replant a vineyard – for example, in 1982 they grubbed up a plot of Beaune Blanche Fleurs planted in 1926 – the soil is rested for at least 2 years before the new grafts are planted. No herbicides are used – 'up to now' – just constant hoeing to keep the soil aerated and the weeds down.

The Tollot cuverie is a model establishment. Neat as a new pin, with a row of open cement *cuves*, each painted in a wash with the name of the wine that goes into it picked out in large wine-coloured capital letters, as if they were so many private front doors in a rather self-conscious surburban street – just another gesture of Tollot friendliness – a sort of vinous 'good-neighbour' scheme.

Everything in the cellar is spotless. The painted vats, though installed in 1949, look almost new, this is the result of almost obsessional cleaning; for example, at the start and end of each harvest all the pipe-work in the cellar has water pumped through it under pressure – probably with a Tollot at either end and a few more in between.

However over the 40 years the expansion of the business has outgrown the space outside the row of front doors. Packing materials, filters etc. are stored there and the vats have started to complain. So a new bottle cellar and shipping hall have been constructed to simplify working and get rid of some of that cuverie clutter.

If hygiene is paramount in the cellars, then yields motivate work in the vineyards. Vines are replaced individually up to 35 years old on relatively low-vigour rootstocks to keep average vine age high. There has been much replanting in the Beaune and Corton in the 1970s, but elsewhere the vines are considerably older.

Évasivage is taken very seriously; in 1990, for example, 3 separate passages were made through the vines to remove excess buds and shoots. However, there is no green-pruning, the collective Tollot belief being that this work is better done before mid-June, rather than being left till later. François is mildly scathing of the much-publicised August green-prunings : 'it is good for photographs for journalists', but not of much value, since it involves cutting out unripe material from the middle of the vines, rather than making random excisions from around the edges.

The moment of harvesting – crucial to grape quality – is determined both by *prélèvements* and by the risks involved in waiting. In 1988 they decided that the risk was worth taking, though the general policy seems to be that it is better to gather in slightly unripe grapes – they can always make suitable adjustments in the cuverie – than to delay unduly and risk a completely spoiled crop. Whenever they decide to pick, the bunches are subjected to 3 separate scrutinies – as they are cut, by the porters on the carts, and again by 8 people manning a sorting-table at the cuverie.

The harvest usually begins with the Beaunes – earliest to ripen – and always ends with the whites – Bourgogne Blanc, Aligoté and Grand Cru Corton-Charlemagne. The whites, though a small proportion of production, are something of a Tollot speciality. The Bourgogne Blanc is usually excellent – plenty of ripe fruit, good acidity, round, complex and mouthfilling. Not cheap, it is a wine which

The Tollot family – at work in their vineyards. Recognise them?

invariably outclasses itself, made with the Tollot thoroughness and concern for quality.

At the other end of the ladder is the Corton-Charlemagne, made from a plot of 25-year-old vines in Le Corton. It begins fermentation in stainless steel and finishes it in cask – SO_2 and manipulations are kept to the minimum. The wine is usually fine rather than overtly muscular – to be drunk perhaps while the succulent fruit of youth is still there rather than waiting too long for the uncertainty of old age. It is invariably an attractive example of the appellation.

All the white wines have a touch of new wood – 25% or so for the Charlemagne – with a preference for Tronçais oak. 'I know the forest of Tronçais and the wood – lovely wood, impeccable; that's what I would like to have in the cellar.' Whatever preference François may express to his tonnelier, he is healthily sceptical about what eventually turns up: 'There is no Appellation Contrôlée for wood,' he laughs, 'so it is probably better to buy the planks from a friend, dry them for 3 years yourself and then stand over the tonnelier while he makes the casks.'

Tollot casks are described as 'assez brulés' – but not by express order; this imparts a noticeable 'toasty' flavour to the whites. However, unusually, they do not rouse the lees in their white wines – reckoning that this is only sound practice with wines which are long in fermenting to high alcohol levels. It is clearly not their style.

The whites are racked twice, once 'well after the *malo* in July' – the lees contact avoids early yellowing – and again at the *relève de col*, just before bottling. 'We have much to learn about white wine vinification,' chuckles François, 'we are just small lots – amateurs.' Highly gifted amateurs, then!

Red vinification is 'très classique'. The bunches are 66–75% destalked and crushed before being transferred to their cement *cuves* – the *régionales* are kept in stainless steel. Fermentation is started as soon as possible and *cuvaison* deliberately short. The temperature does not exceed 30–35° C and the vats are *saignéed* if needed (as it was in 1989 and 1990). The wine is decanted when a match lit in the *cuve* fails to extinguish – in other words there is no more CO_2, and thus no further fermentation.

Once the press- and free run wine have been assembled, 2–3 weeks of *débourbage* follows, with the *cuves* covered to prevent loss of aroma and oxidation. This seems an excessively long period of settling without the prospect of much gain in quality.

The wine then passes into casks – '33% new wood for Grands and Petits Crus alike – we're very socialist here,' muses François. There are 3 rackings, first cask-to-cask in February or March, with aeration by spraying over an umbrella-shaped contrivance to

Not all, but a selection of Tollots

maximise air contact. Some fine lees are left with the wine to keep it going until the next racking, generally 4 months after the first. Here the wines are unified and pre-filtered with kieselguhr before being returned to cask where they remain until the day before bottling, when they are given a light plate filtration. Up to 1974 they fined the wines, but decided that this battered them more than a gentle second filtration.

For the Tollots, the production of a truly fine wine is an amalgam of a multitude of small inter-related details. Their reds are highly individual, accentuating the ripe, succulent, almost sweet flavours of which the Pinot Noir is deliciously capable. 1985 and 1989 for example are vintages which well compliment this style of wine-making.

The 1989 Chorey – an appellation which deserves to be better known – is attractively perfumed with a succulent distinctly moreish flavour. Of the two Savignys, the Lavière, from less humid soils than the Champ Chevrey, had more power and muscle, with aromas of 'petits *fruits rouges*', highish acidity and quite light, round tannins. The Champ Chevrey, from stonier soil, seems denser and better structured, with greater depth of flavour and generally more vinosity. However, when these wines age the Lavière, from older vines planted from *sélection massale* by Tollot Père in 1945, usually develops more complexity than its sibling.

The pair of Beaune Premiers Crus are wines from relatively young vines. However, both have good depth and finesse. The Clos du Roi is not the easiest of vineyards, containing large moisture-absorbing limestone boulders. In dry years, such as 1990, maturity can be a problem. However, the 1989 has an attractive mid-garnet colour, with a most promising array of aromas and flavours – plenty of wine here, with the Tollot succulent ripe crushed fruit showing through – perhaps it lacks a little concentration, but will nevertheless make a delightful medium-weight bottle in the mid-1990s. The Grèves, from 4-year-older vines, has more depth and centre. Probably the best of all the Beaune Premiers Crus, it invariably shows its class – a bit more of everything, longevity included.

The *cuvée* of Aloxe-Corton is an *assemblage* of 4 separate Villages *climats* and 2 Premiers Crus – Les Vercots and Les Fornières. The sacrifice is worth it – the Premiers Crus have a dimension of depth and richness which would be unusual from simple Village *climats*. The democratic 33% of new wood tends to dominate the wine when it is young – so it needs several years maturation; in addition, the high percentage of iron in the vineyards – a characteristic of Aloxe-Corton, deriving from both the soil and from small brown stones – contributes an earthy depth which takes time to round out.

The 2 red Grands Crus – Corton and Corton Bressandes – are both substantial, powerful wines. The Corton, whilst good, is generally eclipsed by the Bressandes, which invariably seems to have more subtlety and finesse. With age, the sheer class of the Bressandes shines through – greater breeding and vinosity – more sensual than the direct and intellectual Corton.

The Tollots are a fine band of brothers and a reliable source of delicious wines – individuals, made collectively, of course.

VINEYARD HOLDINGS

Commune	*Level*	*Lieu-dit/Climat*	*Area*	*Vine Age*	*Status*
Aloxe	GC	Le Corton (Charlemagne)	0.24	25	P
Aloxe	GC	Corton Bressandes	0.92	37	P
Corton	GC	Les Combes	0.61	10–60	F/P
Aloxe	PC	Vercots/Fournières	1.50	45	P
Aloxe	V	(Several climats)	1.89	45	P
Beaune	PC	Grèves	0.60	14	P
Beaune	PC	Clos du Roi	1.10	10	P
Beaune	V	Blanches Fleurs	0.28	6	P
Savigny	PC	Les Lavières	1.95	45	P
Savigny	PC	Le Champ Chevrey	1.47	35	P
Savigny	V	Les Ratosses	0.26	37	P
Savigny	V	Aux Champs Chardons	0.40	1992	P
Chorey	V	(Several climats)	6.30	25	P/F
Chorey	V	—	1.20	1991	P
—	R	(Bourgogne Rouge)	1.25	27	P/F
—	R	(Bourgogne Blanc)	0.69	18	P
—	R	(Bourgogne Aligoté)	1.25	19	P
—	R	(BGO)	0.35	43	P
		Total	**22.26 ha.**		

Domaine Jacques Germain

CHOREY-LÈS-BEAUNE

This is one of those medium-sized self-taught Domaines which one comes across from time to time, producing wine which, if not up to top-class levels, is sometimes of exciting quality.

The setting is perfect: a fine, if slightly crumbling, seventeenth-century Château surrounded by a deep moat containing a modicum of water and some fish, all enclosed by an ancient stone wall and screened by a pleasant, attractively wooded, park.

This is the home of François Germain and his family. François, a friendly cheerful, excitable man in his forties and one of two brothers in a family of 5 children, took over on the death of his father in 1968. His training was both in the commercial side of his father's négociant business and, because he believed in the importance of practical experience, in the Domaine's vineyards and cellars learning the vigneron's art. In addition, he spent a few years in a larger establishment, which he chiefly remembers for its policy of filtering the red wines through kieselguhr, then plates and finally through a membrane. There was probably very little of the original left for the customer.

François draws his lines of policy with firm, uncompromising strokes: 'you must extract the best – Grand Vin', adding: 'it's not always easy.' He is sharply critical of those vignerons who, driven by what their customers can afford, make wine to a price and not to a standard. An ebullient extrovert whose own enthusiasms shine through, he confesses a passion for good food and fine wine and makes no secret of his search for perfection.

He seems to be more than master of his 16 ha. Domaine. Apart from 2.5 ha. of regional appellations, this consists of 3 ha. of Pernand Blanc, 5 ha. of Chorey Village and no fewer than 6 different Beaune Premiers Crus. François feels that this is a comfortable size for him to oversee, with the help of 4 workers.

In the vineyards healthy, ripe grapes and low yields are the aim. 'With the Pinot Noir,' he explains, 'you must not exceed a certain yield – 30 hl./ha. for the Premiers Crus and 40 hl./ha. for the Village appellations.' To this end, old vines, good quality clones, short pruning and an '*évasivage* très sérieuse' are all germane. Although he dislikes green-pruning in principle, in 1990 an entire month was spent in removing excess buds and in August there were further excisions – 'exceptionally; I haven't done this since 1973.'

François has also given thought to the best form of training for his vines. Whilst most viticulteurs are content to use the *Guyot simple* pruning – a single *baguette* with up to 10 eyes on it and a spur with 2 eyes for next year's wood – since 1988 François has trained his vines *en cordon de Royat*, using a cane of 1 m. length with just 3 eyes and a spur with just 1 eye. This gives both lower yields and a degree more of potential alcohol, in the form of grape-sugar. 'Even with the best clones, classically trained, you get too much fruit. The *Guyot baguette* was invented first to lower the level of the fruit and second to increase yields, not to reduce them.'

Vinification is conducted on somewhat modified classical lines: 'I start from the premise that stalk tannins are hard and skin tannins are fine, but difficult to extract.' The solution, introduced in 1983, is complete destalking and a good week of post-fermentive maceration to leach out these fine tannins and to fix the colours extracted before fermentation.

Once vatted, a larger than normal dose of SO_2 is administered. This is intended both to minimise volatile acidity produced during *malo* and to allow 2–3 days pre-fermentive maceration to maximise extraction of glycerol and aromas. If fermentation is sluggish, François simply borrows a bucket of ferment from a friend and inoculates.

After fermentation at up to 32° C in one of a variegated rank of well-kept, medium-sized open wooden *cuves*, housed in a newly acquired cellar in the village, the wine is left for its maceration with the *cuves* firmly closed. The Chorey, being a lighter wine which naturally matures relatively rapidly, has only 10–12 days total *cuvaison*, whereas the Premiers Crus have 18–22 days.

Thereafter, an *élevage* in cask – 50% new oak for the Premiers Crus and 25–30% for the Choreys followed by 2 rackings and a kieselguhr filtration. François is 'bowled-over with delight' by the kieselguhr system – it excoriates the wine much less than fining, which, in any case, doesn't seem well adapted to his cold cellar. *Elevage* is topped off with a light plate filtration to remove any kieselguhr left in the wine and bottling after some 18 months for the Premiers Crus and 12 for the Chorey.

The results are a range of well-made wines of moderate depth and sound structure. The Beaune Premiers Crus make a particularly interesting group – showing how much the soil varies within the appellation. The Boucherottes and Cent Vignes, from moderately sandy soils are the lightest, generally quite soft and supple. The Vignes Franches, from 40-year-old vines on a higher clay soil, is more solid – broader with more structure and depth. The Les Cras and Les Teurons are the most *charpente* of the group – much more of Pommard than of Savigny in style. The Cras was at one time considered by some as a 'Tête de Cuvée' among the Premiers Crus and its heat-retaining, stony soil usually ripens grapes well, giving a wine of very typical Pinot character.

François Germain's whites are particularly interesting. In contrast to his reds, they get only the minimum SO_2 and are fermented in 15% new Vosges casks, using a selected strain of Montrachet yeast. The Pernand Blanc, from 3 ha. of south-facing land near Echevronne, is quite masculine in character with a pronounced *goût de terroir* and a characteristically crisp acidity. The vineyard, to François' eye, has much the same soil as the Pernand sector of Corton-Charlemagne but, despite his animated protestations that 'it's exactly the same, exactly the same – that makes superb wines' – the wine is not of Grand Cru quality. The Beaune 'sur les

VINEYARD HOLDINGS

Commune	*Level*	*Lieu-dit/Climat*	*Area*	*Vine Age*	*Status*
Beaune	PC	Les Boucherottes	1.00	20	P
Beaune	PC	Lès Vignes Franches	1.00	40	P
Beaune	PC	Les Cras	1.30	40	P
Beaune	PC	Les Teurons	2.00	40	P
Beaune	PC	Sur les Grèves	0.12	40	P
Beaune	PC	Les Cents Vignes	0.60	40	P
Chorey	V	(Several climats)	5.00	20	P
Pernand	V	Plante des Champs + Combottes	3.00	20	P
—	R	(Bourgogne Rouge)	2.00	40	P
—	R	(Bourgogne Blanc)	0.50	4	P
		Total	**16.72 ha.**		

Grèves' Blanc has more richness – in 1989 almost an exotic fruit quality – a good solid wine, needing some 2–5 years to reach its peak.

In 1989 there was a third, rather unexpected white produced. Believing them to be hopeless, François abandoned a few rows of Bourgogne Chardonnay, from the walled vineyard opposite the Château gates. Returning from holiday in November, he found perfect *noble rot*, picked the grapes and made a couple of casks of 'sélection des grains nobles'. He telephoned a vigneron friend in Alsace to find out what he should do with the juice, which had 50 grams per litre of residual sugar. The result is a remarkably fine wine – a good natural acidity, from a blocked *malo* – and a sweetness which does not cloy. The wine is long and stylish – with plenty of attractive *botrytis* to balance its natural structure. Trying to repeat the performance in 1990 was a failure – the rain came in October and washed his hopes away.

This is an interesting Domaine; one from which to pick and choose, but certainly well worth watching.

PARIS
Savigny-lès-Beaune
SAVIGNY-LÈS-BEAUNE
BOUZE-LÈS-BEAUNE
A6
300
Les Vies d'Arnay
Les Vies d'Arnay
Les Vies d'Arnay
Montbatois
Montagne de Rochetin
Montagne de Rochetin
Montagne de Rochetin
Les Topes Bizot
Les Montbatois
Dessus des Marconnets
Montbatois
Les Topes Bizot
Les Marconnets
En l'Orme
Les Perrières
En Genêt
Clos du Roi
Blanche Fleur
Clos du Roi
A l'Écu
A l'Écu
Les Fèves
Dessus de la Grande Châtelaine
La Grande Châtelaine
Châtelaine
Pierre Percée
Creux de l'Ane
Chaume Gauffriot
La Grande Châtelaine
Les Mondes Rondes
Les Mondes Rondes
Les Pierres Blanches
Les Bressandes
Les Bressandes
Les Cents Vignes
Les Chilènes
Champagne de Savigny
Les Mondes Rondes
Les Toussaints
Les Boiches
Les Mondes Rondes
Les Monsnières
Les Mondes Rondes
Sur les Grèves
Les Grèves
Les Mariages
Place St.-Pierre
Chaume Gauffriot
Les Rôles
Au Coucherias
Sur les Grèves
Les Longes
Les Longes
Au Coucherias
Clos de la Feguine
Les Teurons
Le Bas des Teurons
La Blanchisserie
Montée Rouge
Ferme de Battaut
Aux Cras
Les Teurons
Le Foulot
Au Renard
Longbois
Les Longes
Les Longes
Montée Rouge
La Mignotte
Les Teurons
Faubourg de St.-Martin
Faubourg de St.-Martin
Champs Pimont
Champs Pimont
Clos des Avaux
Les Seurey
Le Clos de la Mousse
Les Teurons
Clos des Avaux
Les Avaux
Montagne St.-Désiré
Siserpe
Les Aigrots
Les Avaux
Les Reversées
La Creusotte
Faubourg de Bouze
Les Sizies
Les Sizies
Les Avaux
Les Sceaux
Les Aigrots
Montagne St.-Désiré
Montagne St.-Désiré
Les Sizies
Les Avaux
Belissand
Pertuisots
Les Vérottes
Les Sceaux
Lulunne
Clos Landry
Les Tuvilains
Les Tuvilains
Les Paules
Les Vignes Franches
Les Montrevenots
Les Vignes Franches
Les Chouacheux
Les Chardonnereux
Le Clos des Mouches
Les Vignes Franches
Les Pointes de Tuvilains
Les Prèvoles
Pommard
Les Boucherottes
Les Bons Feuvres
Les Levées et les Pirolles
Les Beaux Fougets
N
Les Epenotes
Les Epenotes
Key
Beaune Premier Cru
Beaune
Côte de Beaune
POMMARD
RN 73
RN 74
Pommard
CHÂLON-SUR-SAÔNE
BLIGNY-LÈS-BEAUNE
SCALE 1/20000

BEAUNE

If Dijon is the administrative capital of viticultural Burgundy, then Beaune is its commercial and historical capital as well as its spiritual home. Encapsulated inside its medieval ramparts is Burgundy's history, from Beaune's beginnings as one of Julius Caesar's encampments in 52 BC, whilst the periphery is devoted to the late twentieth-century industrial sprawl, stimulated by the opening of the 'Autoroute du Soleil' in 1970.

The centre of Beaune is an amalgam of smart shops, restaurants and wine houses, crammed into a maze of narrow streets and attractive squares. This is principally the territory of the grand négociants – Jadot, Drouhin, Bouchard Père et Fils, Bichot, Patriarche and more. They vary in style, the grander hidden discreetly in elegant old houses behind high walls, whilst the less grand deploy large 'dégustation' signs, netting coach-loads of people to visit, taste and buy. Below the tourists' feet winds a honeycomb of cellars full of bottles, casks and cobwebs.

Each November, Beaune becomes the focus of the Côte, when the Hospice auctions the 1,000 or so casks of new wine made from its vineyards. Since its foundation in 1441 by Chancellor Nicolas Rollin and his wife Guigone de Salins, the Hospice has used donations of money and land to fund a charitable hospital. Today, the grounds of the magnificently preserved medieval Hôtel de Dieu are occupied by a modern, well-equipped medical centre, which depends on the wine sale for its income. Some 33 *cuvées* are offered, from a dozen different communes; the wine is variable in quality and invariably expensive. Those who buy are motivated more by charity and publicity than by any expectation of a bargain.

The commercial development of Beaune has spawned acres of brick houses and corrugated warehouses round its outskirts swallowing up much good vineyard land in the way. What is now the Lycée Viticole is partially built on the former Clos Maire, requisitioned just after the war, though the old airstrip has now been returned to vines. Whilst the town planners are doing their best, visitors driving by might be forgiven for concluding that industry has won.

Beaune's vineyards are dispersed widely over a band of gently sloping ground in the north-west quadrant beyond the town. These cover 51.97 ha. of Côte de Beaune, 128.13 ha. of AC Beaune and 321.66 ha. of Premiers Crus, of which there are 39–45, depending on how one counts the various Clos.

The wines of Beaune, although long known and appreciated, are Cinderellas among Burgundy-lovers, with an unshakeable collective image of rather dull neutrality. This is a pity, since the 132,000 cases produced annually include some fine wines.

The vineyards bisected by the N 470 meandering towards Bouze-lès-Beaune are mostly well-exposed to the south-east and, although the soils vary, the Premiers Crus are generally on a mixture of clay and limestone, which becomes thinner and more ferruginous as the slope increases. Those in the western section – Les Aigrots, Les Pertuisots and Les Vignes Franches in particular – have lighter soils, whilst those on the old Pommard road – Les Boucherottes, Les Chouacheux and Les Tuvillans and the lower lying Village land – have damper ground, with more clay, which increases the risk of spring-frost damage.

The cream of the Premiers Crus lie beneath Les Mondes Rondes, a hill to the north-west of the town. Whilst individual fine Beaunes can be found from the westerly sector, it is these 8 or so vineyards which produce the deepest, richest and most complex wines. This was recognised during the last century, with the designation of 7 vineyards as 'Têtes de Cuvée': Champs Pimont, Clos des Fèves, Les Perrières, Les Bressandes, Les Grèves, Les Marconnets and Le Clos des Mouches (the only one from the westerly section).

A small quantity of Chardonnay is produced – in particular, Drouhin's excellent Premier Cru Clos des Mouches and an attractive Beaune du Château from Bouchard Père et Fils. White Beaune accounts for only 6,000 cases per year, some 5% of red output.

The reds vary widely in style, from vineyard to vineyard and grower to grower. Outside the Domaines profiled here, excellent examples can be had from Tollot-Beaut and Jacques Germain in Chorey, Faiveley and Arnaud Marchard de Gramont in Nuits, Michel Ampeau in Meursault, Lafarge in Volnay and André Mussy in Pommard.

Where Beaunes lack depth and complexity this reflects, more often than not, over-production rather than any deficiency in the quality-potential of the vineyards. Wines from Domaines with well-sited old vines, low yields and long *cuvaison* give the lie to the image of Beaune as intrinsically dull wine. A mature example from Drouhin, Jadot or Albert Morot should convince anyone.

Unfortunately, a number of prestigious houses produce wines which keep the old criticisms alive. Bouchard Père et Fils, the largest owner of Beaune Premiers Crus, turn out a range of charmless wines lacking in real depth and finesse. However, they are not beyond the occasional flash of brilliance; their Beaune Vigne de l'Enfant Jesus, from Les Grèves, can be excellent given time to evolve, and elsewhere, their Corton-Charlemagne and Chevalier-Montrachet are sometimes fine. They also make a delicious Aligoté from the Ancienne Domaine Carnot in Bouzeron.

Other Domaines producing mediocre wines from good vineyards are Chanson, Jaboulet-Vercherre, Patriarche and – apart from their Domaine Clos Frantin in Vosne-Romanée – Albert Bichot.

Perhaps the high proportion of Beaune vineyards in the hands of a relatively small number of producers contributes to the commune's poor consumer image. Fortunately, the handful of top Domaines make enough fine wine to redress the balance.

Beaune is often festooned with flowers

Domaine Joseph Drouhin

BEAUNE

Until recently, the great négociant houses of Beaune and Nuits dominated the international Burgundy market. The volume they commanded, and the limited exposure of growers' wines, generated the belief that their produce represented the best to be had, and for many wine-lovers négociant Burgundies provided their introduction to the region's wines.

However, the advent of a more sophisticated market, Domaine bottling and marginally tighter controls gradually transformed the picture. The négociant stranglehold is now broken; their original sources of supply – the small growers – are bottling and selling more of their own wine, so what is left for négociant buyers is frequently of indifferent quality. Some of the best growers continue selling to the négoce as a matter of financial expediency, but what fine wine there is, is fiercely fought over and prices are high.

The lower end of the négociant business continues to churn out badly made, nondescript wines which have little to do with real Burgundy. That these wines obtain appellation certificates discredits the certification process and devalues the AC system.

At the top of the ladder, a handful of quality conscious négociants strive to maintain quality and to ensure supplies by taking the only realistic course open to them – buying their own vineyards. In fact, these Houses now compete on equal terms with their erstwhile suppliers, the growers, who are generally seen by international markets as setting the yardsticks for quality.

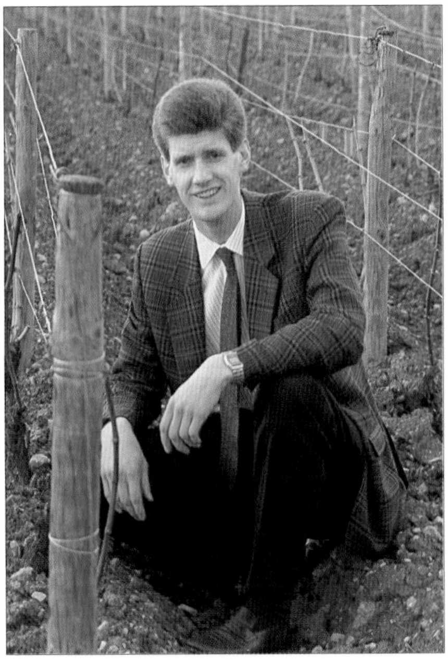

Philippe Drouhin in the vineyards – here the soil is ploughed up round the vine roots for frost-protection

Drouhin is one of Burgundy's top-level négociants. More importantly, it is also one of Burgundy's finest Domaines, owning some 25.3 ha. of vineyards from Puligny to Gevrey. Not an old House, at any rate by Burgundian standards, it was founded by Joseph Drouhin in 1880, as a general négociant. After the First World War Joseph's son Maurice Drouhin decided to specialise in Burgundy and started to buy some vines. The exigencies of working with horses confined his purchases to the locality of Beaune where he acquired the 13.7 ha. Beaune Clos des Mouches which remains the kernel of the Domaine.

Much of what Maurice bought was *en friche* – land entitled to appellation status, but, for one reason or another, not planted. In 1938 he added 0.9 ha. of Clos de Vougeot 'pour le plaisir' – though Vougeot was rather far from his usual ambit and probably not then a viable proposition.

The Domaine is now run by Joseph's grandson Robert, a tall, somewhat autocratic man in his middle fifties. Although intended for 5 years formal oenology training, he was pitched into the deep end in 1957 at the age of 24, when his father suffered a stroke.

His lack of formal training is compensated for by a formidable tasting experience, not only of post-war Burgundy but of wines from every part of the globe. You are just as likely to come across him in Alsace, California or on the banks of the Douro, as in Beaune. An articulate, knowledgeable and courteous man, he is also a media favourite .

Whilst technical administration of the Domaine is in the hands of a small team helped by 'old friends' from the Station des Végéteaux and the Station Oenologique, the wine-making is in the hands of their full-time oenologist Laurence Jobard.

Robert's reign has seen important expansions. Between 1959 and 1962 he extended the Domaine's holdings in the Côte de Nuits, principally in Chambolle-Musigny, and in 1968 he bought vines and unplanted land in Chablis from which he has built a 37.7 ha. Domaine. An important recent purchase was 40 ha. in the Willamette valley in Oregon, USA – 'at the same latitude as Burgundy, on the same altitude and with broadly similar climate'. Robert has great hopes for the Pinot Noir he has planted, though admitting that the soils are rather higher than ideal in acidity. He has put his daughter Véronique in charge of the project and seems very satisfied with her first vintage which was released in mid-1991.

At the Domaine, he aims to produce Burgundies which reflect their origins as closely as possible and is distrustful of trends which lead people to imitative folly. 'What may seem to be an improvement may turn out not to be one' – faults may only become apparent after many years, so it is essential to wait until a wine is mature before you can sensibly evaluate it: 'One must be prudent.'

Robert attributes much of the increased quality he has achieved to his ability to control viticulture. A vine, in his view, produces well, on average for 35 years; so 'to do good work' the quality of any plant material is of prime importance. For the grafts, experience has convinced him that clones are less good than his own *sélection massale* 'They seem to give less complexity, but I can't prove it.' Now some 66-75% of replantings are generated from a *vigne mère* of 1935 vines from the Clos des Mouches, the rest coming from a mix of selected clones.

Rootstocks also need careful choosing. Experience in the 1960s with the much-touted SO4 was not satisfactory – the rooting system was shallower and less long-lived; it produced to excess, especially in young vines, and was more susceptible to the absence of soil magnesium, in part the result of excess potassium used in fertilisers. The current favourites are 41B, 161/49 and sometimes Riparia.

The Domaine's vineyards are managed on the over-riding, quasi-homoeopathic, principle that the physiology of the vine must be seen as a whole, not merely as an amalgam of leaves, roots, wood bunches etc. Foliage control, short-pruning, fertilisers and treatments should not be isolated from their effects on the rest of the plant.

Part of the equation relating fruit to quality is density at which vineyards are planted – in the Côte d'Or usually 10,000 vines per ha. with 8 buds per vine. However, many growers, among them Robert Drouhin, are experimenting with denser planting in the belief that this will produce an all-round improvement in fruit quality. Now, the Domaine plants 12,500 vines per ha.– one of the highest densities in Burgundy – which encourages root-systems to delve deeper and thus to compete for nutrients.

Since Robert Drouhin took over, the firm's wines have improved dramatically, in part as the result of a serious fire which destroyed the new bottling plant in 1976. This was something of a watershed, causing him to rethink his wine-making philosophy and to admit that many of his wines were of less than top quality. A period of reflection resulted in longer *cuvaison* for the reds – from 10–18 days – and a lower fermentation temperature for the whites (18-22° C).

Installed in the Domaine's new cuverie and cellars just outside Beaune, Laurence Jobard reigns over the firm large array of red and white wines, superintending their vinification and *élevage*. Included in her charge is the precious produce of 2 ha. of Le Montrachet – the largest plot in single ownership – and some Chassagne-Montrachet, both belonging to the Marquis de Laguiche. These wines have been made by Drouhin since Maurice and the Marquis became friends just after the Second World War. Knowing the *climats* of the Côte inside out, Robert Drouhin is well aware of what to expect from each.

During vinification much emphasis is laid upon tasting, to decide for example the right moment to rack, or the appropriate proportion of new oak for a given *cuvée*. A well-equipped laboratory provides analyses, but in the end, the palate is pre-eminent.

The white wines are fermented in cask, after a light pressing and 8-12 hours *débourbage*. Only natural yeasts are used and each cask is roused periodically, especially towards the end of fermentation, to ensure that all the sugar is fermented out. Lees contact being an important quality-factor, racking is delayed until early summer to extract maximum finesse and richness into the wine.

Depending on the characteristics of the vintage and the Cru involved, the white wines are given 20-40% of new oak. Drouhin buys its own wood and dries it outside where rainwater extracts much of the gross, aggressive tannins. Robert Drouhin is convinced that careful natural drying has more impact on quality than the particular provenance, and adds that it is important to know the age of any casks which are not new – the oldest in his cellars are 5 years.

Although the precise *élevage* is dictated by constant tasting, in general the firm's white wines are bottled 7-15 months after the vintage. The naturally richer and more powerful wines – Montrachet, Corton-Charlemagne and Bâtard-Montrachet – spend the longest time in cask and are bottled without cold stabilisation, but with a minimum bentonite fining in cask and a kieselguhr filtration.

The red grapes are partially destalked, since Robert Drouhin holds the somewhat unconventional belief that without some stalks a wine lacks complexity. The remaining undestemmed grapes are put into the vats as whole bunches, which promotes both a more regular fermentation and colour stability. The *cuves* are cooled to 14–15° C to allow 48 hours pre-fermentive maceration, after which fermentation starts naturally with the temperature rising to a maximum of 35° C – 'then we start to worry', admits Laurence.

In addition to traditional wood *cuves*, and double-jacketed stainless-steel *cuves*, there is an impressive battery of *cuves auto-pigéantes*. Encouraging trials with rotating *cuves* in the early 1980s generated an enthusiasm for the method which both automates vinification and enables an extended maceration. Laurence is emphatic that these *cuves* are not a means of shortening fermentation nor a substitute for traditional *cuvaison*, but rather a modern way of achieving the same end. Drouhin's red wines used to be criticised for a lack of extract – a charge which would be difficult to sustain today.

Depending on the vintage and on how they evolve the Premiers and Grands Crus spend 12-18 months in cask. Trial finings determine the appropriate dose and fining agent for each wine and this process is followed by filtration and bottling. As a neat concession to information technology, each cask is labelled with a strip of bar-code, so that its contents can be readily identified; at least they don't have to worry about where they left the chalk.

The Domaine produces some 20 wines from its own vines, and a vast range from juice and grapes it buys in and vinifies; it also buys young wine for *élevage*. In common with most top-rank négociants Drouhin treat wines from others' vineyards with the same exemplary care as those from their own. Robert Drouhin claims equal pride in being a négociant as in being a wine-maker, although he is well aware that for many, 'négociant' has pejorative undertones. All his wines are important to him, from the humble Aligoté to the greatest Musigny or Montrachet. However, if one is perhaps a shade closer to his heart than the rest, it is undoubtedly the Clos des Mouches.

This vineyard – part of his father's inspired purchases – produces both a red and a white wine from vines planted on several small plateaux. Interestingly, there is no attempt to determine parcels which might better suit Pinot or Chardonnay, although the produce of young and old vines is vinified separately so that any casks which are not of the requisite quality can be weeded out and sold as Beaune Premier Cru.

In good vintages the Clos produces very fine wines – which develop well over the medium term. These are never blockbusters, but wines of breeding and finesse, backed by solid fruit, some from very old vines. This is consonant with the Domaine's overall style of wine-making, which tends to emphasise elegance rather than brute size.

Drouhin's wines are invariably honest, reliable Burgundy – good, occasionally exciting. The Domaine wines are distinctly better than the négociant offerings, where weaknesses sometimes appear; e.g. some rather uninspiring 1986 reds. Their structure is generally sound and the wines age capably; however, their 'femininity' could sometimes do with a dollop more concentration and depth, a flaw more obvious in vintages where natural ripeness is lacking.

Robert Drouhin relies much on his experience, which he encapsulates as 'the sum of past mistakes. I don't know whether I am a man of experience,' he confesses, 'but I've certainly made enough mistakes.' None the less, his experience has led him well and he has every reason to be proud of his achievements. His unremitting quest for quality has rubbed off on the producers of the Côte d'Or and on many around the world who are discovering what really fine Burgundy is all about. Those who already love the Côte and its wines have much to thank him for.

VINEYARD HOLDINGS

Commune	*Level*	*Lieu-dit/Climat*	*Area*	*Vine Age*	*Status*
Beaune	PC	Clos des Mouches (White)	6.90	27	P
Beaune	PC	Clos des Mouches (Red)	6.80	24	P
Beaune	PC	Grèves	0.80	7	P
Beaune	PC	(Several)	1.60	16	P
Volnay	PC	Clos des Chênes	0.30	22	P
Chorey	V	—	2.70	33	P
Aloxe	GC	Corton-Charlemagne	0.40	11	P
Aloxe	GC	Corton-Bressandes	0.30	20	P
Chambolle	GC	Bonnes Mares	0.30	24	P
Chambolle	GC	Musigny	0.70	16	P
Chambolle	PC	Les Amoureuses	0.60	30	P
Chambolle	PC	—	1.50	17	P
Flagey	GC	Echézeaux	0.50	25	P
Flagey	GC	Grands Echézeaux	0.50	18	P
Vougeot	GC	Clos de Vougeot	0.90	10	P
Gevrey	GC	Chambertin Clos de Bèze	0.10	—	P
Gevrey	GC	Griotte-Chambertin	0.50	10	P
Puligny	GC	Bâtard-Montrachet	0.10	—	P
		Total	**25.50 ha.**		

Maison Louis Jadot

BEAUNE

The fusion of Domaine and négociant is nowhere better exemplified than in the Maison Louis Jadot. Since its foundation in 1859, by the man whose name it bears, this House has grown into both one of the largest proprietors of Premier and Grand Cru land in the Côte d'Or and one of the handful of utterly reliable sources of wine throughout the entire region, from Chablis to Beaujolais.

Its heart, however, is firmly in the Côte. Here, over the years, it has carefully acquired and tended land to produce wines which exemplify at a uniformly high level the typicity and character of their origins.

This did not happen all at once; in fact, its development was distinctly fitful. Louis Jadot started with a parcel of vines in the Clos des Ursules bequeathed to his uncle by his father, a local négociant who had bought it in 1826. With this, and a broad education from his father, he built up a successful négociant business. Purchases of vineyards in Beaune Theurons and Clos des Couchereaux followed. Upon his death the business was taken up 'enthusiastically' by his son Louis Baptiste Jadot who reinvested his profits to acquire more Premier and Grand Cru land, including some Chevalier-Montrachet Les Demoiselles.

Louis Baptiste died in 1939 leaving the firm to his eldest son, Louis Auguste, who had assisted his father since 1931, opening up significant export markets including those of the USA, Great Britain, Holland, South America and New Zealand. In 1954, he took on a young assistant, André Gagey, who was at that time working in his father-in-law's négociant business. Gagey had qualified in commerce and business administration in Dijon before marrying Marie-Hélène Tourlière in 1947. He admits that the alliance of someone from nearer to Dijon with a girl from Beaune was rather frowned upon in those days, but her father clearly minded sufficiently little to give him invaluable experience in viticulture and cellar work which stood him in good stead when he joined Louis Auguste.

Upon the death of Louis Auguste in 1962, his widow asked André to run the firm, with full responsibility for its operations, until her son Louis-Alain should come of age. Sadly, Louis-Alain was killed in a car crash in 1968 at the age of 23. André was then appointed General Manager, and subsequently Managing Director. In 1985 the Jadot family sold the business to the Kopf family, owners of their American importers, Kobrand. Today, André Gagey retains complete discretion to continue the policies of development which he began in 1962 and has been able to extend the firm's vineyard holdings significantly.

In addition to its négoce activities, Maison Louis Jadot is in fact 4 separate viticultural estates, as well as having long-term contracts with 3 other important estates to vinify and market their wines. The Jadot estates are:

1. Domaine des Héritiers Louis Jadot: a 15.32 ha. holding of Premier and Grand Cru land in Corton, Beaune, Pernand-Vergelesses and Puligny including Corton-Charlemagne and Chevalier-Montrachet 'Les Demoiselles'.

2. The 16.8 ha. owned by the Maison Louis Jadot: comprising the fine Domaines of Clair Däu in Marsannay, purchased after unfortunate Clair family quarrels in 1986 precipitated the sale of the Domaine and the smaller Champy Domaine, purchased in 1989 – principally for its excellent cellars adjoining those of Jadot beneath the Couvent des Jacobins in Beaune, for its vineyards and for a marvellous collection of ancient Burgundy dating back to the 1820s. Together, these Domaines provide André Gagey with a superlative portfolio of vineyards including important parcels of Musigny, Bonnes Mares, Chambertin Clos de Bèze, Chapelle-Chambertin, Gevrey-Chambertin Clos St.-Jacques, Chambolle-Musigny Les Amoureuses, Clos Vougeot and much besides.

3. Domaine André Gagey: consisting of 2.42 ha. of Premier Cru land in Beaune and Nuits-St.-Georges.

4. Domaine Robert Tourlière: 2.86 ha. of several well-sited Beaune Premiers Crus and some Clos de Vougeot.

In consequence, the firm now has under its control 37 ha. of the Côte d'Or, of which 8 are Grands Crus. In addition, it makes and markets 80% of the wines of the Duc de Magenta which includes fine parcels of Puligny, Chassagne and Auxey-Duresses, 90% of the Clos des Corvées in Nuits-St.-Georges, share-cropped by Michel Thomas who has a contract with Jadot, and the 7 ha. Santenay Clos de Malte in Santenay.

Pierre-Henri and André Gagey enjoying a glass of their own Burgundy

André Gagey, a charming man full of the gentlest of old-fashioned courtesy and worldly wisdom, is gradually handing over control of the house to his son, Pierre-Henri, who was trained not as a wine-maker, but as an engineer and business administrator. André will tell you proudly how he refused his son employment in the firm, despite his notably successful education, until he had gained wider experience elsewhere. Returning from his banishment suitably broken in, he is now following in his father's distinguished footsteps. According to André, Pierre-Henri is 'passioné du vin' and 'un très bon dégustateur' to boot.

The technical direction is in the capable hands of Jacques Lardière, who joined André Gagey in 1970 to understudy him in that role. He in turn is supported by a young oenologist, Christine, and a team of Chefs de Culture to look after the 4 Domaines. Lardière, who might easily be mistaken for Vladimir Ashkenazy, is an articulate and highly competent wine-maker who believes that his mission is to interfere with nature as little as possible; consequently pumps, filters, and the rest of the technical impedimenta of the inept are, as far as possible, kept out of the way. He is, above all, concerned to retain in each wine the typicity of its appellation, and moreover of each *lieu-dit* within the appellation. 'Le *terroir*, c'est une mémoire,' he explains,waving his arms round galvanically at a cellar full of casks as if they were instruments in some sort of private vinous orchestra he was engaged to conduct.

The Domaine wines are generally forceful expressions of their respective *terroirs*. The négociant wines, however, when they come from less specific origins – a commune or region for instance – will express a different, broader, typicity. A Jadot Meursault, for example, being an *assemblage* of wines from 12 or so different proprietors, will sink the individual style of each within that of the generality. With 300 casks of Meursault, or 90 of Chassagne Village, it can only be so.

André Gagey and his son have built and carefully nurtured close relationships with the growers who provide them with grapes, juice or wine. These are based firmly on 'gentlemen's agreements' – and trust. By and large a Jadot grower, once his quality and competence are proven, is left to get on with his job without interference. If he needs advice it is there, but otherwise there is no attempt to exercise more than a watching brief over his activities. The House is under no obligation to buy anything that is not up to its own standards, which are well-known among the growers; equally, the grower is presumably under no obligation to sell what he has to the House, if he feels that he can do better elsewhere. However, as Pierre-Henri points out, the policy of buying grapes or juice at finished wine prices and the lack of technical expertise among the smaller growers, together with the certainty of payment and the freedom that such an arrangement gives them, puts the balance of financial advantage with the grower as well as helping Jadot ensure continuity of supply. A secure network of provision of this sort is a fundamental part of any successful négociant – even if he also owns 37 ha. of his own vineyards.

The great increase in prices in the 1983 and 1985 vintages, especially for Côte d'Or white wines, temporarily kinked the supply lines. A fragile equilibrium has now been restored, according to Pierre-Henri, and the focus has shifted to the red and white Grands Crus, where the pipes appear to be showing signs of spluttering. However as Pierre-Henri optimistically adds, 'there is progress to be made in areas where the wines are not as good as they should be.' Whether this ambiguous pronouncement is meant to reflect the need to improve the quality of wine-making in poor Domaines with otherwise good land, or else the desire to bring out the inherent qualities of lesser-known communes fringing the Côte, is not clear. Either way, increases in demand from old and new markets alike will require négociants like Louis Jadot either to increase the flow through the existing pipes or else to find somewhere else to pipe from.

For the present, supply and demand seem precariously balanced – except perhaps for the rarer Grands Crus, where rationing is the inevitable consequence of scarcity. In this climate, there is ample room for diversity – for example, Jadot are able to market 5 different Beaune Premiers Crus and 7 different Gevrey-Chambertin Premiers Crus. This strong desire to bring into consumer consciousness the individuality of each *lieu-dit* thrives on an increasingly sophisticated trade and public, who are prepared to take the trouble to attend to what others might regard as distinctions without differences, and is a cornerstone of the Jadot policy.

In the cellars, Jacques Lardière watches over his 62 *cuves* and his battalion of casks with infinite care and patience. He knows each village and each *climat* well – its soil,

The engaging Jacques Lardière, at work in the tasting room

exposition, vine age and ripening characteristics. He knows the way its grapes behave in the fermenting vats – whether they lose acidity or work better at this or that temperature – and takes considerable pride in letting each wine express to the fullest extent the character of its origin.

His philosophy of wine-making is courageously simple: the less you intervene, the better the expression of typicity. 'Men are afraid; they do not dare follow nature,' Jacques remarks – a pungent imprecation on many of the viticulteurs who interfere too much with their *cuves* and their casks. For his own *cuves*, the lightest of sulphuring, neither heating nor cooling, and a pre-fermentive maceration of 4–7 days – until nature is ready for the yeasts to work.

Jadot's reds invariably need time to blossom. Jacques Lardière is not a man dedicated to short *cuvaison*: a remarkable 25–33 days 'en *cuve*' to extract the very maximum of colour and aroma is about average, where everyone else is content with half that time, probably fearing *volatile acidity* and excess tannins. Jacques regards this, and his almost 100% destalking (except for the smaller parcels such as Chambolle-Musigny Les Amoureuses and the Musigny where a small proportion of stalks are left) as important elements of making a fine, long-lived wine. 'Tiens,' he exclaims, with yet more orchestral gesturing, 'aromas come from the dynamics of yeasts and bacteria; *cuvaison* is like charging a battery – the longer you let it charge, the more aromatic and gustatory power you will have at the end.'

Not daunted by a month or more of *cuvaison*, he is proud to announce that he generally ferments at 35–40° C. Most vignerons would break out in a muck sweat at the thought and warn that beyond 32° C you are courting disaster – the fermentation might stick, *volatile acidity* may rise and heaven knows what else may befall. Jacques is quite content: he has fermented some 1,200 *cuves* in two decades of wine-making and not one has 'stuck'. In any case, if one day it happens, then 'c'est facile', you simply decant the wine off its solids, press the pulp, put the whole lot back in the *cuve* and off it goes once more. 'There is no danger in the *cuves*,' argues Jacques, 'the potential danger is in the imbecility of man.' There are many estimable vignerons who would not subscribe to this view of things.

As you might expect with this modern traditionalist, cultured yeasts have no place in his scheme of vinification; that would be unwarrantable intervention. It is pretentious to interfere with nature. 'Selected yeasts?' says Jacques scornfully, 'selected for what, why? Selection means nothing at that level since we don't really know what the micro-organisms are.' There are more than 500 different aromas detectable in wine and the extraction of the maximum possible from this great diversity is so important, and only achievable with indigenous yeasts.

Tasting with Jacques Lardière is an education. Wine, as he sees it, has a definite role to play in people's lives – it is there to bring a little imagery, a little magic. People pay for a fine bottle not simply to spend money but to have a far-off shaded window opened – a glimpse of something magical, of something special. 'We are working with the imagination, the emotions, the unconscious.' He clearly has little patience with those who prefer to spend their time nit-picking over sterile descriptions, instead of enjoying what is in their glass.

Jacques' open wooden *cuves* are *pigéed* twice daily to keep the cap moist and to help extraction – but there is no *remontage*; this deprives the yeasts of oxygen and thus lengthens fermentation. The wines are then put into cask – about 15% new wood for the Premiers and Grands Crus and older casks – 'des bons' – for the Village and regional appellations. Traditionally, the Jadot wines were racked 2/3 times before bottling; Jacques has reduced this to a single racking, in September to December of the year after harvest. The racking is carried out from cask-to-cask within the same population of casks for each wine. Whether the wine is racked new to old or new to new depends entirely on tasting; there are no fixed rules.

After 18–22 months in wood the wines are racked clear of their lees and unified; 2–3 weeks later they are bottled with neither fining nor filtration. The exceptions to this are the regional wines which are very lightly filtered – 'it is less tiring for the wine than a racking,' argues Jacques.

The Domaine's white wines are fermented in cask direct from the presses. No time is allowed for the juice to settle since Jacques is convinced that once you clarify a juice you remove something from its aromatic organisation which has an impact on typicity; you end up making a wine rather than producing it. The wines spend anything between 12 and 20 months in cask, with only one racking. In naturally leaner years such as 1987 and 1988 some 15–20% of new oak is used and cask ageing is prolonged to add more fat to the wine. In better years – 1985 and 1983 for example – the white wines have no new wood at all since they are considered to have enough natural structure without adding more. A skimmed-milk fining and a plate filtration precede bottling.

The results of all Jacques' conducting are stunning – a range of wines with individuality, depth and consistently high quality. The whites have both finesse and depth of fruit, from the attractive, sappy, regional Bourgognes, through the ripe, earthy Auxey-Duresses to the heights of the Chevalier-Montrachet Les Demoiselles and the Montrachet. Whilst the négoce wines are well-made and correct, the Domaine wines are among the best of what one might expect to find in growers' cellars. The Duc de Magenta's Chassagnes are impeccable – with considerable vinosity and depth; the Grand Cru whites have a complexity and power which need years of cellaring to develop but which are well worth the wait. A Chevalier Les Demoiselles 1978, tasted from a magnum in 1988, was everything one might expect from a wine of such pedigree – a deepening golden colour with a fully developed honey and grilled almonds aroma of great complexity and a superb spectrum of flavours which kept one sniffing and sipping with fascination and pleasure.

The range of reds is no less impressive. Long *cuvaison* inevitably results in a deep colour – more or less dense Victoria plum in youth – evolving into a lighter garnet 'tuile' with progressing age. Each Village wine admirably evinces the typicity of its origins – from a somewhat rustic Marsannay and Fixin in the north to a Santenay Clos de Malte of some depth and finesse in the south.

From the vast range of the Domaine's Premiers and Grands Crus the Beaunes stand out – not just for their overall quality, but for the differences between the various individual *climats* spread throughout the commune. The *Monopole* Clos des Ursules – part of the Vignes Franches vineyard originally owned by the Ursuline Convent at Beaune in the seventeenth century – is the Jadot flagship; its wine is generally quite perfumed and relatively forward, never a blockbusting Premier Cru but one which has no difficulty ageing. Of the others, the Grèves and the remarkably deep Les Avaux from the Champy Domaine stand out. In December 1990, the 1989 Avaux was almost opaque black-cherry in colour; the very old vines clearly contributing to a huge concentration of fruit – wholly atypical of most young Beaunes one is ever likely to encounter. This wine seems set fair to last a quarter of a century without turning a hair.

The range and overall quality of the Domaine's red Grands Crus is equally impressive. Of the 1989s, some are more concentrated, others more elegant – but there are none which would cause one to question for a moment their ranking as Grands Crus. Among those from Gevrey, the Charmes-Chambertin was most exciting with a density of extract and flavour, and a balance which makes one wish that one could vault 20 years hence to see what will become of it. The Musigny, although recently racked, was pure silk – a slender aristocrat compared with the albeit taut but distinctly muscular Gevreys.

André Gagey has built up Louis Jadot into a firm of uncompromising quality. As with any Domaine not everything is invariably wonderful, but competence and integrity make it a thoroughly trustworthy source of yardstick Burgundy.

VINEYARD HOLDINGS

DOMAINE ANDRÉ GAGEY

Commune	*Level*	*Lieu-dit/Climats*	*Area*	*Vine Age*	*Status*
Beaune	PC	Les Chouacheux	0.67	20	P
Beaune	PC	Les Cents Vignes	0.42	12	P
Beaune	PC	Les Grèves	0.84	4	P
Nuits	PC	Les Boudots	0.50	15	P
		Total	**2.43 ha.**		

DOMAINE ROBERT TOURLIÈRE

Beaune	PC	Les Grèves	0.65	15	P
Beaune	PC	Les Grèves (White)	0.13	40	P
Beaune	PC	Les Toussaints	0.89	25	P
Beaune	PC	Les Tuvilans	0.56	35	P
Vougeot	GC	Clos de Vougeot	0.64	27	P
		Total	**2.87 ha.**		

DOMAINES DES HERITIERS LOUIS JADOT

Aloxe	GC	Corton Charlemagne	1.88	20	P
Aloxe	GC	Corton Pougets	1.54	25	P
Pernand	PC	Clos de la Croix de Pierre	1.50	15	P
Beaune	PC	Les Bressandes	1.03	14	P
Beaune	PC	Les Theurons	1.03	12	P
Beaune	PC	Clos des Couchereaux	1.93	25	P
Beaune	PC	Les Boucherottes	2.57	22	P
Beaune	PC	Les Chouacheux	0.39	17	P
Beaune	PC	Clos des Ursules	2.74	30	P
Puligny	PC	Les Folatières	0.21	15	P
Puligny	GC	Chevalier-Montrachet Les Demoiselles	0.51	37	P
		Total	**15.33 ha.**		

DOMAINE LOUIS JADOT

Gevrey	GC	Clos de Bèze	0.42	38	P
Gevrey	GC	Chapelle Chambertin	0.39	30	P
Gevrey	PC	Clos St. Jacques	1.00	30	P
Gevrey	PC	Les Cazetiers	0.12	20	P
Gevrey	PC	La Combe aux Moines	0.17	22	P
Gevrey	PC	Lavaux St. Jacques	0.22	28	P
Gevrey	PC	Etournelles St. Jacques	0.38	35	P
Gevrey	PC	Les Poissenots	0.19	23	P
Beaune	PC	Les Avaux	1.43	25	P
Beaune	PC	Clos des Mouches	0.28	30	P
Savigny	PC	Les Dominodes	2.01	25	P
Morey	GC	Bonnes Mares	0.27	5	P
Chambolle	GC	Musigny	0.17	30	P
Chambolle	PC	Les Amoureuses	0.12	5	P
Chambolle	V	—	0.04	30	P
Vougeot	GC	Clos de Vougeot	2.58	10	P
Marsannay	V	(White)	0.56	48	P
Marsannay	V	(Red)	2.78	22	P
Marsannay	V	(Rosé)	2.38	35	P
—	R	(Bourgogne Aligoté)	0.92	28	P
—	R	(BGO)	0.42	30	P
		Total	**16.83 ha.**		
		Grand Total	**37.46 ha.**		

Domaine Louis Latour

BEAUNE

Louis Latour, one of the most respected and traditional Domaines in Burgundy, is in fact an amalgam of two distinct but closely related enterprises. The older arm of the business, Maison Latour, represents the development of an established wine négociants, Lamarosse, founded in 1797 and acquired by Louis Latour (III) in 1867. It buys both grapes and juice from growers throughout Burgundy, making and marketing a complete range of wines through its international importers, and was responsible for putting the quality of more modest Chardonnays such as Mâcon-Lugny and Chardonnay de l'Ardeche onto the world's wine-lists.

The younger part of the business is the Domaine Louis Latour which started when the Latours, a family of vignerons since the early seventeenth century, arrived at Aloxe-Corton in 1768. Plying their trade as schoolteachers, vignerons and coopers, the Latours retained their handful of hectares until Louis (III) increased it to 10 ha. in the 1860s.

The Lamarosse négociant business thrived to the extent that in 1891 Louis Latour had amassed enough capital to profit from the family squabbles of the Comtes de Grancey and buy their magnificent 35 ha. Domaine in Aloxe-Corton. Since then each successive Louis Latour has been Mayor of Aloxe, the physical and spiritual heart of the Domaine.

Up until the appearance of the fourth Louis Latour (1874-1941) a series of only sons had ensured an unproblematic succession. However, not content with adding vines to the Domaine by marrying some, Louis IV broke the rules and sired 6 children. In the 1960s when 5 of them decided to withdraw their share of the vineyards, the Domaine was unable to buy them out, so by 1970 it found itself some 15 ha. the poorer.

Nonetheless, impoverishment is relative, and the Domaine today is owner of some 44 ha. of vines, the majority being Premiers and Grands Crus. Apart from 0.8 ha each of Chambertin and Romanée-St.-Vivant, bought in 1898, all the land is in the Côte de Beaune.

The tradition continues – the Domaine is now directed by Louis V's son Louis-Paul Latour (b.1931), who has recently been joined by his son Louis-Fabrice (b.1962) as finance director. Louis V's brother, Jean Latour, now 85, who looked after the Domaine for nearly half a century (1925-1974), continues to provide a living link with the past.

The Domaine's day-to-day fortunes are in the hands of the lean, intense Denis Fetzmann, a qualified agronomist and

The Domaine's Château de Grancey at Aloxe-Corton gives its name to the firm's finest Corton

oenologist, who heads a small technical team which looks after the vineyards and the cellars. His formidable expertise ensures maximum care goes into every stage of the production process and provides an element of cross-fertilisation between the different responsibilities.

In the vineyards, the Domaine has a history of being innovative. During the *phylloxera* epidemic of the last quarter of the nineteenth century, it was the wit of Louis III, who realised that one could bypass the disease by grafting on to resistant American rootstocks, which prompted him to buy vineyards cheaply, whilst most vignerons despaired. In the 1890s he planted some 17 ha. of the Grancey Domaine on to new roots and encouraged other vignerons to use the same technique. He was also instrumental in planting Chardonnay in place of Aligoté and Pinot Noir in limestone-dominated sections of the southern slopes of the Corton hill, which remarkable insight paved the way for the appellation Corton-Charlemagne.

Denis Fetzmann and the Chef de Culture, Michel Magnien, take the care of their vineyards very seriously. 'Culture traditionelle' is the policy, which means resting the soils for 2–3 years before replanting. Since the Domaine is replanted in total every 47 years, this represents a permanent sacrifice of several years production on one hectare of vines.

Whereas the Domaine's Pinot Noir is a mixture of *sélection massale* from their own vineyards plus 33% clones to preserve as far as possible the originality of each *climat,* new plantings of Chardonnay are now exclusively in clones. The difference reflects the difficulty of finding suitable indigenous Chardonnay plant material which has a low disease risk. In this respect, Pinot Noir is less problematic than Chardonnay. When clones are used, their progress is followed closely, from vineyard to bottle. The Domaine procures suitable rootstocks from propagators in the south of France – 161/49 and Riparia for Pinot, S04 for Chardonnay – and makes all its own grafts, for planting each spring.

Throughout the Domaine, and especially in the steep vineyards behind the cuverie at Aloxe-Corton, soil erosion presents a constant problem. Constructing special drainage conduits to collect soil washed down by the rain is one line of attack, whilst a person working full time to maintain the Domaine's kilometres of stone walls is the other. The authorities will not allow eroded soil to be reconstituted with earth from anywhere – especially in a Grand Cru, so retaining what is already there is a sensible priority.

Since the vine is a naturally rambling plant, health by itself will not produce high quality fruit – one has to limit its yield. Denis Fetzmann is proud of the fact that in the Domaine's Corton vineyards, the average yield over the last 20 years has been 30 hl./ha. Against a normally permitted maximum of 35–42 hl./ha., this hardly appears excessive. The keys are well-known: old vines, careful *sélection massale* from low-yielding vines, short pruning and the minimum doses of fertiliser.

To this formula, Denis Fetzmann adds a

green-pruning of bunches when he considers it is necessary. In 1990, despite restricting each vine to some 6–8 bunches, a perfect flowering presaged a huge harvest. Between 20 July and 15 August, a team was sent in to remove half the crop from 12 ha. of the Domaine's vines. In 1989, some 15 ha. were scoured to remove a second generation of grapes, which threatened to sap sugar production for the main bunches and would have added unwelcome acidity had they found their way into the vats.

All the Domaine's wines are vinified by their oenologist, Jean-Pierre Jobard; the reds in their superb vaulted cuverie, built in 1830 at Aloxe-Corton in the middle of the Les Perrierès vineyard. The red grapes are destemmed and crushed, then transported by a splendid system of large shiny copper bowls on overhead rails – installed by the inventive Louis III – to their respective vats, each of which represents a particular parcel of vines selected by age, appellation or plant origin.

By the next day fermentation is generally under way, mediated by the natural yeast population. There is no pre-fermentive maceration and *cuvaison* lasts a mere 8–9 days. This follows the principles of Dr. Guyot, set out in the 1850s, who counselled a rapid fermentation which did not pass 30° C. Temperature is controlled by a system of heat-exchangers which can be lowered into the *cuves,* whilst a thrice-daily *pigéage* helps by keeping the cap of skins broken up and moist.

The press-wine, expressed by an ancient pneumatic membrane press which serves for both red and white grapes, is added to the free-run wine, and this is followed by 24 hours *débourbage* before the new wine is transferred to casks in the magnificent cellars beneath the cuverie.

Such abnormally short vinification has attracted its share of criticism. It is said that one cannot extract enough 'matière' in 8 days to give a wine sufficient structure and typicity. The defence is that this is no more than traditional Burgundian practice, and moreover, that what is sought is finesse rather than sheer size. After 10 days *cuvaison,* says Denis Fetzmann, you extract tannin at the expense of finesse. In any case, Jean Latour vinified the wines for the Hospices de Beaune from 1925 to 1975 in exactly the same way as his own, and no-one complained about those.

The red wines remain in cask – 20% new oak only – for about 18 months. They are racked after the *malo* cask-to-cask and again just before the vintage, when a selection is made for each *cuvée.* Whether a wine is fined depends on the vintage; however, there are 2 filtrations – one after the second racking and another 2 months or so later, just before bottling.

In between these, the Domaine's red wines are subjected to a process which has caused considerable controversy – they are flash-pasteurised for 3 seconds at 72° C. This practice, instigated by Louis IV at the end of the nineteenth century, is intended to protect the wine's colour and aroma, to increase its stability and to guard it from bacterial spoilage. It does not, according to the Domaine, 'prevent wines ageing, improve poor wines or make all wines taste the same.' It is felt to be the 'gentle option' – less tiring for the wine than a harsh filtration or fining.

Whilst pasteurisation may not prevent a red wine from ageing, it may change the way in which it does so. Wine contains a host of naturally volatile elements – so it is not inconceivable to conjecture that even as little as 3 seconds at 72° C might dramatically alter their balance. Louis Latour have not, as far as one can ascertain, followed the evolution of the same wine bottled with and without pasteurisation – it would be a simple experiment and would kill the controversy once and for all. Commentators have too often noted rich, opulent fruit in cask and rather less excitement in bottle for the controversy to be quelled with a colour pamphlet. The Domaine doth, perhaps, protest too much.

Latour's explicit preference for finesse and their short *cuvaison* results in wines which generate controversy. For many, their Corton-Grancey – a brand representing the best of each vintage's Cortons – their Chambertin and Romanée-St.-Vivant, represent the summit of what fine red Burgundy is all about; for others the wines, whatever else they may have, simply lack depth and interest. Argument is superfluous; it is in the end a matter of taste.

Whilst the Village wines and some of the Premiers Crus have often seemed pleasant but lacking in precision, the Grands Crus in great years can make fine bottles. However, in many cases they seem to develop a flat and uninspiring aspect as if stunted from birth. Bottles of Corton-Grancey from the 1953, 1959 and 1962 vintages tasted recently have been dull and insipid – certainly not what one expects from mature Grand Cru of such pedigree.

Whatever the doubts about the Domaine's red wines, there can be none about its whites, which represent some of the finest Burgundies available. Apart from the grapes from Montrachet and Corton-Charlemagne, which are pressed at Aloxe-Corton and the *musts* transported to Beaune, these are vinified in toto at the Domaine's new cuverie in Beaune.

There, the juice is put into tank and controlled at 29° C. until fermentation has begun when it is transferred to cask. Latour are very particular about their casks – all are made from their own Allier oak, selected for its fine grain and dried naturally at Aloxe. Whilst the reds only see 20% of new wood, the Domaine's whites are fermented in about 80% new casks.

After a minimum of 4 months on their fine lees, the wines are racked, cask-to-cask, followed 9 months or so later with a fining and light filtration, before being bottled – a total of 12–15 months in wood.

The 3,000 cases of Corton-Charlemagne and the pitiful 180 cases of Chevalier-Montrachet Les Demoiselles represent the totality of the Domaine's white wine output. The grapes are deliberately harvested late, ripeness rather than acidity being the principal consideration. They are invariably great wines, which start life tight and budded but which, with age, blossom into supreme aristocrats.

Although both share immense power and complexity, they are very different in character. The Corton-Charlemagne tends to have a more masculine elegance, slightly reserved austerity, underpinned by concentrated, ripe fruit, whereas the Chevalier seems to express the plumper, more feminine charm one associates with Puligny. There is also an equally fine Montrachet, but not from the Domaine's own vines.

As a substantial Domaine-owning négociant, Louis Latour's reputation stands high. Controversy over its red wines should not detract from its achievements in bringing fine Burgundy to a much wider public.

VINEYARD HOLDINGS

Commune	*Level*	*Lieu-dit/Climat*	*Area*	*Vine Age*	*Status*
Aloxe	GC	(8 Climats)	17.00	N/A	N/A
Aloxe	PC/V	(3 PCs + Village)	6.00	N/A	N/A
Pernand	PC/V	(1 PC + Vlillage)	2.30	N/A	N/A
Beaune	PC	(5 PCs)	5.50	N/A	N/A
Volnay	PC/V	(1 PC + Village)	0.70	N/A	N/A
Pommard	PC	Epenots	0.50	N/A	N/A
Aloxe	GC	Corton-Charlemagne	9.50	N/A	N/A
Puligny	GC	Chevalier-Montrachet	0.50	N/A	N/A
Gevrey	GC	Chambertin	0.80	N/A	N/A
Vosne	GC	Romanée-St.-Vivant	0.80	N/A	N/A
		Total	**43.60 ha.**		

Monsieur Denis Fetzmann was unwilling to provide proper details of vineyard holdings; those given are approximations.

Domaine Albert Morot

BEAUNE

The abiding dream of most wine buyers is one day to stumble upon some sleepy little Domaine producing delicious wines that doesn't seem to be overburdened with customers and just happens to have a few bottles of older vintages. At a time when the Côte d'Or is one of the best mapped and researched viticultural areas in the world, it stretches one's credulity to find that such Domaines still exist, but they can be found and it is this element of exploration which contributes to making Burgundy such an exciting place to sniff around, in a way that Bordeaux will never be.

A chance bottle with a friend in Chablis several years ago provided the spark for an introduction to the Domaine Albert Morot in Beaune. Having tasted excellent wine, the first visit was something of a shock. The Domaine's headquarters – the whimsically neo-gothic Château de la Creusotte, on the periphery of Beaune – must rank in the top flight of Burgundy's architectural curiosities. It appears to represent no particular style, but strongly resembles the kind of 'hatters castle' mixture popular with wealthy industrialists in northern England at the turn of the century.

Probably the last word in modernity and fashion when it was built in 1890, the Château has clearly been subjected to the sternest test any building might be expected to undergo – neglect. For the past century or so, bits have been falling off it: chimney-pots missing, shutters hanging at rakish angles – rather as if the house had made the mistake of opening an eye to the sun one day and then found it couldn't shut it again; tiles missing off the roofs; plants sprouting out of water-hoppers long unkempt; and a veritable snakes and ladders of a guttering system which cascades water in every conceivable direction; in short, a museum of bad maintenance. Fortunately, things have now been taken in hand and the Château is slowly being put together again.

However, this is not a Domaine to be judged on appearance. While it is rarely mentioned in books and its wines seldom seen at tastings, quality is uniformly high and its Beaunes among the finest in the appellation. This is due largely to the enthusiasm and dedication of the Choppin family who have owned and managed the Domaine for nearly 70 years.The present generation comprises Guy and Françoise Choppin, grandchildren of Albert Morot, a late nineteenth-century Beaune négociant. Guy, now in his sixties – who looked after things

Françoise Choppin watching casks being topped up in her cellars

so competently from 1952 – sadly became ill in 1984, suffering from a progressive malady which has left him house-bound and withdrawn. Fortunately his younger sister, Françoise, a charming and efficient lady in her early sixties, stepped in and took charge of both Guy and the Domaine. She is a remarkable person – short, wiry and energetic – with a passion for her wine and a deep feeling for quality and how to produce it. With the help of a single 'ouvrier' for the heavier work and the part-time services of a couple of ladies, she now runs the entire operation – vineyard, cellar and business. She does not drive and seldom leaves the estate – 'in case a customer calls – they even come on Sundays, you know'. In 1990 her furthest excursion was to her barrel-maker in Meursault; 'abroad' probably means Santenay.

A visit here is always an eccentric delight. A dilapidated, cock-eyed sign propped up against a tree on the edge of the walled park surrounding the Château extends a permanent invitation to 'visite et dégustation'. The courtyard is generally presided over by a large, harmless, hyper-active, noisy dog which seems to be everywhere at once – almost as if feeling obliged to represent a small canine army, the remainder being temporarily absent.

The cellars, reached from a raised ground-level cuverie, are old and exceedingly cold. Tasting raw, young wine from the cask here on a January afternoon is likely to impact more on one's feet than on one's teeth. But it is worth the discomfort, for the 100 or so old oak *pièces* neatly stacked along the main cellar aisle contain the results of a tradition with no intention of compromising on quality.

Françoise believes that quality begins with the vine. This is fortunate, since 80% of the Domaine's wine is the product of its own vineyards acquired between 1893 and 1894 principally from the then owners of the Domaine de la Romanée-Conti and the Domaine de la Pousse d'Or – a patchwork of holdings scattered around the southern and better end of the Beaune appellation; almost 7 ha. of land comprising 6 of the finest Beaune *climats* and a *Monopole* of 1.81 ha. of the Savigny Premier Cru Clos la Bataillère. This results in a total annual production of about 4,000 cases, all Premier Cru.

Within these fine vineyards, the Pinot vines are allowed to reach an advanced age. Françoise has no doubt that, although yields are commensurately reduced, quality of fruit improves dramatically with increasing vine age. Although her vines are rigorously pruned to further reduce production and increase concentration, this is sometimes not enough. In 1990 a woman was employed for the entire month of August to green-prune much of the Domaine. This resulted in substantially reduced yields, and a 'very contented' worker.

It is fair to say that one can learn much about a vigneron's attitude to quality from their attitude to vine ageing. Those who are too ready to grub up vines before their fiftieth birthday, or who think that a vine produces its best quality fruit when it is 30 years old, say more about the quality of their own wines than they might imagine. The unmistakable contribution to taste of very old vines is a hallmark of Françoise Choppin's wines.

Vinification is thoroughly traditional: since 1926 the grapes have been completely destalked. 'Stalks, they're bitter, they fill up the *cuves* every year, that's all; they bring nothing good to the wine,' is Françoise's uncompromising statement. *Cuvaison* lasts up to 3 weeks - with plenty of *pigéage* to prolong fermentation and maximise the extraction of colour and flavour compounds. No cultured yeasts here: 'one tries to be as natural as possible'.

The press-wine is normally added to the free-run wine. A new Vaslin press acquired in 1982 presses gently, leaving a rich pulp for the distillery to make into the Domaine's excellent Marc (one of the best in Burgundy). The wine then is put into cask and taken down to the depths of the cellars.

Françoise is not blindly enamoured of new wood – about one third seems right to her. However, in 1990 her new bottling-machine broke down while bottling the 1989s. This resulted in a shortage of casks, so she had to buy new ones. Thus the 1990s have an indeterminate amount of new wood: '50%

easily, easily – I made a very great effort, I had to find a place for those wines,' chuckles Françoise, surveying the line of bright new barrels with evident pleasure.

The wines are usually kept in cask for about 12–14 months. Some American critics have tried – unsuccessfully thank heavens – to persuade her to bottle later. However, she is adamant that they have always bottled early, 'to keep the perfumes, the freshness'. Tasting her 1972s, 1971s and 1949s there is no doubt that she is entirely right.

For all her experience, Françoise Choppin is not an oenologist, so has to rely on her experts. Thus all the wines are fined, with albumen.'Some tell you "no fining" – those are the people from the Côtes de Nuits who like tannic wines – others tell you 10% or 20% fining, or half' – a laugh and a shrug. What does it matter, the results are magnificent.

The wines are also filtered, until recently through an ancient plate filter; now it's kieselguhr, followed by a passage across a light membrane to remove any gross particles which may still be left.

Bottling used to be by hand, but in 1986 Françoise – seeing the travails of the man bottling the large 1985 harvest – took pity and bought a small bottling machine. Telling you this, she adds, in case you might be assailed by doubts: 'this is not a factory, you know, we take our time to do things.' The results are impressive – wines with plenty of depth and flavour, each expressing the individuality of its *climat* and, above all, ageing superbly.

The Savigny Bataillère, apart from being the most delicate of the range, is also something of an oddity. It is not in fact a designated vineyard site, but rather a triangular enclave at the base of Les Hautes-Vergelesses (Savigny, not Pernand). As far back as anyone can remember, it has always been known as Savigny-Vergelesses 'dit Bataillère'. Until recently it also carried the designation 'Clos', being enclosed with a wall on two sides, the third being the track dividing the Haute from Basse Vergelesses. However, the authorities took exception to this, hotly contested of course, possibly because part of the wall had collapsed. So for the moment it is simply 'Savigny-Vergelesses, la Bataillère'. In 1987 the officials had another go and tried to suppress the 'Bataillère', but Françoise was on the telephone straight away: 'Écoutez ! . . . ' She won her point.

The Bataillère is generally harvested late, the vines being relatively young (planted 1958 and 1972; they had finally to grub up the 1945 vines). In character it has great perfume and finesse and plenty of extract – almost a junior Beaune Cents Vignes. 'It's a ladies' wine, this,' remarks Françoise with a smile. Maybe, but it is also the best Savigny.

The Cents Vignes itself tends to be deeper in colour than the Bataillère, with plenty of stuffing on the palate and an attractive nose which develops early. The vineyard was replanted during 1958/9, so the vines are approaching an age of interesting quality.

The Toussaints, replanted in 1969, is often rather tight at first, with a good natural acidity and plenty of firm fruit. Often quite a meaty wine, it needs a decade or more to show its true colours, in a fine vintage such as 1985, 1988 or 1990.

The Marconnets – planted half in 1950 and the rest in 1958 – is rather more Pommard or Corton in style than Beaune. It has the finesse of a Corton but the depth and breadth of a Pommard. It can be quite soft (e.g. 1989) with an individual nose of more animal character, and is particularly long-lived.

If Marconnets is Corton, then the Teurons is decidedly Gevrey – a firmly-structured wine, with overtones of meat-extract and a distinct hint of *fruits sauvages* – on the nose. It keeps especially well in great vintages.

The last two of Françoise's remarkable range of Premiers Crus, Grèves and Bressandes are, in great vintages, among the best wines to be found in the Côte de Beaune. The Bressandes typically starts off closed up like a clam, giving little for 5 years, then gradually emerging from its shell to reveal a silky opulence of aromas and flavours of great distinction. The major part of the vineyard was last replanted in 1946, so there is no lack of delicious, concentrated old-vine fruit. A 1971 tasted in 1990 was still seductively youthful, but with a richness and depth which made one think of a mature Vosne-Romanée or even an Echézeaux.

The Grèves, from a mere 12.53 ares of vines planted in 1948, is sensationally good. Sadly, the vineyard was grubbed up after the 1990 harvest, so the supply has dried up entirely for the present. The wine is usually among the deepest in colour of the range, with a nose of *fruits sauvages,* liquorice and almost sweet fruit. On the palate it manages to combine the depth of the Bressandes with the finesse of the Cents Vignes.

This is fine wine-making by any standards. If the great vintages are excellent, the 'in-betweens' are no less successful in their own way. In 1982,1979 and 1967, for example, the wines are delicate but also full of nuances and lingering flavours with, invariably, a touch of tannin and enough acidity to keep everything alive. Wines to enjoy whilst waiting for the grander vintages to mature.

The Château de la Creusotte's newly restored exterior

However, it is the 5-star vintages which really put this Domaine at the top. For Françoise, 1971 is so far the real vintage of the century. Her 1971s have a dimension of ripe complexity and breed which puts them in the same league as the best Côte de Nuits.

Guy Choppin certainly knew what he was doing. His 1949 Beaune Grèves, tasted in 1989, was remarkably fine, having all the concentration and depth of that fine vintage allied to an exceptional length and grandeur.

It is difficult to understand why Beaune has always been something of a Cinderella among cognoscenti. Given the choice between a Premier Cru Volnay and a Premier Cru Beaune, most would choose the Volnay. This implied indictment is unjustified, particularly with wine from properties such as this to testify in Beaune's favour.

This is a great Domaine which is well worth following. Its wines are invariably modestly priced and made to last – ideal for anyone looking to stock a cellar without developing cirrhosis of the wallet.

Sadly, the succession is uncertain. Neither Guy nor Françoise has children, so there is no knowing who will inherit this fine estate. They have already refused predatory offers from the USA and elsewhere, but how long they can keep going is a matter of guessing. One thing, however, is certain: as long as they are in charge, there will be no compromise on quality.

VINEYARD HOLDINGS

Commune	Level	Lieu-dit/Climat	Area	Vine Age	Status
Beaune	PC	Les Teurons	0.99	1963	P
Beaune	PC	Les Grèves	0.13	1992	P
Beaune	PC	Les Toussaints	0.77	2969	P
Beaune	PC	Les Bressandes	1.27	1946/60/82	P
Beaune	PC	Les Cent Vignes	1.28	1958/59	P
Beaune	PC	Les Marconnets	0.68	1950/58	P
Savigny	PC	Clos La Bataillère	1.81	1958/72/92	P
		Total	**6.93 ha.**		

POMMARD

The vineyards of Pommard begin at a fork in the road, 2 km. south of Beaune at a spot marked by a prominent stone cross. Branching to the right the road follows the wall of Les Epenots for a further half kilometre, passing the solitary, disused railway station and the imposing Clos of the Château de Pommard on the left, before reaching the village itself.

Here, in a small square, a couple of pleasant 'routier' style bar/restaurants, one on each side of a small bridge, represent the complete extent of the village's gastronomy. Beneath the bridge meanders l'Avant-Dheune, a dispirited little water-course which descends from the Combe high above the vineyards, peevishly given to overflowing, flooding houses and cellars and causing general inconvenience. The village is further animated by a dress shop, a patisserie, and a newly-opened wine shop owned by a consortium of local growers.

Until quite recently, Pommard enjoyed a reputation for producing big, heavy, heart-warming wines, a sort of vinous central heating, with plenty of guts and not much finesse – which Harry Yoxall aptly characterised as 'pleasant drinks without much authority'. Producers, both inside and outside the commune, climbed onto this gallopingly profitable band-wagon, with wines which were either dismally dilute, or else cut with something distinctly un-Burgundian, to satisfy a seemingly insatiable demand for Pommard.

This was known and noted in the 1930s and continued, despite the introduction of AC controls in 1936, until well into the 1960s. Pommard seems to have been favoured because it had an easily pronounceable name. Things have changed since then; the runaway popularity, and prices, have now abated and there are presently several top-class Domaines producing affordable wines of considerable quality.

The vignoble, much reduced since the early nineteenth century, now covers some 337 ha., of which 211.62 ha. are designated AC Pommard and 125.19 ha classified as AC Pommard Premier Cru.

The commune wines, from vineyards either on higher ground above the village or else on the flatter land between the RN 73 and RN 74, encompass a broad spectrum of styles and qualities. The rockier, thinner soils of the upper slopes give wines with more finesse but less depth than those from the heavier, clayier soils lower down. The vineyards at the eastern end of the commune, which continue Les Epenots, have stonier, better drained soils and give commensurately finer wine.

However, it is with the 29 Premiers Crus that the wines of Pommard become serious. These are sited on a belt of hillside, flat at the bottom and steep at the top, on either side of the village.

On the Beaune side of Pommard, the best are Les Pézerolles, L'Argillière and Les Epenots, which is divided into Les Grands and Les Petits Epenots. Straddling the two Epenots is the Clos des Epeneaux (sic) of Comte Armand, whilst the part of Grands Epenots closest to the village contains the 2.92 ha. Clos des Cîteaux, which belongs to Jean Monnier of Meursault.

In this sector, a south/south-east exposure combines with stony, red clay-limestone soils to produce wines of power and muscle. They tend to have noticeably more tannin and less delicacy than the Premiers Crus of next-door Beaune, and the best need keeping for 10 years or so to develop their potential.

On the Volnay side of the village lie Les Rugiens, Les Jarolières and Les Fremiers (which reappears as Les Fremiets in adjacent Volnay). Les Rugiens is divided into the excellent Rugiens-Bas and the less good Rugiens-Hauts, although the distinction is never made on labels. The vineyards here are steeper, on rockier soils, and well exposed to the south-east. The wines have more finesse and less rustic muscle - often with hints of the silky delicacy of the best Volnays about them. The Rugiens, however, is often among the richest of the Pommards. If there were a re-classification, then Les Rugiens-Bas and parts of Les Epenots would be credible candidates for Grand Cru status.

Profiled here are a handful of exciting

50% of Pommard's gastronomy; the other half is next door

Domaines. In addition, one talented vigneron who is creating much interest is Jean-Marc Boillot. Jean-Marc, the first wine-maker at Olivier Leflaive, runs his 10 ha. Domaine from his grandfather Henri Boillot's splendid house, on the edge of the village. Despite plenty of old vines, long *cuvaison* and 40% new oak, the wines are designed for early drinking. The Pommard Jarolières and Rugiens are the pick of the bunch, with Puligny Premiers Crus Champs-Canet, Combettes, Truffières and Referts, which arrived 'en partage' from the Sauzet Domaine in 1991.

Outside the village, Hubert de Montille's Pézerolles and Rugiens are wines of great distinction and Mme. Armande Douhairet's Pommard Chanlins is often excellent, especially in ripe vintages such as 1985 and 1989. The Château de Pommard make a respectable Pommard from a 20 ha. Clos – the largest in single ownership in the Côte – which is matured in 100% new wood. Drouhin and Jadot both produce good *cuvées* of Les Epenots, and Arnaud Machard de Gramont a fine Pommard Le Clos Blanc. The Domaine Parent is highly regarded in some circles, but in recent tastings their wines, though tannic and solid, lacked both charm and class.

Many vignerons in Volnay are also good sources of Pommard – Joseph Voillot, Regis Rossignol, Jean-Marc Bouley and Yvon Clerget in particular – albeit on a small scale.

Apart from the attractions of the dress-shop and the patissier, Pommard boasts no fewer than 3 separate Châteaux, and a fine eighteenth-century church with a 32 m. tall bell-tower. This forms the centre-piece of the quiet tree-lined main square, and is surrounded by fine Domaines – de Courcel, Gaunoux, Clos des Epeneaux – and the village school.

Of the Châteaux two, the eighteenth-century Château Micault and the 1802 Château de Pommard, both belong to the family of Jean-Louis Laplanche, professor of psychology at the Sorbonne. The third, on the north-eastern side of the village, is the Château de la Commaraine which, with its 3.75 ha. Clos, is the property of Jaboulet-Vercherre. The wine invariably sound but generally uninspiring.

For the rest, Pommard has a quiet, monastic history. Probably named after Pommone, the goddess of fruits and gardens, its best *climats* were owned by a variety of religious orders from the thirteenth century onwards.

The cross of Pommard used to mark the site of a muddy ford until a bridge was built in 1670. Here, between the two Routiers, the 'diligences' would stage, and passengers would have to traverse on foot. If successful, a hole in the base of the cross – still there in the replica – was provided for a suitable contribution. For most visitors, however, the vineyards and growers are the main attraction, and here there is increasingly enough to justify an exploration.

Domaine du Clos des Epeneaux

POMMARD

Among the Domaines in these pages, the Clos des Epeneaux shares the distinction with the Clos de Tart in Morey-St.-Denis of producing but one wine – a Pommard Premier Cru from which it takes its name. It is further unusual in that its vineyard is in one single piece – a weather risk that many hardened vignerons would not care to contemplate.

The Domaine originally belonged to the Marey-Monge family, one of the greatest of nineteenth-century Burgundian proprietors. When in 1855 one of the Marey-Monge daughters married Comte Armand, the Domaine – being part of her dowry – passed into the 'patrimoine' of the Armands.

However, the Armands were not by tradition vignerons, so *régisseurs* were employed to manage the estate. This system, common among the grander Burgundian land-owners, was open to abuse, especially if the *régisseur* had his own vineyards to tend and the landlord was frequently absent. In January 1985 the present Comte Armand, an international lawyer in Paris, appointed a young French Canadian, Pascal Marchand, to sole charge of the estate.

The choice of Pascal was unusual. Already 'passioné du vin', he had arrived to explore Burgundy in 1983 from Montreal. 'I had never seen a vineyard or cuverie,' he confesses, 'but wanted to visit Burgundy as it was the region I knew least.' After helping to vintage the 1983 and working for a few months in the cellars, Pascal returned home. He enrolled for a viticulture and oenology course in Beaune, returning in November of the following year to take up his place.

In June 1984 he went to work for Bruno Clair in Marsannay, and whilst there met, by chance, his future employer. Quite what inspired the Comte to put this inexperienced young man in sole charge of his precious Domaine is not clear, but he did, and the result has been eminently successful.

The Domaine Pascal took over was, to use his description, 'a bit faulty'. Whilst the vineyard was acceptable, the cellars needed tidying up and much of the stock of casks required renewing. Apart from looking after the ripening 1985 grapes, there were the entire 1983 and 1984 vintages still in cask in the cellars to be seen to.

With the 1985 vintage out of the way, Pascal started to work out policies for maintenance. Without a fragmented vignoble as an insurance aganst frost, storm or disease, any innovative plans had to be tempered with a degree of caution.

To keep vine age high and maintain a sensible production level, *répiquage is* preferred, although limited to vines less than 40 years old since digging individual holes into solid rock is very hard work. Replanting larger parcels of the 5.2 ha. Clos is also kept to a minimum – since 1985 only 1 ha. has been grubbed up. Pascal chose to replant this on a mixture of selected clones but, seeing the result, decided that the next substantial planting will use a *sélection massale* from the Domaine's own vines.

The current vine population ranges 5–56 years in age. Whilst the older plants are mostly on S04 roots, apparently defying the conventional wisdom that they are short-lived, newer plantings are on the fashionable 161/49. Although the vineyard is virtually flat, it has a moderate lime content to which 161/49 is well-adapted.

The soil profile – studied with care by Pascal – shows a rather meagre topsoil, with a high stone content, giving on to a substantial bedrock of marne calcaire. Curiously for Pommard, the iron content is not high; however, it is well drained, which is important on flat ground.

Pruning is kept short. Young vines are trained *en crochet* up to 6 years old, making a gradual transition to the conventional adult *Guyot* training by adding one 'eye' each year.

Much reflection has gone into developing a strategy for treating the vines during the growing season. Pascal admits that in this he is still feeling his way. The main problem is the grape-worm, a miserable, useless insect which fractures the skin of the berries and renders them prone to rot through the open wound. The vigneron's dilemma is that if he simply blankets the vines with effective but perforce strong insecticides, he kills the insects at the expense of problems later on – spray resistance, alterations in the soil microflora etc.; however, not treating the vines risks extensive rot resulting in low yields and a possible reduction in quality.

The solution may lie in new sprays which destabilise the grape-worm's reproductive cycle. These act by destroying the odour compounds on which the species relies to attract and thus reproduce. Although much less harmful to soil and vine these products do not seem to eliminate the worms entirely. They can breed, but are 'invisible' and do not puncture the grape skins. To detect them one has only to put a grape in a bowl of warm water, when they materialise quite rapidly.

As far as other treatments go, Pascal is more sure of his ground. He has banished all systemic products and is considering putting an embargo on *pénétrants.* This will only leave contact sprays – which are effective until the next shower washes them off the leaves. These exclusions include herbicides, so the soil has to be worked by hoe and pick to uproot grass and weeds. Until there is more information on how synthetics affect the vine and on their patterns of degradation in the soil, he is happier working without them.

Of equal importance to healthy vines are low yields. In this struggle, fertilisers are the key. Growers these days, Pascal will tell you, are rich; they can afford to buy whatever they want to put onto the soils. However, he limits himself to very careful doses of organic fertilisers, simply to adjust *trace elements* when necessary. The plants must suffer – 'it is necessary to understand the soil and the needs of the vine. Sometimes, when you see, elsewhere, the leaves green until November, you know that there is too much nitrogen in the soil.'

The point Pascal makes is important. The uniqueness of each small vineyard in Burgundy is a function of its soil. For the wine it produces to express that uniqueness, it must nourish itself – not from artificially enriched surface soils but from deeper down, where *trace elements* are leached into the water-table. For this to happen, growth of the naturally proliferous lateral roots must be restricted, so that the main, tap-roots are encouraged to seek sustenance further down. However, to achieve this it is necessary for the vine to have enough vigour of its own, so it needs adequate surface nutrition, provided largely by a balanced cocktail of well-known essential elements – phosphorus, magnesium, potassium, nitrogen etc. This is why the use of fertilisers is critical. The temptation to over-fertilise, producing masses of healthy green foliage and kilos of juicy, ripe grapes, is too much for many Burgundian vignerons, who no doubt feel their coin-laden trouser pockets sagging in sympathy with the pendulous vine branches. The dilute wine such grapes produce, even if the grower bothers to *saigner* the *cuves,* pleasant though it may be, does nothing to express the typicity and character of its origins, which the Burgundians with all their 'réunions' and 'confréries' constantly swear to uphold.

Whatever his decision about treatments and fertilisers, there is one misfortune from

Pascal does most of the work on his own

which Pascal's vineyard seems to be miraculously immune – hail. Hail is by no means uncommon in Pommard – from May to August the risk is there. However, the Clos des Epeneaux, at the northern end of the commune, escapes while its more southerly neighbours suffer. The storms seem to come up from the south-east, cross the village and then turn sharply north-west, no doubt funnelled by the Combe behind the vineyards. This is indeed a stroke of fortune for a single-vineyard Domaine.

When it comes to harvesting, there is another advantage – the Grands Epenots (of which the Clos des Epeneaux is a part) invariably ripens early. Other viticulteurs with several plots in Pommard and nearby tend to harvest their Epenots first if they have any. With only one plot to consider, Pascal Marchand can afford to wait until the grapes are fully ripe – but not over-ripe – before picking.

The vinification sequence is broadly traditional. The grapes are entirely destalked, given a moderate dose of SO_2 in *cuve,* homogenised with an anaerobic pumping-over and then left to ferment on their own yeasts. Pascal tries to mix cooler morning grapes with the hotter afternoon harvest to avoid artificial cooling. Fermentation usually starts after 3–4 days; a further *remontage,* this time with air, helps to multiply the yeasts and start the process off. Fermentation proceeds at temperatures up to 33° C, with a total *cuvaison* of 10–17 days, depending on the speed of fermentation and on the vintage.

Following a 2–3-day *débourbage* in tank – 'clarification problems,' contends Pascal, 'come from what one puts on the vines' – the wine goes into casks, 30% of which are new. He prefers a mixture of Allier, Nevers and Vosges wood to any single oak, but believes that 'the provenance . . . says nothing, it is the quality of the barrel-maker which is most important.' His casks are medium charred – having tried a very strong charring and found that this tended to lock in any *goût de réduit* the wine might have.

In any case, he does not want to mark the wine too much with wood flavours, so after the first racking, at the start of the following summer, the wine in new casks is assembled with that in older casks - the original 4 *cuvées* now becoming 2 – and then put back entirely into 3–5 year-old casks. The wines are fined in cask, in December of the second year, and then left *sur col* until their second racking any time between January and April. The 1989s were, however, not fined – they were clear and would certainly have lost valuable tannins in the process.

The two lots are re-unified at the second racking and then left for 3 weeks in tank before bottling by gravity, without filtration. No timetables are fixed for all these operations, much depending on the style and needs of each wine.

It is worth stressing that the Clos des Epeneaux is made from an *assemblage* of different wines from vines of different ages grown on a single plot of land. The grapes are harvested by vine age and vinified in 3 lots: young vines, less than 12 years old; 12–20-year-old-vines and finally vines older than 30 years. The point of this is that, when the wine is finally assembled, there are 3 or more individual 'palette-colours' which can be used, in greater or lesser proportion, to enhance the complexity of the Grand Vin.

In especially good vintages, there may be a Cuvée Vieilles Vignes, made exclusively from the older vines. However, fine as this is, extracting the best wine inescapably diminishes the concentration of the standard blend.

Tasting sample casks of each 'lot' from the 1990 vintage, the differences are striking. The younger vines give a wine of greater delicacy – aromas of *fruits sauvages* – with goodish concentration, quite a firm structure, and almost tarry flavours.

Wine from the 12–20-year vines – macerated for 17 days, the longest yet – is virtually black in colour with a layer of aggressive tannins dominating concentrated ripe fruit underneath. The 30-year-old vines produce an opaque wine, black cherry in hue, with yet more concentration. The natural balance of old vine fruit shows through here, with a layer of firm but far less aggressive tannins covering a mass of rich fruit.

The 1989s, already one stage on towards final *assemblage,* are more tractable – the younger vines giving a relatively light wine, for a Pommard, with aromas of *fruits sauvages* and some firm tannins. The 12–20-year vines show more colour, with aromas of *fruits rouges* and liquorice, quite spicy – with a round, softish profile and some ripe supporting tannin. The old vines produce the most opulent and well-integrated wine – a liquid of power and depth, yet disarmingly soft. The blend of these constituents promises well – a wine for the next 5–20 years.

The style of the finished wine tends to be very structured, even for Pommard which is often regarded as the Nuits of the Côte de Beaune. The old vines contribute significantly to the depth of the wine, especially in fine vintages such as 1988 and 1985. The 1988 is particularly successful – deep in colour with an attractive nose of wild blackberries beginning to open out and succulent, ripe concentrated fruit underneath. The tannins are beautifully balanced with the fruit, though firm enough to suggest long-distance maturation.

Despite his relative inexperience, Pascal Marchand already produces fine wine. It will be fascinating to see what emerges from this Domaine as he, and his vines, increase in maturity.

VINEYARD HOLDINGS

Commune	*Level*	*Lieu-dit/Climat*	*Area*	*Vine Age*	*Status*
Pommard	PC	Clos des Epeneaux	5.20	5–56	P

Domaine de Courcel

POMMARD

It is comparatively rare, among the numerous small Domaines of the Côte d'Or, to find one of high quality which is not operated by its owner. In Pommard there are two: Comte Armand's Clos des Epeneaux and the Domaine de Courcel.

This latter is an 8.30 ha. exploitation which has been in the hands of the de Courcel family for four centuries. Its present owner, Gilles de Courcel, took over the Domaine with his sister on the death of their aunt, Mme. Betrand de Courcel, in 1976. Now a Paris banker, he is 'passioné du vin', having worked variously at Bichot in Beaune, Piper Heidsieck in Reims and then in the export department of Calvet in Bordeaux.

Meanwhile, his Domaine is in eminently capable hands. Yves Tavant, a slender, jockey-like man in his late forties, with a mischievous twinkle, is the third generation of his family to take charge of the cellars. Since 1966 he has been responsible for the wines, in which he exudes justifiable pride. Unfortunately, his son is developing more in a literary than scientific mould, so Yves may be the last Tavant at Domaine de Courcel.

The heart of the Domaine is 5 ha. in the Grand Clos des Epenots, where the vines range from 5 to 60 years old, averaging about 45 years. The rest are Pommard Premiers Crus Rugiens, Fremiers, the rarely seen Croix Noires, a patch of Pommard Villages and some Bourgogne Rouge.

Despite Yves' quarter of a century at the Domaine, there is no evidence of things falling into the rut which elsewhere is usually referred to as tradition. Gilles de Courcel is bent on quality, and flexible enough to adopt innovation where he believes it beneficial.

While both soil and leaf analyses are enlisted to inform the fertilisation programme and to help determine rootstocks for replanting there is relatively little *repiquage;* rather, half a hectare of vines is grubbed up every 3–4 years and then replanted. Only clones are used, but de Courcel is experimenting with several different individual clones to see which gives the best quality wine. He is also finding – as are many other Domaines who care to try – that *cordon* training is a positive quality influence, keeping yields down and giving smaller berries. Experimental rows of *cordon*-trained vines in Les Epenots produced better-quality fruit than those trained conventionally.

The separate treatment of younger vines from pruning to harvest is an integral part of the Domaine's search for quality. Although de Courcel does not yet green-prune, he is considering this for young vines which tend, however rigorously they are pruned, to be over-productive. Younger vines, especially in the Grands Epenots, are generally picked later than the older vines and vinified separately, only being amalgamated at the first racking if considered to be of suitable quality. Otherwise, their produce is sold to the local négoce.

In the vineyards, soil erosion, though perhaps less marked now than in the past, is a continuing problem, particularly in the steeper parts of Les Rugiens. Yves Tavant remembers his grandfather struggling with hods of earth on his back trying to replace some of the topsoil washed down by heavy rains. Yves himself did not escape the toil – in 1969 he spent 15 days carting soil back to the top of the vineyard – but he concedes that what you replace is rarely what has been washed down, most of this finding its way irretrievably into gullies and drainage ditches.

Harvesting is a matter of picking each parcel as it becomes fully ripe. They generally start with the old vines in Grands Epenots, followed by the steeper Rugiens, going on through the 35-year-old Epenots vines, to Fremiers and so on. There is a severe *trie* in the vineyards – especially in years such as 1984, when much of the unripe harvest was left on the vines for the birds.

In parallel with the vineyards, there is evolution in the cellars. Normally, Yves likes to leave 33–50% of the stalks with the berries for fermentation, but in 1990 the exigencies of space caused by the size of the harvest forced him to destalk completely. In that year, he wanted to try a short, cold maceration before fermentation to extend the *cuvaison* beyond its usual 14–15 days. However, despite his best efforts the yeasts were so healthy that they started to work at 14° C, even though he had added 50% more sulphur than usual to delay the onset of fermentation.

Even with his desired maceration truncated, Yves found that a cooler, slower fermentation extracted more fat and glycerol into the wines. This is a procedure which, given a healthy harvest, he will continue.

The year 1990 was obviously one of experiment for Yves Tavant and Gilles de Courcel – apart from the voluntary cold maceration and the involuntary destalking they tried adding pectolytic enzymes during fermentation, to help subsequent clarification and also decided to leave the wines on their lees after the *malo* before their first racking. Whilst it is refreshing to see innovation, one wonders why they needed enzymes in a year which was noted for the health of the harvest. Perhaps the local Station Oenologique was behind the decision?

In 1975 the Domaine sold all its wine to the négoce. Now at least 50% is bottled and sold by them, and the proportion is increasing. Yves believes that the methods he is using are reverting, with some modifications, to what his father and grandfather did 'dans le temps'. However, some things have changed, seemingly for good. 'Dans le temps', they used to heat the cellars to get the *malos* going – the bacteria work better in a warm environment; now, they just put the casks downstairs and leave the bacteria to their own devices. They also used to leave the wines upwards of 2 years in cask; now the realisation that wines, especially from lighter vintages, desiccate rapidly if left too long in cask, has led to a reduction in *élevage* to a more fruitful 15–18 months, depending on the wine and the vintage.

Another common practice 'dans le temps' was to excoriate wines by excessive filtration. Gilles is currently striving to eliminate filtration altogether – hence perhaps the experiments with enzymes – except when the state of the wine renders it essential as, for example, in vintages such as 1983 where rot was prevalent. At present the wines are fined in bulk and then subjected to a very light plate filtration 'above all for the USA'. It would be encouraging to hope that, at some time in the near future, wine-makers would have the courage to treat their wines as they think fit, without regard to the demands of their jittery clientèle.

Whatever one's reservations about the *élevage,* there are none on the quality of what ends up in bottle. The de Courcel wines are carefully crafted, designed to typify their appellations and above all fashioned to be kept. At the back of Yves' mind is the precept that the Pinot Noir is not a highly coloured *cépage,* so there is no attempt to extract unnatural depths of colour by an exaggerated fermentation temperature or unduly long *cuvaison,* although it should be remarked that their 14–15 days is longer than one generally finds in Pommard or Volnay.

The range starts off with a Bourgogne Pinot Noir made from 33-year-old vines and matured entirely in old wood. More Volnay in style than Pommard, this wine has a clean, ripe strawberry nose and plenty of solid fruit. The 1989 was rather raw and somewhat four-

Yves Tavant checking the condition of a bottle from the Domaine's library of older vintages

square, but with a year or two in bottle should make a good example of its appellation.

Of the Pommards the lightest of the Premiers Crus is the Fremiers, made from vines planted in 1970 and 1974. In 1988 and 1990 all the Domaine's vats were heavily *saignéed* – some 2,400 litres in total, mostly in the young vines – to further concentrate the juice; however, it appears that there was no *saignée* in 1989, despite its being a prolific vintage in the Côte. This shows up in the Fremiers, which seems to be somewhat dilute. It has considerable finesse, and good acidity (some acidification took place in 1988,1989 and 1990) so may well flesh out.

There are no such reservations over the Epenots and Rugiens. The former (1989), though not exceptionally concentrated, is beautifully perfumed – violets, red fruits, liquorice – with notable length. A wine which will give pleasure from about 1995 onwards. The 1989 Rugiens has a markedly deeper hue and is more concentrated and structured. The soil, although not deep, is richer in clay than the Epenots, and this gives the wine a more typically Pommard profile which will take longer to evolve. The 25% of new oak adds to the natural structure without dominating it in any way. A wine to keep until the year 2000 or so under ideal circumstances.

The yields here are kept deliberately low. However, in 1990, despite a rigorous *saignée,* they just breached the *PLC* – the level above which distillation is obligatory. This system, originally designed to punish systematic over-producers, is falling into disrepute for treating good and bad wine alike. It is depressing to see fine wine going for distillation when demand so far outstrips supply. There is an overwhelming case for a tasting test for surplus production, so that fine wine can stand on its merits.

Like much of the best of Burgundy, and indeed everywhere else, de Courcel wines are made to be kept and should not really be finally judged until they have had a chance to settle down and mature. The Rugiens 1985, for example, is just beginning to show itself. Not deep in colour, no obvious signs of premature ageing, but a superbly opulent and complex nose, starting to emerge from its slumber; turning from the primary, fruit-based aromas, to the distinctive Pinot *sous-bois,* with violets and spice superadded. On the palate it is relatively delicate for a 5-year-old Pommard but with enough fruit and tannin to keep it going for several years, and supreme finesse. A Côte-Rotie which appeared similarly forward at so young an age might give cause for anxiety, but for a Pommard this is nothing untoward.

The great vintages from this Domaine are wines of elegance and depth. A 1978 Epenots tasted recently had an opulent, really magnificent visceral, gamey, nose, with a hint of vegetal *sous-bois* and an equally opulent range of flavours. A wine of ripe, fat fruit, with a thin line of tannin holding it up. A marvel, but not surprising from only 20 hl./ha. and from the talented hands of Yves Tavant.

VINEYARD HOLDINGS

Commune	*Level*	*Lieu-dit/Climat*	*Area*	*Vintage*	*Status*
Pommard	PC	Grand Clos des Epenots	5.00	45	P
Pommard	PC	Rugiens	1.00	45	P
Pommard	PC	Fremiers	0.65	18	P
Pommard	PC	Croix Noires	0.60	13	P
Pommard	V	Vaumuriens	0.35	7–19	P
Pommard	R	(Bourgogne Rouge)	0.70	12–33	P
		Total	**8.30 ha.**		

Domaine Michel Gaunoux

POMMARD

Mme. Gaunoux is a lively, articulate lady, seemingly in her early fifties, who has fought a battle for her Domaine and is quite determined to keep it at the top. The battle arose when her husband Michel died suddenly in 1984.

Her legacy was a 10 ha. Domaine, sited principally in Pommard, but with some Beaune and Corton, founded by her late husband's grandfather, Alexandre Gaunoux, in 1895. He had arrived somewhat haphazardly, having visited the Château de Volnay for a wedding and there met a local négociant's daughter whom he later married. Michel subsequently took over from his father (Alexandre's son) in 1960. Fortunately, in addition to his capable wife he left a son and daughter who will eventually inherit the Domaine.

Mme. Gaunoux setting out a tasting

Although she had worked with Michel selling their wine, Mme. Gaunoux knew little more than the broad descriptive details of how he set about producing it. Nonetheless, she decided to continue to build on what he had achieved rather than giving up the struggle and selling. Replacing Michel's skills was not easy – there are legions of newly-minted wine-makers pouring out of the various educational establishments in Beaune and Dijon, but real talent is rare. When those who applied for the job of wine-maker turned out to be no-hopers, Mme. Gaunoux decided to go it alone, with the caviste, who had worked closely with Michel, taking over the wine-making. As long as he was able to tell her that 'Michel would have done it like that', she was content.

This single-minded lady has indubitably won her fight. The wines from her cellars are of a quality and consistency which others might do well to emulate. Part of the secret lies in the high proportion of vines which are between 30–60 years old. Major replanting is virtually unheard of here – the policy being to replace vines which expire individually rather than grubbing up whole patches.

However, when yields eventually dwindled to economically unviable levels, some replanting became inevitable. In 1990 they dipped their toes into the water and replaced 0.25 ha. of very old vines in the Pommard Les Arvelets vineyard. Instead of the traditional *sélection massale,* Mme. Gaunoux decided to consider clones. She admits to having experienced some difficulty in finding plant-material of sufficient quality, but finally chose 4 different clones – 2 selected for quality and 2 for productivity. This seems a curious sort of compromise since the cream of currently available clones has been repeatedly selected for optimum quality and productivity. It is rather like buying two separate trouser legs – one chosen for crease resistance and the other for colour-fastness; you could still end up looking like a dis-coloured concertina.

Before planting, the soils are carefully analysed and any base mineral or element deficiencies adjusted. The ground is then left fallow for 12 months before the chosen grafts are planted out. The Domaine is very concerned to minimise the use of fertilisers – in fact, only guano is used, in very small doses. 'What frightens us is that too much is put on to vineyards.'

Every major decision made by Mme. Gaunoux is taken after considerable thought and discussion. Much of the technical input which helps her comes from information provided by an organisation of which the Domaine is a member. Entitled 'Domaines Familiaux de Tradition', this is a federation of high-quality Côte d'Or Domaines, of which Olivier Leflaive is currently the President. Seminars, expert lectures and study visits keep the 20 or so member Domaines informed of technical advances and encourage a free exchange of information and experience. They have also made representations to the Ministry of Finance in Paris, demonstrating that the current tax laws render the passing to the next generation of even a small Domaine virtually impossible.

In addition, Mme. Gaunoux subscribes to the local co-operative – an excellent organisation run by a retired French army colonel, which marshals useful information on viticultural hazards and disseminates it urgently if need be. The recommended treatments are based on a variety of modern synthetic products but 'when we can jump a treatment, we do – for the sake of quality, not to save money,' explains Madame.

In the cellars everything is, as one might imagine, thoroughly traditional – 14 large open wooden vats stand in a well-disciplined row (they probably know about the colonel) and what stainless steel there is sits disconsolately in corners, no doubt trying to pretend that it is traditional too. Vat number 4 is an impostor – stainless-steel carefully camouflaged with a wooden-clad exterior.

Vinification is 'the most intellectual part of our work; each year, everything is re-examined.' The bunches are completely destalked, but, Mme. Gaunoux adds confusingly, 'we might leave 20–25% of stalks in the vats.' Fermentation proceeds traditionally with natural yeasts – although she does admit that, in 1980, when they built a new wall in the cuverie, they were obliged to use a *pied de cuve* to get the first vat going – presumably because the builders had unwittingly battered the indigenous cellar yeasts to extinction.

Although Madame was willing to talk about her *cuvaison* – an equally traditional 15–17 days – she was somewhat coy about the temperature to which her fermentations are allowed to rise. 'Everyone has their own methods; you have to know how to take risks,' was offered to start with; then, under a little gentle pressure – 'let's say 32–34° C'. The true figure is may be a good deal higher, but it seemed ungentlemanly to press the point – rather like asking her to disclose her age. Let's say 32–34° C.

One thing is not in doubt – Mme. Gaunoux does not like 'push-button' vinification. 'Each cask behaves differently – like a patient who is ill, they have to be treated as individuals. It's no good just pressing a button and going off to bed – you have to be prepared to get up at 3 a.m. if necessary.' So every night during fermentation, each of Madame's traditional vats – even number 4 – is carefully tucked up and covered with a plastic lid, to retain aromas and alcohol.

The wines are left in tanks for their *malos,* since this simplifies monitoring and control; thereafter, they are kept in cask for 18–24 months – with 33–50% new Allier oak ('plus a little Tronçais'). Less naturally structured years see more new oak and better years less. 1989, for example, saw none at all, whereas the 1986, which was entirely sold to negoçiants, had a fair ration of new wood. 'We are not particularly in favour of new casks,' says Madame, with an air of someone who has no intention of being swayed by popular trends, adding, as an afterthought, 'It's fashion, snobbism.'

When they are ready, the wines are unified in bulk, fined with egg-whites and then filtered 'à plaques Suisses'. Whether Swiss filter-plates are better than the rest is obscure, but Madame clearly considers them to be so.

Throughout *élevage* the minimum of sulphur is used. Mme. Gaunoux confesses herself flabbergasted by what she finds when she visits the Côte de Nuits: 'I won't say the names, but some people put in six litres per tonne!' This, she is convinced, has nothing to do with real Burgundy.

Another indication of the Domaine's rigorous attitude to quality is their stout refusal to bottle any vintages which they consider indifferent: 'the consumer must never be disappointed by a bottle of our wine,' she argues. Thus not a single bottle of Domaine Gaunoux was produced in 1970, 1975, 1980 or 1986 and precious little in 1977. How inspiring it would be if one or two other producers were prepared to make a similar sacrifice in what they all claim is the undying pursuit of quality.

The marketing of the Domaine's wines is somewhat individual. Tasting in cask is not allowed, nor is any wine made available until it has had at least 2 years in bottle. In addition, Madame never lists fewer than 5 vintages at any one time, keeping back stocks of each wine to be sold later to her regular clientèle – one of the very few Burgundy Domaines to offer older vintages.

If her marketing displays a charming but welcome eccentricity, her sales are no less so. Not a single bottle, she explains, has been sold to the USA since 1983, nor has she yet an importer in the UK; 'We have enough clients in France' – mostly the top echelon of starred restaurants and regular 'particuliers'. She faces the fact that none of her wine finds its way on to the two greatest Burgundy export markets with pragmatic equanimity. 'We do not go out looking for clients, they come to us,' is the essence of her approach.

Mme. Gaunoux is a proud and clear-headed lady. She dislikes journalists and is suspicious of anyone whom she considers will not appreciate what she is trying to achieve. She need have little anxiety – her wines are deep, brooding, concentrated animals, of very fine quality. There is nothing blowsy about them, however – just discreet, exemplary complexity and great class. The yields of the Domaine are low: 'We don't often reach 35 hl./ha. – it's very rare.'

The Pommards are especially fine, with impressive power and depth. The style is deliberately oriented towards *vins de garde* – wines which accentuate the mature expressions of the individual *climats* rather than the more youthful, aromatic Pinot flavours. The Pommard Grands Epenots, for example, tends to a very rich, almost over-ripe *figué* aroma in vintages such as 1983, but more typically Pommard spices in years such as 1985. Underneath there is plenty of ripe, sturdy fruit of remarkable density – the contribution of the old vines and a long *cuvaison* to extract maximum flavour – and a dimension of breed and length seldom seen in other wines from this commune.

Pommard can be rustic and ungainly – but not here. Mme. Gaunoux considers that the lesser vintages – for example 1984 – invariably need 10 years in bottle before becoming fully mature, whereas the greater years need at least 15. The 1987 Grands Epenots, for instance, is a wine of splendid potential from a vintage which is marked by extremes of quality. After 24 hours open, it began to develop most seductive, almost pine and garrigues provençale aromas, and to show a lovely concentration of deep, ripe, old vine fruit – another bottle to lock away for a decade. These wines may not have the strength of vintage port, but seem to demand the same sort of ageing.

Mme. Gaunoux and her excellent wines deserve more international recognition. She is a redoubtable lady who probably cares more for acclaim than she will readily admit. Her apparent distaste for overt publicity may have contributed to her low profile, but anyone who wants some of the best in Pommard should stroll up to the Place de l'Eglise and see what delights lie beyond the high wall in its north-eastern corner.

VINEYARD HOLDINGS

Commune	Level	Lieu-dit/Climat	Area	Vine Age	Status
Pommard	PC	Les Rugiens (Bas)	0.69	40	P
Pommard	PC	Les Grands Epenots	1.76	45	P
Pommard	PC	Les Arvelets	0.26	1990	P
Pommard	PC	Les Charmots	0.26	35	P
Pommard	PC	Les Combes	0.25	50	P
Beaune	PC/V	(4 climats)	2.04	35–40	P/M
Aloxe	GC	Corton Renardes	0.65	30–35	P
Pommard	R	(Bourgogne Rouge)	1.00	30	P
		Total	**6.91 ha.**		

Domaine Girardin

POMMARD

Beneath the grand ranks of the greatest Domaines there lies a solid band of less prestigious, but no less hard-working, estates which provide those drinkers and merchants who are not quite so mesmerised by labels with excellent Burgundy at affordable prices.

The Girardins are such a Domaine. A small exploitation of some 6.70 ha. wisely spread across Pommard, Beaune and Meursault, with a little Aligoté and a little more Bourgogne Pinot Noir included for good measure. No fewer than 7 different red Premiers Crus, 2 in Beaune and 5 in Pommard, provide the kernel of the estate.

This is a truly family undertaking. Henri and Hélène Girardin, now not far off retirement, and their talented and knowledgeable daughter Aleth work hard to keep the vineyards healthy and the vine age as high as possible and to bring up their wines to best advantage in the cellars beneath their respective houses, which stare at each other across the small road leading from Pommard towards Volnay.

Aleth's marriage in 1988 to an actor, and the subsequent arrival of children, has temporarily put her out of action. However, she continues to help and advise her parents and to teach her interested, but as yet not entirely tutored, husband the mysteries of wine in general and of Pommard in particular.

Unlike the larger Domaines of the Côte, financial stringencies ensure that the ideal rarely matches the actual. For example, they can't yet afford a destalking machine, so they have to manage with an ancient crusher which, according to Aleth, swallows everything. Thus, whether or not to destalk a given vintage or *cuvée,* is mere theorising. The essential *pigéage* is done by human feet; folkloric and charming as this may seem, the hard cake of stems and skins makes the going 'like concrete', especially at the start. Pressing is equally 'artisanale'; a 1906 vertical press does the work but takes all night about it, and presumably requires several man-hours after the vintage to clean it thoroughly.

Undaunted, they soldier on. Only the Premiers Crus are given a ration of new wood, and then only 10%, probably because the casks cost so much. After some 18–20 months in barrel, a contract bottler is summoned – they can't possibly afford the investment in even the smallest of bottling machines for one week's work a year – and the wine kieselguhr filtered and bottled.

For the American market things are slightly different: their importer requires them to put all the wines he buys into 100% Allier oak – a policy which the Girardins would never dream of employing for their own wines, even assuming they could afford it. Presumably they are not at present in a position to refuse a good order, but perhaps when they have established a broader base of clientèle, they will be free to insist that the wine is made in the way they want. As might be expected, the new wood *cuvées* were completely dominated by the oak, effectively stifling much of the rich fruit underneath.

Despite these constraints, the wines are generally excellent, sometimes superb, although on occasion the enforced full quota of stalks shows through, giving the wine a taint of greenness. However, this is offset by the high average vine age and a *cuvaison* of 10–12 days at up to 35°C., which endows the wines with real depth and concentration. In cask they tend to have deep, limpid Victoria-plum or black-cherry hues and plenty of densely packed, structured fruit.

Whilst the village Pommard, from a mixture of *lieu-dits,* is usually authentic and very well made, it is the Premiers Crus from Beaune and Pommard which constitute the pick of the cellar, with the Rugiens and the Grands Epenots being the 'Crème de Tête', as it were.

The Rugiens comes from 35 ares of vines planted in 1910 in the late ripening lower section of the vineyard, where the soil is deep and high in red iron oxides – hence the name ' R(o)ugiens'. The 1989 and 1990 both had virtually opaque, very dense tones and a magnificent depth of fruit. The former was already quite round, with ripe and almost soft tannins covered by concentrated, sweet fruit; in contrast the 1990 seemed to have firmer tannins and yet more power. Both are wines of great length and quality which will amply reward long keeping.

Pinot Noir vines in full summer leaf at Pommard

The Grands Epenots comes from 53 ares of vines planted a decade earlier than the Rugiens, in a section of the vineyard between the Clos des Epeneaux of Comte Armand and the Clos de Cîteaux belonging to the Monnier family. The rootstocks are divided between rupestris and riparia – both in wide use at the end of the nineteenth century – and in some years vines will fail to produce anything at all, so the yields are very low indeed. The wine is yet denser than the Rugiens, with even more guts and stuffing and an appealling nose of *fruits noirs.* Both the 1989 and 1990, still in cask, are wines of exceptional quality, some of the best to be found in the appellation, with a concentration and richness of extract which promise to develop into something remarkable in the years to come.

This is a very fine small Domaine; no pretension, no self-aggrandisement, just unremitting hard work and great attention to detail. It is pleasant to speculate on what Henri, Hélène and Aleth could do if some fairy godmother bestowed on them a destemmer, a bottling machine or perhaps a clutch of new casks. One never knows . . .

VINEYARD HOLDINGS

Commune	*Level*	*Lieu-dit/Climat*	*Area*	*Vine Age*	*Status*
Pommard	PC	Les Rugiens	0.35	80	P
Pommard	PC	La Refène	0.40	20	P
Pommard	PC	Les Charmots	0.57	50–55	P/F
Pommard	PC	L'Argillière	0.08	45	F
Pommard	PC	Les Epenots	0.53	55–80	P/F
Pommard	V	(Several climats)	1.63	40–45	P/F
Beaune	PC	Clos des Mouches	0.35	35	P
Beaune	PC	Les Montrevenots	0.41	45	P
Beaune	V	Les Bons Feuvres	0.09	30	F
Meursault	PC	Les Poruzots	0.26	1990	F
—	R	(Bourgogne Pinot)	1.38	35	F
—	R	(Bourgogne Pinot)	0.35	1991	P
		Total	**6.40 ha.**		

Domaine Mussy

POMMARD

André Mussy is a Burgundian original. The tenth generation of Mussys in Pommard, he is now a hearty 77-year-old and, having personally vinified no fewer than 63 vintages (and helped to harvest a mere 66), shows no signs of the decline that might afflict other septuagenarians lacking his passionate devotion to fine wine and to their work.

This is a one-man Domaine – created, developed and still run by this kindly, old-fashioned man – consisting of 6 ha. spread over Pommard, Beaune and Volnay.

In 1981 André suffered a great misfortune when his only son was killed in a tractor accident in the vineyards. His voice falters and he gently wipes his eyes as he recounts finding his son's remains, crushed. There is no bitterness, just sadness, vivid memories and wild regret.

The keys to great wine, as André states them, are low yields and traditional vinification. The first is achieved by careful selection of the finest clones – 113/114/115/677 and 777 – short pruning, 6 eyes on the *baguette* plus 2 on the *courson,* an *ébourgonnage* each May and old vines. He believes that July or August green-pruning is folly: it is far too late and in any case a conscientious vigneron would notice any excess earlier and act then.

The method of looking after his precious vines is deliberate and consistent. The soil is hoed in the old-fashioned way rather than given herbicides – this helps absorb rainfall and thus combats soil erosion, especially in dry summers. Fertilisers are only used to replace essential nutrients, which the vines have taken from the soil, and then only in small, organic doses. Foliage is kept as high as possible to encourage maximum photosynthesis at the end of the ripening season and to prevent the bunches being cooked by direct exposure to the sun. Finally, André tries to harvest as late and as speedily as possible; 2 teams of pickers can apparently do the job in 6 days – starting with the Bourgogne, then the Volnay, the Beaune Epenottes, Pommard Épenots, Pézerolles and Saucilles, and finally the Gamay and Aligoté.

Treatments are classic – emphasising copper and sulphur-based products. No systemic or anti-rot sprays are employed because the oily residue they leave on the bunches delays fermentation and affects the wines capacity to take fining and filtration.

Vinification is 'truncated traditional'. Years ago, André says, *cuvaison* lasted 3 weeks – largely because fermentation took some 8 days to get going, the proportion of juice being much less than today. Now, however, *cuvaison* averages 8–10 days, with 2 or 3 *pigéages* a day to extract colour and aromas: 'le secret de vinification, c'est le *pigéage'.* He allows the temperature to rise to 32° C., using a heat exchanger to cool the *must,* if necessary, to 29° C.

When the free run wine has been decanted, the residue is pressed in a splendid 1946 Demoisy press Unfortunately, this apparatus has the disadvantage of not being readily repairable and more importantly necessitates cutting up the 'cake' by hand between each pressing – this takes an hour or more. Perhaps his son-in-law who now works with him will take pity and buy him a new Vaslin press for his seventy-eighth birthday.

After a 36-hour *débourbage,* the assembled wine is put into casks – 17–25% new, depending on the analysis of the wine and its taste qualities. Interestingly, richer vintages such as 1988 and 1989 see no new oak, and 1990 only get 20%. Following this logic, the 1990 Village wines have more new oak than the Premiers Crus – 25% instead of 20%.

In former times, André explains, his wines spent 2 years or more in cask before bottling. Modern Mussy wines spend about 18 months in cask – in 1989 part of the crop was vinified in tank until after *malo* and only then put into cask for *élevage.* After 2, or even 3 rackings, the wine is re-unified, fined with egg-white, left 2–3 months *sur col* before being filtered (7 vintages out of 10) and bottled.

André is most careful to avoid manipulations which disturb the wine; he is particularly hot on only using piston pumps and not rotating pumps which aerate the wine as they work: 'We don't want to make mayonnaise,' he adds drily.

Trotting briskly round the 1786 cellars, Andre draws samples from the casks, formally announcing each wine in turn, rather in the manner of a toast-master. Both the Beaune Montremenots (Mussy's idiosyncratic spelling has it as Montrevenots) and the Beaune Epenottes have a Pommardish slant to them. The Epenottes has more finesse – albeit with a definite *goût de terroir* – than the Montremenots which is ripe, a touch rustic, with flavours of wild fruits.

The Pommard Pézerolles and Saucilles are usually amalgamated into one *cuvée* and sold as Pommard Premier Cru. Tasting the 1989 one *cuve* was slightly touched with *volatile acidity;* a second cask turned out to be fine, with a better spectrum of aromas and some depth, though with a rustic edge and lots of substance.

The best wine in André Mussy's cellar is the Pommard Epenots, from a parcel of vines in the Petits Epenots section of the vineyard. The 1989 was delightfully round, with tannins to lose, while the 1990, still in tank awaiting transfer to casks was altogether bigger and richer.

André attributes the quality of his wines largely to his low yields. 'We got 39 hl./ha. in 1990,' he muses, 'but in the last 10 years we have averaged 35 – barely.' Like him, the wines age superbly. The Pommard Epenots 1983 was just beginning to show its qualities – a lovely old Pinot nose supported by ripe fruit with good length.

He is in no doubt about the best of his 63 vintages – his second, the 1929. It froze during the winter to minus 22° C., and there was snow in the vineyards until March. They had to replant extensively afterwards but some of the old vines remain to contribute to André's Epenots in 1990. 'With a glass of wine like the 1929,' André beams, 'you need one girl on each knee. It was the best of all my vintages – probably because I was young . . . that counts.'

Leaving the cellar with this finest and kindliest of Burgundians, we had to agree that the 1990 Pommard Epenots was the wine for his hundredth birthday – in magnums.

VINEYARD HOLDINGS

Commune	*Level*	*Lieu-dit/Climat*	*Area*	*Vine Age*	*Status*
Pommard	PC	Epenots	0.58	22	P
Pommard	PC	Pézerolles	0.20	43	P
Pommard	PC	Les Saucilles	0.45	49	P
Pommard	V	—	0.63	30	P
Beaune	PC	Les Epenottes	1.00	20	P
Beaune	PC	Les Montremenots	1.43	40	P
Volnay	V	—	0.20	3	P
Pommard	R	(Bourgogne Pinot)	1.50	50	P
		Total	**5.99 ha.**		

VOLNAY

The wines of Volnay are the Chambolle-Musignys of the Côte de Beaune – elegant, full of finesse and lacy delicacy, but with a depth and structure which can keep them alive for several decades. If the wines of Pommard sometimes seem like a truck-driver's interpretation of Pinot, then those of Volnay are a ballerina's.

As usual, this has more to do with the soil than with any quirk of wine-making. Much of Volnay's vignoble sits on slopes underneath which runs a band of Bathonian limestone, overlaid with either marls of various geological origins or with stony, well-drained scree materials. Even the lower, Village, vineyards contain less clay than those of Pommard, so the broad character of finesse is maintained.

The village itself is a compact little borough, tightly encircled by its vines, leaving no room for trendy architects to try their hand at scarring the view. From many of the houses, one has an uninterrupted vista over the vines to the plain and hills beyond. Even the telephone box on the terrace outside the rather drab Mairie enjoys this pleasing prospect.

The name 'Volnay' apparently derives from Volen, the god of water, worshipped, according to Henri Cannard, for some obscure reason by the Gauls. In 1195, this became Vollenay – still preserved on the Marquis d'Angerville's elegant labels – just before the Dukes of Burgundy started to use Hugues IVth's Château as a summer retreat.

Royal patronage continued into the sixteenth century, when Louis XI took a particular fancy to the Volnay, acquiring several of the best vineyards – including Champans, Fremiet, Bousse d'Or, Caillerets, Clos des Chênes and Taillepieds. He even despatched a royal official to make an inventory, presumably to make sure that they were all still there. The Sun King – Louis XIV – is also recorded as an 'amateur' of Volnay, perhaps because the Faculty of Medicine of the period extolled its high qualities.

With all this exalted hype Volnay became something of a cult drink, and prices rose accordingly. When the time came to classify the Côte, in 1860, those responsible were 'very generous' (Henri Cannard) in their classification of Volnay, 'probably for reasons of commerce'. This might explain why almost 54% of the commune's land is designated Premier Cru, significantly more than most other communes, with the exception of Beaune, the home of the committee looking into the matter.

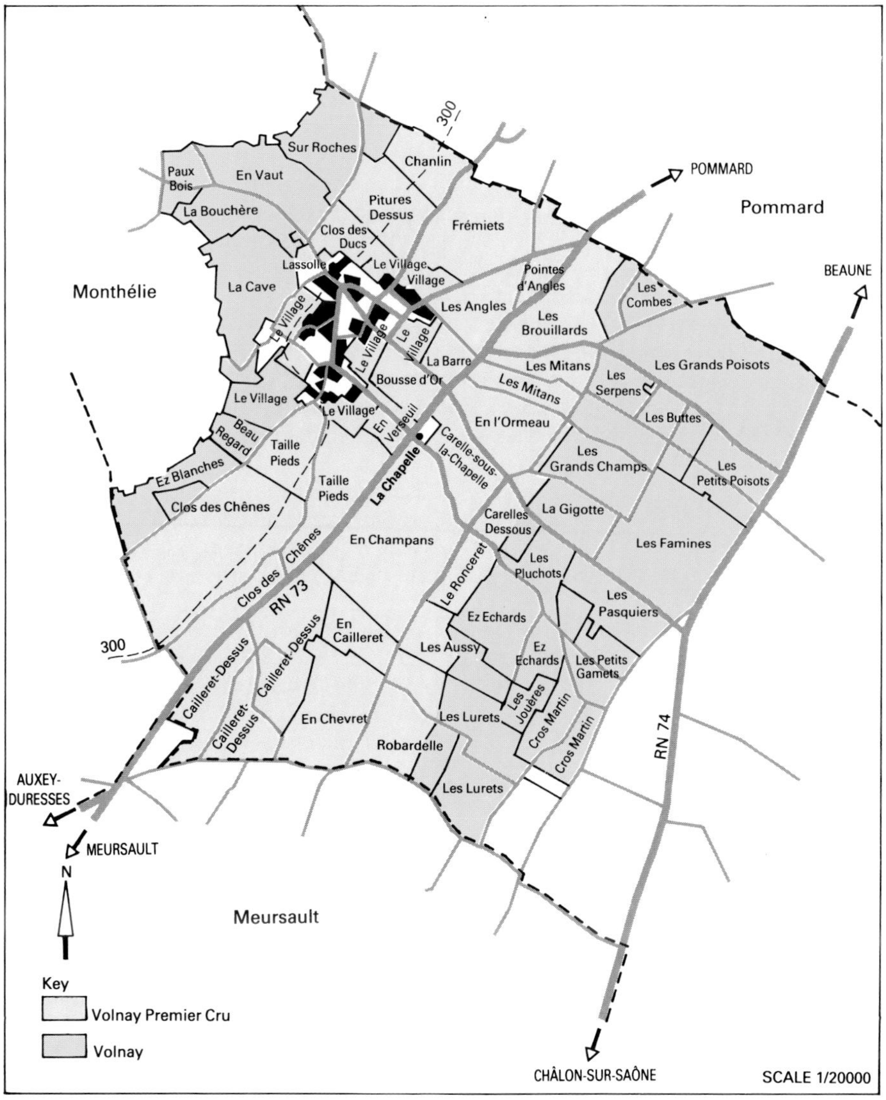

Volnay's vineyards extend to 213.27 ha., of which 98.37 ha. are AC Volnay and the remaining 114.90 ha. Premiers Crus, comprising some 33 individual *lieu-dits*.

As at Pommard, the Villlage vineyards are either on the higher, more exposed slopes, or else on the lower and flatter sections between the RN 73 and the RN 74. These form the upper and lower bounds of the Premiers Crus, which occupy a narrow band below and to either side of the village itself.

These can be broadly classified into 5 geologically distinct sections: firstly, those in the centre of the village – the Clos des Ducs, the Bousse d'Or, Le Village and Les Taillepieds are planted on relatively hard marls, with a high proportion of white chalk admixed. This gives wines of both vigour and finesse; some of the best in the commune.

The second section consists of vineyards due south of Volnay – Champans, Caillerets, Ronceret and En Chevret. Here the vines are on moderately steep slopes, well-exposed to the south and south-east, with stony soils and rusty topsoils giving onto a vein of quite friable Bathonian limestone. Further down these vineyards, away from the RN 73, the rock disappears and the soil deepens

The Clos des Chênes, just above the RN 73, consists of pure limestone soil, very thin and stony, with the terrain becoming steeper the further one gets from the road, making soil erosion a recurring problem.

The fourth section comprises the Premiers Crus to the north-east of the village which adjoins Pommard – Fremiets, Chanlins,

Pitures Dessus and Les Angles. Here the limestone is less evident, although the soils are relatively stony, with a covering of loose shale which detaches itself and washes down in the rain. These wines, the Fremiets in particular, generally emphasise finesse rather than structure.

The final section, the 29.07 ha. of Premier Cru Volnay-Santenots, is something of a peculiarity, being located entirely in the commune of Meursault. The soils vary widely, from limestone to *terre rouge,* stones to no stones, slopes to flat, giving wine which is least typical of Volnay. Its situation is one of those administrative aberrations which cause needless confusion. The vineyard is divided into 5 individual *lieu-dits* each of which is entitled to the appellation Volnay-Santenots (Premier Cru), provided the wine is red. If, however, white wine is produced, the relevant appellation becomes Meursault, or Meursault Premier Cru depending from which *lieu-dits* it emanates. The paperwork involved must keep several important officials in Dijon permanently on their administrative toes.

Pitiot and Poupon list 85 individual growers and 11 larger Domaines who operate from Volnay and, whilst numbers by themselves are no indication of quality, the standard of wine-making is high. Although the Domaines profiled here excel, there are several others who are consistently reliable sources and should be considered seriously by anyone in search of good wine.

Yvon Clerget, with no fewer than 5 separate Premier Cru Volnays in his 5.10 ha., produces wines which are agreeable to drink young but have the structure for age. The Volnay-Santenots, from 52-year-old vines, the Caillerets from 53-year-old vines and a fine Carelle Sous la Chapelle deserve mention.

Jean-Marc Bouley turns out rather more overtly muscular wines, with plenty of stuffing from his 12 ha. spread principally between Pommard and Volnay. Late harvesting and long slow fermentation, followed by light filtration but no fining, results in concentrated, well-defined wines of depth and style. His use of 60% new oak seems to have spawned him a particular following in the USA. The Volnays Clos des Chênes and Caillerets and the trio of Pommard Premiers Crus – Pézerolles, Fremiets and Rugiens – are the cream of this cellar. The quality can be excellent but is still uneven, so it is essential to taste carefully.

Regis Rossignol, a short, animated man with dark, swept-back hair, manages to combine a passion for excavating cellars and other do-it-yourself tasks with skilled wine-making. His policy of not destalking produces tannic wines which need bottle-age, but his meticulous attention to detail and willingness to keep back wines which are unduly hard amortise the effects. A Pommard Village and a Volnay Premier Cru are his best *cuvées.*

Finally, Joseph Voillot, a charming older vigneron, steeped in the traditions of the land, produces a near-exemplary range of Volnays and Pommards from some 10 ha. of 20–30-year-old vines. 8–12 days *cuvaison* of 30–100% destemmed bunches and a 15–18 month *élevage* in up to 33% new wood results in wines which are complex and characterful. In good vintages, his Volnays Fremiets and Champans and the Pommards Pézerolles and Rugiens (this deliciously rich in 1989 and 1990) would hold their own against examples from grander Domaines.

It was hoped to include a profile of the Domaine de la Pousse d'Or, highly thought of in some circles. The manager, M. Potel, chose not to honour a long-standing appointment, so this is not possible.

Volnay and its vines, looking south towards distant Meursault

Domaine Marquis d'Angerville

VOLNAY

D'Angerville is among the greatest names of Burgundy. It became so in the late 1920s when the father of the present Marquis became dissatisfied with the négociants, who then controlled virtually all Burgundy sales, and began to criticise them openly for their corrupt blending practices. Getting nowhere, he and a few other courageous growers, including Henri Gouges, decided to dissociate themselves from the négoce and started to bottle and sell their own wine. Others joined them, and thus Domaine bottling was born.

The present Marquis, Jacques d'Angerville. does not pretend to such iconoclasm. He is content to enjoy the peace and quiet of his delightful eighteenth-century home, and to produce superlative Volnay for the world to share his pleasure.

The family house, which came into Angerville hands in 1804, when Baron du Mesnil, then Vice-Governor of Autun, bought vineyards in 'Vollenay', is an imposing country manor situated on a small elevation at the northern end of the village. Whoever built it chose the site with care: a handsome terrace faces south and east over the vineyards, and this, together with the more recent swimming-pool, enjoys sunshine, when there is any, all day long. Indeed, the Marquis will tell you that in summer he can swim in the evening sunlight until 8 o'clock.

The vineyards, comprising just under 14 ha. in production, have remained intact since the days of Baron du Mesnil. They include no fewer than 8 Volnay Premiers Crus, some Meursault Santenots and Pommard Les Combes. The pearl in the oyster is the 2.40 ha. Clos des Ducs – a *Monopole* – which lies adjacent to the northern wall of the house, effectively forming part of the garden. The wine is ripe, smoky and, in great vintages, capable of considerable ageing.

The Marquis is uncompromising in his quest for quality. As he sees it, the keys are low yields – generally 27–33 hl./ha. – and a significant proportion of old vines. Since he came to work with his father in 1950, he has never asked for a *PLC*. Of course, yields see-saw naturally: in the disastrous 1975 they sank to 18 hl. /ha., peaking in 1990 at 43 hl./ha. Equally, he rarely grubs up vines; the last occasion was in 1984 when a small parcel of very old vines ceased to be viable. Only this, or severe soil erosion, would cause him to replant to any significant extent. Otherwise vines are simply replaced one by one as they die or are enfeebled by age.

In the steeper vineyards the soil is systematically worked rather than treated with herbicides. The Marquis believes that hoeing aerates the earth which encourages the penetration of any surface water, thus holding the soil together and so minimising erosion. This contradicts the usual view, namely that hoeing the soil makes it more friable and thus more prone to erosion.

The vineyards are tended on the principle of minimum interference – yields being kept down by using only 'plants fins' – a *sélection massale* of his father's, short *Guyot* pruning and severe *évasivage* when the growing season begins. In 1990, for the first time, grapes were removed in August, just at *veraison,* to further reduce yields. There is, however, some doubt in the Marquis's mind as to whether this really produces the desired results – the timing is so precise: 'too early and the vine catches up, too late and, well . . . it's too late and the operation is useless.'

Otherwise the viticultural regime is fairly classical but adaptive to circumstance. Treatments, both preventive and curative, especially for the grape-worm, tend to be administered together. *Court-noué* – the dreaded fan-leaf virus endemic in Burgundy – is dealt with by using specially vaccinated clones from the research station at Colmar in Alsace. *Eutypiose* is also becoming a serious threat – in one of the Angerville vineyards, for example, a recent count found the incidence to have already reached 1.34%. Given its destructiveness and its 7-year incubation period, it is under constant surveillance.

Jacques, Marquis d'Angerville – one of Volnay's and Burgundy's most respected vignerons

There is no systematic order of harvesting at the Domaine, picking depending entirely on the state of maturity of each Cru. In 1976, for example, the Meursault Santenots was so ripe that it was harvested in August. Of all the Volnays, however, the Clos des Ducs is generally harvested last, because the vines on this harder, limestone-rich soil require a longer ripening cycle.

Vinification is as traditional as the Marquis: 'The less one puts this and that in the wine, the better. I don't do anything – just wait for the fermentation to start.' In other words, don't interfere with nature. The grapes are completely destalked, lightly sulphured, and then vatted and left to ferment.

There is, unusually, virtually no standard *pigéage,* rather twice daily *remontage* using powerful jets to break up the hard cap. For the 1990 vintage the Marquis tried out a couple of *cuves auto-pigéantes* for the Volnay Champans – something of a break with tradition! He considers that the results of this essai more closely resemble a lesser than a great year, so presumably the experiment will not be repeated. He does admit that these new-fangled *cuves* give better extraction and tannins but warns that one has to know how to use them: 'you mustn't turn them round and round like coffee mills – just a couple of minutes each way, twice a day, will do.'

Jacques d'Angerville is not in favour of *saigner* – although he did *saigné* a little in 1984 and again in 1990. He will tolerate a maximum of 10% if really necessary, but considers that it brings no real benefit, removing both sugars and aromas as well as the intended water. He is, however, following closely the experiments of Potel at Domaine de la Pousse d'Or, who is trying an apparatus which extracts water by evaporation. If this technique is perfected, it may well spell the end of widespread *chaptalisation* in the Côte.

The 'less you put things in the wine . . .' principle precludes the use of enzymes. However, *chaptalisation* is inevitable in Burgundys marginal climate – and sugar, when it is needed, is added in several small doses during the active phase of fermentation rather than the widely regarded optimum period, towards the end.

The temperature is allowed to rise to 35° C during the *cuvaison* which lasts for 8–10 days. After press- and free-run wine have been assembled, the *cuves* are covered and left for 2–3 days for the gross lees to settle out before the wine is transferred to cask.

For a Volnay, whose finesse might so easily be submerged under new wood, Jacques d'Angerville defends his decision to use 'never more than 35% new oak – one shouldn't abuse it'. Moreover, the wine only remains in its new barrels until it is racked and unified after the *malo* some 3–10 months later. The remainder of its *élevage,* 15–24 months in total, is spent in older oak. In preparation for bottling, each cask is fined, without further unification, and given a light plate-filtration.

The Marquis has no more dealings with the négociant fraternity than did his father; the entirety of the Domaine's 100–200-cask production is sold in bottle – either to export markets, which take some 65%, or within France, particularly to the great restaurants which lap up all they can get. No doubt the Marquis comes across his bottles in the course of the long-distance peregrinations of which he is especially fond.

Jacques d'Angerville worked closely with his father until the latter's death in 1952. This experience and the years that followed have turned him into a fine wine-maker with a sure touch. Strolling round the neat rows of barrels in the cellars under the house, one becomes aware of his passion for the estate and its wines – undiminished after nearly half a century. He pronounces a preference for wines which are 'distinguished and long; unctuous and ripe', wines which, defying the general misconception about the Côte de Beaune, are generally more rewarding after 10 years than after 5 years.

Of the Premiers Crus, the Clos des Ducs stands out, followed north to south by the Fremiet, Taillepieds, Champans and Cailleret. The Fremiet vines are planted in a poor, thin topsoil on 'lave calcaire' – a marne limestone. Being on the Pommard side of the village, the wine tends to be quite broad and muscular. The 1989, still in cask, showed ripe, rich fruit and a hint of rusticity – no more than the merest glance at Pommard – with a fine balance of acidity and tannin.

In contrast, the Taillepieds, on the same band of soil as Fremiets but with a more southerly exposure, and at the other end of the village, Côte Meursault, has greater length and distinction. In 1989 it was more concentrated with a classy smoked bacon nose and seemed set fair for a fine future.

The Domaine's mouthwatering 3.98 ha. of Champans, just below the road to Meursault, is divided into 2 separate strips running north-east to south-west at either end of the vineyard. The wine is generally characterised by greater *charpente* than the other Premiers Crus – more sinew and tannin. The 1989 played true to form – being noticeably deeper and meatier than either Fremiet or Taillepieds but still retaining its seductive length and class.

The Marquis refers to the Champans, together with Fremiet and Cailleret, as 'Têtes de Cuvée'. The Cailleret, planted in the top, 'dessus' section of the vineyard, abutting the Meursault road, is arguably the finest of the trio. It seems to combine the power and strength of the Champans with the exuberant finesse of the Fremiet. A 1964 Fremiet tasted in 1989 was still in great form – plenty of ripe, old vine fruit with a marvellous, thoroughly seductive mature Pinot nose. It combined delicacy with power and considerable length – a remarkably complete and enjoyable wine.

Among this magnificent array of Premiers Crus the Clos des Ducs stands out for its unbridled distinction; it just seems to have an extra touch of class and depth. The 1989 from the cask had an attractive deep, limpid colour, smelt distinctly of gently smoked bacon and new wood – a fine and complex nose in the making – and showed precocious charm and finesse on the palate. An extraordinary equilibrium marked it out from the others, fine as they undoubtedly are.

The Clos des Ducs from that much (and unjustly) criticised vintage, 1987, was still closed up in December 1990 – not a block-buster (these wines rarely are) but plenty of wine nonetheless, with a touch of raw tannin to lose. It has both depth and vinosity and will make a good bottle for the mid-1990s. The 1983 Clos des Ducs was, in contrast, beginning to release its aromas – with a touch of *sous-bois* and a distinct point of *surmaturation* which shows as a slight 'figginess' on the nose. The ripeness comes through on the palate – a deep wine, with incipient complexity and a slightly dry edge; hint neither of rot nor of the excessive dryness which marked some wines of this patchy vintage.

The time will come, perhaps in the next decade, when this kindly nobleman will seek to extend his travels and to let go of the reins which he has so capably held for nearly half a century. Of his 3 children, the most likely successor is a daughter, married to an agronomist, who lives nearby and, with her husband, helps from time to time at the Domaine. The next Marquis is a banker in London; apart from enjoying the occasional shipments he presumably receives from Volnay, he seems unqualified to replace his father. The third child, a daughter, lives in Paris and does not appear to be interested in the estate.

The entrance to the 18th-century Domaine

Such is the anatomy of one of Burgundy's great estates. It is a shame that many people who buy fine Burgundy seem to confine their purchases to the Côte de Nuits, in the mistaken belief that the Côte de Beaune does not produce wines capable of ageing. Whilst it may be true that the soils in the Côte de Nuits tend to produce longer-lived wines, there are many estates in the Côte de Beaune producing wines of great longevity.

The Marquis d'Angerville's wines are marked by exemplary typicity and exceptionally high quality – Volnays which may be equalled, but rarely bettered. They more than merit their space in the cellar.

VINEYARD HOLDINGS

Commune	*Level*	*Lieu-dit/Climat*	*Area*	*Vine Age*	*Status*
Volnay	PC	Clos des Ducs	2.40	25	P
Volnay	PC	Champans	3.98	25	P
Volnay	PC	Fremiet	1.57	25	P
Volnay	PC	Cailleret	0.45	25	P
Volnay	PC	Taillepieds	1.70	25	P
Volnay	PC	L'Ormeau	0.65	25	P
Volnay	PC	Les Angles	0.53	25	P
Volnay	PC	Pitures	0.31	25	P
Meursault	PC	Santenots	1.50	25	P
Pommard	V	Les Combes	0.38	25	P
		Total	**13.47 ha.**		

Domaine Michel Lafarge

VOLNAY

Michel Lafarge produces some of Burgundy's most precise and penetrating wines. From his base in Volnay – a neat but unpretentious house in a quiet back-street hiding some splendid thirteenth-century cellars – he tends and vinifies the produce of nearly 8 ha. of vines, just over half of which are in Volnay. Although the Domaine dates back to the early nineteenth century, its present size is largely attributable to Michel and his father who have added parcels of land as and when suitable opportunities have come their way. Michel's own contribution has been the small plots of Premiers Crus Beaune Teurons and Pommard Pézerolles.

This tall, grey-haired and thoughtful man has been running the family estate since 1960, for the last 10 years with his equally tall son to help him. As Mayor of Volnay he combines civic duties with his wine-making and clearly enjoys both. However, he has been heard to say that he won't stand for election again because he wants more time to be with his wine and his family, but, no doubt, someone will try to persuade him to carry on when the time comes round.

From his house, perched on one of the highest points of this pleasant village, the Lafarges can see right across the vignoble. It is here that Michel believes the quality of wine is made or lost. Listening to him talk about his vines and to his exposition about how they should be looked after, it is clear that, despite advancing years, he has not become embedded in any of the tradition or dogma which vignerons so often use as excuses for sloppiness or incompetence. He is quite prepared to think things through afresh, with an open mind, although he places a high value on the traditions of transmitted experience.

Michel is convinced that the initial selection of plant material is one of the most important decisions a vigneron has to make. For his own vines, he uses a *sélection massale,* although he has tried mixing a few different clones among a row or two to see what they will give. His hesitancy about clones stems from the feeling that too much about their performance remains unknown. Also, even if one prunes short, debuds severely and takes all the usual steps to restrict yields, clones simply over-produce.

This over-production is an amalgam of 2 factors: firstly, the health of modern plant material means that each vine in the row produces regularly – unlike the pre-war

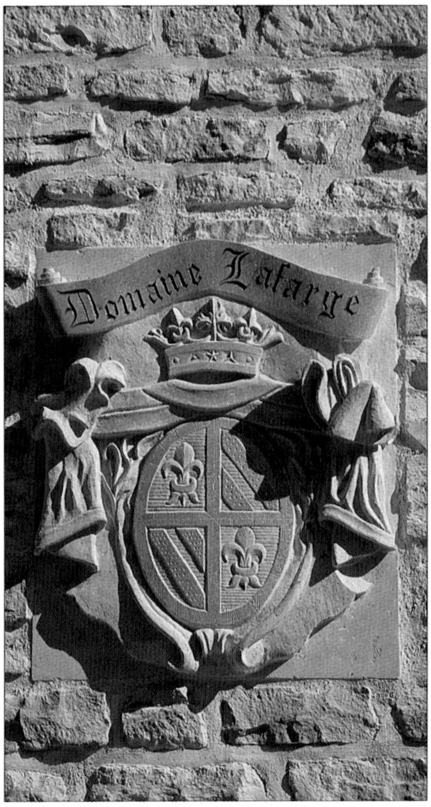

The family escutcheon

pattern of say 7 out of 10. Secondly, each plant is generally more prolific than its predecessors. The result is invariably higher yields all round, and the only sensible remedy, less productive clones.

While Michel Lafarge is waiting for these to appear, he is content to observe his own plants producing reasonable, but rarely excessive, yields. In passing, he observes that the same clone planted on the same rootstock will produce differently, both in quality and in quantity, in different vineyards. He concludes that there is an urgent need for a much wider variety of roots and clones to suit Burgundy's multifarious *terroir.*

The Lafarge vineyards are tended with expert care. There has been what Michel refers to as a 'twinge of conscience' among the vignerons of the Côte in recent years, towards the micro-flora and fauna of their soils. A more ecological attitude has led to the use of less noxious products in smaller treatment doses, rather than a blanket blitz-spraying. His own policy is to 'observe, see what is going to happen, then work parcel by parcel'.

However, the ideal policy may sometimes be impractical; a vigneron with 6 ha. can't afford the luxury of excessive experimentation if failure means a damaged harvest; equally, in such highly fragmented vineyards, the options, even for the vigneron who can afford it, may be limited by outside factors. It is difficult, for example, to go 'biodynamic' if neighbours continue to use conventional sprays.

None of these considerations prevents Michel from pursuing his own policies where he can. For example, he is passionately in favour of *cordon* pruning – a system which consists of a single spur from which several shoots are trained. In his view, this has distinct advantages: it limits the harvest, by producing more grapes, but these much smaller and more concentrated; furthermore, by spreading out vegetation and bunches – which is not possible with the traditional *Guyot* pruning – rot is reduced and made more tractable in the event of an outbreak. Finally, it makes the winter pre-pruning much easier, although the essential spring *ébourgonnage* is much harder.

Given his ecological stance, it is not surprising to find that Michel Lafarge uses only organic fertiliser, and as little of that as possible. His mistrust of advice, especially from product salesmen, meant that he was one of the few vignerons not to overdose their vines with potassium in the 1960s. 'You must never throw yourself at once into everything they tell you', is a piece of wisdom kept permanently in the background and dusted off from time to time, particularly no doubt, when fertiliser salesmen appear at his door.

On treatments of the vine, he is succinct: 'you should always be careful – if you can't, then at least limit it as much as you can.' The Lafarges have used traditional remedies, based on copper and sulphur, for as long as he can remember and have no intention of changing without a very good reason. Not satisfied with the standard product, they make up their own Bordeaux mixture – a laborious procedure – which is worth it because 'it has a better action'.

One of the greatest problems of quality in Burgundy is the *verjus* – that second crop of grapes which appears from time to time, especially in hot years, and which has to be kept out of the vats at all costs because the grapes are incompletely ripe and would only contribute green acidity and dilution. They are often hard for pickers to distinguish from ripe bunches since their skins may be equally black, so the Lafarges weed them out at the cuverie. Growers who do not take such care only add volume at the expense of quality.

When necessary, there is a green-pruning. However, Michel Lafarge is hesitant because he has yet to be convinced of its value. At present, it is only his young vines and clones which are affected, but he realises that timing is critical if the remaining bunches are not to compensate with large, dilute berries.

If the vineyards are worked on the principle of 'watch then act', vinification is no different; nothing is systematic. The broad guidelines are as follows: the crop is 80–100% destalked – the less the better the health of the bunches, since stems lengthen fermentation; there is a short pre-fermentive maceration in good years, whilst in poor vintages the fermentation is started immediately with a *pied de cuve.* Commercial yeasts are never used because 'they give a much more fragile fermentation'.

As for the fermentation itself Michel and his son ask themselves the same question every year – how long and at what temperature. The answer is reached by scrutiny of the charts for previous vintages and trying to reconcile what they did then with the results before deciding how to ferment this year's crop. 'The only way of improving quality is to review what has been done and achieved before.' Generally, they prefer a longer fermentation at a lower temperature to something shorter and hotter – a procedure reserved for rotten or unripe years. Michel admits that the process of deciding is a most enjoyable one – working closely with his son.

Avoiding pumps and enzymes is also a matter of policy. 'Every pump is bad', Michel declares roundly, adding that the need for enzymes indicates a problem in clarifying the wine which in turn indicates poor raw material, which in turn indicates 'above all, poorly maintained vinification equipment', excessive pressing or the presence of spray residues in the must. 'No one had enzymes thirty years ago', he argues.

There is a vigorous dislike of automation not just because it's untraditional, but because it can so easily destroy the precious raw material. For example, many vignerons use a pump to transfer the pulp left in the *cuves* to the presses. Chez Lafarge it is removed by hand. 'Don't forget, the harvest is fragile,' one is reminded.

Cuvaison lasts up to 14 days, with a temperature bracket of 28–33° C. Michel is not a great partisan of the *saignée,* believing that it unbalances a wine, although he is prepared to bleed up to 10–15% if necessary, as in 1990. 'It's not a panacea, but it can help from time to time,' he suggests.

Looking at the vignerons around him Michel finds that many of them are constantly being surprised by the quantity of grapes that arrive at their cuveries. He thinks that they would do better if they took the trouble to match their harvesting to their style of vinification and the capacity of their *cuves.* For him, it is better to reduce the number of pickers and spend a few more days harvesting than to have to speed up or shorten vinifications because you are constantly being knocked down by yet another load of grapes.

Having exercised themselves forking the pulp from the vats, the Lafarges are not going to compromise that effort by using an automatic press. For them a manually driven extraction is best – since they see too much possibility of prolonged or excess pressure with the modern machines. 'If you go away and leave a manual press for two minutes, it is still in the same place when you return. With the automatic ones, it may have gone berserk and crushed the pulp to death.'

Once the result of the first, gentle pressing has been amalgamated the wine is run into cask. Generally the Lafarge wines have 25% new wood, perhaps a little more for the Premiers Crus, but Michel is somewhat bemused by those who declare a firm policy on this matter. 'When you order your casks,' he observes, 'you know neither the quantity nor the quality of the crop, so it is impossible to match the new casks to the harvest.'

What happens to his wines thereafter depends entirely on how they evolve and in particular on how they taste. 'Laboratories are all very fine, they provide control, but you can't vinify by numbers,' chants Michel, adding, 'yes, oenologists are precious, but they are never very good vinificators.'

If the lees are healthy the first racking may be delayed by a month or so. The second racking will equally depend on the date of the *malo* and the type of wine. The Lafarges like to bottle their Volnays before the second summer, even earlier in less structured vintages, so *élevage* typically lasts 15–20 months. Filters are used as little as possible they prefer to fine instead.

The results of the Lafarges' skill are usually stunning – wines of a concentration and purity which seem to exemplify the spirit of Volnay. Even their basic Pinot Noir has a raspberryish Volnay nose which makes one want to take a mouthful. Although a touch rustic on the palate, with a few years in bottle it softens into a fine wine for its appellation.

The Lafarge wines are characterised by a finely-tuned combination of finesse and structure. Whatever the vintage, the balance is always there; in the greater vintages – 1985, 1988, 1989 and 1990 for example – although the styles differ, there is a distinct thematic continuity, a House style almost, which emphasises the delicacy of Volnay, or the meatier genre of Pommard or Beaune.

The Pommard Pézerolles is more lively than the Beaune Grèves or the Volnays – in 1989 supple with a firmish structure and great finesse. A Volnayish Pommard, as it were.

The Beaune Grèves – from 50-year-old vines – is altogether different; the 1989 is all finesse, albeit supported by ripe, concentrated fruit and round balancing tannins, with a superb long finish. This is a wine which will give enormous pleasure in 5–10 years.

The Volnay Village *cuvée* is an assemblage of the produce of 8 or 9 different parcels of vines. The 1989 has a medium deep colour of crushed strawberry hue, aromas of violets, a touch of liquorice, and a lively yet soft flavour with a fair depth of fruit and sufficient acidity to keep it for several years. Not a big wine, but fine and interesting nevertheless.

There are 3 excellent Volnay Premiers Crus to choose from. The 'Premier Cru' itself is an amalgam of Chanlins and Mitans from 20–40-year-old vines. The Clos du Château des Ducs is from 57 ares of 16–55-year-old vines and the Clos des Chênes from 90 ares of vines ranging 12–50 years in age. The Clos des Chênes is usually a complete wine, with more spicy overtones than the Clos du Château des Ducs. This latter has more finesse – violets and *fruits rouges* on the nose, different profile, different characteristics.

The Lafarges make fine wines. They are one of those few Domaines that can be relied upon to turn out interesting wine in almost any vintage. These are the sort of wines which give immense pleasure when they are young, plump and succulent, but which turn into something infinitely more interesting if you can bear to keep them for half a decade.

VINEYARD HOLDINGS

Commune	*Level*	*Lieu-dit/Climat*	*Area*	*Vine Age*	*Status*
Volnay	PC	Clos des Chênes	0.90	12/30/50	P
Volnay	PC	Clos du Château des Ducs	0.57	16/55	P
Volnay	PC	Mitans + Chanlins	0.36	20/40	P
Volnay	V	(Several climats)	2.48	Various	P
Pommard	PC	Les Pézerolles	0.14	30	P
Beaune	PC	Les Grèves	0.38	50 +	P
Beaune	V	Les Teurons	0.20	35	P
—	R	(Côtes de Beaune Villages)	0.28	12	P
—	R	(Bourgogne Pinot)	1.00	20/35	P
—	R	(Bourgogne PTG)	1.50	20/45	P
		Total	**7.80 ha.**		

Domaine de Montille

VOLNAY

Hubert de Montille combines the dual callings of lawyer and vigneron with apparently effortless ease. From his cellars come some of the finest Pommards and Volnays, wines which attest his dedication to quality and his skill in producing it.

The de Montille family have lived in Volnay since before the Revolution and, despite the inevitable expansions and contractions that the inheritance laws have wrought, generations have managed to maintain a viable viticultural Domaine.

Hubert was born into wine in 1930, just after his grandfather had divided his Domaine between his children. In 1947, his father died and he was propelled into managing the Domaine with his mother and an uncle. The years spent shadowing his father in the vineyards and cellars stood him in good stead when, in 1954, a year after his uncle's remarriage, his aunt gave birth to a son during the vintage, and he was left to make the wine on his own.

However, wine was not as profitable then as now, so a vigneron had to supplement his income where he might. For the young de Montille, the law was the chosen path. After completing his studies, Hubert followed the family tradition of advocacy, developing a thriving general practice which he runs from an office in Dijon.

During the summer the furniture in the spacious, shady house in Volnay is dusted off and the family moves in for the season. Between the Hospices sale in November and early summer, the place is shuttered up and left in the custody of a couple who inhabit a small wing next to the large red gates. Hubert and his wife meanwhile repair to Dijon where he continues his law practice, making no more than occasional visits to Volnay to keep an eye on his estate.

Together with a young apprentice, the guardians are responsible for the vineyards and cellar work. Since 1984 Hubert's son, Etienne, has been working part-time at the Domaine, taking time off from his job with an accounting firm to vinify the wines. In 1990 he vinified solo for the first time.

The Domaine which Hubert de Montille inherited consisted of just 3 ha. of vines. By careful acquisition, this has more than doubled to nearly 7 ha. covering a fine spread across Volnay and Pommard. When he started taking an interest in the 1950s, before clones were available, vignerons used to select their own plant material from the best in their vineyards – *sélection massale* – which was then grafted onto *phylloxera*-resistant rootstocks; Hubert de Montille remembers marking some 2,000 plants for possible selection in his own vineyards. Eventually he became persuaded, although he can't remember how, that clonal selection was an improvement on tradition, and started planting clones in 1978, together with a touch of *massale* for insurance and variety. This early plot of clones was one of the first trial plantings in the Côte. Now all new plantings are with clones, predominantly on rootstock 161/49.

Before this, in the 1960s, Hubert de Montille had decided that *cordon* training, still widely used for the Pinot Noir in Chassagne and Santenay, was maladapted to modern viticulture, principally because the necessity to lengthen the *cordon* each year makes it impossible to return to the main vine-stem. The only option was to revert to the more usual *Guyot* system, which is the manner in which all de Montille vines are now trained.

Although a lawyer, Hubert de Montille does not share that profession's supposed insensitivity to practical realities, being well aware of the consequences of the theories he expounds so eloquently. For example, although he is in favour of a selective green-pruning to remove excess grapes, he realises that this should only be done in August – when his workers are on holiday. The operation requires highly skilled labour, so is out of the question for practical reasons.

One gets the impression that Maître de Montille is at his best when there is a problem to solve. The care of his vineyards is a constant challenge, which he tackles with relish and urbane intelligence. Much as he might prefer to run a wholly organic regime for dealing with pests and diseases, he realises that in the fragmented environment of the Côte, preferences have to be tailored to what happens around you. Nothing is achieved, for example, by using up-to-the-minute 'biodynamics' if the vines on either side of you are drenched in a constant shower of systemic sprays and powerful insecticides.

The local Station des Végétaux provides detailed assessments and prescriptions throughout the growing season, which most vignerons follow more or less slavishly. Hubert de Montille was not fully convinced of its seriousness until 1983, when the Côte experienced an attack of grape-worm of such intensity as had not been seen for many years. The Station began to investigate with more than its customary vigour, resulting in a greater understanding than hitherto of the life cycle and susceptibilities of this insidious pest, since when treatments have become much more precise and effective.

The aim of each year's vineyard work is to achieve the ripest, healthiest grapes. To this end, the de Montilles invariably take the significant risk of a late harvest – 'compared to others'. However, whilst each additional day of sunshine adds to a grape's quality potential, a few hours of a Burgundian autumn storm can mean a rapid dilution of the juice or, worse still, rampaging rot.

Even given ripe grapes the vigneron has to decide how best to extract their potential. According to the type of vintage, stalks are removed before vatting, up to a maximum of 60%, a higher proportion of stalks being retained in years when the wood is riper.

At present there is a distinct vogue for a period of cool maceration before fermentation starts – this is said to extract both colour and aroma from the skins into the juice. Hubert de Montille is sceptical: he admits that maceration adds power and aroma, but believes that these are relatively ephemeral. His own preference is for a short maceration, followed by fermentation at a relatively high temperature (up to 34° C) and 6–8 *pigéages* each day. This, together with *a cuvaison* of 15–17 days, will give maximum extraction of durable colour and aromas.

One of Hubert de Montille's 'bêtes noires' is excessive alcohol in wines which he considers, above all, to be delicate. Thus for him, over about 12 degrees the subtlety of a wine risks being masked by the alcohol. *Chaptalisation,* a necessity for all Burgundian vignerons, must therefore be kept to the minimum compatible with the appellation requirements and with balance. He is watching with particular interest the trials being carried out by Potel at the Domaine de la Pousse d'Or and by Michel Delon at Château Leoville Lascases – whose wine he admires greatly – with an apparatus which extracts water from the juice by evaporation. While it remains to be seen whether concentrating sugar by extraction is the converse of adding it, there is hope that it might be possible, by such means, to reduce *chaptalisation* further, if not to eliminate it entirely.

The *élevage* is thoroughly traditional, although Hubert de Montille's dislike of wines which are too solid and his corresponding desire to retain as much natural delicacy and purity in his wines as he can, means that

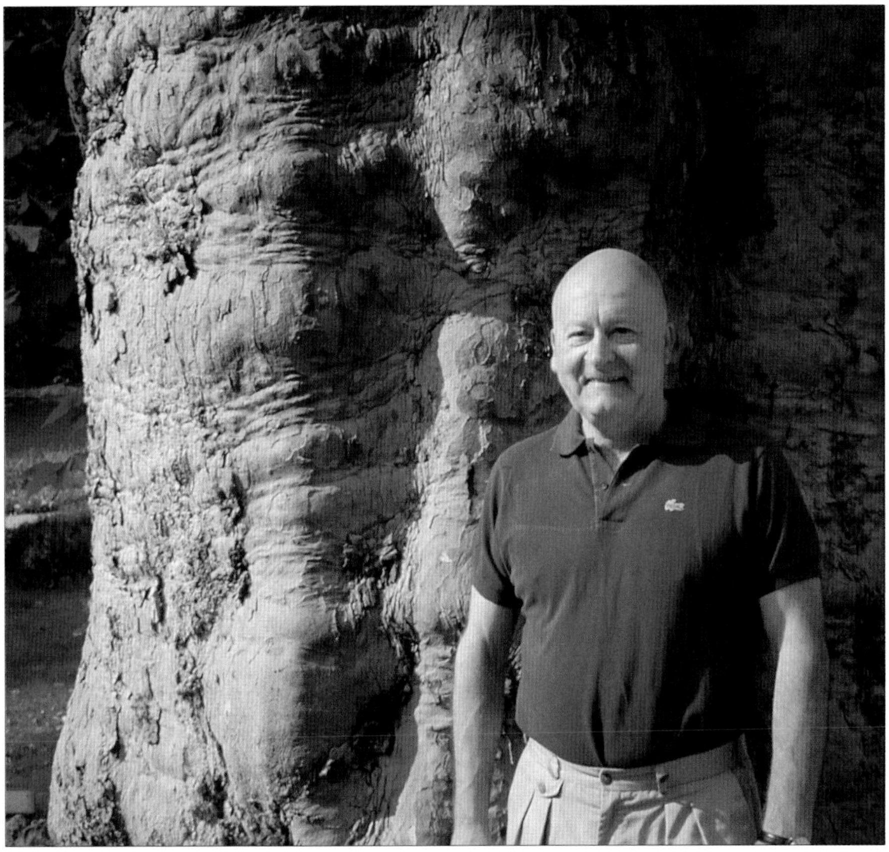

Maître Hubert de Montille dwarfed by a large oak tree in his park

there is no excess of new wood – just 20–33% each year plus a cocktail of 1–3 year-old casks for the rest. 'If our wines were Chambertin or Richebourg, we would put them all into new wood, but for Volnay the wood would dominate the wine.'

His experience with different sorts of wood has led to a preference for Nevers, Chatillonais and especially for Vosges; Tronçais is undesirable, 'too much vanilla', but Vosges gives an element of 'finesse and distinction'. The Domaine buys its own wood and leaves it at Volnay to dry for 18 months. It is then delivered to the barrel-maker who gives it a touch of steam to further dry it ('15 minutes of steam saves 4 months of natural drying') before it is fashioned into casks.

By and large, nature is left to work the wines at her own pace. In particular, Hubert stresses, the *malos* must be allowed to happen naturally; 'the later they are the less I am displeased,' he adds. The second of two separate rackings, each into tank to unify the wines, is followed by fining in cask. The wines remain *sur col* for 3–4 months and are then bottled, generally without filtration; this means a total *élevage* of 20–24 months. There have been occasions when a light plate filtration was deemed necessary but 'that is not my cup of tea', confesses Hubert.

The Domaine's wines are yardstick examples of what fine Volnay and Pommard should be. Although concentrated in flavour and generally beautifully parfumé in youth, these are not wines designed for early consumption. On the contrary, they give of their best after some years in bottle.

Of the Volnays, the Village *cuvée* is, as one would expect, the least complex of the range. Nonetheless, it is a serious wine and repays keeping in all but the lightest vintages. There is a Volnay Premier Cru which is a mixture of the produce of several different small plots of vineyards, none of which is large enough to justify bottling on its own. This is usually quite a rich, firm wine, with plenty of meat under a positive, well-developed nose.

There are 3 separate, named Premiers Crus. The Taillepieds, situated opposite the Champans on the southern, Meursault side of the village, produces a wine of great finesse, generally softer and rounder than the others. In contrast, the Champans is a much bigger wine, with almost Pommardish muscle, yet with the finesse of the Taillepieds. The Mitans comes somewhere in between the two in style, with attractive plump fruit and considerable delicacy, especially when it has the chance to mature.

The Pommards are a superb pair: the Premier Cru Pézerolles typically showing the depth and complexity derived from its *terre rouge,* whereas the Rugiens, also on *terre rouge,* seems to have greater structure and depth combined with notable finesse, perhaps from the relatively poorer soils of its more sloping situation.

It is, however, with age that de Montille's wines really show what they are made of. After a few years in bottle, the 1985s are just beginning to open out – still young, but starting to show the transition between the fruit-based aromas of youth and the liquorice, *sous-bois* and vegetal smells of maturity.

The 1972 Taillepieds and the 1971 Pézerolles, tasted at the Domaine in January 1991, were both very fine wines. The 1972, picked on the 10 October, the latest in Hubert de Montille's memory, has blossomed but slowly. Virtually untasteable in its early years, by virtue of its overwhelming acidity, it has developed a magnificently distinguished mature Pinot nose – with a hint of faded flowers, which he particularly likes – and a soft, stylish complexity of flavour which is thoroughly seductive.

The 1971 Pézerolles is even more alluring, with an almost creamy ripeness preceded by an attractive touch of *surmaturité* and offset by a layer of fine, delicate aromas. Its depth and complexity of fruit well covers its 13 degrees natural alcohol. A very fine bottle by any standards.

Hubert de Montille's Volnays are sometimes criticised for being rather too plump for typicity. What one feels about that is a matter of personal judgment. With a Domaine capable of producing such consistently fine bottles, it would be churlish to cavil.

VINEYARD HOLDINGS

Commune	*Level*	*Lieu-dit/Climat*	*Area*	*Vine Age*	*Status*
Volnay	PC	Les Champans	0.66	1/15/30	P
Volnay	PC	Carelles Sous Chapelle	0.20	5	P
Volnay	PC	Les Brouillards	0.38	3/4	P
Volnay	PC	Les Angles	0.15	30	P
Volnay	PC	Le Village	0.15	30	P
Volnay	PC	Les Taillepieds	0.79	11	P
Volnay	PC	Les Mitans	0.73	13	P
Volnay	V	—	0.15	13–25	P.
Pommard	PC	Les Rugiens	1.01	8/15/30	P/M
Pommard	PC	Les Pézerolles	1.09	10/25/50	P/M
Pommard	PC	Les Grands Epenots	0.23	5	P
Pommard	R	(Bourgogne Rouge)	0.75	20	P
Pommard	R	(BGO - Les Sorbins)	0.06	50	P
		Total	**6.35 ha.**		

Monthélie

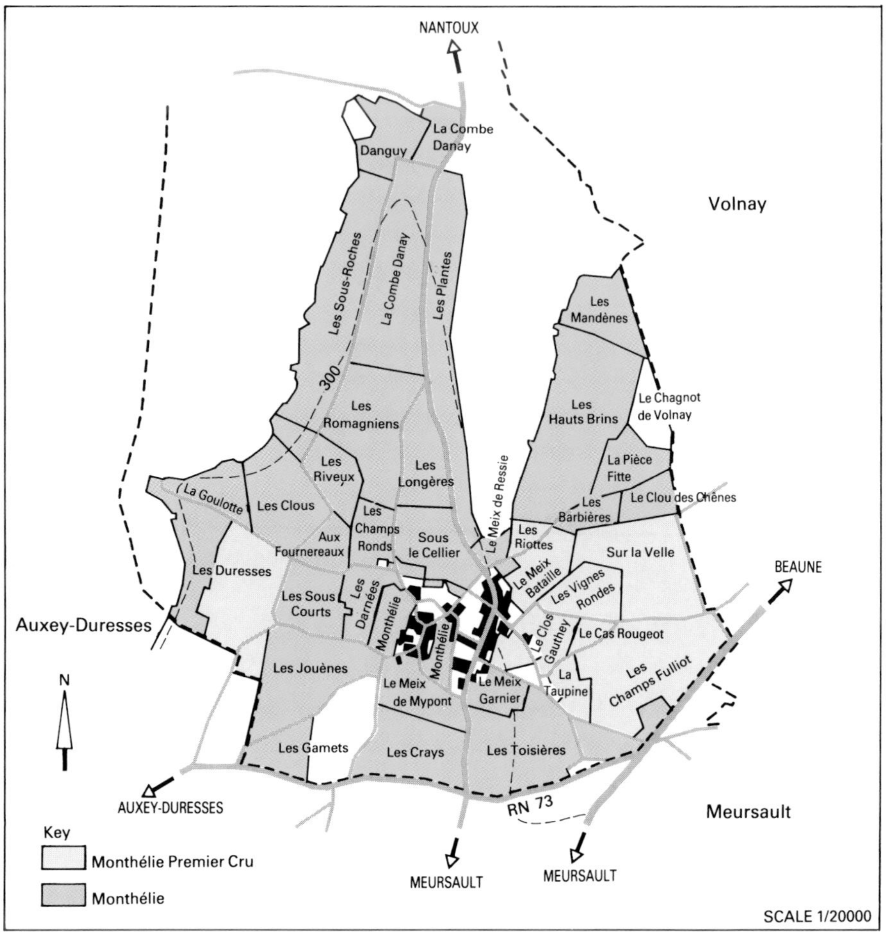

Tucked away behind Meursault, at the top of a hill, is Monthélie, one of the most under-rated communes of the Côte d'Or. It is odd that this delightful, picturesque little village, perched above its vines as though it were keeping some sort of perpetual eye on them, should be so neglected. This may have something to do with the fact that much of its excellent red wine is sold in bulk to négociants, reaching the market as Côte de Beaune-Villages rather than as Monthélie. The time has come for a revival.

Although overlooking them, Monthélie lives in the shadow of Meursault and Volnay, which bound it to the south and east respectively. As if to ensure that it has no chance whatever of expanding, and thereby regaining the pre-eminence it enjoyed between the eleventh and sixteenth centuries, when it belonged to the Abbey of Cluny, the siege is completed by hills to the north and Auxey-Duresses stationed to the west Thus are the 200 inhabitants of Monthélie, and their vines, ineluctably encased.

Fortunately what they have is good: their village, a maze of steep, narrow streets and alleys, some leading somewhere, others going nowhere, has barely changed since much of it was built during the eighteenth and nineteenth centuries. Wandering these quiet byways, one would not be entirely surprised to encounter a sedan chair ferrying a noble de Suremain back to his Château, or a crier in frock-coat and stove-pipe hat proclaiming Napoléon's defeat at Waterloo.

Monthélie has recorded history dating back to the ninth century when the Gauls occupied the land, and unrecorded history back to the Romans. The remains of a Roman encampment are to be seen on the west side of the village, and an assortment of Roman artefacts has surfaced over the years to embellish the story.

Recent times have been relatively tame; apart from the *phylloxera* which devastated Monthélie as it did the rest of the Côte in the last quarter of the nineteenth century, nothing much happened until 1913, when a parish war broke out with Auxey-Duresses over the provision of water from which Monthélie, having only three small wells, suffered particular deprivation. The arguments were somehow settled and a permanent water supply finally arrived in 1919.

In September 1944 a squadron of French troops, sent to liberate Monthélie, ran out of petrol. It took them several days to find it and when they came to leave, they departed with many enduring friendships and plenty of wine. Every two years since, veterans have returned to the village to renew the ties – and to replenish their cellars.

Monthélie is one of the smallest communes of the Côte, second only to Vougeot. Some 42 individual growers are listed, together with two Domaines, for a total of 172.21 ha. of vines. Of these, 108.72 ha. are AC Monthélie and 31.18 ha. are Monthélie Premier Cru, whilst the remaining 42.31 ha. are *régionales.*

Most of the AC Monthélie vines are on more or less steep slopes to the north, south and west of the village. These hillsides are equally varied in exposure, but are well-drained and do not have the heavier soils found elsewhere. That most of Monthélie's vignoble is on slopes is a distinct advantage.

There are 11 Premiers Crus. Of these, 3 account for two-thirds of the total surface: Sur la Velle (6.03.01 ha.), Les Champs-Fuillot (8.11.22 ha.) and Les Duresses (6.71.34 ha.). The best – Sur la Velle and Les Champs-Fuillot – are due east of the village, contiguous with Les Caillerets and the Clos des Chênes of Volnay. The soils, as those in this sector of Volnay, are mainly Bathonian limestone, with an admixture of marls and iron-bearing rock, particularly in the higher sections, giving the ground a reddish hue.

The only Premier Cru outside this section is Les Duresses, situated in the Auxey valley and oriented on a north-south axis. This gives an exposure to both the east and west, far less favourable than that of the Volnay sector. The soil contains markedly less limestone, which makes for wines with more structure but commensurately less finesse.

Although there is a tiny quantity of Monthélie Blanc, made from 100% Chardonnay – on average some 660 cases each year – it is on the reds that the reputation of Monthélie is founded. From the best Domaines, these are wines of depth and structure, with great longevity. In a good vintage, they tend to start off rather austere, with high acid and tannins but with plenty of ripe, fleshy fruit underneath. In character, the best combine the finesse of Volnay with the body and structure of Auxey.

The finest Monthélies come from the de Suremains at Château de Monthélie and from the engaging nonagenarian, Mme. Armande Douhairet; elsewhere, there are excellent *cuvées* from Jadot in Beaune and from Jean-François Coche in Meursault.

Monthélie deserves wider recognition, both for its wines and for its pretty village. The Château, with its magnificent wrought-iron gates and splendid carriage-sweep, is well worth a look. Although slightly faded, it exudes a noble defiance, with the air of a building seemingly saying 'I've seen it all and had enough; if you don't look after me, I reserve the right to fall down altogether.'

Elsewhere, there is La Ferme du Majorlet, between Monthélie and Volnay, which also belongs to the de Suremain family. This has a curious place in the village's history. In 1765, as Henri Cannard recounts, the farmer's wife, driven next door by a leaking roof, gave birth to a child. Unfortunately, her neighbour's house being in the commune of Volnay, there followed an epic struggle between the priest of Volnay and the seigneur of Monthélie for the soul and taxes of this brand-new parishioner. It took 25 years to finally decide the matter, in favour of Monthélie.

The wines of Monthélie are under-valued. Anyone who seeks to buy good, often excellent, sensibly priced red Burgundy could do worse than investigate this attractive, friendly commune.

Monthélie – a quiet, picturesque village surrounded by its vines

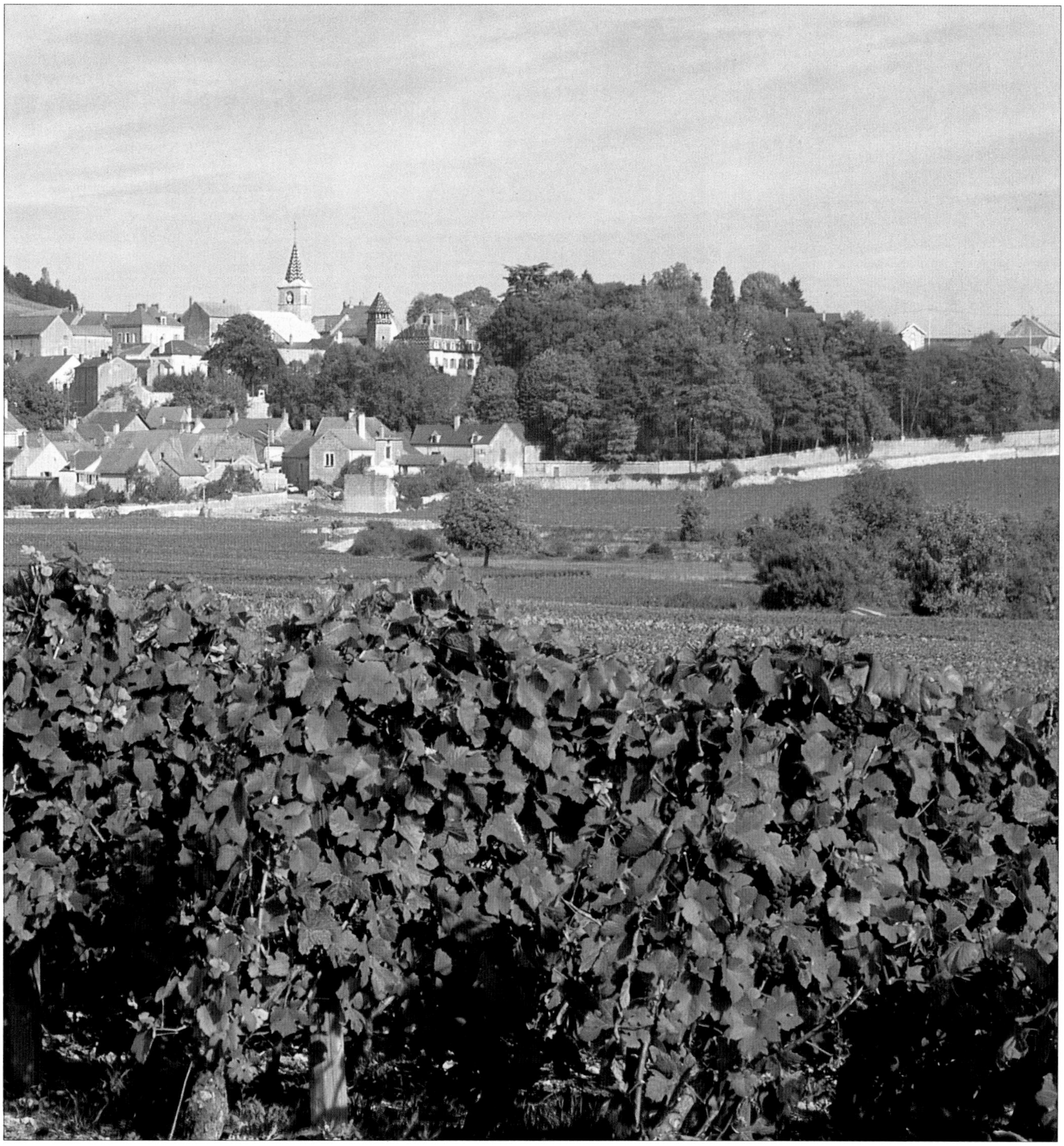

Château de Monthélie

MONTHÉLIE

The Château de Monthélie is one of the few substantial buildings of the Côte d'Or. Of mainly early and mid-eighteenth-century construction, it sits perched on the edge of an escarpment, above Monthélie's southerly extremity. Although once fine and noble, it has, through decades of neglect, degenerated into a state of slightly scuffed aristocracy.

This eccentric establishment originally belonged to the de Monthélie family who built it. It finally came to Robert de Suremain just before the last war. Since 1983, his grandson, Eric de Suremain, together with help from his mother, has run the estate. Eric's grandmother – Mme. de Malibran – is Vincent Leflaive's elder sister, so his mother also helps out in Puligny. Relationships in Burgundy tend to be convoluted!

With an oenology diploma from Beaune preceded by a short spell at Chalone in California in 1976, Eric is well qualified to look after his future inheritance – and his 3 ha. of vines in Rully, where he and his wife live. He clearly enjoys his responsibilities .

After extensive replanting in the late 1970s, every endeavour is made to keep vines as long as is practicable. Of 2.7 ha. of Premier Cru 'Sur la Velle', for example, nearly 0.75 ha. were planted in 1928.

Yields are kept down by widespread use of the low vigour rootstock 'Riparia Gloire', and by leaving grass between vine-rows untreated, using only spot herbicide applications directly beneath each plant.

His viticulture is a blend of ancient and modern. Clones were tried but, since 1985, he has reverted to a *sélection massale* from their own, old vines. He is also contemplating the revolutionary *biodynamics* – perhaps waiting to see the outcome of current trials at Domaine Leflaive.

In the cellar, Eric's orientation is firmly classical. Well aware of the latest techniques, he is yet sceptical of much that passes for 'progress'. He especially eschews automation, preferring personal contact to get the feel of each of his *cuves;* so twice daily he strips off, jumps in and starts treading. *'Pigéage* gives one the aspect of the *cuve',* he explains.

In advance of Eric's immersion, the bunches are completely destaked and lightly crushed. In 1988, 1989 and 1990, he added 2–5% of whole bunches to each vat, although he seems uncertain what this achieves. The pulp is cooled to control both speed and temperature of fermentation, which normally rises to 30–32° C.

Part of the enamel-tiled roof of the de Suremains' Château de Monthélie

The 8 days *cuvaison* is surprisingly short for the depth of extract in Eric's wines. However, as *décuvage* occurs before all the sugar has been converted – a practice which 'gives more finesse to the wine' – this figure is somewhat illusory. Four further days' *débourbage* finishes off fermentation.

Neither Eric nor his predecessors have favoured new oak. With new plantings becoming productive, the proportion of new wood inevitably increased – to about 20%; but this is now declining. 5% is seen as ideal – but Eric is still tinkering with the problem. 'Excessive new wood denatures the wine'.

In the cold, dripping cellars beneath the terrace (the roof leaks) the *malos* proceed slowly. In July or August the wines are racked, unified and returned to cask. Thereafter the time they spend in wood is determined by the vintage; the shortest total *élevage* was for the 1984/86 and 1987 vintage, which were bottled in February of the second year. The longest – for most of the 1982, 1985 and 1988 Premiers Crus – is 2 years. The wines are 'never, never' fined but, since 1984, are kieselguhr and plate filtered before bottling. Eric is trying to eliminate these particular filters, and experimented with cartridges for the 1989s. A trial with kieselguhr, just before the *malo* in 1984 and 1986, gave 'dramatic results with the wine's colour'.

The Domaine's wines are highly individual, and very fine. In youth, they have a deep, impenetrable appearance, almost the black-cherry aspect of young Syrah, but this rapidly lightens. Low yields – well below 40 hl./ha. – and old vines combine to endow even the Monthélie village *cuvée* with a firm, ripe, almost sweet concentration.

Interestingly the Château was one of the rare Domaines to record lower yields in 1990 than in 1989 making the entire range of 1990s highly promising. Meanwhile, the 1989s are becoming deliciously 'tendre', though still quite big-framed wines.

Although the Champs Fuillot is generally regarded as the commune's finest Premier Cru, the Sur la Velle is not far behind. Eric's version of the latter ages well – gradually developing secondary and tertiary aromas of *sous-bois* and strawberries. The 1987 was still youthful in 1991 – needing a further 2–4 years to integrate its acidity and tannins. The 1986, by contrast, was much softer and riper, from a small harvest which gave natural potential alcohol levels of up to 15.7 degrees.

The 1985 Sur la Velle is typical of its vintage – quite a soft, mouthfilling wine, smelling of ripe wild strawberries; complex and harmonious, but without much residual tannin. The 1984 is again different: lighter in tone than either the 1985 or 86 but with a darkish hue. On the palate the wine is soft and forward, with a hint of pine resin.

These wines are some of the best in Monthélie, an achievement Eric attributes to low yields and to his habit of finishing fermentation in the absence of skins. If he follows Robert de Suremain's precept – 'there are no petites années – it is the just balance that counts' the Domaine cannot but progress from strength to strength.

VINEYARD HOLDINGS

Commune	*Level*	*Lieu-dit/Climats*	*Area*	*Vine Age*	*Status*
Monthélie	PC	Sur La Velle	2.81	1928/60/80/84/90	P
Monthélie	PC	Le Cas Rougeot	0.16	1972	P
Monthélie	V	En Remagnien	0.88	1972/85	P
Monthélie	V	Les Hauts Brins	0.51	1976	P
Monthélie	V	Les Clous	0.72	1987/91	P
Monthélie	V	Les Barbières	0.18	1984	P
		Total	**5.26 ha.**		

Domaine de Monthélie-Douhairet

MONTHÉLIE

The fortunes and style of this 300-year-old Domaine are directed by the delightful nonagenarian Mme. Armande Douhairet. This personable, chatty lady, the last surviving member of the family, presides over the reception of visitors from her cosy, first-floor apartments, taking a lively interest in whoever passes through the arch into her courtyard. She still tastes, now preferring mature wines to younger ones.

When she took over, after the death of her uncle in 1945, the estate consisted of some 12 ha. of vines. Her sister soon decided to sell her half-share, so Madame was left with 6 ha., which is how the Domaine remains today. Although it is known principally for its red and white Monthélie, this accounts for only just over half the total production.

Since 1988, the day-to-day vineyard and cellar work has been in the hands of a young vigneron, Francis Lechauve, and his girl-friend. Francis, who learnt his wine-making skills with André Mussy and Bernard Fevre, is starting to make an impact on the quality of Mme. Armande's wines.

In the vineyards, the policy of replacing individual vines continues. Many of the Domaine's vines are in their late thirties or forties, and it is intended to keep the average age high. Francis has stopped using systemics to treat disease, preferring penetrants or contact products which engender less plant resistance. There have been no anti-rot treatments for many years, although insecticides deal with grape-worms and the copper content of Bordeaux mixture hardens the berry skins, each of which helps reduce the incidence of rot.

The Domaine's vineyards are mostly on hillsides – especially in Monthélie, where the half-slopes are generally regarded as producing the best wine. The soil is rotivated to mulch in grasses – herbicides only being used on particularly stubborn patches. *Évasivage* is considered an essential quality factor: 'If you do the job properly the first time, there is no need for any green-pruning,' is Francis' philosophy.

Careful selection of 'plants fins' ensures sensible yields and a good balance of solids: liquid in the grapes. Yields are normally low – the Village appellations produce some 45–8 hl./ha., and the Premiers Crus 35–40 hl./ha. – 'often less', adds Mme. Armande. Vinification is of the 'revised classical' variety – the principal revision being the systematic introduction of about 17% whole bunches into the otherwise destalked

A living testimony to the benefits of good wine – 90-year-old Mme. Armande about to enjoy something from her personal reserve

pulp. These tend to prolong fermentation, whilst the stalks act as drainage ducts for the juice thus making the *chapeau* rather less jammy and easier to work.

The pulp is cooled to 14° C, which delays the onset of fermentation by 3–4 days, during which time colour is extracted. Fermentation proceeds with natural yeasts, and the temperature rises to 33° C; above this, Francis believes, there is significant loss of aroma

Élevage lasts some 18 months for the red wines – with about 40% of new oak for the Premiers Crus, and little or none for the *Village cuvées;* two rackings, a fining and a light kieselguhr filtration precede bottling.

Under the aegis of Francis Lechauve the quality of the wines is gradually improving, so looking at vintages before 1988, although interesting, is of limited value. However, the 1988s, 1989s and 1990s are most promising.

The Domaine has always made *vins de garde.* The Monthélies generally start out quite deep and succulent, with enough tannin to keep them going. Of the Domaine's two Premiers Crus, Le Meix Bataille tends to have more finesse; its clay-limestone soil and its situation on the Volnay border seems to impart roundness and delicacy. The Duresses, on the border of Monthélie and Auxey-Duresses, is quite the opposite in character – greater rusticity, more closed up and tannic – a wine which in good vintages must be kept for at least 5 years to come together and to begin to show its paces.

Mme. Armande's recent Pommards and Volnays are also excellent. The Pommard Fremiers – which touches its Volnay namesake – is more typical of Volnay than of Pommard; more lively, but perhaps less structure; a wine more of lace than muscle. The Pommard Chanlins, which adjoins the Rugiens, also on the Volnay border, has more obvious depth and structure. The 1990 Chanlins is a remarkable wine – with real profundity and concentration, backed by a layer of well-integrated tannins – a wine to keep for a decade or two.

The Pommards are deliberately given more new oak than the Volnays – 'they can support it,' argues Francis. Whilst the Volnay Village *cuvée is* good, the Champans is significantly better, combining both the delicacy of Volnay with elements of the structure of Pommard.

If the quality of Mme. Armande's wines has been variable in the past, this indomitable and charming old lady and her Domaine seem at last set on course for a bright future; she is well assured of some magnificent drinking for her 100th birthday .

VINEYARD HOLDINGS

Commune	*Level*	*Lieu-dit/Climat*	*Area*	*Vine Age*	*Status*
Monthélie	P	Les Duresses (R)	0.21	24	P
Monthélie	PC	Les Duresses (W)	0.26	8	P
Monthélie	PC	Le Meix Bataille (R)	0.43	22	P
Monthélie	V	(R)	2.05	25 & 40	P
Monthélie	V	(W)	0.17	8	P
Meursault	PC	Les Santenots	0.30	38	P
Meursault	V	—	0.17	30	P
Volnay	PC	En Champans	0.94	25 & 40	P
Volnay	V	—	0.13	30	P.
Pommard	PC	Les Fremiers	0.17	30	P
Pommard	PC	Les Chanlins	0.30	P	
—	R	(BGO)	0.22	45	P
—	R	(Bourgogne Aligoté)	0.51	45+	P
		Total	**5.86 ha.**		

AUXEY-DURESSES

Auxey from the slopes of Montagne du Bourdon – with its best-known Premier Cru, Les Duresses, in the foreground

Auxey-Duresses is another of the small communes of the Côte de Beaune which is undergoing something of an image transformation.

Until relatively recently, its vignerons provided an excellent source of Côte de Beaune-Villages and Bourgogne Rouge and Blanc for the main négociant houses. However, with escalating prices of the better-known appellations, buyers have been sniffing round in Auxey and elsewhere for sound red and white Burgundy at sensible prices. Today, as more Auxey is being bottled and sold by growers directly, under the Village label, merchants are making a long overdue re-appraisal of this commune. A distinct air of incipient prosperity abounds.

The village has long had a reputation for no-nonsense wines, which are straightforward but without a great deal of character. Post-*phylloxera,* and until the AC system arrived in the late 1930s, much of Auxey's red output went to augment the insatiable thirst for Volnay and Pommard, whilst the whites no doubt stood in for Meursault. Given the difficulty of finding the genuine article, the conclusion must be, not that Auxey was considered as good as Pommard etc., but rather that the consumer's ignorance allowed duplicity on an egregious scale.

Despite its erstwhile role of compliant understudy, Auxey is a small pleasant, rather elongated village sitting peacefully in the valley between a pair of gentle, green hills. Here the roads from Beaune, Meursault, St.-Romain and Autun converge, giving the place an air of bustle which belies the reality.

This strategic location made it an ideal site for ancient settlers, of which prehistoric encampments on Mont Melian and a Druid temple in nearby Petit-Auxey are evidence. Petit-Auxey – 'Hauxiacum' – is thought to be the earlier settlement, since it controlled not only the traffic along the valley but also essential water sources.

Vines have been planted on these hillsides for centuries. The monks at Cluny owned vines here between the tenth and fourteenth centuries, until the Abbey of Maizières took over. A contemporary inventory shows them as proprietors, in 1692, of most of the *climats* which are still considered the finest.

Auxey is not a large vignoble. Some 169.63 ha. of Village and Premier Cru land are spread out over 3 geographically separate areas: Le Mont Melian to the south-east, La Montagne du Bourdon to the immediate

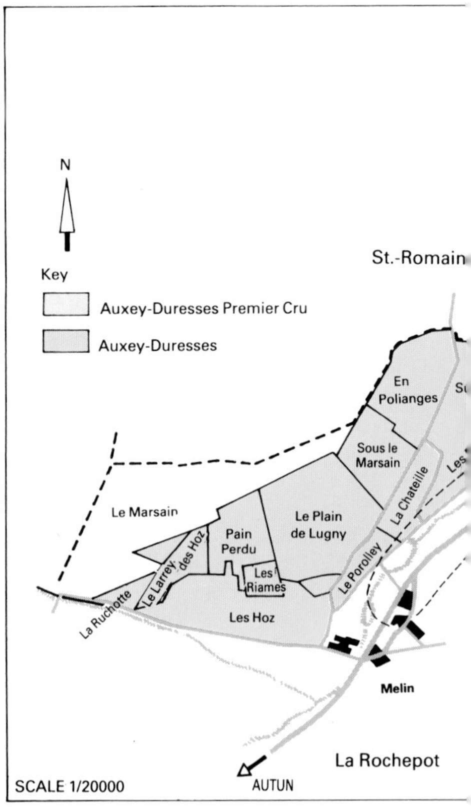

north and the Hameau de Melin, a kilometre or so down the RN 73 towards Autun.

Although red and white wine is produced on each site, most of the commune's white output – which accounts for approximately 25% of the total – comes from grapes grown on the Mont Melian. Until the Chardonnay took over, this cluster of 10 vineyards was planted extensively with Pinot Blanc and Aligoté. What Aligoté there now is comes predominantly from lesser, *régionale,* land round the base of the hill.

The vineyards of Mont Melian face north or north-east which makes ripening difficult. However, being a continuation of Meursault their soils add an element of class in years when the grapes do ripen fully. Underneath a few centimetres of stony, thin topsoil, there is a layer of easily dislodged shale. There is virtually no Pinot Noir in this sector.

On the northern side of the village, adjoining Les Duresses of Monthélie, on a swathe of 31.76 ha. of moderate and steep-sloping ground, directly beneath La Montagne du Bourdon, lie Auxey's 7 Premiers Crus. Apart from its protective properties this hill faces almost due south, giving an excellent chance of bringing Pinot Noir to full ripeness.

A charming feature of these vineyards is the little 'clochetons' – small, wrought-iron fret-work follies with painted white roofs – which serve as shelters in hot weather from where owners can both admire their vines and oversee their workers.

The soils here are generally deep, with varying proportions of limestone. Much of the topsoil is stony scree, which makes soil erosion a constant problem, especially in the steeper sections of Les Duresses and Reugne. Several viticulteurs are experimenting with sowing selected grasses to retain the soil, which otherwise they are obliged to take back up the slopes after rain has washed it down.

The third section of 13 vineyards lies above the hamlet of Melin, on the Autun road. From a mainly easterly exposure come both red and white wines, in about equal quantities.

In 1961 Auxey took to the viticultural leading-edge. Under the auspices of the *INAO,* a couple of vignerons planted an experimental area in vines trained on the high, spread, Austrian Lenz-Moser system. This was modified into a 'Lyre' configuration in 1965, and there are now some 20 ha. planted thus. Spreading the vegetation in this way promoted better photosynethsis, and therefore higher sugar levels, particularly valuable in this marginal climate.

The wines of Auxey continue to become better known; this enables the vignerons to sell more in bottle and thus to invest more in vineyard maintenance and vinification equipment. Whilst the wines of lesser vintages tend to suffer from a lack of roundness and charm and are generally best avoided, those from riper years can be excellent. The whites might almost be taken for junior Meursaults, with aromas of hazelnuts and lime-blossom and often a pleasant, fat flavour with a noticeable *goût de terroir.* The reds tend to muscular robustness, with aromas of 'petits *fruits rouges'* and plenty of guts. They benefit enormously from keeping for a few years – 10 or more will do no harm in top-notch vintages.

Apart from the mildly eccentric Jean-Pierre Diconne, profiled here, the best wines come from the estate of the Duc de Magenta which are now vinified and marketed by Louis Jadot in Beaune. These are invariably yardstick wines of high quality – the white especially, is usually deliciously ripe and fat – setting the standards for the rest of the commune's vignerons and admirably demonstrating the class of which Auxey is capable.

In addition, Domaines Michel Prunier, Leroy and Roy Frères are excellent sources, and there are fine Auxeys to be had from Michel Ampeau (white), Jean-François Coche (red), François Jobard (red) and André Pernin-Rossin (red).

The village is not bereft of humour: in 1971 the chef-patron of the local restaurant, La Cremaillère, Jean Camilleri, and some German customers founded La Confrérie du Pot au Feu, to mimic a more illustrious and older organisation, the Chevaliers du Tastevin, at Vougeot. There are now over 400 members in several countries, presided over by a Grand Sénéchal, swearing undying and constant allegiance to the Pot au Feu. Since this estimable dish is probably accompanied, to perfection, by copious quantities of Auxey-Duresses, what started as a prank is doubtless helping the commune to market its increasingly good wares.

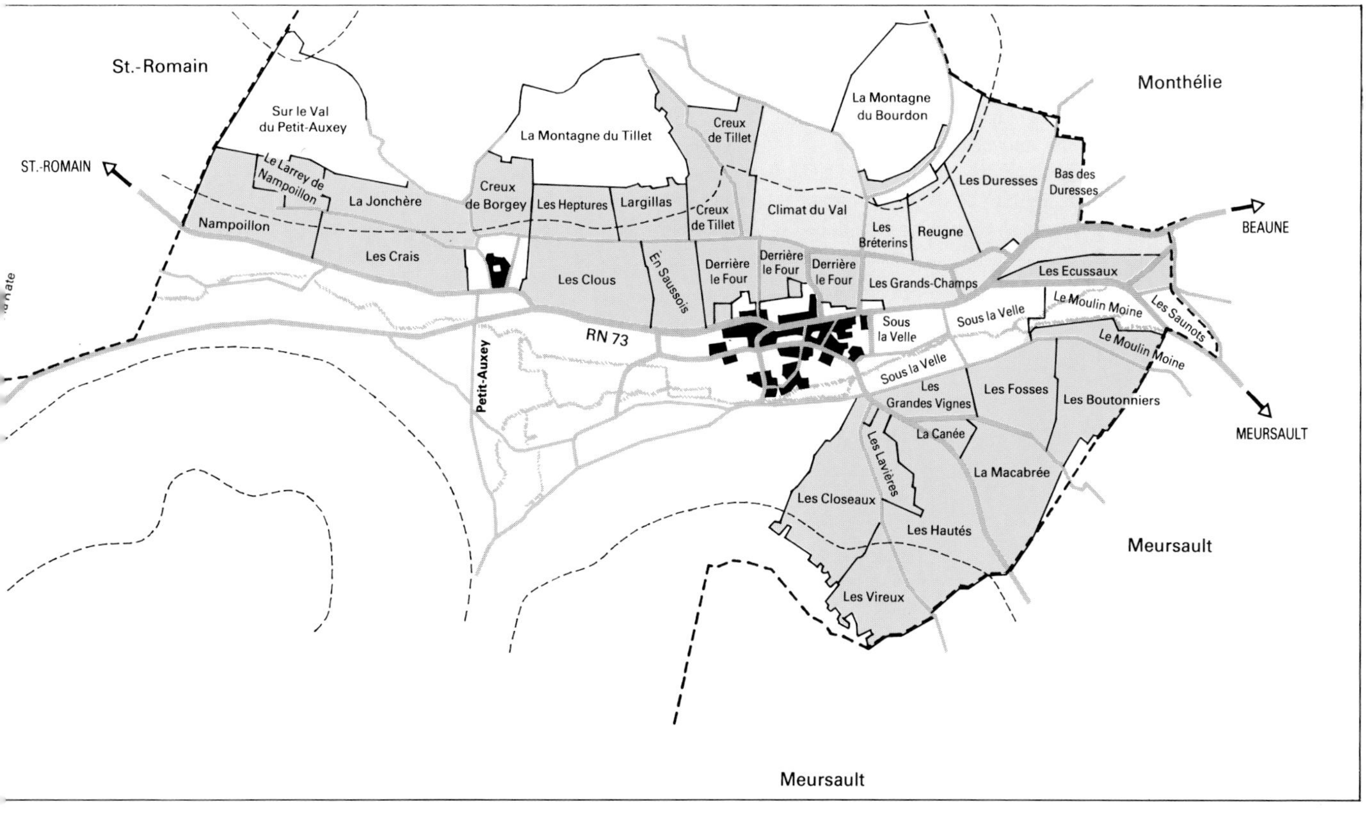

Domaine Jean-Pierre Diconne

AUXEY-DURESSES

Of the few producers of note in Auxey-Duresses, Jean-Pierre Diconne is one of the most individual. An angular, rather animated and galvanic Burgundian, he took over the family vineyards from his father in 1972, having worked with him from 1960 when he was 15. His parent, in turn, had worked as a paid employee at Meursault before moving to Auxey to work for the proprietor of some vines which were bequeathed to him in 1927.

Jean-Pierre is not a man to be influenced by what goes on around him. He operates on the belief that knowing your vines is the best route to quality, and is clearly cynical of much of what currently passes for improvement. He likes to have old vines – among the oldest being a patch of Chardonnay in Les Duresses, planted in 1927. However, when the time does come to grub up a parcel of vines, there is no question of replanting the land straightaway. His father believed in allowing the land to rest before putting it to work anew. Jean-Pierre recalls one plot of Auxey-Duresses which was finally replanted in 1955 after some 25 years fallow. More recently, he replanted a parcel which had been without vines for 14 years. This is clearly not a Domaine in which decisions are taken with undue haste.

The trick of keeping vines into old age is apparently to stress the vine and make it suffer. He is strongly in favour of low yields, although he remarks dryly that you get the lowest yields of all when part of the vineyard is not planted. Nonetheless, a tiny patch of 1893 Chardonnay vines in the Meursault Les Luchets vineyard is still going strong, so they must be doing something right.

When all else has failed to keep yields within acceptable bounds, Jean-Pierre sends his wife into the vineyards to remove excess bunches. In 1990, however, even though 'the wife had taken off 6 bunches per vine, the yield was still very large'. The trouble appeared to be that Mme. Diconne was despatched on her mission too early – if she had waited until August instead of going out in July, perhaps the vines would not have been able to compensate for their loss. Jean-Pierre grumbles that he is not at all sure that the large berries he harvested were as well structured as the smaller ones he normally gets. 'The journalists, the writers, the media believe it works, but, in the end, it's more complicated,' he comments.

Since his vines in Meursault ripen a few days before those in Auxey, he usually starts picking there. However, 'one can make a mistake', he admits somewhat ruefully, recalling that in 1990 'everyone harvested too early. 'The problem, in his eyes, is that people erroneously count 100 days from the start of the flowering in calibrating the date of full maturity, instead of waiting until at least 50% of the flowers have developed.

The Domaine's production is divided about equally between red and white wine. Jean-Pierre works to a limited extent with négociants – especially Ropiteau and Olivier Leflaive. The négoce *cuvées* are generally separated out before the wines are transferred to cask.

The white wines start their fermentation in bulk and once the temperature is stable, are put into cask – 25% or so new Allier and Tronçais oak. Cask hygiene is of great importance to Jean-Pierre, especially since his whites spend a minimum of 15 months in cask, on their lees, without being racked – 'our *malos* are slow to happen', he explains with unaccustomed understatement. If the casks are not cleaned thoroughly, the wines can develop off-flavours and, as he has noticed with certain of his neighbours' 1988s, can desiccate and lose their fruit.

After this abnormally extended sojourn in cask, the wines are vinified in tank, fined with bentonite and, 6 weeks or so later, kieselguhr filtered before bottling by a contract bottler.

Wandering around tasting among the rather disorganised honeycomb of cellars scattered around the Diconne Domaine provides a salutary experience in not judging by appearances. Although order does not appear to be one of Jean-Pierre's highest priorities, the wines are, by and large, excellent.

A 1989 Auxey Blanc, unracked in its cask in January 1991, showed no signs of lost freshness or of suffering from the experience. It was remarkably ripe and rich in fruit, with excellent acidity, a touch of oak on the palate and deliciously long and stylish – altogether a complete and complex wine.

A Meursault Les Narvaux 1989, withdrawn from its original cask and proffered for tasting after Jean-Pierre had drawn the pipette across his nose and approved a modest sample squirted directly into his mouth, was distinctly bigger and burlier than its Auxey cousin. The vineyard, on the Puligny side of the village, is composed of a thin topsoil giving onto almost impenetrable rock, which imparts finesse and acidtiy to the wine.

A Meursault Les Luchets tasted alongside the Narvaux was entirely different: much finer, leaner, showing more 'race' and style. The one-third new wood seemed well integrated without dominating in any way. This vineyard is situated a mere 500 m. from the Auxey boundary, and consists of relatively deep red earth, with a high proportion of stones and 'lave' – a sort of porous rock.

The red wines are equally individual in their vinification: a strong dose of SO_2 is given to delay fermentation by 3 days – an innovation since 1988. In 1990 this dose amounted to 1.5–2.5 litres per tonne. There is no destalking and 12–14 days *cuvaison* at high temperatures – above 35° C in 1980, 1984 and 1985 and very high in 1982. 'Temperatures are getting lower,' comments Jean-Pierre ruefully, 'on the advice of all these prestigious oenologists.' He prefers not to *piger* but to work with a *chapeau immergé*: 'only one good *pigéage*, just up to my elbows'.

The press-wine is tasted before being added, or not, to the free-run wine which is then transferred to cask to spend at least one

VINEYARD HOLDINGS

Commune	*Level*	*Lieu-dit/Climat*	*Area*	*Vintage*	*Status*
Auxey	PC	Les Grands Champs (R)	0.42	1962/67	P
Auxey	PC	Les Duresses (R)	0.42	1927	P
Auxey	V	Les Grandes Vignes/Les Vireux/ Les Closeaux (R)	1.07	1945/71/75	P
Auxey	R	Les Grandes Vignes/ Les Closeaux (W)	0.89	1927/55/71	P
Auxey	R	(Bourgogne Rouge)	0.42	1950/72/73	P
Meursault	V	Les Narvaux Dessous	0.77	1970/81.86	P
Meursault	V	Le Limozin	0.45	1954/55/70	P
Meursault	V	Les Luchets	0.71	1930/1950	P
—	R	(Bourgogne Aligoté)	0.92	1930/52/88	P
—	R	(BGO - Gamay)	0.63	1938/50	P
		Total	**6.70 Ha.**		

year on its lees. Having tried Nevers oak and wood from Buxy and the Morvan, Jean-Pierre has settled on Allier as 'beaucoup plus fin'.

The *malos* proceed very slowly in the ice-cold cellars – 'in 1988 some casks took two years to complete their *malos,'* remarks Jean-Pierre by way of illustration. If on completion of the *malo* he is not ready to rack the wine, each barrel is given a half-dose of SO_2 and left until he has the time. In principle, each *cuvée* is racked but once – into a bulk container. However on rare occasions the wine is fined and thus demands a second racking. It is never returned to cask. The last time Jean-Pierre fined his red wines was in 1985.

Unlike the white wines, the reds are filtered by Diconne himself, not by the bottler. A light pre-filtration precedes a second, tighter plate filtration. The entire process from vat to bottle usually exceeds 2 years: 'on a une vinification longue, nous,' remarks Jean-Pierre phlegmatically.

As one might expect, the Diconne reds are not for early consumption. The Auxeys tend to be quite raw and unapproachable for the first years, opening out slowly over a decade or so to reveal their real qualities. Sadly, as people do not generally think of Auxey-Duresses as producing *vin de garde,* much of the Domaine's wines are drunk too soon.

This doggedly old-fashioned style of winemaking, albeit modified to suit Jean-Pierre's own perceptions of Auxey, produces distinctive, but interesting wines. If you like the style, then this is as good a source for red as it is for white.

Golden slopes – autumn vines at nearby Monthélie

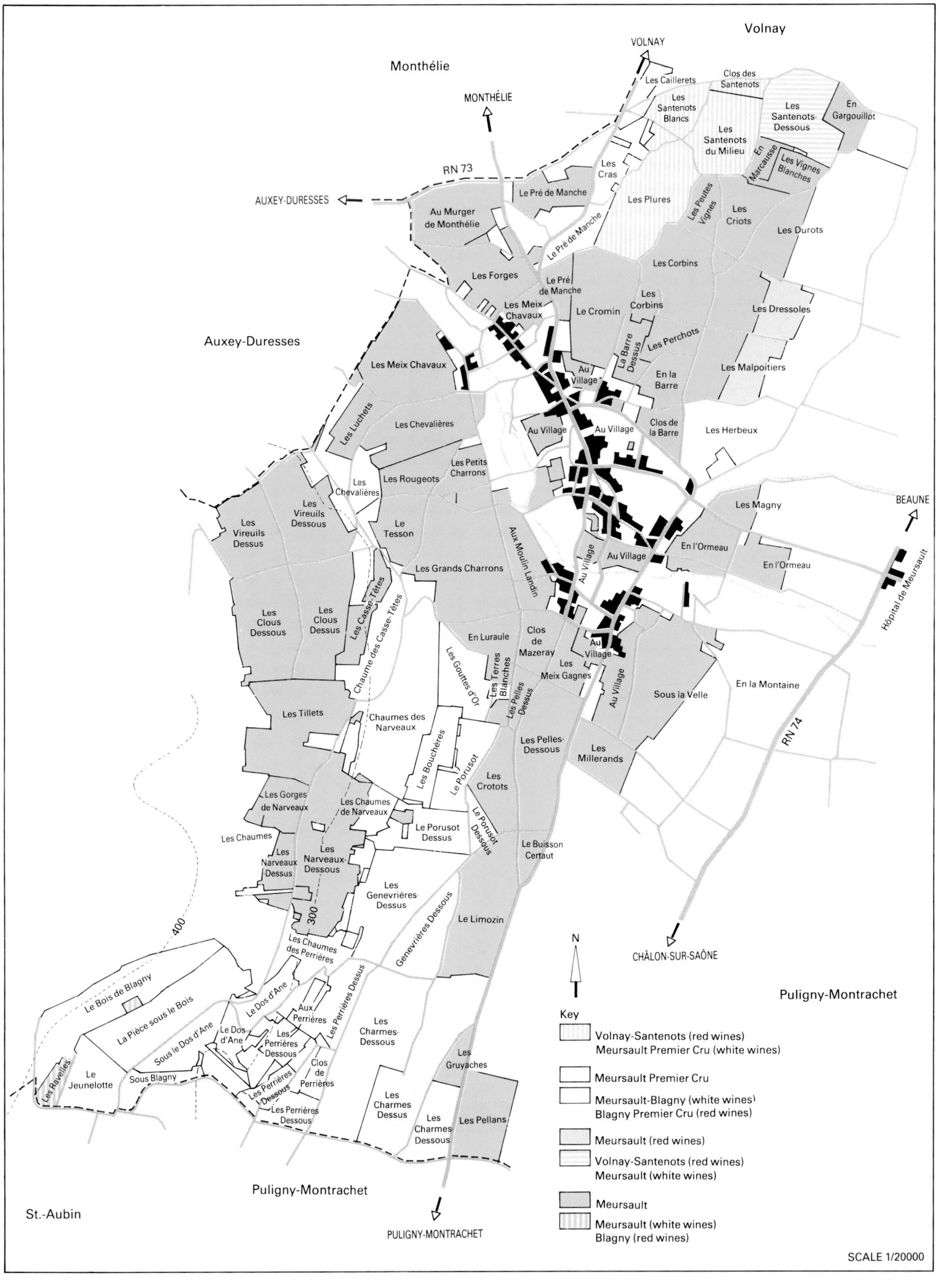
Volnay
VOLNAY
Monthélie
MONTHÉLIE
RN 73
AUXEY-DURESSES
Auxey-Duresses
Les Caillerets
Clos des Santenots
Les Santenots Blancs
Les Santenots du Milieu
Les Santenots-Dessous
En Gargouillot
En Marcausse
Les Vignes Blanches
Les Cras
Les Plures
Les Peutes Vignes
Les Criots
Les Durots
Le Pré de Manche
Au Murger de Monthélie
Les Forges
Le Pré de Manche
Les Corbins
Les Meix Chavaux
Le Cromin
Les Dressoles
La Barre Dessus
Les Perchots
Au Village
En la Barre
Les Malpoitiers
Les Meix Chavaux
Les Luchets
Les Chevalières
Au Village
Clos de la Barre
Les Herbeux
Les Petits Charrons
Les Rougeots
Les Chevalières
Les Vireuils Dessous
Les Vireuils Dessus
Le Tesson
Les Magny
BEAUNE
Aux Moulin Landin
En l'Ormeau
Les Grands Charrons
Les Casse-Têtes
Chaume des Casse-Têtes
Les Clous Dessous
Les Clous Dessus
En Luraule
Clos de Mazeray
Les Gouttes d'Or
Les Terres Blanches
Les Meix Gagnes
Les Pelles Dessus
Sous la Velle
En la Montaine
Hôpital de Meursault
Les Tillets
Chaumes des Narveaux
Les Bouchères
Le Porusot
Les Pelles-Dessous
Les Millerands
Les Crotots
RN 74
Les Gorges de Narveaux
Les Chaumes de Narveaux
Le Porusot Dessous
Les Chaumes
Les Narveaux-Dessus
Les Narveaux-Dessous
Le Buisson Certaut
Les Genevrières-Dessus
Genevrières Dessous
Le Limozin
300
400
Les Chaumes des Perrières
N
CHÂLON-SUR-SAÔNE
Le Bois de Blagny
La Pièce sous le Bois
Le Dos d'Ane
Aux Perrières
Les Perrières Dessus
Sous le Dos d'Ane
Le Dos d'Ane
Les Perrières Dessous
Les Charmes-Dessous
Clos de Perrières
Les Gruyaches
Les Ravelles
Le Jeunelotte
Sous Blagny
Les Perrières Dessous
Les Perrières Dessous
Les Charmes Dessus
Les Charmes Dessous
Les Pellans
Puligny-Montrachet
Puligny-Montrachet
St.-Aubin
PULIGNY-MONTRACHET
Key
Volnay-Santenots (red wines)
Meursault Premier Cru (white wines)
Meursault Premier Cru
Meursault-Blagny (white wines)
Blagny Premier Cru (red wines)
Meursault (red wines)
Volnay-Santenots (red wines)
Meursault (white wines)
Meursault
Meursault (white wines)
Blagny (red wines)
SCALE 1/20000

MEURSAULT

About half-way between Beaune and Santenay lies Meursault. Radiating outwards from the main square on top of the hill, roads lead to Monthélie and Volnay, to Auxey and St.-Romain, through vineyards to nearby Puligny or by a more arterial connection to Autun or Châlon.

Immobile, at the centre of all this to-ing and fro-ing is Meursault's solidly gothic townhall with its multi-coloured roof, from where the affairs of the commune's 1700 inhabitants are administered.

The village reeks of prosperity, mostly derived directly from wine, but tangentially from the services it provides. Meursault is a place for wandering; attractive narrow streets leading to small courtyards, or out into the vineyards, contrast with broader thoroughfares syphoning off heavier traffic to more exotic destinations.

The imposing Château de Meursault, standing among its own vineyards, is also worth visiting, especially as the entry fee allows you to amble through its splendid cellars and taste ad volente.

The village is nothing but vignerons – some 170 in all – many proclaiming their existence with elaborate signs outside of the gates of their Domaines. With some 170,000 cases to dispose of annually, outbreaks of 'vente directe' are hardly surprising.

The commune, divided into Village (304.94 ha.) and Premiers Crus (131.88 ha.), is the largest producer of fine white in the Côte.

Pinot Noir accounts for about 6,000 cases of red Meursault per year from three separate appellations: Meursault Rouge (and Premier Cru), Blagny (and Premier Cru) and Volnay-Santenots. Each has its designated vineyards – Blagny's two surrounding a picturesque hamlet divided between Meursault and Puligny, and the Volnays coming from an administrative hiccup of six vineyards at the northern end of the Meursault.

Meursault's vignerons evidently enjoy making red wine, but are less successful than at making white. In ripe years, such as 1985, 1988, 989 and 1990, the reds are fleshy and attractively perfumed; those who destalk invariably perform better than those who do not.

Administrative buffoonery extends its confusion to the white wines. White grapes planted in Volnay-Santenots vineyards make Meursault Santenots (Premier Cru) and Meursault 'tout court', whilst that from Blagny becomes Meursault-Blagny (Premier Cru) or straight Meursault.

Several of the Village *climats,* while not Premiers Crus, are becoming sufficiently known to have their names added to labels. The principal Premiers Crus lie on south-east facing slopes to the south of the village. A lone pair – Les Cras and Les Caillerets – stare across the Volnay border, just above Les Santenots Blancs.

Of these 6 principal Premiers Crus 4 – Les Charmes, Les Poruzots, Les Genevrières and Les Perrières – are each subdivided into 2 or more *climats,* the quality and qualities of each differing enough to justify a distinction. Dramatic soil variation within this narrow band, and experience, has evolved what amounts to an informal hierarchy. With the constant proviso that the vigneron's contribution can submerge that of the vineyard, the dominant characteristics of each Premier Cru can be broadly described.

At the northern extremity, Les Bouchères (4.41 ha.) and Les Gouttes d'Or (5.33 ha.) produce wines of less finesse but fuller structure. They last well, without developing the complexity of a great Genevrières.

Next in rank, Les Charmes, the largest Premier Cru, is a 31.12 ha. slab of vines occupying most of the slope's vertical extent. Effectively in three sections, the lower two have richer soil and make broader, fuller wine, whilst the upper 14.27 ha. produces wine of complexity and 'rondeur', often with a curiously soft, minerally undertone. The wine exemplifies its name.

Les Poruzots (11.43 ha.) is also tripartite: Le Poruzot, Les Poruzots Dessus and the tiny Les Poruzots Dessous – are all on sloping stony soil, which gives wine with a strongly flinty bouquet and high natural acidity.

Les Genevrières (16.05 ha.) is quintessential Meursault – lime-blossom, honey and nuts on the nose, subtle on the palate.

Finally, Les Perrières (12.91 ha.), adjoining, like Les Charmes, the commune of Puligny, sits on a band of limestone, with an overlay of heat-reflecting stones. From here come the finest Meursaults – steely, yet rich and elegant, full of backbone, less open and forthcoming when young but with time, developing a majestic aristocracy. More the understated Puligny than warm Meursault accessibility. A mature Perrières is a fine experience.

There is a wide variety in style and competence among the commune's Domaines. An apparently insatiable demand for Meursault in the 1970s and 1980s led many growers to excessive yields. A fine Meursault should have concentration, grip and backbone, in addition to its natural open, 'peaches and oatmeal' tones, characterised by Harry Yoxall as 'ingratiatingly soft'. Flat, flabby, over sulphured and cardboardy wines discredit this noble Appellation.

Among under-achievers, the wines of Domaine Jacques Prieur, in particular, have been notably disappointing in recent vintages, with Meursaults, Pulignys and even Montrachets disgracefully lacking in definition and concentration. Martin Prieur, who has taken over from his peripatetic father, seems to realise that much work is needed, especially in the vineyards, to restore a potentially top-class Domaine to its rails.

Nevertheless, there is a wealth of fine winemaking in Meursault. Apart from growers profiled here, good wine is to be had from Pierre Boillot who has just separated from his nephew and erstwhile partner, Frank Mikulski. They produced a fine, rich Charmes from 60–75-year-old vines and an excellent, but rather looser-knit Gouttes d'Or. It is to be hoped that some of their joint spark survives the split.

Meursault is renowned for the feast it provides each November during Les Trois Glorieuses, on the Monday following the Hospices auction. The Paulée is a magnificent lunch, to which the commune's growers invite friends and customers. No wine is provided, but 'according to tradition . . . each brings his bottle'. This amounts to a gargantuan bottle party. Lasting well into the afternoon, the Paulée is the most relaxed gathering of the Burgundian year and a splendid tribute to the spirit and purpose of wine.

Meursault from Les Grands Charrons; the colourful roof of the Mairie is clearly visible

Domaine Robert Ampeau et Fils

MEURSAULT

Domaine Ampeau is one of the few establishments in the Côte d'Or where the quality of red wine-making is on a level with that of the white. Most growers in Meursault and Puligny will tell you that they have more difficulty crafting their reds than their whites, and even the best seem to be mildly baffled by the intricacies of destalking and *cuvaison,* variables peculiar to red vinification. However, because they are talented people, most manage to make a respectable shift of things and, although the Pinots are distinctly less consistent and interesting than the Chardonnays, red Pulignys and Meursaults are by no means to be written off wholesale.

Ampeau is a noteworthy exception; a Domaine where the quality of its reds – from Volnay, Blagny, Pommard, Beaune, Savigny and Auxey – has improved to the point at which it might almost rest its reputation on these wines. Nonetheless, it is with their Meursaults that the Ampeaus have made their name, and they continue to excel.

By Burgundian standards the Domaine is not old, having been created by the grandfather of the present manager, Michel Ampeau, at the turn of the century with the acquisition of a few vines in the locality: Village Meursault, the Premiers Crus Charmes and Perrières and a parcel of Volnay Santenots. Michel's father, Robert, took charge in the early 1940s and added significantly to the Domaine's holdings, firstly by marrying a Mlle. Bobey who brought with her vineyards in Beaune and Savigny, and then by careful purchases of suitable land that came up for sale.

The parcels of Puligny Combettes, Pommard, Auxey-Duresses (rouge) and some more Volnay Santenots were added during the early 1950s, and the 1.6 ha. of La Pièce sous le Bois in 1973. Robert remained firmly at the helm until Michel took over in 1985, and both he and his wife live at the estate to make sure Michel continues the traditions of two generations. In 1980 a Société Civile was created to exploit the vineyards, although the vines themselves continue to belong to Robert.

Whilst the wines are made in a separate *cuverie* in Meursault, the Domaine's headquarters are in the Rue du Cromin, one of the many narrow feeder roads skirting the village. Here, behind a line of white-painted posts fencing off a small courtyard, are the offices and principal cellars, adjoining a row of sheds and garages along one side of the courtyard. Beneath the house, rather like a lopsided mouth waiting to be fed, gapes a ramp leading down to the cool vaulted cellars.

Michel Ampeau where he most enjoys being – among his vines

This is the charge of the young-looking 52-year-old Michel Ampeau – a lean, energetic bachelor, whose infectious humour masks an intensity and single-mindedness which, combined with his passion for his vines, are the talk of many of his peers. On winter days of an inclemency which would drive even the most conscientious of growers indoors to their paperwork or to their firesides, on the pretext of a bout of stock-control or urgent tasting, Michel, more often than not, will be found muffled up and hard at work in his vineyards – pruning, ploughing or whatever needs doing.

Not only is he a fanatical viticulteur, but also a highly skilled one – not a man to cut corners or to espouse the soft option. His way of looking after his vineyards is direct, careful and labour intensive. When it comes to replacing vines, every effort is made to adapt clones and rootstocks to the microclimate. Only the finest clones are used, several in each vineyard for complexity and equilibrium, as Michel believes that selection has honed them to a fine pitch of excellence, unmatched by any possible *sélection massale.* 'It's like running a race,' he explains, 'if you have trained athletes they will finish in say two hours and still be fit; but if you asked the growers of Meursault to run, they would take all day and some would still be going.'

The Ampeau viticultural regime has one point of particular interest; namely, that each July Michel carefully sows seeds of Ray-Grass in between each vine row. Along with a handful of other growers, the Ampeaus have been doing this for 20 years. The belief is that the grass, which continues to grow to a height of 10–12 cm. by harvest time, serves the dual function of opening up soil which may have become compacted by the passage of machinery or by geological adhesion and of stabilising it against erosion in years which may be especially wet or windy. The grass is allowed to grow until December and then destroyed with a herbicide treatment. If by remote chance some gets forgotten, any still in situ in January becomes stubbornly tenacious and virtually ineradicable.

Michel is as attentive to detail in the cellars as he is in his vineyards. What he is after are wines which will keep. This is not simply a matter of high initial acidity for the whites and brutally aggressive tannins for the reds, but the more difficult achievement of an equilibrium which will hold and not fracture as others do because one constituent happens to dominate the rest.

Built-in longevity is an integral part of Michel and Robert Ampeau's philosophy, since theirs is one of the few Domaines on the Côte which does not release its wines until they are deemed ready to drink. Not a bottle, neither red nor white, is generally sold until it is 5 years old – and many are kept even longer. In 1991, for example, small quantities of 1979 Meursaults were still being offered to their regular clientèle, whereas the 1987s were still 'in reserve' waiting, presumably, to grow the distinctive Ampeau mould.

Vinifications are broadly traditional, with natural yeasts and plenty of *batonnage* to extract the maximum richness and complexity into the wines. Although only 10–25% of new wood is used, to avoid an excess of oak flavours, Michel believes that fermenting his whites in new rather than old oak casks harmonises the flavours derived from the wood with the wine more successfully than would be the case if the wine was put into new oak after fermentation. In addition, fermentation in casks, old or new, produces wines which age more slowly than those fermented in bulk.

He also considers it important to leave any necessary *chaptalisation* until the last practicable moment to prolong fermentation and to extract greater finesse and complexity, whereas most vignerons add their sugar either at the beginning or just after the moment of highest temperature. *Chaptalising* in this way requires considerable precision of judgement and carries the attendant risk of unwanted residual sugar remaining in the wine after the yeasts have given up working. However, whilst he is fully aware of the dangers, Michel believes that the rewards more than outweigh the risks.

After the *malolactic fermentation,* around May following the vintage, the new wine is racked into casks which are then moved to a cellar at 13°C. A month later the wines are fined with bentonite and then given a light plate filtration (a pity, because it is unnecessary and because filtration, however delicate, cannot help but remove some of the natural guts and acidity from the wine) before being bottled by a small bottling machine. *Élevage* of only 9–10 months seems unusually short; however Michel Ampeau considers that early bottling helps retain the youthful fresh grape aromas and flavours and, above all, the acidity so necessary for the long period the wines are destined to spend in the Ampeau cellars.

The Domaine's wines are highly individual in character. Tasting a range spanning several different vintages, one is struck by a distinct House style – lean, taut Chardonnays and Pinots, not immediately flattering to the palate but rather endowed with an intellectual austerity which it takes a little time to appreciate. Ampeau wines give one the impression that they are busy cogitating in their bottles and will decide for themselves how much they are prepared to reveal. If you are discourteous enough to interrupt them at the wrong moment, then you cannot expect much by way of response. If, on the other hand, you tap into an Ampeau bottle while it is in a state of relaxed communicativeness, then you may expect, and get, much.

Especially interesting are the so-called 'off-vintages'. Not only do Ampeau's 1974s, 1977s, 1980s, 1984s and so on last long after practically everyone else's seem to have been consigned to the vinegar jar, but they often provide interesting and delicious drinking. Trying to guess the vintage of an Ampeau Meursault, however, can reduce the most experienced of tasters to despair, so well are they made that the vintage identity markers are frequently nowhere to be found, leaving the taster fog-bound. This is the result of infinite pains in putting only the healthiest, ripest fruit into the fermenting vats.

However fine the lesser vintages, they are naturally overshadowed by the well-known great ones. The high initial acidity of Ampeau wines means that even longer is needed to soften and harmonise them, especially with vinifications which emphasise not fat and flesh, but the lean and intellectual form where acidity long remains obtrusive.

By refusing to sell their wines young, the Ampeaus avoid the danger that premature consumption will lead to their wines being misunderstood or tasted in an incomplete state. However, keeping back every vintage, good and less good, apart from having a devastating effect on their cash-flow, runs the individual risk that one wine or another will fail to develop as expected, especially in less good years where the balance of constituents in a wine tends to be more fragile. Michel Ampeau seems unconcerned – he knows his wines and has a good idea of how they will age in bottle; he also benefits from an impressive track record to bolster his confidence, should his nerve start to falter.

However, while tradition plays its part in his thinking, he is not averse to a little modernisation now and then, when it seems appropriate. For example, the Domaine used to press with a Mabille press, which tended to give a rather murky juice requiring long settling before fermentation started; now a pneumatic Willmes press has been installed, incorporating a relatively new internal drainage system for running off juice, which Michel considers gives a much clearer must. However, balanced against this is the greater time taken to press a pressful of grapes 2–2.5 hours which brings an attendant risk of oxidation. Again, Michel is prepared to accept this in the cause of quality.

The production of red wine now accounts for some 60% of the Domaine's total. Over the last decade Michel's meticulous wine-making skills have greatly improved their quality which, although perhaps not quite as consistent or exciting as the whites, makes Ampeau reds wines of typicity and substance and well worth seeking out, especially in good vintages . It would seem that, at last, Mlle. Bobey's dowry is coming into its own.

Michel Ampeau's Meursaults are gloriously austere and delicious wines. The 1979s are beautifully structured and now approaching their apogee. After an hour open, the 1979 La Pièce Sous le Bois had an attractive Meursault nose of honey, nuts and lime-blossom with a firm, long flavour, plenty of grip and depth, and a good concentration of fruit; a great success in what was a notably high-volume vintage. Here is a wine which would partner to perfection a plain, or even a strongly sauced dish of sea-bass or sole, not to mention a noble crustacean.

VINEYARD HOLDINGS

Commune	*Level*	*Lieu-dit/Climat*	*Area*	*Vine Age*	*Status*
Puligny	PC	Les Combettes	0.75	35	P
Meursault	PC	Les Perrières	0.60	35	P
Meursault	PC	Les Charmes	0.30	P	
Meursault	PC	Volnay Santenots	1.51	25	P
Meursault	PC	La Pièce sous le Bois	0.80	35	P
Meursault	V	Les Crotots	0.45	12	P
Meursault	V	Sous la Velle	0.42	25	P
—	R	(Bourgogne Blanc)	0.40	30	P
Pommard	V	Les Vaumuriens	1.10	25	P
Beaune	PC	Clos du Roi	0.32	20	P
Blagny	PC	La Pièce sous les Bois	0.80	35	P
Savigny	PC	Les Lavières	0.55	35	P
Savigny	PC	Les Fournaux	0.80	25	P
Auxey	PC	Les Ecusseaux	0.90	20	P
		Total	**9.70 ha.**		

Domaine Boyer-Martenot

MEURSAULT

Yves Boyer runs a fine small family Domaine from an unpretentious house and cellars in the La Velle Quartier of Meursault. As with most Burgundian Domaines, its extent has variously sprouted and been chopped down by inheritance since the Boyers started owning vines in the 1850s. Presently, it stands at just over 6.5 ha., mostly *en métayage* or *en fermage* from either parents or in-laws, and is thus small enough to be managed by Yves and his wife.

The wine made here is some of the best in the commune – mouthfuls of real depth and complexity, not the mouthfuls of fruit without any genuine substance so often found elsewhere. To achieve this, Yves tries to keep his vines as old as possible and to avoid using clones – although he has planted a few to see what they produce. In addition, he takes the decision on when to harvest with great care – making his own measurements throughout the Domaine to determine the most propitious moment for each parcel.

The white wines, which form 83% of the production, are fermented in cask with natural yeasts. New wood accounts for about 33% in the Bourgognes and Village wines, with a touch more for the trio of Premiers Crus. Yves prefers Vosges and Allier – 'plus fin' – with a greater than average charring.

Although there is no control over temperature in cask, the *musts* rarely climb above 20–22° C: 'they don't overheat in small quantities'. *Batonnage* once or twice a week helps to keep the lees evenly distributed but this is discontinued after *malo* to allow settling before the wines are racked in May. They remain in cask until bottling, usually in September, before the new vintage. The wines are prepared with a bentonite/casein fining, re-unified in bulk and given a light plate filtration.

Yves is a quiet, thoughtful man – a contrast to his extrovert wife who looks after the 'côté administratif' and the customers from her small office in the courtyard. He clearly cares deeply about what he produces and is one of a relatively rare breed of vignerons who take trouble to think their wines through, rather than relying on habit or worse still, 'tradition', from year to year.

The white range starts with a ripe, well-concentrated Bourgogne Aligoté. This has a hint of the variety's hallmark *goût de terroir* and an harmonious nerve of natural acidity kept fresh by *élevage* in stainless steel; altogether excellent for its appellation.

The Bougogne Chardonnay, vinified in cask, is equally good in its class; the 1989 had plenty of fruit, good length and concentration, and a touch of real complexity.

Meursault Village is represented by a trio of very attractive wines: the Narvaux, planted mainly on calcaire magnesien – a soil with virtually no clay – is concentrated and fat with noticeable power. The 1989 seemed a trifle four-square in early 1991, but was delicious, none the less. The Pré Manche, situated just beneath Patrick and Katherine Javillier's splendid new house at the top of the village, beyond the camp site, is altogether different – the 1989 showed positive aromas redolent of exotic fruits and orange peel. On the palate it was somewhat austere – a characteristic of this vineyard – but had real concentration and excellent length under this slightly forbidding young mantle. In this location, the vines suffer badly from drought which might in part account for the character of this vintage.

The third Meursault is L'Ormeau – from vines surrounding the Boyers' house at the bottom end of the village. Deep soil here gives the wine much more power, but perhaps a little less complexity. Despite this, the 1989 is excellent – slightly tighter bud than its brothers, but promising to open out into a delicious bottle in 5 years or so.

The Premiers Crus constitute the cream of Yves' production. The Charmes vineyard is generally considered as 3 distinct plots of land – upper, middle and lower; Yves has vines in each, but most are in the sector nearest to the Puligny border, which probably accounts for the complexity and finesse which he manages to extract from his grapes. The 1989 Charmes tasted in January 1991, although suffering from recent bottling, showed hints of fine depth and complexity, with unmistakable power; a bottle to keep for many years, into a nutty old age.

The Perrières is a vineyard which has a deep layer of 'pierre pourri' which helps retain moisture in what is otherwise unusually dry soil. Yves' Perrières generally has charm and puissance with richness and opulence. Less 'Puligny' than the Charmes perhaps, but none the worse for that.

The reds – from Auxey, Pommard and Meursault – are made to suit Yves' personal preference for big, tannic wines. His somewhat curious logic is that you can't get sufficiently high tannin levels from skins alone. However, his policy of going to the other extreme and leaving all the stalks in the fermenting vats, irrespective of the ripeness of the wood, seems a misguided expedient, especially in sunless vintages when the greenness of the unripe wood shows through. Although Yves tries to absorb some of the shock which his customers might feel if they were to drink these meaty mouthfuls prematurely, by keeping the wines back for a couple of years or more, there is no doubt that this inflexible vinification removes some of the delicacy and finesse one expects from these appellations. The wines are by no means bad, but lack balance. Neither is late harvesting of the Pinot Noirs, to ensure maximum ripeness of both berry and wood, a sound solution. A longer *cuvaison* than the 8–10 days Yves presently allows, without stalks, would both extract the tannin he wants and give the wines a much better balance.

There have been criticisms of sloppy *élevage* in recent vintages. However, things looked perfectly in order in late 1990 – casks properly topped with clean bung-holes and nothing to indicate poor hygiene. But failings are relatively easily hidden – so perhaps an element of caution is advisable.

On the evidence presented, Yves Boyer is making excellent wines, thoughtfully put together with real depth and complexity. This is a fine source of Meursault.

VINEYARD HOLDINGS

Commune	*Level*	*Lieu-dit/Climat*	*Area*	*Vine Age*	*Status*
Meursault	PC	Les Perrières	0.63	30	F
Meursault	PC	Les Charmes	0.67	35	M
Meursault	PC	Les Genevrières	0.19	1956	M
Meursault	V	Les Narvaux	1.23	25	M
Meursault	V	L'Ormeau	0.64	1925	F
Meursault	V	Pré de Manche	0.22	1960	P
Meursault	V	(Red)	0.24	1978	P
Auxey	V	—	0.51	34	P
Pommard	V	—	0.54	1943	M
—	R	(Bourgogne Aligoté)	0.87	1947	F
—	R	(Bourgogne Blanc)	0.50	1965/80	F
—	R	(Bourgogne Rouge)	0.33	1972	P
		Total	**6.57 ha.**		

Domaine Coche-Debord

MEURSAULT

Alain Coche – a cousin of Jean-François Coche-Dury – lives with his family and 86-year-old father, Julien, in the La Velle quarter of Meursault, not far from Bernard Michelot. A short, stocky man, with greying hair and a slightly harassed manner, he seems to have too much to do and to be generally dragged along by events rather than being in charge of them.

A high proportion of the vines on the estate are old – Alain claims that 60% have seen their sixtieth birthday and that the average age is 30–40 years. With such a high percentage of older vines, large-scale replanting has hitherto been unnecessary, but now that some of the oldest are nearing the end of their useful life, larger parcels must be grubbed up and the land rested and replanted.

Alain buys clones from the nursery and plants them on carefully chosen rootstocks 161/49 for the hillsides, and 3309 for the 'demi-coteaux' – literally the half-hillsides. These, he feels, help give a regular crop and are best adapted to the different soils. He talks forthright sense about rot: 'eliminate the puncture of the grape-worm and you have eliminated 80% of rot'. Therefore he uses chemical sprays against these caterpillars, although against the other principal cause of rot – humidity – there is little to be done except ensure that excess foliage is removed regularly during the summer to allow the air to circulate around the bunches.

Harvesting is generally as late as possible: 'I usually pick a week later than the others!' The grapes are pressed in a Vaslin press, dosed with SO_2 and then given 24 hours to settle. This is done whether or not the lees are clean, 'because if the wine is to spend 2 years in cask then only the fine lees are needed.' A long slow fermentation in cask ensues – lasting up to 3 weeks. There is no attempt at temperature control except that *chaptalisation,* when necessary, is left until the last practicable moment, when the *must* density reaches 1,000–1,010, both to prolong fermentation and to help maintain a low ambient temperature.

The Meursaults are then put into casks, the lesser appellations going into larger wood. Twice a week they are *batonnée* – a process which is continued for as long as necessary. For the 1988 vintage *batonnage* lasted 18 months, until the spring of 1990!

Unusually, the whites at this Domaine are not racked after the *malolactic fermentation* but kept on their fine lees until bentonite fining during the second year. Shortly afterwards the wine is racked, left for about a month, then bottled with a light plate filtration. This amounts to a total *élevage* of 2 years – at the extremity of what most regard as prudent, especially in less ripe vintages.

Red wines, accounting for about 50% of the Domaine's production, are vinified somewhat idiosyncratically. There is no *égrappage,* although in 1990 Alain admitted to experimenting with a 25–40% destalking, the results of which are still being evaluated. After light crushing, a litre of SO_2 per barrel is added, then the pulp is cooled and left to macerate for 5 days. Once a day the cap is broken up *(pigéage)* to extract more glycerol and thus give the wines more roundness. The cellar is then warmed to help fermentation start. Each large *cuve is* covered with a plastic tarpaulin to minimise the loss of volatile alcohol and a long, slow fermentation ensues. The pulp is then pressed by hand in a Demoisy piston press and the *vin de presse* added back to the *vin de goutte.* Because the SO_2 has removed colour, Alain believes a long post-fermentive maceration is necessary to restore it.

Following alcoholic fermentation, the *cuves* are allowed a further week to settle before the wine is put into oak – 25% new from the Nievre/Allier. After the *malolactic fermentation* is over (March – April the following year) the wines are racked and returned to cask. In January – February of the second year they are dosed with egg-white – the usual fine red wine fining – and left *sur col* until a month before bottling in August – September.

This red vinification has more in common with Bordeaux than with Burgundy and one senses that Alain is experimenting with his reds to discover what works best.

Tasting in one of several cellars scattered round the village – he seems to collect them, as a hobby – surrounded by unlabelled bins of old vintages, it was instructive to see how 100% of stalks and long maturation affected the structure and overall balance of a range of red 1989s. Those, such as a *cuvée* of Auxey-Duresses, which had not seen new oak were supple, with reasonable length and soft, ripe fruit. However, those reared in new oak – a *cuvée* of Monthélie Les Duresses for example – seemed over-balanced by tannins. Unusually ripe grape-wood in 1989 may help restore these wines to some sort of equilibrium.

The best red is probably the Pommard La Platière, which contains the produce of a patch of Premier Cru insufficient to produce its own *cuvée.* This, plus Alain's 40-year-old Platière vines, adds a touch of extra finesse and concentration. In short, Coche-Debord reds are defunitely constructed as all-in wrestlers rather than prima ballerinas.

The Domaine's white wines are kept in another building near the Chevaliers vineyard. These are decidedy masculine in youth, with firm acidity and plenty of sappy sinew. Alain wants his wines to last '10 years at least for a Meursault to start drinking well'. The Goutte d'Or, Limouzin and Charmes are the best of the Meursaults, with the Chevaliers and Ormeau close behind.

Alain Coche puts much thought into his wines. They are, in truth, highly individual in style, but nonetheless, for those prepared to be patient, represent excellent examples of their origins, which after all is what great Burgundy is about.

VINEYARD HOLDINGS

Commune	*Level*	*Lieu-dit/Climat*	*Area*	*Vine Age*	*Status*
Meursault	PC	Les Charmes	0.29	50	P
Meursault	PC	Goutte d'Or	0.19	50	P
Meursault	V	Les Chevaliers	0.31	30	P
Meursault	V	Les Limouzin	0.25	50	P
Meusault	V	L'Ormeau	0.37	30	P
Meursault	V	—	1.00	30	P
Meursault	V	—	0.40	35	P
Auxey	V	(White)	0.21	10	P
Auxey	R	(Auxey Côte de Beaune)	0.40	35	P
	R	(Bourgogne Blanc)	0.80	25	P
	R	(Bourgogne Aligoté)	0.79	30	P
Pommard	V	La Platière	0.26	40	P
Monthélie	PC	Les Duresses	0.30	15	M
Monthélie	PC	Les Duresses	0.30	15	M
Monthélie	V	—	0.23	15	M
—	R	(Bourgogne Rouge)	1.50	15	P
—	R	(PTG)	0.64	15	P
		Total	**7.94 ha.**		

Domaine Coche-Dury

MEURSAULT

It would be inconceivable to discuss the important Domaines of Meursault without, in almost the same breath, uttering the words Coche-Dury. For at least a decade, this estate has been considered by many to epitomise the finest of which the appellation is capable.

This runaway success has been the personal achievement of Jean-François Coche, who took over from his father in 1972. On first acquaintance he gives the impression of a dedicated, thoughtful scholar who happens to find himself in a *cuverie* rather than a library, although he would probably be equally happy in either. Closer scrutiny reveals beneath the apparent scholarship a real scholarship allied to a quiet but indefatigable devotion to quality.

Jean-François is the third generation of his branch of the family to run the Domaine. The first generation Coche, his grandfather, acquired 6 parcels of vines after the First World War: Bourgogne Chardonnay Les Belles Côtes, Meursault Blanc in the *lieu-dits* Les Vireuils and Les Petits Vignes, Auxey-Duresses Blanc Les Boutonnières, Monthélie Les Crays and a very small parcel of Bourgogne Pinot Noir. Initially grandfather Coche employed vignerons to make the wine, but later started to do it himself, selling wine in bottle as well as 'en négoce'.

Jean-François' father took charge in 1964, remaining at the helm until 1972 and finally retiring in November 1989. During his custodianship a further 16 individual parcels of vineyards were added to the Domaine's holdings, bringing the total up to almost 9 ha. These, most notably in the Volnay Premiers Crus Clos des Chênes and Les Taillepieds, and in Meursault Premier Cru Les Perrières (Dessus), added significantly to the Domaine's commercial viability.

On assuming responsibility Jean-François set about buying outright the parcels of vines which were *en métayage* – that is to say those being share-cropped for other owners. This system – well established in Burgundy, where vineyard holdings tend to be small, and frequently commercially unviable by themselves – allows the owner and the farmer to divide the crop in an agreed proportion, usually 50/50. Sometimes the rent is paid in wine, sometimes (as with M. Coche) in fruit.

The most recent acquisition is a parcel of Meursault Chevaliers, a Village vineyard, bought in 1986 to supplement an adjoining holding. Although soaring land prices

Jean-François Coche, his wife and their daughter Marie-Hermine; as usual young Rafael was out on his bicycle

virtually preclude expansion, Jean-François is keen to snap up any parcels of vines coming on the market which happen to abut his own.

It is hardly surprising to learn that here, quality begins in the vineyard. Jean-François is emphatic that, to give of their best, vines must be severely pruned. Traditional *guyot* pruning, even with a short fruiting cane, tends to produce larger and less concentrated grapes than those from vines trained *en cordon.* So 30% of his vines are trained *en cordon de Royat* – with 3 fruiting canes off the main *cordon,* pruned to 2 buds each. This system regularly produces smaller grapes, reducing yields by up to 50% obtained with *Guyot.* Which vines are treated in which way is up to the pruner, who will take into account the natural vigour of the vine. Jean-François feels that this balance is about right

As with any conscientious grower, vine age is also a critical quality factor. Coche's policy is to replant as and when individual vines die rather than grubbing up a designated area each year. He has novel views on the effect of vine age on wine: 'You can make a good wine with young vines, but you must be severe in limiting the number of bunches you leave on each plant. Wine from younger vines tends to evolve more rapidly and to have a shorter life, but can be very 'flatteur' to begin with.' Rigorous pruning also encourages a sound, deep, root system – a key to drought-resistance and wine complexity.

To this end, his young vines are hoed throughout the year to plough in grass and weeds, whilst the older ones are hoed twice, in March and April, and then given a dose of herbicide to keep them weed-free during the growing season. 'This way we are free of worry through the summer, when there is so much else to do.'

His pursuit of quality has engendered a dislike of commercially produced clones – they are over-selected, 'too uniform, too little finesse'; instead, he selects plant material from his own vineyards, which is then delivered to the nurseryman who prepares the grafts. This *sélection massale* leads to a greater diversity in the vineyard, and thereby to greater complexity in the wine.

Whilst normal vine afflictions are easily controlled there is much concern over a new malady which is making its presence felt in most wine-growing areas of France, not least Burgundy. *Eutypiose* is an insidious infection, since after the early, visible symptoms outward manifestation may disappear altogether for up to 7 years, by which time the vine is irrecoverable and the disease has probably spread to other parts of the vineyard. Two randomly selected parcels in the Coche vineyards studied in 1990 by the local research station showed 4.48% of Chardonnay with symptoms of *eutypiose* in one and 0.45% in the other. Jean-François can only speculate on this difference: the most affected parcel, Meursault Les Luchets, is on a hillside with dry, stony, rocky soil, whereas the untouched vines are on flat land with richer, more humid soil. This latter was badly affected by the great frosts of 1985, which he believes killed off the disease, whereas the sloping vines escaped frost damage, possibly allowing the fungus which spreads *eutypiose* to live on. Vigilance and instant removal and incineration of affected vines is the only hope.

In the modest, modern cellar, vinification for both red and white wines proceeds along broadly traditional lines. Coche believes in adding sulphur to the grapes as soon as they are picked to avoid any possibility of oxidation. American experiments showing that this procedure protects the final wine against eventual oxidation less than not doing so, are dismissed with a disbelieving shrug which recognises the contradiction without being able to account for it.

Alcoholic fermentation, with only natural yeasts, is in up to 50% new Allier oak for the whites and up to 100% for the reds. The precise proportion of new wood is determined by the wine and the vintage – no formulae here! Jean-François is adamant that the longer the fermentation the finer and richer the wine; so he is delighted when some casks continue fermenting well after the usual 10–14 days – often up to 3–4 weeks. The *malolactic fermentation* gives relatively few problems. On the rare occasions when a cask fails to start its *malo,* it is given an inoculation of some fresh lees from a cask which has just finished – a trick which usually produces the desired result.

Another tradition which Coche believes enriches a wine is rousing the lees in a cask by simply stirring with a stick. *Batonnage is* common practice among white Burgundy makers during the winter following fermentation. It should not be excessive, but enough to give an even distribution of lees within the cask. Lees indeed nourish the wine, but excess can produce undesirable off-flavours, so care has to be taken to avoid over-feeding.

Coche's white wines spend some 10 months on their lees until their first racking in July following the vintage. A second racking 4 months later – and fining with bentonite to deposit smaller particles suspended in solution which would otherwise remain – is followed by a further 6 months of rest. After some 20 months in cask, the wine is bottled by hand without filtration, direct from its fining.

Apart from his magnificent and much sought-after whites, Jean-François Coche produces some of the finest red Meursault to be found. However, his main problem is finesse, since in his experience, and somewhat contrary to common belief, Pinot Noir is more susceptible to loss of aromas than Chardonnay. So, 'To have finesse in a red wine is difficult . . . very difficult'.

Being a talented man, he manages it. His Pinot Noir is completely destalked and fermented for 10–12 days before being transferred to cask, of which 20% are new oak. In contrast with his white wines, there is only 1 pressing, instead of 2, and the first racking is in March or April, 2–3 months earlier. The wine remains on its fining throughout the following winter and is bottled directly from cask after some 18 months' *élevage* with neither further racking nor filtration. All this, and scrupulous topping up of casks, helps keep oxidation at bay and retains freshness and finesse in the wines.

From a well-structured, concentrated Bourgogne Pinot Noir from 6 different *lieu-dits* in Meursault, through a ripe, succulent, Meursault Rouge, a Monthélie and an Auxey-Duresses, to a fine pair of Volnay Premiers Crus, the Coche reds are beautifully crafted wines and well worth looking out for.

Remarkable complexity and richness characterise Jean-François' white wines. From a superlative Aligoté (vinified in second- or third-year oak) to a noble Meursault Perrières (50% new oak) they have a depth and structure which are, sadly, all too rare. Ask him what really matters in the achievement of quality and he will tell you that one must start with a fair proportion of old vines, severely pruned for low yields (35 hl./ha. in Perrières in 1989, more in 1990). '45 hl./ha. is ideal for making a Grand Vin,' he reflects, although 40 hl./ha. is more often the reality – except in 1990 when yields rose to 60 hl./ha. Thereafter it is a matter of putting a cool juice into the fermentation casks and allowing as long a fermentation as you can. Then, provided you disturb things as little as possible – you have a fair chance of making fine wine.

There is no doubt as to the quality of the Coche product. The Meursaults are characterised by great richness with a firm backbone of harmonious acidity which ensures them longevity. The wines have flesh but it is taut rather than flabby which gives an athletic charm rather than fragile elegance – Betjeman's Joan Hunter-Dunne rather than Dickens' Dora Spenlow.

Even the humble Aligoté is here ennobled with an uncommon and most attractive veneer of finesse. Coche's only Premier Cru, Les Perrières, is a delight from colour to nose to aftertaste – honey and flowers when young developing into hazelnuts and toast with age. In style it is more redolent of Puligny, next to whose northern border it lies, than of Meursault, where there is more clay in the soil. Some claim to smell the stones from which the vineyard takes its name, but this smacks of pretension. Jean-François also produces 385–450 cases of a magisterial, firm-framed Corton-Charlemagne – one of the best in the appellation.

All these wines are intended to be kept, even in lesser vintages. In late 1990, Coche was heard explaining to a Swiss customer that the 1984s were just beginning to approach their rightful drinking age, and that the 1985 reds might also be started upon.

As with the wines, so with their creator: an understated, refined complexity and dependable firmness, with much beneath the surface for those caring to search it out. Jean-François is not an extravert, but has charm and undeniable quality.

He clearly cares where his wines end up, bemoaning the restaurateurs who pass greedily from one vintage to the next, regardless of their differing maturities, without the slightest pretence at keeping the bottles a year or so before letting their uncomprehending clientèle loose upon them. There are some who make an effort,' says Jean-François with evident exasperation, and one has only to glance round his office shelves at menus from Girardet, L'Auberge de l'Ill, Troisgros, Lameloise and the rest to know the level of quality he's talking about.

The Domaine's clientèle is faithful and fortunately, for the most part, comprehending. One third of each vintage – the same *cuvées* every year – is sold to the négociant houses Louis Latour and Louis Jadot – both justifiably proud of their white wines. The remainder goes to individual customers, approved restaurants and increasingly abroad. Buyers around the world clamour for stocks and those lucky enough to succeed know that they have yardstick bottles on their hands.

When, in the distant future, Jean-François' son Rafael assumes his father's fine mantle, it seems fair to assume that nothing much will have changed.

VINEYARD HOLDINGS

Commune	*Level*	*Lieu-dit/Climat*	*Area*	*Vine Age*	*Status*
Aloxe	GC	Corton-Charlemagne	0.34	1960	F
Meursault	PC	Les Perrières	0.23	1947	P
Meursault	PC	Les Perrières-Dessus	0.29	1960–74	F
Meursault	V	Moulin-Landin	0.43	1972	P
Meursault	V	Chevaliers	0.12	1956	P
Meursault	V	Les Rougeots	0.65	1943/62/74	P
Meursault	V	Les Dressoles	0.44	1930	F
Meursault	V	Les Narvaux	0.38	1965/85	F
Meursault	V	Clos des Ecoles	0.51	1973	F
Meursault	V	Les Vireuils	0.61	1947–1984	F
Meursault	V	Les Luchets	0.32	1930/73	F
Meursault	V	Les Peutes-Vignes	0.19	1938	F
Meursault	V	Les Durtos	0.12	1961	F
Meursault	V	Les Malpoiriers (Red)	0.14	1981	F
Meursault	V	Les Caillerets	0.18	1937/71	F
Meursault	R	(Bourgogne Pinot Noir – 5 difft. parcels)	1.21	1954–72	F
Meursault	R	Les Pacriots (Aligoté)	0.39	1951	F
Meursault	R	(Bourgogne Chardonnay – 4 difft. parcels)	1.23	1972–75	F
Volnay	PC	Le Clos des Chênes	0.16	1960	F
Volnay	PC	Les Taillepieds	0.21	1989	F
Auxey	V	Les Fosses (Red)	0.27	1982	F
Auxey	V	Les Boutonnières (White)	0.23	1928	F
Monthélie	V	Les Crays	0.28	1987	F
		Total	**8.93 Ha.**		

N.B. The vineyards marked F. (=fermage) are *en fermage* to Jean-François Coche from his father.

Domaine des Comtes Lafon

MEURSAULT

The Domaine des Comtes Lafon is, without doubt, the finest estate in Meursault. It has the advantage over most of its competitors of a litany of land-holdings which it warms the heart to read: 12.5 ha. of superbly sited vineyards including no fewer than 4 Meursault Premiers Crus, over 3 ha. of Meursault Villages, some of the most favourably located plots of Volnay and Volnay Santenots, 1 ha. of Monthélie Premier Cru and 0.33 ha. of Le Montrachet. Not only these vineyards, but a talented wine-maker whose consummate skill, year after year, extracts from them something exceptional.

Dominic Lafon is the latest in line of an interesting family. His great-grandfather, Comte Jules Lafon – who incidentally founded the annual Paulée at Meursault, the final feast on the Monday after the Hospices de Beaune sale – was an unusual man. By profession a lawyer, he amassed a great fortune marrying on the way a Mlle. Boch from Meursault who probably had vineyards and certainly had no money. Jules was a bon viveur who enjoyed eating and drinking well, and a collector of everything from fine paintings to fine china. He circumnavigated the globe twice before finally dying in 1940.

In the meantime, being a man of rare quality only interested in the best parts of the best vineyards, he had sold off the inferior parts of his wife's vineyards to buy something better. Thus today the Domaine has vines among the choicest parts of Meursault Perrières – generally regarded as the best of the Premiers Crus – Meursault Charmes and a large chunk of the kernel of Volnay Santenots, the Santenots du Milieu – a vineyard referred to in 1855 by Lavalle as a 'Tête de Cuvée'. In 1935 Jules acquired 0.33 ha. of Le Montrachet in the Chassagne section, between the holdings of Baron Thenard and the Domaine de la Romanée-Conti. The fine house in which Dominic's parents still live, with the magnificent 2.10 ha. Clos de la Barre for a garden, was in all likelihood part of the Boch patrimoine.

Jules had two sons – Pierre and Henri. Pierre, who died in 1944, never had charge of the estate, which was taken in hand by Dominic's great-uncle Henri in the early 1940s. Unfortunately, Henri had an aversion to work, and soon sold much of his inheritance – priceless paintings, furniture, china, land, farms and houses all went to subsidise his extravagant lifestyle. Fortunately the Domaine remained intact, though Henri preferred to sell the grapes because he could not be bothered to vinify them.

In 1954 matters came to a head when uncle Henri and Jules' wife – an indomitable old lady – decided to sell the estate. However, Dominic's father, René, intervened to stop the sale, undertaking to manage the estate despite being put under an injunction neither to make capital expenditure nor to borrow against the assets. Clad in this extraordinary pecuniary strait-jacket, he set about putting the Domaine back into good order. At that time much of the land was let out to 2 families of viticulteurs – the Bouleys of Volnay and the Moreys of Meursault – so it was possible to oversee the upkeep of the vineyards without having day-to-day care of them. In addition René, an engineer by profession, was living in Paris and unable to spend much time in Meursault, although he somehow managed to vinify his own wines, with the help of an employee. Gradually, however, he restored the vineyards to proper condition.

In 1967 René moved back from Paris to live in the family home with his wife and 4 children, Dominic – then aged 9, his younger brother Bruno, aged 8, Jean-François and Anne – and began to take full charge of vinifying the grapes which came to the Domaine under the 50% share-cropping agreement.

In 1978 Dominic went to the Lycée Viticole in Beaune to study viticulture and oenology and a year later started to be involved in the estate, helping out during the vintage. After graduating he went to work for the courtier Becky Wasserman in nearby Bouilland, saving his holidays so to be at the Domaine during the harvest. During the early 1980s, he became more involved with decision-making, being partly responsible for the 1981 and 1982 vintages and finally taking full responsibility for the 1984s. The same year his brother, Bruno, arrived to help with matters financial and administrative, and remained until after the 1989 harvest. He now works with the Beaune négociants, Drouhin.

Meanwhile the Domaine had become a Société Civile, the shareholders being René and Jacques Lafon and Marie-Thérèse d'Armaille: Dominic's father, uncle and aunt.

In April 1988 Dominic married Anne Roumier, sister of Christophe of Domaine Roumier in Chambolle-Musigny (he had to look at his engraved wedding band to remember the year and date – such is the hierarchy of importance to a dedicated vigneron) and now has a daughter Lea. His parents still live in the fine house next to the *cuverie* and *chais* in the Rue de la Barre, whilst he and Anne live 'two minutes away' in the village.

Dominic has worked indefatigably to create the worldwide reputation for excellence that the Domaine presently enjoys. Much of what he learnt at viticultural college was useful, although he subsequently found out that theory and practice do not always coincide. Nonetheless, he learned to recognise what was valuable and discard what was likely to be of little use, and that has stood him in firm stead thereafter.

This Domaine not only produces exemplary wines but, with Dominic at the helm, is a model of how such an estate should be run. The overriding impression here – and indeed from most of the top-class producers in Burgundy – is that there are no formulae. Each decision is taken on its merits against a background of experience of possibilities and consequences. One also gets a strong sense of flexibility – wine-making not ossified in mindless tradition but undertaken with at least one eye on ideas to improve quality.

In technical matters, Dominic Lafon is immensely able. He discusses wine-making techniques and innovations with friends of his own generation up and down the Côte d'Or, but given a problem he will make a dozen telephone calls for advice on how to solve it – a refreshing readiness to admit difficulties which is less evident among the older generation. Equally, he is always willing to help out friends with problems – a fining which has not worked, stuck fermentations, how to fine, whether to filter – all important decisions needing careful consideration.

His own vineyards are expertly tended, with a distinctly organic orientation. Traditional products – chemical sprays, herbicides for two-thirds of vines etc. – are still used, but the aim is to shift as much towards organic materials as possible. Dominic has visited the producer of his organic fertiliser – a fermented amalgam of racehorse straw, high in carbon, sheeps' skin and hair, wood dust etc. – to see how it is made, and now uses only this. He is considering alternatives to chemical sprays, which he continues to use, though in the minimum doses possible, meticulously directed at the parts of the vine where they are most needed.

Dominic is very aware of rot, and believes that it is important to try and eradicate this early, instead of waiting until the harvest to excise affected grapes. He believes that much of the incidence of rot is attributable to the grape-worm, which punctures the skins and opens the berry to *botrytis* infection. Among several interesting experiments he has on hand is the introduction of specially bred flies known to feed on grape-worms. They have no detrimental effect themselves but have to be introduced on an annual basis, in egg form.

The thrust of Dominic's viticulture is firmly aimed at maintaining healthy vines to an old age and with reducing yields. The latter is achieved by short pruning, low levels of fertilisation and planting carefully selected clones onto rootstocks which themselves have low vigour (predominantly 161/49). Training is *Guyot simple* with a small amount of *cordon de Royat* for older vines.

When replanting, the preference is to replace individual vines in vineyards which basically are in healthy shape; otherwise, where an entire parcel has to be grubbed up – as in the Goutte d'Or where Dominic found old vines badly degenerated by *court noué* when he took it back from the farmer who had share-cropped it – replanting is made with 4 or 5 different selected clones. Chardonnay clones show less quality variation in taste than Pinot Noir, so there is less need for a wide variety.

Choosing plant material in Pinot Noir is a complex process, since there are numerous available strains. The two main sub-species are the Pinot Fin (also called Pinot Tordu) used by all good growers, and the Pinot Droit, growing taller and straighter, which one often sees planted in the 'arrières Côtes'. Although Droit is much easier to work with, can be trained high and mechanically harvested, its quality is greatly inferior to its twisted brother.

Dominic uses two sources of Pinot Noir – firstly selected clones 113/115/667 and 777 – the newest and finest low-cropping clones available – and secondly, a *sélection massale* from a plot of 65-year-old vines in his Volnay Champans vineyard. He has just started a further trial with a few vines from friends he respects – Michel Lafarge in Volnay, Patrick Bize in Savigny, Christophe Roumier in Chambolle-Musigny and Étienne Grivot in Vosne-Romanée – to see how they work in his soil.

Lafon generally harvests later than his neighbours. The order of picking each parcel is determined by ripeness and seems to change every year. Unlike other growers in the village, he is not especially concerned with acidity levels – 'a green apple is not as good as a ripe apple' – but with maximising sugar. He claims that he rarely has problems with acidity because his viticultural regime keeps vigour low and restricts yields. Only those with larger yields have acid deficiencies, especially in riper years. The pH level, which he regards as the most useful measure of acidity, settles at around 3.5 for his reds and 3.35 for the whites – in the finished wines. As far as yields go, 45-50 hl./ha. is regarded as an acceptable maximum for Meursault Village wine, 40 hl./ha. for Premier Cru whites and 35 hl./ha. for reds.

In 1990 he decided to leave a plot of Meursault Village en la Barre, just below the Clos de la Barre, to harvest late. About 3 weeks after the general harvest he induced some friends with the promise of a good lunch and some interesting bottles to help him pick. They worked well during the morning, but after lunch experienced some difficulty focusing. Notwithstanding, they managed to totter around harvesting – 'quite well', says Dominic – and the Domaine's first late harvest Meursault is now safely in bottle.

On arrival at the cuverie, the hand-picked grapes are put into a pneumatic Bucher press (acquired in 1983) and pressed slowly and gently for 2–2.5 hours. The maximum pressure is 2 bars, but Dominic programmes the press cycle so that the minimum time is spent at this pressure to avoid extracting harsh tannins from stalks and pips.

The juice is then given a sanitising dose of SO_2 at the lower end of the normal level – a maximum of 5 g. per ha. for whites and 7 g. per ha. for reds. Excision of rotten fruit in the vineyards obviates the need for excessive sulphur. The juice is allowed to settle to eliminate the gross lees. The length of *débourbage* depends on the vintage; in clean years such as 1985, 1988, 1989 and 1990, 12 hours is allowed; in less healthy years, longer.

The *must* is then cooled to 12–14°C before being put into barrels for fermentation. The Premier and Grand Crus go into 100% new oak – a mixture of Vosges and Allier from the Damy, Raymond and François Frères tonnelleries – where they remain for 6 months; the Village Meursaults are put into second-year wood from the previous vintage.

After their *malolactic fermentations,* the Premier and Grand Crus are racked into older wood and into a cooler cellar, the racked Village wines remain in their casks. Once a week each cask is *batonné,* to give a better extract and richness; this process also helps the *malolactic fermentation* and aids final clarification of the wine. *Batonnage* normally ceases during February or March following the vintage, when tasting indicates that the flavours are correct

Six or 7 months after harvest, the first racking occurs. At this stage the wines are assembled and a *cuvée* made up in tanks from the various lots of each wine. The fine lees are retained and the wines then passed by gravity into casks in a yet cooler cellar. There they remain until the following spring when they are racked clear of their lees.

Fining is a matter of much concern to Dominic Lafon. Realising that different fining agents can have noticeably different impacts on aroma and flavour, he is very careful to find the most suitable agent. In addition, since he has found that unfiltered wines taste better than filtered, special care is needed in fining to obviate the need for subsequent filtration. The system is simple: samples of all the wines are taken and sent to a speciaiist laboratory where they are analysed for proteins and other matter in suspension and subjected to sample micro-fining. Three or 4 days later Dominic and the oenologist assess the results for clarity and taste. Provided the wine is reasonably clear, taste quality takes preference over clarity. With these results, Dominic is able to judge which wines require which finings. The options are usually: 1. Casein and bentonite – casein adjusts undue yellowing in the colour and rounds out the wine, especially if it contains harsh wood tannins, and bentonite aids ithe precipitation of suspended proteins. 2. Isinglass and bentonite – isinglass is a fish fining which is neutral in taste impact and just clarifies the wine. 3. Bentonite alone – for proteins. 4. Isinglass alone – a polishing fining. Thus after 20–24 months of cask age, the Lafon Meursaults and Montrachet are finally bottled.

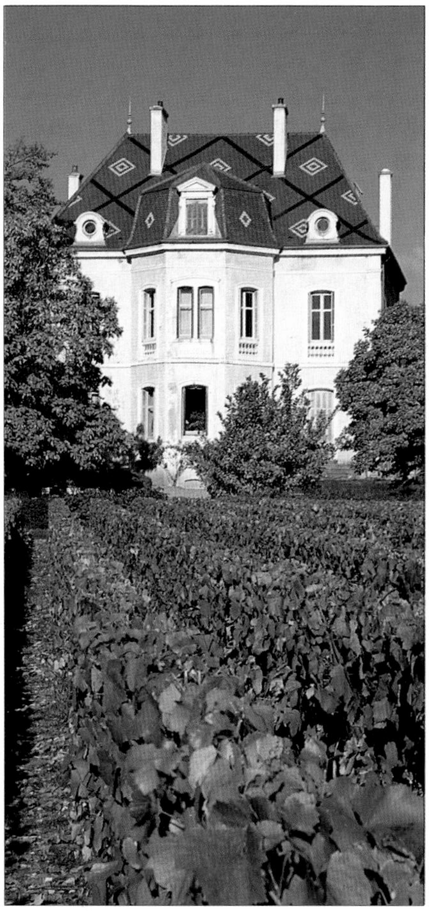

The Domaine's residence seen from its garden – the Clos de la Barre

Dominic's red wines are also models of their kind, therefore worth considering more closely. The aim is to harvest as ripe as possible to avoid the need for additional stalk tannin. After 90–100% destemming and a light crushing, in a machine designed to simultaneously eliminate dry rot, the pulp is cooled to 16° C in tanks and then left to ferment with natural yeasts. Dominic denies that this is a deliberate pre-fermentive maceration but considers the process as a development of the traditional belief that cooler grapes make better wine. Cooling the pulp delays fermentation by 3–4 days, since yeasts function very slowly at this lower temperature, giving time for better extraction of fruit components. The final aim is to ferment the red wines at anywhere between 16° C and 30–32° C, and a heat exchanger is on hand to lower temperatures a second time should they rise too far.

The theory of fermentation is complex, but it is known that an important element of the coloured pigments, the anthocyanins, are soluble in water, so are extracted effectively by a maceration of skins and juice before fermentation (grape juice is about 95% water and contains no alcohol at this stage) . However, these anthocyanins – essential to the continued colour development of a red wine – are chemically unstable. Fortunately they are made stable when in the presence of tannins; but tannins are only extracted in sufficient concentration by alcohol. Dominic considers that the higher temperatures of fermentation further aid extraction of tannins and colour pigments. Artificially heating the pulp before fermentation was an option to maximise colour extraction, but this did not fix or stabilise the colour thus extracted – they rapidly degenerated and browned.

Finally, Dominic concluded that his regime of cooling the red pulp and allowing it to rise gradually to fermentation temperature both aided the extraction of water-soluble colours and, by slowing down the onset of fermentation, extracted better fruit flavours and finer, less harsh tannins which worked well in stabilising the inherently unstable anthocyanins.

Once the free-run wine is run off, the remaining pulp is pressed for 45 minutes at a gentle 1.5 bars to extract a relatively supple press-wine which is then added to it before removal to tanks for 24 hours to sediment out the unwanted 'gross' lees. The wine is transferred into casks, 33% of which are new oak, for 20–24 months. They are racked once in the following spring after *malolactic fermentation* – less fine lees being retained than for the white wines – and again after fining with egg-whites a month or two before bottling.

Yields at the Domaine are small – on average 35 hl./ha. for the white wines – a reflection of deliberately severe pruning and the high proportion of old vines. The average production is increasing because land formerly share-cropped by others is now coming back into the Domaine's control. About 30,000 bottles were produced in 1988 and 45,000 in 1989. The anticipated maximum is nearer 60,000 bottles per year.

The Domaine seems to have cellars everywhere: two under the house, one under the cuverie and a new cellar, for palletised bottle storage, recently excavated to connect them all together. Interestingly, the digging revealed a splendid vertical 6 m. soil profile of the Clos de la Barre, which abuts the south-eastern side of the house. Beneath barely 1 m. of rocky soil lies a bed of solid calcareous rock. Through this tightly knit and seemingly impenetrable foundation, thick healthy vine roots were clearly visible. It is the natural ability of this rugged plant to penetrate such terrain that gives the produce of its fruit such absorbing yet inimitable qualities.

There is no particular style which Dominic aims to achieve. However the wines invariably have remarkable concentration and plump succulence which makes them most attractive at first, with length and well-nigh impeccable balance. Long fermentation and lees contact give a softness and complexity to even the Meursault Village wine and to the Clos de la Barre which make them quite seductive and approachable from an early age. The Meursault Desirée (an individual vineyard site, but not a Premier Cru) is characterised by marked aromas of exotic fruits – mangoes and pineapples – and dried apricots. Dominic refers to this as his 'Viognier', and proudly presented it as such to Marcel Guigal who makes one of the finest Condrieus from that unusual grape.

The Charmes is a rung up the quality ladder, with a much tighter structure and generally greater power than the Desirée. The second Premier Cru, Genevrières, is very different – less obvious power and far greater elegance. It tends to be rather closed up for the first couple of years and shows less attractively than the Charmes to start with. The Perrières is acknowledged as the finest of the Premiers Crus and would probably be upgraded to a Grand Cru if the authorities could manage to do so without too much contention and fuss. The wine, at least in the Lafon interpretation of it, seems to combine the structure and thoroughbred power of the Charmes with the elegance and finesse of the Genevrières. It has more style and complexity than either, also more concentration and length.

These are of course generalisations; the style of each wine varies from vintage to vintage and changes with age. Lafon wines are made to be kept and indeed, repay cellaring and patience. The Le Montrachet is without doubt the finest wine in the Lafon stable. According to Dominic, it is never big or powerful but a wine of finesse, elegance and above all astonishing length. If you are looking for power, he advises, go for a Bâtard-Montrachet, not for Le Montrachet The Domaine's 1989 Montrachet, still in cask, was by no means a blockbuster, rather a mouthful of style and elegance supported by a line of firm, harmonious addity. However, it was set apart from the Meursaults of that excellent vintage by an extraordinary concentration and persistence combined with a multi-dimensional finish which remained on the palate long after the wine itself had left.

When Dominic took over, many in the commune predicted that he would not make a go of it and that the Domaine would be sold within a few years. Later, when he began to reclaim land from *métayeurs* whose contracts had expired, he was faced with calumny and open abuse. It is a pleasure to see his confidence and single-mindedness succeeding against what must have appeared insuperable odds, and also encouraging to find a supremely talented wine-maker showing his less able peers what can be done with meticulous care and considerable dedication.

VINEYARD HOLDINGS

Commune	*Level*	*Lieu dit/Climat*	*Area*	*Vine Age*	*Status*
Chassagne	GC	Montrachet	0.33	25/45	P
Meursault	PC	Les Charmes	1.75	35/65	P
Meursault	PC	Les Perrières	0.75	35	P
Meursault	PC	Les Genevrières	0.55	40	P
Meursault	PC	Goutte D'Or	0.33	1990	P
Meursault	V	Clos de la Barre	2.10	30	P
Meursault	V	En la Barre	0.60	35	P
Meursault	V	Desirée	0.50	20	P
Meursault	PC	**Volnay Santenots Du Milieu	3.75	28/35	P
Volnay	PC	**Clos des Chênes	0.33	15	P
Volnay	PC	Champans	0.50	2/3:65 1/3:3	P
Monthélie	PC	**Les Duresses	1.00	4/15	P
		Total	**12.49 ha.**		

** Part, or all, of these vineyards are leased *en métayage* and will revert to the Domaine in 1993.

Domaine Patrick Javillier

MEURSAULT

Patrick Javillier has built up this small, high-quality Domaine since returning from military service in 1974 armed with a Diplome Nationale d'Oenologie from Dijon. In 1982 his father Raymond gave him 4 ha., 3 *en fermage* and 1 *en métayage*, to which he added parcels of Meursault Les Tillets, Puligny, Pommard and Bourgogne Blanc. Marriage to a charming parcel of Savigny Blanc brought the estate to its present 8.5 ha. He is an amalgam of conscientious detail and refreshing willingness to experiment – at heart, a small boy with a new chemistry set.

His viticultural regime is organically oriented, though he avoids excessive use of copper-based solutions which can cause a copper 'casse' in the wine – manifesting itself as a brown stain in the bottle but with little impact on the flavour – and too much organic material which increases the risk of rot at harvest. Grass is checked by an organic treatment or a light herbicide.

Patrick stresses the effect of pruning on the strain of vine used. Normally both Chardonnay and Pinot Noir vines are pruned to a short *Guyot simple*; but a patch of Pinot in the Pacriots vineyard in Meursault, thus pruned, mysteriously ceased yielding. The same vines pruned less severely responded with a healthy 50–55 hl./ha. and *must* weights of 13.5 potential alcohol. Patrick attributes this to the strain of vine – Pinot fin de Santenay – which is found widely in Santenay, Volnay and Pommard.

Much thought is given to the choice of plant material. Rootstocks are normally 161–49 on slopes and 3309 at the base of hillsides because they give a better acidity in these richer soils. Experimental vinifications of grapes from different roots found S04 to give more dilute wine with lower acidity, so it is no longer used in the Javillier vineyards.

Efforts are made to maintain a high average vine age; against conventional wisdom, Patrick doubts whether old vines by themselves can produce a really well-structured white wine. They may add to the concentration but it is far from certain that they give better structure or complexity than younger vines. The ideal is to have both.

Conscientious and careful as he is, Patrick clearly enjoys experimenting when he believes something profitable can be learned. For example, he is presently trying different levels of new wood, with a view to reducing the proportion for his Meursaults from 25–30% to about 15–20%. He has also tried low temperature fermentation, but dislikes the results: 'It gives neutral wines – no perfume' – and has mixed feelings over long fermentations: 'they produce more glycerol but are not always beneficial.' Essays with fish finings have not been felicitous – they tend to give yellower wines lacking freshness.

The origin of his new oak has been the subject of investigation: until recently equal proportions of Vosges, Allier and Tronçais were used. Tasting the wines, it was felt that while the Vosges and Tronçais gave better structure and more immediate impact on flavour, the Allier imparted greater finesse and subtlety, though these qualities took a year or two to emerge.

The vinification itself might be called modified classical. A gentle nudge on the next-lowest pressure of which the Javillier Vaslin press is capable is followed by immediate sulphuring to prevent premature oxidation, always a greater risk with white juice than with red. Each lot is then divided: part is fermented in tanks at a relatively cool 20–22° C, and part ferments in cask at 26–28° C. When the density of the tank *must* reaches 1,008, it is also transferred to cask to complete fermentation.

A hint of idiosyncrasy comes in when he explains why he is so cautious about *batonnage* of his young wines. Most growers in Meursault enthuse over the practice, which involves introducing a stainless-steel instrument into the cask (or an old stick if you are completely traditional) and giving the lees at the bottom a good stir. The frequency of this operation varies, according to taste, from once a month to 3 times a day, and lasts from a week or so to 6 months or more. In theory, this distributes the lees through the wine ensuring an even uptake of their undisputed nourishment. Patrick disagrees, considering that it degasifies the wine – which has natural $C0_2$ dissolved in solution – robbing it of freshness and perfume. He therefore limits *batonnage* to once or twice a week, and then only up to the onset of *malo*.

The wines are fined with a very light dose of casein-bentonite, stronger in years with touches of rot. Patrick believes that fining refines a wine and is essential to white wine vinification. Equally, a light filtration is beneficial since it removes gross particles not entrained by the fining. However, efforts are being made to reduce filtration to a minimum.

The Javillier range starts with Bourgogne Blanc. Even here, there is no let-up on experiment: a couple of 1989s, one filtered, the other not, showed plenty of attractive, ripe fruit and style.

Tasting a range of 1990 Bourgogne Blancs demonstrated that, even at this basic regional appellation level, there is individuality in each *climat* if you take the care to extract it. Patrick's Bourgogne Blancs are among the best to be had. However, it is his Meursaults which have made his reputation. Though without Premier Cru land, he is achieving wonders with his individual Village *climats* from which Les Tillets, Clos du Cromin and Les Narvaux stand out. Relatively lean and firm in structure when young, these have plenty of solid fruit underneath waiting to show itself when enough time has passed to integrate the new wood, as older vintages eloquently witness. Blind tastings have confirmed Patrick Javillier's Meursaults as some of the finest in the appellation.

He and his delightful wife Katherine have worked hard to build up their Domaine and deserve their success. Anyone in search of genuine quality would do well to seek out Patrick Javillier – if not at his newly-opened shop, you will probably find him in the tasting-room of his splendid new mansion on top of the hill. Let's hope that no one is trampled in the rush!

VINEYARD HOLDINGS

Commune	*Level*	*Lieu-dit/Climat*	*Area*	*Vine Age*	*Status*
Meursault	V	Les Tillets	1.50	25	P/F
Meursault	V	Clos du Cromin	1.00	50	M
Meursault	V	Les Clous	0.38	10 & 50	P
Meursault	V	Les Casses-Têtes	0.15	15	P
Meursault	V	Les Narvaux	0.24	35	P
Puligny	V	Les Levrons	0.18	35	P
Pommard	V	En Boeuf	0.19	35	P
Savigny	V	Les Grands Liards (R)	1.00	55	F
Savigny	V	Le Mont-Chenevoy (W)	0.65	1991	P
Meursault	R	(Bourgogne Rouge)	0.39	30	P
Meursault	R	(Bourgogne Blanc)	2.75	1 & 20	P/F
		Total	**8.43 ha.**		

Domaine François Jobard

MEURSAULT

François Jobard is a particularly difficult man to pin down. He works his 4.91 ha. of vines virtually single handed with the help of one occasional labourer, his wife and a very new straddle tractor and never seems to be at home. This machine, which arrived in his courtyard during the summer of 1990, was forced upon him because, although his old open tractor was still in good working order, he could no longer stand the ravages on his face and eyes of the chemicals which he had to spray on his vines. He was, justifiably, not prepared to keep the vines in good health at the expense of his own. Now, with a bright sky-blue-covered cab – it even has air-conditioning – he is clearly a much happier viticulteur.

The estate about which he drives this expensive model of modern farming hardware is itself a model of a high quality small Domaine. The land holdings, although entirely in Meursault, comprise a good, varied spread of some dozen different *climats* divided between 5 Premiers Crus, Meursault Village, Aligoté and some Bourgogne Blanc and Rouge. However, with so little help, it is hardly surprising that François' neighbours regard him as a workaholic.

He is a man of thoughtful, rather shy, demeanour. Talking to him in the dining room of his spacious house just below the Clos de la Barre, communication was at first rather one-sided. However, avowing a reasonable acquaintance with his wines as a London wine merchant resulted in a noticeable thaw in the temperature, monosyllabic responses giving way to virtually complete sentences. Once he realised that the sacrifice of 2 hours of his precious time was to result in something other than just another magazine article, conversation positively buzzed along.

François' shyness hides a great depth of understanding of wines and the intricacies of their creation. Brought up in the house in which he now lives, surrounded by wine and its trappings, he is imbued with a devotion to what he has. A man whose instincts are for traditional practices, he looks with some suspicion on those of his colleagues, both young and old, who 'rush off to their oenologist every five minutes'. It is this same tradition which dictates that technology should be kept firmly in its place – at the service of the vigneron; technologists may have designed and built his new tractor, but on no account are they allowed to drive it.

The land he farms is, with the exception of 2 small plots, all his own. His great-grandfather, or great-great-grandfather – he can't remember which – started the whole enterprise going in the 1860s and on the way constructed the house he now (with convenient modifications) lives in. His wife looks after him and their 3 children – 2 girls, 20 and 16, and a boy aged 13. The eldest girl is studying pharmacy and does not, at present, seem particularly interested in the vineyards; perhaps now her father's swollen eyes and blistered face have abated, her perception of the vigneron may become more favourable, but that remains to be seen.

François' style of wine is individual. His aim is to do as much as possible naturally, without interfering. 'Let nature do the work; co-operate with nature, don't try to fight it,' is his guiding principle. In practice this amounts to as near an organic regime as he can get; although it is still necessary to use standard chemical treatments, these are stopped at the beginning of August to ensure that no trace of product finds its way into the wines.

Originally, François would replace dead vines by selecting particularly healthy and sturdy vine stocks in the vineyards and taking cuttings from them. These would then be

François and his colourful new tractor

grafted by hand on to American rootstock and planted out the following spring. Since 1975 the practice has been to buy virus-indexed clones instead – less risk and presumably less labour. Nowadays, replanting is parcel by parcel, letting the soil rest for 3–4 years in between. Wherever possible, soil adjustments are made organically, with a dose of natural, powdered manure super-added for good measure.

Young Jobard vines are pruned very severely, only half a *baguette,* until their fourth flowering. 'If,' says François, 'the charge on the young vine is excessive in relation to its strength, it gives nothing interesting.' Pruned thus, the fruit is of excellent, usable quality. Of the mature vines about half are trained in the classic *Guyot simple* and half in the less seen *cordon de Royat* which is better suited to more feeble, less productive vines. Which vines are trained *Guyot* and which *cordon is* a matter for instinctive judgement, the general aim being to restrict yields and maximise fruit quality.

When to harvest is also a matter of instinct François discounts the value of *prélèvements* 'These,' he tells you, 'give the barest of indications of maturity, which are usually wrong,' and, in any case, maturity levels can alter dramatically in 48 hours, so they have little value. His own method is to walk through his vineyards to see when the grapes are ready. This is a time when he is delighted to subjugate technology to instinct.

Although he vinifies traditionally, there are a couple of interesting nuances of technique which illuminate the style of wine François produces: a long, slow pressing – some 3 hours in a Willmes press; no *débourbage* – he is against it – rather, a vigorous *batonnage* before the wine is transferred to a mixture of casks and larger *foudres* for fermentation, to ensure an even distribution of lees.

The rest is deliberately traditional: no cultured yeasts; no control of fermentation temperature – the key is to press the grapes immediately they are received, which avoids the need for temperature-control afterwards. *Chaptalisation is* made as late as possible to prolong fermentation and to keep down the ambient temperature in the fermenting casks.

A Jobard wine spends a long time in the cellar before being allowed out in a bottle dignified with a Jobard label on it. François' policy is to keep wines on their original lees for some 12–18 months, when they are given a first racking and unified. In his experience, any *goût de lie* apparently disappears at racking and, in any case, 'wines without lees won't keep well.'

They are then returned to cask for a further period of maturation of up to 3 months, after which they are fined with casein and a little bentonite (casein to clear up any colour defects and bentonite to

Bottles maturing undisturbed in the cool Jobard cellars

precipitate out any suspended proteins). They are allowed to settle for a further 1–2 months before being given a final polishing filtration and bottled on the small, rather ancient Jobard bottling line.

The end of this rather absorbing mixture of tradition and instinct is a range of impressive wines. The House style tends if anything to a rather refined rusticity and a certain dryness – presumably from the length of time the wines spend in cask. New wood is deliberately underplayed, with no more than 15–20% new Vosges oak, which François finds more discreet and less violent in its impact on the wines.

Set against this slightly austere side of Jobard's wines, there is an amplitude on the palate, and with age a superb development of aromas – particularly on the Genevrières and Charmes – to which long fermentation and extended lees contact no doubt contribute. The style is distinctly old-fashioned Meursault, muted with considerable finesse – but none the worse for that.

The 1989s and 1990s show great promise – the former being particularly opulent and fleshy with Premiers Crus which will be delicious in the mid-1990s.

Having offered a remarkable, honeyed, decadently over-ripe 1983 Genevrières, François disappeared into a small mycelium-wreathed bin in a corner of the cellar and carefully extracted a black candy-floss-covered bottle. The wine emerged a bright green-tinged gold with an immediate and attractively rich honeyed nose, redolent more of lime-blossom and spices than fruit or flowers. Guessing the vintage was a challenge; as wines develop, they tend to lose their more obvious, youthful, vintage markers and to present themselves with tertiary aromas of mushrooms, undergrowth and spices. The wine turned out to be a 1979 Charmes, which was too easily mistaken for a 1978. We were all told how wonderful were the 1978s, and how less fine by comparison were the 1979s – a large, dilute crop. However, the passage of time has proved these judgements premature. Jobard was proud of his 1979 Charmes, with good reason.

The Domaine's 2,000 or so cases are avidly snapped up by its restaurant and private clientèle. François could so easily increase his yields and give himself more to sell, but that would never be his way. This is one of the best Domaines in Meursault, run by a man of fine quality who inspires confidence.

VINEYARD HOLDINGS

Commune	*Level*	*Lieu dit/Climat*	*Area*	*Vine Age*	*Status*
Meursault	PC	Les Charmes (Dessus)	0.16	27	P
Meursault	PC	Les Genevrières	0.54	16	P
Meursault	PC	Les Poruzots (Dessus)	0.77	20	P
Meursault	PC	La Pièce sous le Bois	0.21	33	P
Meursault	V	En la Barre/Corbin	1.18	28	P
Meursault	V	En la Barre	0.13	25	F
Meursault	V	Les Tillets	0.74	40	M
Blagny	PC	La Pièce sous le Bois	0.29	33	P
Meursault	R	(Bourgogne Blanc)	0.32	20	P
Meursault	R	(Bourgogne Aligoté)	0.19	4	P
Meursault	R	(Bourgogne Rouge)	0.38	20	P
		Total	**4.91 ha.**		

Domaine Joseph et Pierre Matrot

MEURSAULT

Thierry Matrot always wanted to be a vigneron. Having absorbed all his father's knowledge, he went first to the Lycée in Beaune to study oenology and then to its sister establishment in Mâcon to learn the commercial aspects of running an estate. In 1976 at the age of 21 he returned to the family Domaine in Meursault, where he is now in full charge.

His philosophy is simple: 'wine is made in the vineyards – and far less than people think, in the cellar.' However talented an oenologist, with poor raw material he's lost before he's even started. With 18 ha. of quality vineyards Thierry has ample scope for putting his theory into practice.

As well as replanting with a selection of virus-free clones, Thierry is careful to maintain a high average vine age by individual replacement of defunct vines and scrupulous soil disinfection. The ideal is a maximum of 20% young vines in any one parcel. This policy is helped by minimising the use of strong toxic sprays which affect the vines and impoverish vineyard micro-flora.

Thierry speaks with some passion on pruning and yields. Some of his colleagues believe yields of 50-60 hl./ha. are compatible with top quality wine; he does not. Whilst in his view ideal yields are 35 hl./ha. for Pinot Noir and 45 hl./ha. for Chardonnay, his own 10 year averages are 30 hl./ha. for Pinot, 40.5 hl./ha. for Village Meursault and 38.5 hl./ha. for Premier Cru. These are achieved by strict pruning – 4 eyes for Pinot and 5 for Chardonnay, with a severe *ébourgonnage* as early as possible after bud-burst each spring.

According to Thierry, the relationship between yield and quality is not the simple inverse correlation that many would have us believe. His own theory is that, up to a certain yield, quantity does not affect quality. However, beyond this level there is a distinct caesura and quality plummets. Although the precise rupture point depends on factors such as vintage, vineyard, etc., in his view the critical level for Chardonnay at about 50 hl./ha. is higher than that for Pinot Noir.

Thierry harvests at optimum ripeness, which for him means about 13.2° potential alcohol. He dislikes the taste of over-ripeness, especially in Chardonnay, preferring to maximise maturity without risking the *botrytised* richness which can result from too late a harvest.

After any rot has been excised – in the vineyard for Pinot, by a destemmer for the Chardonnay – the harvest is given a dose of SO_2 or not, depending upon the health of the bunches. The grapes are then pneumatically pressed for 40 minutes at low pressure and for the same duration at higher pressure for about 90 minutes in total. A period of settling follows to remove unwanted gross lees before the wine is cooled to 15–16° C and transferred to casks for fermentation.

The Aligoté is treated differently, being given a dose of bentonite to eliminate the gross lees and one of the two usual rackings. This accelerates its progress into bottle so it is ready for sale earlier, and is gentler than racking for the Aligoté's fragile juice.

Apart from eliminating a deleterious pumping, cooling in bulk ensures that white fermentations do not rise much above 20° C. Thierry is disbelieving of vignerons who claim to ferment at a specific temperature – the magic number is usually the ambient temperature of their cellars, so their policy reflects nothing more than necessity.

The aim is to start the fermentation as quickly and to keep it active for as long as possible; the first to avoid oxidation and the second to maximise extract and flavour. Cultured yeasts are generally used to get the pot boiling both because speed is essential and also because anti-rot products used in the vineyards have destroyed much of the micro-flora, including the natural yeasts essential to fermentation.

Thierry unconventionally refuses to use new wood. All his wines are vinified and matured in second year or older oak. New casks were formerly broken in by a friend for the first year; now they fill them with Bourgogne Chardonnay, which is then sold to a négociant. Whilst oak flavours are strenuously avoided, Thierry is anxious to retain control of the casks.

His idiosyncrasies extend to not believing in *batonnage,* considering this 'stirs up good and bad lees alike', giving too much power to the wines and making them heavy and lacking in finesse. 'In any case,' he argues, 'the carbonic gas in the wines distributes the lees quite well' without his help. However, he expressly seeks a long period of lees contact and therefore only racks once – a month or so before bottling between August and the beginning of September – in any event before the next vintage arrives.

Although broadly traditional, Matrot's vinification is, if not revolutionary, then certainly iconoclastic. Tasting together in the quiet, cool cellar beneath the house gives him the chance to explain what he is trying to achieve in a fine bottle of Meursault. His aim is to maximise the fruit in the wine, to allow the *terroir* to express itself through the grape and to retain as much elegance as possible.

The wines themselves have excellent balance – and although some may appear at first to lack acidity, it is there, masked by a rich overlay of ripe (but not over-ripe) fruit. The Meursaults are fine, though deliberately restrained – as if being brought up intellectuals rather than chorus-girls. There is no obvious House-style, but a distinct touch of understated class and considerable potential for ageing.

Although Thierry is no great amateur of very old white wines, he reported that a 1947 Matrot Meursault tasted recently was in excellent health – attractive and vigorous. His own wines are definitely not designed to be drunk young: it would be culpable infanticide to tackle the 1988 Meursault Premiers Crus, for example, before their fifth birthday, though you might be forgiven for going at a bottle of the excellent, ripe and succulent Premier Cru red Blagny, 'La Pièce sous le Bois', while you were waiting.

VINEYARD HOLDINGS

Commune	*Level*	*Lieu-dit/Climat*	*Area*	*Vine Age*	*Status*
Meursault	PC	Les Charmes	1.12	30	P
Meursault	PC	Les Perrières	0.53	30/50	P
Meursault	PC	Blagny	1.80	30	P
Meursault	V	(Several climats)	4.70	30	P
Meursault	PC	Volnay-Santenots	1.40	30	P
Blagny	PC	La Pièce sous le Bois	2.35	30	P
Puligny	PC	Les Chalumaux	1.32	30	P
Puligny	PC	Les Combettes	0.31	30	P
Auxey	V	—	0.57	30	P
—	R	(Bourgogne Chardonnay)	2.00	30	P
—	R	(Bourgogne Aligoté)	1.75	30	P
		Total	**17.85 ha.**		

Domaine Michelot-Buisson

MEURSAULT

Bernard Michelot, now well into his sixties, presides over one of the largest estates in Meursault – 22 ha. of well-sited vineyard land – with amiable geniality. This, as many Burgundian Domaines, originated at the end of the last century when the devastation wreaked by *phylloxera* and *oïdium* drove vignerons from polluted land in search of more profitable pursuits.

The Domaine is housed in modest buildings on the southern extremity of Meursault, with a triangular corner pointing directly towards Puligny. The visitor is ushered into a small office at the back of the house, with an attractive terrace facing the small family-owned Clos St.-Felix. A proclamation affixed to the door announces: 'Direction'; however, within it is debatable whether Bernard Michelot is directing the office, or the office has taken charge of Bernard Michelot – streamers of paper pour disconsolately from a small calculator like unwanted Christmas decorations and rejected paper screws carpet the floor.

Bernard enjoys talking about his philosophy which, in general, is firmly directed towards the consumer. His aim is to make wines at once 'sec' and 'moelleux', with fine green-gold colours evincing the true character of their *cépage* and *terroir,* which are above all 'a pleasure to drink' – wines not for the intellect but for the soul. However, his wines are *vins de garde* and he is severe with those who draw their corks too soon.

Emphasis is laid on careful pruning. All Michelot vines are pruned *Guyot* to 5–6 buds maximum. If a vine is not producing well it is rested for a year or two, virtually unproductive. Alternatively, if the new wood is not vigorous and healthy, the pruners cut the existing cane down to 2–3 buds and use a spur to lengthen the *baguette.*

Bernard Michelot's average yields of 50–55 hl./ha. have aroused criticisms of excess. He replies that he does not aim to maximise yields by generous pruning but, on the contrary, prunes severely, for him, the weather is the final determinant of yield. What matters is the quantity of grapes per vine, rather than the yield per ha. His argument is bolstered by comparison with the Bordelais: he has 11,000 vines per ha., Bordeaux has 5,000 so there must be fewer grapes harvested per vine in Burgundy to give the same yield per ha. as Bordeaux.

An historical argument is also wheeled out to justify greater yields in modern vintages: mechanisation has greatly facilitated

Bernard Michelot tasting in his cellars; note the ceiling light – bottles (one hopes not full of Meursault)

replanting – a tractor makes 150 holes in the time it takes to dig 10 by hand. Vines were thus replanted less often and so less productive. In a modern vineyard one expects to find 98% of vines regularly cropping, whereas 30 years ago the proportion was nearer 80%; ergo, greater gross production. While he may have convinced himself, the question Bernard has to address is how he manages some 5–10 hl./ha. more than his colleagues.

In the vineyard, Michelot replants a parcel of vines each year, using 4 clones, selected after visits from Raymond Bernard and microvinification of grapes from many different vines. The results convinced both expert and vigneron that whilst each wine was good, the assemblage was infinitely more complex.

Michelot's vinification is relatively traditional: 2–3 pneumatic pressings are followed by fermentation in oak – about 25% new, irrespective of the *climat* or vintage. The remainder of the casks are less than 5 years old: 'You can't make good wine in 10–15 - year-old casks.' There is no attempt at temperature control since, according to Bernard, 'fermentation directs itself'. *Chaptalisation,* where necessary, is performed at the start of fermentation, which then continues at its own pace – the longer, the better, in Bernard's view. No sulphur is added in the vineyard, but the presses are filled quickly – a white Michelot grape waits no more than 2 hours before being pressed and the fermenting casks filled up immediately the tumultuous phase ceases, to prevent premature oxidation.

The wines are racked at the start of the new year, unified and returned to cask. In July or so, they are given a bentonite and casein fining and bottled 2–3 months later, usually just before the new vintage.

Michelot's Meursaults are interesting, well-made wines. Their style is somewhat individual, usually powerful and fleshy, but with a distinctive touch of old-fashioned rusticity which may not appeal to everyone. The wines are not built for long ageing, being best within a decade or so of the vintage. Although the Premiers Crus are the pick of the crop, the village Meursaults are also excellent. Bernard Michelot's wines can be bought with confidence, and are particularly well worth looking for in second-rank vintages, at which he seems to excel.

VINEYARD HOLDINGS

Commune	*Level*	*Lieu-dit/Climat*	*Area*	*Vine Age*	*Status*
Meursault	PC	Les Perrières	0.20	8	P
Meursault	PC	Les Charmes	1.38	19	P
Meursault	PC	Les Genevrières	1.65	24	P
Meursault	V	Les Narvaux	1.30	26	P
Meursault	V	Les Tillets	0.83	40	P
Meursault	V	Les Grands Charrons	0.85	33	P
Meursault	V	Clos du Cromin	0.98	19	F
Meursault	V	Clos St.-Felix	0.82	30	P
Meursault	V	Les Limozins	0.68	31	P
Meursault	V	Sous La Velle	1.98	40	P
Meursault	V	(Various climats)	2.12	35	P
Puligny	PC	Les Folatières	0.16	20	P
Puligny	PC	La Garenne	0.10	18	P
Puligny	V	Les Grands Champs	0.28	34	M
Santenay	PC	Les Gravières	0.41	N/A	P
—	R	(Bourgogne Chardonnay)	5.18	20	P
—	R	(Bourgogne Aligoté)	1.18	40	P
—	R	(Bourgogne Pinot Noir)	1.12	32	P
—	R	(Bourgogne Grand Ord.)	0.32	56	P
		Total	**21.55 ha.**		

Domaine Pierre Morey

MEURSAULT

Pierre Morey is a remarkable man. In his early forties, he has a smallish estate of his own in Meursault, and has recently been awarded the ultimate accolade of being invited to succeed the talented Jean Virot as wine-maker at Domaine Leflaive in Puligny. He will say that the omens were not good – he was born in a relatively poor vintage (1948) but mercifully conceived, as he may cheerfully add, at the end of the harvest in 1947, an exceptional year.

The Moreys, an established Meursault family – only tenuously related to the Moreys of Chassagne-Montrachet – arrived in Meursault under somewhat unorthodox circumstances during 'La Terreur' in 1793. Apparently, during the Revolution, though the Meursaltiens' republican distaste for the clergy deprived Meursault of its priest, there was an equally strong popular desire to remain good Catholics. The problem was finally solved by Alexis Morey, from Chassagne, who managed to persuade a priest to make night-time visits to Meursault to celebrate mass in wine-cellars there. Whilst on these nocturnal peregrinations, Alexis met and fell in love with a Mlle. Millot. They married, had several children and built up a small viticultural estate.

Unfortunately, frequent subdivisions under the Napoleonic inheritance laws left virtually nothing of the original family 5 ha. when Pierre's father, Auguste Morey-Genelot (born in 1912) came to inherit in 1930. He finally abandoned life as a viticulteur in 1934 to become a travelling representative for a pharmaceutical company. During this wilful absence the little remaining land was run by his father – Pierre's grandfather. Being an old soldier, wounded in the FIrst World War, he soon became physically and spiritually tired of keeping things going and issued an ultimatum to Auguste to return or see the estate abandoned. Auguste returned in 1936.

In those days, it was common practice either to rent vineyards or to farm them on a share-cropping basis. Auguste refused to buy vineyard land because he regarded the prevailing prices as excessive, and therefore set about finding suitable vineyards to share-crop. He ended up in 1937 with 4 ha. of superb land including the Meursault Premiers Crus Perrières, Charmes and Genevrières and 33 ares of the Grand Cru Le Montrachet – in the Puligny section. All these belonged to the Domaine des Comtes Lafon. Sadly for Pierre, the agreement has now expired so the vineyards have to be returned. After 'friendly discussions – we have mutual respect for each other', it was agreed that the land should be handed back in stages, starting in 1987. So the last Morey Genevrières vintage was in 1988, the last Charmes in 1990 and the last Montrachet, 1991. One can imagine the sadness of handing back these incomparable vineyards, after more than half a century of tending them and enjoying their produce, when there is no realistic expectation of replacing them.

Although he and his wife – who teaches physical education – have just moved to something rather larger, with a good garden for their 2 children, for most of his life Pierre and his family lived in a pleasant but unpretentious house in that part of Meursault known as the 'Quartier Neuf', built just after the twin miseries of *oïdium* and *phylloxera* at the turn of the twentieth century. Money being scarce, building started, then stopped in rather a hurry.

The First World War came, followed by the great Depression of the late 1920s and then the Second War. All these momentous events left little cash for grandiose building, hence what had become the New Quarter in 1890 was very much the same in 1945. Today Meursault is considerably expanded and it would probably be the grand custom-built mansions up on the hill behind the camping site which would be entitled to the desirable appellation of 'Quartier Neuf' – if anyone bothered any more.

Pierre is a tall, dark man, with a manner combining a university professor with an incipiently mischievous schoolboy. Confident in his abilities to make and judge fine wine, he has the humility to be aware of the tightrope a conscientious vigneron is expected to walk. Brought up surrounded by vineyards and wine, his art is second nature; although he and his brother were both expected to join in at vintage time, he recalls that his brother's co-operation was only forthcoming with considerable reluctance, whereas he couldn't wait to help.

For Pierre, as for most great wine-makers, nothing is dogmatic; everything has its reason and is thoroughly thought through. If tradition is upheld it is only because it produces the best results. He admits that his methods are little changed from his father's day. There is more technical insight into why things work as they do and help is available to put them right if they go wrong, but these only serve as back-up for instinct and experience, for which there is no substitute.

Since much of the family land has usually belonged to someone else, and been farmed on their behalf, Pierre admits to no great expertise in matters of viticulture. Regimes of treatment for the vines, replanting policy, clonal selection or *sélection massale* were all questions which were ultimately decided by the landowner, not the farmer. However, he will shortly have to make such decisions himself, since vines originally planted by Auguste now require replacing.

On matters of annual maintenance, things are more straightforward: prune quite short – *Guyot simple* to 8 eyes; be very severe in *ébourgonnage* – the spring pruning of unwanted buds and shoots; remove excess grapes after flowering to restrict yields; very small doses 'by comparison with some of my colleagues' of mostly organic treatment products and positively no rootstock S04 – it is too precocious and productive – use 161–49 on hillside vines and Riparia gloire on plains and flatter land.

On yields, Pierre's views are unexpected: for Chardonnay yields of up to 60 hl./ha. are compatible with Grand Vin, 'without enormous risk', and the Pinot Noir will support up to 45 hl./ha., provided one is prepared to *saigner* in years where natural abundance and rainfall have left the juice too dilute (e.g. 1982).

He supports the trend towards less use of herbicides and more hoeing. At present his practice departs from his theory in that he continues to use herbicides for all but his young vines; that, he says, is merely 'provisional'. Herbicides are to be discouraged in favour of hoeing because they tend to proliferate lateral roots on the vine, thus discouraging the important tap-root from seeking nutrients and water further down in the soil; they encourage rot in wet or humid years; they change the natural development of the vine and they infect and destroy the structure of the soil. In addition – just in case any of the pro-herbicide lobby are still standing after this sustained battery – herbicides are the progenitors of other undesirable weeds and grasses which are much more difficult to eradicate than those you started with. One has the distinct impression that herbicide salesmen are among the least successful tradesmen at Domaine Pierre Morey.

Aware of the ready charge that it is useless to criticise unless one is prepared to offer an alternative, Pierre has embarked on some experiments with the new control regime

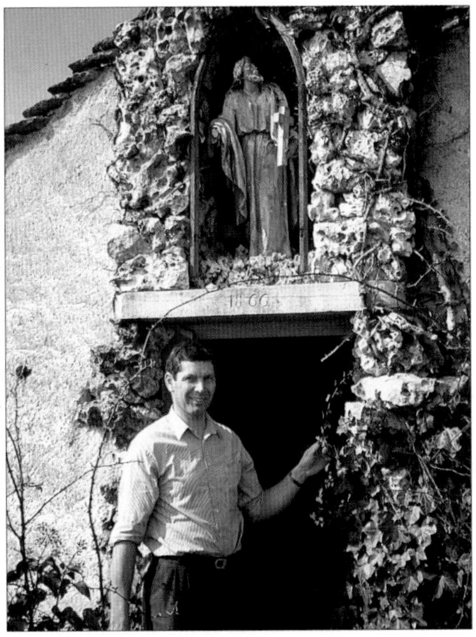

Pierre Morey in front of his little summer-house – in search of divine inspiration?

called 'biodynamie'. This revolution is the result of work by Rudolf Steiner on plant extracts at the end of the nineteenth century. The products now being proposed to viticulteurs rely on the ability to apply treatments to either vines or soil at precise times of the day. The doses are of relatively high potency, in the homoeopathic sense in which greater potency accompanies greater dilution of the original re-agent. An experimental hectare was put to the test during the 1990/1991 growing season.

As far as vinification goes, nothing is skimped. According to Morey, 'the only great decision is choosing the right day to pick.' In practical terms, it is of course necessary to decide on the vintage date in advance – firstly to have enough pickers at hand, and secondly so as to move quickly should the weather suddenly deteriorate. Morey visits each vineyard several times in the days up to the vintage to determine the exact ripeness of grapes. What is sought is not maximum ripeness, but that elusive equilibrium between sugar and acidity which will put balance and finesse into the final wine.

Apart from the decision on when to pick, one of Pierre's greatest responsibilities is to decide in what order the various parcels should be harvested. This decision is always taken with an ear to the weather forecasts, which reflect the one element of the equation over which he has no control. Whilst a late harvest is not his policy, he does admit that 'we are not among the first to pick'.

With his new responsibilities at Leflaive, Pierre has had to completely reorganise his home team to ensure that everything is properly looked after if he is down in Puligny. He has a couple, M. and Mme. Lete, living above the cuverie and cellars at the old Morey house – she looks after visitors and deliveries, while he helps with the vineyards and cellar work. In September 1990, Pierre engaged a young Californian, Dean de Korth, with 3 years' work experience at Domaine Olivier Leflaive in Puligny. De Korth's role is to understudy Pierre in the cellars. However, since Domaine Leflaive is but 5 minutes by car, and the telephone has now reached Puligny, there is no real risk of things suffering if anything goes awry in Meursault.

The vinification over which Pierre presides is robustly classical. The grapes are pressed in an old Vaslin press, proudly operated by his father Auguste, who has done the job for years and clearly knows its foibles. Pierre is contemplating a pneumatic model, but one suspects that the risk of antagonising a valued member of the labour force may delay his decision. His brother, now a reformed character as far as wine and wine-making are concerned, also appears eagerly at vintage time. He is an engineer with the French aircraft company Dassault and his skills are invaluable when anything stops working

As the juice runs from the presses it is given a dose of SO_2. If there is *botrytis,* or the juice is not reasonably clean, it is allowed to settle before being run into casks for fermentation. The Morey cellar is constructed on 3 levels, so that the wine can be moved from press to fermentation to maturation casks without being aerated by a pump. The casks used for the regional appellations are all second year or older; the Village wine goes into about 25% new oak, and the Premier and Grand Crus into 33% new oak. Experiments have led Morey to conclude that Vosges wood is better for Meursaults whereas Pulignys harmonise better with Allier. If there is enough volume of any single *cuvée,* he prefers to have a contribution from each type of oak in the final *assemblage.*

Pierre's wines are *batonéed* three times each week up to the winter equinox, since he is convinced of the value of lees contact for the development of a young white Burgundy. Thus, at first racking, after the *malolactic fermentation,* he only racks off the gross, heavier lees, leaving the finer lees to nourish the wine during the summer. However, at the second racking in September, the wines are racked completely clear all of their lees.

After tasting and analysing each wine, a decision is made on whether to use fish fining or bentonite as a fining agent. In some vintages the former works better, in other years the latter, here especially when there is residual protinaceous matter still in suspension. Wines which are unduly yellow may also require some casein to be added to the bentonite to clarify them properly.

After a light cartridge filtration, the wines are bottled in February or March of the second year – about 18 months after the vintage. This is relatively long compared with what happens elsewhere, but Pierre Morey believes that these additional months in cask give a much better evolution to the wine, adding a structure and richness which make for longevity . He tried bottling at 11 months, but the results were manifestly inferior.

As one tastes at the third, deepest, level of this quiet, cold cellar, with bins of mycelium-covered bottles tucked into obscure corners, the value of all the care and thought devoted to a Morey white wine becomes apparent. Their overriding characteristic – from the Aligoté made from a patch of 30-year-old vines, shortly to be grubbed up and re-planted, to the Montrachet – is aristocracy. The wines have ineffable breed, backed up by firm, fleshy fruit. Nothing lean or ascetic here but glorious opulence, especially evident in the young wines, still in cask in October, when most of their contemporaries at other Domaines are beginning their lives in bottle. Pierre believes in waiting: 'You need great patience in the *élevage* of a wine', and, moreover 'often the courage to do nothing'.

Every stage in the production of these wines is approached with skill, care and, above all, diligence. As so often with quality, it is details which make the difference between magic and mediocrity. From the simple expedient of filling each cask as soon as the first tumultuous phase of fermentation is over, to keeping a slow fermentation going as long as possible, to delaying bottling until that precisely chosen moment, nothing is left to chance or undertaken thoughtlessly. Pierre Morey is a consummate artist and his wines are a worthy tribute to the co-operation between man and the land.

VINEYARD HOLDINGS

Commune	*Level*	*Lieu-dit/Climat*	*Area*	*Vine Age*	*Status*
Puligny	GC	Bâtard-Montrachet	0.48	25	M
Meursault	PC	Les Perrières	0.52	22	P
Meursault	V	Les Forges/Les Tessons	1.00	24	P/M
Meursault	V	Les Durots (Red)	0.26	16	P
Monthélie	V	(Several climats)	0.78	30	M
Pommard	PC	Les Grands Epenots	0.43	25	M
—	R	(Bourgogne Aligoté)	1.85	30	P/M
—	R	(Bourgogne Blanc)	1.20	18	P/M
—	R	(Bourgogne Rouge/PTG)	1.49	29	P/M
		Total	**8.01 ha.**		

Domaine Rougeot

MEURSAULT

Marc Rougeot was born in one of those vintages that Burgundy, indeed most of viticultural France, would rather forget – 1956. Through effort of will, he overcame this congenital misfortune and is now installed as the Domaine's winemaker and the fifth generation of Rougeots in Meursault.

Land ownership began with Marc's grandfather who possessed a small Domaine selling wine in bottle under the Rougeot-Latour label. Marc's father, who took over in 1955, soon realised that there was not enough land to provide a sensible living, since most of the 20 ha. were situated in scattered plots of lesser appellations. He therefore decided that his viticultural activities would have to be subsidised by something more profitable, and promptly invested his business skills in founding a firm of public works contractors.

This enterprise prospered, finding rich nourishment on the autoroutes and other major development projects of the 1960s and 1970s. The 'travaux publics' enabled Rougeot Père to add 3 ha. of Ladoix in the 1960s and a further 1 ha. of Pommard in 1975. The vineyards in Meursault, however, remain those of Marc's grandfather. In addition, until the late 1980s, the Rougeots farmed vineyards for the Château de Meursault; 6 ha. of Premier Cru land which one suspects they would dearly have liked in their portfolio.

When Marc took charge in 1975 much of the wine was sold in bulk. In the intervening years he has gradually weaned the Domaine off this practice and built up the private and export sales to the point that wine is now all sold in bottle under the Domaine's own label. Thus he finds himself in the fortunate position of having as much custom as stock in normal vintages, and in the invidious position of having far less stock than custom in less abundant ones. In the event of a disparity, a system of rationing is applied so everyone gets vintage B in proportion to their purchases in vintage A. The income to replant and re-equip is assured, and Marc is left to concentrate on producing top-quality wine.

Like many of the new wave of young Burgundian wine-makers, Marc Rougeot lives over the shop – in this case an elegant seventeenth-century village house bought by the family in 1981 – thank heavens for autoroutes! This quiet, substantial dwelling is entered from the street by a pair of solid automatic steel gates which would have given Monsieur Hulot endless scope for mishap. Within, there is a delightful secluded garden with pear and apple trees which adjoins a small walled vineyard – the Clos des 6 Ouvrées – from which comes a soft, attractive Bourgogne Chardonnay.

Underneath the house is a maze of cellars terminating in a steel-encased library of older bottles. Browsing through this small, but growing, treasure-house you should not be surprised to find bottles of claret and Sauternes, and a couple of cases of Romaneé-

Marc Rougeot trimming grafts for his plants

Conti walled up for future feasts, while a bottle of Château Yquem 1937 props up a little pile of older Sauternes. In contrast, there are very few of the Domaine's own mature wines to draw upon, since the purchase of two Willmes presses in 1985 and major works in the cuverie depleted its resources. However, now that the financial position is more favourable, Marc intends to begin accumulating a library.

In the vineyards, hoeing-in weeds and grass is preferred to herbicides which can engender resistance; soil is also ploughed up round roots in the winter as a measure of frost protection. Any vines that, despite this care, manage to die, are grubbed up in the autumn and replaced the following spring. They used to select clones from an old 'mother vine' at Ladoix, but abandoned these for more reliable and virus-indexed quality from the nurseryman.

To keep pests and diseases at bay Marc favours the traditional Bordeaux mixture, a copper sulphate based brew which is a proven but non-toxic anti-mildew and anti-*oïdium* treatment, plus specific insecticides as they are needed. Marc is aware that the copper tends to harden the grapes, and thus to delay maturation, since the sun penetrates harder matter less easily, so some care is taken to spray no more than necessary.

Once at the cuverie, the grapes are dosed with SO_2 at the rate of 0.5–1.0 litre per tonne before being pressed in the new Willmes presses. These were chosen by Marc after considerable experimentation. This involved vinifying 2 separate *cuvées* of Meursault in 3 different presses – a Vaslin press consisting of a pair of stainless-steel plates which gradually approach each other squeezing the grapes in between, and Bucher and Willmes pneumatic presses which operate on the principle of blowing up an expandable balloon which gently crushes the grapes.

He then invited all the viticulteurs of Meursault to blind taste the results. The Willmes press won. Moreover, he discovered that the Vaslin press produced twice the volume of lees of the Willmes and that those lees were much coarser and less easily settled. Lees are important in the first months of a wine's life, since the young wine feeds on them, gaining in complexity and structure. It is also generally considered that the finer the lees the more finesse in the wine.

In addition to these advantages, the Willmes press has a series of programmes which give finely-tuned control over total pressing time, maximum pressure, the time to reach and remain at maximum pressure and the time during which the press drum turns. It is possible to have a pressing so gentle that it is like crushing the grapes in one's hand.

After pressing, the *cuvées* of each vineyard are unified and the juice allowed to settle at 6–7° C for 12–15 hours. If necessary, dirty juice is clarified with bentonite – but this is rare. Alcoholic fermentation takes place in bulk, with twice-daily *batonnage* to ensure even lees distribution. This frequency is greater than one normally finds in Burgundy, but the particularly cold ambient cellar temperature makes it necessary, according to Marc. After fermentation at 19° C. in large oak *foudres* and having reached a density of about 1,008, all but the Aligoté is put into oak casks.

After much experimentation it was decided to use 35–40% of new Vosges oak. The exception is the Meursault Charmes which, being a Premier Cru, it was felt had the natural power to support 100% new wood.

The *élevage* is designed to allow slow maturation with minimum interference. Hence, the least possible number of rackings – 2: one after the *matolactic fermentation* and a further racking after fining (with bentonite), just before bottling. Filtration is used only when absolutely necessary, and then with kieselguhr and not plates, which would take acidity and stuffing out of the wine. Bottling takes place after some 15 months in cask.

Whilst there are many Domaines in Meursault with a more prestigious catalogue of vineyards – there is a lone Premier Cru, Les Charmes – what is achieved here is very impressive. Marc Rougeot has a horror of Meursaults which are fat, heavy or over-blown, preferring rather wines which have 'subtlety, finesse, elegance and vinosity'.

The result is a range of wines with considerable style and harmony. Wood is used with great care to avoid making the wine with dominating oak flavours, and by and large the wines exhibit remarkable balance and finesse. Many are stored under Marc's parents' house, a modern building next to the profitable 'travaux publics' depot on the outskirts of the village. This is in the Monatine vineyard which produces one of Rougeot's finest Meursaults.

Tasting in the cellars beneath the vineyard brought to mind a magnificent bottle of Rougeot Meursault Charmes from the distinctly unmagnificent 1975 vintage. Apparently, it was the first vintage for which Marc had sole responsibility and he remembers well being continually shouted at by his father while he was making the wine. For its first year or so it was deemed undrinkable and consigned to a corner as not being fit for sale, accompanied no doubt by further imprecations from Rougeot père. Then it began to emerge into a truly remarkable wine, not just for the vintage, but for Meursault of any vintage – a deep yellow-gold colour with an exotic fruit aroma and an almost over-ripe richness – an immensely seductive wine and thoroughly delicious mouthful. Apologies were apparently forthcoming!

The younger wines show considerable promise. From a rather floral Aligoté – 'I prefer to make an Aligoté rather than a Meursault Charmes', more of a challenge presumably – through a 9-month bottled Bourgogne Chardonnay with an attractive lemony richness and a firm structure, to the Meursaults – characterised by their amplitude and length in the mouth and, in the case of the Charmes 1900, overtones of pepper and spice rather than the acacia-honey and grilled hazelnuts one expects.

The reds are less inspiring, though Marc says emphatically 'I am learning, I am learning, I am learning with reds.' His policy of using 100% new oak for his Pommard and Volnay in 1990, together with 100% of the *vin de presse,* may have been just too much for the rather delicate Pinot fruit to stand. But this is essentially a white Domaine.

Marc Rougeot is doing an excellent job with quiet confidence. His family – an agglomeration of 12 horses, a charming wife who is descended from a quality printing business in Beaune and works there from time to time, and two children, Pierre-Henri aged 9 and Alexandre aged 5 – have every reason to be proud of him.

VINEYARD HOLDINGS

Commune	*Level*	*Lieu-dit/Climat*	*Area*	*Vine Age*	*Status*
Meursault	PC	Les Charmes (Dessous)	0.38	1968	P
Meursault	PC	Volnay Santenots (Red)	0.85	1976/82	P
Meursault	V	Sous la Velle	1.68	1969-86	P
Meursault	V	Le Pellans	0.39	1978	P
Meursault	V	Monatine	0.39	1974/75	P
Meursault	V	Les Grandes Gouttes	1.41	1974/79	P
Meursault	V	Au Village	0.33	1971	P
Meursault	R	(Bourgogne Rouge)	1.98	1967-85	P
Meursault	R	(Bourgogne Aligoté)	1.49	1980-81	P
Meursault	R	(PTG)	1.42	1973	P
Meursault	R	Clos des 6 Ouvreés	0.26	19731	P
St.-Aubin	V	Le Banc (White)	0.25	1956/86/91	P
Pommard	V	(Several climats)	0.99	1950–80	P
Ladoix	V	(Several climats – Red)	2.89	1956	P
Monthélie	V	Les Tossières (White)	0.31	1990	P
		Total	**11.85 ha.**		

Domaine Guy Roulot

MEURSAULT

Despite a somewhat turbulent recent history, this 12.5 ha. Domaine is among the finest in Meursault. Since the premature death in 1982 of the creator of the estate, Guy Roulot, there have been no fewer than 3 wine-makers: Ted Lemon, from California,was responsible for vinification from January 1983 to January 1985; he was succeeded by Franc Grux, who was in charge during the 1985, 1986 and 1987 vintages, leaving during the 1988 harvest to become the wine-maker for Olivier Leflaive in Puligny; and finally, the present co-manager, Guy's son Jean-Marc Roulot, who assumed full responsibility with the 1989 vintage.

The business is a truly family affair – Jean-Marc and his sister Michèle Javouhey-Roulot run the Domaine, together with their mother Mme. Geneviève Roulot, Guy's widow, from a modern house-cum-cellars on the periphery of the town. Jean-Marc is a somewhat serious person who regards visitors, especially writers, with a degree of caution amounting to downright suspicion. However, when one establishes one's credentials and gets to know him he is a man of warm amiability.

He does not seem to mind that his professional career as a classical actor has had to take second place to running the Domaine. His mother and sister manage the financial and office departments and wisely leave him to get on with the viticultural and cellar work. Mme. Roulot senior, who is a delightful and elegant lady, mans her computer in the small Roulot office, whilst Michèle takes firm charge of financial management with the air of someone entirely capable of getting her own way with recalcitrants – be they customers or bank managers.

The Domaine is of post-war construction built up by Guy Roulot during the late 1950s and early 1960s, with purchases of vineyards in Meursault, Auxey-Duresses and Monthélie. Jean-Marc learnt the ropes from his father and more or less continues in the fashion set at that time. He believes that the general standard of wine-making in Meursault is by and large good, and that the most dramatic improvements will come from the vineyards rather than the cellars.

There is no doubt that sloppy wine-making and careless cellar practices are now less widespread than hitherto, vignerons having realised that a better educated wine trade will not pay top prices – or any prices – for badly vinified wine. Equipment and technical support are readily available to any vigneron who wishes to make use of them, so that there is no excuse for over-sulphured, heavily oxidised or flabby, corsetless wines.

With a younger generation of trained, conscientious wine-makers installed in some of the Meursault's most important Domaines, quality levels are high. Problems tend to be shared, wines are critically evaluated in blind tastings and the spirit of co-operation abounds; meanwhile, those who routinely over-crop will doubtless continue to do so.

Roulot is a model of careful viticulture: short pruning and two separate spring *évasivages,* the first to remove suckers sprouting on the lower part of each plant and the second to cut off any double shoots which sap strength from the vine, to limit yields and ensure that the available photosynthetic power is concentrated where it is most needed – in the young bunches.

Deliberate reduction of herbicides to the bare minimum by rotary hoeing and herbicide regimes gives the soil the best chance of avoiding both infection from ever more powerful chemical products and compaction from repeated passages of heavy machinery through the vineyards. Fortunately there is a strong element of continuity with the past, in the person of a full-time vigneron who worked with Guy Roulot for many years.

Jean-Marc believes that vine replacements are best carried out individually, although when the need does arise to replant a particular parcel of vines a thorough soil analysis and suitable nutrient adjustment is effected, together with a full year of fallow rest. Three clones are used in each parcel replanted, giving greater complexity in the final wine. Soil is ploughed up round the roots *(buttage)* each winter only on those parcels which have been worked by hoe, rather than treated with herbicides.

Harvesting is particularly careful; vintagers are never left alone to harvest, because they tend to cut bunches indiscriminately. Instead, an experienced member of the Roulot team shadows them to ensure that only fully ripe bunches are harvested and, more importantly, that any *pourriture sec* (dry rot) is excised. Limited amounts of *pourriture humide* are acceptable as this tends to add a degree or two of alcohol to the wine, and thus, especially in leaner years, a little more richness and amplitude.

Once harvested, the grapes are pressed in a pneumatic Bucher press. Unlike many other high-quality Domaines, the pressing only lasts an hour and a half – some 20–30 minutes less than normal elsewhere in the commune, which results in less juice, but juice of a much higher quality.

Jean-Marc firmly believes that too long at maximum pressure extracts skin and pip tannins which are detrimental to wine quality. His press fortunately enables him to programme the total duration of each press cycle, the time taken to reach maximum pressure and the time spent at both ends of each cycle, giving him total control. A tangential advantage is that the cake remaining after pressing is much more amenable to distillation of a quality *marc,* on which this Domaine prides itself: 'we have no wish to distil straw'.

Alcoholic fermentation is preceded by a period of *macération pelliculaire.* This is a relatively new idea, pioneered outside France, whereby the grape juice is left on the skins for between 24 hours and several days to extract flavour and aroma compounds, many of which, situated just beneath the grape skin, are not readily extracted by normal pressing. Since there is no alcohol present, the extraction of undesirable harsh tannins is kept to a minimum. In addition, this maceration delays the onset of fermentation which Jean-Marc considers beneficial.

Another practice on which he has strong views is that of *batonnage* – the practice of rousing the lees in cask with an old stick or broom-handle, if you are doggedly traditional, or with a specially bent stainless steel tool if you wish to be modern. Although practised elsewhere, this is a particularly Meursaltien habit whose value and application are much discussed locally. In Burgundian lore, 'A woman, a Puligny and a walnut tree, the more you beat them the better they be' may indeed hold good, but there is a sight more beating done in Meursault than in its illustrious neighbour. The most beneficial beatings are normally administered between the termination of alcoholic fermentation and the end of December following the vintage.

The frequency of *batonnage* is a matter of judgement, not of science. Tasting a wine before and after, one is aware of a distinct change in flavour, in particular a gain in richness. Some, including Jean-Marc, claim that there is a compensating loss in finesse, but this is by no means certain. Some growers rouse as many as 50 times during the weeks following fermentation, others twice weekly or just once a month. Jean-Marc favours the latter on the grounds that it maximises gains whilst minimising losses.

The whites are vinified in 20–30% of new

oak, the proportion being determined by the character of the Cru and of the vintage. Whilst fermentation proceeds more rapidly in new than in older oak, it is generally felt that the qualities imparted by new wood harmonise better with the wine when fermentation, rather than just subsequent maturation, is carried out in new oak. So there is a balance to be struck.

After the *malolactic* fermentation in February, the different lots are assembled and sulphur levels adjusted. The wines are once more put into cask where they remain until the following June. The lees, meanwhile, are kept for making Fine – a brandy distilled from wine – another speciality of the house. After fining, they are racked a second time, filtered with a plate filter and then bottled. Jean-Marc is anxious to replace his plate filter with a more sensitive carbon filter to minimise the deleterious effects on flavour and acidity levels that filtration often brings. The total *élevage* is about 10–11 months; this may seem short, especially for the better wines, but he considers that his cellars are not cold enough to justify keeping his wines longer in cask.

There has been much experimenting with different fining agents since Jean-Marc discovered that the traditional fining with bentonite tended to give a rather broader style of wine, whereas fish protein produced markedly different results. He also found that some of his vineyard sites produced wines which were more compatible with fish fining than with bentonite. Tasting the 'fish' wines, one noticed a much tighter, leaner spectrum of flavours – this was evident in the Vireuils and Tessons *cuvées* – whereas with bentonite the profile was much more diffuse – particularly for the Charmes, Meix Chavaux and Perrières. There will undoubtedly be more experimentation before any final decisions are made, but it is interesting to note that whereas the bentonite-casein finings are much more common in Meursault, *col de poisson* is more widely used in Puligny. One is led to speculate on whether similar comparisons have been made by anyone in Puligny.

The Roulot style is midway between the overtly riper wines of Dominic Lafon and the more austere, intellectual style of Michel Ampeau. The wines have frank aromas, not masked by either oak or lees, and a marked richness, even in less opulent years, which in time develops the classic nut/honey character so often found in Meursault. However, there is a lean, cerebral quality in these wines which gives them depth and interest.

The basic Bourgogne Chardonnay, from 1 ha. of vines in Meursault, is usually excellent – plenty of richness and concentration backed by a firm structure which derives in part from contact with new oak. In 1989, Jean-Marc decided to mature part of this *cuvée* in large, old wooden *foudres*, after the *malo*, instead of keeping it entirely in small casks, to avoid wood flavours dominating. The result is a delicious mouthful, which will drink well into the mid-1990s.

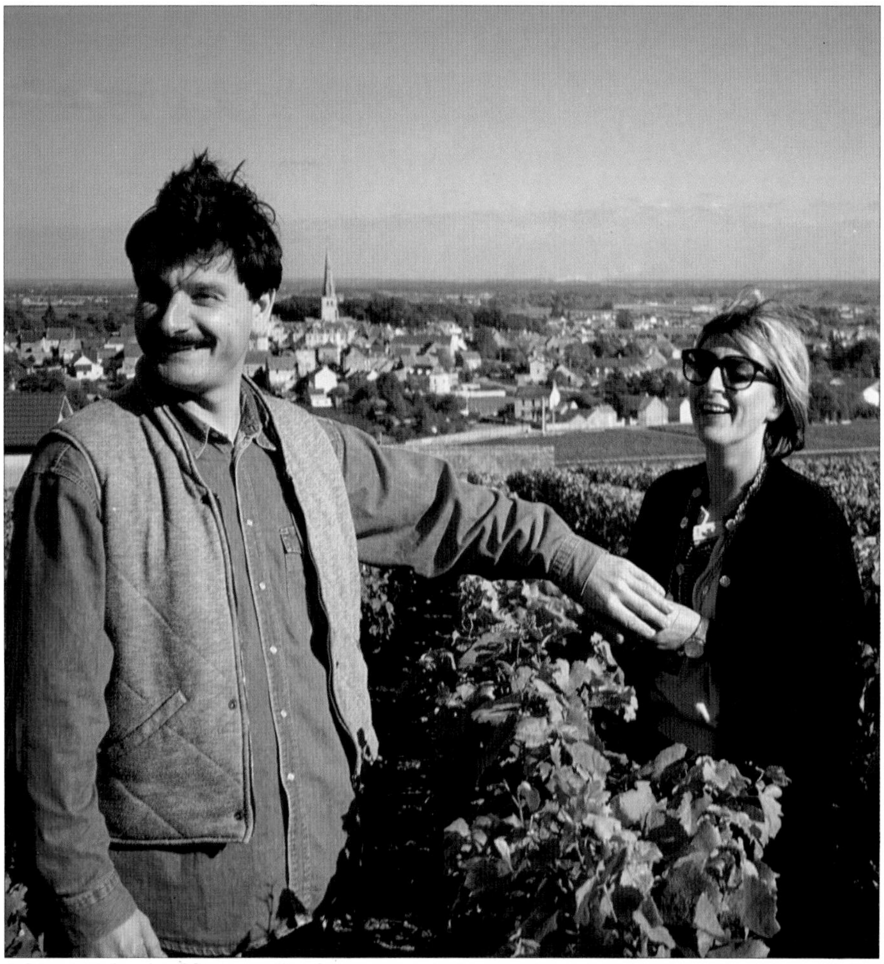

Jean-Marc Roulot and his sister Michèle

The *cuvées* from the various Meursault Village *lieu-dits* are equally well made and interesting, varying from a rich, yet tight Meix Chavaux to a long, rich, warm Tessons – in good vintages such as 1988 and 1989 of undoubted Premier Cru quality.

The Domaine's two Premiers Crus are invariably excellent wines. Les Charmes – open, ripe, with a broad, well balanced structure, develops well over a decade or more. Les Perrières is yet finer: a powerful, complete wine, with all the richness, length and class one expects from this great vineyard and, in vintages such as 1983 and 1988, potential longevity.

This Domaine is back in skilled and conscientious Roulot hands and, despite the vicissitudes of the 1980s, remains one of the finest sources of Meursault in the village.

VINEYARD HOLDINGS

Commune	*Level*	*Lieu-dit/Climats*	*Area*	*Vine Age*	*Status*
Meursault	PC	Les Charmes	0.25	25–35	P
Meursault	PC	Les Perrières	0.25	25–35	P
Meursault	V	Les Tessons	0.80	25–35	P
Meursault	V	Les Luchets	1.00	25–35	P
Meursault	V	Les Tillets	0.50	25–35	P
Meursault	V	Meix Chavaux	1.80	25–35	P
Meursault	V	Les Vireuils	0.66	25–35	P
Meursault	R	(Bourgogne Chardonnay)	1.00	25–35	P
Meursault	R	(Bourgogne Aligoté)	1.00	25–35	P
Auxey	V	—	1.50	25–35	P
Monthélie	V	—	0.50	25–35	P
—	R	(Bourgogne Pinot Noir)	2.00	25–35	P
		Total	**11.26 ha.**		

PULIGNY-MONTRACHET

The attractive, self-confident yet unpretentious village of Puligny-Montrachet lies at the foot of a band of vines 2 km. wide and 1.5 km. deep, from which come some of the world's most concentrated, complex and sought-after dry white wines.

Here one finds the Village, Premier and Grand Cru vineyards which have made Puligny a place of near pilgrimage, not just for grateful drinkers but for frustrated Chardonnay producers from elsewhere who strive, although probably loathe to admit it, to imitate the Grands Vins of Puligny from less propitious *terroir*.

The village reeks of prosperity: neat, discreet, manicured houses and cellars, hidden from view by simple glossy wooden gates, a few offering half-hearted invitations to 'visiter les caves', attest to the commercial success which Puligny's vignerons have long enjoyed. Nothing fancy or ostentatious, however, to show for astronomic land values and high wine prices; the only expensive cars are those in the square next to Le Montrachet, the village's sole hotel.

Prosperity has not, however, bred laziness. The growers are hard-working individuals who dislike any distraction from their daily routine. The most extravagant frivolity to which they might be persuaded to succumb, usually at the insistence of their wives, would be a week or two's exotic holiday. Otherwise they stay firmly put, to mind their Domaines and to receive a relentless stream of international visitors.

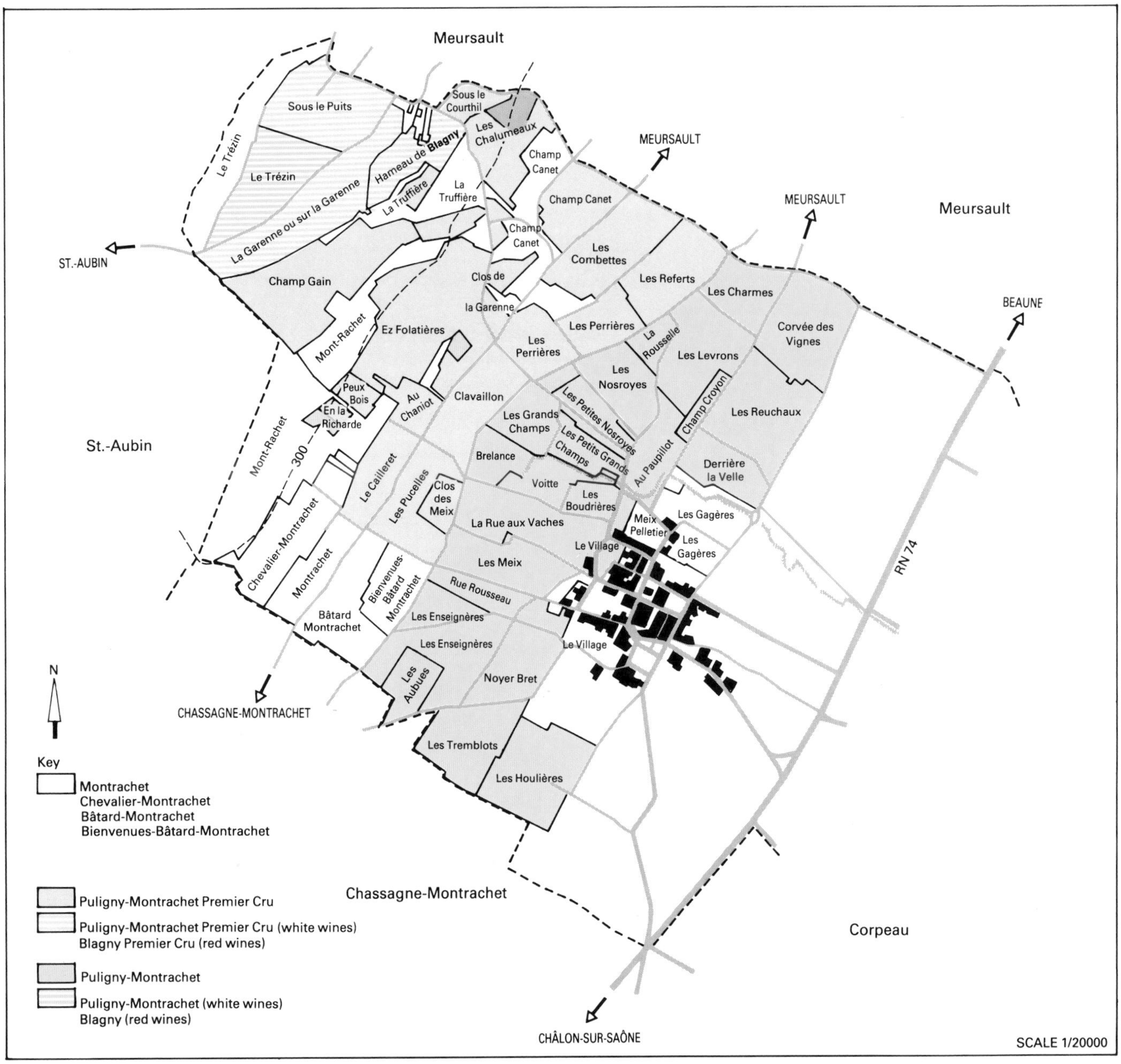

The fief for which Puligny's 75 viticulteurs and 3 Domaines are responsible consists of 114.22 ha. of AC Puligny-Montrachet, 100.12 ha. of Premiers Crus, and 21.09 ha. of Grands Crus. These produce annually, on average, 88,000 cases of white wine and 3,200 cases of red wine. This may seem abundance, until one realises that 50% of total production belongs to négociant houses and a further 50% of what remains is sold in bulk; thus, not much more than 25% of Puligny is bottled and sold by the growers.

It is not, at first, easy to accept that the wines of Puligny – especially the Premiers and Grands Crus – differ from those of neighbouring Meursault or, indeed, from each other. After all, they share broadly similar soils, a common *cépage,* are grown on equally well-exposed hillsides, and have equally skilled vignerons.

However, differ they do – a phenomenon largely attributable to changes in soils and subsoils, often within the space of a few metres. Stand in Grand Cru Bienvenues-Bâtard-Montrachet, where the vineyard tracks cross, facing the village: a couple of metres below is AC Puligny-Montrachet (80–110 francs per bottle); to the left is Premier Cru Les Pucelles (150–200 francs); and the Bienvenue you are standing on will fetch 250–300 francs. This is the result of soil, not cupidity, and is as striking a demonstration of the importance of *terroir* as can be found anywhere.

There are 12 Premiers Crus in Puligny and 3 in Blagny, the hamlet above the village which, owing to a characteristically Gallic muddle which no one seems willing to simplify, divides its 54 ha. of vineyards between Puligny and Meursault.

These Premiers Crus vary in style and status. Those closest to Meursault – Champ Canet, Chalumaux, Les Combettes and Les Referts – are planted on thin soils dominated by scree and rock, with patches of slate; these produce lighter, more floral wines, with less power and richness than those nearer Chassagne.

In the middle of the Premier Cru band are Clavoillon, Les Folatières, Clos de la Garenne and Les Perrières, with Champs Gains and La Truffière above them. These also represent a mixture of soils – varying from the deeper ground of Clavoillon through the stony Perrières to the steep, easily eroded limestone scree of Folatières. If it makes any sense to generalise, one might characterise these vineyards as producing the most masculine wines of Puligny, they begin life rather austere, but develop beautifully over 5–10 years or more.

The finest of the Premiers Crus are, without question, those adjacent to the Grands Crus. Here, Les Pucelles and Le Cailleret produce wines of abundant power and concentration which, in good vintages, are of Grand Cru quality. Indeed, part of Le Cailleret is now incorporated into the Grand Cru Chevalier-Montrachet and sold as Les Demoiselles, so named after two Mademoiselles Voillot who owned it in the 1880s. Domaine Leflaive owns a commanding 2.9 ha. of Pucelles, producing some 1,500 cases of superbly concentrated, complex, opulent wine, which outshines many others' Grand Crus.

Puligny has 4 Grands Crus, all superbly exposed to the south-east, two of which it shares with the commune of Chassagne-Montrachet. Unfortunately, these have become heavily fragmented, with some owners having no more than a few rows each. Apart from practical difficulties – if you only have two barrels what do you use to top them up? – small volumes are difficult to work with and rarely make top-class wine. Selection is therefore 'de rigueur', if one is paying Grand Cru prices.

The smallest of the quartet is Bienvenues-Bâtard-Montrachet, so christened by outside workers who farmed these vines *en métayage* during the nineteenth century, and were known as Les Bienvenues. Although Bienvenues is no more than an administrative enclave of Bâtard-Montrachet, there are those who claim to detect differences between the wines – the Bienvenue being, allegedly, lighter. It is more likely that any differences are due more to vine age and vinification than to systematic differences in soil or micro-climate.

Of Bâtard-Montrachet's 11.86.63 ha. only 6.02.21 are in Puligny. The wine is slightly more open than either Le Montrachet or Chevalier-Montrachet but, in the hands of masters such as Leflaive and Sauzet, it is something of exuberant power and weight needing years to open fully. Interestingly, the Domaine de la Romanée-Conti own nearly 0.2 ha., but sell their wine en négoce.

Chevalier-Montrachet occupies 7.36.14 ha. of sloping ground just below the Mont Rachet. The soil is thin, with a layer of marl and scree covering seemingly impenetrable limestone. Somehow the Chardonnay's root-system works its way into this rock, to produce wines of immense presence and concentration. The respects in which an individual Chevalier may differ from an individual Le Montrachet are better ascribed to differences other than those of soil,

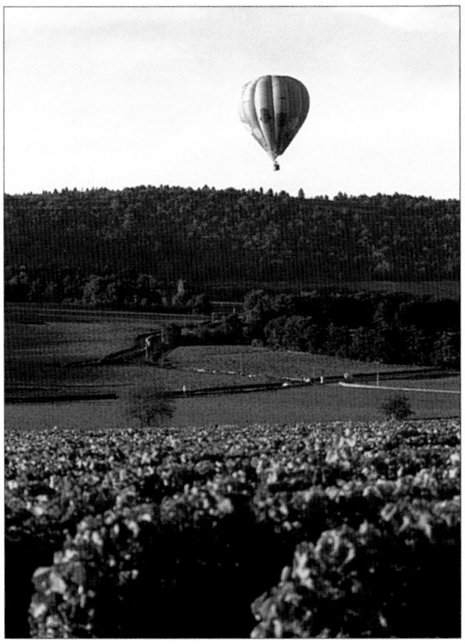

Precious vines at Puligny – looking over Les Grands Champs and Clavoillon up towards Blagny. Hot-air balloons are a popular attraction for tourists seeking a different perspective

although being on slightly higher and steeper ground may account for marginally less richness which some experts claim to detect. The best wines come from Leflaive, Latour, Jadot, Chartron and Niellon. Bouchard Père, who own a princely 2.028 ha., produce a wine which invariably seems to lack the concentration and depth one expects from a Grand Cru.

Le Montrachet, the most expensive and precious dry white wine in the world, comes from a 7.99.80 ha. strip of vines, no more than 100 m. wide, with one end just below Chevalier-Montrachet and the other adjoining a Village vineyard in the commune of Chassagne. The 4.01.07 ha. in Puligny is divided among 5 proprietors, of which the largest by far is the family of the Marquis de Laguiche with 2.062 ha. Other important proprietors in the Puligny sector are Domaine Ramonet (0.259 ha.) and Bouchard Père et Fils (0.889 ha).

Whilst the Montrachets from Ramonet, Romanée-Conti, who own 0.676 ha. in the Chassagne section and from Comtes Lafon, invariably outclass the rest, the *cuvée* Marquis de Laguiche, made and sold by Joseph Drouhin, and that of Marc Colin are usually fine examples. The best of the Chevaliers are just as good. It is interesting to note that not a single vine of this fabled Montrachet is owned by a grower in Puligny!

THE GRANDS CRUS OF PULIGNY-MONTRACHET

Lieu-dit	*Area*	*Props.*	*Av. Prod.*
Montrachet	7.99.80	17	2600 C/S
Bâtard-Montrachet	11.86.63	49	4400 C/S
Bienvenues-Bâtard-Montrachet	3.68.60	15	1300 C/S
Chevalier-Montrachet	7.36.14	16	1950 C/S
Totals	**30.91.17 ha.**		**10250 C/S**

Domaine Louis Carillon et Fils

PULIGNY-MONTRACHET

The Carillons are a splendid family – delightful, welcoming, enthusiastic and, moreover, producers of some of Puligny's finest wine.

They are absorbed by their family history and have recently been digging around in the local archives in search of distant Carillon ancestors. Whilst they already knew of a Carillon viticulteur at Puligny in 1632, the latest bout of excavation has unearthed a Jehan Carillon, of similar calling, who worked in Puligny in 1520. Perhaps now that they have traced their history beyond the 1580 reached by the Leflaives, they will ease up on genealogy, but somehow one doubts it.

Fortunately, there are plenty of Carillons to do the digging: Louis, the present head of the house, succeeded his father Robert after the war, in turn bringing in his two sons – Jacques in 1980 and François in 1988 – to help him. Grandfather, now aged 71, is still much in evidence, if a neat plot of leeks and other vegetables behind one of the many Carillon cellars is trustworthy testimony.

Although the Domaine's headquarters are nominally in the Rue de l'Eglise in Puligny, the village's proximity to the water-table has made underground cellars unviable, and obliged it to extend sideways. Thus the visitor is conducted out and about the locality, through a gate here, a door there, up this flight of steps, down that, to taste from tanks and barrels hidden in the the most unlikely corners. Opening a door of a fifteenth-century courtyard, you may well find yourself facing a battery of late twentieth-century stainless steel, or an up-to-the-minute computer-controlled press; in another building one finds a confessional grille set into a wall, used during the Revolution when religion was banned; the flight of steps behind enabled the priest to escape across grandfather Carillon's vegetable garden in the event of a search. Another small cellar was used during that period to store valuable religious artefacts from the church opposite, and blocked up with a cupboard to avoid detection.

In spite of external appearances, the Domaine is thoroughly modern. The Carillons are masters of their craft, using technology judiciously to back up tradition, and producing wines of great depth and purity. The heart of their 12 ha. Domaine is in Puligny – with a patch of Bienvenues-Bâtard-Montrachet, Premiers Crus and 5 ha. of Puligny Villages, spread over 11 separate *lieu-dits.* In 1981 a Société Civile was formed to run the vineyards for grandfather, Louis and his two sons, who own them – a saving in administrative time and expense.

Anyone with vines in Puligny has to remind himself constantly that the soils, especially around the village where the ground is flat, are only a few centimetres from the water-table, and thus very humid. This will influence choice of clone and rootstock, and make for greater vigilance in case of mildew or rot. On the slopes, away from the village, the risks diminish.

The soils are ploughed twice a year – once in the autumn to mulch in fertilisers and even out the ground, and again in the spring to destroy the roots of any indigenous grasses. Nourishment is carefully calculated to ensure a healthy working vine, which will produce of its best between 15 and 50 years of age.

The most besetting diseases are mildew and *oïdium* – rose growers' nightmares – particularly for the Chardonnay, which is especially susceptible to *oïdium.* Whilst traditional copper-based treatments are preferred, they are used only at the end of the vegetative cycle since copper tends to retard the growth of a young vine and sulphur is only effective if the weather remains both hot and dry. Recent years have seen a shift towards modern products, both preventive and curative, to control pests and diseases.

Periodically, patches of vines are grubbed up and replanted to ensure a good mix of vine ages. Whilst older vines are more desirable, a vigneron who had only old vines would sooner or later be obliged to replant and thus find himself with no wine for several years. Carillon replantings are infrequent, the most recent being in 1980, 1982 and 1989.

Sadly, the entire 0.47 ha. plot of Combettes, originally planted by Grandfather between 1935–40, was grubbed up after the 1986 vintage; the soil remained fallow for 6 years, before replanting in 1992. Since the produce of young vines is not entitled to the appellation for 3 years, this means a loss of 9 years' production – a total of some 2,000 cases of Premier Cru Puligny – a vivid testament to their dedication to quality. 'We like it best if the soil rests a little, to re-establish its structure,' Jacques explains.

Since 1982, new plantings have been 50:50 clones and *sélection massale* with a carefully chosen mixture of clones and rootstocks. 'Only 50% of clones are any good,' reckons Jacques, adding that the widely used 161/49 rootstock is maladapted to Puligny's humid soils, so they have used less of this and more of others such as 3309, 5BB and 101/14.

The date of harvest is carefully studied – acidity as well as sugar levels being taken into account. Unfortunately, although the *ban de vendanges is* normally calculated as 100 days from the flowering, an extended period of flowering because of rain or lack of sunshine can result in widely different levels of maturity in a single vineyard. As well as noting the information given by the village *prélèvements,* the Carillons make their own assessments before starting to pick, preferring in general not to harvest too late: 'We don't have grapes which are adapted to Vendange Tardive here.'

The wines are vinified in what the Domaine describes as a 'semi-traditional' manner. The 'semi' component refers to their practice of keeping the wines in cask for only 9–12 months, and then decanting them into tanks for a further 3–6 months before bottling. This is more a practical expedient to release casks for the new vintage than a matter of preferred style.

After a light *débourbage* to conserve as much of the fine lees and indigenous yeasts as possible the Bienvenues and the Premiers Crus are fermented in cask, with a maximum of 20% new oak. However only 66–75% of the produce of their 5 ha. of Puligny Village wine ferments in small oak, depending on the casks they have available. Louis Carillon dislikes both the 'fruits exotiques' flavours produced by low temperature fermentation and the use of too much new wood, so his wines ferment at around 25°C. He also believes that too much new oak dries out a wine and can destroy its typicity – 'The wine tastes delicious when it is young, but not when it becomes older.'

The Puligny Village *cuvée,* about 100–120 casks altogether, is assembled in tank and bottled, in September, just before the harvest. The wine is fined with a mixture of bentonite and casein, and then filtered twice, first with kieselguhr and then through a membrane, which may or may not be of sterile porosity, depending on the vintage. The aim of what might be regarded as severe filtration is to remove any risk of deposit – much more visible in white wine than in red – and to ensure stability for wines which are destined for export to hot and cool climates.

The Premiers Crus and the Bienvenues are left in tank for a further 3–6 months before similar treatment and bottling. Quite what this extra period of ageing adds to the wine is not clear, although being in tank rather than cask risks drying out the wine less.

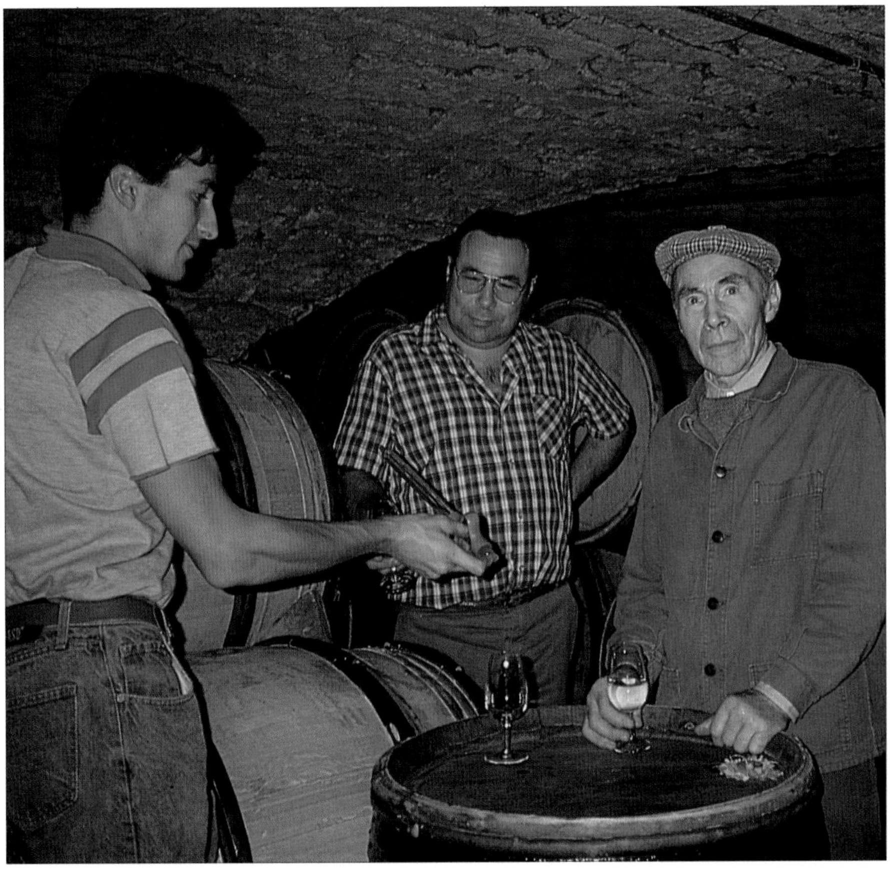

3 generations of Carillons: Robert, Louis and François

One-third of the Domaine's production is red – 1 ha. each of Mercurey, Bourgogne Rouge, Chassagne-Montrachet and Côte de Beaune-Villages. The Carillons destalk 80–100% and prefer a relatively long *cuvaison* of 10–19 days, arguing that this is necessary to unlock colour and to extract the 'more difficult' but finer tannins. They ferment at up to 35° C, with a few days' pre-fermentive maceration 'if the grapes are not too hot'.

An interesting, and sensible, part of the vinification is to vinify the press-wine apart until the following September and then to taste it before deciding whether and in what proportion it should be assembled with the free-run wine. This latter is kept on its lees until September, whereas the press-wine, having more gross lees, is racked after its *malo*. The wines are assembled in tank just before the vintage, given an albumen fining, then a membrane filtration and bottled between January and March of the second year.

Some of the Domaine's red output, notably a proportion of the Puligny Village, the Mercurey and the Côte de Beaune, finds its way on to the négociant market. The rest is bottled by the Carillons and sold either to one of their export customers or to a growing band of private and restaurant clients.

The reds tend to be well-made examples of their origins, the long maceration giving a good depth of structure and plenty of concentration. The Chassagne, from vines planted between 1955 and 1964 on the Puligny side of the commune, is undoubtedly the best of the bunch, with an attractive strawberry perfume, plenty of ripe fruit and a soft and stylish open texture, underpinned with tannins. The Mercurey is also worth looking out for – a more 'sauvage' masculine wine, but one which in 1988 and 1989 will develop into an excellent bottle if it is given 5 years or more to do it.

The Carillon whites exude purity – almost extract of Chardonnay, with plenty of depth and complexity. The keys to their style, according to Jacques, are low yields (that is below 50 hl./ha. for Premiers Crus), and minimum racking, preferably without air. They also attribute the aromatic typicity of their wines to their care in fermenting at the right temperature.

The Puligny Village is an excellent example of their style: direct pure fruit, opening out in the mouth to show a lovely, understated richness with a hint in 1989 of *surmaturité*. A wine which will benefit from a few years' keeping.

The Champ Canet is the most delicate, most feminine of all the Premiers Crus; it has aromas and flavours which are above all fine, rather like intricate lace, backed by a gentle richness which gives it substance underneath the rather fragile exterior. It is always the first of the Carillon Premiers Crus to open out after bottling.

The Perrières is a complete contrast: an altogether richer, broader wine, from less stony soil from vines lower down the hillside than the Champ Canet. Its heavier skeleton makes it a wine for longer keeping.

The Referts is different again: here a more stony and shallower soil gives the wine a characteristic mineral flavour, with a marked acidity at the outset. A less round and supple wine, often with a nose reminiscent of dried oranges and apricots, it starts off with power and complexity which develop into quite a rich, fat wine with age – more of a Meursault with Puligny overtones than the converse.

The 0.12 ha. of Grand Cru Bienvenues-Bâtard-Montrachet produce a characteristically very firm and closed-up wine but one through which can be discerned an inherent power and richness. Tasting it young, one has to look for the aromas and guess how all the rather disparate elements will fit together, but its class is never far below the surface.

If the Carillon whites are not quite as seductive as those of Etienne Sauzet, nor as magnificently aristocratic as those of Leflaive, this is not to deny them a place in the top league. They have their own individuality and profound purity which, although different in style, is something to be prized and savoured; a tribute to this excellent family's skill and art.

VINEYARD HOLDINGS

Commune	*Level*	*Lieu-dit/Climat*	*Area*	*Vine Age*	*Status*
Puligny	GC	Bienvenues-Bâtard-Montrachet	0.12	1959	P
Puligny	PC	Les Combettes	0.47	1992	P
Puligny	PC	Le Champ Canet	0.55	1/2:1959 1/2:1972	P
Puligny	PC	Les Perrières	0.94	25/15/4	P
Puligny	PC	Les Champs-Gains	0.23	1964/65	P
Puligny	PC	Les Referts	0.24	1961	P
Puligny	V	(Various climats)	5.00	1952–1990	P
Puligny	R	(Bourgogne Aligoté)	0.25	1961	P
Puligny	R	(Bourgogne Rouge)	1.00	1955/68/70	P
Chassagne	V	—	0.25	1955/63/64	P
Chassagne	V	(R)	1.00	1955/63/64	P
St.-Aubin	R	(Côte de Beaune-Villages)	1.00	1977/78	P
Mercurey	V	—	1.00	1970/76	P
		Total	**12.05 ha.**		

Domaine Jean Chartron

PULIGNY-MONTRACHET

Jean Chartron is a short, amiable, diplomatic man, who clearly enjoys the good things of life and is content to be counted among those privileged enough to produce some of them.

Until 1989, when he gave up the mayoralty of Puligny-Montrachet after 12 years in office, his life as a grower was inextricably entwined with the community in which he lived and worked. Now free of parochial duties, he devotes his considerable energies to the Domaine, which he took over when his father died in 1983. This is a fine estate, founded by his grandfather in 1860, consisting of some 10 ha. of vines all in the commune of Puligny.

The jewel in Jean's crown is probably not the 0.71 ha. of Grand Cru Chevalier-Montrachet, enviable as that is, but the 3.33 ha. swathe of the Clos du Cailleret – a magnificent enclosure within the Cailleret vineyard, forming the northerly extension and sharing the same broad geology of Le Montrachet Both this and the 1.09 ha. Clos de la Pucelle – a similar enclosure within the Pucelle vineyard – are wholly owned by the Domaine, which permits them to add *Monopole* to their labels.

Together with this Domaine, Jean Chartron is an equal partner with Louis Trebuchet in the négociant business founded under their joint names in 1984. Louis' experience in the Burgundy négoce – 10 years with Jaffelin and a short spell with Laboure-Roi – and Jean's Domaine combine to make what their publicity describes as 'une alliance féconde'.

Chartron et Trebuchet have built up a large range of wines which are sold mainly for export, and are the only house to offer no less than ten different Crus of Puligny-Montrachet. Of their average 1,000-cask output, some 200 casks are attributable to Domaine Jean Chartron.

The Domaine's wines are carefully wrought by their recently installed winemaker, Michel Roucher, who together with Louis and Jean forms the triumvirate which takes all the major decisions. Overall policy is based on the over-riding principle of minimum intervention.

The vinification is a mixture of tradition and innovation. Although he is not a revolutionary Jean is a born experimenter. Up to the 1990 vintage the grapes were pressed, sulphured, the juice left for 24 hours to settle and then put into cask to ferment. However, in 1991 he tried macerating the grapes with their skins for some 15–18 hours before

Mural painted on the cuverie for the 1991 St. Vincent tournante. St. Vincent is the patron saint of wine and villages take turns at hosting the festivities

fermentation. This *macération pelliculaire is* designed to extract greater aromatic richness and depth of flavour. Many believe it also destroys the wine's typicity, so it will be interesting to see how Jean's 1991s evolve.

Fermentation is carried out in cask, with an inoculation of selected yeasts. It is unusual for a Domaine of this quality to use cultured yeasts, but Jean insists they provide an important element of control on both the start and the progress of fermentation. 'Indigenous yeasts are a mixture of good and bad; bought yeasts are only the good ones.'

The white wines receive a maximum of 40% new Allier and Vosges oak for the Grands Crus and 33% for the Premiers Crus. A rotation ensures that none of the Domaine's casks is more than 3 years old. Once in cask, the wines are *batonnés* twice a day, which further adds richness and ensures homogeneity. This continues to the end of alcoholic fermentation, when seeds of lactic bacteria are introduced to induce the *malo.*

Since the aim is to leave the wine on its fine lees as long as possible, the first racking in April is never completely clear. The wine is unified in tank, then returned to casks. In general, the Premiers Crus are bottled just before the summer to preserve typicity and finesse and the more powerful, structured Grands Crus some 12 months after vintage.

Preparation for bottling consists of a light bentonite-casein fining followed by a filtration. Jean Chartron's eventual aim being to eliminate both processes completely, he has replaced a double filtration (kieselguhr plus millipore) with a new single form of less abrasive sterile filter.

Each of the Domaine's wines is a distinct individual, designed to reflect its origins as closely as possible. Although, especially in ripe vintages such as 1983, 1989 and 1990 they have undoubted power, the overall style emphasises finesse rather than size.

The Puligny Premier Cru Les Folatières is a vineyard at the northern, Meursault, end of the commune with thin, limestone-rich soil. This gives a wine of steely finesse, with a good nerve of natural acidity which is perhaps less 'flatteur' to start with than, for example, the Pucelles, but develops well given a few years in bottle.

The Pucelles is altogether different – much richer generally than the Folatières, less floral on the nose with greater fatness and power. In a good vintage Chartron's Clos de la Pucelle might be mistaken for a Bâtard-Montrachet – a junior version, perhaps.

The Chartron Caillerets was originally 2 distinct parcels of vines until 1974 when Les Petits Caillerets, a 0.71 ha. plot at the northern end of the Chevalier-Montrachet vineyard, was, after pressure on the authorities, re-classified as Chevalier. The Clos du Cailleret produces a wine of distinction. As with all great white Burgundy, the best usually begin life as a rather compact bundle – one can see the underlying finesse and can taste the power and fruit, but they need slow evolution in bottle to decode their charms.

The Domaine is producing better and better wine as the years go by. In greater vintages their balance and depth nearly put them into the top flight, but in less ripe years, they seem to lack something of the class found, for example, in a Leflaive or a Ramonet. This should be seen as no more than a minor quibble with a fine Domaine.

VINEYARD HOLDINGS

Commune	*Level*	*Lieu-dit/Climat*	*Area*	*Vin Age*	*Status*
Puligny	GC	Chevalier-Montrachet	0.96	23	P
Puligny	PC	Clos de Cailleret (W)	3.33	27	P
Puligny	PC	Clos de Cailleret (R)	0.74	26	p
Puligny	PC	Les Folatières	1.24	18	P
Puligny	PC	Clos de la Pucelle	1.16	21	P
Puligny	R	(Bourgogne Blanc + Rouge)	2.00	16	P
Puligny	R	(Bourgogne Aligoté)	0.23	29	P
		Total	**9.66 ha.**		

Domaine Henri Clerc

PULIGNY-MONTRACHET

The Côte d'Or is strewn with Domaines capable of producing superb wines but, for various reasons, not quite managing it. Whilst some fail through over-production or sheer laziness, there are a few which, try as they will, seem unable to break out of the 'good but not great' mould. Henri Clerc comes into this category.

Bernard Clerc took over the Domaine, inherited from his mother (a Mlle. Patriache), in 1965. Although he takes great trouble to produce the best, recent performances have fallen well short of top quality and one is driven to enquire what is going wrong.

The raw material is superlative: some 26 ha. of fine land – including Grands Crus Chevalier-Montrachet, Bâtard-Montrachet, Bienvenues-Bâtard-Montrachet and Clos Vougeot, and Premiers Crus in Puligny, Meursault and Blagny.

The search for likely sources of difficulty leads in several directions. First, the vineyards: all but 1.5 of the 27 ha. are tended by *tâcherons* – often people with no real interest in doing the best possible job. Bernard says the only task they can be relied upon to do well is removing excess buds, since this saves them time later at winter pruning.

One gets the feeling that if he could sensibly lighten his acreage, particularly in the 16 ha. of *régionales,* he would gladly do so. At present he rents out these vines to young vignerons who need the appellations, but this is a slow process.

Bernard harvests partly by machine, mostly for the lesser wines but also for about 20% of the Crus. This probably causes a diminution in quality and a reduction in the next year's yield from damage to new wood by the pulsating rods which knock the grapes from the vine. In 1990, a loss of some 1,500 litres was attributable to this.

Neither lazy nor incompetent, Bernard seems to have got himself into a rut of vinification practices which, although labour-saving, can only detract from the quality of his wines. He reasons, justifiably, that his customers like his style, so why change?

Tasting his wines, one is immediately aware of a thematic continuity characterising them – from the basic Chardonnay up to the exalted Chevalier-Montrachet. This thread is an austere dryness, a slightly shrivelled undertone, even in ripe years such as 1989. As they age, often somewhat prematurely, they appear irremediably wrinkled and never quite blossom.

Bernard gives his wines as much lees contact as possible by putting them into cask before fermentation and leaving them there, without racking, until they are bottled some 10–11 months later. But centrifuging the juice beforehand cannot help but remove much of the valuable fine lees along with grosser impurities.

Unlike many fellow vignerons, he is not much in favour of *batonnage.* 'We *batonné* our wines once or twice, just at the end of fermentation to make sure it is finished properly.' Perhaps earlier, more frequent rousing might add extra richness and fat.

The wines are kept in 33% new oak, the Grands Crus having up to 80%. This is mostly Tronçais, with from 1990 a touch of Vosges. However, Bernard orders casks which are 'very well charred', a preference shared by few growers, especially for more delicate wines. In vintages such as 1988 these give wines which, he admits, are dominated by a burnt/bitter taste.

The wines ferment up to 30–35° C, without any attempt to cool them. Bernard explains: 'I do not like low temperature fermentation; it's good if you like bananas or exotic fruits – good for little wines.' Again, he is out of step with most of the top-class Domaines who normally ferment at 20–25° C. A more moderate temperature would make for a richer, less austere character in what should be delicately balanced wines.

Once clear of fermentation, further problems ensue. Bernard ruefully admits that he has difficulty with his *malos.* Perhaps the cellar is too cold; perhaps it is the over-use of SO_2, added in the vineyard, again at the cuverie, and adjusted before and after fermentation; perhaps the important bacteria have been removed by the centrifuge before they get the chance to work?

The final nail in the coffin is the wine's preparation for bottling. Bernard is against fining unless an excess of iron, protein or copper renders it quite unavoidable. Instead the wines are given no less than 3 separate filtrations through a coarsish kieselguhr, then a finer kieselguhr and finally a sterilising plate filter. The reasoning is that these procedures supposedly tire the wine less than a very fine millipore filtration but Bernard seems barely aware of what he is doing: 'I could perhaps rack the wine and avoid these filtrations,' he muses, unconvincingly.

The final wine quality is probably a result of some or all of these small eccentricities. The Pulignys which form the majority of the non-regionals are clean and correct, often quite spicy and not without interest, but they tend to be too austere for genuine appeal.

Bernard Clerc is a charming, dedicated man who deserves success. It would be good to see him dispose of 12 ha. of *régionales,* sack the *tâcherons* and employ a small, dedicated workforce to tend the vines and help in the cellars. Next, he should turn the centrifuge over to making candy-floss, increase the frequency of *batonnage,* decrease fermentation temperatures and the charring on his casks and, finally, try a light bentonite-casein or fish fining instead of three filtrations, however delicate they may be. He could then depart on a well-earned holiday, certain that there would be a queue of customers at his imposing gates in the Place des Marronniers on his return.

VINEYARD HOLDINGS

Commune	*Level*	*Lieu-dit/Climat*	*Area*	*Vine Age*	*Status*
Puligny	GC	Chevalier-Montrachet	0.15	5–21	P
Puligny	GC	Bâtard-Montrachet	0.18	46	P
Puligny	GC	Bienvenues-Bâtard-Montrachet	0.65	13	P
Puligny	PC	Les Pucelles	0.08	27	P
Puligny	PC	Les Folatières	1.49	25	P
Puligny	PC	Les Champs-Gains	0.32	26	P
Puligny	PC	Les Combettes	0.67	28	M
Puligny	V	Les Charmes (W)	0.26	7	P
Puligny	V	(Several climats) (W)	2.62	14	P
Puligny	V	(R)	0.27	5	P
Meursault	PC	Sous le Dos d'Ane	0.55	15	M
Blagny	PC	Sous le Dos d'Ane	0.93	20	M
Vougeot	GC	Clos de Vougeot	0.31	N/A	P
Beaune	V	Chaume Gaufriot (R & W)	0.44	4	P
—	R	(Bourgogne Aligoté)	1.66	20	P
—	R	(Bourgogne Blanc)	6.08	20	P
—	R	(PTG)	3.09	19	P
—	R	(Bourgogne Rouge)	5.60	20	P
		Total	**26.35 ha.**		

Domaine Leflaive

PULIGNY-MONTRACHET

The hamlet of Blagny just visible from the vineyards at the north-east edge of Puligny, near the Meursault border

Whilst experts might argue the relative merits of one particular bottle of white Burgundy over another, there is rare unanimity among them over the Domaine which consistently produces Burgundy's finest white wines.

For years Vincent Leflaive has supplied his neighbours and the rest of the world's producers with yardstick examples of what can be done with the raw materials of prime vineyard land and the Chardonnay grape. The results are inspirational – Premier and Grand Cru wines of immense depth and concentration, raw power combined with great complexity, yet with that dimension of aristocratic breed which defies description.

If the village of Puligny-Montrachet is self-effacing, no less is its greatest estate. The visitor in search of the source of his marvellous bottles will find little enough to help him. If he walks round the main square, the Place des Marronniers, and heads for the western corner, he will come across a pair of black iron gates giving on to an inner courtyard. Nothing as prosaic as a nameplate informs him where he is, nor is there a bell to ring to tell anyone that he's there; all but the most intrepid would probably give up at this point and go off to Le Montrachet on the southern side of the square for a consolatory glass or two or, better still, for lunch.

If, however, our visitor keeps going and passes through the small white-painted postern gate, he will find himself in another, larger, courtyard facing a substantial old manor house, with doors everywhere but rarely anyone to be seen either coming in or going out of them. Having got this far, the only course is up one of a pair of stone staircases to the first floor. While the right-hand stair leads nowhere, its twin arrives at a small, paperless office manned by a computer which appears to be working away in an appropriately respectful manner, all on its own.

It is fair to say that the Domaine does not encourage visitors to turn up hoping for the best. However much you love Leflaive's wines, you are more likely to succeed if you come armed with an appointment, or at least with an introduction from one of their importers, than by trying the 'I've come 10,000 miles just to be here' approach.

This is an estate with a great deal of fascinating history behind it. As described in an excellent booklet produced with great flair by Vincent's wife, Mme. Liliane Leflaive, there have been Leflaives in the area since 1580 when Marc Le Flayve (sic) turned up at nearby Cissey. However, it was not until his great-great-great-grandson Claude Leflaive came to live in the Domaine's present headquarters on his marriage to a widow, Nicole Vallée, on 3 February 1717, that Leflaives came to Puligny.

In 1835 his son, also Claude, divided up his 5 ha. (including a plot of Batârd-Montrachet) among his 5 children. Only one of these legatees, again Claude (when you've got a good name, stick to it), kept his patrimony and it was his grandson, Joseph Leflaive – who inherited the family house and a mere 2 ha. of vines in 1905 – who is the real founder of the Domaine as we know it. The estate had dwindled, not because vineyards had been lost, gambled or sold, but because of French inheritance laws which require all property to be divided equally among descendants, making it almost impossible to keep important Domaines intact.

Between 1905 and 1925 Joseph gradually built up the Domaine's vineyards by careful acquisitions which were made possible in many cases by the desire of vineyard owners to leave viticulture after the *phylloxera* and *oïdium* epidemics of the late nineteenth century. As well as acquiring about 25 ha. of prime vineyards, he added another 25 ha. of land in and around Puligny and numerous buildings, including the cuverie, in the Rue de l'Eglise, and the chais.

With his régisseur and friend, François Virot, Joseph instituted a plan of systematic replanting on to selected rootstocks, taking the opportunity to replace plots of Aligoté and Gamay with Chardonnay.

Having divided his vineyards between his 5 children in 1930, with a legal instrument which prevented them from further selling or subdividing, Joseph died at Puligny in 1953. In 1955, 4 of his children decided to cooperate in continuing the family tradition by keeping the Domaine intact. It is three of these – Vincent, Anne and Jeanne – together with their descendants who are the major co-proprietors of the Domaine today.

Vincent and his brother Jo took over the Domaine in 1953 and ran it together until Jo's death in 1982. There being a family tradition of always having two managers at the Domaine, Jo's son Olivier was put in joint charge with his uncle Vincent in 1986. Vincent, a man of forceful zeal, finally submitted to formal retirement in 1990, after a winter of illness, and put his daughter Anne-Claude in his place.

Thus flows the history of a great estate. Now, firmly in the hands of an eminently capable younger generation, Domaine Leflaive seems set for a future no less illustrious than its past. Anne-Claude is an intelligent and articulate woman who, having undertaken a short apprenticeship at the Domaine in 1979, is now in full-time charge. She is assisted by her cousin, Olivier, who also runs his own successful Domaine in Puligny and divides his time between the two enterprises, receiving clients and travelling widely. There is also a monthly council of 25 of the Domaine's principal shareholders, to discuss major policy decisions and to keep everyone informed.

Anne-Claude and Olivier are backed up by a formidable technical team: Pierre Morey, from Meursault, who was appointed wine-maker on the retirement of Jean Virot (François' son) after the 1987 vintage, and Jean Jafflin, who replaced the talented Michel Mourlon as Chef de Culture in the same year.

The vineyard holdings of the Domaine are awe-inspiring: in Grands Crus 1.75 ha. of Chevalier-Montrachet (out of a total of 7); 1.88 ha. of Bâtard-Montrachet (out of 12) and 1.12 ha. of Bienvenues-Bâtard-Montrachet (out of 2.3). In Premiers Crus nearly 3 ha. of Les Pucelles; 0.7 ha. of Les Combettes and almost 5 ha. of Clavoillon, plus Village land in Puligny and some red Premier Cru Blagny.

In October 1990, Anne-Claude added a further 6 ouvrées (0.25 ha.) of Puligny Premier Cru Les Folatières to 4 ouvrées of the same acquired in 1989. This will enable them to make a respectably-sized *cuvée* of Folatières and it will be interesting to see what emerges here in the forthcoming years. All this makes Leflaive the single largest owner of Premier and Grand Cru vineyards in Puligny – a total of 20.0 ha.

Sadly, they own no Le Montrachet. The Domaine attempted to buy some when a plot became available some years ago, but gave up because the price was too high and because they did not then believe that white wines would ever be in great demand. This is probably one of the few mistakes they have made! They and their customers can take comfort from the fact that their Chevalier-Montrachet not only equals most Montrachets, but frequently out-distances them.

The accession of a younger generation to the management of the Domaine has brought a spirit of re-evaluation and research to its activities. Nowhere is this more evident than in the vineyards. The widespread incidence of the fan-leaf virus, *court-noué,* especially in Bienvenues-Bâtard-Montrachet and other Chardonnay plantings, has remained an unresolved problem since the war. This virus, which takes many forms, degenerates the leaf and thus inhibits effective production of grape sugars by photosynthesis. Traditional treatments with chemical sprays have ceased to work, as vines have grown more resistant; so ever stronger products have had to be developed.

Anne-Claude Leflaive believes strongly that to continue with increasingly powerful chemical regimes is undesirable, both ecologically and for the long-term health of these precious vineyards. After much research, she has instituted trials – on 1 ha. of vineyards drawn from all levels of quality – of a system of treatment known as 'bio-dynamics'. This, in essence, follows work of Rudolf Steiner at the turn of the century, who used dilute doses of plant-based compounds to treat vines and soil. The aim is to stimulate a disproportionate response by encouraging the vine to develop its own resistance mechanism to parasites and viruses and to treat the soil, not so much for mineral deficiencies, but in a way which maximises the activity of benevolent micro-flora.

This is effectively a form of homoeopathic treatment which is relatively new in vine-yards. There are growers in the northern Côte du Rhone and in Vouvray who have experimented successfully with such a regime, but its long-term efficacy and consequences are as yet unknown.

Biodynamics requires the application of treatments on precise days and at precise times, calculated in part by reference to the lunar cycle. In one case Leflaive was asked to treat just before sunrise, which required workers to be up and about at 5 a.m. This, in addition to asking them to mix a teaspoonful of powder to 500 litres of water, rather than the usual 5 kilos of chemical, must have come as something of a shock. No doubt, the reduction in the miserable effects of chemical sprays on their faces and eyes will more than compensate for the odd early hour, should biodynamics be adopted in full. As long as they are not asked to dress in white and chant mystic canticles over their watering-cans, whilst bent double and facing due east, little difficulty is envisaged in getting them to accept what must be something of a novelty. However, until the trials are complete, the traditional chemical regime will continue.

Elsewhere, great effort is put into reducing yields. Pruning is *Guyot simple* – that is, one branch pruned to 6 eyes and a spur, pruned to 2 eyes, for next year's wood, which Anne-Claude is trying to reduce to 5 eyes. In 1988 the practice of *ébourgonnage* was introduced at the Domaine; as soon as is practicable after bud-break, workers are sent through the vineyards to remove excess buds – both on the main branch and on the spur. This reduces the number of bunches and thus limits yields.

In incipiently prolific years, a further, special passage through the vineyards is made during the summer to remove further bunches. This green-pruning is painful but necessary to maximise the concentration of flavour and sugar in the bunches that finally come to ripeness.

In the knowledge that the consequences of a mistake will last half a century or more, the choice of plant material is made with considerable care. The rootstocks onto which a Leflaive scion can expect to be grafted are those low-vigour standards used by most other conscientious growers: 161/49 for the Premiers and Grands Crus (with the exception of the Bâtard-Montrachet which is planted on 5BB) and the somewhat less common Riparia and a little of the congeni-tally vigorous S04 for the Puligny Village vineyards. The Chardonnay clones to which they are attached are either B77 or B95 – the qualitative best of what is currently available.

The Domaine has a policy, which borders on fanaticism, for putting only the healthiest fruit into the presses. To this end, they like to harvest just a few days after the official *ban de vendange* – the earliest permitted picking date. Since the *ban* frequently coincides with the autumn equinox, they fear that any further delay might bring an unwelcome seasonal change of weather – rain followed perhaps by rot.

Preparations for harvest begin a couple of weeks earlier, when 200–300 individual grapes are harvested from different parts of the estate and pressed in small hand-presses. From this juice the ratio of sugars to acids is computed which enables Pierre Morey and Jean Jafflin to follow the evolution of maturity in each parcel of vines and thus eventually to determine the precise moment of harvesting. When the time comes, the pickers are despatched with specific instructions to pick neither rotten fruit nor fruit which is towards the top of the vine, as this is likely to be much less ripe than that lower down.

Once the grapes reach the Rue de l'Eglise, they are immediately pressed in each one of two new pneumatic Bucher presses of 3,600 litres capacity. These give a throughput of about 40–45 228-litre barrels per day. The juice is dosed with SO_2, to prevent premature oxidation and to help settle gross lees during the 24 hours *débourbage* which follows.

When necessary, the *must is* then *chaptalised,* whilst still in bulk and before the alcoholic fermentation. Anne-Claude looks for a final balancing alcohol level of 13–13.5 degrees for Grands Crus, and 12.5 degrees for Premiers Crus and Village wines.

Fermentation takes place in large wooden *foudres* for the Bourgogne Blanc and Puligny Villages lots, and in small casks for the Premiers and Grands Crus, 33% of which find their way into new wood – mostly Allier, with a touch of Vosges. As far as possible, indigenous yeasts are used, to maximise typicity and complexity; in some vintages, for example 1987, cultured yeasts were necessary to kick start the first fermentations.

Whilst a long, even fermentation is preferred, no artificial means are employed to prolong it beyond its natural limits. Pierre Morey has recently instituted some trials with yeast husks which are thought to give a longer, more regular fermentation. Throughout, twice-daily *batonnage* ensures an even distribution of lees throughout each cask.

Following a lead from Patrick Bize in Savigny, the Domaine is now buying its own wood. The worldwide demand for French oak casks has led to misgivings, shared by Anne-Claude, about the quality of the wood used by tonneliers and in particular about the accelerated methods of drying which often lead to green, sappy flavours in the wine. She is now buying her own wood from the Forest of Bertranges, in the Nièvre region, and drying it naturally at Puligny for at least two years. It is then given to a small tonnelier to fashion into casks. The ability to pursue this policy makes the Domaine the envy of many growers who lack only the financial resources to follow suit.

Until 1988, the grapes from any one vineyard were amalgamated and vinified as one wine. However, Pierre Morey and Anne-Claude have decided to vinify each lot separately until it has finished its *malolactic fermentation* and been given its first racking. This enables them to follow more closely the evolution of the wine from each patch of vines. There are already dividends in the form of systematic, recognisable differences between different vine ages, rootstocks, soils and locations within a single vineyard.

Although the practicalities of such a policy are daunting – many small volumes of wine to be kept apart and scrupulously recorded – the experiment has been extended to keeping individual lots apart until bottling. It is hoped that eventually this work will enable them to further improve quality by fine-tuning the *élevage* of each *cuvée.*

A further racking takes place after the *malolactic fermentation* – usually no later than April – and the wine is then transferred from the Rue de l'Eglise to the cellars beneath the offices in the Place desMarronniers. Here, in a row of pot-bellied stainless steel tanks with legs that appear to be far too short for them, giving the impression of a sort of overfed metallic 'corps de ballet' waiting mischievously until no one is looking to break into a vigorous 'pas de dix', the various lots are unified, 10 casks to a tank, and left throughout the following winter.

The purpose of this transfer is to conserve freshness and structure in the young wine and to release cask space for the vintage to come. A fining with casein and bentonite (fish fining was tried but found to be less conclusive) and a single cellulose plate filtration before bottling between February and April of the second year, completes the bringing up of a young Leflaive Puligny.

There is nothing particularly revolutionary or remarkable in this vinification of some of the world's greatest Chardonnays, except perhaps for the unusual expedient of a long period in stainless steel before bottling. What the Domaine stresses is the necessity for infinite care to obtain the best fruit and to handle it delicately with an obsession for hygiene. A clinically clean environment – clean tanks, picking baskets, floors, hands, pipes, air, in short clean everything – leads to clean wine. In turn, clean wine requires less disturbance and handling, and above all less sulphur. Less disturbance, less handling and less sulphur in their turn mean that one destroys less of the delicate natural flavours and aromas of the grape. The principle may be blindingly simple but in practice demands obsessive vigilance at every stage of production.

Tasting a range of Leflaive wines in the small, informal tasting room off the main courtyard is as much a philosophical exegesis on what constitutes a fine wine, as a survey of the characteristics of whatever vintage is being offered. Understanding the spirit of the Domaine is a prerequisite of understanding its wines, and the better they are understood, the more will they be enjoyed. A Bach fugue may be appreciated for its power, or its sonority, but will yield much more to someone who is aware of the principles of contrapuntal construction and can therefore appreciate what has brought about such a sublime combination of external simplicity with inner complexity.

The Leflaive concept of a great white wine is one of elegance and harmony combined with finesse. A wine may exhibit a multiplicity of different aromas and flavours, but if they do not combine harmoniously, the wine is unbalanced and therefore flawed.

However, this deceptively easy harmony, which characterises all Leflaive's wines, belies their true nature. Even the simple Puligny Village wine has a structure and class that others would be content to emulate in their Premiers and Grands Crus.

What is the secret? According to Vincent Leflaive there is no magical alchemy by which a bunch of ripe Chardonnay grapes is transformed into exquisite wine. He is adamant that care and control are necessary at every stage of production – from the clonal selection and pruning in the vineyard through to deciding on the precise moment to bottle each appellation.

However, while they may be necessary to the production of great Pulignys, care and control are themselves by no means sufficient. A vigneron may be able to control the temperature of his fermentation vats, and may be infinitely careful in doing so, but this will not by itself produce the quality of Leflaive or Ramonet. The skill is as much one of knowing what to do as of knowing how to do it. Behind the judicious use of technology there must be a feel for what goes into a fine bottle of wine. This is the vigneron's true art – a talent beyond the power of teaching.

What are the results of such toil and skill? A range of wines which make one's mouth water just thinking about them. The red Blagny from the picturesquely named Sous le Dos d'Ane (Under the Donkey's Back) is a wine full of seductive, ripe fruit with, as one might expect, balancing acidity and tannin. Not a wine for great feasts or for analytical sipping but a delicious mouthful to enjoy with simple dishes. It is reasonably priced and usually excellent value.

The Pulignys begin with the Village wine – bags of fruit, superb balance and, for its level, remarkable complexity. Of the Premiers Crus, the Clavoillon, geographically midway between Puligny and Meursault, is usually ripe, stylish and several notches more complex than the Puligny tout court. Vincent Leflaive believes this to be the most masculine of his trio of Premiers Crus, combining the nuttiness of Meursault with the elegance

Olivier, Vincent and Anne-Claude Leflaive in the Domaine's courtyard at Puligny

of Puligny. The Combettes vineyard, situated two-thirds of the way up the Côte on the Meursault border, produces wine of a different character: a touch more earthiness, with distinct tones of grilled almonds, peaches and honey.

Fine as these two undoubtedly are, they are invariably overshadowed by the Pucelles – a vineyard just below Les Caillerets and adjacent to the Grand Cru Bâtard-Montrachet. In a great vintage, such as 1983, this wine has a depth of flavour and concentration which are truly sensational. It also has a dimension of class and vinosity which have led many to declare it as Grand Cru in quality.

The Grands Crus themselves are no less exalted. Each has its individuality and spectrum of aromas and flavours, the richness and complexity of which vitiate descriptions which soon begin to sound like pretentious rubbish. Leflaive's Grands Crus have so much nuance and interest in them that every sniff begs a sip and every sip is sheer delight. His wines are fine testaments to the wine-maker's art.

Vincent Leflaive will tell you, if you give him the chance, that his wines are usually drunk too young. They need time to evolve to unpack and show their qualities. After 5 years the Premiers Crus will begin to drink well, but one should wait 8–10 years before making a tentative foray at the Grands Crus. A 1979 Bienvenues drunk in 1990 was just beginning to show its real class, and a 1983 Chevalier tasted in the same year was still an infant. Less opulent vintages, recently 1987, 1982 and 1981, invariably exhibit the same spectrum of qualities as richer vintages, but in less degree. You should not buy Leflaive's wines by the vintage chart – there are no disappointing bottles here.

Great white Burgundy has the potential, if properly stored, to keep for a long time. Anne-Claude cites a bottle of the Domaine's Chevalier-Montrachet, 1949, which she tried recently: 'I am always a bit puzzled over the qualities of old wines from our Domaine; but I assure you, this was oooh! ex-tra-ord-in-ary, with aromas of kernels and walnuts – ex-tra-ord-in-ary.'

Pierre Morey and the Domaine are lucky to have each other – a talented wine-maker in a privileged environment. Anne-Claude and Olivier seem to be putting down sound roots in their magnificent heritage, so everything seems set fair for a refulgent future, at this greatest of Burgundy Domaines.

VINEYARD HOLDINGS

Commune	*Level*	*Lieu-dit/Climat*	*Area*	*Vine Age*	*Status*
Puligny	GC	Chevalier-Montrachet	1.75	20	P
Puligny	GC	Bâtard-Montrachet	1.88	17	P
Puligny	GC	Bienvenues-Bâtard-Montrachet	1.12	32	P
Puligny	PC	Les Pucelles (Clos du Meix)	2.92	22	P
Puligny	PC	Les Combettes	0.71	26	P
Puligny	PC	Les Chalumeaux/Les Folatières	0.50	3 & 7	P
Puligny	PC	Les Clavoillons	4.67	20	P
Puligny	V	Brelance/La Rue Au Vaches/ Les Grands Champs/ Les Nosroyes/Les Tremblots	3.21	Various	P
Puligny	R	Les Houlières	1.75	9	P
Blagny	PC	Sous le Dos d'Ane	1.58	33	P
		Total	**20.09 ha.**		

Domaine Étienne Sauzet

PULIGNY-MONTRACHET

It is not easy – nor perhaps is it necessary – to be thoroughly objective about a Domaine which, year after year, turns out a range of superlative white Burgundies. A bottle of Sauzet Puligny rarely fails one's expectations and frequently surpasses them.

Apart from a cellar full of mouthwateringly fine wine, the Domaine has a view which most serious wine-lovers would be happy to gaze at for hours; from the windows of their headquarters, on the westerly extremity of Puligny, one looks directly out onto the magnificent saddle of the Grands Crus. From her office, when the routine of 'declarations' bores her, Étienne Sauzet's grand-daughter, Jeanine Boudot, can simply raise her eyes beyond Les Pucelles towards Bâtard, Bienvenues, Les Chevaliers and Montrachet itself. This must rank among the world's most pleasurable prospects, especially with a glass of her husband Gérard's Puligny in one's hand. In such circumstances, a lack of enthusiasm for the authorities and their witless stream of paperwork would be entirely understandable.

The vignoble is substantially that built up by Étienne Sauzet in the 1920s He started with around 3 ha. at the turn of the century and then married some more vineyards in 1924. Additions, largely in Premier and Grand Cru land, followed during the 1950s, bringing the Domaine up to its maximum size.

It prospered until 1909 when Jeanine's mother – Étienne Sauzet's daughter, who owned the vineyards – decided, largely for tax reasons, to divide them between her 3 children. However, she failed to stipulate that the Domaine must remain intact, so when Jeanine's brother Jean-Marc Boillot signified his intention to extract his share, the problem of equitable division arose and, with it, domestic dissension. Although resolution of the problem was not simple, it was achieved, and its impact amortised by the agreement of the other brother to contract his share of vines to the Domaine for 20 years.

The result was that in 1991 the Domaine lost all its Premier Cru Les Truffières, some Puligny Villages, and part of Les Referts, Champ Canet and Combettes. Whilst this is naturally a severe blow to Gérard and Jeanine, their own wine will not suffer in quality – there will just be one-third less of it, and the Grand Cru holdings remain intact.

Under Gérard's hand the Domaine has become one of the finest in the Côte. Initially great efforts were needed to re-establish the condition of the vineyards, which were what he describes as 'a veritable mine of potassium' following the wild excesses of potassium-based fertilisers lavished on them in the 1960s. It took constant soil analyses and 10 years of repeated small doses of potassium-munching magnesium to restore some sort of equilibrium.

As well as being an important determinant of the Domaine's fertilising programme, soil analyses are used to help decide the appropriate rootstock for new plantings. Vines die, often of old age, sometimes from hail or storm damage, but frequently from disease. Virus diseases such as *eutypiose* and leaf-roll are particularly savage, since long incubation and gradual, almost imperceptible degeneration make early detection virtually impossible. The choice of root is critical to the maintenance of a healthy vineyard, and the adaptability of root to both soil and vine variety an integral part of that choice.

Although Gérard relies as much as possible on replacing vines individually, there comes the time when a larger parcel of vines has to be grubbed up and replanted. The present policy is to use 50% clones and 50% *sélection massale* from the Domaine's own vines on rootstock determined by soil-type. Rootstock 161/49 is excellent on sloping sites, with a moderate active lime content; otherwise 3309 is used for patches of Bourgogne Blanc on flatter land since it is relatively late ripening.

As with any top-quality estate, there is an annual struggle to rein in the natural exuberance of the vine, to keep yields down at levels compatible with high quality. Much work is done while the vine is growing to concentrate its vigour, in particular a very strict *évasivage,* especially with the young vines, to remove double shoots and excess buds. Gérard considers this operation to be even more important than the pruning, especially for the Chardonnay where a green-pruning, to cut off excess bunches, is not regarded as a credible option. The reason is that if you green-prune the Chardonnay, while you may indeed end up with fewer bunches, these are likely to contain too much juice – the vine puts any additional energy at its disposal into swelling the berries, whereas the Pinot Noir will thicken the skin.

Much of what is done in the vineyards is based on the principle that one observes first and acts afterwards. In deciding when to harvest, for example, it is essential to know what has happened at flowering – 100 days or so earlier. If there has been wet weather, the flowers tend to *couler* - they drop off, thereby diminishing the potential yield of grapes, since it is the flowers that eventually turn into bunches. The less charge a vine has on it, the sooner it is likely to ripen, and so the flowering may partly determine the order in which the various vineyards are harvested.

The aim is to pick when the grapes are at their maximum maturity, which usually means leaving the plantings on 3309 roots, such as Les Truffières, until last. However, delaying unduly risks over-ripeness, which

Gérard and Jeanine Boudot with their children

may add an element of richness to the wine but tends to detract from its aromatic purity and thus from its typicity. This *surmaturité*, which, in a damp autumn can easily become the *noble rot* so important in the great sweet wines of Sauternes, Germany and elsewhere, often masks the underlying qualities of any wine it affects, with its own distinctive aromas and flavours. Gérard Boudot quite justifiably describes choosing the right moment to harvest as a lottery.

After the intricacies of the vineyard, the process of vinification is relatively uncomplicated. After dosing with just enough sulphur to kill the natural yeasts, the intact bunches are pressed in a pneumatic press and the resulting juice left for 12–18 hours to deposit its gross lees. Bentonite and enzymes may be added to help clarification in difficult years, for example in 1983 when there was widespread rot.

Following any necessary *chaptalisation*, fermentation takes place in cask – provided there is enough space – otherwise, the Village Puligny is fermented in tank. For the last 10 years, Gérard has used selected strains of cultured yeasts to ferment his *must.* Experiments carried out then, and repeated more recently, suggest that fermentation is more regular and complete with these than with the indigenous population. In particular there is less risk of being left, at the end of fermentation, with residual sugar which refuses to ferment. This is a wine-maker's nightmare, since if the bacteria which mediate the *malolactic fermentation* manage to attack the sugar, the result is 'piqure' – acetic acid – which smells and tastes unpleasant even in modest concentrations and moreover is ineradicable.

In order to maintain the temperature of fermentation at 18–20° C – not so easy in Puligny where the high water-table precludes naturally cool underground cellars – the ambient temperature of the cuverie is lowered to 14° C ten days before the harvest is expected.

After fermentation, Gérard's aim is to leave the wine on its lees as long as possible, provided these are healthy. To achieve the finest quality of lees, a prolonged *débourbage* of the press juice is essential. The finer the lees, the less the risk of a *goût de lie* which can so easily dominate and spoil a wine. To get the best out of a wine's fine lees, most – though by no means all – white wine-makers, including Gérard, consider it important to ensure their even distribution throughout the cask by periodically stirring them up – *batonnage.*

At Domaine Sauzet this process starts whilst the wine is still fermenting, during which time it is roused every 2 days. When fermentation has finished, the frequency is reduced to fortnightly up to the *malo,* and thereafter to monthly until the wine is racked.

In a normal year, when the lees are healthy, the wines are given just one racking – after some 12 months on their lees and 2 months or so before bottling. The Puligny Village, Chassagne Village, and Puligny Premiers Crus Referts and Perrières are usually bottled before the following harvest, the Combettes, Champ Canet and Grands Crus being left until November.

To prepare the wine for bottling, they are racked from their lees into *cuves* and then given a dose of fish fining for 15–21 days. Gérard has found that this particular fining agent retains more of the purity and finesse of a wine than the widely used casein – which he regards as more of a specific treatment for wines which have become prematurely yellow. Moreover, 'the wines often taste better after fining than before – much finer,' so this is not just a matter of clarification. They are then given a kieselguhr filtration, using the lighest earth – 'terre rose' – which Gérard has found to tire the wines less than the traditional plate filter, which he ceased using in 1982.

The Sauzet wines exude finesse and elegance. Part of the secret, according to Gérard, is the judicious use of new wood which he emphasises is there not to impart its own qualities to his wines, but rather to support their natural aromas. He prefers wood from the Vosges, Allier and Tronçais, with no more than a medium char, allowing a maximum of 50% new wood for the Grands Crus, 33% for the Premiers Crus and 25% for the Puligny Village. 'Never above, but often below: the proportion must not be higher than that necessary to keep the wine consistent – that is the way to work.'

The Sauzet range starts with a delicious Bourgogne Blanc, made from vines within the commune of Puligny but without its appellation, yielding about 30 hl./ha. This generally tastes well above its official class, being full and ripe, with plenty of soft, fleshy fruit and good length.

The Puligny Village is invariably fresh and beautifully balanced with a floral elegance and Puligny power which are most attractive. Even in leaner vintages, such as 1981, or dilute vintages, such as 1982, Gérard manages to achieve a grip and balance in this *cuvée* which give style and interest. Undoubtedly, the lowish yields of around 45 hl./ha. contribute a helpful element of concentration.

In 1989 the harvest was virtually perfect: 'The best raw material I have ever seen,' volunteered Gérard. The quality of the wines is remarkable, surpassing even the fabulous 1983s, some of which were touched with discernible *botrytis*, especially in the *cuvées* emanating from the flatter Village vineyards. In his opinion, 1989 is the best vintage in Puligny for 30 years.

The Referts is the most masculine of the Premiers Crus – opulent, ripe, with a nose of dried orange peel and a long, powerful flavour in 1989 – yet often with a distinctive *goût de terroir* and muscle which are strikingly reminiscent of Meursault.

The Combettes is a complete contrast – with a honeyed mouthfilling panoply of fruit coupled with nuance, power and length which generally brings it within a hair's breadth of Grand Cru quality – unquestionably the 1989 is of Grand Cru quality.

The hallmarks of Gérard Boudot's wines are richness and class. They seem to combine Puligny breed with an almost exotic concentration of fruit, yet there is nothing clumsy or overblown about them. Both the Grands Crus evince these qualities in fine measure, although in different styles.

The Bienvenues, from a patch next to Les Pucelles, seems more often than not to emphasise the Pucelles finesse rather than the power and structure of Bâtard – brains not brawn, perhaps. The Bâtard, on the other hand, has noticeably greater richness and breadth – a big wine, but not lacking in finesse and style. The Sauzet 1989s are magnificent specimens and undoubtedly destined to become collectors' pieces.

The contraction of Gérard Boudot's vineyard holdings can only be seen as a tragedy for the wine-drinking world – as if Ashkenazy were somehow reduced to half a piano or Menhuin restricted to a two-stringed violin. The inevitable frustration for such a talented wine-maker will perhaps find some other means of expression. Meanwhile, one can only marvel at what he has achieved and enjoy what there is.

VINEYARD HOLDINGS

Commune	*Level*	*Lieu dit/Climat*	*Area*	*Vine Age*	*Status*
Puligny	GC	Bâtard-Montrachet	0.14	17	P
Puligny	GC	Bienvenues-Bâtard-Montrachet	0.12	25	P
Puligny	PC	Les Combettes	0.97	38	P
Puligny	PC	Le Champ Canet	1.00	30	P
Puligny	PC	Les Perrières	0.48	5	P
Puligny	PC	Les Referts	0.70	25	P
Puligny	V	—	2.59	22	P
Puligny	R	(Bourgogne Blanc)	0.52	4	P
Chassagne	V	Les Encegnières (W)	0.49	43	P
		Total	**7.01 Ha.**		

CHASSAGNE-MONTRACHET

Chassagne-Montrachet – a long, straggling village just over the old Paris–Lyon road, the RN 6, from Puligny – is by no stretch of the imagination exciting, but a solid, workaday commune without Puligny's compact charm or Meursault's open, commercial bustle. However, the excellence of the wine amply compensates for the somewhat pedestrian ambience.

Chassagne's origins are Roman. Human remains unearthed in Les Caillerets suggest that early settlements were further up the hill – beyond what is now the older part. If so, the village has gradually expanded down to its present position, newest manifestations of which are a grand 'Salle de Réunion', a 'Caveau des Vignerons' and a large, rectangular, brick bus-shelter.

Despite Chassagne's somewhat unprepossessing exterior, there are outbreaks of delightful little courtyards and mellow old

stone buildings. Many families whose names have for centuries been associated with the community – Colin, Delagrange, Gagnard, Morey and others – have rooted here and spread their matrimonial tentacles; anyone trying to sort out the different affinities may sometimes need genealogical tables to ensure they are dealing with the right Domaine. Adding a spouse's surname, though designed to help identification, often generates more confusion than it dissipates.

A popular but erroneous belief is that Chassagne produces mainly white wine. However, in an average year, only 42% of the 120,000-case production is white, the remainder being red; in the years just after the last war, the red proportion was nearer 80%. The false impression probably arises from the strong international market for white wine, particularly in the 1970s and 1980s, which enabled growers to charge considerably more for this than for red.

The change in fashion has led to extensive replanting, to meet the demand for white wine. However, whilst most Chassagne vineyards are entitled to produce red or white, there are sound geological reasons for preferring some *climats* for one or the other. Unfortunately, much recent planting has been on flatter land, whose high-yielding rich soils are unsuitable for Chardonnay; resulting wines are dilute and generally mediocre.

A few years ago, Bernard Morey and others tried to draw up a Chardonnay 'map' of Chassagne, in an effort to limit plantings to suitable soils. The initiative failed, through lack of co-operation. In the interests of their appellation's good name, growers should ask the *INAO* to revive and supervise this worthwhile project.

The vineyards are even more elongated than the village. Starting just over the RN 6, they extend, generally with a good south-easterly exposure, for some 2.8 km. before reaching Santenay and Remigny. The degree of slope varies from the flatter land below the Santenay road to the steeper hillsides 1.5 km. above, under 'La Grande Montagne' – 300–400 m. high.

The Chassagne Village appellation, embracing both red and white wines, covers 179.51 ha. of land, almost all below the Puligny-Santenay road. Most of the Chassagne Rouge is also produced here, though some excellent red Premiers Crus are made, particularly the Clos St.-Jean and Clos de la Boudriotte from Ramonet and a range of interesting Morgeots.

The soils designated as best suited to Pinot Noir tend to have more depth and a higher iron-oxide content. These are concentrated below the village, mainly on Village AC land.

There are no fewer than 18 principal Premiers Crus, covering 158.79 ha.; many are subdivided into 2, 3 or 4 individual *climats*; the wine may thus bear the name of the principal *lieu-dit* or else that of the *climat*, so there is ample scope for confusion. The most frequently encountered are: La Boudriotte, Les Vergers, En Remilly, Morgeot (58.11 ha. divided into 22 *lieu-dits),* Maltroie, La Grande Montagne, Clos St.-Jean (14.16 ha.), Les Chenevottes, Les Chaumées, Les Champs Gain, Les Caillerets, Les Embrazées and Les Grandes Ruchottes.

Fortunately Chassagne's wines are more complex and aesthetically interesting than its parochial architecture. This is the new bus shelter . . .

Two of the 3 Chassagne Grands Crus – Le Montrachet and Bâtard-Montrachet – are dealt with under Puligny-Montrachet, since they straddle both communes. The third, and smallest of the 6 white Grands Crus of the Côte de Beaune, is Criots-Bâtard-Montrachet. This rather forlorn patch of land, entirely within Chassagne, extends to only 1.57.21 ha. and produces some 550 cases per year. The largest owner, with a holding of 0.62 ha., is the Domaine St-Joseph in Santenay, belonging to Joseph Belland, Adrien's brother.

Mme. Bize-Leroy has recently acquired some 600 sq. m. of Criots-Bâtard-Montrachet, in appalling repair, for what local gossip puts at 1,600,000 French francs; at this rate, 1 ha. of this least prestigious of the Grands Crus is worth 27,000,000 Ff. One wonders whether this is commercially viable.

The cream of the white wines derives from the broad band of hillsides above and either side of the village. Here the rock is mainly oolitic limestone, a fish-fossil substance imparting nerve and vinosity. Across this band, soils vary from *terre rouge,* with some clay in the Les Vergers and Les Chenevottes sector, through the white marls of Morgeot, Boudriotte and Champs Gain to the red, ferruginous earth either side of the Santenay road and the very hard clay and stony ground of Clos Pitois and Les Embrazées, on the commune border.

As with Puligny and Meursault, much Chassagne is dilute and disappointing. Equally, there are excellent wines to be had from every sector of the vignoble; as usual, vine age, yields and the grower's skill are as important as the appellation.

Apart from the Domaines profiled here, fine Chassagnes are made by Laurence Jobard for Drouhin from the Marquis de Laguiche's estate, and by Jacques Lardière at Louis Jadot from the vineyards of the Duc de Magenta. These are yardstick, classy Chassagnes; expensive, but well worth it.

White Chassagnes from top growers and good vintages will keep for years. Wines from the 1960s ands 1970s are still delicious and the best by no means fading. The reds do not, usually, have the longevity of their white counterparts – being quite soft and plummy after 5–10 years and developing a lean, pinched character thereafter.

THE GRANDS CRUS OF CHASSAGNE-MONTRACHET

Lieu-dit	*Area*	*Props.*	*Av. Prod.*
Croits-Bâtard-Montrachet	1.57.21	7	550 C/S
Bâtard-Montrachet	5.84.42	See Puligny	—
Le Montrachet	3.98.73	See Puligny	—
Totals	**11.40.36 ha.**		**550 C/S**

Domaine Blain-Gagnard

CHASSAGNE-MONTRACHET

Unlike his brother-in-law Richard Fontaine (Domaine Fontaine-Gagnard), Jean-Marc Blain comes from a family of viticulteurs; when in 1980 he married Jacques Gagnard's younger daughter Claudine, whom he had met while they were both studying oenology at Dijon, and moved to Chassagne, wine-making did not come as a complete novelty. Jean-Marc and his wife now have some 6.5 ha. of vines including Grands Crus Bâtard-Montrachet and Criots-Bâtard-Montrachet plus 5 white and 2 red Chassagne Premiers Crus and other Village and Premier Cru.

Jean-Marc is a shy, diffident man who works hard at his job. He strives to keep his vineyards in top condition and to maintain a high average vine age by replacing individual vines where practicable. He stresses the importance of mixing vine ages because a vineyard composed entirely of old vines will one day have to be grubbed up with the consequent loss of several years' production. In 1989 and 1990 a new pneumatic press enabled the separate unification of grapes from young and old vines from his two Grands Crus. The results indicated that the young vines gave finesse and fruit, whilst wine from older plants was noticeably fatter and richer. A mixture of the two was best of all.

Yields are maintained as far as possible at 40–45 hl./ha. for Chardonnay and rather less for Pinot Noir. Apart from a careful *ébourgonnage* each spring, the method of pruning helps significantly, particularly for red vines, which are trained *en cordon*. The *cordon* spreads out the vegetation, limiting the number of spurs to 2 on each of 3 eyes, each pruned to 2 buds, giving a maximum potential of 12 bunches per vine. One curious feature of *cordon* training is that individual berries tend to be large at Chassagne and Santenay and small at Volnay.

The harvest is of great concern to Jean-Marc – and indeed, to all the Gagnard clan. Richard Fontaine-Gagnard is the fortunate possessor of a refractometer, which is shared during the run-up to picking to add to their own assessments of sugar levels in each vineyard. Jean-Marc often starts by picking his 'tête de cuvée' reds – the Premiers Crus Morgeot and Clos St.-Jean, deliberately leaving the most important vines of all – the 'battle engines' of the Premier and Grand Cru whites – until they are at optimum ripeness. However, being the only Gagnard without cooling apparatus, he tries to harvest early in the day before the grapes become too hot. The Gagnard harvest tends to be a cooperative family effort, with pickers moving between all three Domaines.

Jean-Marc's aim is to make *vins de garde* – wines with sufficient depth and structure to be kept. To achieve this, SO_2 is kept to a minimum and lees contact to a maximum, with regular *batonnage*. He gives each cask a sharp tap, now and then; the resulting shock-wave keeps the lees on their toes, as it were, and is especially efficacious in promoting a regular *malo*.

The whites are fermented in cask, 25–33% new Allier oak with a moderate charring. Jean-Marc tried Vosges and Cher oak but found the Allier more satisfying. He breaks in new casks with hot water, to remove excess tannins, a practice which his barrel-maker considers akin to putting ice-cubes into a glass of Montrachet.

The wines are racked twice, once in the spring when they are unified, and again cask-to-cask just before fining in the autumn. The fining agent is milk or casein – bentonite takes too much out of the wine. Bottling takes place just before the vintage – 6 months earlier than his father-in-law, whose colder cellar gives a slower evolution in wood.

Jean-Marc's whites are invariably copybook Chassagnes; sharply defined, generally on the richer side, but with a careful balance of constituents – essential to proper ageing. Apart from the pair of Grands Crus, the best are Les Caillerets, Morgeot and La Boudriotte. Of these, Caillerets is the most elegant and feminine – though it can start off closed and unyielding. The Morgeot, from *terre rouge,* is distinctly heavier, with a broader frame and more obvious muscle. If there is a hierarchy, then the Boudriotte would probably just win; it combines the 'primeur' aspects of Morgeot's Caillerets with structure – a wine lovely when young, but which soon closes up and may not emerge for several years.

If the keys to a fine white Chassagne are plenty of *batonnage,* good casks, minimal oxidation and scrupulous cellar hygiene, coupled with a well-balanced soil and small yields, fine reds are no less exacting. Jean-Marc systematically destalks his bunches before vatting, a *cuvaison* of 12–14 days is the norm, with the temperature rising to 35° C. Yields are so low that there is never the need to reduce the volume with a *saignée de cuve* and *chaptalisation,* when necessary, is preferred in small doses, as late as possible, prolonging the fermentation by up to 4 days.

A peculiarity of the Blain-Gagnard red wine *élevage* is that only 10-year-old white wine oak is used. 'Chassagnes are savage enough,' says Jean-Marc, 'better to have finesse than adding more hardness with new casks.'

The wines are fined after the second racking, just before or after the new vintage, lightly plate filtered and bottled in January or February of the second year – with the jointly-owned bottling machine.

Of the 2 red Chassagne Premiers Crus, the Clos St.-Jean – from well-drained soil, with a lowish clay content and stony topsoil – has indubitably greater finesse. The 1978 Morgeot tasted in 1991 was still young, with a deep, sustained ruby colour and a nose which suggested that it was starting to emerge from hibernation. His wines may start life with his reticence but seem to end up with his smile.

Jean-Marc Blain is a fine wine maker – a conscientious man who cares about quality.

VINEYARD HOLDINGS

Commune	*Level*	*Lieu-dit/Climat*	*Area*	*Vine Age*	*Status*
Chassagne	GC	Bâtard-Montrachet	0.34	5 & 35	P
Chassagne	GC	Criots-Bâtard-Montrachet	0.21	15 & 40	P
Chassagne	PC	Les Caillerets (W)	0.37	25	P
Chassagne	PC	Morgeot (W)	0.86	25	M/P
Chassagne	PC	La Boudriotte (W)	0.46	30	P
Chassagne	PC	Clos St.-Jean (W)	0.22	1987	P
Chassagne	PC	Morgeot (R)	0.49	23	M/P
Chassagne	PC	Clos St.-Jean (R)	0.22	30	P
Chassagne	PC	Les Champs-Gains (W)	0.12	10	P
Chassagne	PC	La Grande Montagne (W)	0.23	1988	P
Chassagne	V	Les Mazures + Les Chaumées (W)	0.47	25 & 40	P
Chassagne	V	Les Gougeonnes + Les Houillères + Les Chaumes	1.05	30	P
Chassagne	R	(PTG)	0.59	25 & 50	P
Volnay	PC	Chanlin	0.37	14 & 60	P
Pommard	V	Combes + La Croix Planée	0.52	4 & 8	P
		Total	**6.52 ha.**		

Domaine Colin-Deleger

CHASSAGNE-MONTRACHET

While Chassagne seems to have a less grand international image than Puligny, it makes up the deficiency with a relatively large coterie of small, but thoroughly conscientious growers, producing wines to a high standard year on year.

Among this band is Michel Colin who owns 11.96 ha. judiciously spread across the commune, with the exception of a pocket-handkerchief parcel of 15 ares of 45-year-old vines in that curiosity of a Puligny Premier Cru, Les Demoiselles. The parcels of Morgeot, Chenevottes and Maltroie came with his wife – marriage is not just a matter of the heart in Burgundy!

Michel is a serious, quietly spoken man in his early 50s, whose family have been viticulteurs in Chassagne for 3 generations. As one might expect, he takes considerable care over his vineyards; each year he replants 20–50 ares, although his policy is to replace individual vines wherever practicable. He used to select his own plant material from among his vines; however, since clones are now fully virus-indexed and guaranteed free of that scourge of Chardonnay, *court-noué,* he has been planting a mixture since 1982/3.

Since many of his vines are on steep slopes, soil erosion is a constant problem. Almost every year, Michel is obliged to collect up topsoil which has been washed down and to carry it back whence it came. To overcome this, he is experimenting with *enherbement* – the sowing of selected grasses between the vine rows. Michel believes that, in addition to soil-retentive properties, grasses may have a disinfectant role and reduce *botrytis* – one of the worst maladies for which there is no effective treatment.

All the usual steps are taken to keep yields within that narrow band between excessive and uneconomic. Michel also summer-prunes relatively high, 1.15 metres; this not only thins out the foliage, but enhances natural sugar production, thus minimising the need for *chaptalisation.*

Vinification of the white wines, which form just under half the Domaine's production, is relatively straightforward: following pneumatic pressing which yields fine lees, thus eliminating the need for *débourbage,* the smaller lots go directly into cask for fermentation; volumes in excess of 8 *pièces* start their fermentation in temperature-controlled stainless-steel *cuves* and are put into cask when the *must* density reaches 1,020 or so.

Some 20–25% of new Vosges and Allier wood is used and the aim is to keep the wines on their fine lees until the July following the vintage – even if the *malo* has finished, in which case the SO_2 is adjusted as necessary. Weekly *batonnage is* administered until Christmas, when the frequency is doubled until the *malos* have finished. The wines are racked into bulk, left on a casein fining for 1–2 months before being plate-filtered and bottled just before the new vintage is harvested.

The policy of longish lees contact and speedy, early bottling is designed to give wines which emphasise their freshness both in flavour and aroma, whilst at the same time having the potential for moderate ageing. Tasting with Michel consists of a delightful ramble through the Crus of Chassagne. La Maltroie and Morgeot apart, all his white vineyard holdings are on the Puligny side of the commune which makes for greater finesse. However, although the wines are generally rich in fruit and, in vintages such as 1989 and 1990, high in alcohol, they do not always have the profundity one expects. This is a cellar from which to pick and choose.

It seems invidious to select any one of the range of Premier Cru Chassagnes above the others; each has its own characteristics and temperament. Perhaps, however, the En Remilly is intellectually the more interesting for its situation at the top of Mont Rachet, at the limit of the Grand Cru Chevalier, on the other side of the hill, where Chassagne and St.-Aubin meet. In style, one might consider Michel Colin's En Remilly as a junior Chevalier – it has both the richness and structure, combined with power and finesse and has an aspect of class which the Morgeot, for example, sometimes lacks.

The Puligny Les Demoiselles is also something of a curiosity, being the first small patch of vines in the Premier Cru Les Caillerets, bordered on two sides by Grands Crus – to the south, Montrachet Chevaliers and above Les Chevaliers; the filling in a somewhat exalted vinous sandwich! The wine has both power and finesse, although with marginally lighter structure than its illustrious neigh- bour. Nonetheless, Michel Colin's Demoiselles is a very fine wine which fills the mouth and begs to be kept for 5–10 years.

The reds are more uneven than the whites. Like many of his colleagues, Michel seems to be less sure of his round vinifying Pinot Noir – still, as it were, feeling his way. Although he seems to be doing all the right things, the wines seem to lack real heart Michel is experimenting with a rototank, which is not intended to shorten the 10 days *cuvaison* he gives his reds, but to automate the strenuous task of *pigéage.* This apparatus endows wines made in it with slightly more tannin than those vinified traditionally.

The Domaine's reds are tough. 'Pretty tannic – ten years, no problem,' is how Michel summarises them. Whether this amounts to an imbalance is a matter of individual taste. The best, in the years when he makes it, is undoubtedly the Chassagne Vieilles Vignes. It appeared in 1985, 1987 and 1988, and again in 1990. The vines average 30+ years, and give a wine of greater depth and complexity than the rest.

The wines from this Domaine are good, sometimes verging on great. Michel Colin's skill is rewarded with a faithful clientèle, both in France and abroad. His wines find their way onto the lists of several grand restaurants where, no doubt, he sometimes eats after a strenuous day at one of his favourite pastimes – skiing and hunting.

VINEYARD HOLDINGS

Commune	*Level*	*Lieu-dit/Climat*	*Area*	*Vine Age*	*Status*
Chassagne	PC	Les Vergers (W)	0.50	40	P
Chassagne	PC	Les Chaumées (W)	1.92	20	P
Chassagne	PC	En Remilly (W)	0.70	3–20	P/F
Chassagne	PC	Les Chenevottes (W)	0.41	45	P/M
Chassagne	PC	Morgeot (W)	0.67	35	M
Chassagne	PC	La Maltroie (W)	0.53	3–30	M
Chassagne	PC	Morgeot (R)	0.23	20	M
Chassagne	PC	La Maltroie (R)	0.15	25	M
Chassagne	V	— (W)	0.85	25	P
Chassagne	V	— (R)	4.00	25	P/M
Puligny	PC	Les Demoiselles	0.15	45	P
—	R	(Bourgogne Aligoté)	0.85	15	P
—	R	(Bourgogne Rouge)	1.00	15	P
		Total	**11.96 ha.**		

Domaine Jean-Noël Gagnard

CHASSAGNE-MONTRACHET

Jean-Noël Gagnard is somewhat out on a limb, both physically and figuratively, from the rest of the Chassagne Gagnards. His house, an imposing edifice opposite Ramonet's cellars at the southern end of the village, is about as far as possible from his brother Jacques and his sons-in-law, and he works completely independently from the rest of his relations.

Jean-Noël and his attractive daughter, Caroline, are the eleventh and twelfth generations of Gagnards in Chassagne, and claim to trace their ancestors back through to 1632. He worked with his father from 1943–1969 before talking full control and now has Caroline, a graduate of the Lycée Viticole in Beaune, working full-time with him, 'doing a bit of everything'.

The Domaine currently stands at 7.65 ha. – beefed up with purchases of Morgeot and Caillerets between 1948 and 1950, and more recently with a further 0.5 ha. of Caillerets, acquired in 1980.

Although Jean-Noël gives the impression of entertaining a rather laid-back attitude to the details of what goes on, he is a quiet, reflective person who runs his estate with care; not an up-to-the-minute technocrat, but someone preferring a system which might loosely be described as 'stuck in transit' – somewhere between old-fashioned and traditional.

In the vineyards, rather than replacing individual vines, parcels are left until they are about 35 years old and then grubbed up. All but the steepest vineyards are treated with herbicides, after a single annual hoeing. Jean-Noël is contemplating *enherbement,* especially in the steep Caillerets, to prevent the worst of soil erosion – a common struggle in Chassagne.

Regular soil analyses provide the meat for a 5-year plan of adjustments in *trace* and *base elements,* and the Service des Végétaux supplies a programme of recommended treatments for pests and diseases. However, for the worst malady of all – apoplexy, in which an apparently healthy vine, through a curious excess of vigour, seems to suffer a sort of botanical heart attack and dies – there is to date no cure.

Fortunately some of the more regular vine-pests seem to be localised. The grape-worm, for example, is much more severe in Volnay and Meursault than in Chassagne and Santenay. Nevertheless, a thorough selection in the vineyard, supervised by Jean-Nöel's wife, is necessary to ensure that only prime fruit reaches the cuverie.

The harvesting date is also decided on the basis of advice from the Service des Végétaux rather than on individual *prélèvements*; this is a somewhat rough-and-ready expedient, since maturity can vary widely between different sections of a commune, especially one so extended as Chassagne. In 1990, Jean-Noël reported finding differences of up to 15 days in vegetal development on a single vine – although he reckons that it caught up by harvest time. Delaying picking beyond the cautious advice of the Service would undoubtedly benefit the wines, especially the reds.

Caroline and Jean-Noël spring-pruning in Les Caillerets

The white juice is sulphured, given a light *débourbage* and put straight into cask, of which 20-25% are renewed annually. Although the *must* is not cooled, the cellar is air-conditioned, and so the temperature rarely rises above 22° C. There are two rackings – the precise timing depending on what other work is on hand. Generally, the aim is to rack as soon as possible after *malo*, unifying in tank, then returning the wine to the same casks. The process is repeated in November, before the wine is fined, plate-filtered and then bottled 2–3 months later – an *élevage* of nearly 18 months: 'We remain traditional,' comments Jean-Noël.

Reflecting on the value of these extra few months in cask – the norm seems to be 11–12 months – Jean-Noël can only offer in justification: 'I think that there is a good result – it's that which counts in the end,' adding that unduly early bottling can sometimes lead to problems with clarification.

Red vinification is based on total destalking and a longish *cuvaison* (12 days or so) at a maximum temperature of about 32° C. If the grapes arrive too hot, then Jean-Nöel throws open the doors of his cuverie to cool them down, otherwise fermentation is left to proceed naturally. In 1988 the crop came in at 29° C, which was beyond the cooling powers of even the widest cellar door, so a heat-exchanger was rapidly acquired; a contrast to the memorably hot 1947 vintage which failed to respond to bags of ice in the *cuves* and had to be flash-pasteurised at 80° C to ensure some degree of stability.

Up to now there has been no need to use either a *saignée de cuve* or enzymes – no doubt low yields and both fining and filtration have seen to that. There is, exceptionally, no *pigéage* of the red *cuves*. This is not some whimsical policy decision, but rather reflects the fact that some time ago the cuverie was divided into two floors leaving only 60 cm. clearance between the top of the *cuves* and the ceiling, making it physically impossible to introduce apparatus, human or mechanical, into the *cuves*.

Another peculiarity of Jean-Noël's red vinification is that his wines see no new wood. This is partly a financial expedient, and partly a matter of family tradition – Caroline and her father amicably disagree on which. Instead, second-year white wine casks are employed.

The remainder of the *élevage* mirrors that of the white wines – 2 rackings, the second in November, fining in cask with egg albumen and a polishing filtration just before bottling in January or February of the second year.

These slight idiosyncrasies do not appear to detract from the overall quality of the Gagnard wines. The reds tend to be quite soft and plump – not particularly long-lived wines, but attractive after 5 years or so. The Chassagne-Montrachet, Clos St.-Jean is marginally the better of the 2 Premiers Crus – with more finesse and elegance than the Morgeot, which has greater power and breadth. This is explained, in part, by the relative richness of the Morgeot soils, especially in the lower sections of the vineyard, which contrast with the lighter *terre rouge* of the Clos St.-Jean.

The whites are delicious: the Chassagne Villages being quite fat and stylish, although noticeably less structured, as one might expect, than the Premiers Cru *cuvée* – a mixture of Champs-Gains, Chenevottes, Les Places and Les Blanchots, which in 1990 was distinctly tighter and more complex.

There are 3 individual white Premiers Crus, of which the Clos de la Maltroye has been recently replanted (1990) and will not return to full production for at least 4 years. However, there are 2 other excellent wines to choose from: the Caillerets and the Morgeot. The latter, from 12-year-old vines in Les Petits Clos Boudriotte, is usually a powerful, plump wine, with plenty of fruit and broad finesse. Both the 1989 and 1990 were showing real depth and length in January 1991, with a nerve of acidity which will keep them alive for many years to come.

In style the Caillerets has less substance than the Morgeot, but distinctly greater finesse. Both the 1989 and 1990 showed well, although the 1990 was noticeably tighter than the 1989, with more grip and less open texture. The 1989s here, as elsewhere, will come forward before the great 1990s.

With the Bâtard-Montrachet, one reaches the summit of Jean-Nöel's range. This wine, from a mixture of 1959 and 1975 plantings, in the Chassagne section of the vineyard, has, as one expects from a well-made Grand Cru, both power and complexity in abundance. The 1990 was almost *surmature* on the nose – a very attractive, rich spectrum of aromas already developing. The new wood was well-integrated and virtually melted beneath the layers of firm, ripe fruit. Paradoxically, a sample from an older cask seemed to have more new wood qualities than that from the new barrel, and was slightly softer and less rich. The natural 13.9 degrees of alcohol give the wine an excellent 'ampleur' without overbalancing it.

The 1969 Bâtard, was still in fine form in late 1991 – mid old-gold in colour, and fully mature, attractive lanolin and hazelnuts nose, and fresh, powerful and complex on the palate.

Jean-Nöel Gagnard's cramped, low-ceilinged cellar is another of the several splendid sources of fine Burgundy in Chassagne-Montrachet. However, his practice of leaving his white wines those extra few months in cask and his rather imprecise attitude to racking bring un-evenness of which buyers should beware. In particular, there is nothing to be gained from bottling these finely-tuned white wines late, and much to be lost. Decisions of this sort should be made individually, rather than as inflexible matters of policy or family tradition. There is something disarmingly 'seat of the pants' about this Domaine - but what classy pants!

Grape set – the moment when embryo bunches become visible

VINEYARD HOLDINGS

Commune	Level	Lieu-dit/Climat	Area	Vine Age	Status
Chassagne	GC	Bâtard-Montrachet	0.36	25	P
Chassagne	PC	Les Caillerets	1.01	20	P
Chassagne	PC	Morgeot (Les Petits Clos – Boudriotte)	0.80	12	P
Chassagne	PC	Clos de la Maltroye	0.37	1990	P
Chassagne	PC	Chenevottes/Blanchots	0.56	30	P
Chassagne	PC	Place/Champs-Gains	0.51	30	M
Chassagne	V	Les Masures/Les Chaumes	0.75	20	P
Chassagne	PC	Clos St.-Jean (Red)	0.33	30	M
Chassagne	PC	Morgeot Clos Charreau (R)	0.14	40	P
Chassagne	PC	Morgeot – Grand Clos + Clos Charreau + Les Boirettes (Red)	0.63	40	M
Chassagne	V	(Several climats)	1.46	35	P/M
Chassagne	R	Champ Derrière (Aligoté)	0.44	-	M
Santenay	PC	Clos de Tavannes	0.29	30	P
		Total	**7.65 ha.**		

Domaine Gagnard-Delagrange

CHASSAGNE-MONTRACHET

Jacques Gagnard, a short, square man, gives you the distinct impression that he does not enjoy sitting still – he prefers to be out among his vines rather than in his self-consciously neat little office. He admits that he is a 'type indépendent', not a team man, and that 'no one would put up with my character'. In truth, he may appear to be a bit of a bruiser, but there is a great deal of friendly charm underneath, not to mention a profound knowledge of the ways of the vine.

With his brother, Jean-Noël Gagnard, Jacques is the head of a confusingly tentacular family of Chassagne viticulteurs. Both his daughters are now married into wine-growing – Laurence to Richard Fontaine and Claudine to Jean-Marc Blain. Jacques' own wife, Marie-Josephe – née Delagrange – has a sister, Andrée, who married a viticulteur, Edmond Bachelet. Each of these worthy husbands decided to award themselves a 'Delagrange', further contributing to the confusion. Apart from shared ownership of some of the machinery, these several Gagnard exploitations are independent and autonomous entities: none more so than Jacques.

His declaration of independence does not extend to the vineyards, where he confesses that 'We use the latest techniques of culture.' That is to say, his 4 ha. are largely cared for in the manner prescribed by the Service des Végétaux to which every sensible viticulteur subscribes. In general, vines, he believes, are like humans – they need a balanced diet: 'If you ate a biscuit with a litre of water for a month, you wouldn't be left with much energy,' is how he explains his philosophy.

Jacques' views on modern improvements are tempered by the pre-*phylloxera* perspective of Mme. Gagnard's grandfather, another M. Bachelet, now dead. Knowledge of traditional methods enables him to resist the blandishments of twentieth-century product salesmen. For example, instead of spraying mindlessly to treat rot, he is content to prune short, to plant less vigorous clones and rootstocks and to control foliage to encourage good air circulation round the bunches. He is also closely following research into the production of strains of Pinot Noir which have less compact bunches than normal; these may diminish the incidence of rot, but could also have negative taste consequences.

Nowadays vines, like humans, live longer. Looking after vines has become as much a matter of adapting the plant to its soil, as of a series of predetermined operations each month of the year. Whilst 'Pruning is the key', how high or wide to prune foliage in the summer and when to harvest all depend upon the natural vigour of the vine and the humidity and general characteristics of the soil. Replanting is not without its share of problems. Apart from what to plant, there is the question of how to clean up the soil.

Vines often die from infectious degeneration, a virus for which the only solution is to grub up the vine, disinfect the soil and replant. However, the malady tends to remain deep down in the soil, so the root system of a new vine will eventually become infected. In times past, the recommended treatment was gas fumigation of the soil, but the gases became trapped underground and released later to damage new plantings. It is hoped that virus-free clones will overcome this problem, but this is by no means guaranteed.

Jacques makes excellent wines, of both colours. The reds, from 100% destalked bunches and an 8–10 day *cuvaison,* are soft, fruity and concentrated. The best are the Chassagne Morgeot, from his father-in-law's 60-year-old vines, which sees no new wood, and a deliciously silky Volnay Champans, from young vines and about 28% new wood.

His whites are even better. The life of a great white Burgundy, Jacques will tell you, depends on its first 24 hours in the cuverie – rapid pressing and plenty of water to keep working tools completely clean. There is no *débourbage:* 'What's the point, you have no lees left,' but 'we stir, we stir.' He likes his wines to gain richness from their lees, rather than from selected yeast strains, which he considers destructive of concentration. So indigenous yeasts and plenty of *batonnage* are de rigueur in his cellar.

He also has a vigorous dislike of new wood, not only because it dominates a wine and masks the individuality of each Cru, but also because the vanillin leached from a new cask will itself ferment, being a sugar, and add further to alcohol levels. Although he uses a maximum of 20% new wood himself, he considers that 'it is barely merited, even in a Grand Cru'; second-year casks have a far gentler and finer effect.

New wood is one of the negative effects of recent prosperity – vignerons can now afford a new cask for its impact on the wine, rather than just to replace something no longer serviceable. Jacques quotes Jean Hugel who apparently in an off-guard moment answered his rhetorical question: 'What is Meursault?' with 'Chardonnay with new oak in it.'

Jacques' white wines are thus bottled 15–16 months after the vintage following fining in cask and a light filtration. The Morgeot, from 35-year-old vines planted on stony soil with a high clay content, gives rich wines with good acidity. It does not give much bouquet to start with, but is quite ripe and fat.

The Boudriotte has less topsoil than Morgeot, and tends to produce wines which are drier and more elegantly perfumed rather close-knit, but with greater length and finesse. There is also a small quantity of excellent Bâtard-Montrachet and even less Montrachet. Jacques has now given this last plot, together with substantial parcels of red Clos St.-Jean and Morgeot, to his daughters, although he retains and vinifies the fruit.

VINEYARD HOLDINGS

Commune	*Level*	*Lieu-dit/Climat*	*Area*	*Vine Age*	*Status*
Chassagne	GC	**Le Montrachet	0.08	25	**
Chassagne	GC	Bâtard-Montrachet	0.27	2/3:8 1/3:20	P
Chassagne	PC	**La Boudriotte (W)	1.15	22	**
Chassagne	PC	Morgeot (W)	0.47	30	P
Chassagne	V	Voillenots-Dessus + Les Crais (W)	0.37	20	P
Chassagne	PC	Morgeot (R)	0.43	60	P
Chassagne	R	(Côte de Beaune (R)	0.33	15	P
Chassagne	PC	**Clos St.-Jean (R)	0.30	35	**
Chassagne	R	**Côte de Beaune (R)	0.25	40	**
Chassagne	PC	**Morgeot (W)	0.26	25	**
Chassagne	PC	**Morgeot (R)	0.25	22	**
Volnay	PC	Les Champans	0.37	10	P
—	R	(Bourgogne Aligoté)	0.15	35	P
—	R	(PTG)	0.19	15	P
		Total	**4.87 ha.**		

** These vineyards are now owned by one or both of Jacques' daughters, although he continues to make and sell the wine.

Domaine Bernard Morey

CHASSAGNE-MONTRACHET

The Moreys, with the Gagnards, are the most important wine-making dynasties in Chassagne. Their history is simple. Albert Morey – now in his seventies – had two sons, Jean-Marc and Bernard. When he retired in 1981 he decided to split the Domaine between them, retaining only his holding in Bâtard-Montrachet – partie Chassagne.

The brothers agreed that their work would be easier if the appellations rather than the vineyards were divided; so now, for example, Jean-Marc has Les Chaumées and Bernard Les Embrazées. The only vineyards they have in common, apart from Village appellations, are Santenay Le Grand Clos Rousseau, St.-Aubin Les Charmois, Beaune Grèves and Chassagne Les Caillerets. Up to 1987 treatments and harvest were undertaken jointly but now they work independently – it seems to be a question of maintaining complete independence for inheritance purposes, rather than anything disagreeable; no doubt they chat from their tractors from time to time when their paths happen to cross.

Bernard Morey is a large, friendly man, with a quiet, modern house in the centre of Chassagne. He works hard and devotes much care and thought to his task. He is one of the few vignerons who still makes his own grafts (about 10,000 in 1991) which gives him complete control, from vine to bottle. Being impishly cynical about the quality of what he might get if he bought his plant material from a nurseryman, he uses 'mother vines' from Les Baudines, a vineyard replanted in clones in 1972.' This is the only way of knowing what you're planting,' he adds with a laugh; 'this way the grafts are freshly lifted and don't spend two months outdoors before being used.'

However, although the health aspect of clones attracts him, Bernard does not believe that they are best for quality: 'It is heresy to try and transform a vineyard into two or three clones; they only give excessive neutrality,' he feels. When he has to replace individual vines, he therefore tends to use a *sélection massale* rather than clones.

To satisfy himself on this point he vinified grapes from clones and from a traditional planting separately, from the same vineyard – and confirmed that the wine was indeed of markedly lesser quality, even with a mix of clones. He contends that the produce of clones from Les Baudines invariably tastes less good than his other Premiers Crus.

What particularly disturbs him is the mounting incidence, over the last decade, of the virus disease *eutypiose,* especially in the Chardonnay. There is no ready cure, except to grub up the affected vines, disinfect the soil and replant. Unfortunately, because they are trained *en Guyot* he has to pre-prune his Chardonnay vines, to remove surplus wood, in the autumn while the sap is descending. This makes it much easier for the micro-organisms which spread *eutypiose* to infect the vine. His Pinot Noir vines, however, being trained *en cordon,* as are many in Chassagne and Santenay, can be left to be pruned until the spring, whilst the sap is rising, and are therefore less at risk.

On the matter of when to harvest, Bernard is characteristically forthright 'I like to harvest quite late'; adding, 'the malaise of this region, is the current tendency to advance the date of the harvest.' He is in no doubt that, certainly over the last decade, the balance of advantage has been heavily skewed in favour of picking late: 'There has hardly been a year when we have not gained from waiting.'

He tells of one colleague who, in 1988, harvested his Chardonnay a full 10 days before he did; the wines had 2 degrees less potential alcohol and had a thin and weedy aspect which even prolonged lees contact failed to redeem. 'You must learn to wait.'

Bernard's illuminating discourse on harvesting terminates with a friendly but scathing attack on those who are over-cautious: 'It's no good falling into the trap of harvesting when the pH is right – this usually means the grapes aren't ripe and will simply result in excess addity. The degree of sugar is more important than the acidity – you must be prepared to take risks. The last 8 days of maturity are those which give the wine more natural alcohol and power.'

Bernard's white wines are classically vinified with about 11 months of *élevage* from the moment they are put into casks for fermentation until they are removed from their fining, filtered and bottled. There are one or two concessions, however, to the twentieth century: a pneumatic press, which presses very gently and gives such fine lees that there is no need for any *débourbage* between pressing and fermentation; also, the juice is cooled to around 15°C so that the fermentation will not heat above 20-21°C. For the rest, the process is thoroughly traditional – lots of *batonnage,* no artificial yeasts and leaving the new wine in cask until the last possible moment before racking off its fining.

On the matter of casks and wood, Bernard becomes mildly cynical: 'Even if you buy your own wood, you must sleep at the barrel-makers to make sure that they use nothing else for your casks.' The question of the provenance of his oak elicits a humorously jaundiced: 'Well, we ask for Allier. . .' While his own casks are normally renewed at the rate of 25% each year, things can go wrong: in 1989 the usual quantity of barrels was ordered, well in advance; in the event, the crop was small, so using all his new wood augmented the proportion from 25% to 30%.

Bernard's whites are fine and reliable. Deliberately long lees contact and naturally highish alcohol (from a late harvest) gives them a fatness and richness which is most attractive. In his view, there is no doubt about the key to a good balance of alcohol, acidity and aroma *élevage* in cask, on the lees'. He confesses himself somewhat bemused by the Californian method, which seems to him to consist of first centrifuging the juice to remove the yeasts and lees and then putting back cultured yeasts to start the fermentation.

The Domaine's white wines are normally fined in the July following the vintage and subjected to a moderately strong plate filtration before bottling just before the new harvest. The subject of filtration brings out evident exasperation in Bernard's tone: 'It's a real saga; people want unfiltered wines but, at the same time, want wines which are clear.' He concludes that this is all a passing fashion which will probably go away sooner or later, if he doesn't ponder on it too much.

Tasting in the 250-year-old cellars beneath the cuverie, one has a feeling that Bernard and his views are all part of a tradition which, like the mould on cellar walls, is not lightly discarded.

Although there is a little generic red and white Burgundy, the serious whites start with the St.-Aubin Premier Cru Les Charmois. This is usually a well-structured wine, with good depth and a distinct *goût de terroir.* The soils here are poor and pebbly, with a highish iron content; this, and vines planted in 1956, both contribute to the wine's concentration.

The Chassagne Village *cuvée* is usually very fine – partly because it contains a proportion of Premier Cru, Les Vides-Bourses, which is next to Bâtard-Montrachet, and partly because it emanates from 30- and 45-year-old vines. In good vintages it tends to start life with a slightly masculine charm, quite firm and 'puissant', which needs a few years to round out and open.

The Premier Cru Les Baudines – 'the famous clones', chortles Bernard – is situated at the southern extremity of the village, on the Santenay border, just beneath Joseph Belland's Clos Pitois. It is in fact part clones and part *sélection massale* and seems, at least in recent vintages, to be more floral and rather four square, lacking the depth of the Village wine. After all the vines are only 18 years old . . . barely adult!

The Embrazées, of which Bernard has 1.25 ha., tends to show best when it is quite young; a charmer, but without the 'fond' of either the Morgeot or the Caillerets. The soil here is quite light, stony and red, which gives finesse but insufficient depth and structure for very long ageing.

Supremacy in this Morey cellar is between the Morgeot and the Caillerets. Both vineyards have rich soil, with significant limestone content, making for big, powerful wines which repay keeping. If the Caillerets can be generalised, it tends more to great 'rondeur' and 'finesse', whereas the Morgeot is 'plus solide', with great richness and power. In good vintages, such as 1989 and 1990, both are heavyweights – not lumpy or out of balance in any way, but just big wines. The Caillerets has a more approachable floral side when young, whereas the Morgeot is slightly deeper in colour and a bit more obviously fleshy. Whatever the nuances, however, both are generally very fine indeed.

Bernard Morey also makes excellent red wines, some 55–60% of his production, from a fairly traditional vinification. The bunches are completely destemmed and allowed to macerate for as long as possible – 'If it lasts 3–4 days I am very pleased' – before being heated to 20° C. to induce fermentation. Cement *cuves* are used; they maintain temperature more evenly and are easier to look after: 'Wooden vats are all very fine for decoration, but what happens during the rest of the year – they dry out, are re-hydrated, dry out again, and so on,' is all Bernard has to say on this matter.

Fermentation temperature rarely rises above 32–33° C., although cooling was needed in 1990 when it rocketed to 36° C. *Cuvaison* lasts for 12–15 days – longer than that of many of his colleagues in this part of the Côte, and the *cuves* are systematically *saignéed* to further concentrate the wine. Enzymes are added just before transfer to cask to help eventual clarification, which is also facilitated by the traditional practice of pitch-forking the *marc* into the presses, rather than pumping it.

The proportion of new wood depends on the vintage and the wine – the Santenay, Beaune and Chassagne Vieilles Vignes see 25% of new Allier, the Chassagne 'jeunes vignes' having somewhat less. Two rackings later, the wine is fined and given a polishing filtration and bottled, usually just before the new vintage or during the second winter.

Bernard Morey – a concentrated sniff

The range of reds is small, but good. The Beaune Grèves, one of the best of all the Beaune Premiers Crus, tends to be quite soft and spicy – an individual wine, a Chassagne interpretation of Beaune. The Santenay Grand Clos Rousseau is invariably of a fine colour, with a slightly 'sauvage-nose', and a long, soft flavour – a wine of great delicacy, but not without structure.

In 1980, Bernard's Swiss importer suggested that instead of submitting samples to the Chevaliers de Tastevin for the lottery which is 'Tastevinage', he should market a 'Cuvée Vieilles Vignes'. Since then, there have often been two *cuvées* of red Chassagne: Montrachet – a Vieilles Vignes, made from 40–50-year-old vines, and a standard *cuvée* made from younger plants. The Vieilles Vignes comes from 2 ha. of vines, mostly on the flatter ground, part of which is on the Puligny side of the village. There is a single plot of one hectare, the other hectare being comprised of 3 separate parcels of vines. 'Not a single vine is missing,' says Bernard proudly, as the pipette disappears into the cask for a sample.

In vintages in which he deems the wine worthy of separate designation, it is a fine example of what red Chassagne should be – moderately deep in colour, soft, plump strawberry fruit, with an overlay of delicacy and succulence which makes you want to keep sipping. The wine needs time to integrate its constituents – to absorb the wood and grape tannins and to come out of its shell.

No Domaine is perfect – perhaps the Beaune and Santenay are not as exciting as one can find elsewhere. Nonetheless, the standard of Bernard's wine-making is very high and his label is a guarantee of quality. Since 1970 all his production is Domaine bottled – except presumably for the odd lot which doesn't meet his exacting standards. He also has an allocation of Albert's fine Bâtard, reserved for favoured customers.

Bernard's interests extend beyond the village – he skis, professes himself a good fisherman and enjoys visiting other growers especially in Alsace and Bordeaux, for which he has a particular affection. He adores Sauternes and has a small stack maturing in one corner of the cellar. He has ensured future supplies by sending one of his sons for a 'stage' to Bordeaux and the other on a similar mission to – where else . . . Alsace.

VINEYARD HOLDINGS

Commune	*Level*	*Lieu dit/Climat*	*Area*	*Vine Age*	*Status*
Chassagne	PC	Les Embrazées (W)	1.25	30	P
Chassagne	PC	Les Caillerets (W)	0.31	15	P
Chassagne	PC	Morgeot (W)	0.64	20	P
Chassagne	PC	Les Baudines (W)	0.37	18	P
Chassagne	V	— (W)	0.28	45	F
Chassagne	V	— (R)	3.10	30	P/M
St.-Aubin	PC	Les Charmois (W)	0.33	35	P
Santenay	PC	Grand Clos Rousseau (R)	0.41	18	P
Beaune	PC	Les Grèves (R)	0.64	25	M
—	R	(Bourg. Red/White)	1.10	20	P/M
		Total	*8.43 Ha.*		

Domaine Jean-Marc Morey

CHASSAGNE-MONTRACHET

Although there are many points of similarity between Jean-Marc and his brother Bernard, which might be expected from 16 years of working and vinifying together with their father, it would be misleading to treat them as a large Domaine with 2 branches.

Jean-Marc is a bluff, friendly no-nonsense man, who lives in a commensurately pleasant, no-nonsense house on the edge of the village. His amiable open charm, however, hides much suffering. In 1990 his wife, who looked after all the administration of the Domaine, died; added to this tragedy, one of his workers was killed in a tractor accident and the other was so shocked that he stopped working altogether. Thus, in the space of a few months, Jean-Marc had much heaped on to his broad shoulders.

Despite all his troubles, he makes superb wine from his 8.5 ha. of vines. His father Albert clearly brought up his sons to take infinite pains, especially in the vineyards. Like his brother, Jean-Marc believes in replanting vines individually, where possible, rather than waiting until a parcel gets too old and then replanting it. He shares with Bernard a healthy disrespect for clones, preferring his own personal *sélection massale.*

Jean-Marc's vines are pruned short. This, together with a deliberate policy of the barest minimum of fertilisation – just fine adjustments of *base elements* for quality, nothing for quantity - and a very thorough *évasivage,* keeps production down to levels that are compatible with top quality. This means an average yield of some 42 hl./ha. for Chardonnay, although in 1990 it soared to nearly 57 hl./ha. He agrees with Bernard that, up to a point, Chardonnay can produce better quality at larger yields than Pinot Noir.

The relatively rich soils of Chassagne mean that without severe pruning, yields, especially for Pinot Noir, would be excessive. This explains why most of the vignoble's Pinots are trained *en cordon de Royat.* By limiting the number of spurs on the *cordon* or branch, and by pruning these short, the yield is controlled. The *cordon* system also spaces out the vine's foliage, which increases natural sugar production and thus concentration. However, Jean-Marc is vociferously opposed to any form of green-pruning to limit production by removing bunches later on in the summer: 'That isn't part of a viticulteur's mentality; people do this more for publicity than for quality; a proper *évasivage is* the best *vendange verte* you can do.'

Jean-Marc's white vinification differs little from that of Bernard. They both agree about the need to use indigenous yeasts and to maximise lees contact before the first racking, to give the wines as much richness and depth as possible. However, he is not in favour of the fashionable *macération pelliculaire.* 'I spent a long time discussing this with Professor Max Leglise, at the time when he became rather obsessed with this "truc", recommending it to everyone from here to California, but I don't think that this is really adapted to my style of wine.'

There is no *débourbage,* but the juice is put straight into casks –15–20% new – for alcoholic fermentation. For his *malos* – a second fermentation mediated by naturally occurring bacteria – Jean-Marc has tried using 30 different strains of lactic-bacteria, without perceptible improvement. As so many growers have found in similar experiments with yeasts, the indigenous varieties give the best results.

Bottling the whites always takes place in September, to conserve freshness and make room for the new vintage. The risks of drying out a young wine in cask increase with time, so unless you have a glacial cellar and thus a much slower evolution it makes sense to bottle sooner rather than later.

The white Chassagne Village *cuvée is* generally good and 'typé'. The 1989 had a nose redolent of lime-blossom, floral, with a hint of grilled nuts.

The Caillerets tends to be closed and somewhat austere to begin with, although it is seductively rich. The fruit beneath is quite 'tendre' – giving a wine which opens out after about 5 years in good vintages.

The other white Chassagne Premier Cru, Les Chaumées, represents a striking contrast – being more 'primeur' in style, more open, but with plenty of guts and ripe fruit. The vines are on the Puligny side of the village, on a steeply sloping hillside, with soil which is very high in limestone which would account for a predominance of finesse over structure.

Jean-Marc is clear about the style of wine he wants to achieve, for both his reds and his whites: 'I look for maximum fruit, but also for maximum keeping, paradoxical, perhaps, but my wines can be drunk young but will keep for 10, 20, 30 years without problem.'

The reds, vinified in much the same manner as Bernard's, are worthy examples of the appellations they represent. The Beaune Grèves is perhaps a shade more elegant than his brother's, with plenty of 'fond' and character. There is only one *cuvée* of Chassagne Village – no 'vieilles vignes' here, it all goes into the same pot. The wine is of medium weight and backed up with a good envelope of tannins to give it longevity.

The best of Jean-Marc's reds is unquestionably the Chassagne Premier Cru Les Champs-Gains – a hillside vineyard at the southern end of the village, just below Domaine Ramonet's cellars. The 1989 example was deeply coloured and beginning to show an attractive aromatic development of cherries and *fruits sauvages.* On the palate, the wine has length and real depth – altogether delicious.

The Domaine exports its wines far afield. Some of the wines are still labelled 'Albert Morey et Fils', but with the name of either Jean-Marc or Bernard added, so one can tell from which Morey it originates. Jean-Marc is as fine and careful a wine-maker as his brother and an excellent source of wine.

VINEYARD HOLDINGS

Commune	*Level*	*Lieu-dit/Climat*	*Area*	*Vine Age*	*Status*
Chassagne	PC	Les Caillerets	0.70	30	P
Chassagne	PC	Les Champs Gains	0.40	1966	P
Chassagne	PC	Les Chaumées	0.33	1951	P
Chassagne	PC	Les Chenevottes	0.11	1980	P
Chassagne	V	(Chardonnay)	0.94	25	P
Chassagne	PC	Clos St.-Jean (R)	0.19	1982	P
Chassagne	PC	Les Champs Gains (R)	0.63	1966/70	P
Chassagne	V	(Pinot Noir)	1.72	1957/68/74	P
St.Aubin	PC	Les Charmois (W)	0.21	1979	P
Santenay	PC	Grand Clos Rousseau	0.412	1972	P
Santenay	V	Chainey	0.32	1978	P
Beaune	PC	Grèves	0.65	60+	M
—	R	(Bourgogne Aligoté)	0.47	1985	P
—	R	(Bourgogne Rouge)	0.49	20	P
—	R	(BGO/PTG)	0.32	1975	P
		Total	**7.89 ha.**		

Domaine Fernand Pillot

CHASSAGNE-MONTRACHET

This is another of the fine Domaines of Chassagne, comprising nearly 8 ha. of well-placed vines, including 6 white and 3 red Chassagne Premiers Crus. Fernand Pillot, now helped full-time by his son fresh from the twin delights of military service and the Lycée Viticole, is one of those vignerons who spare no trouble to make the most of their unique land.

A short dark-haired man with a wry smile, Fernand is in no doubt as to what determines quality: low yields, minimum fertilisers and an obsession with hygiene. Fifteen years working with his father have given him a thorough grounding in the vigneron's art. He still does his own grafts, although the use of *sélection massale* has largely given way to 'clones fins', and is a stickler for careful pruning and a thorough *évasivage*. 'We cut off masses of embryo bunches'.

As is the custom in Chassagne and Santenay, the Pinot vines are trained *en cordon* and the Chardonnays *Guyot simple.* Fernand likes to prune his vines short – especially the *Guyots* which are cut back to 6 eyes. This helps to avoid the need for a subsequent green-pruning, which he believes takes some of the vine's natural vigour.

As with many producers in Chassagne and St.-Aubin, Fernand Pillot's white wines are of considerably higher overall quality than his reds. Growers will often admit that they find it much more difficult to vinify red grapes than white – the Nibelung hordes of fermentation, maceration, destalking and *élevage* seeming to conspire against them.

The principal problem is generally the management of tannin – a factor virtually absent in white wines. The naturally less structured style of red Meursaults, Pulignys and Chassagnes in particular makes the achievement of a balance between fruit, alcohol, acid and tannins a very precise matter, since the delicacy of the fruit is so easily upset by an excess of any of the remaining three constituents.

Fernand's method is to limit the stalks left in the vats to 30% – even this is probably too high for real finesse – to avoid more than a day or two of pre-fermentive maceration and to use a relatively high temperature (up to 35° C.) as the preferred means of extracting colour, which he regards as the principal difficulty with the Pinot Noir.

Cellar manipulations are kept to a minimum, using gravity where practicable to move the wines from cask to cask, rather than pumps which tend to aerate and thus oxidise the wine. Red wines from Chassagne, Meursault and Puligny seem peculiarly prone to the development of a flat, cabbagey taste from premature oxidation.

The wines are kept for about a year in cask, of which 25% is new Allier oak: 'fine grained, above all'. This amounts to a total cask maturation of some 15 months – before fining with dried egg-white and the plate filtration which precede bottling.

Fernand reasons that fining gives a certain element of finesse to his wines and is therefore necessary. However, if you fine and don't filter then you are obliged to remove the wine from its fining and leave it for a further month or so to rest – an additional racking which is undesirable. Ergo, he both fines and filters. The logic may be impeccable but the argument is not: if enzymes were added at fermentation the wines would clarify naturally and could thus be bottled with a light polishing filtration in all but the most difficult vintages – a better solution altogether. Fernand has been experimenting with enzymes; so perhaps there is a change on the way.

His red wines are sound, but frankly uninspiring. The Chassagne Premiers Crus are the pick of the crop but seem to lack real density. Tasting his wines both in Chassagne and elsewhere confirms this impression.

The whites, however, tell a different story. Here, Fernand is clearly a master of his craft. After pressing and sulphuring, the juice is put into either enamelled or stainless-steel vats to begin its fermentation. When there is no longer a risk of over heating it is transferred to cask with its fine lees; 25% of the casks are new Allier oak, with a strongish charring. Infrequent but regular *batonnage* ensures that these lees are kept in suspension.

The wines are racked twice, with or without *égalisage* depending on the particular *cuvée.* Larger lots are fined in bulk at second racking, with casein, smaller 'more important' lots being treated in cask.

Bottling takes place just before the new vintage – generally with a moderate plate filtration. Fernand Pillot believes that, as with his reds, fining adds significant finesse to the wines and this, together with a deliberately early bottling, conserves the maximum of fruit, freshness and aromatic complexity.

The cream of this cellar undoubtedly lies in the splendid range of Chassagnes. They are invariably fine examples of their vintage and excellent expressions of their individual origins. Chassagne is a geographically extended commune, so a Morgeot, from one end of the village, will taste entirely different from a Clos St.-Jean from the other.

The noblest of these fine whites is unquestionably the Grandes Ruchottes. This vineyard consists of relatively heavy, deep soils, and lies closest of all the Chassagne Premier Cru vineyards to the Grand Cru Bâtard-Montrachet. Fernand's Grand Ruchottes has a pronounced green-gold colour with a ripe, positive nose. In its youth this tends to evince lime-blossom and the more floral aspect of the Chardonnay grape; with a few years ageing in bottle, however, this changes to aromas more redolent of nuts and honey. The wine is usually ripe and powerful, with mouthfilling substance and considerable length – invariably a sign of quality. In essence, this is Fernand Pillot's junior Bâtard, and a more than worthy testament to his wine-making skills.

VINEYARD HOLDINGS

Commune	*Level*	*Lieu-dit/Climat*	*Area*	*Vine Age*	*Status*
Chassagne	PC	Grandes Ruchottes (W)	0.37	18	F
Chassagne	PC	Les Vergers (W)	0.87	1/2:7 1/2:35	P
Chassagne	PC	Morgeot (W)	0.52	12	P/F
Chassagne	PC	Vide-Bourse (W)	0.45	20	P
Chassagne	PC	Champs-Gains + Macherelles	0.05	25	P
Chassagne	PC	Champs-Gains (R)	0.33	35	P
Chassagne	PC	Morgeot (R)	0.38	25	P
Chassagne	PC	Clos St.-Jean (R)	0.10	36	P
Chassagne	V	— (W)	0.63	4	P
Chassagne	V	— (R)	1.52	30	P/F
Santenay	V	—	0.32	25	P
St.-Aubin	PC	—	0.41	18	P
Puligny	V	—	0.50	1988/9	P
—	R	(Bourgogne Aligoté)	1.07	30	P/M
—	R	(BGO)	0.43	23	P/M
		Total	**7.95 ha.**		

Domaine Ramonet

CHASSAGNE-MONTRACHET

If there is one Domaine which can challenge Puligny's Leflaive and Sauzet for the overall consistency and excellence of white wines, it is Domaine Ramonet in Chassagne. Although there have been eccentricities and hiccups, principally due to uneven bottlings rather than poor wine-making, this Domaine regularly produces remarkable wines at every level, from superb Village Chassagnes to masterpiece Grands Crus.

This is not, however, an old-established estate by Burgundian standards, being no more than a third-generation parvenu. Started by Pierre Ramonet during the late 1920s, it came briefly into the hands of his son André before passing to the present custodians – André's sons Jean-Claude and Noël. Pierre Ramonet had married a Mlle. Prudhon, so for a time the wines were sold under their joint names or, confusingly, as Domaine André Ramonet – only the label differed. However when the brothers created a Société Civile to exploit the Domaine's vineyards, the name was changed to Domaine Ramonet, which is presently the sole denomination.

The vineyards have been acquired gradually since the first purchase – in 1934 a parcel of Chassagne Premier Cru Les Ruchottes. The most recent acquisition was the Montrachet in 1978. Interestingly, all the Ramonet Grands Crus are in the commune of Puligny, although the Domaine has its headquarters and cuverie in Chassagne.

The visitor to the Domaine, in the corner of a quiet little square tucked away at the far end of Chassagne, will find no signpost to tell him where he is, just an undistinguished modern building, housing the cuverie, with rather plain, functional cellars beneath. The office, if it can be called that, consists of a partitioned-off cubicle at the top of the building, next to a grindingly noisy labelling machine. The Domaine's administration is handled elsewhere in the village.

Pierre Ramonet vinified his last vintage in 1983 with André; the following year Noël and his brother took over full control. Although both brothers appear to take joint responsibility for everything, in fact there is a firm division of labour: Noël concentrates on the cellar work whilst Jean-Claude looks after the vines and, being computer-literate, superintends the office-work. However some jobs, such as pruning and tasting, are done by them both, which makes for an integrated operation. 'From graft to bottle – we do it all,' barks Nöel, horrified at the suggestion of

Noël, André and Jean-Claude Ramonet outside their cuverie

anyone else taking on the vineyard work; 'the patron is in the vineyard, in the cellar, everywhere!'

Noël Ramonet, a shock-haired, tracksuited, studiedly eccentric individual in his early thirties, is the more vociferous of the two brothers. Although he appears to disdain publicity, he clearly relishes the opportunity to air his views, a proceeding carried on in short, ballistic sentences from which the principal verb is frequently omitted as if, shorn of unnecessary verbiage, they might be expected to travel faster: 'No stainless-steel here; personal policy!'

In the vineyards efforts are directed to keeping vine age high and yields low. Up to 30-year-old vines are replaced if they succumb to frost or disease; thereafter the parcel is left until the time comes for it to be completely replanted. The Ramonets consider not only the average age of the vines, but also the minimum age at which a vine will produce wine of sufficient quality for their high standards, to be of equal importance. Produce of 'jeune vignes' – that is to say of vines up to 18 years old – is not incorporated into the Domaine's wines, but vinified and *élevé* apart.

The vines are pruned short – the Chardonnays to 2 x 7 eyes *en Guyot* and the Pinots *en cordon de Royat* – that is with 3 fruiting canes of 2 eyes each trained off a single cordon, with a spur of 2 eyes on the main stem.

Although clones are used for replanting, these are chosen personally by the Ramonets, and then grafted on to whichever rootstock is deemed best adapted to the soil concerned. The vines are treated according to whatever prescriptions are handed down by 'the person who comes from the Service des Végétaux' in Beaune so there is, presumably, no deliberate attempt to attenuate the doses of whatever products are used.

Beyond the somewhat general statement of uncontentious principles, Noël Ramonet is relatively imprecise on details of their vineyard management. One gets the impression that he regards viticulture as unsophisticated outdoor farming work – a necessary but irritating step in obtaining raw material for him to work on in the cuverie. The analogy being perhaps the starred chef who has also to look after his kitchen garden; the work really starts when he gets the vegetables into his pots.

The Ramonet pots, however, produce nectar. For all his apparently bluff indifference, Nöel knows perfectly well what supremely fine wine is about. If the office decor is anything to judge by, he seems to relish tasting whatever is finest from around the world. Apart from a scarcely credible, anatomically record-breaking, pneumatic nude stuck on the back of the door – 'Miss December' on what appears to be a tractor-driver's calendar from a fertiliser company –

the only embellishments of this depressingly spartan enclosure consist of photographs of various rows of bottles with Noël standing contentedly behind them. Any spare shelf space is consecrated to more tangible memorabilia, in the form of empties from bygone tasting epics. These attest to an eclectic palate – Grange Hermitage, old Vendange Tardive from Alsace, 1947 Cheval Blanc, Petrus of various vintages, New World Chardonnays and so on. It is interesting that, more often than not, where you find the finest wine you also find the wine-makers who taste most widely outside their own region.

There is an element of practicality about the Ramonet harvest: they start with the older Pinot vines which take some two days to pick. Whilst these are fermenting – a period of some 8–10 days – they get on with picking the Chardonnay. The harvest ends, traditionally, with the younger red vines.

The reds from this Domaine tend to be supple and soft, for relatively young consumption. The *régionales,* the Bourgogne Grande Ordinaire and the Passe-Tout-Grains, are vinified in autovinificators. The results have not encouraged Noël who finds that the wines made in this way lack finesse. The Chassagne reds are, however, vinified differently – with 50% destalking and a species of *carbonic maceration* in 'semi-closed' cement *cuves,* with two *pigéages* and two *remontages à la pompe* daily for about 8 days.They then pass into cask – with 35% of new Vosges and Tronçais oak for one year. Then, whether or not the *malos* are completed, the wines are racked, unified in tank and fined with albumen. Three weeks later they are filtered through wide pore plates – which Noël does not regard as filtration – and bottled.

Both the Clos de la Boudriotte, from low-yielding old vines on predominantly clay-limestone soils, and the Morgeot, from younger vines on soils with a higher clay content, are quite ripe and stylish. Never aggressive, the tannins always seem to balance the fruit and acidity. The Boudriotte is the more concentrated of the pair, typically smelling of *fruits rouges,* griottes and, according to Noël, Kirsch cherries. The 50% of whole bunches undoubteddly contribute to the characteristic softness of the Ramonet red wines. Perhaps they would profit in extract and structure from a day or two longer *cuvaison* and possibly a few more stalks in riper years.

The white vinification is started off in stainless-steel or enamelled *cuves,* where the *must* is *chaptalised* if necessary. Once fermentation has started, the wines are put into cask – again 35% of new wood, but Chatillonais and Tronçais, lightly charred, where it is completed. There are generally 3–4 days of strong fermentation at 22–25° C. If the temperature appears to be getting out of hand, the means are there to control it.

Unusually for white wine-making in the Côte de Beaune, Noël Ramonet does not *batonner* his wines. Apart from being a 'tradition familiale', he argues that stirring the lees risks mixing good and bad lees together. 'If you do this eight or ten times a year, your wine will not be well nourished . . . personal policy,' he adds, omitting the verb from the sentence as his customary form of emphasis.

The wines do, however, remain on their lees for some considerable time before their first racking when they are assembled in *foudres.* After a total of 12–15 months in cask, they are racked again and then fined with a mixture of casein and bentonite, left a further 21 days, and bottled directly off their fining with a light plate filtration.

Until recently some of the wines – particularly the white Chassagnes – were bought in cask by Delaunay, a broker from L'Etang-Vergy in the Arrière-Côte, and bottled by him with the Ramonet label. As a result, there were often striking differences between Domaine and broker bottlings of the same wine, so it is important to check the label for confirmation of 'Mise au Domaine' if there is any doubt. Since 1987 only Domaine bottled wine has carried the Ramonet label, so the problem should not recur.

The Ramonet cellars are a doubtful example of order – rather like those at Jacques Reynaud's superlative Château Rayas where the wines are reared in something of a jumble. In neither case does the experience do them any apparent harm. On the contrary, year after year these cellars nurture and bottle some of the most stylish and concentrated white wines which vineyard land is capable of yielding.

When young, the Ramonet Chassagnes have a glorious green tinge and a modestly exotic spectrum of fruit-based aromas. The Morgeot, from a part clay/part limestone soil, is usually the most delicate of the 3 Premiers Crus, whilst the Caillerets, being more on hillsides and the soil having more limestone content, is richer, with greater depth and underlying structure. The Ruchottes, also from hillsides, with a higher proportion of clay than the Caillerets, is fuller and more supple. It is worth noting that nearly a hectare of the Domaine's Ruchottes contains vines which are almost 60 years old, adding further to its concentration of fruit.

Noël Ramonet has no time for those whose wines he finds unbalanced for want of acidity – a problem especially in the ripe years of the 1980s – 1983, 1905, 1988, 1989 and 1990. 'Too much crop,' he snaps back, adding that low yields and old vines are the only solution. He tastes critically, whether his own or anyone else's wines, and has little patience for people who cut corners or overcrop.

Good as the white Chassagne Premiers Crus are, the Grands Crus are several leaps up that rocky ladder leading to absolute perfection – whatever that elusive chimera may turn out to be. The quantities are pitifully small – 7 300-bottle *pièces* of Bâtard-Montrachet, 9 of Bienvenues Bâtard-Montrachet and finally, huddled together in a far corner of the cellar for mutual society, a rather disconsolate pair of barrels containing the riches of Montrachet itself.

Noël finds no great or systematic difference between his Bâtard and his Bienvenues 'barely a metre between them', he explains. However, any similarity may also be accounted for by the fact that the grapes from both parcels are vinified together and only separated at the moment when they are put into cask. The Bâtard is put into Chatillonais barrels – 'more violent, masculine, hard,' chants Noël – while the Bienvenues go into Tronçais – 'much finer!'

Both wines are as rich and powerful in impact as one would expect from Grand Cru from such a Domaine. Finely-crafted as the Chassagnes are, these have deeper colours, much deeper concentrations, altogether greater complexity, and considerably more

DOMAINE RAMONET VINEYARD HOLDINGS

Commune	*Level*	*Lieu-dit/Climat*	*Area*	*Vine Age*	*Status*
Puligny	GC	Le Montrachet	0.25	70	P
Puligny	GC	Bâtard-Montrachet	0.40	40	P
Puligny	GC	Bienvenues-Bâtard-Montrachet	0.50	40	P
Puligny	PC	Champ-Canet	0.40	1993	P
Chassagne	PC	Les Ruchottes (W)	1.03	40	P
Chassagne	PC	Morgeot (R)	0.50	25	P
Chassagne	PC	Morgeot (W)	4.00	30	P/M
Chassagne	PC	Clos de la Boudriotte (R)	1.00	50	P
Chassagne	PC	Les Caillerets (W)	0.40	25	P
Chassagne	PC	Les Chaumées (W)	0.25	0	P
Chassagne	PC	Les Vergers (W)	0.50	30	P
Chassagne	PC	Clos St.-Jean (R)	0.70	60	P
Chassagne	V	— (R)	2.50	30	P
Chassagne	V	— (W)	0.90	35	P
Chassagne	R	(Bourgogne Aligoté)	0.40	50	P
Chassagne	R	(Bourogne Grande Ordinaire)	0.23	20	P
		Total	**13.96 ha.**		

power and profundity. These are wines which, with effortless ease, fuse the seemingly immiscible characteristics of finesse and power, into an integrated ensemble which far exceeds their original constituents. Perhaps the Bâtard is a shade more masculine in form than the Bienvenues, but there is really very little in it.

Unable to meet the demands of 35% of two casks, the Montrachet is put into 100% new Chatillonais oak. The wine is difficult to judge when young – being temporarily knocked out by its wooden surroundings. Although not appearing to be more concentrated than the other Grands Crus, it does have an extra dimension of complexity and completeness which sets it apart. The Domaine has only been making Montrachet since 1979, so it remains to be seen how the wine develops with age. If the Chassagnes are anything to judge by, the results should be spectacular.

Ramonet's wines are as near to the apotheosis of Chardonnay as one is likely to get. Fine as they often are from the cask, they are not intended for drinking young, but are made to be kept for 10 years or more. Ruchottes 1970 and Morgeot 1971 were magnificent, complex and elegant wines 20 years on, and the Ruchottes 1978 was still evolving. Old white Chassagne turns into a delicious amalgam of honey and hazelnuts, with touches of lime-blossom and toast on the nose.

Although the wines are much in demand, the prices for the Chassagnes are not exaggerated, and they are well worth buying and keeping, if you have cash and patience.

Noël believes that the best way to enjoy one of his fine white wines is 'en aperitif' or, if you must eat, then with the simplest of dishes. He is firmly against attempts to match fine wine to fine food – neither ends up enhancing the other and there is invariably a loss of quality on both sides.

Jean-Claude and Noël Ramonet's wines are invariably a joy – perhaps even enhanced by the Domaine's mild eccentricities. In common with many of the Côte's more individual vignerons, Noël dislikes correspondence and visitors in equal measure. Even if you surmount the difficult hurdle of making contact and manage to secure an appointment, it is likely not to be kept.

If you do go visiting, your reception may be unusual. One visitor, rendezvous arranged, turned up to find Noël – whom she had not met before – stationed outside the cellars to tell her that he wasn't in and, furthermore, that in all probability he would not be back for several hours.

When you are as dedicated as Jean-Claude and Noël to the all-consuming task of making great wines, then the unwelcome distractions of administration and visitors inevitably take second place. In the nature of things, one can merely smile at the lapses, although one has a sneaking feeling that they are not invariably forgetfulness but more correctly ascribed to . . . 'personal policy.'

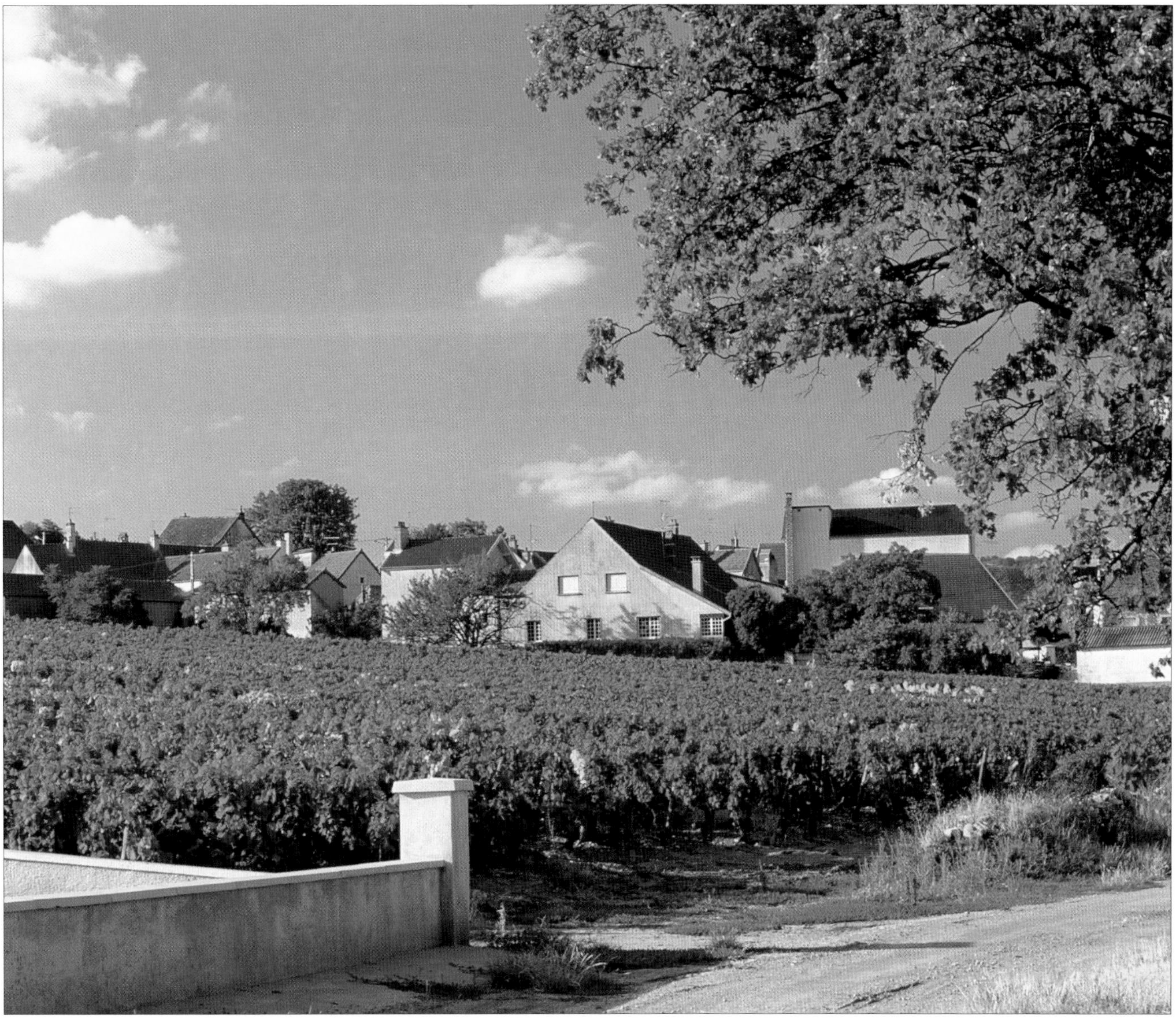

Chassagne-Montrachet

St.-Aubin

St.-Aubin is a pleasantly tranquil, compact village, nestling under a band of gently sloping limestone next to a bend in the RN 6 Chalon–Avallon road. Although only a few kilometres from both Puligny and Chassagne, the visitor may well feel that he is exploring, off the beaten track as he meanders through its narrow, convoluted streets. Just under 300 souls inhabit St.-Aubin, most of whom doubtless toil in the service of wine.

The origins of the village date back to the turn of the second millennium, although recent archaeological discoveries seem to confirm that the site was inhabited during the Bronze and Iron Ages. Henri Cannard records that in 1890, in the Champ de la Vigne a great number of ancient human bones were found; further excavations in 1973 revealed a number of contemporary tools in addition to the bones of mammoths and hyenas.

The commune also comprises nearby Gamay – a small working village – which was a site of strategic prominence up to the beginning of the twentieth century. The old Roman road from St.-Aubin led to a Maison-Forte thus making the village an important crossroads. At the turn of the century, a local priest counted no fewer than 43 'activités commerciales' in the village including 'a barrel-maker, two cafés, an hotel, a garage, an ironmonger, a cobbler, a grocer and a barber'.

Its illustrious past has gone, but Gamay remains an attractive hamlet, more noted perhaps for the grape-variety to which it gives its name than for its Maison-Forte. This grape was brought to Burgundy by Seigneur du May in the Middle Ages and widely planted along the Côte until this century when it was superseded by the Pinot Noir and its produce declared ignoble.

The vignoble of St.-Aubin is extensive – some 80.15.81 ha. of Village wines and no less than 156.46.09 ha. of red and white Premiers Crus. The reds of the village are entitled to be marketed either as St.-Aubin-Côte de Beaune

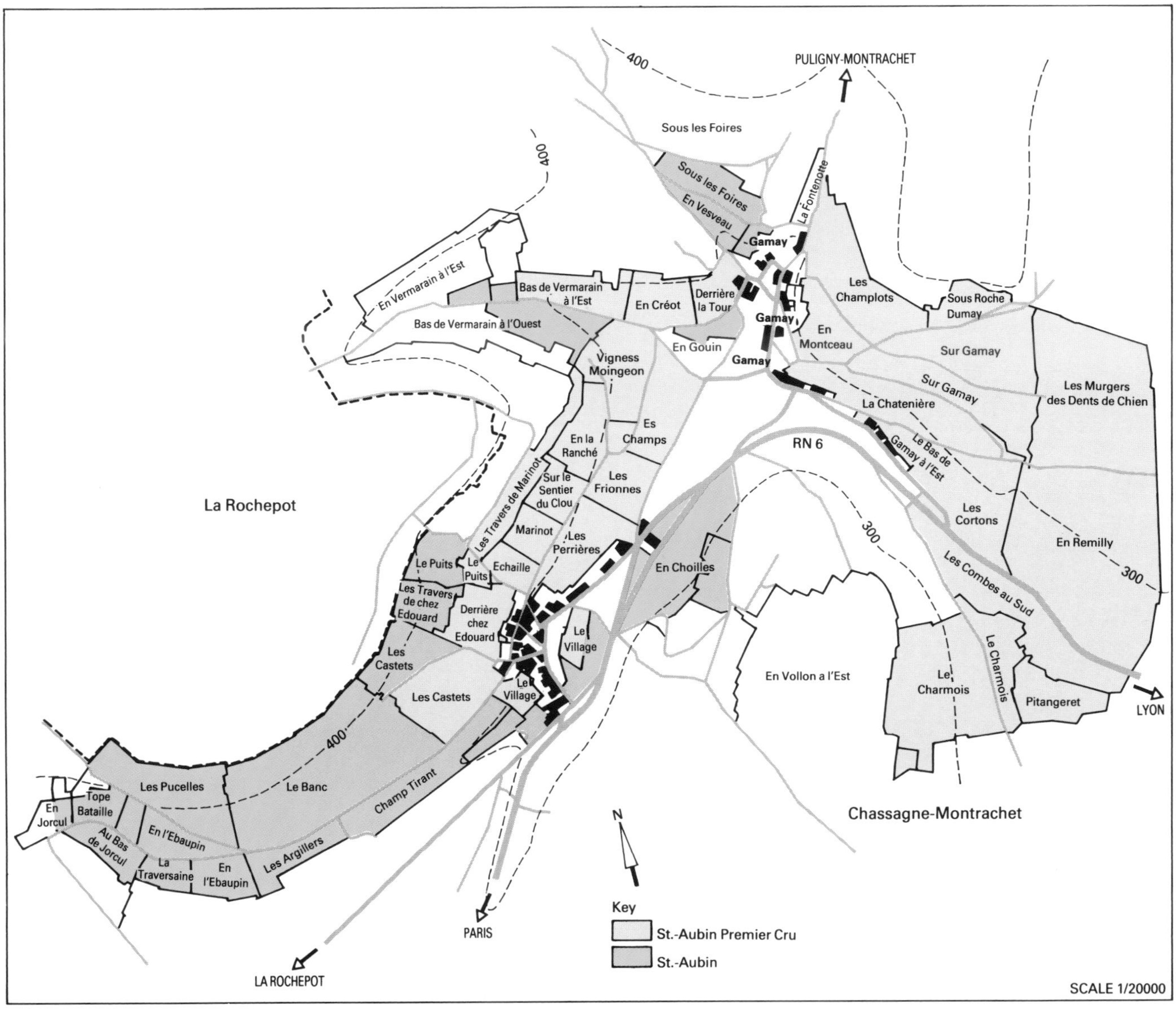

The compact village beneath the bare outcrop of Le Rochepot

or as Côte de Beaune-Villages; however, much of the commune's output is also sold as Bourgogne Rouge and Blanc. This will no doubt change as people come to appreciate the quality of St.-Aubin and as the Premiers Crus become individually recognised.

There are two separate vineyard sites: one, the Montagne du Ban, is situated on an east-west axis immediately behind the village, with south, south-east and south-west expositions. Here are to be found some of the better Premier Cru vineyards: Les Castets, Les Frionnes and Sur le Sentier du Clou, planted on soils which are mainly limestone marls.

The second swathe of vineyards, all Premiers Crus, lies on the Roche du May, above Gamay, at an altitude of 240–300m., and extends across the RN 6 to the Chassagne border. Expositions, although mainly south-westerly, seem to embrace all points of the compass. Here the soils are more varied, with brown limestones admixed with clay on the lower slopes and more obvious limestones on the higher sites, especially on those immediately backing on to the Mont Rachet. Here are the finest of the white Premiers Crus, namely Les Murgers des Dents de Chien and La Chatenière on the Puligny side and Le Charmois on the Chassagne slope.

It is worth finding your way up on to the top of the Mont Rachet – if you can discover the right track – from where a short walk through 100m. of snake-infested scrub (it's safe in winter) brings you out just above the Puligny Grand Cru Chevalier-Montrachet~ This is the nexus of 3 communes – St.-Aubin, Chassagne and Puligny – and a perfect vantage point over the entire sweep of Puligny and its vines.

The band of limestone rock continues on both sides of the hill – indeed, the continuation of the St.-Aubin Premier Cru Dents de Chien, having lost Les Murgers along the way, reappears as a Chassagne Village appellation. The two St.-Aubin vineyards at the top of the hill are exposed to the drying influence of winds and are generally cooler than those lower down, protected by the hillside. This means that they ripen later and thus, in marginal years, are less successful.

The wines themselves are well worth investigation. The reds, especially from the better Premiers Crus, are generally robust and earthy in character, developing into attractive wines over 5–10 years in a good vintage. Growers who do not destalk tend to make wines which are over-tannic and thereby out of balance.

The white wines reach higher peaks than the reds. They have a distinctive *goût de terroir,* definitely an acquired taste, which threads through their maturation, and the ability to last. A 15-year-old white St.-Aubin will probably smell of lime-blossom and have a nutty, earthy flavour which goes well with good fish and white meat dishes. It is worth sticking to the better vintages since the situation of the vineyards means later ripening than Chassagne or Puligny and consequently wines which in naturally unripe vintages are green and lacking in finesse.

The commune of St.-Aubin is fortunate in having a band of hard-working, skilful growers whose efforts, until relatively recently, have passed lamentably unrewarded. However, with prices of more exalted white Burgundy beyond most people's reach, merchants are beating a path to their doors for wines which, while never great, are generally sound, with abundant character and a bearable price-tag.

The best sources in St.-Aubin itself are: Gérard Thomas, Hubert Lamy, Roux Père et Fils and Henri Prudhon. Growers and négociants outside the viillage making good St.-Aubins are Jadot, Chartron et Trebuchet, Olivier Leflaive, Jean-Marc Morey, Bernard Morey and Marc Colin.

With this deservedly increased recognition, more wine is being sold under the Village label, and individual Premier Cru *climats* are beginning to establish their own identities. Provided prices remain sensible, this welcome trend is likely to continue.

Domaine Hubert Lamy

ST.-AUBIN

Hubert Lamy is a large, open, deliberate man who, with a handful of other quality-conscious growers, is establishing the reputation of St.-Aubin as a source of attractively priced, sound Burgundy.

There have been Lamys toiling away in the village since 1640. Indeed, the last generation toiled indoors as well as outdoors, producing 7 children among whom the vineyards were divided when Hubert took over from his father – who still lives in the village – in 1973. His Domaine now extends to some 7 ha. of red and 5.6 ha. of white, spread over St.-Aubin, Chassagne, Puligny and Santenay.

While his two children are still too young to work full-time, Hubert's wife looks after the commercial side of the Domaine. 'My treasurer', as he delightfully refers to her, ensures that her husband does not overspend on some shiny, up-to-the-minute piece of equipment which might take his fancy. The treasury has been recently unlocked to the extent of an impressive new cellar and smartly shut up again so, for the present, severe economy is in force.

There is no doubt that Hubert's wine-making skills and his vivacious wife's budgeting have combined to create a solid success. Their wines are reasonably priced and among the best in the village.

Hubert clearly relishes being out among his scattered vineyards. This is where quality begins. Minimum fertilisers, plenty of *répiquage,* carefully chosen rootstock, short *cordon* training for the Pinot Fin, with the indispensable aid of 'precise soil analyses – the clay content of a vineyard can differ within a few metres'. Hubert is not generally in favour of removing grapes later on in the season to further reduce crop size. However, he did make a limited *vendange verte* in 1982, which caused some incomprehending derision among his colleagues. The wines, apparently, were much the better for it.

Hubert's red vinification has recently undergone an important change. Since the 1989 vintage the bunches have been destalked to a greater extent than before. This change is not seen as permanent, but it is to be hoped that the improved quality of these wines will cause him to reflect seriously on the wisdom of leaving any significant proportion of stems in his vats in future.

A more durable change has, however, taken place in the length of *cuvaison;* formerly 8–10 days, Hubert has wisely decided that a further 4 days is rewarded with much greater extraction. This reinforces the argument for fewer stems. Selected yeasts are used – heaven knows why: there is nothing wrong, and everything right, with the natural yeast population.

Hubert finds it difficult to decide on an optimum temperature for red fermentation: wanting to extract colour, but believing that this inevitably detaches tannins. He might prolong his current 3–4 day pre-fermentive maceration at 15–16° C. by a further day or so. This would extract enough colour and should avoid any imbalance of tannin.

The wines are given more or less press-wine, depending on its quality, and then kept in cask for about 15 months, fined with albumen (or gelatine in the case of aggressive tannins) and plate-filtered before bottling. Only the *cuvées* of Santenay and St.-Aubin Les Castets see any new oak: 'We must go slowly on these expensive casks,' Hubert announces, adding with a smile at his wife, 'I must first persuade my treasurer to give me the money! 'Yes,' adds Mme. Lamy, 'if he has a new destalker, he can't expect too many casks as well,' turning an invisible key on the invisible cash-box.

Hubert's 1989s are definitely better for these changes. Earlier vintages seem to have suffered from excess astringency and a marked leatheriness which mars their ageing. He tried a 24-hour maceration à chaud (40° C.) for the Chassagne village *cuvée* which resulted in a softer, warmer wine, with more harmonious tannins. The St.-Aubin Premier Cru Les Castets and the Chassagne are the best of the red bunch.

The whites start their fermentation in bulk, so that the temperature can be controlled at 20° C. When the density of the *must* reaches about 1,020, the wines are transferred to cask to continue their fermentation. The St.-Aubins and Pulignys see about 33% well-charred, new wood, the rest being raised in older oak. 'I would like to use more new wood, but casks are expensive – the client must pay for it in the end; when I see them making excellent white wine in Chablis, without any wood, I ask myself if I am doing the right thing.'

Fining, either with casein if the wine has a tendency to oxidise, or with fish fining if not, precedes a moderately tight filtration and bottling between June and August – deliberately early to retain the wine's freshness.

If the quality of the reds is still evolving, the whites have already established a level of excellence. Four different St.-Aubin Premiers Crus form the heart of the production; these tend to start with a touch of austerity, with every sign of being built to last. Of these, the Frionnes and En Remilly are particularly good – fullish, sappy, wines with plenty of depth and interest. The En Remilly comes from young Chardonnay vines, planted on crushed-up rocks, on top of the Mont Rachet.

Outside the commune, Hubert makes a village Puligny, Les Tremblots, and a Grand Cru Criots-Bâtard-Montrachet – only one solitary cask here. These are both excellent, and more than worthy of their appellations. The 1989 Criots is a firm, well-constituted wine, with plenty of depth and concentration; despite the small volume (what on earth does he top up his cask with?) Hubert has managed to retain a good nerve of acidity, something lacking in many 1989 whites.

Hubert Lamy deserves to be better known. He is a fine source of attractive, quality wines at more than reasonable prices.

VINEYARD HOLDINGS

Commune	*Level*	*Lieu-dit/Climat*	*Area*	*Vine Age*	*Status*
Chassagne	GC	Criots-Bâtard-Montrachet	0.04	15	F
Chassagne	PC	Les Macherelles (W)	0.13	3	F
Chassagne	V	La Goujonne (R)	1.90	38+	F
Puligny	V	Les Tremblots	0.89	21	P
St. Aubin	PC	Les Frionnes (W)	0.45	28	P
St. Aubin	PC	Les Meix (W)	0.52	48+	P
St. Aubin	PC	En Remilly (W)	0.87	3	F
St. Aubin	PC	Les Cortons (W)	0.57	2	P/F
St. Aubin	PC	(Several climats) (W)	0.55	N/A	P
St. Aubin	PC	Les Castets (R)	1.58	18	P
St. Aubin	V	La Princée (W)	0.66	5	P
St. Aubin	V	Le Paradis (R)	0.95	15	P
—	R	(Bourgogne Aligoté)	0.95	37	P
Santenay	V	Les Hôtes	0.60	43+	P
—	R	Côte de Beaune-Villages	0.77	N/A	P
—	R	(Bourg.Hte.Côte de Beaune)	0.76	N/A	P
—	R	(Bourgogne Rouge)	0.54	N/A	P
		Total	**12.73 ha.**		

Domaine Roux Père et Fils

ST.-AUBIN

The Roux, like many other of the local families, have been in the village for two centuries or longer. However, it is only since 1960, when Fernard Roux left his son Marcel the curate's egg of a legacy of 4 ha. of vines, but neither stock – hail and frost in 1956/57 and 1958 – nor customers, that the modern enterprise began. Marcel added 21 ha. to the Domaine's land and is now the largest vineyard owner in St.-Aubin. In 1975 Marcel's eldest son, Christian, an oenologist, joined his father, and in 1980 his second son Régis came into the business; there is a third little brother waiting in the wings!

By 1984 the Roux discovered that they were in a perpetual state of having more customers than wine to sell them, so they set up a négociant business, which specialises in the appellations of Puligny, Chassagne, Meursault and, of course, St.-Aubin.

The Domaine's wines are stored in some 20 small cellars dotted around St.-Aubin and elsewhere, in all sorts of curious, anonymous corners. Its principal address, at the top of the village, consists of a narrow arch, some cellars, and what seems a very small office for the administration of such a large enterprise.

Although the Roux seem determined on quality, one gets the impression that they approach it by somewhat idiosyncratic methods. They entertain a healthy distrust of officialdom and particularly of the idea that the law can sensibly intervene in nature.

In the vineyards, the Domaine continues its practice of 15 years of leaving vine prunings to mulch into the soil as humus – which also helps degrade any herbicide residues. This is disturbing, since it is well known that the disease *eutypiose* is spread by spores from infected wood. Unless prunings and dead vines are incinerated immediately, the probability that the disease will become widespread approaches certainty.

The wine-making is careful and, by and large, traditional. The white Crus, and a part of the Bourgogne Blanc, are fermented in cask – 20–33% new – at 20° C for up to two months. This long, slow transformation of sugar helps extract secondary aromatic compounds and glycerols. Natural yeasts are used, and *chaptalisation* is kept to the minimum: 'The wine expresses its finesse better and is more pleasurable with less alcohol,' explains Christian.

After a first racking in February or March, after the *malo,* the wine is returned to cask and fined a week later. The fining remains with the wine for up to 3 months, since the Roux contend that the *malade de mise* is in fact attributable to the fining and not to the act of bottling, so the longer the wine remains on its fining, the less it will suffer at bottling. Cold stabilisation – chilling to precipitate out excess, harmless tartrates – and a sterile filtration at 0° C., to keep the aromas in the wine, complete the *élevage.*

The style of the Roux whites is deliberately aimed at a clientèle who want wines which are approachable young but which will benefit from some ageing. For their own part, the brothers, collectively speaking, prefer wines which have a delicacy and freshness (e.g. the 1979s), rather than the old-fashioned, heavier, oxidative style (the 1978s). Their St.-Aubins, in particular, tend to have a fine nerve of acidity, plenty of fruit and a distinctive *goût de terroir.* The best of the whites is their Premier Cru La Chatenière.

The Roux red vinification has undergone a major change since 1987 – possibly as a result of criticism which focused on an imbalance of harsh tannins. Up to the 1986 vintage, most of the stalks were left in the vats since, as Christian admits, they believed that tannins added ageing potential to a red wine. However, it was gradually borne in upon them that what was needed were small yields and long *cuvaison,* rather than simply putting anything they could think of that might leach out tannins, into their *cuves.* From the 1987 vintage, therefore, the bunches are virtually 100% destemmed.

The provision of a new cuverie has given their reds a further advantage, in that as they now have more *cuves* there is no longer the pressure on vat-space there was before, so they can leave the wines on their skins for longer. A maximum of 8 days *cuvaison* has now become 12–15 days.

Christian and Régis have also been trying out a roto-*cuve* on their Auxey-Duresses and Premier Cru St.-Aubin reds and are impressed with the results. These closed fermentation vessels seem to help retain aroma and concentration and add roundness without appearing to remove any of the wine's typicity. The St.-Aubin Rouge now consists of a blend of 60% roto-wine and 40% traditionally vinified wine, and the balance is much finer for it.

The desire to keep the tannins in equilibrium has also led to a reduction in the proportion of new wood used – now about 20–25% with the balance being third- and fourth-year casks from the white cellar. After their *malos* the wines are removed from St.-Aubin to a cooler cellar at nearby Nolay where they remain until ready for filtration and bottling, some 12–18 months after the vintage.

These changes have made a dramatic difference to the quality of the Roux reds. Formerly rather lean wines with an unyielding nerve of green tannins, they now have much greater balance and concentration.

The Domaine's sales are almost entirely within France, leaving exports in the hands of the négociant arm. This is a pity because the wines, especially those of St.-Aubin, deserve to be more widely known. Whilst the rise in prices for the Chassagnes, Pulignys and Meursaults is bringing the white St.-Aubins into merchants' consciousnesses, marketing the reds is a slower process. They are all well worth trying, and for anyone feeling adventurous, Roux Père et Fils is one of the best sources of supply.

VINEYARD HOLDINGS

Commune	*Level*	*Lieu-dit/Climat*	*Area*	*Vine Age*	*Status*
St.-Aubin	PC	La Châtenière (W)	1.00	15	P
St.-Aubin	PC	Les Cortons (W)	1.00	10	P
St.-Aubin	PC	Les Frionnes/ Les Castets (R)	2.50	40	P
St.-Aubin	V	— (R)	1.50	40	P
St.-Aubin	V	— (W)	3.00	25	P
St.-Aubin	R	(Bourgogne Chardonnay)	3.00	10	P
Corpeaux	R	(Bourgogne Rouge)	4.00	40	P
Corpeaux	R	(Bourgogne Aligoté)	2.00	20	P
Chassagne	PC	Les Macherelles (W)	0.60	1991	P
Chassagne	PC	Clos St.-Jean (R)	0.50	30	P
Chassagne	V	— (R)	1.00	40	P
Chassagne	V	— (W)	1.00	45–50	P
Puligny	V	—	0.50	60	P
Meursault	PC	Les Poruzots	0.45	15	P
Santenay	PC	La Comme/Beauregard	2.50	40	P
		Total	**24.55 ha.**		

Domaine Gérard Thomas

ST.-AUBIN

Gérard Thomas is one of the best sources of St.-Aubin. From his 9 ha. of vines, all but 2 ha. of which are in the commune, the bluff, weather-beaten Gérard produces a range of 10 carefully made wines which are invariably of good to very good quality and particularly good value for money.

The Domaine was created after the last war by Gérard's father who rented and bought vines. On his retirement in 1982, Gérard took over and started to rationalise what was a highly fragmented estate. In 1986 he added the Premier Cru Les Murgers des Dents de Chien to the estate and the following year bought a plot of the white Premier Cru La Chatenière.

Both whites and reds are made more or less traditionally. The whites are kept in cask for about one year, and bottled after fining and two separate filtrations. However, nothing is immutable, so when a *cuvée* of St.-Aubin Premier Cru 1988 failed to complete its *malo,* it was simply kept in cask for an extra year until deemed in a fit state for bottling.

Gérard Thomas's St.-Aubins are usually ripe, quite plump wines, with good, stylish flavours. His habit of jumping from vineyard to vineyard during harvesting to pick at optimum ripeness seems to pay off with a good concentration of fruit in most wines.

The amount of new wood used depends as much on cash-flow as on anything else. In 1989 he managed 10–15%, but in 1988 had to be content with renewing a few cask staves to give a sort of partial new oak.

The cream of the St.-Aubins are the Premiers Crus Les Murgers des Dents de Chien, which is just below the satellite hamlet of Gamay, and La Chatenière which is just above it. Les Murgers, which is in fact also just behind the Mont Rachet, is an exposed vineyard with poor soil giving on to hard bedrock. The wine is characterised by aromas of dried fruit and lime-blossom and with plenty of ripe fruit and finesse. Both the 1988 and 1989 are mouthfilling offerings which need keeping for several years to reach their prime.

Thomas sells much of his output to private clients and to restaurants, so he deliberately aims at wines which have the fruit and charm for early drinking but which can yet be kept to develop in the medium term; a difficult fence to straddle, but he does it with aplomb.

The Meursault Blagny and the Puligny Premier Cru La Garenne are also neatly crafted wines. The Meursault often has a touch of the St.-Aubin rusticity underneath its powerful exterior, but is none the worse for that. The 1988 and 1989 Blagnys are both excellent efforts – the latter having more obvious flesh and richness, whilst the former is tighter and distinctly more masculine.

The La Garenne has plenty of the elegance one would expect from a Premier Cru Puligny – with a dimension of power which derives from the relatively high clay content of the soil. Here the 1988 is noticeably more successful than the 1989, which seems to lack definition and length.

Gérard is busy extending his small production of reds; at present, apart from a Bourgogne Rouge, there is only a St.-Aubin, Côte de Beaune and 30 ares of St.-Aubin Premier Cru Les Frionnes. A further 70 ares of Frionnes were planted in 1991.

The reds are vinified in cement *cuves,* without any pre-fermentive maceration and with about 10 days of *cuvaison.* Wisely, Gérard avoids anything more than a touch of new wood – this may make financial sense as well – preferring to *saigner* his *cuves* to concentrate the wine rather than to add any artificial structure. Much of what is poor in Auxey-Duresses and St.-Aubin reds can be attributed to an excess of stalk or wood tannins.

The wines spend 18–24 months in cask; precisely when they are fined, filtered and bottled depends, according to Gérard, on when he has time to spare, space to spare and cash to spare. Having said this, he was shocked to be asked whether or not he used a contract bottler – after all, many estimable growers do. The answer, of course, was an emphatic 'Non!'

Gérard's reds tend to be quite sizeable wines – not delicate, fruity mouthfuls for the faint-hearted. The Frionnes is, with Les Castets, arguably the best of the St.-Aubin Premiers Crus. Both give wines which are naturally high in tannin and acidity to begin with but which, if carefully vinified, will last well for up to a decade in the best vintages. The 1988 Frionnes, with 2 years of cask ageing behind it, but no new wood, had an attractive, positive nose redolent of strawberries and blackberries. On the palate it had a soft attack, which gave way to a mouthful of rather astringent youthful tannins. Perhaps, 2 years in cask was just too much. Gérard's customers will need at least 5 years to find out.

Vines in full flower

If you are looking for modestly-priced white Burgundy, the amiable Gérard Thomas is an excellent source. St.-Aubin will never reach the aristocratic heights of its neighbour on the other side of the Mont-Rachet, but it can provide plenty of interesting wines for those prepared to lower their sights a little.

VINEYARD HOLDINGS

Commune	*Level*	*Lieu-dit/Climat*	*Area*	*Vine Age*	*Status*
Blagny	PC	Meursault-Blagny	1.00	20	M
Puligny	PC	La Garenne	0.50	25	P/M
Puligny	V	— (W)	0.50	25	M
St.-Aubin	PC	Murgers des Dents de Chien (W)	1.30	15	P/M
St.-Aubin	PC	La Chatenière (W)	0.40	10	P
St.-Aubin	PC	Les Frionnes (R)	0.30	25	P
St.-Aubin	PC	Les Frionnes (R)	0.70	1991	P
St.-Aubin	PC	(Several climats) (W)	1.80	20	P/M
St.-Aubin	V	— (R)	0.30	4	P
St.-Aubin	R	(Côte de Beaune) (R)	1.25	30	P
—	R	(Bourgogne Rouge)	1.25	25	P
		Total	**9.30 ha.**		

Hubert Lamy and his team winter pruning

SANTENAY AND REMIGNY

Santenay's imposing Château of Philippe le Hardi

Although not strictly the last wine-producing commune in the Côte d'Or – that honour falls to Cheilly-Les-Maranges – Santenay is generally regarded as its southernmost outpost. For years, buyers have come here in the hope of some sound quality, reasonably priced red Burgundy to fill the gap between the grander communes and the Rullys, Givrys and Mercureys of the Côte Chalonnaise.

Apart from these considerations, Santenay is an old and attractive village more obviously oriented towards its community than to the tourism which infects the ambience of much of the Côte. The place is in fact two villages: the most recent and largest part, which sprang up with the advent of the Chagny-Nevers railway line in 1861 and is now home to many of the larger Domaines and most of the local commerce, is Santenay-le-Bas.

A kilometre or so up the hill is Santenay-le-Haut, a much older hamlet with narrow, steep, winding streets and an air of immutable isolation. Here are two of Santenays main tourist attractions – the Casino and the thermal springs.

The former is the town's largest earner, employing some 40 people throughout the summer to cater to a heterogenous clientèle from the 'jeunesse dorée' of the Côte to crusty old gold-veined Swiss travellers. It operates from a splendid 1914 building, with large small-paned windows, which looks as though it has been lifted, brick and beam, from Le Touquet or Deauville, fashionable French seaside resorts of the 1920s.

The thermal springs have long been part of Santenay's history. They were almost certainly used by the Romans, who settled on the Mont de Senne, a magnificent vantage point 500 m. above the valley, and by the early seventeenth century, were documented for their curative properties. In the late nineteenth century they were so popular that the single spring was inadequate and another was sought, and found, by the local pharmacist. This artesian well produces water high in lithium which is especially recommended for stress-related complaints.

The heyday of Santenay as a spa, according to Henri Cannard, came in 1891, when some 10,000 came to take the waters which, like those of many spas, had broad curative properties, claiming success with everything from constipation to corns. A 100-bed hotel was built and they even tried bottling water to increase sales. Sadly, the hotel survived only one year; it was bought in 1946 by French railways as a retirement home. A new hotel was opened in 1979, and the cures still contribute to the local economy.

The wines of Santenay have never figured prominently on the map of Burgundy, enjoying a reputation for reliable robustness rather than for elegance or finesse. Of the 113,000 or so cases produced annually, 111,000 are red, made from 378.18 ha. of vineyards covering a large area between Chassagne to the north-east and Cheilly-Les-Maranges to the south-west. Of these, 124.29 ha. – nearly 33% – are Premiers Crus, the majority, and best, of which lie in a single band of hillside above the main road.

Although there are 11 Premiers Crus altogether, only 5 are encountered with any regularity: La Comme (22.07 ha.), Clos des Tavannes (5.32 ha.), Les Gravières (23.40 ha.), La Maladière (13.58 ha.) and Clos

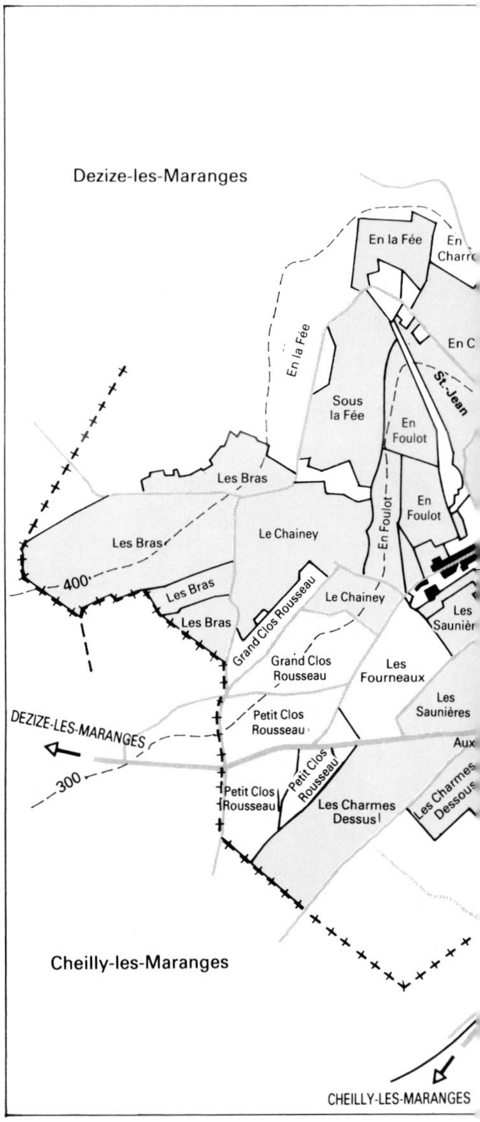

Rousseau (23.84 ha.). Of these, the first three are in the heart of the appellation, in the sector nearest to Chassagne.

Here marly, limestone soils, stony and thus well-drained, give wines an earthy robustness, of which the best need 10 or more years to develop. While Santenays rarely appear as charm-school graduates, they do, with time, take on a certain bawdy elegance which, whilst not quite the real thing, will pass muster for a sort of seductive refinement; the clothes may be expensive but you can still glimpse the tattoos underneath.

La Maladière, a south-east facing vineyard to the west of the others, has more limestone in the soil which combines with a higher elevation to produce more perfumed but lighter wines. The négociant house, Prosper Maufoux, is the largest owner here, offering a wine which is usually light in colour and rather evanescent in flavour.

The Clos Rousseau – divided into Grand and Petit– although on deeper, brown limestone soils, richer in clay and iron oxide, which are not best suited to fine wine production, can give wines of excellent richness and genuine depth.

There are two viticultural matters of note about Santenay: first, there is a species of Pinot Noir known as the Pinot Fin de Santenay, which growers often refer to as that planted here and in Chassagne, and well adapted to the local soils. Whilst there may have been such a strain in years past, what is now planted are conventional clones, although there may be pockets of *sélection massale* from older strains of Pinot.

Secondly, Santenay Pinot Noir vines are trained *en cordon de Royat,* to limit their vigour from naturally productive soils. This has both advantages and disadvantages – the foliage is more spread out, giving better photosynthesis and better ripening, and pruning can be delayed until the spring, since there is no *baguette* to train. However, reinstating a *cordon* after frost damage is difficult, and *cordon* training is known to increase the risk of the acariose mite, which eats both fruit and leaves, and of red spider.

Whether or not a bottle of Santenay is likely to be interesting and age-worthy, depends as much on the producer as on the vineyard. Much that is produced is light, often stalky and tannic wine which, whilst perfectly quaffable with well-flavoured stews and roasts, is not worth buying and keeping.

However, there are some pockets of excellence where old vines, small yields and careful wine-making combine to produce wines which have much merit. In addition to the two Domaines profiled here, good Santenays are made by Pousse d'Or (Clos des Tavannes) and by Maison Drouhin.

Santenay Blanc is little seen. However, from good producers such as Louis and René Lequin, who make their white from Pinot Blanc rather than Chardonnay, it can be delicious – for drinking within its first few years.

Santenay well deserves a renaissance. There is much worth drinking from the best growers in the commune – and from one or two, some seriously fine wine.

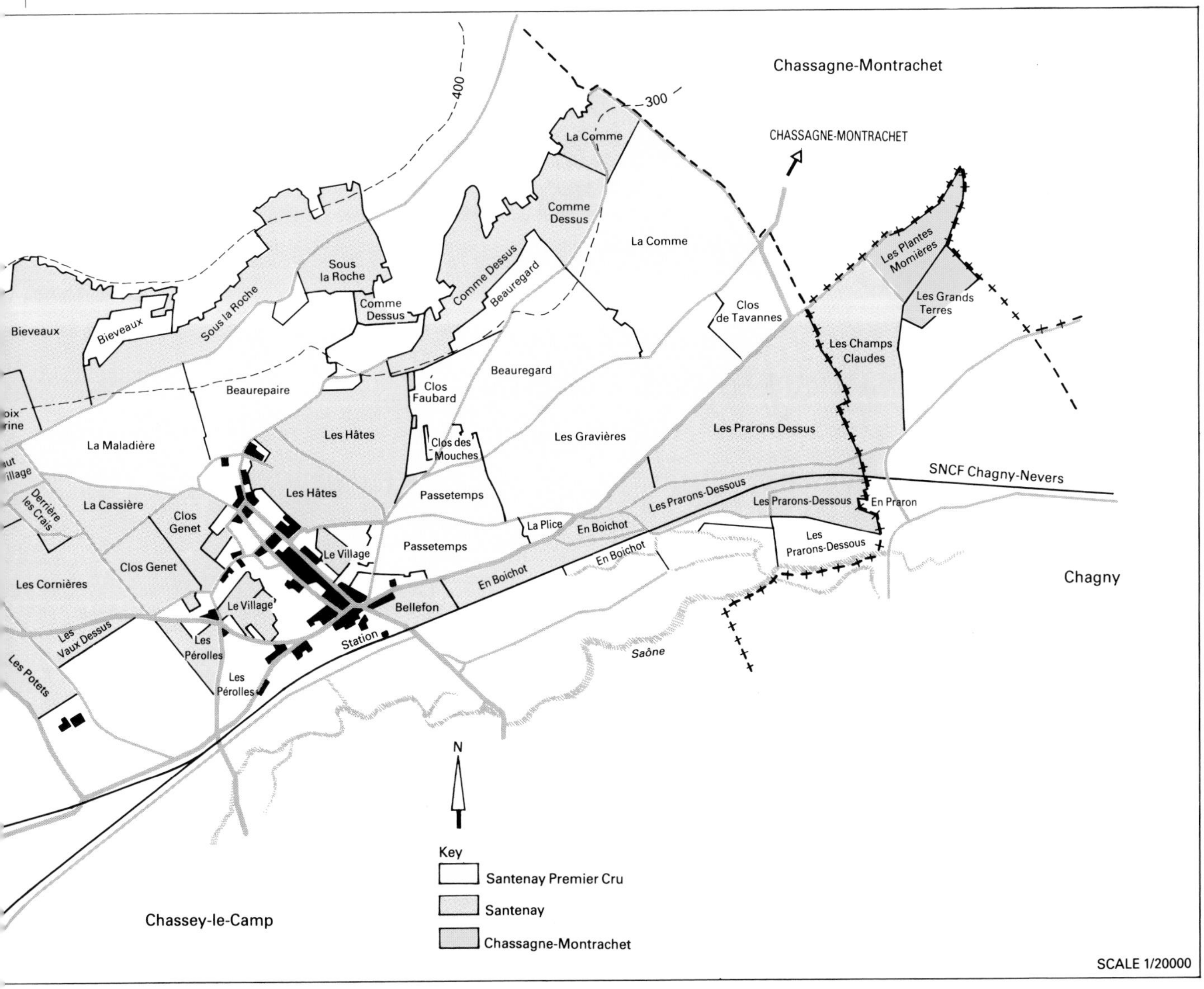

Domaine Adrien Belland

SANTENAY

The Côte d'Or is such a fragemented mosaic of smallholdings that, even now, one should not perhaps be surprised to find a long-established Domaine making wine of exceptional quality, apparently still largely unrecognised. Yet it still seems odd, so much extolled are the virtues of the top estates that there remain discoveries to be made.

Adrien Belland may not see himself in the light of a discovery – after all his family have been vignerons at Santenay for several generations, and he has been making wine on his own account for nearly 40 years. As long as his wine sells well, what do the plaudits of critics or the glare of international publicity matter – he would probably regard them as more of a nuisance than anything else?

Yet Adrien Belland, lowering his substantial frame into one of his cramped office chairs, does concern himself with what others think of his wines. A large book, propped up behind the wash-basin which doubles as a spittoon, is soon lifted down to show off the numerous medals which his wines have won over the years at fairs in Mâcon and Paris – acclamation in gold, silver and bronze, for Santenays, Cortons and Chambertins.

The medals are well-deserved by this distinguished wine-maker. His old parents, both still alive, produced 4 children, all of whom took their share of vineyards when the division came. Adrien started with 3 ha. and added to them, principally by marriage to a girl from nearby Autun who, fortuitously, was of the Latour family. With her came prime parcels of Grands Crus Cortons, Perrières and Clos de la Vigne au Saint, plus Aloxe-Corton Village vines and some Chambertin. In 1975 he added a further 55 ares of Corton Grèves, bringing the Domaine up to its present 11 ha.

Many dismiss the wines of Santenay as being light and definitely not for keeping. Tasting with Adrien Belland might change their mind; he builds his wines on the architectural principle, from solid timber, and is not someone who would contemplate, for the slightest instant, the use of plywood.

Visiting the Domaine, situated in one corner of the torpid little main square of Santenay, is something of a trip into history. Behind the rather neat façade, leading on to a small courtyard, lie the cellars. Here one might get the impression, from the litter of bric-à-brac which bestrews the floor, that wine-making is an ancillary activity which vies for attention with gardening, restoring pre-war heaters and cycle repairs. This would be a profound mistake.

The first wine offered is a 1990 Santenay Village, from a large enamelled vessel in the ground-floor cuverie, with '12' proclaimed on it. The wine is extraordinary: impenetrable and virtually black, with masses of fruit and layers of ripe tannins. A clearly startled look elicits from Adrien: 'It's all in the vines – even the power,' which he regards as enough of an explanation. Comment at an end, the remains of the wine are expectorated into an ancient wheelbarrow, full of old grafts, which just happens to be nearby. Adrien plants them out in the garden which slopes away to the railway line at the back of the house. Those that don't take are brought in and abandoned in the cuverie – emergency supplies of firewood presumably.

Flicking with a wooden stick at an exposed bundle of bare wires on the wall of one of the many small cask-lined underground galleries, Adrien crackles the lights into action and starts drawing off samples from the various barrels. If the Santenay is black, what, the visitor might be forgiven for silently wondering, is the Chambertin like?

Next, however, comes the 1990 Corton Grèves, equally impenetrable black/purple. Tasted blind, one might easily guess at a young Syrah, although it seems to have a ripe warmth which perhaps would make one hesitate. There is yet more complexity and extraordinary depth and class underneath its mask of tannins.

The cellars are more than two centuries old; they are certainly very bleak on a glacial January afternoon, although Adrien is content to wander round in an open-necked shirt. 'I never touch my wines, neither here nor there,' he explains, waving his stick at a bank of barrels, an oblique reference to his policy of long vinification. No pre-fermentive maceration, just a *pied de cuve* to get the yeasts working and 12 days or so of *cuvaison* at a maximum of 34° C.

Adrien believes in *pigéage*: 'I attach great importance to that,' he avers, adding that he tried fermenting with a submerged cap – the principal alternative to *pigéage* – but found that it gave less character and less colour to his wines.

However, there is no pumping-over. 'The yeasts work perfectly well without oxygen,' Adrian explains, rummaging fruitlessly round

The Domaine's unobtrusive entrance. Which way to the Casino?

the cuverie in search of the Domaine's instrument of *pigéage,* of which he is particuarly proud. This device, when it finally turns up, propped up behind a vat against a table full of tools, turns out to be an elaborate sort of rubber lavatory plunger, with the inverted conical end section perforated with small holes. These are covered with flaps, so that they open up on the way down through the cap, to break it up, and close on the way up to suck up the wine – more effective than foot-treading, and eliminating the need for *remontage.*

Another small vault houses the 1990 Chambertin which comes from vines at the Morey-St.-Denis end of the vineyard. It is *élevé* in 50% new Allier oak but, like all the other wines, is kept in tank until after the *malo* before being transferred to cask – in March. Surprisingly, it has a shade less colour than the Corton, although this does not herald any relaxation in the structure. The wine has an opulent griotte cherry nose, masses of ripe, densely-packed fruit and extraordinary complexity. The new oak is beautifully integrated and barely noticeable.

The wines generally spend a year in cask before being racked back into the *cuves* where they are fined, filtered and bottled between March and September of the second year – a total cycle of some 18–24 months.

This is uncompromising tradition for which Adrien Belland's customers ought to be thoroughly grateful. Although he sells a little Santenay in cask en négoce, the rest is bottled at the Domaine, 60% going to export and the rest within France.

The 1989 Corton Grèves and 1989 Chambertin are next on the list. Despite being at ambient cellar temperature, 7° C., both wines taste remarkably fine. The Corton has the characteristic depth of colour, and an attractive aroma of *fruits sauvages* mixed with liquorice. Quite a wild wine on the palate – big, a touch rustic in the best sense, yet long and complex. The Chambertin is dense, although less so than the 1990; the temperature has muted its nose, but on the palate it is a big, spicy wine, strongly liquorice, quite supple and 'flatteur'; a wine of beautiful balance which but for a touch of hollowness would be Grand Vin. At 15° C . . . who knows?

Two vintages of Santenay Les Gravières are produced to show how the wines evolve in bottle. The 1985 is of deepish mid-Victoria plum hue with a rich, almost burnt tarry nose – liquorice and viscera. Although a touch rustic, the wine is deep and tarry in flavour, a big wine with plenty of concentration; still youthful, it needs at least until 1996 before the next bottle is brought out. Les Gravières is generally less tannic and structured than La Comme – probably the best of the Santenay Premiers Crus.

The 1971 Gravières is still in its prime – moderately deep in colour, with no exaggerated signs of age, a gorgeous open spicy nose and a decidously delicate, yet positive, Pinot flavour, again hints of spice, coffee and liquorice. A very fine wine which will still last for years.

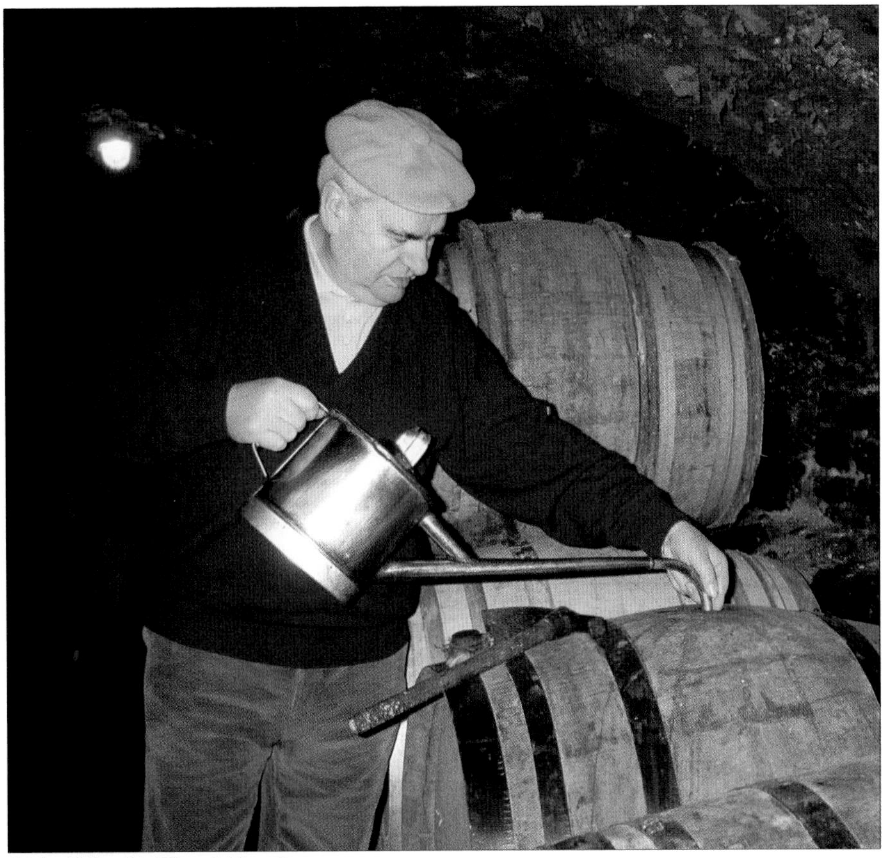

Adrien Belland topping up his casks

As to the secrets of making his wines, Adrien has nothing particular to suggest. 'We make *vins de garde,'* he offers, stating the glaringly obvious. No differences in vinification or *élevage* distinguish a Village Santenay from Grand Cru Chambertin – except that the latter gets some new oak, whereas the former will probably be raised in an older cask. Adrien believes that destemmed grapes from old vines impart enough natural structure and character, especially with his long vinification, without the need to add more, artificially, with new barrels.

His son Jean-Claude, now in his early thirties, does much of the cellar work, although since 1991 he has had his own Domaine to look after, including 33 ares of Santenay La Comme and 36 ares of Corton-Charlemagne from his aunt. With plenty of tannic, slow-maturing red wine in his father's cellar, he must occasionally feel like a refreshing glass of something white. His father certainly does – in 1980 he bought 45 ares of Puligny-Montrachet!

VINEYARD HOLDINGS

Commune	*Level*	*Lieu-dit/Climat*	*Area*	*Vine Age*	*Status*
Gevrey	GC	Chambertin	0.41	25	P
Aloxe	GC	Corton, Clos de la Vigne au Saint	0.49	20	P
Aloxe	GC	Corton-Perrières	0.69	40	P
Aloxe	GC	Corton-Grèves	0.55	25	P
Aloxe	V	Les Boutières	0.58	35	P
Santenay	PC	Clos des Gravières	1.21	35	P
Santenay	PC	La Comme	0.85	22	P
Santenay	V	Clos Genet	1.56	28	P
Santenay	V	Les Hâtes + Les Charmes-Dessus	2.12	30	P
Chassagne	PC	Morgeot (R)	0.48	30	P
Puligny	V	La Rue aux Vaches (W)	0.45	35	P
—	R	(Côte de Beaune-Villages)	0.99	35	P
—	R	(Bourgogne Rouge)	0.58	30	P
		Total	**10.96 ha.**		

Domaine Lequin-Roussot

SANTENAY

Sitting in their traditional office, in their traditional house, next to the level-crossing in Santenay, Louis and René Lequin, whilst not entirely the very type and model of each other, bear sufficient resemblance in their openness and manner to Charles and Ned Cheeryble – the kindly, generous pair who befriended Nicholas Nickleby – as to make other description superfluous. They are not in fact twins – Louis is the younger by 2 years, and the larger of the pair, whilst his brother exemplifies a leaner version of the mould.

They obviously enjoy each other's company, and take great pride in the firm, which they run for themselves and their mother. This is an old Domaine since there were definitely Lequins in Santenay in 1679 and probably before. Armfuls of ancient parchment – indecipherable deeds, attestations, warrants, declarations, assignments, inventories and other legal memorabilia – are produced to illustrate the depth and respectability of the family lineage.

The Domaine was born when their great-great-grandfather, Louis Isidore Lequin, married Thérésine Roussot in the late nineteenth century and came to live by the level-crossing. Interestingly, the house was built by Isidore's father from the proceeds of selling snails which he paid local children to gather and crush; he also owned mines of silica which was sold for glass production. The Domaine presently comprises some 13 ha., concentrated in Santenay, but with enviable parcels of Chassagne Morgeot (Blanc), Bâtard-Montrachet and Corton-Charlemagne. The vines are virtually all owned by Louis' and René's mother and farmed, *en fermage,* on her behalf.

When the brothers took over in 1969, much replanting of very old vines was needed, so there was little cash to spare for new acquisitions. However, they did subsequently manage to add parcels of Pommard and Nuits to the patrimony. At that time, most of the wine was sold 'en négoce,' since the wines of Santenay were little known and appreciated, although, interestingly, some of their Bâtard-Montrachet was sold in bottle to the USA, by Alexis Lichine, between the wars. This arrangement came to an abrupt end when Lequin Père refused to accede to a demand from the 23-year-old Lichine that the wine be bottled immediately, despite the fact that it was still 'en plein *malo*'.

René and Louis decided to turn their skills to producing a 'produit de luxe', and therefore started to bottle more of their production – a further drain on cash. Although some of the still finds its way to the local négoce, most is now bottled and sold by the Domaine.

Vigneron's yoga. René and Louis Lequin at work. Note Louis' inventive way of carrying his secateurs

Their vineyards are particularly healthy, a fact which they attribute to a lack of money in the Côte de Beaune in the 1960s and 1970s; higher prices in the Côte de Nuits meant more disposable cash which vignerons spent on fertilisers and treatments. This meant more systemic spraying and thus greater resistance to new products. Generations have been sorcerers' apprentices in this respect.

This is above all a traditional Domaine. *Sélection massale* is still used for plant material – although there was a trial planting of clones 113/114/115 in 1986 – and the vines are treated with contact and penetrating products, but never with systemics. The aim is to cure rather than to prevent disease – except for *oïdum* and mildew where the reverse is the case. 'We are not particularly ecologist,' claims Rene, 'but we respect nature.'

One peculiarity of the Lequins' viticulture is illustrated by Louis staggering into the office preceded by a vast bundle of vine trunks. 'We train all our mature red vines *en cordon de Royat',* as is the custom both in Santenay and in Chassagne. However, the peculiarity is that this practice extends to the vineyards in Nuit-St.-Georges and Corton Languettes, the latter being planted with plant material selected from the Santenay vines. In Corton this gives the vines a different aspect from those at Santenay – both in leaf colouring and in tighter bunch structure.

Louis and René demonstrate the *cordon de Royat* with their vine branches: 'We can prune later because there is no *baguette* to bend,' says Louis. 'The later you prune the less the seepage from the cut – whilst the *cordon* only bleeds for 14 days, the *Guyot* (used widely elsewhere in Burgundy) bleeds for 50 days.' This also lessens the risk of *eutypiose,* the virus disease which is causing concern throughout France, and which is propagated by air-borne spores entering the vine's metabolic system via pruning wounds.

Their wine-making philosophy is one of unbridled optimism: 'Everything is in the grape.' This is said more as an expression of faith in their raw material, and a refusal to tinker with what nature has given them, than as an advance absolution for any failings which might befall.

Since *cordon* training tends to give more tannic wines and Santenays are, in René and Louis' view, naturally well structured, vinification is relatively short. A total *cuvaison* of 9–12 days in enamelled cement *cuves,* closed to retain aromas and even drops of water which they claim also contain aromatic substances, is preceded by total destalking of the crop.

Only natural yeasts are used – the *cuves* being heated if fermentation doesn't start naturally after 3–4 days' maceration. 'I think we have got a packet of yeast somewhere,' says Louis, and René nods, 'but we haven't used it yet; we have a marvellous micro-flora on the grapes and in the cuverie, so we don't need selected yeasts from Narbonne or somewhere else.' Enzymes are frowned on and only used, for clarification, if essential.

Pigéage is an integral part of the brothers' vinification. For years Louis, who abandons the vineyards for the cuverie at vintage time, lowered himself into each vat in turn and trod down the cap. However, becoming understandably tired of this exertion, he went off, with René, to inspect an automatic apparatus. 'We were horrified,' he confesses, 'because we couldn't smell anything at all in that cuverie – all the aromas had escaped.' That ended the search for automation – Louis dons his shorts and continues to immerse his sizeable self in the *must* . . . and tread.

Fermentation temperatures rise to about 33° C: 'I have no fear,' says Louis. This is followed by 4–5 days *débourbage* with the *cuves* closed. The Corton and Nuits excepted, the *malos* generally take place in bulk to ensure uniformity – 'a better development and no bad surprises' – and are normally finished by December or January, 'but not in 1990,' the brothers chorus.

Once the *malos* are over, the wine is racked, given a strong dose of SO_2 – to avoid having to use too much at bottling – and then divided, half going into cask and half into inert bulk. The same division is made once more after the second racking in the following September.

The Lequins are not against wood – they renew some 20% of their cask population annually and use up to 50% of new wood for any given wine. However, they feel that keeping part of each *cuvée* in tank helps retain the wine's natural freshness and balances out the characteristics obtained from some 18 months' wood ageing. The wines are both fined, with egg albumen, and lightly plate-filtered – they used to filter more strongly for export markets, but this practice ceased in 1988 with growing acceptance of natural deposits in red wine.

René and Louis state their aims succinctly: a de luxe product, retaining the typicity of origin and with the capacity to age. Tasting with them in their cold cellars underneath the house is a long but cheerful process. They are anxious to show the interested visitor as much of their wares as possible – each brother disappearing alternately to dip into one bin or another and reappearing like some sort of vinous conjuror, with a bottle of this or that which 'might be interesting to try'.

The young wines tend to be quite tough and tarry – not light-coloured and weak, as Santenays are so often characterised. The Premier Cru La Comme, from a vineyard which has 40 cm. of clay-limestone topsoil giving on to a band of hard rock, is undoubtedly the best of the Lequin Santenays. In more open years, such as 1989 and 1987, it tends to be marked by a positive perfume of *petits fruits rouges* with an attractive feminine streak. In naturally tougher vintages, such as 1988 and 1990, the wine seems to show a different facet – a spicier character, but always quite soft, even when the fruit is still masked by an envelope of tannins.

The other *cuvées* of Santenay are made with equal care and can be broached somewhat sooner than the Comme. The Santenay Le Clos Genet - one of the original vineyards of the house - although only a Village appellation, is also noteworthy. The vineyard has considerably more clay than La Comme, giving a wine of greater breadth and softness – sometimes with a distinct touch of spiciness, but generally less structure than its Premier Cru cousin.

Of the Domaine's other reds, the Corton is well worth seeking out: 0.20 ha. of 30 year-old vines producing in better years a firm, stylish wine of good depth and ripeness. The Chassagne Morgeot seemed for some reason to be less successful than either the Santenays or the Corton.

The brothers like their wines to be kept, and are not averse to doing this themselves if they consider that a particular wine is likely to be misjudged if consumed prematurely. Thus it was that in 1991 they still had 25,000 bottles of 1983s which were considered too hard at present to be let loose on the market.

The new policy of lighter filtration will undoubtedly add balance and ageing potential to the Domaine's wines; Louis and René believe that, for example, their 1988s will outclass the 1978s.

The white wines, which account for 9% of the total production, are both well made and interesting. The vinification consists of fermentation in metal *cuves* and then decanting into casks when the density reaches 1,020. Racking is avoided, provided the lees are clean, and the wines are bottled after 12 months or so. In 1987 they tried fermenting the Chassagne at 18–20° C. but found that this gave a less authentic result than fermenting at around 25° C., which is what now happens.

Although there are minuscule quantities of Bâtard-Montrachet and Corton-Charlemagne (they grubbed up half their holding in En Charlemagne to plant Chardonnay which had its first vintage in 1992), the Santenay Blanc from the Premier Cru Clos Rousseau is the most interesting of the Domaine's white wines. This vineyard, situated towards Dezize, is planted not with Chardonnay but with Pinot Blanc Vrai, and contains a high proportion of clay and iron oxide which tends to give its wines an attractive broad 'ampleur'. In opulent vintages, such as 1989, the wine is soft and stylish – to be drunk within its first 5 years or so, whilst in tighter years – 1988, for example – it will repay keeping for longer.

The brothers chatter away contentedly about their wines, dipping again into this bin or into that, bringing out yet another vintage to compare with the preceding or to see how it is getting along. Their willingness to taste and to criticise their own wines is refreshing – perhaps stemming from the day when René, then aged 5, being given two glasses of white wine to compare by his grandfather, expressed a decided preference for one of the pair. It was a vin de table – the other was Bâtard-Montrachet. Each brother has his own personal bin of Bâtard-Montrachet of his birth year, continuing a family tradition which Louis and René have extended to their own offspring. Apart from this anniversary store, these children will inherit a fine, thriving and conscientious Domaine, when the time comes for two of the Côte d'Or's most engaging vignerons to leave the level-crossing and pass on their mantle.

VINEYARD HOLDINGS

Commune	Level	Lieu-dit/Climat	Area	Vine Age	Status
Chassagne	GC	Bâtard-Montrachet	0.24	15	F
Chassagne	PC	Morgeot (W)	0.59	12	F
Chassagne	PC	Morgeot (R)	0.62	18	F
Aloxe	GC	Corton-Charlemagne	0.18	1990	F
Aloxe	GC	Corton-Languettes	0.19	30	F
Pommard	V	Les Noizons	0.15	7	F
Nuits	V	Les Brulées	0.30	27	F
Santenay	PC	Le Passe-Temps (R)	1.20	22	F
Santenay	PC	La Comme (R)	1.87	20	F
Santenay	PC	Clos Rousseau (W)	0.29	43	F
Santenay	V	Les Hâtes (W)	0.27	3	F
Santenay	V	Le Clos Genet (R)	0.58	25	F
Santenay	V	Les Charmes (R)	1.19	3 & 42	F
Santenay	V	(Several climats) (R)	4.32	18	F
—	R	(Côte de Beaune-Villages)	0.18	23	F
—	R	(Bourgogne Rouge)	1.02	16	F
		Total	**13.19 ha.**		

Appellations and Quality Control

The Côte d'Or's 8,000 ha. of vines are divided into no fewer than 116 different appellations. With so many in such a relatively small wine region, it is worth clarifying what is meant by an appellation and discussing their significance for the wine drinker.

The first thing to be made clear is that although colloquially referring both to an area of vines and to the name of the wine produced there, appellations are primarily granted to land. Only in a secondary sense do they attach to wine which must pass certain tasting and other tests before becoming formally entitled to an appellation.

The French system of Appellation Contrôlée (AC) did not spring ready-made from the mind of some enlightened law givers, but evolved over nearly 4 decades before being progressively codified from the 1920s onwards. Its aim was to provide a legal framework for delimiting and controlling areas of wine production and to set up a structure of local, regional and national committees first to create the appellations, then to police them.

In the Côte d'Or, appellations are precisely mapped plots ranging in area from vast acreages of Bourgogne Rouge and Blanc to the 0.85 ha. of La Romanée. The large number of individual appellations reflects the fact that over the centuries certain vineyards throughout the Côte have been found regularly to produce better wine than others. So, when the AC system was set up, each designated vineyard site was graded on its quality potential into one of four categories – in ascending order:

1. **Regional:** (e.g. Bourgogne Rouge, Passe-Tout-Grains, Côte de Beaune Villages).
2. **Village:** (e.g. Pommard, Nuits-St. Georges, Beaune); obviously Pommard can only be produced from vines in Pommard, and so on.
3. **Premier Cru:** specific vineyards considered to be capable of consistently producing wine above the level of Village quality, on the label these are designated as 'Village + Premier Cru', (with the option of adding a specific vineyard name if the wine comes solely from that *climat,* e.g. Volnay, Clos des Ducs).
4. **Grand Cru:** crowning the pyramid are the Grands Crus – 32 individual vineyards of particular excellence, scattered throughout the Côte, each with its own AC (e.g. Chambertin, Montrachet, Corton-Charlemagne). Grands Crus, for which the rules specify lower yields and higher minimum natural alcohol, have the distinction of only using the vineyard name on the label, without the usual accompaniment of the village to which they belong. So, for example, wine from the Grand Cru Chambertin – a single plot of land in the village of Gevrey Chambertin – would simply be labelled Chambertin, whereas wine from the Gevrey-Chambertin Premier Cru vineyard Les Cazetiers would be labelled Gevrey-Chambertin, Les Cazetiers.

AC classifications are not immutable and changes do occur. Processing applications for new appellations or for upgrading vineyards is the job of the Institut National des Appellations d'Origine *(INAO).* From their office in Dijon, a staff of four administers the affairs of the entire Côte d'Or. In conjunction with local committees, they also decide the earliest permitted date of harvest for each commune.

Although the *INAO's* principal mission is not control, but delimitation, its inspectors have considerable powers. In addition, two other government services keep a constant eye on the Côte's vignerons: the Direction Générale des Impôts field three inspectors to ensure that wine taxes are paid, and thus have an interest in harvest declarations and sales.

However, it is to the Direction Générale de la Concurrence, Consommation et Répression des Fraudes' trio of inspectors that the task of policing the Appellation regulations principally falls. These are wide-ranging, covering viticultural practices, harvesting, permitted grape varieties, plant density, pruning etc., and laying down rules for vinification: *chaptalisation,* acidification, blending, sulphur etc.

According to a senior official of the Répression des Fraudes, apart from overseeing that the *ban de vendange* is respected and permitted yields are not exceeded, the most important controls are those undertaken in vignerons' cellars. Spot checks and inspections are used to ensure that vinification practices are observed and that stocks tally with harvest declarations or paper-work for any wine bought in.

The main aim of all this grading and control is to preserve the authenticity, typicity and quality of AC wines. Before an AC is granted, certain qualifying conditions must be met – including a minimum level of natural alcohol and a maximum yield per hectare of vines. Thereafter, growers are required to present each wine for which an AC is sought – *agrément* – for analysis and tasting. If a wine fails, then it may be submitted twice more. Inspectors also have the powers to visit Domaines unannounced and to take random samples.

For the buyer, the significance of the AC system is that, other things being equal – vintage, grower etc. – the higher the vineyard's classification the better, in theory, the wine. Thus a Pommard – Premier Cru Les Epenots – from this single vineyard in the commune of Pommard should be a finer, more complex and generally better wine than a Village Pommard which, in turn, should outclass a Bourgogne Rouge made from grapes grown within the boundaries of Pommard.

Unfortunately, things are rarely equal and this neat hierarchy is all but vitiated by the growers the system seeks to regulate, since they themselves differ widely in competence. A Village wine from a top grower will, more often than not, outclass a Premier Cru from a less gifted hand. The system is also devalued by the failure of the authorities to enforce the regulations available to them.

A hopeless lack of manpower makes theory and reality widely divergent. The 'Fraudes squad' is up against unbeatable odds, with some 4,400 annual declarations of harvest in the Côte – each comprising several wines – and only three unqualified, part-time inspectors to police them.

In recent years the operation of the appellation controls have been trenchantly criticised, both inside and outside the region, by customers dissatisfied with the standard of many AC Burgundies regular appearing on the export market. In particular, fire has been directed towards the practice of over-*chaptalisation,* either to increase volume or to cover up faults, and to the apparent tolerance of excessive yields, especially in Premier and Grand Cru vineyards.

Control of yields is no better. The system of base yields, which sets a maximum for each AC, has a built-in mechanism for authorising increases whenever it is deemed fit. This plafond limite de classement *(PLC)* – typically providing for an extra 20% on base yields – was only intended to be invoked in exceptionally abundant vintages. However, in recent years growers have been demanding, and getting, the *PLC* in vintages where the case for it has been, at best, marginal.

There is also a strong case for much greater vigilance in the vineyards to scrutinise yields of individual plots. A yield of 50hl./ha. may be acceptable in a well-maintained vineyard, with every vine producing, but not if one-third of the vines are missing and the other two-thirds are in a degenerate state. Anyone with their eyes open can see the problem in vineyards up and down the Côte.

In an authoritative exposition of the AC legislation, Anthony Hanson (1982), in a chapter subtitled 'The Buyer Deceived', pointed out that, although the laws have been tightened in recent years, loopholes give any grower with a gram of imagination the ability to drive a coach and horses through them, with apparent impunity. He concluded that, 'the good old, bad old days when any rosé can call itself Clos de Vougeot, Chambertin or Corton, so long as it comes from the right soil and vines and fulfils a few conditions, are still with us.'

The vigneron still has considerable scope for cheating. He can over-produce, declare what is authorised and then bottle the surplus for cash sale. The 'second cellar', run on a strictly cash basis, is endemic in the Côte. Alternatively, any production over the legal limit can be declared as a surplus for a lesser AC. Since declarations of harvest need not be presented until 25 November there is plenty of time for the unscrupulous vigneron to arrange his casks, knowing full well that the inspectors have insufficient time to taste everything. If this sleight of hand gives him an extra barrel of Grand Cru, his trouble is well recompensed.

According to the rules, any wine produced over the maximum limit must be sent for distillation into industrial alcohol – it cannot be bottled or sold as wine. In other words, part of a single vat of wine is given the AC and part refused. This is absurd. If the wine is of AC quality then it should all be released for sale; if not, then the whole lot should be declassified or sent for distillation. In any case, there seems little to prevent a pragmatically-minded vigneron with a surplus of Grand Cru from sending the same quantity of Village or Regional wine to the distillery and keeping the better wine for himself.

Fortunately, there is evidence of change. Pressure from a variety of sources has led to a scheme whereby a vigneron presenting for *agrément* a wine which is judged to be of borderline quality will be given the benefit of the doubt for one year, on condition that his cellar practices are monitored by an independent oenologist. However, since he has the right to appoint the oenologist, cynics might consider that there is plenty of scope for collusion. Nonetheless this is a welcome development.

What is the significance of all this for the consumer, perhaps faced with a row of Burgundies on a shop shelf thousands of miles away from the Côte d'Or? Buyers, who cannot always taste first, look to an appellation as a guarantee both of authenticity and of quality. For the first, one expects the contents of the bottle to correspond to what is printed on the label, and this is generally the case. For the second, those relying on an appellation for a certain level of quality will often be disappointed – a poorly vinified, dilute Chambertin is, unfortunately, still a Chambertin.

One widespread practice, which compromised the quality of much post-war Burgundy, has thankfully largely disappeared; *coupage* – the blending of a proportion, usually small of the genuine Burgundy with something cheaper, flourished in the 1950s and 1960s. As André Simon commented: 'Blending is to some extent like kissing – it may by quite innocent, but it may lead one away from the narrow path of duty and propriety.' Many Burgundians were led away!

The principal difficulty faced by the authorities is that growers, particularly those regularly producing at or near the maximum yields, form a powerful pressure group with a vested interest in the status quo. At present, for example, tastings for the *agrément* are conducted between 15 November and 15 April following the harvest – i.e. when the wine is a few months old. As anyone with even a nodding acquaintance with wine-making knows, much can happen to change a wine in the year or more between then and bottling, even assuming that the grower is honest and careful.

Furthermore, only carefully selected samples of each wine are tasted. This allows a grower with several casks of one wine to submit a single sample to gain the AC for the entire quantity, leaving the door wide open for all sorts of malpractice. For example, in 1983, a year notable for rot in the Pinot Noir, many buyers discovered that the wine they received in bottle bore scant resemblance to what they remembered tasting in cask. Wily growers, knowing that buyers could not taste every cask of each wine, had presented the best casks for tasting and added the contents of the rotten casks just before bottling. The hapless clients had little recourse, except perhaps the sanction of non-payment, whilst the AC officials seemed reluctant to intervene.

Moreover, the official tasting-panels are barely independent of the producers and their interests. There is still no representation of export markets which, as Hanson points out, form the principal output for many of the greatest AC names. The incidence of wines failing their tasting test on grounds of quality is negligible – standards are obviously set so low that all but vinegar passes. Such nonsense strengthens an already irrefutable case for more vigorous use of the existing powers enabling substandard wine to be declassified to a lower appellation. Making clear to growers that poor wine would be downgraded would be a powerful spur to improving overall quality.

One can only conclude that there is still no real will to control either yields or quality. The requisite laws and powers exist, but are ineffectually policed with the inevitable result that substantial volumes of indifferent wine, much with the cachet of exalted appellations, continue to pour on to a gullible export market. This tarnishes the reputation of the region and its appellations and compromises the efforts of the many conscientious Domaines who strive tirelessly for quality. An appellation system is only as good as its enforcement.

In the end, the customer's only real safeguard is a sound knowledge of what constitutes good and bad Burgundy. If he dislikes what he is being offered, he should vote with his feet and buy elsewhere.

Appellations in the Côte d'Or

	Côte de Nuits		*Côte de Beaune*	*Total*
Grands Crus	24		8	32
Commune & Premier Cru	7		18	25
Communes	8		20	28
Sous Communales	1		15	16
Volnay Santenots	_		1	1
Régionales		14		
Totals	**40**	**14**	**62**	**116**

Note: 1. The Côte d'Or comprises c. 8000 ha. of vineyards (=20,000 acres) spread over 45–55 kms. (28–35 miles) between Dijon and Sampigny.
2. Sous communales appellations are: 14 'Village plus Côte de Beaune', Côte de Nuits-Villages and Côte de Beaune-Villages.

Maximum yields and minimum alcohol levels

	Red Wines		*White Wines*	
Appellation	*R de B*	*Alc.*	*R de B*	*Alc.*
Communal/ Village	40	10.5	45	11.0
Premier Cru	40	11.0	45	11.5
Grand Cru	35	11.5	40	12.0

Notes: 1. R de B refers to the *Rendement de base,* the normally permitted maximum yield, expressed in hl./ha.
2. Alc refers to the minimum alcohol requirement and is expressed in degrees.
3. The above figures are those normally set for most appellations of the Côte d'Or.

Climate and Microclimates of the Côte d'Or

An old vigneron's saw proclaims that 'mieux vaut saison que laboraison', which loosely translated means that, when it comes to wine quality, the weather usually has the final word. Whilst modern technology may have muted the effects, its general purport remains valid: that, between bud-burst in spring and harvest in autumn, weather contributes significantly to the character of a wine.

The Côte d'Or lies on the 47th parallel, near the northerly limit for regular viticulture, in a zone of continental, temperate climate. Here, away from maritime influences, the vines enjoy relatively short, warm summers and long, cool winters. In most years, this pattern promotes an even vegetative cycle, but irregularities at either end of the season give the weather an important and frequently decisive influence.

Paradoxically, the vine produces its best wines in marginal climates rather than its preferred habitat – the Mediterranean or the tropics. Thus in more northerly vineyards of Burgundy, Bordeaux, Champagne and Germany, a long, slow ripening contributes to lower alcohol and greater aromatic finesse. Further south, regular hot summers give higher alcohol and greater uniformity, vintage variations having less importance.

The vine has specific minimum needs to fully ripen grapes; broadly these are: 1,400 hours of sunshine during the growing season, 685 mm. of rainfall, a temperature of 15° C. during flowering, an average summer temperature of 22° C., a winter average of 3° C. and an annual average of 10° C. (although the ideal is nearer to 15° C.). In the Côte d'Or these minimum conditions are generally met; average rainfall exceeds 700 mm. and sunshine averages 2,000 hours, providing some compensation for a lower than optimum average summer temperature of 19–20° C. In May the temperature can rise rapidly, helping the vine's buds to swell; in June an average of 16–18° C. usually ensures trouble-free flowering, provided there is no rain to damage the fragile flowers and disrupt pollination.

These three critical parameters – sunshine, rainfall and temperature – work together; but how they are distributed throughout the growing season is just as important for quality as their totals or averages. Rainfall, in particular, is more beneficial in small regular doses than as a few memorable downpours. Similarly an even, hot summer is better than a few weeks of searing heat followed by prolonged cool weather. Viticulteurs have to remember that two equally analytically ripe grapes may disguise completely different patterns of development.

The vine's needs can be considered separately:

Light: the vine needs daylight for its most important process – photosynthesis, converting carbon dioxide and water to sugar and oxygen. Although sunshine is the most important provider of infra-red and ultra-violet light for this purpose, the process can continue in total cloud cover given reasonable warmth.

How much sunlight a vine receives depends on its gradient and exposure. In the Côte, south and south-east sloping sites are favoured, vines being usually planted down the fall line. But sunshine hours vary greatly from one vineyard to another; Pinot Noir grapes in Corton vineyards in west-facing Pernand-Vergelesses invariably ripen much later than those planted in south-facing Aloxe-Corton.

Pruning and trimming the foliage also affect the amount of direct sunlight that reaches the bunches later in the year. The current fashion is for higher summer-pruning, leaving a much taller canopy of leaves, which has been found to increase sugar levels by up to 2 degrees of potential alcohol. This has sometimes resulted in over-shading the ripening bunches, affecting skin ripening from direct contact with sunlight. Regular sunshine is also essential – the even distribution of sunshine hours being just as important as the total.

Heat: sunshine is also related to temperature – providing heat as well as light. Direct heat from the sun is, however, only one source of warmth: heat can be reflected off the soil or can arrive as convected heat from a warm air-flow – e.g. from low to higher ground.

However, while heat and light are known to be important in viticulture, the optimum balance between them is less certain: can more light compensate for less heat or more daylight for less sunlight? Longer days in northern Europe make this of more than academic interest; what is known is that overall temperature is proportional to the sugar content of grapes and inversely proportional to acidity levels.

While extreme heat, which can cook the grapes, is relatively rare, extreme cold is less so. The Côte has on average some 60–70 days of recorded frost annually, which in memorable years such as 1956 and 1985 reached –27° C. Although the vine is a hardy plant and can tolerate short spells at around –25° C, prolonged exposure kills even the dormant vine.

Spring frosts are also a distinct risk in these northerly latitudes. Cautious growers make allowance for frost damage when pruning, but this is no help when several nights of late frost start scorching early buds. In the last fortnight of April 1991, for example, widespread damage – up to 100% in some lower-lying vineyards – was caused by several nights of severe frost. This presents little risk to the vine's long-term life, but reduces that year's potential crop size. Further north, Chablis growers have long used a variety of frost-protection measures from smudgy oil-stoves to sprays which coat the young buds with a protective layer of ice – this works because the latent heat of freezing acts as insulation. Vignerons of the Côte have yet to take such steps.

Water: water is needed both to keep the vine's vital functions going and for photosynthesis. It is absorbed directly through the leaves – although in very small quantities – and by osmosis through the roots, reaching the plant in a variety of forms: snow, hail, fog, rain, humidity and from spraying. In dry years the vine survives because its deep roots are able to pick up moisture from the bedrock, and it is the *trace elements* and minerals leached out from soil and rocks which supply most of its essential nutrients.

The importance of using rootstocks which rapidly establish a sound deep rooting-system, and cutting proliferous surface lateral roots to encourage this is appreciated by most better Domaines. In years such as 1976, 1988 and 1990, when drought, consequent on prolonged intense heat, put photosynthesis at risk, older vines with well-established roots were much less affected than younger plants. Although much of the Côte is on solid, seemingly impenetrable rock, the vine manages to insinuate its roots to depths of 10 m. or more; such is the survival instinct!

As with light and heat, the distribution of rainfall, particularly just before the vintage, is as important as the annual total. In dry years, enough rain to balance the volume of juice to skins and ensure a viable concentration has often meant the difference between a good and a great vintage. On the other hand rain at flowering will cause *coulure,* when the flowers fail to set, and will disrupt pollination. Equally, cxcessive rain at harvest may swell the grapes and over-dilute the juice, or in severe cases cause the berries to burst and thus rot. Rain at almost any time may wash off protective sprays and make life difficult for the harassed vigneron.

In an area as diverse as the Côte, it is impossible to specify an optimum precipitation; so much depends on the soil drainage – one plot of gravel will effortlessly absorb several times what would waterlog a patch of clay. So not all vignerons view approaching rainclouds as a blessing.

Light, heat and water are thus the main climatic variables – how these are distributed in any given year constitutes that season's weather. As far as wine quality goes, it is not just the absolute levels of each but how they interact which matters.

Specifically, the ratio of damp to warmth seems critical in determining balance and harmony in a wine. In wet, cool years, wines are dilute and unripe and not much will save them. However, in wet but warm years, when the grapes may be ripe though dilute, wines often have considerable bouquet and finesse. A determined *saignée* will often restore the equilibrium (1982 was an excellent example). Conversely, years of excessive heat and low rainfall produce harsh, tannic, sometimes jammy wines, needing long bottle age: there is nothing the vigneron can to do put things back in balance; 1976 is a fine example of this sort of vintage. Best of all is normal dampness combined with great warmth – conditions which usually betoken a great vintage.

So often in such a marginal climate as Burgundy's, freak weather will cause scattered damage somewhere or other. Hail is the most frequent culprit, arriving with little advance notice at any time between April and August. The storms tend to be highly localised – often just a few hundred metres across – cutting savagely through anything in their path. Sheltered sites are far less hail-prone than more exposed vineyards on open plains or hillsides.

Hail is devastating: it can destroy flowers, scar leaves or split the grapes, provoking rot. In the worst cases it splits the wood, killing the plant. There are rockets which seed hail clouds with potassium iodide to disperse them, but these are expensive and of limited efficacy. In the face of a hail-storm the vigneron is virtually helpless.

High wind is less of a risk along the Côte. Winds prevail from several directions – the best known and coldest being the northerly Bise. However, deleterious effects are usually confined to drying out the vegetation and cooling higher exposed sites, retarding maturity.

Against this array of potential destruction, the vigneron has only limited protection. Over the centuries fragmentation of the vineyards, which forces vignerons to have holdings scattered throughout one or several communes, has proved his best defence.

In addition, the variety of micro-climates up and down the Côte play an important part in the quality of what is produced. Essential to understanding the Côte d'Or is the realisation that, as well as being a complex geological mosaic, it is also a vast patchwork of micro-climates. Growers who know their vineyards will talk of peculiarities and susceptibilities of each little plot as though they were a collection of eccentric humans: some are late developers, some capricious, some early ripeners, some frost- prone, some prone to dampness at the bottom, whilst others suffer unduly from wind.

Micro-climates occur above, below and on the soil. The micro-climate of the bunches may differ from that of the soil or roots – how the leaves are trellised or summer-pruned will alter one, whereas clay

Combes play an important part in the Côte's weather. Here the limestone outcrops of the Combe d'Orveaux form a striking back-drop to the vineyards of Chambolle- Musigny

or gravel subsoil will affect the other. Both will be influenced by whether the soil is hoed or simply treated with herbicide and compacted by heavy machinery on its routine passage between the rows.

The major factors determining micro-climate are aspect, altitude, shelter, drainage and gradient. These, to a greater or lesser extent, modify the vine's environment. Elevation is also important: higher ground will have lower average temperatures than lower – adjusted by a lapse rate of 3 centigrade degrees per 1,000 vertical feet of displacement.

Looking along the Côte, all these variables play a part. Although the vineyards are mostly exposed south or south-east, a multitude of smaller variations must be considered. Many of the best vineyards are on slopes of different gradients, some exposed, others well sheltered by woods or hills. An almost infinite variety of soil types ensures a varied distribution of drainage, from hollow gravel to thick clays.

One of the most significant geographical features of the Côte is the series of recurrent 'combes' which bisect it laterally, generally on an east-west axis. These act as conduits for rain, and for small rivers, as well as forming efficient wind-tunnels which accelerate the air-flow, catching exposed vineyards in their path. Some are wider than others; all play an important part in the micro-climate of nearby communes.

Equally significant is the micro-climate round and within each bunch of grapes. Bunches near the top or edges of the foliage will mature at a different rate from those more densely shaded towards the centre, and those closer to the soil will enjoy a different heat regime from those further away.

As growers well know, it is a profound mistake to regard a bunch of grapes as a homogeneous, evenly-ripe entity. The Pinot Noir in particular often produces very tightly-packed bunches which impedes free air-circulation, reducing cooling in hot weather and encouraging the spread of rot in damp conditions. Also it is not unusual for the outside of a bunch to be fully ripe while berries on the inside are still underdeveloped and high in acidity. Careful picking and sorting is thus essential.

A harvested grape represents the sum of a particular growing season. Two successive vintages may yield grapes of equal ripeness from the same vineyard but the final wines may differ strongly. Analytical ripeness is therefore only the broadest indication of the likely result of vinification. Against extremes of weather, there is little the grower can do; however his management of soil and foliage, in particular, can significantly influence the quality of the harvests.

THE ENIGMA OF SOIL

Together with climate and grape variety, soil is among the most important determinants of wine quality. In Burgundy, unlike anywhere else in Europe except perhaps for Alsace and Germany, the classification of vineyard land depends as much on soil as on anything else. Nowhere is this more important than in the Côte d'Or. Looking at a map of the vineyards, it is apparent, though often barely credible, that no more than a few yards may separate a Grand Cru and a humble Village vineyard. These seemingly arbitrary divisions reflect the fact that centuries have convinced wine-makers and tasters that there are systematic differences in wine quality between grapes from one plot and those from another. It is on such detailed differences that the AC classifications are based.

Noting differences does not mean that you can necessarily explain them. After all, a vineyard is more than just its soil; it is also *terroir,* a much discussed concept which comprises topsoil, subsoil, slope, exposure and micro-climate, each of which contributes to a wine and thus might possibly account for any observed differences in quality. Furthermore, interactions between these various factors probably mean that the totality is more than simply the sum of its constituent parts and, consequently, that it is meaningless to discuss the influence of one aspect of *terroir* without considering the others.

Nonetheless, experience in Burgundy suggests that, even when other factors have been eliminated, differences remain, for which soil is the most plausible explanation. Specifying the mechanisms involved has fascinated geologists, vignerons and tasters for decades.

Soil is a diffuse concept. In common speech it signifies whatever you put your spade or hoe into, but to the geologist it refers only to the top layer of a vertical profile of the vineyard, those beneath being the underlying superficial sediment and the substratum of solid rock. The way the earth has evolved makes it shaky to conclude that all the layers are of the same composition; on the contrary, each has its own particular properties. What is clear is that soils perform two quite distinct functions for the vine: they have physical properties which affect its water regime and heat-retentive environment, and chemical properties which influence its nourishment and growth.

The optimum physical properties of soils for fine wine are those related mainly to their drainage. The balance is delicate: vines die rapidly in places where their roots are waterlogged, but equally need a reservoir of accessible water into which deep roots can tap in years of drought. However, surface damp and consequent high humidity in soils, such as those on plains near the RN 74 which are notably high in clay, are undesirable, since they create frost-pockets which can lead to damage. Most of the vines lost in the Côte in the great frosts of 1985 were on this flatter, frost-prone land which, fortunately, is zoned mainly for Regional and Village AC.

As a general rule in the Côte d'Or, the favoured vineyard sites are those on well-drained hillsides, where excess water and cold air can spill off and where exposure to heat and light are maximised. However, the soil at the top of these slopes is generally too thin – giving finesse and subtlety to wines, but without much structure; whilst that at the base is the opposite – too rich and deep, excellent for structure but producing little by way of finesse. Hence the finest vineyards tend to lie in the heart of the hill, where the soils produce an optimal balance of structure and elegance.

In addition to good drainage, the heat-retentive properties of the surface soils play a small, but useful, role. By storing up heat, which is radiated back into the surrounding air, stony soils can, for example, make a difference to the vulnerability of buds to a snap late spring frost, or even raise sugar levels and tip the balance towards success in a marginal vintage.

Among the physical properties of soil, the size and cohesion of topsoil particles are of particular importance. Many Premier and Grand Cru *climats* along the Côte are on slopes as steep as 20 degrees, where rainstorms can easily dislodge large amounts of loose earth, which the unfortunate grower is then obliged to take back up again. This instant soil erosion is particularly destructive, since the finer particles which are invariably the most easily washed away, are those consid- ered to be among the most important for quality. Fortunately, there is a high proportion of stones and pebbles in many vineyards, which helps with soil retention.

Soil erosion is not confined to the steep slopes; even in vineyards such as Le Montrachet or the lower part of Romanée-Conti, on slopes of 5° and 3°40' respectively, rain can remove topsoil to an extent which necessitates replacement. Whatever the soil, if enough continuous rain fails to saturate the topmost few centimetres of the topsoil, it will erode.

To combat this, some growers are experimenting with grasses, sown between vine rows, to act as soil retainers. These are effective, but tend to compete with the vine for water – which is undesirable, especially in hot dry years such as 1976 or 1988 when water is at a premium. Grasses also change the reflectivity of the soil and are notoriously prodigious potassium consumers, so such regimes can also affect the nutrient balance.

Soil is, however, more than just an inert, more or less cohesive, growing medium for the vine; it is also the means by which it obtains much of its nourishment. The overriding need is for water – there is no chemical reaction of the vine which is independent of it – and, apart from minute quantities picked up directly from the leaves during rain or spraying, the vine relies principally on its roots tapping into reservoirs in the subsoil and rock for its supplies.

This ability of roots to delve down and extract water from the subsoils has a further benefit. Since many substances necessary for plant growth are water-soluble, they may be leached out of the soil by water and transferred to the vine by osmosis. However, although the precise mechanisms by which plants extract nourishment from soils are imperfectly understood, it seems likely that more is gained from direct contact between root and soil than from water-borne transfer.In a region such as the Côte d'Or, however, making great wine is more complex than simply planting a vine in sites which are neither waterlogged nor frost-pockets. Widely different soil-types support a large variety of vine-types, so it is a matter of finding which are best adapted to any given soil. For example, Pinot Noir and Chardonnay perform magnificently in the limestone soils of the Côte d'Or and Champagne, but would be a poor choice for the gravels of the Medoc.

In addition to the appropriate fundamental soil-type, certain *base elements* – principally nitrogen, potassium and phosphorus – are essential to support proper plant growth. Other useful *trace elements,* mostly minerals, may also be present in greater or lesser quantities. It is known that the vine can use either sort of element to meet its needs. What is not known is whether, or how, a particular substance will intervene to affect wine quality. The best the vigneron can do is to commission regular soil analyses and use these to fine-tune his soils through sensible use of fertilisers. Once a reasonable balance has been established, fertilisers are largely unnecessary.

Keeping soils properly balanced is skilled work, serious mistakes often having long-term and costly consequences. Vignerons on the Côte well remember the 1960s and 1970s when cash-rich growers were persuaded by eloquent fertiliser salesmen to over-indulge their vineyards in potassium. The results, which are still being felt some 30 years later, were disastrously low wine acidity levels and thus wines which disintegrated far too early. Unfortunately it is known that potassium never fully degrades; a classic study in the UK (Warren & Johnston, 1962) showed that even after 56 years, an application of potassium fertiliser was still having a marked effect. It seems, in any case, that potassium once taken up by the vine will be held there until loss through the grapes and through pruning gradually removes it.

Although soil undeniably contributes to the taste of a wine, the mechanisms are poorly understood. What is clear is that there is no simple correlation between soil-type and taste; for example, a high iron content does not bring a taste of iron, nor a chalky soil a taste of chalk. The influences appear to be infinitely more subtle.

What, therefore, can be said about the quality of soil which is most likely to produce fine wine? There is a common belief that 'vines, like poets, produce their best when they must struggle for survival . . . in the anaemic soil that is typical of the best growths' (Lichine, 1982). Vignerons also believe this; how often does one hear them declare that 'the vine must be made to suffer' – and 'vine stress' is common New World currency.

However, the relationship between viticulture and poor soil is far from universal. Whilst it is true that the meagre, nitrogen-less soils of the Médoc would support little else, except perhaps forest, much of the Côte d'Or is perfectly adaptable to other culture. Until just after the last war, for example, blackcurrants were harvested commercially in Puligny, from what is now vineyard land.

What is probably true is that, historically, vines being long-term plants requiring minimum maintenance were planted on soils that were of little use for much else, or too hard to work. Also, because the vine needs a long, warm ripening season, the further north one goes, the more likely it is that vineyards are to be found on hillsides to catch as much sunlight as possible. This, together with naturally greater erosion on slopes, means that soils tend to be poorer than those on plains, where alluvial deposits and river silts have collected. Hence, perhaps, the enduring myth of poor soils.

The real importance of a relatively nutrient deficient topsoil is, however, to encourage the vine to establish a deep root system, both as a means of extracting nourishment from the subsoils and also as an insurance against drought.

Professor Hancock, the eminent British geologist, in a personal communication, points out that 'modern vines based on American rootstock obtain most of their nourishment from relatively shallow roots, often not more than 0.4 m. deep . . . However, within many regions of fine wine production, the natural soil layer is very thin, only of the order of 0.2 m.; on the other hand, many of the regions that produce largish quantities of mediocre wine have thicker soils.' Thus, he concludes, the common belief in the importance of poor soil 'has an element of truth, but is a somewhat misleading simplification. It is more a matter of the balance that is suitable for the vines.'

Geologists have long known that the entire Côte sits on a bedrock of limestone, formed around 170–150 million years ago during the Jurassic period. At that time there was a warm shallow sea lapping against the ancient rocks of the Massif Central, a short distance to the west. Limestones, sometimes alternating with various amounts of clay, accumulated slowly in this sea. Since the Jurassic period, sea-levels have oscillated many times, but with the lower sea-levels of today the Jurassic limestones and clays are exposed at the surface. In many places the strata have collapsed downwards towards the valley, along fractures parallel to the hillside.

During the last glaciation, the remnants of which can still be seen around the Poles, the Côtes were subjected to deep freezing every winter. During each summer thaw, the surface sediments slid down the hillsides over the frozen rocks beneath, even on slopes of only a few degrees. Many of the famous vineyards are located on these slide-deposits, although some, such as Chevalier-Montrachet, are underlain by solid limestone. In addition, over the millennia water has permeated the underlying rocks, removing soluble limestone, leaving the insoluble sand-like and clay impurities, the proportions of which in the topsoil have therefore progressively increased.

Against this broad geological background, the soils on the Côte d'Or have been intensively studied, partly to understand better which vines are best adapted to which soils, and partly to see if there is any discernible correlation between wine quality and soil-type. What has been found is that limestone is particularly favourable to the production of *vins de garde* whereas, for example, granitic soils tend to produce more rapidly maturing wines. Differences between Riesling sites in Alsace provide striking demonstrations of this.

In a classic study, published in 1957, Mme. Rolande Gadille analysed extensive soil samples from all over the Côte, but, although many interesting relationships emerged, she found no obvious correlation between soil-type and wine quality.

A later study by a group of eminent French geologists (Meriaux et al., 1981) attempted to relate various physical characteristics of the villages of the Côte – slope, stoniness, clay and total limestone content – to quality levels. They found that the better vineyards – i.e. Premiers and Grands Crus – tended to be on slopes of more than 3%, with average stoniness of 5–40% and a clay content which is finer than that of Regional AC or Bourgogne land. Higher limestone contents were also noted in the better sites.

To date, the available studies have yielded little useful information for anyone hoping to list the soil ingredients – either necessary or sufficient – for a Côte d'Or Grand Cru. However, it still seems highly probable that soil is an important determinant of the typicity of the various communes and *climats* up and down the Côte, since, removing variables which blur the picture – grower, micro-climate etc. – there remain significant and systematic differences between wines produced in adjacent vineyards and in different communes.

Soil is only part of a complex equation on the Côte. While geologists and other experts are cautious in their conclusions, others generalise and misrepresent its properties and classification in an attempt to unravel the fascinating enigmas of the region. So far, it would seem that it is the physical properties of vineyard soils and rocks which play a greater part in influencing wine quality than any obvious differences in chemical composition.

For anyone tempted to over-simplify the difficulty of disentangling the role of soil from other influences, a neat experiment by Professor Ravasse at Montpellier might just dissuade them: he concreted over half a plot of vines and compared its wine with that produced from the other half. Over 27 years, he found no significant differences in either productivity or in richness of sugar. However, the concreted vines tended to wilt rather more when it became very hot!

In the words of the eminent French geologist, Professor Noël Leneuf, 'there must always be an element of mystery', this is what drives curiosity. At the same time, one cannot help but agree with Professor Hancock that whilst 'geology is only a matter of theoretical interest to the drinker, it is of vital importance to the grower.'

Pinot Noir

The Pinot Noir is the most capricious of all grape varieties – invariably demanding from the grower, wine-maker and drinker the utmost forbearance and respect. It is highly sensitive to climate, soil, pruning and training, and especially to how it is handled and vinified. At its best it produces wines which are sensuous, magnificently perfumed and seductively fleshy, at its worst, meagre, angular offerings with charmless, raw, stalky flavours and enough acidity to run a car battery.

One might ask why people persevere with such a mischievous, moody grape; after all, there are plenty of alternatives. On the Côte d'Or growers sometimes express frustration at its unpredictability, but cling like gamblers to the fascination it provides in the face of an attainable, but irritatingly elusive, jackpot.

They have certainly had plenty of experience. Pinot Noir's long history on the Côte began with its debut as a named variety – Pinot Noirien – around 1375, although plantings of a similar vinifera variety were documented as far back as the first century AD. Philippe the Bold, Duc de Bourgogne, saw the need to plant better varieties for the soils in his vineyards to give of their best and, persuaded of its value, issued an edict in 1395 in favour of the Pinot Noir, banning the more prolific and less noble Gamay.

Custom and the law have since enshrined the pre-eminence of Pinot Noir as the noble red grape of the Côte. However, it is wrong to think of it as a single variety. Not only has it been heavily cloned since the late 1950s, it has also spawned a healthy population of spontaneous genetic mutations. Henri Gouges, for example, started his Nuits-St.-Georges Blanc in the 1930s when he found vines in his Perrière vineyard with both red and white grapes sprouting from the same plant.

Most of the Pinot vines planted on the Côte, whether clones or individual *sélection massale,* have the Pinot Fin as parent. This strain – also known as the Pinot Tordu because of its misshapen trunk – is considered the only Pinot variety suitable for producing the finest Burgundies. But there is another, less fine, strain – Pinot Droit. So named because it grows straight upwards, it is more prolific than the Pinot Fin and much easier to work with. Many growers, seduced by the prospect of less labour and more wine, saw the Pinot Droit as a ready means of increasing their incomes. Plantings mushroomed in the 1960s and 1970s, until the disparity in quality became apparent. Any remaining are gradually being replaced with Pinot Fin, especially in the better sites as the vines expire.

Physically the Pinot Noir is characterised by small, tight, bunches and a small, mid-green leaf. The compact, pine-cone shape of the clusters is thought to be the origin of the name Pinot (it means pine in French). Compared with the Cabernet Sauvignon, for example, the Pinot bunches are some 40–50% smaller and the leaves some 4% smaller in overall dimension. In warm, humid conditions this compactness provides an ideal micro-climate for rot to develop and spread, so clones with looser clusters tend to be favoured.

The grape also has a fragile skin, difficult to ripen fully, which is partly responsible for the Pinot's reputation for giving a relatively light-coloured wine. More seriously for the grower, a thin skin provides easy access for the grape-worm, a perennial nuisance in most Côte d'Or vineyards. This insect punctures the grape, leaving a wound which then rapidly becomes rotten; if the rot spreads, it severely affects the quality of the wines.

The Pinot's susceptibility to both mildew and grey rot accounts for at least some of its awkwardness. It is also highly vulnerable to the fan-leaf virus *(court-noué)* which, in the years of neglect both during and immediately following the last war, ran riot through many of the best vineyards. Transmitted by a root-sucking worm, and by grafting, it appears to be encouraged by over-tired soil and enfeebled vines. Its effects are clearly visible: the leaves turn yellow and fall off and their veins spread out into a fan-shape. Degeneration and finally the death of the vine are inexorable consequences, without the possibility of a cure. Where vines are infected, the only realistic solution is to grub up, disinfect the soil and replant with virus-free grafts.

The Pinot Noir is a notoriously early budder, making it particularly susceptible to spring frosts. For this reason many growers prune their vines generously to ensure that at least some buds come to fruition. It needs a long, reasonably even growing season to ripen fully, and abhors extremes of heat. Those with plantings in the hotter regions of California and elsewhere have found that no amount of cool fermentation will restore finesse and delicacy, once the grapes have been ripened to their jammy maximum.

There has been much study of the best methods of training and pruning Pinot Noir in the Côte. In Santenay and Chassagne, in particular, it is trained *en cordon de Royat,* experience suggesting that in their rich soils the grape performs better with extended vegetation and a less productive bud distribution. Although no-one can satisfactorily explain why, the strain planted here is also different from elsewhere on the Côte. The 'plante fin de Santenay' seems well adapted to its environment, and growers know how to coax the best from it.

The Pinot's capriciousness extends to its taste. Although adaptable to a variety of methods of vinification, it exhibits a much greater diversity of style than either the Cabernet Sauvignon or the Syrah. Whilst these manage to retain their fingerprints almost wherever they are grown, the chameleon Pinot puts on a different expression for each origin. Tasters faced with a line of Pinots from around the world might be hard put to identify the common denominator, so complete are its disguises.

In Burgundy, Pinot Noir responds well to a marginal climate and well-drained, meagre soils predominantly high in limestone. It performs best when vines are old and yields low. However it is truculent and fussy about where it shines. Because of its relative fragility (Pinot skins are in fact more robust than is generally believed) it needs to be fully ripe before it will vinify into a balanced wine.

However, wines made from low yields of ripe Pinot will support a good larding of new oak, and can age magnificently. Tantalising glimpses of the majesty of which Pinot Noir is capable are enough to keep growers everywhere, not just on the Côte, struggling to emulate. The greatest of Burgundies will continue to inspire those for whom, whether openly admitted or not, that ravishing silky opulence and extraordinary complexity remain an enduring goal.

The quest for a Pinot Noir wine which comes near to matching a Côte d'Or Grand Cru has become like a Holy Grail, especially for many New World wine-makers. To date, Parsifal has yet to appear.

CHARDONNAY

In contrast to the Pinot Noir, the Chardonnay is a model of obedience and good behaviour. Not only is it versatile, resilient and content to grow in a variety of soils and climates, it is adaptable to almost any vinification to which it is subjected. At best opulent, rich and concentrated, with a remarkable longevity, Chardonnay represents for many the epitome of what dry white wine should be. Wherever it is planted, it seems to wear its heart on its sleeve and to present an attractive personality, whatever the adversities. In short, whether for producer or consumer, Chardonnay is exuberantly user-friendly.

The history of Chardonnay is less well documented than that of the Pinot Noir; there is an obscure little village in the Maconnais called Chardonnay, which may have something to do with its origins, but whether it has, or indeed whether the grape pre-dated the village or vice versa, remains a mystery. When it first arrived in the Côte is also uncertain. Although the nobilityof some of the great Grand Cru sites, such as Montrachet and Corton, was recognised as long ago as the eighth century, their plantings were then a mixture of indigenous varieties rather than a single *cépage*. Aligoté was widely planted until the end of the last century, even in prestigious vineyards.

If the origins of Chardonnay are blurred, so is its ancestry. Constant references to 'Pinot Chardonnay' reflected the widespread belief that it was a white mutant of the Pinot Noir. Although this has now been disproved, growers still talk of it and believe there is a link.

In the vineyard the vine flourishes without giving the vigneron undue trouble. It buds early, which renders it susceptible to spring frosts, but is well able to support prolonged winter cold without suffering. However, together with their colleagues in Chablis, the growers of the Côte remember the winter of 1956, when the thermometer plunged to –27° C. and stayed there long enough to destroy a high percentage of the Côte's vines, both Pinot Noir and Chardonnay.

Provided it can enjoy a long, even growing season, with reasonable warmth, the Chardonnay will consistently ripen well. It has a knack of attaining high sugar levels in conditions which would leave other varieties wanting and therefore needs less *chaptalisation,* although it can become flabby if it is harvested too late, or with low acidity.

Left to its own devices the Chardonnay will proliferate foliage in every direction. Whilst this may look healthy, it dissipates the vine's energies into leaves rather than bunches. This natural vigour makes it imperative for the vigneron to prune short and to take scrupulous care in removing excess buds and shoots early on in the summer if he wants to harvest a crop of balanced, concentrated grapes. The Chardonnay vine is also very susceptible to *oïdium* and to *court-noué.*

In the Côte, ripening depends very much on the individual site – the cooler westerly expositions of Pernand and Savigny, for example, or the higher, more exposed slopes of St.-Aubin or Chassagne, needing an extra week or more to bring grapes to maturity than south or south-east facing *climats* of Puligny or Meursault.

In its desire to please, the Chardonnay is not at all fussy about soils – doing well, if not spectacularly, on the high pH, acid-neutral soils of the Mâconnais and performing to perfection, if differently, on the Kimmeridgian clays of Chablis. However, the better adaptability of the soils to Pinot Noir means that there are no significant plantings of Chardonnay in the Côte de Nuits. The few plots that do exist – Musigny and Morey in particular – suggest that it would probably perform respectably if given the chance.

A ripe bunch of Chardonnay grapes. Mottled skin discolours the wine if the juice is left in contact with it for too long

In the Côte de Beaune the best sites, including the Grands Crus, are those with well-drained, predominantly limestone soils; however, attempts to correlate soil-type and quality have so far produced nothing more than a plethora of inconclusive statistics. Montrachet has obviously no intention of devolving its secret.

One of the great virtues of Chardonnay is its ability to produce fine wine at yields at which the Pinot Noir would taste positively watery. Top growers who would put an upper bound of 35 hl./ha. or so on Pinot Noir will show no sign of undue discomfort if their Chardonnay brings in half as much again. This may have more to do with not needing to balance solids to liquids in white vinification than to any special characteristic of Chardonnay.

In the cellar, the Chardonnay is equally malleable. It will deliver fine quality whether fermented cool or warm, whether vinified in new oak, old oak or stainless-steel, and will be happy bottled early or after a year or more in cask. It supports *élevage* in virtually any type of new oak barrels, rarely becoming unduly tannic or *boisé* in flavour.

However, its tendency to develop high sugar levels, particularly during the final stages of ripening, usually occurs at the expense of acidity. So in exceptionally hot vintages, such as 1983, it can become clumsy and alcoholic, unless steps are taken to retain natural acidity. Growers who are tempted to delay picking can find themselves with very rich, soft, super-ripe wines which appear over-blown and deficient in grip; in short, too much fat and no stays!

For the wine-lover, the greatest of the Chardonnay's attributes is its ability to age. Whilst a young Grand Cru may be pleasant to drink, it is with years in bottle that it really begins to express its origins and to show its breeding. The balance between youth and age is, however, finer with white wine than with red – the absence of significant tannin bringing even the slightest hint of over-oxidation into sharp relief.

Although growers throughout the viticultural world have scaled notably greater heights with Chardonnay than with Pinot Noir, their untiring efforts to match the restrained depth and power of the Côte's white Grands Crus continue to meet with limited success. There is a dimension of understated elegance and class in a fine Corton, Meursault or Puligny, which seems to defy mimicry.

Choosing What to Plant

However sophisticated one's vinification techniques, quality ultimately depends on the raw material – the grapes. These, in turn, are determined by the location of the vineyard, the climate and, above all the type and quality of the plant.

A European vine plant consists of two distinct halves grafted together: a scion, the top section which determines the grape variety, and a rootstock, the lower section, which establishes the rooting-system and contributes to the adaptability of the plant to its soil and to its general growth characteristics. Both halves are important to the vigneron deciding what to plant in his vineyard.

Half a century ago he had little choice; he could either buy plants ready grafted or *phylloxera*-resistant rootstock, make a selection of scion from his own vines *(sélection massale)* and cobble together his own grafts. Even though most conscientious vignerons preferred their own grafts, the results were haphazard; if these survived the first year or so, they could not be relied upon either to be disease-free or to produce regularly.

It was not until the late 1960s that the science of plant selection and breeding turned its attention to the vine: by 1969 it was able to offer growers a choice of individually selected and bred clones of Pinot Noir and Chardonnay, together with a range of rootstocks to suit a variety of soil types. Gradually, as the results of these early clones were studied and the industry developed, growers were persuaded to abandon home-made selections in favour of the commercially produced alternative.

Today, most have confidence; but the Burgundian vigneron is not to be rushed, so there are still those who distrust the quality of standard clones and continue to produce their own plant material.

Clones: A clone is 'a group of individuals produced by means of vegetative propagation of a single organism' (Becker, 1982). In fact, both the Pinot Noir and the Chardonnay one sees in the vineyards are not one genotype but a population – thousands of clones and mutations – from which some few hundred have been studied intensely to produce the handful currently marketed.

To establish an individual variety it is necessary to start from a single pip, bud or eye from the vine; however, efforts are now being made to propagate direct from genetic material, to refine the selection further. Developing a clone takes 12–15 years, since at each stage the propagated plants have to be observed and further culled before they can be multiplied in commercial quantities.

The original impetus for cloning was the widespread virus degeneration, especially of Chardonnay, which ravaged the Côte in the 1950s. Once virus-free strains had been developed, the emphasis changed to selecting for varietal purity and for quality.

The aim of cloning is not to change the spectrum of a grape variety but to refine the strain so that there is less variability. This means maximising both the strain's state of health and its varietal purity. In developing a clone, selection is made both for positive attributes – higher sugar levels and better sugar/acid balance, stability of performance, resistance to frost, pigment quality, date of budding and ripening, berry size, leaf and wood development etc. – and for absence of negative qualities – disease and viral infection.

In Europe, emphasis is placed on obtaining disease-resistant stock, whereas in the USA it tends to be on developing disease-free stock – these are not the same. Disease-free stock has been found to produce better yields and sugar levels which in the end result in better wines.

At each stage of clone selection – there are usually three 3–5 year stages in all – as well as consideration of observable qualities of the kind outlined above, account is taken of such matters as soil and exposure requirements and how the vine will be pruned and trained. In addition, grapes from each population of clones are micro-vinified to determine what qualities each imparts to a finished wine, and some 5 years tasting allowed to establish consistency of quality and ascertain how the wine stands up to bottle ageing.

The final stage in clonal development is to ensure that each individual plant is virus free. Originally the entire vine would be heat-treated to achieve this, but modern techniques rely on irradiation of just the shoots. However, freedom from viruses is no guarantee that once in the hurly-burly of the vineyard, a vine will develop none. So once planted out in the real world, clones are closely observed and periodically overhauled and re-selected.

The grower can remain blissfully ignorant of all this – 'you don't have to know how the tractor works to drive it,' remarked one. However, most on the Côte take a keen interest in clones and their habits, and the matter of *sélection clonale* versus *sélection massale* is much discussed in café society.

When it comes to choosing what to plant, the careful grower must take several factors into account. Some varieties of Pinot Noir yield markedly more than others – for example, the infamous Pinot Droit strain has several permitted clones which are responsible for much of the over-production in Burgundy; although eschewed by most top- quality growers, it is still quite widely planted.

Furthermore, it is generally believed best to plant several different clones of one variety in each vineyard rather than just one. This encompasses two important ideas: firstly, that a single clone will yield a rather standard wine, whereas three or four mixed together will produce greater complexity, and secondly, that if you rely on a single clone and it happens to develop a fault or a disease, then you have lost your production in that vineyard until you replant – an unacceptable risk.

The second idea is perhaps sound sense. The first, however, is false – according to Professor Raymond Bernard, who was one of the developers of clones in Burgundy in the late 1950s. His experiments have shown that a single clone will often produce the best wine. In his view, clones are often blamed for poor quality, when the true culprit is excessive yield. Growers are also perhaps operating on the mistaken belief that the best quartet is a combination of the best four soloists. Whatever his planting policy, a grower must realise that each clone has its own characteristics: some give higher sugar/alcohol levels whilst others ripen earlier or give more even ripeness, and so on.

The Burgundian vigneron is a distinctly cautious species. Although many are devout partisans of clones, others, whilst grudging converts, continue to regard them as a mixed blessing. Some, perhaps persuaded by their neighbours, are just beginning to try a few clones to see what happens, whilst a few Domaines remain steadfast in their refusal to countenance clones under any circumstances.

However, after a quarter of a century of experience, there is much for which growers along the Côte may thank Raymond Bernard.

Fresh grafts, ready for planting

Degenerative viruses – especially *court-noué,* which severely attacked the Chardonnay plants of Puligny and Chassagne after the Second World War – are under control and in consequence, a vigneron can now be sure that some 90–95% of his vines will produce every year, whereas before the proportion was no greater than 60–75%, a factor which partly accounts for today's higher yields.

Whilst new clones appear and established ones are taken in for routine maintenance, much is being done to improve what there is, particularly in the area of virus susceptibility. Experiments in Colmar, Alsace, with vines which are given a low dose of virus and then planted out in a plot affected by that same virus, seem to indicate that it may be possible to effectively 'vaccinate' plants against specific infections. However, the emergence of new strains of virus make such a programme more complex than it might at first appear.

Out in the field, some 80% of vignerons are now using Chardonnay clones, whereas only 50% have accepted clones of Pinot Noir. Among the experts, there is concern that the variety of commercially available clones in both varieties has become too great. There is a compelling argument for adding to the *INAO's* controls a list of approved clones for planting on AC land, especially in the Premier and Grand Cru *climats* where the temptation to go for high yields most needs to be restrained.

Rootstocks: Before the epidemic of *phylloxera* which progressively destroyed some 75% of viticultural France from about 1863 to 1900, and much of the rest of Europe's vineyards later, vines were planted on their own roots. However, after considerable misery and fruitless experiment, it was discovered that the only effective protection against this disease was to plant vines on to phylloxera-resistant American roots. Thus was the rootstock born.

Today, except for some New World plantings and a handful of surviving pre-*phylloxera* vineyards in Champagne, the Douro valley and elsewhere, vines are customarily planted on to selected resistant rootstock. However, choosing a suitable rootstock is almost as complicated as choosing the scion on to which it is to be grafted. As Kunkee and Goswell noted in 1976 'selection of . . . rootstock for use in control of nematodes and *phylloxera* is far more complicated than merely assessing resistance and making the graft.'

The most commonly used rootstocks, developed by much the same techniques as clones from crossings derived from two of three American parents (vitis rupestris, vitis riparia or vitis berlandieri), have their own strengths and characteristics. From these, further crossings of European vines with American rootstocks are made to produce the ideal roots for various combinations of soil, climate, graft etc. . . The result is a wide variety of acceptable resistant roots from which, theoretically, the vigneron can choose.

However, years of experiment and observation have narrowed the sensible choice down to a handful of practicable affinities. It would be a foolish grower indeed who ignored decades of distilled collective wisdom and planted his vines on something wildly heterodox.

The principal considerations in choosing suitable roots, for the Côte d'Or or for anywhere else, are the vigour of the root, the soil into which it is to be planted and adaptability to the scion and the microclimate. It is important to realise that the rootstock is not inert, but interacts with the scion during their life together and, as with any marriage, success is due as much to compatibility, however ill-suited they may sometimes appear, as to income – i.e. yield.

In particular, the vigour of the roots must balance that of the scion: too much and the flowers may abort or unwanted foliage abound – the headless chicken phenomenon; too little and the grapes will not mature properly. The S04 rootstock, of which there are still significant plantings in all parts of the Côte d'Or, produces high vigour to start with and then seems to degenerate, probably because of low resistance to active lime in the soil; however, some growers have older plots of vines on S04 which are still producing superbly.

Soil affinity is also critical – some roots have a high tolerance of calcium, excess salinity, acidity, etc. whilst others are less successful in richer soils with a high clay content. This is especially important in the Côte d'Or where soils can vary significantly within the space of a few metres. For example, the latest strain of 161/49, which is now replacing the S04 on sloping sites, is particularly well adapted to soils with a high active lime content whereas other, less adaptive roots result in the development of *chlorosis.*

Not all roots are suitable partners for all scions. This is not a matter of gross incompatibility, rather of fine tuning. For example, an inappropriate rootstock could lead to uneven development of sap, too early a flowering or too late a ripening, all of which matter in the marginal, continental climate of Burgundy.

The conscientious grower will also take account of the microclimate of the individual site which is to be planted. Is it excessively humid, a frost-pocket, or perhaps particularly wet or windy? If it is low-lying, as is much of the Côte, and thus near to the water-table – as at Puligny-Montrachet or in the lower parts of the Clos de Vougeot – then a shallower-rooting stock is preferable.

Along the Côte d'Or a handful of clones and roots are currently in widespread use. Of the Pinot Noir clones, 113, 114 and 115 – all developed from a mother vine in Morey-St.-Denis and first marketed in 1971 – are popular, as are 667 and 777 which became available in 1980. For Chardonnay, B75, B76, B77, B95 and B96 are common, as is the B548 propagated from a *vigne mère* at La Vineuse in the Saône-et-Loire and first marketed in 1978.

The most widely planted rootstocks in the Côte are the 161/49, which performs best on well-drained sloping terrain, the 3309, a *chlorosis*-prone rootstock which prefers soils with less active lime and is used in semi-sloping vineyards where the soil is richer, and the S04 which is still used by some growers who seem able to make it work. There is also a renaissance in the use of Riparia, which is particularly adapted to deeper soils and is effective in limiting vine vigour.

The distillation of all this is that there are a great number of factors to be considered before planting a vineyard. Fortunately for the vigneron there is much free expert help at hand, so he does not have to cudgel his brains to disentangle the intricacies. Provided he remembers that you cannot make an inappropriate grape-variety succeed by the expedient of grafting it on to an 'appropriate' rootstock, he is unlikely to make any earth-shattering mistakes.

Maintaining the Vine

The vigneron who has chosen and planted his vines with care must then coax them into producing the best possible fruit. In deciding how to achieve this, he must project his thoughts beyond the short-term, extrapolating the effects of each treatment or practice beyond one growing season, over the life-expectancy of the vine. There are two undisputed keys to producing quality wine: healthy vines and low yields. These are not alternatives: it is no use having exuberantly healthy plants over-producing, or tiny yields from diseased vines.

How a plant performs depends as much as anything upon the soil it grows in. Neither in chemical nor in physical structure is the soil beyond the vigneron's sphere of influence. Chemically, repeated use of strong, toxic sprays will destroy the fragile balance of yeasts and bacteria which constitute the soil's micro-flora, and can alter soil-pH. Physically, modern heavy machinery will gradually break up and compact the topsoil, altering its drainage properties.

Many of the Côte's finest vineyards, for example the hill of Corton and the top sectors of Vosne-Romanée, are on steep slopes. Not only does this make mechanical working difficult, it also increases the likelihood of soil erosion, when heavy rain washes down valuable topsoil which the wretched vigneron then has to take back up again. To combat this, he may allow natural grasses to grow or consider planting special grasses to help retain the soils. This *enherbement* is still experimental; whilst it appears to be an excellent preventive the grass tends to retain moisture which both increases frost-risk and also takes valuable water from the vines in dry summers.

Under normal circumstances vignerons have to decide whether to hoe their vineyards or to use chemical herbicides to eradicate grass and weeds. The former aerates the soil but also makes it sticky, restricting access to the vineyards after rain. Furthermore, the mechanical hoes used may physically damage the vine trunks, which can lead to Esca – a sort of vine apoplexy which kills the plant. The alternative is to use herbicides, but these contaminate the soil. There is significantly less erosion when the soil is hoed since water penetrates more easily and binds the topsoil. Twenty years ago, only 10% of the Côte's vineyards were treated with herbicides – hence less erosion; nowadays the proportion is estimated at 85%.

The growth and health of the vine, as well as the structure of the soil, are also affected by fertilisation. In the 1960s and 1970s fertiliser salesmen and prosperous vignerons combined to saturate much of the Côte with potassium-rich fertiliser. Thirty years later, the soils are finally shaking off this imbalance, which led to wines with high pHs and low acidities. Vignerons are now more enlightened, and the best only use the minimum of organic humus, manure, or nothing at all.

Even the minimum may be a mistake since, some 80% of commercial organic fertilisers have no nutritive value beyond adding unwanted nitrogen to the soil. Nonetheless, a well fermented humus may help prevent soil erosion and can act as a small water reservoir, which is especially valuable on hillsides. Some vignerons mulch vine prunings back into the soils, for much the same reasons, but this merely re-cycles the potassium they contain.

In short, vignerons need to take much greater care with their soil management than they do at present. Neither excess plant vigour nor destabilised micro-flora contribute anything positive to wine quality.

Left to itself, the vine is a rambling plant and a notoriously irregular producer – a few bunches one year and perhaps a glut the next. To work with it in areas such as Burgundy, to reduce its proliferousness and to ensure that foliage and bunches receive maximum insolation, it must be trained and pruned. Vines are also individuals – some are more vigorous than others, some mature their fruit better etc. – so, within the limits laid down by the rules of each appellation the vigneron must adapt his work to his vines.

There is no doubt that the severity of each winter's pruning, how many eyes per vine the grower leaves, is fundamental in determining the potential quality of the wine he makes. In the Côte d'Or the law sets a limit of 80,000 buds per ha. – i.e. 8 buds per vine, assuming the usual vine-density of 10,000 per ha. This corresponds to a yield of some 40–45 hl./ha. – too much, at least for Pinot Noir in Grand Cru sites. Growers for whom quality really matters, prune more strictly, realising that this entails a risk, should there be frost or hail.

Once the vine has started to grow, the vigneron must remove any double shoots or excess buds from each vine. This task, *évasivage/dédoublage,* normally undertaken in early spring, is an essential operation in limiting yields; how many passes a grower makes through his vines is an indicator of quality; some are noticeably more conscientious than others. Research at Dijon University indicates that if more than 6 buds remain on a vine, then only quality drops, whereas below 6 there is a progressive diminution in quantity.

Throughout the summer, excess foliage is removed to avoid humid micro-climates for the bunches and to ensure that they get as much sun as possible. Nowadays, the tendency is to train and summer-prune the vines higher because this increases maturity and sugar levels. There is much research into the precise shape and height of *palissage* which is proving valuable in Burgundy's marginal climate. However, too high a trellis entails a risk of creating patches of shade, preventing sunlight from reaching bunches at the centre of the vine.

In some years, despite his best efforts at pruning and thinning, the grower may still have too many bunches and decide to remove some. The theory is simple: the more bunches per vine, the less it is able to ripen them, so reducing the charge will restore the balance.

However, there is heated disagreement as to whether this green-pruning works. Some growers believe it is nothing more than gimmickry since, when the time arrives, most of the potential has passed from the vine into the bunches – which are then cut off; in any case, the antagonists argue, the vines just compensate, so you are effectively back where you started. Others claim that the process works perfectly well, provided that you do it at the right moment – at *veraison,* when the grapes are turning from green to black.

Green-pruning is very fashionable at the moment: local newspapers are full of photographs of people bent double, hard at work removing bunches from famous vineyards. Those who disagree scathingly counter that if you need to remove bunches then you had too many buds to start with – a self-inflicted excess. This controversy splits even top Domaines, and seems set to last for some time.

Whatever he decides to do about any excess bunches, the vigneron will probably be more preoccupied with keeping his vines free of the multifarious infestations which threaten them from bud-burst to harvest. The problems are not simple – viruses may remain undetectable until it is too late to save the vine; pests rarely announce

One cure for soil erosion is to plant soil-retentive grass between the rows – as here in Domaine Gouge's Les Vucrain's vines in Nuits

their arrival in advance; an overnight storm can cause an outbreak of rot; the berries may swell and burst or the man next door may forget to spray, leaving your vines vulnerable; the catalogue is endless.

A grower must determine a treatment policy and plan the skeleton of his annual regime in advance. He must decide whether to use only surface, contact products, which are the least harmful but which wash off at the merest drop of rain, or whether to opt for products which penetrate the vine or for systemics which remain active for much longer. He can either opt for the security of preventive treatments which may turn out to be unnecessary, or wait for the signs of infestation and then treat curatively with one of the excellent new products which, at least for *oïdium* and mildew, work recursively. Each system has its benefits and disadvantages.

In formulating his policy, the vigneron should take account of the longer-term effects of what he does. Problems of resistance and toxicity have caused a major reassessment, with many growers backing off from the ever-stronger synthetic products, which select out all but the most virulent forms of a disease, and turning towards a more natural, organic regime. Beyond promoting the immediate health of the vines, products may also leave residues which can significantly affect the course of fermentation.

Understandably, most growers are by nature cautious – preferring an extra treatment or two to the risk of disease – and having prospered, can afford to be so. However, many blatantly over-treat, which encourages rot and is beneficial neither for their wine nor, in the long term, for the vines. Others are making strenuous efforts to reduce treatments – in particular for rot. Problems with an effective, widely used anti-rot product containing the procymidone molecule, have forced a complete rethink, since there is as yet no viable alternative.

At present, the annual invasion of pests can only be contained with insecticides.These breed their own resistance problems, so products with greater specificity are being researched in order that ecologically beneficent fauna are not indiscriminately destroyed along with the unwanted spiders and larvae. Fortunately, favourable weather over the last few years has allowed growers who treated curatively to greatly reduce insect sprays, saving both time and money.

Most growers subscribe to the Service de Protection des Végétaux – an organisation which disseminates specific advice on risks and treatments throughout the Côte, by means of regular bulletins. Its aim is to persuade viticulteurs to limit treatments and to point them in the direction of ecologically friendly products. So once a Domaine has its broad treatment strategy in place, much of the detailed decision-making is taken out of its hands.

Despite all the up-to-the-minute offerings from the chemical companies, many growers are returning to the traditional copper- and sulphur-based treatments for mildew and *oïdium*. Copper is a useful substance but needs careful usage: it tends to provoke *coulure* at flowering, slows down vegetation and tends to accumulate slow-degrading toxic residues in the soil. However, if used towards the end of the season, it hardens the somewhat naturally fragile Pinot Noir skins, preventing the dreaded grape-worm from puncturing them and getting in. It is thus, indirectly, a valuable aid in rot control, since the wounds made by this worm rapidly turn rotten. However, copper and sulphur are both contact products which are readily washed off.

There is one disease which is causing justifiable concern along the Côte – *eutypiose*.This malady is particularly insidious since, after brief but visible early symptoms, it can take 7 years to reappear in an infected vine, by which time it is too late. *Eutypiose* is spread by air-borne spores, especially in damp windy conditions, and enters the vine through pruning cuts and other wounds. It is virtually untreatable, although sealing cuts immediately after prunng seems to help.

Many older growers refuse to take *eutypiose* seriously, ascribing it either to prolonged sunshine or to the inventiveness of chemical companies, short of business. Sadly, it is all too real. Studies in 1990 indicated that 83% of Pinot Noir and 90% of Chardonnay vineyards throughout the Côte were affected to some extent. The highest level with Pinot was 23.2% and with Chardonnay 25.9%, and the incidence is increasing. The only solution is to grub up affected vines and burn them immediately, and it is encouraging to see that communes have taken the role of policeman into their own hands to ensure compliance.

With all the difficulties and problems of maintaining the vine, it is good to note some promising new developments. There is much research afoot into alternative ways of dealing with insects, especially the grape-worm. Mimetic, growth-regulator sprays, which disrupt the musk odours which are essential to mating and so destabilise insects' reproductive cycles, are currently on trial in several vineyards, with apparent success. These are of much lower toxicity than conventional insecticides. The use of glue pads to trap grape-worm moths is also proving useful in determining the precise moment to treat larvae, thus minimising the strength and number of treatments needed. Finally, there is some hope of increasing the level of benign predators on a variety of species – including red and yellow spiders, which pump sap from the vine; this would remove the need for most treatments without destroying the eco-balance.

On a more general level, there are significant trials of a system of vine maintenence known as 'biodynamie'. This is based on the nineteenth-century work of Rudolf Steiner, and consists of using very low doses of product, applied at highly specific times – a sort of viticultural homoeopathy. A group of Burgundy growers recently visited the Domaine Huet in Vouvray, where Noël Pinguet is using the method with considerable success. A few Domaines, including Leflaive and Leroy, are now dipping their feet into this rather revolutionary water, and many others seem eager to go paddling.

On the hardware front, mechanical harvesters have been spotted in Meursault and Gevrey, and elsewhere on the Côte. These are of doubtful benefit – research suggests that up to 3 years old, machine and manually harvested wines do not differ, whereas thereafter the machine wines start to age more rapidly. Also, there are serious concerns about the long-term effects, on their root-systems and general health, of shaking the vines to dislodge the grapes.

There is undisputed consensus that the most significant improvements in quality will derive from better viticulture than from changes in the cellar. However, although most of the Côte's 4,000-plus vignerons are more confident growers than wine-makers, there is still far to go, especially in persuading them to reduce yields further and to limit the number of products and the frequency of individual treatments. Many viticulteurs still cling to the belief that a lush, abundantly green vineyard with neatly trimmed foliage is invariably preferable to one less manicured. Perhaps they are just gardeners at heart.

The Importance and Use of Wood

For more than 2,000 years, the wooden cask was the only serviceable medium for bulk liquid storage. Herodotus records the use of palm wood casks for transporting wine to Babylon and artefacts and documents provide further evidence of barrels in widespread use in wine-making. With no sensible alternative, the barrel became part of the tradition of wine-making in much of Europe.

However, the 228-litre casks one sees in any worthwhile Burgundian cellar represent not only the legacy of history but also recent advances in the understanding of how a wine develops. Only since the late 1970s has serious attention been devoted to understanding the effects of wood on wine, but these few years of research suggest that the subject is much more complex than generally supposed.

The principle of storing young wine in cask is based on the value of a gradual contact with oxygen – slow oxygenation, rather than rapid oxidation – which does not occur with an inert storage medium such as stainless steel. In this respect, wood has two important sets of properties: those related directly to the nature of the cask itself, and those related to the oxygen chemistry of wine.

It is now well-known that the make-up of a cask – shape, size, ratio of wood surface to wine volume and method of cooperage – contributes to a wine's development. Equally important is the type of wood used, the age of the tree from which the staves are hewn and how they are treated before the cask is made up.

Historically, the predominance of oak and chestnut merely reflected availability. Nowadays, choices are more sophisticated, with extensive research devoted to codifying differences attributable to the provenance of the wood and to the way it is treated.

The current feeling is that the importance of wood provenance has been overstressed – tastings revealing diminishing differences between wood from different forests as a wine ages. Growers realise that what matters is the fineness of the grain and how the wood is treated. Moreover, soils and climates differ from forest to forest, resulting in significant differences – especially in the tightness of the grain and its porosity; so mere provenance, by itself, can mislead.

Tastings also indicate that the tighter the grain the better the wine. Tight-grained wood from Nevers will impart a finer, more subtle flavour to a Chardonnay than more loose-grained Limousin. Heart wood will give a different taste from wood from the outside of the trunk which contains more sap. In general the wider the pores the greater the extraction of oak compounds into the wine, thus the greater their contribution to its aromatic and flavour development. Also, wood from a younger tree will not have the same physical and chemical characteristics as that from an older one.

The matter is further complicated by the fact that, as with grape varieties, each species of tree has multiple clones, some producing better wood than others. It has even been suggested that a system of Appellation Contrôllée be introduced to control the provenance and quality of any wood sold for wine casks; this initiative is being supported by research to develop a system of 'finger-printing' oak from different forests. Experts also distinguish summer from spring wood, since a tree-trunk only grows during the summer, emphasising that the proportions of each matter as much as precise provenance. Tannins are localised in summer wood, so the fact that Tronçais oak contains less of this than Limousin is essential to deciding which to use.

The amount of sap (undesirable) in the wood depends on when the tree is felled. Wood cut when the sap is rising perforce contains more. So autumn and winter are the best times to fell, when it is descending.

Whatever the wood, how it is dried and prepared can determine its contribution to a wine. Many growers, realising this, are now buying their own wood and arranging for it to be dried naturally rather than in kilns, since this removes the harsher tannins more effectively and ensures complete dryness, reducing the risk of *volatile acidity* in the final wine. It is generally considered that one year's exposure to the open air is necessary for each centimetre thickness of the plank; so, on average 2–3 years outside is desirable.

Before a cask is assembled, the individual staves must be heated to bend them into shape. Whether they are lightly, moderately or heavily toasted modifies polyphenol compounds and thereby affects the intensity of oak flavours imparted to the wine. In general, a light toast produces more complexity and heavy toast more roundness. Classic trials by Robert Mondavi in the Napa Valley, putting the same base wine into differently coopered barrels, demonstrated not only this effect but also that hand-splitting staves versus sawing, the specific means of heating, toasting versus charring and the thickness of the staves all produced marked variations in wine character.

The age of the wood must also be considered. New oak tends to impart more vinosity to a wine; older wood will give a riper spectrum of flavours.Tastings of the same wine aged in different casks strikingly demonstrate the effect of each of these factors.

Finally, to these complexities one must add the cooper; each works in his own individual fashion, so even given identical ingredients one would hardly expect identical results.

Most wine-makers remain blissfully unaware of these intricacies. They tend to deal with one cooper and, whilst the more sophisticated might specify the provenance of their wood or try out casks from several forests, the only constant factor affecting their calculations is how many to buy each year.

Too much new wood, too high a proportion or too long in cask, can ruin a wine. A careful vigneron will judge these factors on tasting alone: a naturally more structured vintage or a Grand Cru will integrate more new wood than wines of lesser pedigree.

If matching the wood to the characteristics of the wine taxes the comprehension, it is no less complex to grasp what goes on inside the barrel once it is full. The cask itself and the air both contribute significantly to a wine's development.

It was long believed that oxygen enters a cask by transpiration across the staves. This is now known to be false: Peterson (1976) convincingly demonstrated that in a full, tightly-bunged barrel, on its side, there progressively develops a vacuum. So if the wine does take up oxygen during its stay in cask, it does not do so through the staves.

What are the alternatives? Oxygen can enter either by absorption from that already dissolved in the pores of the wood or in the wine, or else – perhaps more plausible in an imperfect world – via either the interstices between the staves which are a less than perfect seal, or through a non-airtight bung. Up to-date cellars may have replaced the old wooden bungs (which tended to warp) secured by rags harbouring zoos-full of microbes, with rubber and glass bungs which improve both hygiene and security, but even these are probably not 100% airtight. In reality, however, far more oxygen finds its way in through routine cellar operations – racking, fining, moving casks, and when the barrel is unbunged to extract a tasting sample – than through any other means.

Whatever its method of ingress, oxygen affects the way a wine develops. Until it is bottled, when it enters a 'reduced' state in which oxygen is virtually absent, wine is prey to the many chemical transformations which take place in the presence of even minute amounts of oxygen. At the limit, a wine completely open to the air will turn into vinegar. However, controlled access to lesser amounts of oxygen over a period of months before bottling is generally beneficial especially for wines intended for keeping.

The role of oxygen is many-stranded: it oxidises tartaric acids, polyphenols and alcohol – all compounds naturally occuring in wine – softens the taste of tannins and stabilises colour pigments. The net effects of all this biochemical activity are a decrease in fixed acids and tannins, the precipitation out of colouring matter and the oxidation of tannins, in both red and white wine, to a brown tint.

The contribution of the cask-wood itself is no less important. Wood adds structure – elements of backbone and firmness. Tannins and other 'phenolic' substances pass from wood to wine in amounts affected by the nature of the cask and the length of time the wine spends in it. However, the effects on tannin structure are generally less pronounced than those on other aroma and flavour compounds. To complicate matters further, the tannins imparted from a new cask are different in character – particularly taste – from those deriving from the grape-skin (their traditional source) and again from those from pips and stalks. Although oak tannins tend to be harder in flavour than skin tannins, they are ideal for wines such as Côte d'Or Chardonnays which benefit from added richness and structure without a harsh, unharmonious backbone.

In each vintage, the grower has to make several key decisions for each *cuvée*: how much new wood, what type and how long should the wine stay in contact with it? If he knows his job, he will seek to add what is attractive without allowing the wood to dominate or destroy the characteristics of grape and *terroir* which make, for example, a Puligny different from a Meursault.

Few top-class Domaines stick unswervingly to a fixed percentage of new oak each year. They have to bear in mind that injudicious use of oak can leave a wine out of balance – the subtle equilibrium between tannin, oak and fruit is easily upset and, once destroyed, may never entirely recover. Too much new wood or too long in cask will often desiccate a wine – it loses fruit and flesh which it never regains. The balance between enhancement and loss is therefore remarkably fine. These judgements can only be made on tasting.

However skilled a grower may be at judging when to bottle his wine, in reality it is often his family finances which determine how many new casks he can afford each year. A new barrel will cost 2,500 francs and he needs 50. They will add 15 francs to the price of every bottle he sells – the market is tight, will he still sell the wine? Perhaps the third-year barrels might just do for a fourth?

He will also be acutely conscious of the 10 per cent loss from evaporation and cellar operations involved in keeping wine in his expensive new casks – and of the costly labour involved in weekly topping-up. He may not, however, realise that there is greater evaporation from an older cask or that the wine in it matures more quickly. Stainless steel vats must often seem an appealing way out; hardly surprising, therefore, that many take the soft option and put less wine into cask and replace them less often.

The proportion of new oak a grower uses will vary from year to year. The unwritten rule is that the potentially finer the wine the more new oak it can support. A Grand Cru will typically be matured in up to 100% of new wood and a Premier Cru up to 40–60%. However, these guidelines must be tempered with others: leaner vintages tolerate less new wood than riper ones, and some communes – for example, Volnay and Chambolle-Musigny – produce more delicate wines which are easily overbalanced by too much new oak. It must also be remembered that the contents of second year and older casks of the same wine will eventually be amalgamated with that of any new barrels to make up the final *cuvée.*

Although it is generally felt uneconomic to put anything less than Premier Cru into new wood some growers put their Bourgogne Rouge and Bourgogne Blanc into a proportion of new oak, often with fine results – and prices to match.

The effect of wood diminishes with each year a cask is used. After about 5 years it has given what it usefully can and will either be resold to someone less scrupulous or sawn up for the geranium tub. The noticeable taste impact of new wood, so evident during the first few years, also diminishes as a wine ages in bottle – the scaffolding somehow integrates with the building. The vanilla and toast aromas and the extra tannins become part of the developing wine.

For white wines, many vignerons now appreciate that the sooner the juice is put into the casks the better, especially if these are new. Not only do white wines fermented in cask have more regular and rapid *malos,* but they also taste rounder and more harmonious than those fermented in bulk and then transferred to new wood.

Wood is thus an important, but highly complex, part of fine wine production. No grower of quality can remain ignorant of its potential or of its pitfalls. Conversely, one can learn more about a grower's attitude to quality from his views on wood and how he uses it, than from any map on the wall vibrantly inked in to demonstrate his exalted land holdings.

A cooper at Maison Louis Latour heating oak staves to bend them into shape

Making Red Wine

One of the features of the Côte d'Or, which makes it so difficult to understand, is that from a small, single vineyard can come wines of such diverse style and quality. How is it that, of two vignerons with vines next door to each other, one can produce something sublime and the other something uninspiring and pedestrian? For example, of more than 80 owners of the Clos Vougeot, a vineyard no bigger than a large field,no more than a handful produce top quality wine.

Unfortunately there is too much indifferent Burgundy leaving growers' cellars for there to be any doubt that much is going awry. While poor quality can often be traced back to ignorance or lack of cash for proper equipment, in many instances it is the direct result of laziness or incompetence. Any grower with healthy, ripe grapes has the raw material necessary for making fine wine; so what is going wrong with the poor performers?

To understand how this happens, it is necessary to get to grips with the broad principles of vinification, which strike more or less common ground. Being aware of the processes involved in transforming grapes into wine increases both the appreciation of wine and also the ability to relate quality to wine-making techniques and thus to pin-point problems.

Top class growers stress the importance of ripe healthy fruit for trouble-free vinification. This entails being prepared to wait for optimum maturity, balanced natural sugar and acidity, and as favourable a ratio of juice to solids as the weather will allow. It also means spending time and money on removing unripe bunches and rotten or damaged berries before they get into the vats, and taking care to use small harvesting containers so that the grapes are not crushed on their way to the cuverie. If growers fail here, then they are in trouble even before they have started making their wine.

In the cuverie, the first important decision is whether or not to separate the berries from their stems – destalking. Stems, which are no more than ripe or unripe wood, absorb colour and contribute little but astringent tannins, which are less noble than those extracted from the skins, so most prefer to remove them. However, this early injection of tannin can help to fix unstable, but valuable, colour compounds – anthocyanins.

Some doggedly old-fashioned growers leave all the stalks in their vats, irrespective of their quality, with the result that, in all but the ripest vintages, their wines have an irremediable raw, unpleasantly herbaceous streak which destroys their balance.

In recent years the prevailing tendency, fuelled by expert opinion, has been to remove more stalks, perhaps leaving 20–30% in particularly ripe years to add structure and also to facilitate the drainage of juice through the cap of skins and pips which forms on top of each vat.

In many Domaines this has resulted in a significant improvement in the quality of wine made, especially in unripe vintages. Some refer to 'old' and 'new' styles of Burgundy; what matters is that tailoring the level of stalks to the vintage makes for a better, more durable, balance. The ability of 'old style' wine to last a century means nothing if all that's left is harsh tannin.

Ripe Pinot Noir grapes contain all the necessary potential for lasting colour, aroma and flavour, mostly located in pigment compounds in and just under the skin, with very few in the pulp. Only to the extent that the vigneron extracts and retains these will his wine succeed.

Extraction occurs before, during and after fermentation and depends on both time and temperature – the longer you macerate the skins with the juice, the more you leach out, especially colour. However, what is extracted before fermentation differs from that extracted during and afterwards. Some growers delay the start of fermentation to increase extraction, either by cooling the pulp or by adding sulphur dioxide (SO_2) to temporarily anaesthetise the yeasts. Others dislike any pre-fermentive maceration and consider inhibiting fermentation to be thoroughly unnatural. Whilst there is no right or wrong, it is beyond dispute that a short period of pre-fermentive maceration gives a more deeply coloured and more intensely aromatic juice.

The heart of wine-making, fermentation, is a complex of processes, at present imperfectly understood, which through the mediation of yeasts transforms grape-sugar into alcohol. It is known to be affected by temperature, size and shape of vat and by whether natural or cultured yeasts are used. Once fermentation is under way, the temperature rises and a cap of solids – skins, pips etc. – is floated to the surface on released carbon-dioxide gas. Both need careful management.

The vigneron has a choice to make: if he ferments his wine at too high a temperature – anything over a maximum of 35° C. is regarded as risky – he may increase the extraction of aroma and flavour compounds from the grapes, but the yeasts may stop working, allowing bacteria naturally present in the juice to degrade any remaining sugar into acetic acid – i.e. vinegar. In high concentrations this *volatile acidity* has an unpleasantly pungent smell and a sharp, sour taste. If, however, he chooses to ferment at too low a temperature, the wine will lack substance and depth.

He also has to decide how often to break up the cap on top of the juice. In Burgundy it is normal to do this – either by jumping into the vat and using your feet or by some automated piston device – at least once or twice daily, to keep the cap moist. The more frequent the *pigéage,* the more extraction from the skins. Lazy vignerons tend to *piger* infrequently, with predictable results.

Many growers, attracted by the security of regular, controllable, fermentations, now use cultured Burgundy yeasts in place of the natural yeast population – the bloom on the grapes. Others contend that each commune and *climat* has its specific yeast population, and that only these are capable of generating real typicity and complexity. Cultured yeasts, they argue, often vociferously, blur these differences and standardise wines.

Although cultured yeasts are being constantly refined to reflect the original yeast populations on the Côte, and sophisticated techniques have been developed for the genetic identification of individual yeasts, there is little research support for the hypothesis of commune or vineyard-specific micro-flora, or for the suggestion that, even if these existed, they would play a significant role in wine typicity. However, security apart, one might justifiably question the need for cultured yeasts when the indigenous ones work perfectly well.

The process of turning red grapes into wine, *cuvaison*, extends from the moment the grapes are vatted to the moment the new wine is run off so that the pulp can be pressed. Each stage has its part to play, extracting different substances from the grapes and transforming others. It is thought that pre-fermentive maceration maximises the extraction of colour pigments which are highly water-soluble, whereas aromatic compounds are mostly extracted during fermentation, during the conversion of grape-sugars to alcohol.

Tannins, so important to a red wine's longevity, are most soluble in alcohol, and are thus maximally extracted during and after fermentation. As they are progressively leached into the new wine, they also act to fix unstable colour compounds extracted by water into the pulp before fermentation started.

There is a wide variation in the preferred length of *cuvaison.* A vigneron with too few vats for his harvest will be forced to shorten it; in other circumstances, if the skins are fragile and not entirely ripe, he may lengthen it to extract more substance and colour. Some growers prefer short *cuvaisons* of 7–10 days, others allow up to 3 weeks and beyond. This vatting time is of prime importance to the character and quality of a wine. Whilst there are no inflexible formulae, it is doubtful whether a wine of serious depth and staying power can be made with a *cuvaison* of less than about 10–12 days.

In the marginal climate of the Côte, the Pinot Noir often fails to reach sufficient ripeness in grape-sugar to produce the legal minimum alcohol necessary for a balance in the finished wine – even in the Grands Crus. In these circumstances a vigneron is permitted to make up the deficiency with sucrose, during fermentation – *chaptalisation* – up to a maximum increase of 2 degrees of alcohol.

In some vintages, growers are faced with a natural imbalance between juice and solids in their grapes. In these circumstances the more conscientious will bleed off *(saigner)* some juice from each vat to restore equilibrium to something approaching the two-thirds to one-third juice-to-solids ratio regarded as ideal for red grapes. Any *saignée* should take place immediately after vatting, since delay will only increase the amount of precious aroma and colour compounds removed with the unwanted pulp-juice.

For some, however, the sacrifice is too much – since the juice *saignéed* represents saleable wine (at 200 francs or more a bottle for a Grand Cru) and is useless for anything but 'vin ordinaire'. A grower's willingness to *saigner* is a good indicator of his attitude to quality.

The *saignée is* a recent, but valuable, addition to the vigneron's weaponry, and many growers now *saigner* on a regular basis, even in ripe, well-structured vintages such as 1990. However it is not, as some seem to consider it, a substitute for failing to prune short, or compensation for otherwise over-cropping.

With a vat full of new wine, the next step is to decant the free-run wine *(vin de goutte)* and then press the pulp which remains. Too harsh a squeezing will express more wine, but this will be higher in tannins and lower in quality, in any case, care must be taken, as *vin de presse* is always higher in tannin and acidity than the *vin de goutte.*

Growers will often claim that they only use wine from the first, gentle pressing to blend in, but their wines often give them away. Asking what proportion of the total press-wine represents is often very revealing – 25% indicates that he is pressing too hard, whilst 5–10% is a more acceptable average.

Once the press-wine has been assembled with the free-run wine and allowed to settle, the new wine is run into 228-litre casks for its *élevage* – literally 'pupillage', or 'upbringing'. It is during these 9–24 months that the vigneron has most scope for destruction. He may use too much, or too little, new wood; he may leave thewine in cask too long so it loses freshness and shrivels up; or he may fail to top up his casks regularly, so oxygen gets into the wine and starts the inexorable progress towards vinegar.

Shortly after alcoholic fermentation, the new wine will undergo a second, natural, *malolactic* fermentation. This is the transformation of harsh malic (apple) acid into softer tasting lactic (milk) acid and is mediated not by yeasts, but by bacteria.

During its *élevage* the wine will be periodically racked, to get it off its lees which after a time impart an unpleasant and individual taste. How often, when and how a wine is racked are of vital importance to its development. In general, red wines are usually racked twice – in the spring after their *malo,* and again about three months before bottling. The important matter is that the precise timing of each racking should not depend on some pre-determined formula, or the need for casks, but on the wine's development, a factor in the assessment of which tasting is essential.

The first racking is so timed because during the *malo* the wine is relatively unprotected from oxygen – there is no $C0_2$ around and the vigneron must not add more SO_2, since this would knock out the very bacteria which break down the malic acid.

If a grower is going to wreck his wine, he is most likely to accomplish this in preparing it for bottiing, when he attempts to ensure that it contains no gross deposits and is generally bright and stable. There are two traditional operations open to him to achieve this: fining and filtration. Fining, by adding a substance which has no taste impact, removes finely suspended particles, often invisible, which would not normally settle by themselves and may, incidentally, reduce tannin levels. Filtration, through a more or less porous medium, removes deposits from the larger visible particles down to the smallest of micro-molecules.

However, these processes often destroy aromatic persistence and finesse, and can take guts and substance from a wine, so many growers strive to avoid them. Others, anxious for the security they bring – knowing they will not be awoken in the middle of the night by an incensed customer on the far side of the world complaining that his expensive Chambertin has become cloudy and started to fizz – fine and filter to excess. Careful wine-making should render all but the lightest intervention unnecessary.

Having reached this far, the grower still has scope for disaster – he must get his wine into bottles. This operation is fraught with danger. First, he must decide when to bottle, for which constant tasting is the only sensible test; a week or two either way can make a massive difference. Then he must cope with the operation of bottling, which is no less full of pitfalls. Many growers, admitting they lack the requisite skills or understandabiy not being prepared to finance sophisticated equipment which they will use for only a week or two each year, entrust bottling to a specialist contractor. Unfortunately, most of these enterprises are remunerated on a piece-work basis, so it is in their interests to spend as little time as possible on the job. This is not beneficial to the wine. The sensible compromise is shared equipment – which is beginning to happen.

Talking to an under-achieving vigneron and looking round his cellar often reveals what is going wrong. Apart from gross incompetence, sloppy hygiene or poor fermentation control, he may makesilly mistakes in the cellar. For example, using the same cask of each wine for tastings – so that it is being constantly un-bunged – lets the air in; or failing to replace the pieces of jute which separate a wooden bung and the cask-hole encourages spoilage bacteria.

One eminent Burgundian vigneron has noted that, whereas some 80% of wines taste good before *malolactic,* only 40% do so after, and a paltry 20%, in his view, still do so at bottling. Although much of the ruination of potentially fine wine is due to high yields, avoidable oversight and workload, much is also due to lack of technical skill. Most vignerons are superb grape-growers, but sadly, all too many are less than competent wine-makers.

Making White Wine

Talking to growers, there is no doubt that most find making white wine considerably more straightforward than making red. It is indeed rare to find one who makes equally fine red and white wine – you are, apparently, either a 'patissier' or a 'saucier' but rarely both.

The most important differences between red and white wine are colour and tannin. White grapes are never truly white, but various shades of mottled yellow and green – which easily discolour wine. So, while red grapes are allowed to macerate with their juice to extract as much 'matière' from the skins before the grapes are pressed, white grapes are pressed immediately, and the juice removed before it can pick up colour from the skins.

Because of his minimal skin contact, white wine contains negligible tannin – an ingredient which adds so importantly to the structure and longevity of a red wine. In order to compensate for this, and to provide a fine white wine with the ability to age, the vigneron must ensure that enough acidity is retained to balance the fruit and alcohol In short, tannin and colour are undesirable and acidity is essential.

Because of its lack of tannin and anti-oxidant enzymes, white juice is more prone to oxidation than red juice. In the same way that a cut apple discolours rapidly unless protected by acidity (lemon juice for example), so white grape-juice will irreversibly brown if exposed to the air. This exacts from the vigneron a high standard of care and hygiene if the wine is to arrive at bottling light-coloured and bright.

This means scrupulous cleaning of everything from cask bungs to the cellar floor and any cellar equipment used. Careful use of $S0_2$ as a disinfectant throughout the life of the young wine also helps the vigneron to this end. However, most of the best growers prefer to concentrate on cellar hygiene in order to reduce $S0_2$ levels to the barest minimum, since beyond a certain concentration this adds an unpleasant, flat dimension to both smell and taste. A few vignerons manage to make excellent wine without using any $S0_2$; however, like cycling with no hands, there is an increased risk of accidents.

Harvest can make or break quality. Sugar and acidity must be balanced to have a hope of success later, and whilst *pourriture humide*, the *noble rot* of the great sweet whites, is of less concern than with reds, grey rot is damaging and must be eliminated before pressing.

The main difficulty at this stage is to ensure that the grapes remain intact. Split berries, unprotected by $S0_2$, rapidly oxidase and discolour in the absence of tannins to buffer the oxidase enzymes which work so fast once juice is liberated. Thus undamaged, ripe and healthy grapes are what the vigneron needs as his raw material. There used to be a vogue, particularly among New World estates, for adding sulphur to bunches of grapes as soon as they had been cut; however, research revealed that this provided wine made from them with less long-term protection from oxidation than simply leaving them unsulphured until after pressing.

Once at the cuverie, the grapes are pressed as soon as possible to extract the juice and remove it from the skins and pips. Research in America and Australia has found that if the berries are simply crushed, just to break the skins, and then macerated at relatively cool temperatures for several hours, whilst undesirable tannins do not leach out, much more by way of aroma and flavour is extracted, since these compounds are located just beneath the skins and are not extracted by pressing.

Some growers in Puligny, Meursault, Aloxe-Corton and Chassagne are now using this *macération pelliculaire* to give their wines greater depth of extract.

Until quite recently, white grapes were pressed in the same type of presses as red grapes – generally devices with a screw-thread which either brought together two horizontal metal plates, or else descended one plate vertically to press the grapes. Modern presses operate on the principle of an expandable bladder which slowly inflates outwards, crushing the grapes against the wall of a cylindrical drum. These allow gentle, controlled pressure, which liberates the juice without extracting undesirable tannins either from the skins or, worse still, from the pips which contain particularly harsh tannins.

Once extracted, the juice is allowed to settle to remove any gross lees before being fermented, in either stainless-steel or glass-lined tanks – or for smaller quantities and better wines, in oak casks. Fermentation in cask is possible with white wine and not with red because there is no cap of skins to be broken up. Moreover, in small volume, the temperature does not rise as high as it would with the same juice in large volume. However, once in cask, the grower has little control over fermentation temperature, beyond cooling the cellar which is both slow and ineffective.

The maximum temperature to which fermentation is allowed to rise decisively affects the character of the wine. Cool fermentation, around 15° C., currently highly fashionable in bulk wine production, gives clean, neutral wines, often with little varietal character. Fermenting Chardonnay at such low temperatures tends to give exotic fruit aromas and flavours which, while pleasant, produce wines which lack individuality. This standardisation also expunges the typicity of each appellation, which is so much part of the interest and finesse of great white Burgundy. Fermentation for Chardonnay seems to work best at 217–25° C. – above this level, the wines rapidly become flabby

Ancient and modern: the galvanised bucket is no less essential than the high-tech Vaslin press

and heavy, and lose freshness.

Growers may ferment wholly in cask or part of each lot in cask, and part in stainless-steel to preserve freshness and acidity and then amalgamate the two parts. If new oak is used, then it is better to ferment the wine in the new cask rather than fermenting elsewhere and putting it into new oak later – the results are more harmonious and both alcoholic and *malolactic* fermentation more regular.

As with red wines, cultured yeasts may be used to replace the indigenous ones and some vignerons are unshakably convinced that the results are better. However, most see no reason to meddle with nature and happily stick to what it supplies. Even though the available selection of cultured yeasts is becoming progressively more refined, there is scant evidence to indicate that they are any better or worse than those harvested with the grape.

Once the new wine is made it has to be nurtured until the time comes for bottling. An important part of this work is ensuring that the wine benefits as much as possible from contact with its lees. The lees nourish the wine, bringing it fatness and aromatic complexity, so the longer the lees-contact the better. However, unhealthy lees or excessive contact can result in an unpleasant *goût de lie*, so constant tasting and vigilance are needed.

Periodically, in order to keep the lees evenly distributed through out the cask, a stainless-steel instrument rather like a scythe with holes in one end, or a length of chain, are put into the wine and rotated with more or less vigour. The frequency of this *batonnage* varies from grower to grower, but once or twice a week up to the *malo* is normal. One grower confessed to his own peculiar system: he simply takes a rubber mallet and taps each cask as he passes; this sends a shock-wave through the liquid and keeps the lees in suspension.

Lees are also important in retaining the fresh colour of a white wine. They absorb colour – keeping a white wine 'white' rather than yellow; it is this property which makes lees undesirable to any great extent in red wine *élevage* and is the reason why red wines are not *batonnés.*

As well as extracting maximum fat from the lees, the vigneron has to take pains to ensure that the balance of acidity is not upset. In very ripe vintages, when natural acidities are low, he may pick some grapes early to ensure part of each *cuvée* has higher acidity; alternatively, he may – with red grapes as well as with white – deliberately harvest a proportion of the second generation of bunches from the vines; these *verjus* are less mature and thus higher in acidity. Alternatively, he can act to suppress the *malolactic* fermentation, thereby retaining some of the crisper malic acid which would otherwise have been converted into softer lactic acid.

If all else fails, the wine can be acidified. This is a strictly controlled operation which involves either adding tartaric acid to the fermenting *must* or adjusting the finished wine with citric acid just before bottling. Neither alternative is particularly satisfactory, for a variety of reasons, but principally because added acid is never entirely harmonious and seems to sit apart rather than integrating with the flavours of the wine.

The lack of tannin makes white wine more fragile than red and more easily upset by too much handling. Top-class Domaines, such as Leflaive, Sauzet or Lafon, stress the importance of both maximum hygiene and minimum interference. The less a wine is moved – racked, oxygenated or pumped, the better. This also reduces the amount of $S0_2$ needed to keep the wine microbiologically stable after bottling.

Two of the vigneron's most difficult decisions are how to prepare the wine for bottling and when to bottle. Clarity and stability are essential if bottles are not to find their way back 6 months later from a dissatisfied client several thousand miles away. Much the same considerations apply to white wine as to red. In deciding his policy, the vigneron has to balance the advantages of fining and filtering with the sure knowledge that too much by way of treatment may irreversibly destroy a wine's delicate equilibrium.

An impressive battery of stainless-steel vats for their Corton-Charlemagne at Domaine Bonneau de Martray

While red wines are fined by adding protein – e.g. egg-white or special milk products – white wines are fined to remove fine protein molecules which can make them hazy, and to correct premature yellowing and render them bright. Filtration comes in varying degrees of harshness, from a light polish to remove anything from old boots to dead wasps to a sterile filtration which removes the smallest of the micro-molecules which are the potential long-term troublemakers. As with red wine, a careful fining can refine a wine's aroma by removing larger tannin molecules (white wine does contain some natural tannin). Overfining or too harsh a filtration may reassure the grower, but invariably removes guts and finesse from the wine.

The decision about when to bottle is critical. A wine may be delicious in cask, with plenty of freshness and fruit and yet be ruined if left to dry out for too long before bottling. Frequent tasting is essential to monitor wines, since they can change from week to week.

In the Côte d'Or white wines are generally bottled any time from a few months after harvest, for a fresh, sappy Aligoté, to a couple of years later, for a powerful Grand Cru.

Although the absence of the need to extract colour and tannin makes white wine-making rather more straightforward than red, mistakes are often made. The most common fault is excessive use of $S0_2$ to protect a wine against discolouring or re-fermenting in bottle. Since $S0_2$ levels are usually adjusted at bottling, an apparent excess may be detected if the wine is tasted within a few months. However, with time, much of this added $S0_2$ will be absorbed by the wine and so will become less noticeable. A serious over-sulphuring, however, is a fault which will result in a flat, irreversible dullness in the wine.

Why do some wine-makers systematically make a better job of the tricky business of turning grapes into wine than others? Whilst there is no straightforward answer, it is clear that much of the abundant poor quality, in both red and white wines, is the result of flaws in vinification or in *élevage* which are easily corrected. Furthermore, a great deal of ndifferent, but correct, wine comes from Domaines who regularly overcrop their vines. There is absolutely no doubt that in many cases, the difference between good and great wine can be attributed to excessive yields.

While all this may be true, there remains the indisputable fact that some vignerons have a gift for wine-making which transcends the mere application of scientific principle. These talented few can ennoble an Aligoté or extract Grand Cru complexity from a humble Village vineyard . This is the difference between skill and genius; fortunately, the Côte d'Or has enough of these stars to illuminate its firmament.

GUY ACCAD

Guy Accad is one of the most controversial, and criticised, figures in Burgundy. Lebanese by birth, he qualified as an oenologist and an agronomist in France, before starting his career as a wine-maker. After working in the Rhône and Provence, he set up a wine-making consultancy in the Côte in 1975. From his office and laboratory in Nuits-St.-Georges he now advises some 40 Domaines.

Accad and his wines inspire both protagonists and detractors to heated debate. In general, the arguments revolve round three specific points: whether or not his method is traditional, whether or not wines made under his aegis reflect the diversity and typicity of their appellations, and whether they have the capacity to age.

Much of the public debate is conducted by critics who have done little more than taste some of his clients' wines. Most have only a superficial knowledge of Accad's methods and virtually none has taken the trouble to meet him and examine his philosophy first hand.

This essay is intended to redress that balance. Its purpose is not to adjudicate on the merits or demerits of what Guy Accad does, but rather to put the debate onto a more informed footing. It is the result of several hours spent with Accad himself and many more talking to and tasting with Jacky Confuron-Cotétidot, Étienne Grivot, Philippe Senard and François Labet, four of his most prestigious clients.

Accad's inspiration derives from his experience of old wines from the Côte which seemed to him to scale heights far greater than those produced today. He considers that, 'If Burgundy was born 50 years ago, it wouldn't have the reputation it does now.' His argument is not that growers are making bad wine, but rather that most are failing to extract the maximum potential from their land.

His philosophy starts in the vineyards: good terrain, healthy vines and ripe grapes are seen as prerequisites of Grand Vin.

Good terrain means the best possible soil-equilibrium – achieved by analysis of soil samples followed by fine adjustments where necessary of the *base elements* (nitrogen, potassium, phosphorus and magnesium). Nothing new, perhaps, but what is different is Accad's insistence on taking soil samples from several parts of each vineyard and indeed from different depths. Those growers who bother to analyse their soils at all are usually content to take a few cursory topsoil samples and leave it at that.

Soil imbalance is known to affect wine: the excess potassium put on the vineyards, especially in the Côte de Nuits, in the 1960s and 1970s led to significantly reduced acidity levels and high pHs. The mechanism involved was complex: potassium led to lower levels of magnesium which, in turn, blocked chlorophyll production, so reducing sugar and acid synthesis. Most growers just shrugged their shoulders and adjusted acidity levels in the affected wines.

Accad's belief in the importance of super-ripe, but not over-ripe, fruit is also a cornerstone of his strategy. He has three lines of attack higher vine density, reduced yields and late harvesting. Many people forget, he argues, that in the last century vines were planted, not in neat rows of 10,000 vines per hectare, but *en foule*, untrained, at a density in Burgundy of some 25,000 per ha. It was only the need for extensive replanting, post-*phylloxera*, which changed things; but from these dense plantations came wines of depth and quality. Why was this so?

He argues that as plant density increases, the ability of the sun to fully ripen grapes, especially in cooler climates, diminishes, whilst at low plant densities, the quantity of fruit on each plant increases, to the detriment of quality. It is therefore necessary to adapt the density to the climate. In general, his rules are that the hotter the climate, the lower the optimal density of planting; conversely, the cooler it is, the higher the density. It is also known that the thinner the soil and the more dispersed its nutrients, better results are obtained at higher plant densities. Accad therefore advises his Côte d'Or clients to increase their plant density to 12,500 per ha.

The second part of the quest for ripe fruit concerns the charge on each vine. In general, beyond a natural limit which varies with site, micro-climate and plant-vigour, the more grapes on a vine, the less ripe they will be. However, careful pruning and, if necessary, removal of excess bunches, can ensure that each vine is burdened with no more than it can handle. So, to harvest ripe bunches, growers should increase plant-density but decrease the charge per plant.

One of Guy Accad's most difficult tasks is to persuade his client Domaines to accept the third strand of his attack and to delay their harvest. Philippe Senard, not by instinct an early picker, was asked to further retard his normal harvest date by two weeks. There is less risk than one thinks,' says Accad, 'if the vine is healthy there is less chance of malady.' He prefers, for example, to have 25% rot in otherwise ripe grapes, which can be cut out, than rot-free grapes which are unripe.

Accad is in no doubt that ripe fruit is absolutely essential for Grand Vin. It contains more, and more complex, aromas than unripe fruit (think of a ripe/unripe apple) and the ripe tannins which accompany it taste rounder and softer. Late harvesting also intensifies colour and minimises the need for *chaptalisation.* In his view vignerons should take more trouble to produce the ripest grapes and to find out what is in them. They will then be in a much better position to decide how to vinify them given, of course, the requisite knowledge.

There is nothing in these views that is revolutionary or that most of the great growers along the Côte would not accept – although some might take issue with the wisdom of a systematically late harvest. The real controversy starts in the cuverie.

Accad stresses that no two vintages are identical and so the broad schema of his wine-making is not to be regarded as an inflexible formula – as some of his critics say. Indeed, he complains that there is too much wine – good and bad – being made on the recipe principle and criticises those who regularly use the vintage as an excuse for poor quality. Most of the variance in wine-quality from year to year is more justly ascribed to the wine-maker than to nature. What it is essential to appreciate is that, even in two analytically beautifully ripe vintages, there will be important differences in grape quality. If the fruit changes, so must the vigneron's way of vinifying it.

It follows therefore that one has to identify, as closely as possible, the characteristics of the vintage. This does not simply mean a crude analysis of acid and sugar levels but rather, for example, determining the thickness of the skins and deciding whether they are the sort of skins which readily give up what they contain or not, because some do and some don't. Only when you know what is in your grapes do you make an intelligent decision about how best to vinify them.

From Accad's perspective, vinification comports a series of choices; you must know what questions to ask and the options opened up by possible answers. Some questions may be answered automatically: for example, Pinot Noir will make red or white wine, but a vigneron with a vat full of Grand Cru Chambertin is unlikely to expend much conscious energy on weighing up these particular alternatives.

Accad's views on what constitutes a Grand Vin are relatively straightforward: 'A Grand Vin is usually a *vin de garde.*' In Burgundy, the notion of a Grand Cru is inextricably linked to the ageing potential of its wines. He tasted a Nuits-St.-Georges 1909 recently and found it to be still deep coloured and sound. To those who counter that such wines were cut with something inferior, he ripostes with the question, 'Cut with what – what could live for 80 years except for a Grand Cru?'

His conclusion is that to arrive at Grand Vin it is necessary, though not alone sufficient, to make *vin de garde*; in short, wines with plenty of colour, aroma and taste. To achieve this, it is necessary to develop a method of vinification which not only extracts the desirable elements from the grapes and rejects the undesirable ones, but which also retains them once extracted. For example, there is little point in extracting a deep colour with a long pre-fermentive maceration, unless you realise that these pigments are inherently unstable and have some plan for stabilising them.

Whilst these goals may be desirable, Accad admits that most growers do not have the detailed knowledge to achieve them: 'you must know the alphabet in order to write . . . there are certain stages at which you must leave me to produce the wine.' This is not arrogance but rather a comment on the difference between intermediates and experts, especially at critical stages of vinification. However, both he and his clients are emphatic that it is not Guy Accad who makes their wines, but they. Although Accad will not work for clients who do not accept his Grandes Lignes of policy, his role is one of consultant, not wine-maker.

These Grandes Lignes are easily stated: the bunches are partially destalked (50–75%), the precise level depending upon intuition and feel, and the grapes sulphured at the rate of 2–3 litres per tonne (2–3 times the usual dose). The pulp is then cooled to 8–15° C. and left to macerate for 5–10 days. Thereafter, fermentation starts slowly and continues, at a maximum temperature of 30° C., until all the sugar is consumed, when the *vin de goutte is* run off without any further maceration. Once the press wine has been added, the new wine is put into cask where it receives a classical *élevage.*

It is important to understand this vinification as an integrated whole, rather than latching on to one or another detail. Accad's strong reliance on colour as a good indicator of a wine's development and his belief that the best colour and aroma compounds are extracted both before and during the early stages of fermentation, in the absence of alcohol, are what actuate his use of both $S0_2$ and cooling to achieve a long maceration.

In fact, the purpose of the high levels of $S0_2$, which many focus on as the hallmark of Accad's vinification, is principally as a solvent, to augment the extraction of colour and tannins, rather than fermentation, since wine yeasts will normally work at the concentrations he employs. However, unlike conventional vinification, where $S0_2$ levels are topped up at each racking and again before bottling, once the initial dose has been added there is no further adjustment.

Accad's doses of $S0_2$ have been criticised as excessive – they lead, it is said, to high levels of sulphites which give the wines a flat, cardboardy taste. His reply is that firstly, if one sums all the small doses of the conventional wine-maker, his are barely higher, if at all, and secondly, that wines so vinified do not taste of sulphites.

Accad's clients are advised to monitor closely both the density and the temperature of their *cuves* and also the speed of fermentation, which Accad believes is a critical determinant of wine quality. Keeping fermentation below 30° C. helps conserve both alcohol and aromas and also minimises the extraction of destructive enzymes.

The rate of change of temperature also plays a part – a slow fermentation will produce different results from a faster fermentation at the same temperature. So whether a *cuve* is *chaptalised* at the start, in the middle or at the end of fermentation must also be considered.

Efforts are made to avoid the common practice of post-fermentive maceration – since the alcohol then present produces a highly unselective extraction leaching out undesirable compounds, in particular enzymes contributing to the irreversible degradation of red wine.

Guy Accad's philosophy is both direct and simple, almost to the point of platitude: since everything one does has consequences, good or bad, it is essential to think through each detail. At each stage, the wine-maker must ask himself: 'Is it necessary to do X?' or, 'Is it a good moment to do X?' or again, 'Why do X at all?' There is too much indifferent wine being produced from unique land and 'tradition' should not be an acceptable excuse for incompetence.

Accad's client-Domaines produce wines which by any unprejudiced standards are impressive – richly coloured, exuberantly aromatic and distinctively individual. Whether these wines can be fairly called 'uniform' or lacking the typicity of their respective appellations must be a matter of individual judgement. Guy Accad and his clients are content to argue that if the wines do have these failings, then so equally do those from conventional growers; but neither he nor they believe that they do. However, some of his clients' wines have been rejected for their *agrément,* on first presentation, so clearly there are those who do find them atypical.

Tasting a cross-section of 1987s, 1988s, 1989s and 1990s from Senard, Grivot, Labet and Confuron left no doubt of substantial differences between *climats* and vintages. The question of typicity is not easily settled in any event; not because the wines are difficult to assess, but because the vast range of styles between the growers in any commune make it impossible to say, in more than very general terms, what constitutes, for example, a typical Corton or Clos de Vougeot. When it comes to individual vineyards, the problem becomes even more intractable. When there are more cold-macerated wines presented, then perhaps the notion of typicity itself will change.

The final criticism concerns the ageing of these wines. There appear to be two separate questions: will the wines last and will they turn into 'typical Burgundy', whatever that may be? There is little doubt from their structure that they will last as long, if not longer, than most conventional Burgundies from similar vineyards. For what they will turn into, there is nothing for it but to wait, since there are no 20-year-old bottles to taste; but, for the 1988, 1989 and 1990 vintages, there seems every chance of a fine future.

Accad's ideas are clearly thought out and cohesive. People will doubtless continue to debate whether his use of heavy doses of sulphur and cool pre-fermentive maceration is genuine innovation or merely a modernisation of traditional practice. The argument is sterile and conclusion immaterial. What needs to be appreciated is that he and his clients are intelligent people, dedicated to improving, as they see it, the quality of Burgundy. Many Domaines who retain Accad's services already enjoy internationally high reputations. Their decision to make fundamental changes in their viticulture and vinification must be recognised as courageous and their motives respected. Inscient critics, who latch on to one or other aspect of the 'Accad method', taste a few wines and find them out of keeping with what they consider to be proper Burgundy, and condemn Accad and his clients, contribute nothing to what is an interesting and important debate for those who care for the Côte d'Or.

Meanwhile, whatever else they may be, many of the wines already produced under the aegis of Guy Accad are indubitably fine. Even if some should evolve lacking a certain Burgundian classicism, would it be heresy to suggest that perhaps it wouldn't really matter?

From Grower to Consumer – How Burgundy is Sold

Although only some 50 km. long and between 500 and 2,000 m. wide, the Côte d'Or is in fact a highly fragmented patchwork of individual small vineyards divided among upwards of 4,000 growers. Each of these growers owns an average of 5 ha. of vines, spread over several appellations, from each of which he will produce a different wine.

So, a typical grower might have in his cellar some ten different wines – a Bourgogne Aligoté, some Bourgogne Rouge or Blanc, perhaps two or three Village wines, several Premiers Crus and one or two Grands Crus if he is lucky . How does all this wine find its way on to the market?

Whilst the wine is still unbottled the grower has 2 choices: either to sell it in bulk or to keep it and sell it in bottle. If the former, his customers are likely to be the négociant houses who in the main own no vineyards, but rely on a network of small growers to supply their needs. It has been estimated that some 60–70% of all Burgundy currently passes through the hands of the négoce, although the proportion will be significantly less in the Côte d'Or because so many Domaines now bottle and sell directly.

If the grower chooses to keep the wine and bottle it, then he can either label the bottles and sell them at his cellar door to private customers, or at less exalted prices wholesale, or he can leave the bottles unlabelled and sell them to négociants who find themselves short of stock.

In practice, there are three stages at which a grower can sell his wine to the négoce – 'sur le marché' as it is called – i) as grapes, juice or very new wine, ii) in cask, or iii) in bottle. Many négociants have annual contracts with a large number of growers offering different appellations throughout the Côte – by this means they make up a list to offer their customers.

These arrangements, which may or may not oblige the négociant to take the crop, are often unwritten gentleman's agreements which have been in place for decades. The good négociant knows his vignerons personally and will give them advice and technical help to ensure they end up with the quality that meets his particular needs.

The better houses will only buy-in grapes or unfermented juice and vinify the wine themselves; this gives them complete control and freedom to make the wine in their preferred style. The less careful tend to buy finished wine and then rear and bottle it in their cellars. The least quality-conscious houses buy unlabelled bottles, 'sur pile', and put on their own labels.

However, most of the finest Burgundy is bottled by the Domaine who made it and sold in bottle. This has been an accelerating trend, even for smaller Domaines from less prestigious appellations. At the turn of the twentieth century, virtually all Burgundy made its way through the négociant system. This remained so until relatively recently: in 1970 only some 5% of all Burgundy produced was sold in bottle by the Domaine which produced it; now, in the Côte d'Or, that percentage is probably nearer to 50.

However, for a variety of reasons, it sometimes happens that a top Domaine has wine which it would prefer to dispose of in bulk. For example, it may have cash-flow problems – great vignerons are rarely talented financiers; or again, in years when the crop is dilute or when, perhaps, a few casks turn out sub-standard, a Domaine may choose, rather than compromise its reputation by selling under their own label, to sell 'sur le marché'.

Although there is nothing in law to prevent a grower and his bulk customer dealing directly with each other, for a multitude of reasons most prefer to use the services of a 'courtier en vins' as a go-between.

Courtiers have been an established part of the marketplace for centuries. They thrived in the Middle Ages, when communications and travel were difficult, going about among the growers and merchants making a market in whatever was for sale. Courtiers were known to have existed in Beaune in 1375 and, despite modern communications, have remained an indispensable part of the trading structure.

There are presently some 60 courtiers in the Côte d'Or. These are independent operators, often just one man and a secretary, without any formal qualifications, holding no stocks, who may be approached by either a prospective seller or buyer – to dispose of the surplus of one or to fill the cellar of the other. The courtier is expected to know the market and to source supplies or find clients. Each Domaine works with a small band of courtiers which it trusts and, conversely, a conscientious courtier will specialise in a limited number of appellations. Since there tend to be periods of intense activity, a single courtier could never manage to cover more than a handful of communes.

Apart from relying on the courtier for his contacts, a purchaser will expect him to oversee each transaction. Curiously, whilst elsewhere in France the courtier invariably works on commission from the buyer, with the large number of small lots he will generally transact in Burgundy, custom decrees that both the purchaser and the seller pay him commission – the usual rate being 2% from the one and 3% from the other.

For this he is expected to deliver tasting samples and to ensure that the wine eventually delivered matches that ordered. However, although he sends the client the bill for his purchase and is responsible for any faults the wine may have, the contract is between grower and purchaser, so, if the grower considers the customer to be a debt risk, then he can refuse to deliver.

Although many négociants value the personal contact involved in dealing direct with the growers who supply them, others prefer the anonymity which courtiers provide. Time-wasting travelling and social pleasantries are dispensed with, and hundreds of samples can be tasted without moving and rejected without embarrassment.

Another species of middle-man, with whom the courtier is frequently confused, is the 'représentant'. This entity – often a company – arranges with Domaines or growers to sell their wines, usually in bottle, on a regular basis. But, unlike a courtier, the 'représentant' will generally produce a catalogue of the wines he has to offer and the larger firms will also have some kind of marketing and distribution organisation. He may also choose to add a profit margin, over and above the normal commission, to cover increased overheads.

Nowadays, the finest Domaines in the Côte find themselves in such demand that, with more customers than stock, they are able to dictate precisely to whom their bottles are sold. Some prefer to concentrate on 'La grande restauration', often measuring their prowess by the number of three-star Michelin establishments featuring their wines.

Many growers take their eating as seriously as their drinking, and enjoy the reciprocity involved in supplying such as Lameloise,

Troisgros, Chapel or Taillevent. Dine, on a Friday or Saturday evening, at one of the more exalted local troughs and you are almost bound to find an uncomfortably overdressed or nonchalantly underdressed wine-grower and his family working their way through the Menu de Dégustation with evident delight, fussed over by the proprietor ever hopeful of an increase in his meagre allocation.

Other growers concentrate on exports and deal only reluctantly with private customers or restaurants. They point to the twin benefits of larger individual orders and less time taken out of over-charged days for social politesse and tasting. Some communes – Chassagne and Pommard, for example – have tried to solve the problem by setting up shops where a number of growers' wines are offered for sale. This saves the customer the trouble of finding and visiting several growers, and the growers the trouble of receiving him – particularly awkward when there is a language barrier which reduces communication between the parties to exaggerated hand-signals and an assortment of inadequate facial contortions. However, such shops undeniably take much of the pleasure out of the transaction.

Even so, there has been a steady trend towards direct sales along the Côte. From Easter to late autumn swarms of wine loving tourists descend on Burgundy to replenish their cellars and to visit their favourite growers. International media attention has turned some of these hard-working sons of the earth into minor celebrities. In many cases, although most wouldn't admit to it, their egos enjoy such frequent ritual massaging and they start to develop modest eccentricities to embellish their act as they expatiate on this technicality or on that vintage, leaning on a barrel or wandering from cask to cask, pipette in hand.

Some, however, are genuinely bemused by all the attention they receive and find it difficult to understand what the fuss is about. However they face the problem of dealing with endless personal callers, most growers welcome the cash and exposure that they bring and there is no doubt that the trend is set to continue. If the astute growercan lever a price advantage out of the process, so much the better.

Many vignerons deliberately sell a high proportion of their production outside France and enjoy taking their families off on exotic wanderings to see where their wine ends up. Such arrangements have sown the seeds of many now long-established friendships between grower and importer over the decades. Others, disliking travel and the anonymity of foreign markets, prefer to sell to French and European customers, with whom perhaps they feel they have more in common. However they eventually distribute their wares, most vignerons take pleasure in the thought that their bottles are finding their way on to tables where they will receive an informed and comprehending appreciation.

In the end, whether a buyer gets anything at all, and indeed how much he pays, may depend on nothing more sophisticated than the whim of the grower. If he doesn't like you, however impeccable your credentials, you plead in vain. Equally, there is always a case or two to be squeezed out of precious stocks for the favoured few. How many buyers have made to leave, after an hour or so of tasting, downcast to find their hesitant request for wine met by an expressive shrug accompanied by the ritual lamentation: 'I have nothing at all to sell,' only to have their spirits uplifted moments later with the vestige of a smile accompanied by, 'but I will go and see if, perhaps, I could find you a few bottles.'

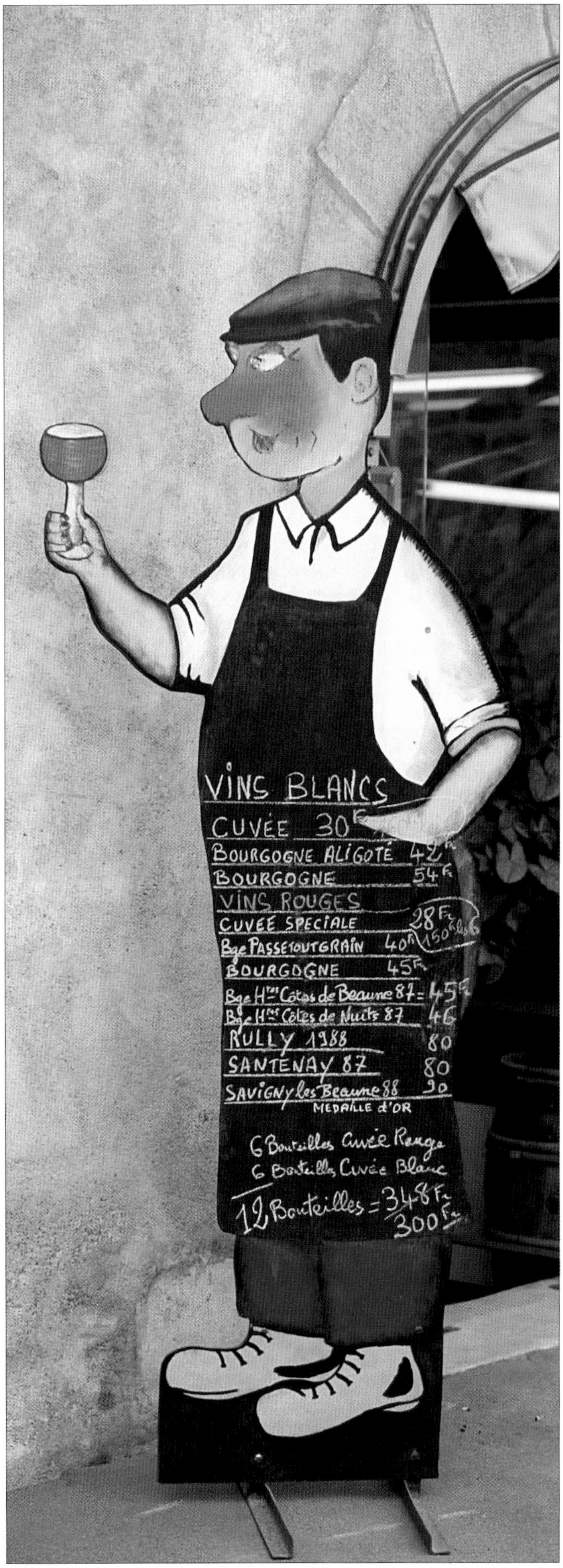

One way of selling your wine – direct to the consumer

Buying and Enjoying Burgundy

In the 1990 vintage, there were 4,400 individual growers declaring a harvest in the Côte d'Or. Assuming each grower bottles 6 wines, one arrives at a total of 26,400 Domaine-bottled wines finding their way on to the market. Among these will be more than 60 different Clos de Vougeots, as many Echézeaux, at least 15 Montrachets, a plethora of Pulignys and a positive tidal wave of Nuits-St.-Georges. How can a prospective buyer hope to find his way through the maze?

Burgundy is a minefield – a buyer's nightmare, where quality often bears little relation to price and where vested interest and ineffectual controls give unscrupulous growers year-round open season on the ignorant or the gullible.

Unfortunately, even if you know which Domaines to buy from, available quantities of the best wines are pitifully small and demand regularly far outstrips supply. What is available, especially in top-flight vintages, is eagerly sought after and rapidly snapped up. This leaves legions of unsatisfied trade buyers wandering round the Côte looking for reliable sources of supply, whilst private individuals find themselves paying their local merchants hefty mark-ups for the golden Domaines, if they manage to get an allocation.

However, whilst supply cannot be increased and there are few bargains, certainly at Grand and Premier Cru levels, it is possible to buy fine Burgundy provided you are prepared to take a little trouble and are not mesmerised by labels.

Recent vintages have seen good crops of excellent wine and recession has left growers with comparatively full cellars, but this modest glut is unlikely to last for long. It only needs a vintage or two of moderate quality to put growers back in the driving seat.

Anyone contemplating building up a cellar of Burgundy, whether traders or private buyers, must ask themselves: where to buy, what to buy, how to buy and when to buy? Fortunately, unlike Bordeaux, in Burgundy larger and smaller customers usually compete on equal terms, since growers have small stocks and tend to enjoy the personal contact which the Bordelais sometimes seem anxious to avoid. Prices are non-negotiable and quantity discounts virtually unheard of – for all but the more plentiful *régionales*. So what is the best strategy ?

Where to buy? If quality matters, then there is no alternative to the type of grower profiled here, or else to one of the handful of reputable négociants. Covering Burgundy by the grower route is both time consuming and costly in shipping and administration if you buy direct, or in locating importers and retailers if you buy locally; the négociants, on the other hand, offer a full range of appellations although rarely of uniformly top quality – in short, a one-stop shop.

In most countries without import restrictions, it is possible to find merchants who specialise in Domaine-bottled Burgundy. For those wanting mixed cases and advice, these can represent an excellent source of supply. However, the range may be restricted and availability limited, so it may be necessary to deal with more than one merchant. Most conscientious merchants will offer periodic tastings – often of single vintages or Domaines – which are a useful means of education and of deciding what to buy. It is important, however, to steer clear of persuasive prose and to make up one's own mind as far as possible, free from a merchant's influence.

For older wines, auction houses are often worthwhile hunting-grounds, but it is important to be sure that fill-levels are acceptable and that storage has been appropriate. For some unexplained reason, Pinot Noir seems to support a greater ullage in bottle (loss of wine) than Cabernet-Sauvignon. Bottles with up to 5 cm. from cork to meniscus can be excellent, provided the colour is sound and the wine clear. Chardonnay, however, is more susceptible to level and older wines should be examined for browning – a sure sign of oxidation.

What to buy? There is no alchemy by which age will transform poor wine into something fine, so laying down indifferent Burgundy, even of a great vintage, is a waste of time, cellar space and money. However, there is much to be said for trying to build up sufficient supplies of young, decent, wine to enable bottles to be kept until they are mature – after all, that is what most growers make them for.

It will be clear from reading the grower and commune profiles that, whilst the top wines are in short supply and beyond the pockets of most people, there is plenty of interesting Burgundy to be found below the stratosphere. The less popular communes, such as Monthélie, St.-Aubin, Marsannay, Auxey-Duresses etc., are well-worth mining for good sensibly-priced wine.

At the everyday level, many of the top growers make sensibly priced *régionales* – Bourgogne Rouge and Blanc, Côte de Nuits or Beaune Villages – which receive much the same skill and care as the Grands Crus. These are not cheap, but there is much more pleasure to be had here than from an incompetently made, and in all probability more expensive, Village or Premier Cru. If in doubt, try a comparative tasting – one sip should convince you.

Once you have found a clutch of growers whose style you like, then there is plenty to be said in favour of sticking with them from vintage to vintage. Certainly, no Domaine is without its failures as well as its successes, and none is immune from the caprice of weather or fate. However, providing you steer clear of really appalling vintages (of which there are very few nowadays), a reputable grower's name on the label is a better guarantee of pleasure than either vintage or vineyard from elsewhere.

The second-rank vintages often offer some of the best bargains – merchants may bypass them because they are anxious to avoid being landed with unsaleable stock, and the grower prices them attractively for similar reasons. The reality is that the best vigneron will make a respectable job of 9 out of 10 vintages, so the chance of encountering a really disappointing wine from a Great Domaine is slender.

Unfashionable vintages, such as 1987, 1986 and 1982, in fact produced some concentrated and delicious wines which, whilst not quite in the top class, are well worth buying and laying down. In any case, it is much more rewarding to be pleasantly surprised by a wine of which one had low expectations than to be disappointed by the unfulfilled promise of a great vintage from a botcher.

We live in an age of gurus. There is no shortage of experts willing to rush into print on a vintage, barely before the vats have ceased to ferment. The growers refuse to judge in this way, but these people seem to know better. Some are qualified and experienced tasters, but most, unfortunately, are not. Unlike merchants, these pundits are rarely answerable for their mistakes. If you find someone whose opinions you trust, then follow them; but, in general, there is no substitute for forming your own judgements.

How to buy? If you are an importer or wholesale buyer, then you can buy either direct from the Domaine, or through a broker. The section on 'How Burgundy is Sold' explains how the system operates. For a private buyer, the best answer is a friendly and trustworthy merchant. Whilst those near enough to visit Burgundy can enjoy the experience of visiting Domaines and tasting first-hand, they soon realise that many of the best growers are reluctant to receive individual visitors – at least without a personal introduction – and even if they manage to breach the front door, they are likely to come away empty-handed.

This reflects neither cussedness nor arrogance, although being turned politely away may often seem like a personal affront, especially if you have come half-way across the globe to worship. The scale on which wine is produced in the Côte means that many Domaines are family operations, run by husband and wife with the help, perhaps, of a couple of workers. Visitors consume a great deal of time, which they can ill afford, let alone the cost of opening expensive bottles for tasting. If, in addition, a Domaine can sell its entire produce several times over with a few telephone calls, there is little incentive to receive visitors. If you feel that there is any risk of rebuttal, come armed with an introduction and an appointment.

However, for many of Burgundy's better Domaines, receiving visitors is part of their way of life and there are few who do not respond warmly to genuinely interested wine-lovers, provided that they are given reasonable notice. Direct sales have grown substantially over the last twenty years, especially to regular Swiss and German clientèle who invade the Côte from Easter to All Saints, re-stocking at advantageous prices and having fun into the bargain.

When to buy? Time was when merchants, unhurried by inflation or demand, would make two or three visits to their selected Domaines, tasting in cask and in bottle, before placing their valued orders. Now, if you are lucky, you receive a fax with an allocation which must be confirmed within weeks, if not days, long before the wine has come anywhere near to seeing a bottle. The price is usually non-negotiable and often carries the unwritten rider that if you don't like it a queue of suppliants are ready to pay up, there and then. Importers who try to skip a disappointing vintage soon find they have forfeited their place in the queue when the next five-star one comes along.

This pressure has found its way to the consumer – if you don't buy 'en primeur', then you risk having to pay more, or worse, getting none of your favourite Domaine's wonders at all.

A succession of over-hyped, over-priced vintages in the Côte has left many buyers disillusioned and overstocked. Following the almost universal media misjudgement of the 1983s, many trade importers have become wary of confirming orders before they have had the chance to taste the wines in bottle. The realisation that a wine which is a well-proportioned, elegant and irresistible maiden in cask, can rapidly turn into a gnarled, shrivelled and thoroughly resistible old witch in bottle, has caused people to rely less on advance press ratings and more on their own convictions – a welcome trend.

Buying 'en primeur' can only be justified when the quality is so high and the market so short of stock that the chance is unlikely to recur. These circumstances being rare – once in a decade possibly – dispassionate caution should override instant gratification.

What of the future? Whilst there may be temporary hiccups in supply and demand which work to the buyers' advantage, the long-term picture is clear – tiny quantities of superb wine from a coterie of top Domaines being chased by an ever-increasing international market. In such circumstances prices must rise. The best wine-makers are becoming cult figures, and their wines demanded by those with the money to pay for them.

For the careful buyer, things are not entirely gloomy. There may be no escape from the price-spiral for the finest Burgundies, but there is much of quality and interest a little further down the pyramid. In addition to the starred growers one knows about, there are many lesser luminaries whose mentality is gradually changing from a policy of quantity to one of quality. Younger, more skilled wine-makers are returning to the Côte, attracted by better prospects and viable returns, to take over from the old guard as they retire, and with them the prospects for finer wines from what are now mediocre Domaines.

However, while lovers of Bordeaux wallow in vast quantities of excellent wine, with plenty of other fine Cabernets to turn to if prices rise too far, the aficionado of Pinot Noir is left with little alternative to Burgundy – *pace* the handful of estates outside Burgundy making respectable efforts to tame this fussy grape.

Cellaring and drinking Burgundy Enough has been written about how to treat wine – even-temperatured storage, laying bottles down, decanting an older wine off any sediment and so on – to make reiteration unnecessary. However, there are some points especially relevant to the wines of Burgundy which are worth highlighting:

1 Fine white Burgundy, although lacking in tannin, needs keeping as much as red. The best of Puligny, Corton and Meursault, whilst often delicious young, will give so much more if they are kept for a few years; how long, of course, depends on the style of wine and on the vintage. In general, Grands Crus will benefit from longer in bottle than Premiers Crus, which in turn mature later than straight Village wines.

2 For all Burgundies, but white wines in particular, the warmer their storage the faster their maturation.

3 Much of the quality of fine white Burgundy is lost if overchilled. This loss is often irreversible. Putting a precious Puligny in the freezer may chill it quickly (even this isn't certain) but will do it little good. Half an hour in an ice-bucket is better for the wine and just as effective.

4 In general, red wine is far more robust than the neurotic anxieties of some collectors and commentators would have us believe. It can withstand a fair amount of moderately rough treatment without too much complaint. While perfect cellarage conditions and service are the ideal, they are rarely the reality. Those with imperfect cellarage, too warm a dining-room or no decanters should take heart. Too often is inherently poor quality attributed to defective handling.

5 Decanting: much pointless hot air has been expended on this subject. What should be remembered, above all, is that wine contains many highly volatile substances which contribute to its complexity and which may be irretrievably lost if a bottle is opened too long before drinking. In addition, decanting aerates the wine, provoking further changes from this contact with oxygen. Whether or not you decant is a matter of personal preference. It helps with young wines artificially maturing them – but is less advisable with older bottles.

6 Too often red wine is damaged by being left in an overheated room before being served. The Pinot Noir is capable of magnificently complex and abundantly subtle perfumes which are easily destroyed by heat which rapidly releases the more evanescent into the surrounding atmosphere. The French term 'chambré', used to describe the room temperature at which red wines are best drunk, reflects a temperature of around 18–20° C., rather than the near tropical Paradise of many modern centrally-heated dining-rooms.

Tasting Burgundy

However much one reads about a wine region, there is no substitute for tasting. And tasting, far from being a recherché art as many believe, is a skill that can be aquired by anyone with normal sensory acuity and the self-discipline to practice intelligently. What matters above all is the willingness to exclude prejudice and to taste honestly.

Taste is many things: in one sense, it cannot be imposed – one person's taste differs from another's; in another, it denotes specific qualities which can be described and discussed. In the sense that one can have good or bad taste, it is also a term of evaluation. All these play a part in tasting wine.

Much has been written by way of introduction to the mechanics of tasting – Broadbent (1970), Spurrier & Dovaz (1983) and Peynaud (1987) all provide useful background material and advice. This short essay is not to supplant these excellent sources, but to indicate what one should be looking for in a wine, and especially in Côte d'Or Pinot Noir and Chardonnay.

It is worth restating the oft-forgotten fact that physiologists only recognise four true tastes: acidity, sweetness, bitterness and saltiness, of which all but the last are important in wine. Beyond these, there are 'taste sensations' – temperature, viscosity, volume, texture, astringency etc. – which also form part of a wine's overall taste profile. Together with a vast array of aromas and flavours, these provide the raw material which the taster has to analyse, describe and assess.

Tasting is complicated by the fact that aromas and flavours do not exist in isolation but interact, reinforcing or masking one another. For example, sweetness masks acidity, alcohol enhances sweetness, tannin can hide fruit etc. These interactions can be powerfully distorting, especially in young wines, since it takes time for a wine's constituents to integrate and for its true quality to emerge.

In any well-made wine, no single characteristic should dominate – fruit must balance acidity, acid must balance alcohol, and in red wine all must balance tannins. This does not mean that the components of taste and aroma cancel each other out, rather that they constitute an active harmony – the dynamic balance of the gymnast, not the passive equilibrium of the sleeper.

What constitutes good balance remains subjective, but one soon develops a sense for wines which are out of kilter. Young wines often appear jagged and unharmonious, which makes them difficult to judge. Only by experience does one learn to recognise an imbalance which is unlikely to be corrected by age.

In addition, a wine's quality is measured by its length (how long the flavours linger after swallowing), persistence (how far back on the palate the taste goes) and complexity (each sniff and mouthful giving something different). However renowned or expensive a wine, if it lacks these qualities then it is not really great.

Tasting blind is a most exacting skill, and the only true test of a wine's intrinsic worth. For anyone learning to taste, it is also invaluable for sharpening the palate and developing an unprejudiced sense of quality. Every effort should be made to taste blind as often as possible.

Making a final quality assessment often provides the taster with the severest test – his ability to exclude the potent influences of reputation, politeness, occasion, or just the opinions of those tasting nearby. It is here that self-deceit creeps in, often bolstered by the fear of being a lone dissenter. All too frequently tasters appear to forget that the quality of a wine is not determined by the label on the bottle, but by what is in the glass.

Whatever the circumstances, one should develop a systematic routine of looking at, smelling and finally tasting wine, in order to discern the strengths and weaknesses of its component parts as a preliminary to deciding its quality level, how well it has aged or will develop, whether or not to buy it, or how it compares with whatever else is being tasted. There is no substitute for tasting and comparing both within and between regions and grape varieties.

In all this ritual, one should never forget that, whatever its individual characteristics, a wine is invariably more than the sum of its constituent parts. Neither should one lose sight of the fact that wine is for drinking, not the raw material for some sort of analytical gymnastics. In general, a wine should be pleasurable to eye, nose and palate; it should have balance between its constituents – acids, alcohols and tannins etc; and above all, it should have a good measure of ripe fruit. Any excess or deficiency compromises quality and risks upsetting a smooth evolution.

Of all the sensory qualities, aroma is especially valuable, since it most powerfully reflects the typicity deriving from *terroir* and grape-variety, its type and intensity are key feactures of wine assessment. Grapes contain two different substances – directly smelling odour molecules and those which are only 'precursors' of aromas. While the former are dominant in aromatic varieties such as Muscat which, as grapes, taste much as they smell, the latter are some 20 times more concentrated in non-aromatic varieties such as the Chardonnay. However, being tied to sugar molecules, these 'precursors' are non-aromatic in their pre-fermentive state and rely upon fermentation to detach and transform them into fully aromatic compounds. During this phase, aromatic concentration rises by a factor of 5–6 as the typicity of the grape begins to emerge.

The temperature at which grapes are fermented is a major determinant of a wine's aromatic quality. Whilst Pinot Noir seems capable of fermenting at relatively high temperatures – up to 35° C. – without undue aromatic distortion, the Chardonnay is more sensitive. Above an ideal band of 17–25° C., aromatic intensity increases sharply, but to the detriment of finesse and freshness; below, fermentation produces some-what colourless, neutral wine, with little varietal characteristics. The importance of temperature also applies to tasting and is not peculiar to wine; many flowers smell different in different conditions – time of day, dry or humid atmosphere, hot or cold temperature. This is nothing more than subtle modification in volatile, organic compounds, common to many forms of plant life, which alters their aromatic profile.

Tasting young wine, especially in cask, is generally more difficult and less gratifying, than tasting something mature. It is also more challenging, since young wines tend to present themselves as an awkward amalgam of unharmonious constituents – rather like a pile of bricks, from which one is invited to imagine the finished building.

In casks, wine changes rapidly from week to week, particuiarly when it is moved, racked, fined or filtered, and dramatically just after bottling – a shock from which it may take months, or even years, to recover. Moreover, different casks of the same wine may taste very different – new wood from old, racked from unracked – so cask samples can only ever be an approximation to the finished product.

It should perhaps be added that, atmospheric as they often are, cellars are physically inconvenient places for tasting, since artificial light and cold distort a wine's qualities. Henri Jayer's uncompromising advice is to taste in the cellar by all means, but to re-taste back home in controlled conditions, and he cautions buyers against the grower's exotic prose and carefully rehearsed asides about dwindling stocks and having sold all but the last few cases yesterday to some illustrious client.

To the eye, Pinot Noir rarely gives the dense, impenetrable appearance one often finds in young Cabernet-Sauvignon or Syrah, although some growers with very old vines, practising long *cuvaison,* may produce extraordinarily dark wines. However, lightness must not be confused with lack of substance – a wine may appear almost rosé yet be packed with concentrated, ripe fruit. Young Burgundy can vary in hue from garnet to black-cherry, and from light to dark in saturation; the spectrum is wide.

Hue and depth are valuable indicators of a wine's age and likely development. Young Pinot often comes with a purple colour component, dervied from anthocyanin pigments which are later transformed into a more stable deep red. In addition, the finest red Burgundies are often accompanied by a limpidity, a softness of tone, which is particularly distinctive and attractive to the eye.

Whatever the hue, it should form a continuous 'robe', from centre to edge of a tilted tasting-glass. A watery meniscus or a degradation of colour is not an encouraging sign. Prematurely brown or brick-edged reds or dull ochre-tinted whites, often the result of too long in cask or over-exposure to oxygen, are unlikely to age satisfactorily. Whilst white wines may be hazy or turbid during *élevage,* in bottle they should be bright and clear and pale straw, green or yellow-gold.

On the nose, young wines may present themselves in a variety of ways. Chardonnays can be flowery or not and Pinots can smell of *petits fruits rouges,* or *fruits noirs* – or, sometimes, of nothing at all. During *élevage* the intensity of aroma may change from exuberantly fruity to dumb and unforthcoming. This is normal and explains why, in assessing young wines, one relies less on aroma and more on basic taste components.

A wine which has spent time in new oak will generally have a marked toasty or vanilla component to its aroma. This often dominates for a year or two, making it important to look underneath to ensure that there is enough fruit to keep the wine alive. The ability mentally to put aside attensive wood or tannin is a skill only developed with practice.

On the palate, because of the absence of significant tannins and 'green', stalky flavours, young Chardonnay is generally more approachable than young Pinot. To compensate, white wines must have enough acidity to ensure a sound development in bottle. Insufficient acidity is a common fault in Chardonnays, especially in very ripe Burgundy vintages such as 1983 and 1989.

Fine Côte d'Or Pinot Noir spans a wide spectrum of flavours – often characterised by a strong element of soft berries – pure, ripe, crushed fruit, mouthfilling and succulent; the wines of the Côte de Beaune, whilst similar in style to those of the Côte de Nuits, tend to have less density and muscle and are not quite so long-lived.

In general, all that can be usefully extracted from very young wine is a rough idea of its underlying structure and depth – acids and tannins being less susceptible to short-term change than aromas and flavours. This provides a valuable guide to overall quality and ageing potential. It is also essential to identify any glaring deficiencies – such

A tasting in progress in London

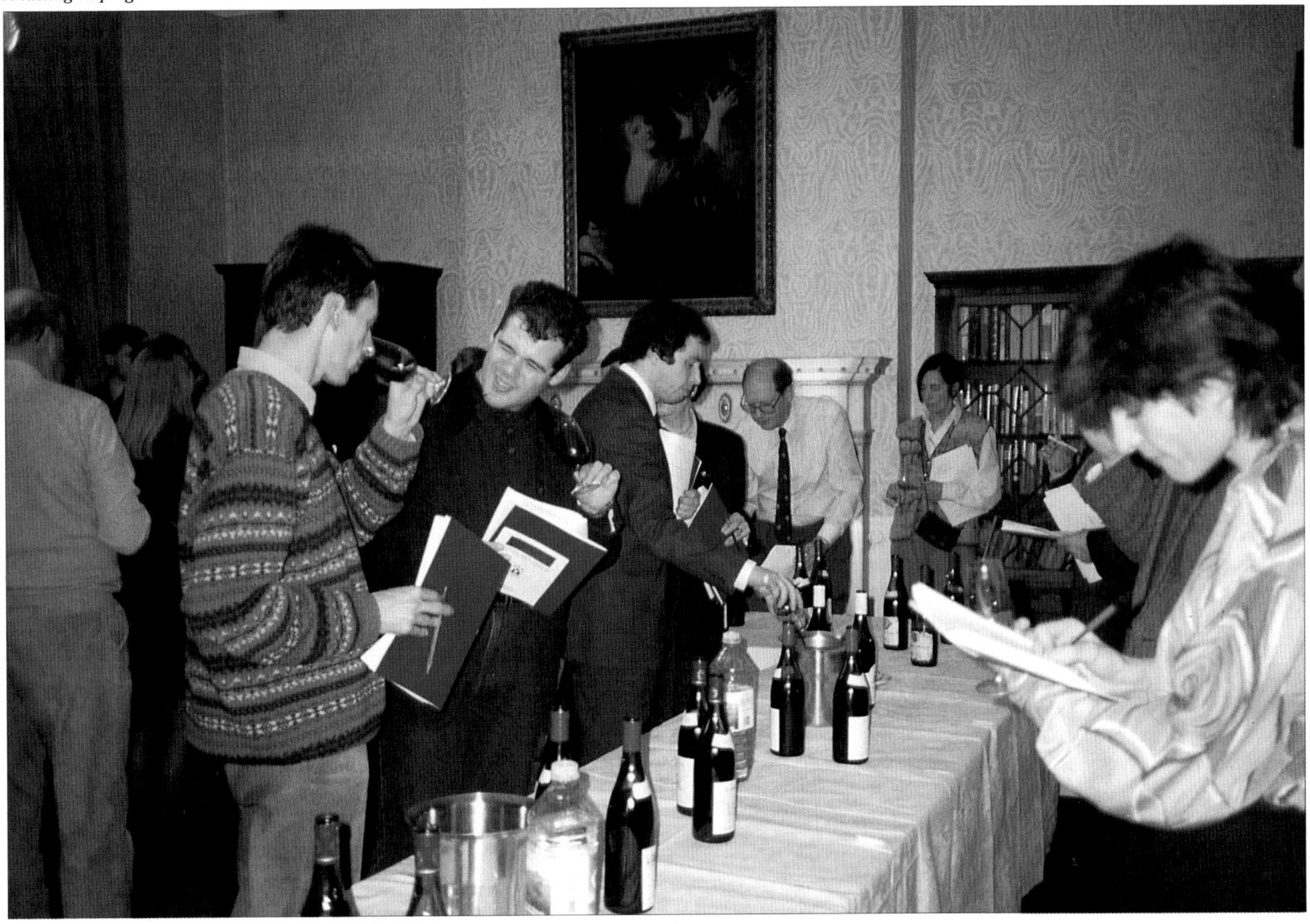

as dilution, a lack of fruit or an irremediable taste of rot – and to be aware that wines change dramatically during their *élevage*, making any early assessments vulnerable.

Although some wines are attractive, even drinkable, from cask, it is with age that great Burgundy comes into its own. Once in bottle, deprived of the opportunity for freely combining with oxygen, a wine undergoes a much slower, more subtle transformation. Reactions between its various chemical constituents – principally alcohols, acids and tannins – gradually alter its colour composition, lightening reds and deepening whites, and produce trace quantities of a variety of volatile, highly aromatic compounds, in particular esters, which contribute significantly to aroma and flavour.

With time, a wine's protection from oxygen lessens and it starts to change. The Pinot Noir, not darkly-coloured by nature, loses redness and develops a brownish tinge, whilst the Chardonnay sheds its youthful green glint and deepens towards yellow or gold. These changes are accompanied by a shift from the primary fruit and floral based smells to more subtle and complex dried fruit and broadly vegetal aromas in the Pinot, often with strong hints of violets and mushrooms, and to those of honey, lime-blossom and nuts in Chardonnay. Wines open out, in both aroma and flavour, and their individual elements integrate. A mature Pinot or Chardonnay should be pure, uncluttered by new wood, and richly fragrant. The time span of a wine's evolution will depend on its individual character; those with more structure – tannins and acids in particular – will be slower to reach maturity and will remain at their peak for longer than those with weaker frames.

Over the years, aromas become more elegant, with notes of animal, visceral and musk in reds and the more oxidative smells of nuts and butter in whites. Pinot Noir can also develop hints of leather, fur and especially *sous-bois* (undergrowth, leaves etc.) and sometimes well-hung game. However, these tertiary aromas do not develop entirely at the expense of fruit – Pinot Noir often reverts to its more youthful fruity aromas (strawberries, raspberries etc.).

The finest of old Pinots have great richness and opulence – fruit which is beautifully ripe, almost sweet, with a silky, velvet texture and complexity and balance which inspire admiration. A great Burgundy should have power and subtlety, depth and delicacy and, above all, something intriguing which makes each sip a revelation.

The great white Burgundies are no less enthralling. After 5–10 years they begin to reveal a richness and elegance, allied to a powerful backbone. The best are invariably understated, complex and intense but never overblown – inviting the drinker to exercise his imagination and to read between the lines, rather than having every detail set uncompromisingly forth.

Tasters should always be on the alert for faults. Whilst nowadays one seldom encounters Burgundy which is defective to the point of being undrinkable, there are many subtle faults, usually indicating laziness or poor wine-making, which can scar a wine for life. A frequent problem in the Côte's marginal climate is a lack of ripe fruit, giving thin and hollow wines. At the opposite extreme, too much over-ripe fruit (e.g. in intensely hot vintages such as 1976 and 1983) gives unpleasant, cooked, jammy flavours – a failing more often encountered in New World Pinot Noir.

Other common faults relate to the use of wood. Excessive new wood will mask the fruit in a wine and destroy its finesse and typicity. Equally, too long an *élevage* in either new or old oak, dries out a wine – it simply loses freshness and the flesh of its fruit – leaving in their place a more less tannic, acidic and meagre skeleton.

Over-chaptalisation either to increase volume or to mask other faults, is responsible for much dreadful Burgundy. Whilst the resulting extra alcohol and glycerol may give wines greater smoothness and thus some initial appeal, to the experienced taster they invariably mask a lack of real depth or interest.

Rot, with its distinctive, musty stamp, is often found in Burgundy. While marginally more tolerable in Chardonnay, it usually indicates a deliberate disregard for quality and an inexcusable carelessness in sorting grapes. In 1983, many growers failed to eliminate rot and their wines are indelibly tainted.

In the cellar, over-use of sulphur ($S0_2$) – in careful doses a valuable aid to ensuring stability – is all too often a sign of sloppy wine-making. Excessive sulphur blunts freshness – particularly in white wine – giving an unpleasant, pungent aroma and a flat, cardboardy taste. A newly-bottled wine may smell strongly of $S0_2$, but this should dissipate with time. With experience one develops a sense for excess.

Mature wines can show additional faults: bottles can be corked – an unfortunate, rare accident; or oxidised – making whites flat and sherryish and reds unpleasantly stale. Wines can be volatile – a distinct whiff of vinegar which may enhance a wine in small quantities but is unpleasant in concentration; or they may be maderised – usually the result of overheated storage.

Superimposed on the general personalities of Pinot Noir and Chardonnay are the individual taste characteristics of the various vineyards and communes along the Côte. However, combining these with the immense diversity of growers' wine-making styles makes the notion of a 'typical' Gevrey, Chambolle, Corton, Volnay or anything else difficult to sustain. Although, by tasting the wines of reliable growers, one does learn to identify broad stylistic differences between communes, for anyone learning to taste Burgundy, it is more profitable to concentrate on the spectrum of flavours and aromas that characterise fine Pinot Noir and Chardonnay than on what to expect from Pommard or Chassagne.

The grading system of the Côte's appellations leads one to expect, above all, a gradation of complexity, finesse and power as one ascends the ladder. What therefore, in broad terms, differentiates Grand Cru from well made Bourgogne ordinaire? Analytically, not much – the main differences lie rather in dimensions which are not susceptible to quantifiable molecular analysis. The grander the appellation the more should its wine have subtlety and nuance, length and persistence, depth and interest, complexity and power, and so on. To the senses, it is aromatic complexity and depth of flavour which provide the most reliable signals of quality. The former is doubly important, since taste contains a strong aroma component.

If a true Grand Cru should be an amalgam of finely-judged balances, for the unofficial accolade of really great wines – Grand Vin – a wine must have something extra. Here, what one is particularly looking for is class – something exciting but indefinable, which cannot be reduced to specific qualities. Class is, arguably, the one element of tasting which cannot be learned through experience – one either has the feel for it or not. What is certain is that if you have to search too hard, it probably isn't there. Even young wines, difficult and gawky though they may be, will show class, paradoxically, through all their youthful rough edges. Class seems to give a wine an indelible stamp – a birthmark which it carries for life. Wines often come near to having class, but fail through trying too hard – with just too much of everything, too ostentatious and revealing; the 'show-it-all' of the body-builder rather than the relaxed, elegant poise of the dancer.

Words, by themselves, can never do justice to the nuances of great wine. This is how it should be – especially in the Côte d'Or, where such rich diversity makes the task of appreciation so challenging. Great Burgundy is rare and expensive, but the effort necessary truly to appreciate it is more than recompensed by what, after all, is the purpose of drinking – the pleasure it provides.

REFERENCES AND BIBLIOGRAPHY

Useful literature on Burgundy is scant. Much of what there is is either general and discursive or else inaccurate. Henri Cannard's Balades en Bourgogne and his series of booklets on individual communes are a mine of interesting historical and social information. For up-to-date tasting notes, Clive Coates' The Vine, a monthly periodical, is authoritative and reliable. On a more technical level, the proceedings of the Institute of Masters of Wine Symposium (1982) on 'Viticulture, Vinification and the Treatment and Handling of Wine' are a useful source of research information. The proceedings of the American Chemical Society's symposium on Alcoholic Beverages (1980) and those of the several Subject Days held at the Long Ashton Research Station, Bristol, Avon, UK in the late 1970s and early 1980s, also provide useful overviews of various aspects of table wine making and handling.

Guy Accad and Philippe Senard where quality really begins – in the vineyard

BECKER, HELMU T (1982) Breeding wine grapes for cool climates in Geisenheim – white and red varieties. *Inst. of Masters of Wine, International Symposium.*

BROADBENT, J. MICHAEL (1970) Wine Tasting. *Wine and Spirit Publications. London.*

BROADBENT, J. MICHAEL (1980) The Great Vintage Wine Book. *Mitchell Beazley, London.*

BROADBENT, J. MICHAEL (1992) The Great Vintage Wine Book II. *Mitchell Beazley, London.*

CANNARD, HENRI Balades en Bourgogne (Tome II). *Imprimerie Pornon, Dijon.*

DUIJKER, HUBRECHT (1977) The Great Wines of Burgundy. *Mitchell Beazley, London.*

GADILLE, ROLANDE (1967) Le Vignoble de la Côte Bourguignonne. *Université de Dijon, Paris.*

HANCOCK, PROF. J.M. (1967) The Geological Controls on Wines *(unpubl. manuscript).*

HANSON, ANTHONY (1982) Burgundy. *Faber & Faber, London. (New edition in preparation.)*

KUNKEE, RALPH E. & GOSWELL, ROBIN W. (1977) Table Wine. *Economic Microbiology, 1 315-386.*

LAVALLE, DR. JEAN (1855) Histoire et Statistique de la Vigne et des Grands Vins de la Côte d'Or.

LEGLISE, MAX (1976) Une initiation de la dégustation des grands vins. *Défense et Illustration des Vins d'Origine, Lausanne.*

LENEUF, NOËL (1988) Terroirs Viticoles en Bourgogne. *Cahiers du Centre d'Etudes Regionales de Bourgogne, No. 4. 27-52*

LENEUF, NOËL (1983) Influence du Sol sur la Qualité des Produits en Viticulture. *Assocn. Intl. des Entretiens Ecologiques, Dijon.*

LICHINE, ALEXIS (1982) A Guide to the Wines and Vineyards of France. *Cassells, London.*

MERIAUX, S., CHRETIEN, J., VERMI, P. & LENEUF, N. (1981) La Côte viticole. Ses sols et ses crus. *Bull. Scientifique de Bourgogne, v.34, 17-40.*

NAUDIN, RENÉ (1989) L'élevage des vins de Bourgogne en fûts de chêne. *BIVB, Beaune.*

PETERSON, R.G. (1976) Formation of reduced pressure in barrels during wine ageing. *Amer. J. Enol. Viticult. v.27, 80-1.*

PEYNAUD, ÉMILE (1987) The Taste of Wine. *Macdonald Orbis, London.*

PITIOT, SYLVAIN & POUPON, PIERRE (1985) Atlas des Grands Vignobles de Bourgogne. *Jacques Legrand, Paris.*

POMEROL, C. (ed.) Geological Journeys. *Robertson McCarta, London.*

ROBINSON, JANCIS (1986) Vines, Grapes and Wines. *Mitchell Beazley, London.*

SIMON, ANDRÉ (1946) A Wine Primer. *Michael Joseph, London.*

SINGLETON, V.L. (1982) Oxidation of Wine. *Inst. of Masters of Wine, International Symposium.*

SPURRIER, STEVEN & DOVAZ, MICHEL (1983) The Academie du Vin Wine Course. *Century Publishing Co. Ltd., London.*

WARNER, R.H. & JOHNSTON, A.E. Proceedings of the Fertiliser Society, No. 72.

YOXALL, HARRY (1968) The Wines of Burgundy. *Michael Joseph, London.*

VINTAGES 1945-1991

These notes represent a general indication of the climate, character and evolution of 45 vintages in the Côte d'Or. In reading them, it must be remembered that the vintage is only one tile in the total mosaic, especially in Burgundy where the grower, vineyard and micro-climate are all of equal, and sometimes greater, importance. With small yields, thorough *triage* and careful wine-making, a skilled vigneron will often surpass the overall quality of the vintage, especially in the more difficult years.

Neither can the differences between individual communes and vineyard sites be ignored; drainage, vine exposition and micro-climate can all distort the general vintage pattern, for good or ill, and when you add fertilisation, vine age, pruning and the difference between an early and a late harvest, the picture becomes unmanageable. This is why the integrity of the grower matters so much.

The localised weather pattern of the Côte can also vitiate any global assessment. A severe hailstorm or snap-frost, in an otherwise good vintage, may mean that the vines of one commune, or even one narrow strip of vineyards, are damaged beyond the redemption of even the most skilled of vignerons.

If a grower cannot buck the weather, neither can the finest of growing seasons compensate for incompetent vinification. A vintage assessment is never more than a large canvas, whose confident broad, brush-strokes hide a wealth of variation between communes and, within communes, between individual Domaines.

In these days of easy travel and instant communication, the international reputation of a vintage is fixed almost before fermentations are over – often earlier. Merchants, who cannot themselves hope to visit all their sources every year, need to 'know', as early as possible, whether the vintage is one to buy or to avoid.

This creates unhealthy pressure on the market, especially on the best Domaines which now demand early reservations if you are to stand a chance of getting a decent allocation of stock. The days of tasting each vintage twice or more in cask and again after a year in bottle before making a buying decision are, in all but the leanest vintages, over.

The public perception of each vintage is largely formed by journalists and commentators. Some are authoritative and reliable, many are not. There is usually nothing tentative about their judgements – the vintage is either black or white – and they wield disproportionate power, particularly over distant markets which seem to relish being led by the nose and lack the opportunity or the spine to judge for themselves.

Unfortunately, these premature assessments seem to cement the rating of a vintage for good and all, which is generally neither accurate, nor good for the consumer. As with harvesting, the benefits of waiting outweigh the disadvantages; growers would do themselves and the public a service if they refused tastings of new wines to all but the bona fide trade, until they were bottled and properly ready to be evaluated.

Reading the assessments which follow, it should also be remembered that after a short time, the storage conditions of a bottle of wine, of any provenance, will play a major part in determining what it tastes like. Bottles of either colour which sit, unsold, in restaurant refrigerators or in sunny shop-windows for long periods will not be improved by the experience, whereas well-cellared wines from distant decades may still be lively and interesting.

With age, bottles progressively develop ullage – that is, wine is lost and the space between cork and liquid increases. Why some wines ullage more than others is something of a mystery, but cork quality and storage undoubtedly contribute. Whilst Chardonnay seems to suffer unduly if the level in the bottle has dropped by more than a centimetre or two (clarity and colour are the best indicators with white wines), Pinot Noir is less susceptible; provided the other signs are good - bright, sound, translucent colour etc. – ullages of several centimetres are perfectly tolerable.

There is an idea abroad that Burgundy does not live for very long. This is a myth. As Michael Broadbent (1980) succinctly put it: 'Well constituted (red) Burgundy will last as long as a good Bordeaux. Lightness of colour and style can be misleading: the key is the intrinsic quality and balance of the component parts.'

These notes, therefore, must be read with all this in mind. At the end, whether one would get more pleasure from a bottle of second- rank vintage from a fine grower than from a bottle of five-star vintage from a botcher, must remain a matter of personal judgement.

1945

Given the lack of materials and the poor state of the vineyards, it is remarkable that wines of such a high standard were made throughout viticultural France in this wartime vintage. In the Côte d'Or, adverse weather conditions greatly reduced the crop size. Severe frosts in March and April were followed by a cyclone which swept through the Côte de Beaune at the end of June. Hot weather throughout the summer, with very little rain, further concentrated an already small harvest. This resulted in red and white wines of considerable depth and extract which have generally lasted well. Much wine was shipped abroad in cask adding to the variability. However, well-cellared wines from this vintage are still providing interesting, and sometimes spectacular, drinking, and show no signs of falling apart.

1946

Having tasted no 1946 Burgundies, it is difficult to comment on their qualities. However, the vintage has the reputation of being a sound one, of reasonable volume. Cold, rainy weather and hail in August were balanced by a late spell of hot weather. The wines appear to have been less well constituted than either the 1945s or 1947s, and most will now have been drunk .

1947

1947 was, and is, an extraordinary vintage. A long unremittingly hot, dry summer ripened and concentrated the grapes to an exceptional degree. One commentator reckons that one has to look back to 1865 to find such high natural sugars in the Côte. Unfortunately the heat at harvest time in mid-September caused many growers difficulty vinifying, since they had no sensible means of cooling the *musts*. In general the 1947s are, as in St. Emilion and Pomerol, rich, opulent wines, with a seductive dimension of fleshy ripeness and extract. High alcohols sometimes resulted in an imbalance and a lack of finesse, but none the less, the reds seem to have held up beautifully – even well-made Village wines continue to give pleasure. This, like 1959, was a vintage to confound the chemists – analytically the wines had so little acidity that they had no business lasting.

The white wines generally suffered from an excess of alcohol and without the prop of tannin, many were blowsy and overblown. Occasionally, though, one comes across a middle-aged delight – a 1947 Hospices Meursault, for example, bottled by Lébègue, was still a mouthfiller, albeit a bit raw and nutty, in 1990. It is worth remembering that many of the négociant reds of this era – up until the 1970s – were beefed up with a dollop of Algerian gut-scorcher or Côtes du Rhone – which significantly added to their richness, although it took away their typicity – A magnum of anonymous 1947 Corton tasted in London in the mid-1980s was nothing other than delicious old Grenache.

1948

Climatically this was an unusual year – a sunny spring followed by cold and rain during the flowering, and a coolish summer with a redeemingly warm and dry September. The grapes were of no more than average ripeness, and gave wines with reasonable fruit and depth. Extrapolating from a limited sample, there may be some pleasant surprises for those with well-cellared bottles. They are, however, overshadowed by the 1947s and 1949s .

1949

Another irregular growing season – a dry and sunny April produced a fine 'sortie' of grapes, which were promptly decimated by prolonged rain during the flowering. Thereafter the summer was notably dry, although some late storms gave much needed moisture to swell the grapes. Picking took place at the end of September giving a crop that was about half the normal, for both reds and whites. This last factor contributed significantly to the overall balance and longevity of the Vintage. The 1949s are characterised by their equilibrium – better acidities and lower alcohols than the 1947s – and by their finesse. For example, a Beaune Grèves from Albert Morot tasted in early 1991 was still deeply coloured, with a fine, complex, old Pinot, nose, intense *sous-bois* and musky aromas, and showed no signs of wanting to put up its feet and relax. In short, a great vintage, of considerable vinosity and finesse, which continues to give pleasure.

1950

Not a vintage to get excited about – humid to start with, then some fine weather up to July when intermittent rain and hail conspired to dilute the crop. Any bottles are best drunk without delay.

1951

1951 is as near to appalling as Burgundy is likely to get; everything – rain, frost, mildew – except hail, had a go at destroying the crop. In general the vegetation was at least a month behind normal. When harvest finally arrived, in mid-October, the juice was miserably dilute. *Saignée de cuve* not then being a weapon in the vigneron's armoury, the inevitable followed.

It is worth bearing in mind that adding wine from a better to bolster a less good vintage was not uncommon, so although any 1950s and 1951s are unlikely to be exciting, they may just be drinkable.

1952

This started off with a warm spring and summer and even flowering – all the early elements of a great vintage. A dry June and a hot July and August would have been too much had not rain fallen on 15 August. The vintage started during the first week in October and a very small crop was harvested. The quality, especially of the reds, was generally very fine, with rich well-structured wines, quite silky in texture, but with enough tannin to keep them from falling apart. Pleasant memories of this vintage include some excellent English and Scottish bottlings throughout the 1970s and 1980s and a magnificent Vosne-Romanée Les Suchots from Gaston Grivot (Jean's father). Romanée Conti – the first vintage after the 1946 replanting – tasted in the mid-1970s, was superbly perfumed, but rather slender and ephemeral on the palate. In contrast, the 1952 La Tâche was rich, complex and gloriously silky.

1953

At the end of May the vines were 3 weeks in advance of their normal maturity. However, normality was restored by a wet and cold June and July, followed by a warm, fine August and September. A late September harvest gathered in a crop of ripe, healthy grapes. This is perhaps the first of the fine Burgundy vintages of which many of the post-war generation of wine merchants have wide experience, since they could still be found with reasonable ease in the early 1970s. The wines apparently started life with considerable charm and 'souplesse' – and, although not structured like Methuselah, seem to have aged remarkably well. The Domaine de la Romanée-Conti produced some stunning wines – the La Tâche tasted on several different occasions in recent years seems still at its silky, seductive best: length, class, and great delicacy.

1954

Late flowering, a wet summer and a cold and humid September meant an October harvest. Despite all these vagaries, the wines have a good reputation. If a solitary example – a fine, complex and well-balanced Chambolle-Musigny from the Barolet Collection – is anything to judge by, there may be some unexpected pleasure in store for anyone with a bottle of 1954 in their cellar.

1955

Up to the middle of August the weather was wet and cold. However, like 1978 in Bordeaux, the vintage was saved by a hot, sunny spell in August and September which continued right through the early October harvest. The wines, although they apparently started life with plenty of attractive, supple fruit, have collectively crumbled. Apart from a few Grands Crus which have kept going – a particularly fine Bonnes Mares from a Lébègue English bottling and a lacy but gently fading de Vogüé Musigny come to mind – bottles from this vintage should be broached without exaggerated expectations.

1956

Growers everywhere in the Côte still talk of the great frosts of 1956, when thermometers plummeted to minus 27° C – and stayed there. This destroyed many vineyards – further north, Chablis was devastated – and was followed by rotten weather throughout the spring and summer. A warm September was not enough to save the vintage, which produced meagre wines of little merit. However, there are always exceptions: a 1956 Domaine de la Romanée-Conti Grands-Echézeaux tasted at the Domaine in 1991, was reported to be complex amd sound, if somewhat transitory on the palate.

1957

There are some delicious, fine and well-constituted wines from this vintage, whose reputation has suffered from the rather hard, charmless 1957 clarets. A fine start to the vegetative cycle and a particularly warm, sunny September and October framed a somewhat uneven summer, see-sawing between heat and cold. The Côte de Nuits seems to have lasted better than the Côte de Beaune, with some very fine wines from the best Domaines. Rousseau's Clos de la Roche is still a splendid, complex wine, with a fine balance and the richness and depth of which that Domaine is so eminently capable. The Domaine de la Romanée-Conti's Echézeaux and Richebourg are both delicious wines with finesse and good length – although the Echézeaux is becoming a bit chocolatey. This is a much underrated vintage; if you find anything from good growers or reputable bottlers, they're well worth a try.

1958

The closest one needs to get to this vintage is its reputation – dilute, charmless wines with little character, even at the outset it was ruined by a cold, watery late summer, which swelled the grapes beyond any hope of reasonable concentration. They certainly will not have lasted; if you have any 1958, try cooking with it.

1959

Rarely a disappointing bottle from a reputable source in this vintage. The growing season was virtually of textbook quality – an even, relatively short, June flowering, followed by dry, sunny and hot weather throughout the summer, punctuated by enough September rain to balance out juice and solids. Picking began in mid-September and continued in fine conditions. The grape-skins were very ripe – in some places the Chardonnay was slightly over-ripe – and the stalks were also brown rather than greenish.

These conditions gave beautifully structured wines, firm and fleshy, with plenty of tannin to sustain them. If there was a general fault, it was a deficiency of acidity. However, although analytic write-offs for this reason, the wines have lasted superbly. Whites, in good condition, are often still magnificent; half a dozen bottles of a Lébègue Bichot Montrachet, drunk (not 'tasted'!) during the 1970s and early 1980s, were without peer – rich without vulgarity, deep without heaviness, *surmature* without figginess and, above all, with inspiring complexity and length.

The reds are just as fine – big, deep wines with both softness and structure, and plenty of nuance and personality. The Côte de Beaune, for once, was not to be outdone by the Côte de Nuits – an Ile de Vergelesses from Chandon de Briailles, drunk in late 1990, although light in colour had all its wits about it and a great deal of charm besides; there was no shortage of either fruit or scaffolding to support this elegant grande dame. There is no reason why well-cellared bottles from good growers should not still have something thought-provoking to say.

1960

As with so many vintages, a promising start to the year degenerated into an uneven summer, chiefly notable for its lack of both sun and warmth. A late harvest, with a high incidence of rot in the grapes, augured badly for the wines. Apparently there were some attractive *cuvées,* if light on fruit and structure, but, unless they were bolstered with some 1959 or 1961, they will have become weak-kneed and decrepit.

1961

Although what happens in Bordeaux has no bearing whatsoever on events in Burgundy, vintages seem to develop an aura of quality from Bordeaux which they never entirely shake off. Whilst 1961 in Burgundy was a good vintage, it was never a great one. An abnormally long flowering, attended by both *coulure* and *millerandage,* significantly reduced the potential crop size. Although an uneven summer, with some very cool spells, threatened to extinguish the promise of an unusually warm spring, a dry, warm end-of-season put the vintage back on its rails. The harvest took place in late September, in excellent conditions, and healthy, if unevenly ripe grapes were delivered to the vats.

This is a difficult vintage to evaluate. For a

start, the Burgundians consider it as a great vintage, of considerable longevity, whereas outside the Côte it is normally regarded as good, but not great. There is no doubt that the whites are fading fast, if they have not expired altogether; there may be the odd bottle of top-class Grand Cru which is still fine, but it must be a gamble.

For the reds, the picture is variable; there are some dreadfully dull and lifeless wines, but some delightful surprises. There appears to be no obvious pattern. A bottle of Domaine de la Romanée-Conti Echézeaux tasted in London in the mid-1970s seemed four-square and rather weedy; however, a Vougeot Vieilles Vignes from Pierre Ponnelle, opened in late 1990, was full of vigour, fruit and charm, and by no means moribund. Anyone with bottles from this vintage would be well-advised to drink them soon; whatever their quality, they won't improve .

1962

This is another vintage for which there is no pattern on which to base any useful generalisation. The vines were sluggish to start because of a cold, sunless spring. However the flowering passed off normally, albeit late, and from then on the weather gradually improved. A hot late season with just enough rain promoted a largish harvest of healthy, well-ripened grapes. Both reds and whites were successful – the reds in both parts of the Côte – with balance and finesse, if not massive concentration and structure. Having tasted very few recently, with the memorable exception of a remarkably fine and opulent La Tâche, the best advice for those with bottles is to drink them. If they are from top-notch Domaines there need be no unseemly haste; if not, go for it!

1963

One might conclude that the only reason for buying, keeping or, still worse, drinking a 1963 Burgundy of either colour is its rarity value. A miserably wet summer following an exceptionally late flowering was beyond redemption, even by a fine 'arrière-saison'. The harvest was barely ripe and highly dilute – qualities which best describe the wines. Although 1963 Bordeaux turn up from time to time in odd corners of the marketplace, 1963 Burgundies do not. Perhaps, as Michael Broadbent diplomatically put it, 'some of the little birds fluttered into congenial nests'.

One wine, however, remains a shining exception. A Montrachet from the Domaine des Comtes Lafon, enjoyed on at least 4 occasions over the past decade, is indeed a remarkable curiosity. For a start it needs a couple or hours or so to breathe – otherwise it gives very little. When it does perform, it doesn't hesitate: a magical nose of distinct *surmaturité* (one top Swiss wine merchant blind-guessed it as an old Sauternes from the nose alone) is followed by a flavour of great profundity; nothing vulgar or 'deshabillé' about it, just a magnificently long, complex mouthful of immense class. Félicitations René!

1964

1964, with 1969, are the best vintages of this decade. A cool spring preceded a short, untroubled flowering, a warm June and a very hot July. There was just about enough rain in August to restore equilibrium and a mixture of sun and rain in September rounded off the season. Drought had been avoided, but the thick skins of the grapes gave red wines with a distinctive, fleshy solidity. The whites have a lumpen, rustic quality about them which is not attractive and which was probably congenital. However the reds have blossomed attractively, throwing off their excess muscle, to reveal finesse and class. A Musigny from Clair Däu, tasted recently, was in splendid fettle – a ripe, complete wine, showing little sign of completing its first quarter of a century and every sign of carrying on for another.

1965

A cold, wet, sunless summer followed by a soggy September left no chance of harvesting ripe grapes. Those that were eventually picked, in mid-October, were dilute and heavily scarred with rot. Even the greatest, most careful, Domaines failed to make anything of merit.

1966

A good, abundant vintage, saved by a fine 'fin de saison'. After an indifferent summer hopes for the vintage were not high. However, September was hot with enough rain to keep photosynthesis going, and a late harvest saw a higher than average crop of ripe, healthy grapes. These translated into quite firm wines, with a sound tannic underlay and, although it took some time to appear, plenty of elegance. There was much that was fine in 1966, from up and down the Côte. The great whites were by and large superb – the good growers in Meursault, Puligny and Aloxe-Corton producing attractive, balanced wines which had both the flesh and the acidity to keep them in trim for a couple of decades, although they are now beginning to show the strain. The reds have become, and are still, charmers. Beautifully perfumed mid-weights, with good fruit and a slightly firm elegance. Well-cellared bottles of Premiers and Grands Crus should still be delicious.

1967

The main climatic features of the year were a late frost which covered the entire Côte on 4 May, a spate of scattered summer hailstorms and nearly two weeks of unremitting rain in September. The frost reduced the crop size, the hail selectively damaged what was left and the rain promulgated widespread rot. Despite these vicissitudes, those who were careful made some good, but not great, wine. The reds seem to be fast losing, or have already lost their initial febrile charm. They were always delicately balanced, with a highish acidity waiting to take over once the fruit began to dry out. From tasting notes, the whites were much more successful, with some delicious Corton-Charlemagne and most attractive Meursaults and Pulignys. However, it would be rash to buy them now, and what remains should be rapidly drunk.

1968

Almost the reverse weather of 1967 – with a cool, rainy July and August and only a marginal improvement in September. Both red and white wines were disastrous. Even the Hospices de Beaune admitted defeat and put no wine up for public sale.

1969

This is a vintage in which there is a wide variance in quality – some wines are very fine indeed, others less so. The flowering, which by and large determines the date of the harvest, was late. Fortunately the weather, a damp, cold spell in September apart, helped the vines catch up, although a significant degree of *millerandage* reduced the crop volume. (*Millerandes* are highly concentrated embryo bunches which never fully develop; however they make a significant contribution to quality.)

The Côte de Beaune produced some magnificent whites – not big, fat wines but wines in the more aristocratic mould, with firm, structured lines and heaps of finesse and vinosity. Well-kept Meursaults and Pulignys, especially the Premiers and Grands Crus from top growers, should still be lively and complex.

On the overall quality of the reds, it is more difficult to comment. While some of the best Domaines made very fine wines, there are some singular disappointments – memories of a weedy and unbalanced Chambolle, Les Amoureuses from de Vogüé, a lifeless, prematurely senile Bonnes Mares from Clair Däu and a rather cooked, uninspiring La Tâche come crowding in. Those with bottles in the cellar should try them and take a view.

1970

A rotten spring, counterbalanced by a warm summer, with a blip in August, and a fine, hot September made for a record harvest which began at the very end of September. If *saignée de cuve* had been common practice, this would be a much more interesting vintage than, in fact, it was. Tasting notes attest, with odd exceptions, to mostly pale coloured, quite pretty wines which have not developed well – insubstantial, uncomplicated and fading fast. The whites have fared no better.

1971

From its youth this was a gilded vintage. Rather like the 1971 in St. Emilion and Pomerol, the 1971 Burgundies, both white and red, started with their hearts on their sleeves. *Coulure* at flowering, which sheds flowers and thus reduces the crop, followed by a long hot summer punctuated by some August hail, resulted in well ripened skins and a fine concentration of juice. The Côte de Beaune, which suffered most from the hail, produced a small crop of superlative whites and some immensely seductive reds. The whites still continue to give pleasure – an Hospices Meursault Cuvée Grivault, French bottled by Lébègue was firm, rich and deep in 1989 – on its way to a delightfully nutty old age and a Chassagne Morgeot, from Ramonet-Prudhon, sampled in early 1992 was magisterially powerful and complex, a fine wine, not just a necrophiliac curiosity.

The reds, provided they have been well cellared, are still remarkable drinking. A warm, opulent and complex Volnay Taillepieds from de

Montille, quite wondrous Beaune Marconnets, Bressandes and Grèves from Albert Morot (an experienced taster thought that the Bressandes was La Tâche, so rich and complex was it), a ripe, youthful, Santenay La Gravière tasted in 1991 with Adrien Belland in his cellars, some fine English bottlings, notably from Averys of Bristol, and a well-nigh impeccable La Tâche from Domaine de la Romanée-Conti – the litany is endless.

This is a vintage which has evolved well – more attractively, in general, than their Libournais counterparts. However, both reds and whites are 'à point' and should not be kept too much longer to catch them before they lose their eminently seductive charm.

1972

This was a vintage which was virtually unsaleable, at least in the UK, until relatively recently. It was initially misjudged – partly, no doubt, because of the weak-kneed 1972 Bordeaux, and also because of the huge size of the crop. The weather conditions demonstrated again the marginality of the Côte d'Or climate – a cold, damp spring, late flowering, followed by a cool, dry summer and then a magnificent September which brought the grapes to relatively healthy maturity and thereby saved the vintage. The white wines never really caught the imagination, although Michael Broadbent reported some to be 'very stylish'.

The reds, however, many of which started out with such mouth-puckering acidity that they were abandoned by their growers as untastable, have, with perverse torpor, thrown this off and quietly evolved into wines of some distinction. Many, tasted with growers during late 1990 and early 1991, are thoroughly worthy bottles for current drinking – a few have real finesse and depth. Most have an attractive old Pinot gaminess, without the opulence and depth of the 1971s. There are probably more surprises than disappointments for those with 1972s in their cellars in the early 1990s. However, they are wines for drinking over the next few years and will not repay much further keeping.

1973

Initially a warm, very dry summer, preceded by a good, even flowering, promised a fine vintage. However, intermittent heavy rain from the middle of July through to the harvest in late September and most of October washed out this hope. Limited experience of the reds justifies their reputation as 'light, pallid and undistinguished' (Broadbent, 1980).

The whites are altogether different – generally firm, structured wines with considerable aromatic development, which have aged well. This is largely attributable to the earlier harvesting of the Chardonnay, thereby avoiding the deleterious effects of autumn rain. A Corton-Charlemagne from Tollot-Beaut, tasted in 1990, was in fine condition with a splendidly deep colour, a nose of grilled almonds and lime-blossom and a tight, masculine flavour of length and distinction. So well-cellared bottles of 1973 white, of respectable provenance, should still be sound and even interesting.

1974

1974 in general is abysmal, for both reds and whites. A moderately good summer was ruined by an atypically cold, wet harvest. The wines were dilute and lacking in both stuffing and balance. From time to time the odd bottle of 1974 red surfaces and surprises – a St.-Romain tasted in 1989 was still alive, though hopelessly over-endowed with acidity and under-endowed with fruit – but the whites seem to have disappeared into oblivion. One occasionally sees wines from this vintage on French restaurant lists, at escurient prices – perhaps they know something we don't?

1975

If anything, the wines were even worse than 1974. A good, warm spring and early summer gave way to miserable weather, which persisted, apart from a spell of dry, sunny weather at the end of August, until the harvest at the end of September. Humidity provoked widespread rot and hail in July and August – especially in the Côte de Nuits (Vosne was particularly affected) – simply made matters worse. The result was a dismal array of wines – many irremediably rot and hail tainted, otherwise dilute and fruitless.

Many Domaines who ought to have known better put out wines under their own labels – it did nothing for their reputations, but after 1973 and 1974 the decision was probably actuated by more than a touch of economic necessity.

The much-publicised report of a tasting of 1975 wines from the Domaine de la Romaneé-Conti in London in April 1980 in which it was generally concluded that, even judged as restaurant carafe wines they all left much to be desired and should never have been sold under the Domaine's label, brought a swift and scathing rebuke from Mme. Bize-Leroy. Her asseveration was that the Domaine's wines need time to evolve and, as she staunchly maintains, much longer in lesser than in greater vintages. The wines, however, are still dismal – how long does one have to persevere before the Domaine admits its mistake?

Oddly enough there are one or two white wines of fine quality. A Meursault Monatine, from Domaine Rougeot, is still drinking beautifully – rich, ripe and round – nothing thin or second-rate about it. Apparently, it was Marc Rougeot's first vintage and when his father tasted the wine he swiftly pronounced on the incompetence of his son, bottled the wine and put it aside. Years later it started to blossom and has continued to do so. No doubt Rougeot père apologised profusely!

1976

A long, hot European summer, when people in cities sweltered, roads melted and the air hung leaden and breathless. The vines, as well as the humans, suffered from the drought and heat, and had to dig deep to pick up moisture and nourishment. Despite a very early *veraison* and an atypical early September harvest, the Pinots were deeply coloured and high in tannins and extract. Many growers found that the concentration of the *musts* made for difficult vinification – thick skins seemed to require a long, slow *cuvaison,* yet they were aware of the dangers of extracting too much tannin.

Those who rushed to snap judgements when the vats were barely empty proclaimed another 1947 or 1959. Unfortunately, as the wines began to develop in bottle it became apparent that they had a serious excess of tannin and would take some considerable time to come round. Growers tell you, in 1991, that you must have patience and wait – even so, there is no certainty that you will end up with something more than middle or upper-middle class.

Many of the reds are still closed up, big, burly, tarry specimens which lack balance and breeding. Some of the whites are still attractive – a Chassagne Les Ruchottes from Ramonet-Prudhon was full and nutty in an old-fashioned sort of way in 1990 – but they tend to have low acidities which have presaged a premature decline. The best advice to those with bottles of either colour is try one and see.

1977

In general, a vintage of indifferent wines. The summer started very wet, but the rot which threatened never appeared; catastrophe was averted by a warm, sunny September. However, the grapes failed to reach reasonable natural sugar levels and much *chaptalisation* was needed to achieve any sort of balance. Limited experience evinces a vintage profile of dilute gutless wines with too much acidity – at best light and lean. There are, apparently, some better structured whites, but they must be falling apart by now.

1978

This is an 'annus mirabilis' both for the weather and for the wines. Cold and rainy weather prolonged the flowering and brought with it both *coulure* and *millerandage,* which reduced the potential crop size. The weather continued wet and cold up to the last ten days in August. The vines, weeks behind normal maturity, needed a fair spell of dry, hot weather for there to be any prospect of a decent vintage. Then the weather changed and there followed two months of just what was needed. The vegetation caught up until by the middle of October, still in hot sunshine, the harvest started.

It is no exaggeration to say that these last weeks of warmth and dryness made the vintage. Clive Coates records a supplier in the Côte Châlonnaise telling him that his vines added an extra 2 degrees potential alcohol (i.e. sugar) in the last fortnight before picking – it was the same up and down the Côte.

From the start, the fine quality of the wines was apparent – attractive positive aromas, quite fleshy, pliable fruit and sound, moderately firm structures. There was an initial elegance and softness which made for rich, mouthfilling wines, without any signs of the hard, tarry tannins which had marked the young 1976s.

The Chardonnay was more prolific than the Pinot Noir but not, fortunately, to the detriment of the wines – the grape can support higher yields than the Pinot without commensurate loss of qliality. However, there is a certain unattractive quality about many of the Côte d'Or 1978 whites which makes it a much less fine vintage than for the reds. Although there are indubitably some fine wines – Leflaive, Ramonet, Ampeau and Lafon stand out – many, even from good stables, lack finesse and have a thick-skinned, overblown character. Some also, including many of Sauzet's Puligny tasted in London in the mid-1980s, had an unattractive vein of 'limey' acidity which left them with a distinctly dirty finish. This is not to put people off trying 1978 whites, but to temper anticipation with a note of caution.

The reds, however, possess no such problems, having evolved and blossomed into wines of great richness and distinction which will continue to give much pleasure. Unlike 1976 or 1969, where one has to pick and choose, the 1978s from conscientious growers are uniformly delicious, from the humblest Bourgogne to the most exalted Musigny. Whilst the *régionales* should have been drunk by now, the Village wines are drinking well although some from the Côte de Beaune are starting to fade.

In contrast, most of the Premiers and Grands Crus have plenty of vigour and life left and will continue to develop over the next few years. At the luxury end of the scale, there are some truly magnificent wines from many of the Great Domaines which are as good a lesson in what fine Burgundy is all about as one is ever likely to get. Some will happily see in the new century, especially in magnums or larger formats, but they do not, by and large, have the structure to last for another generation. How long you keep them depends somewhat on how you like your Burgundy – with the softer, tender flesh of youth, or leaner and thoroughly well hung.

1979

This was a year of plenty – a huge 'sortie' of bunches and an almost perfect flowering presaged a large crop and although the summer was not particularly hot, neither was it particularly wet. Apart from damage from some severe, but thankfully localised, hailstorms which wreaked havoc around Nuits and Vosne, the bunches remained intact and came slowly to what was, if not perfect ripeness, an acceptable level of maturity. (There are two aspects of ripeness which are often confounded: first, ripeness of the individual components of the bunches – skins, wood and pulp etc.; and secondly, the ratio of solids to liquid in the berries. Analytical ripeness – acids, sugars etc. does not address this second aspect. Both are important for quality.)

This is a vintage in which individual growers' yields were a major factor in determining quality – too high and the wines were hopelessly dilute; moderate, and there was the chance of an acceptable balance. Unfortunately, many of the red wines, especially from the Côte de Nuits and often from impeccable Domaines, have turned out dilute, deficient in both stuffing and tannins.

However, there are some attractive wines about throughout the Côte; Pommard, Volnay and Beaune seem to have been more successful than most communes, but this was a year when try as they might some growers just failed to produce anything more than short-lived, unbalanced wines.

The whites are another story. Here again is demonstrated the ability of the Chardonnay to succeed at relatively high yields. Although they lack the structure and concentration of the white 1978s, the 1979s are noticeably finer. They tend to have an elegance of both flavour and aroma which the former lack. Both Leflaive and Sauzet produced much more stylish and suave wines in 1979 than in 1978, which are about at their peak. Whether, in time, the 1978s will prove to be the finer white vintage must be in some doubt, but meanwhile the 1979s continue to give immense pleasure to those still fortunate enough to have them.

1980

Qualitatively, 1980 is the mirror of 1979 – with the red wines generally eclipsing the whites.

A cold, thoroughly inclement, spring caused the latest harvest of the decade – most growers waiting until the middle of October to pick. Fortunately August and September had been hot and dry, so although the crop was small, it was healthy.

The vintage was generally written off by those who comment in advance on such things. Matters were not helped by Louis Latour, head of the Maison Louis Latour, who gave it out that he had not bought a bottle of 1980. While it is true that most of the white wines were flabby and charmless, the reds have turned out to be delightful and in some cases, superb wines. They are characterised by elegance rather than ample roundness – Gainsborough rather than Rubens. There are some yardstick wines from Dujac and Rousseau – deceptively pale in colour but lacking nothing in power and concentration. Such wines will keep for a few years yet; the rest need drinking.

1981

Louis Latour's vintage report well encapsulated the background to this vintage: 'The 1981 vintage ranks among the smallest of the century, especially for red wines . . . From the outset, meagre quantities of fruit were to be seen on the vines, but successive climatic accidents further reduced the projected size of the vintage.' Specifically, although the vegetative cycle started off well, despite some spring frost, it was not until September that there was any really warm and settled weather. This continued into October, but then storms and hail struck – in particular the northern section of the Côte de Nuits. This both physically damaged the grapes amd diluted the juice. The result was less than half the normal crop.

The white wines fared markedly better than the reds. There are some excellent, if rather skinny, offerings from Leflaive, some attractive wines from Ramonet and Sauzet – a fleshy and beautifully balanced Champ Canet, in particular. They will not be long-lived and should be drunk sooner rather than later.

The reds are generally indifferent. The exigencies of removing all traces of rot and the need for heavy *chaptalisation* put growers to the test. Most failed the challenge. Within the somewhat dismal totality there is the odd bright spot from the obvious perfectionists. A Village Gevrey from Joseph Roty, tasted in February 1991, was quite dark in colour, with a rather imprecise, unctuous sort of nose and a soft pulpy flavour which developed well enough in the glass – perfectly drinkable and respectable, but only grudgingly interesting. Nevertheless, with his customary care, François Faiveley managed to transcend the general mediocrity with a fine, rich and mouthfilling Echézeaux, and elsewhere Jacques Seysses, Charles Rousseau amd Domaine de la Romanée-Conti produced complex and worthy wines. However, in the ensemble, 1981 is not a vintage to be taken too seriously.

1982

This was a year in which, as far as the weather went, nothing negative happened. A warm, sunny spring and early summer produced a full flowering, without significamt *coulure* or *millerandage* and the months which followed did nothing to disturb this embryo bumper crop. Rain in August added to the volume which continued to ripen until the middle of September, when the harvest began.

There were two principal problems growers had to face. Firstly, for many the sheer volume of the crop presented acute problems of storage. There was simply not enough vat-space in the cellars to house the fermenting juice. Anything that could hold grapes was pressed into service – one grower even confessed to be fermentmg some grapes in a bath-tub. Unfortunately, this meant that many growers shortened their vinifications to empty vats for the next batch, with consequent loss of depth, colour and extract. Although the vintage was naturally abundant, the problem of excessive *rendements* is generally self-inflicted. Any grower who is serious about keeping yields within levels compatible with top quality is perfectly capable of doing so.

The second and more damaging problem was the high temperatures at which much of the harvest reached the cuveries. Growers who had the means of cooling their *musts* avoided spoilage; those who did not, and worked on the 'we'll manage somehow' principle, were faced with soaring temperatures in the vats, stuck fermentations no doubt – though it is a matter of pride never to admit to it – and high levels of *volatile acidity.* As a result of this experience, there are now many shiny new heat exchangers to be seen lurking in the corners of cellars or poised above the *cuves.*

The wines have nothing of the qualities of 1982 in Bordeaux. In general the best are well-constituted, with plenty of succulent soft fruit and good depth, though sometimes deficient in acidity. The worst are dilute, over-*chaptalised* and charmless; in short, corsetless pap.

The whites are also a mixed bunch. The top Domaines by and large produced fine wines not for long ageing, but with good ripe fruit and an easy charm. Bottles from Leflaive – especially the Premiers and Grands Crus – Lafon, Coche-Dury and Ramonet have all been interesting and enjoyable experiences.

In short, if you are lucky enough to stumble upon a good wine, there is some attractive drinking from the 1982s; though much of what remains is more or less instantly forgettable.

1983

This is a thoroughly inconsistent and enigmatic vintage, especially for the red wines. The key to understanding it lies in the weather during the growing season. Spring was late in arriving, cold and wet, delaying the rise of the sap in the vines and thus the start of the vegetative cycle. However, May saw a distinct improvement and flowering took place in excellent conditions. From then, until the end of August, the weather was largely hot and dry. However, in July severe hailstorms struck the area bounded by Chambolle-Musigny to the north and Vosne-Romanée to the south, including Echézeaux and Vougeot in between. Then in the early days of September the rains came – nearly three weeks of relentless torrent which, despite some protection from their heat-thickened skins, caused widespread rot throughout the entire Côte. The end of the growing season saw a period of extreme heat, which concentrated the grapes to the point of *surmaturité.* The harvest, which started on 25 September, passed off in fine conditions.

There are several factors in this pattern which it is important to emphasise. Firstly, rot: unless rotten grapes are excised at harvest, then they will irreversibly taint wines made from them. This affects white wines less than reds, since whites are vinified without their skins. Once in situ, rot spreads and is difficult to treat. However, an element of protection is provided by the physical thickness of grape-skins, hardened by the use of copper-based vine treatments and by intense heat, as in 1983.

Secondly, hail: this splits berries and taints wines. Low concentrations of rot and hail can be masked by blending with sound wine, but this is not particularly satisfactory and the taint may sometimes disappear with aeration. The impact of hail on taste depends on when it occurs – before *veraison,* when berries change from green to black, is less damaging than after, when the skins are more vulnerable.

Thirdly, *surmaturité:* when grapes are subjected to prolonged heat they become more concentrated and raisiny. The volume of juice is reduced, the skins thicken amd the sugar, acids and extracts in the grape are all increased at the expense of their water content. This can make for difficult fermentations, and for a cooked, figgy flavour which, in moderation, can be attractive.

All these factors contributed in one way or another to the diversity of the 1983s. In cask the wines generally tasted excellent – good concentration, ripe, if not over-ripe, fruit with plenty of depth and extract; in short, a great vintage in the making. However, between cask and bottle something appeared to go wrong. The wines lost their flesh, hardened, and became tough and often astringent. Many curiously developed a taste of rot – probably because prospective buyers were only given samples from clean casks, the tainted wine being blended in later. This, especially from fine Domaines, was nothing less than dishonesty and is unforgivable.

However, whilst as Clive Coates has eloquently summarised them, the 1983s continue to 'excite, disappoint, amaze, infuriate and mislead', the prognosis is not entirely gloomy. Although there is no future for wines which are badly rotten or hailed, those that are simply hard have a reasonable chance of softening, provided there is a balance of fruit and acidity to weigh against the tannins.

Even among the better Domaines there is a wide diversity of quality. Some cut short their *cuvaisons,* for fear of extracting off-flavours and too much tannin; others did the opposite, aiming to extract more richness. Fining, especially with gelatine, was often overdone by growers desperately trying to reduce tannins – the wines were thereby badly eviscerated and now lack balance – and clumsy filtrations frequently made things worse.

Nonetheless, there are some remarkable wines from this heterogeneous vintage – very fine Romanée-Contis, some splendid Ponsots, and attractive harmonious Jadots. There are equally many growers on whose wines only time can make a sensible judgement – wines which seem hard and unyielding and of uncertain future. The only course for those who bought heavily in 1983 is to hang on and hope.

The white wines are less heterodox. Over-ripeness in Chardonnay produces wines of abnormally high alcohols, but does not impact on the taste in the same way as it does with Pinot. The 1983s tended to excess alcohol and some are rather lumpen and clumsy. However, there are some superlative wines – especially from the likes of Sauzet, Leflaive, Ramonet, Lafon, Drouhin and Jadot. The Leflaive and Sauzet Grands Crus are inspirational and will keep for a very long time.

1984

Sandwiched between a heteregeneous 1983 and a uniformly ripe and plush 1985, 1984 seems like a vinous dwarf. The summer was unremittingly cold, with some sunshine but no great warmth to ripen the grapes. It rained for much of September, although cool temperatures kept rot at bay. When the harvest was finally gathered those who picked last benefited, whilst the rest did their best with a large volume of unevenly ripe bunches

In the cellars, growers who were tuned in to the practice of bleeding the vats, to increase the ratio of solids to liquids, made a better fist of things than those who simply blundered on in whatever way they were used to.

In such conditions generalisations are worthless. However, what can be safely said is that as always, the reputable, conscientious growers made good, acceptable wines Some eight years on, the best bottles are showing a medium-weight, elegant, flavoury ripeness and good balance, almost as if they were developing structure as they went along. Judicious use of new oak has, in some cases, added gentle stuffing to wines which by themselves would have been ineffably meagre. In this, as in other vintages, individual vineyard sites with their particular micro-climates played an important role in the relative maturity of the grapes – so the Cru is important as well as the integrity of the grower. Buying Burgundy is no easy business.

1985

Whatever the quality of the wines, the growers will remember 1985 for the savage frosts which hit the Côte d'Or during January and February, destroying a significant area of vines outright and leaving many others weakened and degenerating. In Gevrey-Chambertin alone, possibly the worst-hit part of the Côte, the estimates of vines lost – mainly in the flatter Village and Bourgogne Rouge vineyards near to the RN 74 – vary from 100 to 150 ha. This is a serious level of damage which has had knock-on effects for several years.

However, the growing season passed off relatively uneventfully, with a dry if not particularly warm summer, followed by a fine and exceptionally hot September and October 'not a cloud in the sky, 25 to 30 degrees centigrade during the day, constant sunshine and soft nights more remindful of the Riviera than Burgundy' (L. Latour, vintage report).

The harvest, which started during the last week in September, produced a normal volume of completely ripe and healthy grapes. Vinification has turned these into seductive, deep, rich wines, of great finesse and silkiness. As with the 1978s, the wines were accessible from their earliest months, and they have lost none of the open, ripe fruit which has characterised them throughout. However, the majority have rather low acidities, which taken with their round, softish tannins must put a question mark over their long-term future. Perhaps, like 1947 and 1959, they will conspire to defy the rules and last for half a century!

The white wines have a similar style – plenty of ripe, soft fruit, rather fat and creamy; lovely drinking up to the middle and late 1990s but not really for keeping much beyond then. There was a significant risk of overheating fermentations from a hot harvest, but most sensible growers had learned the lessons of earlier difficult vintages and invested in cooling equipment. The most common deficiency – it would be misleading to term it a fault – is low acidity. However, growers with older vines and thus smaller yields seem to have made wines with a good, firm enough belt for a lack of braces to be of little consequence.

1986

This, and 1987, are vintages when the skills of the grower were, as the French say, 'primordial'. Firstly, he had to choose whether to pick early – the harvest started in the third week of September – or to risk waiting. An uneven growing season had been further disrupted by cold and wet weather from the middle of August onwards; however, in September, which was exceptionally wet, humidity had led to the spread of rot, which persuaded many growers to harvest as soon as possible. These early pickers found themselves with volumes of dilute, characterless wine. Those who were prepared to take the risk and wait were, as is so often the case in Burgundy, well rewarded. A spell of dry, breezy weather, which both dried off the grapes and added a little concentration enabled many to harvest – from the beginning of October – fruit which was both riper and more concentrated than that garnered by their more cautious colleagues.

Secondly, having picked his grapes the grower had to take considerable pains to ensure that nothing rotten found its way into the vats. The best Domaines spent heavily on personnel sorting through bunches and removing rotten berries. Those who were slipshod produced wines which taste of rot.

In dilute years such as this and 1982, if the

cuves are left to ferment by themselves the wines will end up with weak frames – too much juice and not enough ripe solids to balance them. Many growers, faced with this prospect, will draw off a percentage of the juice from each vat – *saignée de cuve*. This process, performed as soon as possible to avoid removing extract as well as juice, depends on guesswork rather than science - one can *saigner* 10% or 60% – you just have to have a feel for what will work. Although it is no real substitute for proper ripeness, a careful *saignée* can help restore a wine's equilibrium. Some growers however, such as Charles Rousseau in Gevrey, believe that this is in effect a defeat – an admission that you have not pruned short enough, or removed enough buds and shoots during the spring.

As a result, the reds from 1986 are a mixture of good – a few very good – and dilute mediocrity. Where the vigneron has taken care, the wines are quite soft in style, well-perfumed and have reasonable fruit. However, despite the care, many could not avoid a layer of rather unattractive dry tannins which are unlikely to round out.

A few growers made very fine wines in 1986 – those of François Faiveley, Charles Rousseau and Daniel Chopin-Groffier coming directly to mind. Christophe Roumier in Chambolle-Musigny is reputed to have made superlative 1986s. The best will keep well – it is difficult to say for how long, because they vary so much in style; however, there may be some pleasant surprises waiting in 5–10 years.

The white wines are considerably more reliable than the reds in 1986. The Indian summer which followed the September downpours transformed sugar levels at, according to one report, 'the rate of nearly half a degree per day', resulting in excellent harvest sugar counts for those who waited. Some grapes even had a touch of *noble rot* which added a dimension of fatness and complexity to the wines.

Those buying 1986 whites to lay down had a wealth of choice. The best Domaines produced delicious wines of finesse and elegance, perhaps reminiscent of the 1979s in concentration and style. These wines should develop over a decade or more and show every sign of a fine maturation. There is much debate as to whether the 1986s will outclass the 1985s – they are very different and, in any case, does it matter?

All in all 1986 was a satisfactory vintage with some good wines to enjoy whilst waiting for the 1985s, 1988s, 1989s and l990s to mature. As always, there are considerable variations in quality between Domaines.

1987

As with 1983, this vintage was rescued from oblivion by an exceptionally hot September. A dismal spring, relieved only by about three weeks of warm, fine weather in March, was followed by an equally dismal summer; the flowering was both late and uneven, with a high incidence of *millerandage* – these are embryonic bunches which never fully develop but which remain small; if they ripen, they are highly concentrated and can contribute much to a wine. Equally, their very presence reduces the overall volume of the harvest, so they are of double benefit. 'August makes the grape, September makes the wine' is a Burgundian saw. This was certainly true in 1987.

The red harvest was some 20% down on 1986, the white harvest nearly 25% less. Fortunately, September was largely dry as well as hot, so rot was minimal and the health of the grapes generally good. This meant that at Domaines where trouble is taken at every stage of the vegetative cycle to keep yields down, concentrations were good and quality consequently high.

However, much of the wine press, as usual, leapt in to judge the vintage and, largely influenced by tales of rain during the harvest, which took place during late September and early October, dismissed it as one of low quality and little consequence. They were wrong.

Although most of the red wines began life with a shell of rather hard tannins from which they are just emerging, they were deeply coloured, with good fruit and extract – helped by the *millerandage* – and had good acidities. Tasting a broad range from both parts of the Côte, during the winter of 1990–91, left an impression of a vintage which has all the elements of quality, but which needs much time to settle down and integrate. Given their high acidities and tannins, it is not difficult to see how people might be led to conclude that they are out of balance. However, one has only to look beneath the wrapping to find good, firm, concentrated fruit. Some growers compare the style and likely evolution with that of 1972 – if so, then there will be some marvellous bottles about in the first decade of the new century.

Among the whites, there are some delicious wines – not immensely charged with fruit, but fine and delicate in style. Most are characterised by a nerve of acidity which in some instances is green and malic. However, by the middle of the decade they should be much more harmonious. The very top estates as one might expect, pulled all the rabbits out of their respective hats and produced wines of great quality – Leflaive, Ramonet, Sauzet and Lafon in puticular.

1988

In 1988 the vegetative cycle was almost a model of regularity: a warm, dry, mid-June saw the flowering pass in ideal conditions. Thereafter, cool, rainy weather gave way to a warm, often hot, summer with lower than normal rainfall which marginally retarded the full maturation of the grapes. A fine September – the month which can make or break a vintage – brought a little rain, but barely enough to produce optimal maturity.

Some growers leapt into their vineyards and started picking in the Côte de Beaune during the third week of September. The results of their haste were grapes which lacked ripeness and which needed heavy *chaptalisation* to generate enough alcohol for balance. Those who took the risk and waited until the end of the month made much richer, more naturally harmonious wines.

This fine growing season produced a large harvest – the reds some 11% more than in 1987 but 12% less than 1986, the whites some 26% more than 1987 but only 2% less than 1986. These figures, however, conceal considerable variation between communes up and down the Côte.

Vinifications were, fortunately, not complicated by excessive heat during the harvest. However, the volume of the crop meant that a *saignée* was obligatory for all but the few who summer-pruned or who had particularly old vines. The red wines are generally deeper and more consistent than their 1987 counterparts in the twin senses that, not only is there overall a higher level of quality in a given grower's cellar, there is also a uniformly fine average along the Côte, from Masannay to Santenay. Although these wines presently lack the obvious 'ampleur' and fleshy charm of the 1989s, there is a general consensus among growers that they will outlast them.

In style, the 1988s started off dominated by a layer of rather austere, though perfectly ripe, tannins. These are beginning to integrate, but the best will need a decade or more for the splendid fruit underneath to really show itself. They present a complete contrast to the 1985s, which have opulent, soft, ripe fruit in abundance. The 1988s have the fruit, but of a more reserved kind. With so many Domaines making excellent wines it would be invidious to select any for particular mention. On the contrary, there should be serious doubt about the capabilities of any grower who failed to produce fine 1988s.

As for the whites, the large harvest also presented problems. Unfortunately, since the skins do not influence their vinification, *saignée* is not an option for white vmification, so growers who over-cropped ended up with dilute wines. Overall, tastings suggest that, whilst this is undeniably a fine, healthy vintage, the whites will not come up to the quality of either 1985 or 1986. Perhaps it is too soon to make more than a tentative judgement, but many wines seem to have a lack of real depth and concentration that no amount of maturation will rectify. However, for the medium term they will provide delicious drinking – with attractive aromas beginning to evolve and quite reasonable acidity to give them balance and life.

Among the white ensemble, there are some notably classy offerings – as usual Leflaive, Lafon, Bonneau de Martray, Coche-Dury, Jadot, Sauzet and Ramonet are perched at the top of the tree, with Pierre Morey, Yves Boyer, Guy Roulot, Jean-Noël Gagnard, Michel Colin and Bernard Morey holding on to the branch below.

1989

1989 was a year of near-perfection for the vine throughout most of the Côte. The vegetative cycle started off some two weeks ahead of schedule, and remained so up to the harvest. March was warm and sunny, with temperatures well above the monthly 5° C average. However the late spring had some surprises: April, though not especially cold, brought nearly 115 mm. of rain; a sharp frost at the beginning of May wrought significant damage in low-lying frost pockets in general, and on the southern, Puligny side of Meursault in particular, and finally, going out with a veritable kick, a hailstorm on 25 May caused widespread damage, especially to the Corton hill and in nearby Pernand-Vergelesses, reducing the potential crop by half.

The flowering lasted for nearly 15 days –

which meant that, within the same parcel of vines, there were to be several different degrees of maturity. Fine weather returned in July and remained until after the harvest, which started relatively early at the end of the second week in September. However, without much rain, some vines, particularly the younger ones on well-drained sites, suffered badly, not having sufficiently deep root-systems to find water elsewhere. Although the grapes were ripe, many vignerons were disappomted that when they looked at the sugar levels at harvest, they had not reached the important 13.5 degrees potential alcohol – the level at which, as M. Duvaud-Blochet, a famous nineteenth-century Burgundian wine grower theorised, natural alchemy turns a good year into a great one.

The drought, hail and frost, together with some *coulure* und *millerandage* reduced the white crop by some 14% on its 1988 level, whilst the red harvest was insignificantly higher than in 1988. Yields in the Côte de Nuits were marginally higher, on average, than those in the Côte de Beaune, accounted for by a late September rainfall, just before the harvest. Such differences in weather patterns between the two parts of the Côte d'Or also explain a small difference in average ripeness – Nuits having marginally less natural sugar than Beaune.

Important differences in ripeness may occur even in a more circumscribed area; for example, in 1989, Le Montrachet reached a natural average ripeness of 12.3 degrees, whereas nearby Bâtard-Montrachet and Criots-Bâtard-Montrachet were harvested at just over 13 degrees.

In cask, both reds and whites shared one overriding characteristic – heaps of fat; ripe fruit; they are mostly opulent, big, soft fleshy wines with enormous charm and elegance; even the reds were almost drinkable straight from the barrel. This exuberant fruit, coupled with low acidity levels, tempted many seasoned hands into comparisons with the 1947s and 1959s. While it is too early to make any definitive assessments, growers are generally of the opinion that the 1989s will make gorgeously attractive bottles for the medium term.

If there is an indicator which sorts out the good from the very good Domaines in a vintage like 1989, it is the yield. In as much as this lies within growers' power (site and vine age making their own important contribution), there are wide variations. Some tell you that they made fine quality from Pinots yielding 50 hl./ha. whilst others talk of excessive yields at 45 hl./ha. Some growers *saignéed* in 1989, although many did not.

However, there are some exceptional wines in the making – Danel Chopin-Groffier's massive, deep, Clos Vougeot, a string of ripe thoroughbred beauties from Méo-Camuzet, a fine 'sortie' from the Domaine de la Romanée-Conti plus a galaxy of other delights from the finest growers in each commune. The best, both red and white, will give an immense amount of pleasure for a dozen or so years from the middle nineties.

In fine, this vintage has a distinct touch of the 'barmaid' about it – plenty of obvious charm and up-front flesh, but perhaps mildly short on intellect.

1990

1990 seems to combine the richness and opulence of the 1989s with the structure and concentration of the 1988s. If so, it will be a very great vintage indeed. However, this is the time for tentative pronouncements rather than 'ex cathedra' assessments.

The early part of the 'periode végétative' was not favourable — an almost summery March was followed by a wintry April with some nocturnal frost. June, average in temperature and rainfall, but deficient in sunshine, saw an uneven, extended flowering, with relatively little *coulure* but significamt *millerandage.* However, from 5 July an anti-cyclone set in, bringing hot, sunny and dry weather, and remained until after the harvest. Unprecedented drought, which threatened the balanced maturation of the grapes was relieved only by a few isolated storms. However, on 30 August when even the most phlegmatic of vignerons was beginning to look anxious, a storm broke – precipitating between 30–60 mm. of rain on the Côte d'Or in little over 24 hours. This was just enough to maintain photosynthesis and effectively saved the crop, since the fine hot weather continued afterwards, unabated.

The harvest started in the middle of September – some 15 days ahead of normal – and the last grapes were brought in around 10 October. In 1990 the vigneron had no reason to delay his picking – the grapes were fully ripe.

Yields were high. In fact many Domaines fearing excess, summer-pruned to further reduce the crop size. Even the authorities were carried away, extending the *rendement de base* for white wines by a full 5% throughout the Côte. In the Côte de Beaune, Chardonnay yields were more than 25% higher than those of 1989 and just over 10% higher than 1988. Despite this volume, sugar levels were excellent, giving white wines of good concentrations with firm, ripe fruit – sometimes noticeably over-ripe with reasonable acidity levels and promising finesse.

Whilst the Pinot Noir crop was prolific, ripe, thick skins and the contribution of super-concentrated *millerands* ensured that the wines did not lack in concentration. Throughout the Côte, the reds are characterised by an excellent depth of almost sweet-ripe concentrated fruit allied to a firm backbone of equally ripe, harmonious tannins. The best Domaines have produced what would appear to be very fine wines indeed, with considerable seductive richness, magnificent length – even at Village level – and a great deal of class. Retasting a cross-section of wines in October 1991, it is evident that 1990 may well blossom into an exceptional Burgundy vintage. Many growers, even those generally given to shrugging understatement, found themselves spontaneously voicing superlatives they had probably forgotten how to use.

Looking at the last two vintages of the 1980s and at 1990, the majority of Domaines rank them, in ascending order of maturity and preference: 1989, 1988 and 1990. However, whilst there are a few who prefer their 1989s to their 1988s it is difficult to find any who rate either more highly than their 1990s.

In short, 1990 seems set to take its place in the annals of great Burgundy vintages.

1991

After several years of mild winters, the 1990/91 Burgundian winter begun with a beneficial freezing-cold spell and a typical November snow. Despite this, vegetative activity started earlier than normal the following spring. March in the Côte d'Or was mild but wet, allowing vegetation to develop apace. However, cold weather re-established itself, blocking normal vegetative development; there was snow in the Yonne on 19 April, and on the nights of 20–21 and 23–24 April – following unseasonally high temperatures at the beginning of the month – severe frost struck the Côte. This destroyed many of the first buds and also some latent growth – not just in the known frost-pockets, but throughout the vignoble. Meursault, Puligny and Prémeaux were particularly affected.

Flowering extended over about 2 weeks from mid-June, presaging at least an uneven ripeness of what crop remained. Then the vigneron's nightmare – summer hail – struck, twice. On 22 June a hailstorm hit the north of the Côte de Nuits, causing severe damage in the Hautes Côtes and in the Grands Crus between Morey and Gevrey. Two months later, on 22 August, a further storm ravaged Ladoix and Hautes Côtes, also damaging Beaune, Chorey, Aloxe, Savigny, Pernand and Corgolion.

The summer was not particularly propitious – a cool June followed by a warmer July, which saw a rapid evolution of vegetation throughout the Côte. *Veraison* was largely complete by the end of August. By the beginning of September however, sugar levels had generally caught up, despite a lack of rain. Pests were less abundant than normal, reducing the need for repeated treatments – either preventively or curatively.

The *ban de vendange* was generally proclaimed for 25/26 September and, as usual, many rushed in to pick, especially where sugar levels were high. Those who waited were rewarded by several days of unstable weather and a downpour over the weekend of 28–30 September. The sun then came out, enabling sugar levels to increase and grapes to be harvested dry. However, by this time rot had spread through much of the Côte and a severe *trie* was necessary to remove this and small, desiccated, hail-damaged grapes. In most communes bunches were of uneven ripeness, so only those who took extra care in sorting their grapes made wines of good balance and concentration.

In parts of the Côte de Beaune, the weather pattern was curious and atypical: in Chassagne – Montrachet, for example, frost damage occurred on the hillsides but not on the plains; in Puligny it tended to be the reverse. Notwithstanding, healthy Grands Crus were being harvested on 1 October at 13.8° natural sugar.

The general picture is consequently patchy; whilst parts of the Côte de Beaune seem normal in crop size and health, much of the Côte de Nuits is rot und hail damaged. As usual, it is the careful growers and late harvesters who are likely to produce the best results.

Glossary

Agrément: the official approval of a wine for its respective appellation. This is based on an analysis and tasting test, carried out between November and April immediately following the harvest.

Assemblage: the process of amalgamating the contents of various vats or casks to unify the wine and to make a single *cuvée* for bottling. This can take place at any time after vinification, but usually occurs at racking or just before bottling. This is also the moment when the conscientious grower will weed out any substandard casks.

Baguette: the principal fruiting cane(s) which remain after pruning.

Ban de vendange: the official proclamation of the start of harvest decided by the local *INAO* committee. Growers who pick before this date are liable to certain vinification restrictions.

Base elements: nitrogen, potassium and phosphorus. These are the essential active soil-ingredients to support plant life. They are not the same as *trace elements.*

Batonnage: the traditional practice of stirring white wines to ensure even distribution of the lees through the liquid. Its frequency and extent vary from Domaine to Domaine.

Botrytis: a fungus which attacks grapes and rots them. It appears in both dry and damp forms and is never desirable in red grapes. In white grapes a touch of damp rot may add quality to a dry wine. The taste of rot, in either form, is ineradicable.

Buttage: traditional practice of ploughing up soil around roots of vines to protect them from winter frosts. Now largely discontinued.

Carbonic maceration: a system of fermentation in which whole, uncrushed grapes are fermented in the absence of air. Colour is extracted without tannin, so the wine is supple and drinkable early. Much Beaujolais and bulk table wine is made in this way.

Cépage: grape variety.

Chapeau: the cap of solids – skins, pips and stalks – which forms at the top of a vat of fermenting red juice, held up by escaping CO_2 gas. If not kept moist, this cap rapidly dries out and sours the entire vat. *Pigéage* both performs this function and also ensures maximum contact between liquid and solids, thereby maximum extraction.

Chapeau immergé: the practice of keeping the cap of skins and pips moist, in a vat of red *must,* by submergmg it permanently underneath a ceiling of wooden planks. Although this eliminates the need for *pigéage,* many growers do not favour it because the cap remains intact. They consider that periodic breaking up of the cap is essential to proper extraction of colour, tannins, aromas etc.

Chaptalisation: the addition of sugar to fermenting *must* to correct a natural deficiency and thus bring the final alcohol level up to the legal minimum. Introduced by Chaptal in 1801, the process is not designed to increase sweetness. The method and amount of *chaptalisation* are subject to legal control.

Charpente: literally 'carpentry'; tasting-term, used to signify structure. Up to a point, the more *charpente* a wine has the better.

Chlorosis: vine disease caused principally by excess calcium in the soil in which leaves turn yellow and cease photosynthesis through lack of chlorophyll. Inappropriate rootstock is a principal cause.

Climat: vineyard site. In the Côte d'Or, *climats* usually have names – Les Cras, Sous la Velle etc. The term is interchangeable with *lieu-dit,* designed to classify wine before bottling.

Col: a *col is* a fining, designed to clarify wine before bottling. A wine remains *sur col* for several weeks or even months, during which period its taste qualities may be distorted.

Cordon de Royat: a system of training vines by laying the main vine stem horizontally along a wire, off which several vertical fruiting canes are taken. This is widely used in Chassagne and Santenay to limit yields and is becoming increasingly popular among top Domaines elsewhere in the Côte.

Corsé: a term of approbation used by tasters which has no precise translation, but generally refers to a wine which is well-constituted and robust. It does not mean coarse.

Coulure: the failure of flowers to set on a vine; often caused by adverse weather conditions which make them drop. Fewer flowers mean fewer bunches and thus a reduced yield.

Coupage: the practice of cutting (blending) one, usually more expensive, wine with something inferior. In the Côte this was common until the 1970s; the cutting wine was usually from the southern Rhône or Algeria.

Coup de feu: the moment of most intense heat during fermentation.

Courson: a short pruning spur, often providing the fruiting wood for the following year.

Court-noué: a virus disease, endemic in Burgundy, especially in white vines. Known as the 'fan-leaf', this malady attacks the vine's leaves, reducing their photosynthetic ability. Grubbing up and replanting is the only solution.

Crochet: method of training the vine, a modified *gobelet,* with fruiting canes pruned short to one or two buds on each. Principally used for very young vines, to limit vigour, or for very old ones which have grown too tall to bend a cane onto the wire without breaking it.

Cryptogams: a family of vine maladies which includes *botrytis, oïdium* and mildew. These are normally treated with specific sprays.

Cuvaison: the process of vatting. The time during which grapes are transformed into wine, starting when the grapes are put into vats to ferment and ending when the new wine is run off to cask. This only applies to red grapes.

Cuve: the vessel in which fermentation takes place. This can be made of wood, stainless-steel, glass-lined epoxy etc.

Cuve auto-pigéante: simply a stainless-steel *cuve* which contains apparatus for automatic *pigéage.* These take several forms – from rotating *cuves* to static ones with rotating paddles. Some growers think that they improve quality; others regard them with deep distrust.

Cuvée: an ambiguous term, referring either to an individual vat – as in 'from several *cuvées* of Meursault he selected one' – or to the bottled wine – as in 'he has a *cuvée* of Gevrey and one of Chambolle'. So a grower might blend several *cuvées* of Meursault to form a single *cuvée* which he then bottles.

Débourbage: the process of settling to allow the heavier, less desirable lees (les bourbes), to precipitate out.

Décuvage: decanting a wine from vat after fermentation. This really only applies to red vinification, where the new wine is run off the residue of solids, which are then pressed to yield the *vin de presse.* The precise moment of *décuvage* involves a delicate decision – which can markedly affect wine quality.

Dedoubler: the removal, during the spring, of any double shoots or buds. This reduces potential yields and spreads out the foliage.

Ébrossage: another word for ébourgonnage, échtonnage, dédoublage or *évasivage.*

Écoulage: running off juice from a vat or press.

Égalisage: the process of unifying several casks of wine from the same vineyard or appellation, to eliminate any differences in taste between them. This usually takes place at racking or at *relève de col* just before bottling.

Égrappage: destalking; separating grape berries from stems either by hand or machine.

Élevage: literally means upbringing. The skilled process involved in caring for a wine between vinification and bottling. Racking, fining, filtration etc. are all part of a wine's *élevage.* The wine-maker and *éleveur* may be different people – e.g. where wine is sold young in cask; hence 'négociant-éleveur'.

En foule: the system of vineyard planting common up to the end of the nineteenth century, whereby vines were densely planted en masse and simply allowed to ramble – their natural propensity.

En friche: unplanted vineyard land, often scrub.

Enherbement: the practice of deliberately sowing grass between vine rows to retain topsoil and prevent erosion.

Eutypiose: an insidious vine infection, probably spread by mushroom-like spores especially in damp, windy conditions Pruning wounds are the most susceptible means of entry. Although most noticeable early on in its development cycle, it retreats, giving the impression that the vine has healed. Thereafter, it can take up to 7 years before any further symptoms appear, by which time it is too late. Some parts of the Côte d'Or are more affected than others. Too many vignerons are failing to take *eutypiose* seriously.

Évasivage: the removal of excess buds from the vine; usually carried out between bud-burst and flowering. An important operation which is essential in restricting growth and reducing yields.

Fermage: a system of vineyard tenancy whereby the tenant farms the land and enjoys the totality of the crop in return for an annual rental, fixed at the cash equivalent of an agreed number of pièces of that vineyard's wine. Even if there is no harvest, the rental is payable. See *Métayage.*

Figué: literally, figgy. Over-ripe Pinot Noir can taste and smell figgy, especially when the skins have been cooked by prolonged hot sunshine in dry weather. Up to a point this can enhance a wine.

Foudre: a large, wooden, fermenting vat.

Framboisé: literally, raspberried; an aroma often found in young Pinot Noir.

Fruits noirs: literally 'black fruits' – a tasting term referring principally to blackberries, blackcurrants, bilberries and plums.

Fruits rouges: literally 'red fruits' – a tasting term referring to strawberries, raspberries, loganberries, redcurrants, cherries etc.

Fruits sauvages: literally 'wild fruits' – a carpet-bag tasting term which tends to refer more to the style of fruit than to the particular variety; it connotes hedgerow smells of freshly picked berries.

Gobelet: system of training a vine with several upright shoots from the main stem – resembling a goblet. Used widely for young and old vines in the Côte, the *gobelet* is particularly associated in France with the Beaujolais, the southern Rhône and Provence.

Goût de lie: a sort of yeasty, cardboardy taste which derives from too much contact between wine and lees and can render a wine flat and disagreeable. A pronounced *goût de lie* is a signal that racking is due – or overdue!

Goût de silex: a particular earthy taste, found especially in white wines from Pernand-Vergelesses and Savigny-lès-Beaune.

Goût de terroir: a tasting term meaning 'earthy taste'. It is often found in Burgundies from lesser communes – e.g. St.-Aubin, Auxey-Duresses – or from vineyards where the soil gives a distinct flavour of its own – e.g. the taste of silex in some Pernand and Savigny whites.

Guyot: system of training invented by Dr. Guyot in the mid eighteenth century, consisting of either a single or double fruiting cane trained laterally off the main vine stem.

INAO: Institut National des Appellations d'Origine. The French governmental organisation which delimits and controls appellations including those for pottery and chickens as well as for wine.

Lieu-dit: this means a specific vineyard site; the term is, to all intents and purposes, interchangeable with *climat.*

Macération: the practice of letting grape-juice or new wine mix with its solids – skins, pips etc. – before, during or after fermentation. *Macération pelliculaire* refers particularly to a pre-fermentive maceration of white juice.

Mâche: a frequently used tasting term; difficult to translate – but has the sense of chewy-gutsiness.

Malade de mise: bottling-sickness. A term referring to the phenomenon where, for a period immediately following bottling, a wine may not taste true to form. Bottling frequently shocks a wine into itself, a state from which it may take up to several years to recover.

Malolactic/Malo: a bacterially-mediated fermentation which turns harsh malic (apple) acid, naturally present in wine, into softer-tasting lactic (milk) acid. It follows alcoholic fermentation.

Marc: (i) the cake of solids left after pressing; (ii) a form of Brandy made by distilling this cake.

Métayage: an alternative system of land rental to *fermage* in which rent is paid, not in cash, but in an agreed proportion of grapes or wine usually one-third, a half or two-thirds. The share-cropper or *métayer* is normally responsible for all the running expenses of the vineyard, except for new plants, posts and wires. The landlord sometimes pays an agreed proportion of fertilisers, sprays etc.

Millerandage: a phenomenon of flowering, when embryo bunches form but fail to develop further. These *millerands* reduce yields but also contain tiny amounts of very rich concentrated juice, which can add significantly to wine concentration.

Monopole: a vineyard in single ownership.

Must: the grape juice before it has finished fermenting and thus become wine.

Noble rot (Pourriture noble): whilst a wholly desirable condition in grapes destined for sweet white wine, a small amount can enhance a dry white wine with its quality of richness both on the nose and on the palate. This is largely derived from botrycine – a by-product of *botrytis.*

Oïdium: powdery mildew; a rapidly spread fungus disease of American origin which attacks new leaves and shoots, and splits and rots the grapes. First observed at the Royal Botanical Gardens, Kew, London, in 1845, *oïdium* ravaged viticultural France in the 1850s. It is effectively treated with sulphur.

Palissage: the training of vine-shoots and foliage onto the upper two strands of wire during summer. At the same time, the middle pair of wires are clipped together.

Pénétrant: a class of treatment products which act by penetrating the vine's capillary system. These contrast with contact products – which don't penetrate the system but wash off easily and systemics which penetrate more deeply. Each has advantages and disadvantages.

Phylloxera: an aphid, 0.5–1 mm. long, with a complex life cycle, which feeds on vine-roots, eventually killing the plant. It multiplies vigorously and is permanently resident in the soils of most European vineyards, which it devastated at the end of the nineteenth century. There is no cure, but planting onto resistant rootstock renders the insect harmless. A few French and other vineyards remain on their original, pre-*phylloxera,* roots.

Pièce: the standard Burgundy barrel, containing 228 litres. The standard Bordeaux 'barrique' contains 225 litres.

Pied de cuve: a starter-culture comprised of artificial yeasts and wine, or which is used to inoculate vats, to induce fermentation.

Pigéage: the practice of breaking up the cap of solids which forms on top of a vat of fermenting red grapes to prevent it drying out. Although traditionally done by human feet, many Domaines use mechanical pistons or hand-wielded plungers to do this task. *Pigéage* also mixes up solids and liquid, thus improving extraction.

PLC (Plafond Limite de Classement): this is the ceiling yield for any given appellation, expressed in hl./ha., and represents a percentage increase – normally 20% – on the *rendement de base.* It is supposedly only authorised in prolific years.

Pourriture: rot, which can come in one of two forms – 'sec' or 'humide'. Neither is desirable, but 'humide' is less disagreeable on the palate than dry rot. *Noble rot (botrytis)* is important in the production of high-quality sweet white wines, but not in Burgundy.

Prélèvement: the practice of taking random samples of grapes from a vineyard to determine maturity/ripeness and thus the right moment to harvest.

Reduit: literally 'reduced' – the opposite of oxygenated. A tasting term for a more or less disagreeable smell brought about by storage in a reduced state – i.e. in the absence of air. The smell is not permanent and is easily eliminated by aeration. When a wine in cask becomes noticeably reduced it should be racked.

Régisseur: the manager or cellar-master of an estate.

Régionales: wines from regional appellations – e.g. Bourgogne Aligoté, Passe-Tout-Grains, Côte de Beaune-Villages, Bourgogne Blanc etc. These come from land in each commune which is deemed unsuitable for a higher appellation.

Relève de col: racking the wine clear of its fining.

Remontage: pumping-over juice from the bottom to the top of a vat during red wine fermentation. This aerates the yeasts and gets them working. It also equalises the temperature in the vat and helps keep the cap moist.

Rendement: yield, normally expressed in hl./ha.

Rendement de base: the base yield. This is the maximum yield set for each appellation, for a normal vintage. It is expressed in hl./ha. – i.e. x 100 litres for each hectare. In prolific vintages, it may be augmented by the *PLC.*

Repiquage: the practice of replacing individually vines which die or get too old, rather than grubbing up an entire parcel. Preferred by many top growers as it helps maintain a high average vine age.

Rondeur: Roundness. A taste-sensation rather than a literal description.

Saigner/Saignée/Saignée de cuve: the practice of bleeding off juice from a vat of red grapes, especially in dilute vintages to concentrate what remains. The later you leave it, the more extract you remove. Many growers maintain that the need to *saigner* indicates over-production in the vineyard.

Sélection clonale: refers (i) to the use of selected clones by the vigneron as opposed to *sélection massale* and (ii) to the highly skilled process of developing clones for commercial propagation.

Sélction massale: traditional process of selecting suitable plant material, by taking wood or shoots from the best and healthiest vines direct from the vineyard. The precursor of clones, and still used by some vignerons.

SO_2: sulphur dioxide. This is widely used in wine-making as an all-purpose disinfectant, since it kills destructive microbes and prevents oxidation. In excessive doses it has a pungent smell and gives wine a flat, cardboardy taste. It should not be confused with bad eggs – that is H_2S, hydrogen sulphide.

Sous-bois: an often used term signifying undergrowth or damp vegetation – an attractive mushroomy smell which is frequently encountered in older Côte d'Or wines.

Sur col: literally 'on fining'. A wine which is in the process of being fined is referred to as *sur col.* In this state, which may last for several months, wines may not taste true to form.

Surmaturité: over-ripeness. Grapes left on the vine in hot dry weather concentrate and shrivel. This gives added depth of flavour but beyond a certain point can bring a tarry, cooked taste to a wine. Over-ripened grapes often have an element of *botrytis* which in white wine frequently results in a special aromatic richness.

Sur pressoir: from the press. A term used to refer to wine sold as juice or in an unfinished state.

Tâcheron: literally, a worker who is paid by task – a piece-worker; however, in current parlance, someone who tends vines for someone else – quite common in the Côte.

Taille: pruning.

Tendre: a tasting term – supple, tender.

Terre rouge: this is red earth, soil often found in the Côte which has been tinted by oxidised iron deposits.

Terre à rouge: soil more suitable for the production of red wine.

Terroir: an elusive but important concept, encapsulating the general physical environment of a vineyard. It includes micro-climate, soil, slope, exposure, drainage etc.

Trace elements: inorganic compounds found in usually minute quantities in soil for example: beryllium, iron, cobalt, manganese, magnesium, chromium. They contribute in different ways to grape-maturity, fertilisation, photosynthesis and sugar accumulation. However, the precise causal relationships are imperfectly understood.

Triage/Trie: the practice of sorting through the crop to pick only ripe, healthy grapes. A *trie* can be done on the vine, or by hand at the cuverie. It is especially necessary in years of rot or hail damage.

Vendange verte: literally 'green harvest' – cutting a proportion of bunches before the proper harvest to reduce the load on each vine. This is a controversial practice, since many believe that the vine simply compensates with larger, more dilute berries.

Veraison: the moment at which the berries of red grape varieties turn from green to black on the vine (usually in August on the Côte).

Ver de la grappe: grape-worm. Insect which punctures the skin of the grape leaving a wound which rapidly turns rotten. There are two generations during each vine-growing cycle, the first harmless, the second not. For no known reason some communes are regularly more infected than others.

Verjus: the second crop of grapes; small and usually unripe, these are mostly found at the top of the vine. They must be removed well before harvest since they both sap vital energy from the vine and also add unripe acidity and greenness to wines if they get into the vats. An important quality factor in Burgundy, since pickers often cannot distinguish *verjus* from the main crop.

Vigne mère: mother vine – the vineyard or set of vines from which clones or *sélection massale* are propagated.

Vin de garde: wine for keeping, as opposed to wine designed for early drinking.

Vin de presse/Vin de goutte: the press-wine is that extracted by pressing the pulp from a red wine vat after the free-run wine *(vin de goutte)* has been decanted. It is usually harsher and more tannic, depending on the pressure used to extract it.

Volatile acidity: acetic acid, vinegar. This comes generally from careless vinification or sloppy hygiene. In tiny quantities it can enhance a wine, but in large doses becomes offensive to both nose and palate.

Measures and Conversions

Measures of area

1 hectare =2.471 acres = 10,000 sq. metres = 100 ares = 24 ouvrées
1 are = 100 sq. metres (100 ares = 1 hectare)
1 ouvrée = 4.285 ares = 0.417 hectares
1 journal = 8 ouvrées = ⅓ hectare (3 journeaux = 1 hectare)

Measures of capacity

0.75 litres = 1 standard bottle
1.5 litres = 1 magnum = 2 bottles
3.0 litres = 1 double magnum = 1 jeraboam
9 litres = 12 bottles = 1 case

1 queue = 2 tonneaux = 456 litres = 608 bottles
1 tonneau = 1 pièce = 228 litres = 304 bottles (the standard Burgundy cask size)
1 feuillette = ½ tonneau = 114 litres = 152 bottles
1 quarteau = ¼ tonneau = 57 litres = 76 bottles

Vat capacity is usually measured in hectolitres:
1 hectolitre = 100 litres = 133.3 bottles = 11.1 cases

Measures of yield

Yields are usually expressed in hectolitres per hectare (hl./ha.)

1 hl./ha. = 100 litres / ha.
1 hl./ha. = 133.3 bottles / ha. = 11.1 cases / hectare
1 hl./ha. - 53.9 bottles / acre - 4.5 cases / acre
40 hl./ha. = 4000 litres / hectare = 444 cases / hectare
40 hl./ha. = 2158 bottles / acre = 180 cases / acre
40 hl./ha. is equivalent to about half a bottle of wine per vine

Measures of production

130 kilograms of grapes produce approximately 1 hectolitre of wine. A plant density of 11,000 vines per hectare and 8 bunches per vine is approximately equivalent to a yield of 55 hl./ha. This is also equivalent to 1 pièce (cask) per ouvrée = 24 pièces per hectare. This amounts to some 650 grams of grapes, or half a litre of wine per vine.

INDEX

Each commune or village featured in this book is referred to in **bold** type. Vineyards indexed under each commune refer to places where they are mentioned in the text and not to maps or domaine holdings, to which readers are also referred. There are often different – equally correct – spellings of vineyard names. We have used the most common.

Acknowledgements

The lengthy preparation of this book has been greatly assisted by many, both in the UK and in France. I am particularly grateful to all the Domaines, whether included here or not, who generously opened their doors, cuveries, cellars and tasting-rooms, gave so much of their time and so freely shared their ideas. Their spontaneous welcome and encouragement will long be remembered.

The following people also gave generously of their time and expertise: Professeur Raymond Bernard of ONIVINS, Dijon; Professeur Michel Feuillat of the Laboratoire d'Oenologie, Université de Bourgogne, Dijon; M. Michel Gormand Courtier en Vins, Beaune; M. Remi Gonin of the Répression des Fraudes, Dijon; Professor Jake Hancock, Dept. of Geology, Imperial College, University of London; Professeur Noël Leneuf, Director of Université, Dijon Research Centre, Marsannay; M. René Naudin of the Institut Technique de la Vigne et du Vin, Beaune; M. Riffiod of the Protection des Végétaux, Beaune; Mssrs. Jean-Luc Servan and PhilippeTrollat of the BIVB, Beaune; Dr. Jean Siegrist, of the Institut National de la Recherche Agronome, Dijon and M. Jules Tourmeau of the INAO, Dijon.

Personal introductions to many growers were obtained through the kindness of merchants and specialist UK importers – in particular: Nick Clarke MW of O.W. Loeb & Co. Ltd.; Simon Cock of Heyman Brothers Ltd.; Claude Giret of Berkmann's Ltd.; Becky and Russell Hone of Le Serbet, Bouilland, Côte d'Or; Robert Rolls of Market Vintners Ltd. and SimonTaylor-Gill of Domaine Direct Ltd.

My special thanks are also due to Don Pinchbeck, Edward Huggins and Shaun Goffe at Epson UK Ltd., who generously provided a fast, reliable Epson PC AX3S portable computer, on which much of this book was written.

Sue Collins at Kyle Cathie Ltd. efficiently copied, collated and despatched mountains of letters to Domaines, and then dealt with their sometimes bemused replies.

Also, this book would not be the same without the photographs of Janet Price. Janet made several trips to Burgundy and spent hours persuading surprised vignerons not to pose in their best suits and encouraging them to relax. The results often say more than my words.

Finally, my special thanks to Dr. Christopher Davenport-Jones, a knowledgeable wine-enthusiast and kind friend, who introduced me to Kyle Cathie, to Kyle herself for her enthusiasm and support, and to my wife, Geraldine, who read and re-read the manuscript, correcting everything from errors of grammar to stylistic infelicities. Without them, this book would never have been.